National Security Law

ASPEN STUDENT TREATISE

NATIONAL SECURITY LAW: PRINCIPLES AND POLICY

GEOFFREY CORN
Professor of Law and Presidential Research Professor
South Texas College of Law

JIMMY GURULÉ
Professor of Law
Notre Dame Law School

ERIC JENSEN
Assistant Professor of Law
Brigham Young University Law School

PETER MARGULIES
Professor of Law
Roger Williams University School of Law

Wolters Kluwer

Printed in the United States of America.

3 4 5 6 7 8 9 0

ISBN 978-1-4548-5274-2

Library of Congress Cataloging-in-Publication Data

National security law: principles and policy / Geoffrey Corn, Professor of Law and Presidential Research Professor, South Texas College of Law; Jimmy Gurulé, Professor of Law, Notre Dame Law School; Eric Jensen, Assistant Professor of Law, Brigham Young University Law School; Peter Margulies, Professor of Law, Roger Williams University School of Law.
    pages cm
    Includes bibliographical references and index.
    ISBN 978-1-4548-5274-2 (alk. paper)
1. National security—Law and legislation—United States. 2. Civil rights—United States. 3. Terrorism—Prevention—Law and legislation—United States. 4. War and emergency powers—United States. 5. Electronic surveillance—Law and legislation—United States. I. Corn, Geoffrey S., author. II. Jensen, Eric Talbot, author. III. Gurulé Jimmy, author.
    KF4850.N38 2015
    343.73'01—dc23
                                                            2015001093

About Wolters Kluwer Law & Business

Wolters Kluwer Law & Business is a leading global provider of intelligent information and digital solutions for legal and business professionals in key specialty areas, and respected educational resources for professors and law students. Wolters Kluwer Law & Business connects legal and business professionals as well as those in the education market with timely, specialized authoritative content and information-enabled solutions to support success through productivity, accuracy and mobility.

Serving customers worldwide, Wolters Kluwer Law & Business products include those under the Aspen Publishers, CCH, Kluwer Law International, Loislaw, ftwilliam.com and MediRegs family of products.

CCH products have been a trusted resource since 1913, and are highly regarded resources for legal, securities, antitrust and trade regulation, government contracting, banking, pension, payroll, employment and labor, and healthcare reimbursement and compliance professionals.

Aspen Publishers products provide essential information to attorneys, business professionals and law students. Written by preeminent authorities, the product line offers analytical and practical information in a range of specialty practice areas from securities law and intellectual property to mergers and acquisitions and pension/benefits. Aspen's trusted legal education resources provide professors and students with high-quality, up-to-date and effective resources for successful instruction and study in all areas of the law.

Kluwer Law International products provide the global business community with reliable international legal information in English. Legal practitioners, corporate counsel and business executives around the world rely on Kluwer Law journals, looseleafs, books, and electronic products for comprehensive information in many areas of international legal practice.

Loislaw is a comprehensive online legal research product providing legal content to law firm practitioners of various specializations. Loislaw provides attorneys with the ability to quickly and efficiently find the necessary legal information they need, when and where they need it, by facilitating access to primary law as well as state-specific law, records, forms and treatises.

ftwilliam.com offers employee benefits professionals the highest quality plan documents (retirement, welfare and non-qualified) and government forms (5500/PBGC, 1099 and IRS) software at highly competitive prices.

MediRegs products provide integrated health care compliance content and software solutions for professionals in healthcare, higher education and life sciences, including professionals in accounting, law and consulting.

Wolters Kluwer Law & Business, a division of Wolters Kluwer, is headquartered in New York. Wolters Kluwer is a market-leading global information services company focused on professionals.

Summary of Contents

Contents

CHAPTER 1

Separation of Powers and the Original Understanding of the Constitution

CHAPTER 2

Modern Separation of Powers: The Framework Cases

CHAPTER 3

War Powers in U.S. History and Practice

CHAPTER 4

National Security Law and the Use of Military Force

Contents

CHAPTER 5

National Security Law and International Law

Contents

CHAPTER 6

Criminal Process and National Security

CHAPTER 7

Intelligence Exploitation

CHAPTER 8

The Power to Detain: From the Framers to Guantanamo

Contents

CHAPTER 9

Military Commissions and the Constitution: From the Revolutionary War to the Aftermath of September 11

CHAPTER 10

Classification and Protecting Vital National Security Information

Contents

CHAPTER 11

Economic Sanctions and Terrorist Financing

CHAPTER 12

National Security Law and Emerging Technologies

Contents

CHAPTER 13

Law and Domestic Security Operations

Preface

The study of national security law is both rewarding and complex. Interest in this field has grown tremendously in the past two decades, reflected in the increasing popularity of the course in law schools and other courses of study throughout the nation. All law disciplines involve both complexity and diversity of pedagogical treatment, as no two texts or professors are the same. However, in this field, there tends to be greater diversity in the primary text used by students, and the prioritization and treatment of materials by the professor, than is commonly experienced in other disciplines of the law.

This student treatise was developed with a very clear objective: provide students with a resource to aid them in understanding what we consider the essential topics in any national security law course. We did not endeavor to produce a comprehensive national security law treatise, nor a textbook in the guise of a supplemental resource. Instead, we focused on key topics of national security law, and within each topic what we believe are the most important sources and authorities. In so doing, our goal was to provide a resource that, while certainly not perfectly synchronized with every national security law curriculum in the nation (something that is probably impossible to achieve), strikes a student-centric balance between the scope of coverage and feasibility of use to enhance the learning experience.

The diversity of the many sub-topics falling under the broad umbrella of national security law suggests to us that there is no uniform syllabus for this broad topic. However, we do believe there are common foundational topics that will almost inevitably be addressed in a national security law course. Accordingly, our text begins by addressing general national security law foundational issues, and then progresses to more specific topical issues. Each chapter, while linked by very broad themes that permeate the subject generally, is intended to stand on it's own. We believe this will facilitate the utility of the text for students who, where appropriate, may selectively utilize topical chapters. This has also led us to tailor the scope and density of each chapter to what we believe is student need, which we prioritized over any effort to provide a consistent tone through the chapters. Ultimately, our mission unifies our chapters: provide a useful resource for students.

We hope we have accomplished our mission, and that students will value the contribution our book makes to their journey through the complexities of national security law. We are especially grateful to colleagues and students who helped us in taking our mission from inception to completion, most notably James Schoettler and Dru Brenner-Beck, both of whom offered outstanding editorial assistance, and the following Research Assistants who contributed throughout the development process:

For Professor Corn: Cynthia Roholt, James "Dennis" Kan, and Raychel Johnson.

For Professor Gurulé: Sabina Danek, Michael Krzywicki, and Mitch Moximchalk.

For Professor Jensen: Grant Hodgson, Caroline Lamb, Court Roper, and Aaron Worthen.

Professor Margulies acknowledges the expert assistance of Roger Williams reference librarians Nan Balliot, Emilie Benoit, and Lucinda Harrison-Cox.

Most importantly, we thank our families and loved ones for their kindness, patience, and support.

Geoffrey Corn
Jimmy Gurulé
Eric Jensen
Peter Margulies

February 2015

National Security Law

CHAPTER 1

Separation of Powers and the Original Understanding of the Constitution

The Constitution's allocation of powers of war and peace sets up a collaboration between the executive and legislative branches. This collaborative view is not the only one. Some have argued that the President has virtually complete power. Others have stressed Congress's authority. The collaborative view, however, best fits the text of the Constitution, as well as the views of the Framers and the lessons of the Founding Era immediately following the Constitution's enactment.

I. THE FRAMERS' CONCERNS

The collaborative model stems from two main concerns of the Framers. First, the Framers were deeply wary of abuses that could occur through placing too much power in a single individual. The Framers viewed King George III of Britain as being in large part responsible for the oppression that the colonists endured before the American Revolution, and for the failure to negotiate in good faith with the colonists regarding their demands for relief from those abuses. Chief among those abuses was the imposition of taxes on the colonists without providing the colonists representation in the British Parliament. "No taxation without representation," patriots like Samuel Adams declared. Indeed, the Declaration of Independence, as written by Thomas Jefferson, was a kind of lawyer's brief proving the stubbornness of the king and the colonists' need to take extraordinary measures to safeguard their liberties. Between the issuance of the Declaration of Independence and the enactment of the Constitution, the United States had a Congress of representatives, but no head of state—no king, queen, or prime minister. This was no accident. While the privileges of monarchy were especially abhorrent to the leaders of the new republic, they also regarded *any* concentration of power in a single individual as unhealthy and unwise.

The Framers who met in Philadelphia in 1787 to draft a new constitution had another concern, however. Entrusting power to the Continental Congress had not been a successful experiment. The federal government under the Articles of Confederation, which guided the new republic before the Constitution's enactment, was weak. It had no power to require the states to obey international law, including basic international rules like the protection of diplomatic immunity. In addition, the Congress had proven ineffectual in making decisions. Many of the Framers who gathered in Philadelphia, including Alexander Hamilton, pined for the "energy" and decisiveness that a single individual wielding executive power could provide.[1] Congress would often be tempted to defer decisions, confident that the people would not be able to hold all members accountable for their failure to take action. In contrast, a single Executive would be immediately accountable for failures, whether those failures involved improvident actions or failures to act.

Moreover, the Framers, including Virginia's James Madison, were wary of granting the new Congress too much power. They were concerned that Congress would run roughshod over any single Executive and over the interests of minorities.[2] The British Parliament, which had in many ways been an equal player in the oppression of the colonists through the imposition of steep taxes, was a case in point. The abuses committed during the "Long Parliament" of seventeenth-century Britain, after the execution of King Charles I, were a reminder that legislative rule could be just as tyrannical as rule by one individual. The task, then, as Madison wisely observed in Federalist No. 51, was to make "ambition counteract ambition"—to construct the federal government so that the executive, legislative, and judicial branches had overlapping responsibilities that required accommodation but not domination by any single branch.

---

[1] THE FEDERALIST NO. 70, at 424 (Alexander Hamilton) (Clinton Rossiter ed., 1961).

[2] *See* JACK N. RAKOVE, ORIGINAL MEANINGS: POLITICS AND IDEAS IN THE MAKING OF THE CONSTITUTION 309 (1996).

II.   THE CONSTITUTION'S TEXT AND STRUCTURE

Engineering the interaction and occasional competition of the three branches was Madison's primary task. To match the legislative branch to the Framers' specifications, further overlapping and division of power was required. This resulted in the Framers' decision to create two houses of Congress—one, the "people's House," a House of Representatives to be elected every two years, and the other, a Senate, designed to be more deliberative and reflective, and therefore elected less frequently: every six years. As we shall see, that deliberative quality in the Senate also encouraged the Framers to lodge within it the power to finalize treaties with other nations that would bind the new republic in the global arena. However, the House of Representatives was not entirely shut out of the lawmaking surrounding treaties. The House would help pass legislation that was sometimes necessary to implement the new republic's treaty obligations.

The Constitution's text tracks the collaborative view, giving Congress substantial power while also granting power to the President.[3] Congress has the power to "declare" war.[4] It also has the power to issue "letters of marque and reprisal," which authorized hostilities short of outright war, legislate regarding "captures,"[5] appropriate funds for war-fighting,[6] and "make Rules for the Government and Regulation of the land and naval forces."[7] Congress can also "define and punish . . . Offences against the Law of Nations."[8] Further, Congress may enact "all Laws which shall be necessary and proper" for executing these powers.[9]

In contrast, the President's only textually enumerated role in war is Article II's designation of the President as "Commander in Chief."[10] In other words, the Constitution expressly grants more powers regarding war to Congress than it does to the President. The best inference from the text is that control over the decision to start a war lies with Congress, while control over the actual *conduct* of war lies with the President as Commander in Chief, subject to Congress's power over appropriations and whatever power Congress has to withdraw authority it has previously provided to go to war.

---

[3] HAROLD HONGJU KOH, THE NATIONAL SECURITY CONSTITUTION: SHARING POWER AFTER THE IRAN-CONTRA AFFAIR (1990).

[4] U.S. CONST. art. I, §8, cl. 11.

[5] *Id.*

[6] *Id.*, cl. 12.

[7] *Id.*, cl. 14.

[8] *Id.*, cl. 10.

[9] *Id.*, cl. 18.

[10] U.S. CONST. art. II, §2, cl. 1.

III.   THE ORIGINAL UNDERSTANDING OF THE ROLES OF CONGRESS AND THE PRESIDENT

The Constitution's text raises questions about the precise distribution of powers among the branches of government. One question concerns the President's authority to deal with sudden attacks on the United States.[11] Another question is the practical meaning of Congress's power to "declare" war. Indeed, because the text of the Constitution is not perfectly clear, the collaborative account has been challenged on both sides. Some scholars believe that the President's power over both war and foreign affairs is virtually complete, except for exceptions that we should read very narrowly. Other scholars believe that Congress is supreme, leaving the President only a modest residue of authority. These two sides also clash on the meaning of developments after the Constitution's enactment, including evidence from the so-called Founding Era that includes the presidency of George Washington. The remainder of this chapter will address each of these questions, followed by a review of the war and foreign affairs power in the Founding Era. The chapter will also briefly note the importance of individual rights as checks on government power in both the original Constitution drafted in Philadelphia in 1787, and the Bill of Rights drafted and enacted shortly afterward.

To consider exactly what the Framers intended by the phrase "declare war," and what residual powers the President might possess, we look first at the debates at the Constitutional Convention in Philadelphia in 1787, and then at ratifying conventions, where the Framers and others dispersed to individual states to argue about the document that the Philadelphia Convention had drafted.

The Constitutional Convention in Philadelphia received a draft document that granted "Executive Power" to a "President."[12] However, the draft did not specify the scope of the President's power, if any, over the decision to go to war. In an important foreshadowing of Congress's authority, the draft granted Congress the power to "make war" and approve taxes for the support of U.S. forces in armed conflicts.[13]

Because the struggle for control over taxation drove the colonists' break with Britain, debates at the Philadelphia Constitutional Convention about taxes clarify the Framers' view of war powers. Virginia governor Edmund Randolph, who had helped write the draft the delegates considered, expressly linked the taxing power with congressional input in the decision to go to war. Understanding that the ability to wage war depended on revenue to support the military, Randolph urged that spending bills originate in the "people's House"—the House of

---

[11] *See* Charles A. Lofgren, *War-Making Under the Constitution: The Original Understanding*, 81 YALE L.J. 672 (1972).

[12] RAKOVE, *supra* note 2, at 257.

[13] 2 RECORDS OF THE FEDERAL CONVENTION OF 1787, at 167-72 (Max Farrand ed., rev. ed. 1966) (hereinafter FARRAND'S RECORDS).

III. The Original Understanding of the Roles of Congress and the President

Representatives.[14] Randolph argued that the President would likely have more influence over the Senate, since Senators served six-year terms and might owe the President because of favors that the President might provide during that time. The House would owe more to the people, Randolph declared, and therefore was less susceptible to presidential influence. The Convention accordingly adopted Randolph's recommendation that all revenue bills, including those on "the means of war,"[15] should originate in the House of Representatives.

Once the allocation of power over taxation was settled, the delegates returned to the decision to go to war. The delegates on a recommendation by Madison and Elbridge Gerry of Massachusetts changed the draft Constitution's grant of power to Congress to "make war" to the power to "declare war."[16] Madison and Gerry stated that they wished to leave the President the "power to repel sudden attacks."[17] However, where the situation did not require immediate action, the delegates agreed that Congress had to authorize the use of military force. Oliver Ellsworth argued that the decision to go to war was a solemn one that should require participation by the legislative branch.[18] George Mason of Virginia, who later played a pivotal role in enacting the Bill of Rights, stated straightforwardly that he was for "clogging rather than facilitating war."[19] The delegates changed "make war" to "declare war" not to take Congress out of the decision-making process, but because they agreed with Rufus King of Massachusetts that the power to "make" war might be confused with the ability to "conduct" a war once it had started—a task that King described as a narrower tactical task and hence an "Executive function."[20] In sum, the proceedings of the Convention demonstrate that the Framers intended a collaborative model in which decisions to go to war and pay for it were made by Congress and tactical decisions about when to attack the enemy were generally the responsibility of the President as Commander in Chief. Highlighting the collaborative nature of war powers, Congress might be able to condition its consent to go to war on the President's use of limited means, especially when the conflict did not involve immediate self-defense.

The collaborative approach is also evident in remarks at the Pennsylvania convention by James Wilson, who later served as a Justice of the U.S. Supreme Court. Wilson noted the importance of avoiding European entanglements for the new republic, and reassured his colleagues that the proposed Constitution would not "hurry us into war."[21] Rather than that decision resting within a single individual's power, Wilson advised, "the important power of declaring war is vested in

---

[14] *Id.* at 279.

[15] *Id.*

[16] *Id.* at 318-19.

[17] *Id.* at 318.

[18] *Id.* at 319.

[19] *Id.*

[20] *Id.*

[21] 2 The Debates in the Several State Conventions on the Adoption of the Federal Constitution 528 (Jonathan Elliot ed., 1836) (hereinafter Elliot's Debates).

5

the legislature at large," including the house of Congress most representative of the people, the House of Representatives. According to Wilson, lodging that power in the legislature would ensure that the decision to go to war emerged not from one person's whim or quest for glory, but instead only from the gravest reasons of "national interest."

Further confirmation of the collaborative approach lies in the meaning of the other powers Congress possesses, including the power to issue "letters of marque and reprisal."[22] This power, which seems almost quaint today, originated in the ability of states of that period to authorize private individuals to attack the shipping of another nation to counter injuries to the vessels owned by their own nationals. Letters of marque and reprisal were designed to give injured parties the ability to obtain redress for such injuries. However, nations' use of such letters to aid private parties had fallen out of favor well before the Constitution's drafting. The Framers more likely wished to permit Congress to authorize military action short of outright war to deter threats by other states. The Framers' grant of this secondary power to Congress reinforces that the Framers intended that Congress be required to approve resort to outright war, should more limited measures prove ineffective.

Some have suggested that any exercise of the congressional power to "declare" war always requires the specific phrase "declare war."[23] However, the Framers almost certainly had a more pragmatic approach in mind that did not insist on particular words such as "declare." The Framers would surely have accepted language such as, "The Congress of the United States hereby authorizes the use of military force." Indeed, the custom of European nations, which the Framers knew well, had shifted away from formal declarations during the eighteenth century. The French and Indian War of the 1750s and 1760s had started in 1754 with regular and substantial uses of force in North America by both Britain and France, yet no formal declaration issued until 1756. Similarly, Britain and France did not declare war on each other as they participated on opposing sides in the American Revolution of 1775-1783. Moreover, international law scholars, such as Emmerich de Vattel, who had profoundly influenced the Framers' thought, did not believe that nations initiating armed conflict had to observe formalities.[24] Vattel took a functional view, observing that international law required only that one nation's decision to use force "be known to the state against whom it is made."[25]

---

[22] U.S. Const. art. I, §8, cl. 11; *cf.* Lofgren, *supra* note 11.

[23] *See* John Hart Ely, War and Responsibility: Constitutional Lessons of Vietnam and Its Aftermath (1993).

[24] *See* Lofgren, *supra* note 11.

[25] 3 Emmerich De Vattel, The Law of Nations or the Principles of Natural Law ch. 4, §55 (1758).

IV. PRESIDENTIAL POWER TO RESCUE U.S. CITIZENS: EARLY HISTORY

A narrow majority of sources believe that congressional authorization is unnecessary when the President acts to protect American persons or property. Jefferson sent war ships to the Mediterranean to defend American commercial vessels from seizure by the Barbary States.[26] However, Jefferson conceded that a larger offensive effort against the Barbary States required congressional authorization. In the mid-nineteenth century, a federal appellate court held that the President could act on his own to retaliate against an attack on an American diplomat stationed in Nicaragua.[27] The President, according to the court, had the power to protect the "lives [and] property" of American citizens. The President also has claimed the power to intervene in other situations involving peril to American nationals; indeed, a few years shortly before the Nicaragua episode, President Franklin Pierce used American naval power abroad to rescue Martin Koszta, a subject of Austro-Hungarian Empire, who had merely declared an *intention* of becoming a U.S. citizen.[28]

V. PRESIDENTIAL POWER AND THE VESTING CLAUSE: A BRIDGE TOO FAR?

Some scholars have gone further, arguing that the designation of the President as Commander in Chief and the Vesting Clause in Article II, which vests "executive power" in the President, confer vast power subject to only limited challenge from Congress and the courts.[29] One can read arguments by Alexander Hamilton as making this point, although Hamilton's arguments also lend themselves to a narrower reading that authorizes the President to act to preserve Congress's options. The Vesting Clause argument stems in part from John Locke's *Second Treatise on Government*, which refers to the Executive's "prerogative power."[30] According to Locke, the Executive has discretion to act for the good

---

[26] Youngstown Sheet & Tube Co. v. Sawyer, 343 U.S. 579, 642 n. 10 (1952) (Jackson, J., concurring).

[27] Durand v. Hollins, 8 F. Cas. 111, 112 (Cir. Ct. S.D.N.Y 1860).

[28] In re Neagle, 135 U.S. 1, 64 (1890); Peter Margulies, *Taking Care of Immigration Law: Presidential Stewardship, Prosecutorial Discretion, and the Separation of Powers*, 94 B.U. L. Rev. 105, 139-41 (2014).

[29] *See* John C. Yoo, *The Continuation of Politics by Other Means: The Original Understanding of War Powers*, 84 Calif. L. Rev. 167 (1996).

[30] *See* John Locke, Two Treatises of Government 393 (Peter Laslett ed., Cambridge Univ. Press 2d ed. 1970) (1690); *see also* Clement Fatovic, *Blurring the Lines: The Continuities Between Executive Power and Prerogative*, 73 Md. L. Rev. 15 (2013) (discussing prerogative power).

of the people, when the laws passed by the legislature are not clear or even when those laws forbid an act that is clearly in the public interest. In such situations, according to Locke, the wise Executive acts in the reasonable belief that the people will eventually ratify the Executive's choice. Locke's example is a decision to raze a building next to one consumed by fire to prevent the fire's spread.

VI. PRESIDENTIAL POWER AND GEORGE WASHINGTON

The Founding Era tracks a more modest view of the President's power, in which the President uses the dispatch and energy that are assets of the office to preserve the status quo and Congress's ability to decide matters of war and peace. One can view Washington's Neutrality Proclamation of 1793 in this light.[31]

The Neutrality Crisis arose because the conflict between France and Britain in the early 1790's threatened Washington's goal of keeping the United States out of European conflicts. The French Minister to the United States, Edmond Genet, argued as a legal matter that the U.S. government was obligated by its treaty of assistance with France to act as France's military ally in the struggle against Britain. Moreover, Genet tried to get U.S. citizens to flock to France's side in the conflict. Washington and his close advisor and Secretary of the Treasury, Alexander Hamilton, viewed both propositions as dangerous, since war with Britain could be ruinous for the new republic. Washington, with Hamilton's advice, issued a Neutrality Proclamation that declared that the United States was neutral in the war between Britain and France and prohibited U.S. nationals from aiding France.

Hamilton, making legal arguments for Washington, cited three provisions of the Constitution in support of the President's power to interpret treaties. First, Hamilton cited the Constitution's Take Care Clause,[32] which requires the President to take care that all the "laws," including the Constitution, statutes, and treaties, are faithfully executed. Second, Hamilton cited the President's power to receive ambassadors,[33] which arguably implied some presidential role in the formation of foreign policy, although it referred expressly only to the President's ability to welcome ambassadors from other countries or decline to receive them if

---

[31] *See* STANLEY ELKINS & ERIC MCKITRICK, THE AGE OF FEDERALISM 332-53 (1993); MICHAEL D. RAMSEY, THE CONSTITUTION'S TEXT IN FOREIGN AFFAIRS 78-80 (2007); Martin S. Flaherty, *The Story of the Neutrality Controversy: Struggling Over Presidential Power Outside the Courts, in* PRESIDENTIAL POWER STORIES 21, 44 (Christopher H. Schroeder & Curtis A. Bradley eds., 2009) (tracing history of controversy over Proclamation); *cf.* Curtis A. Bradley & Martin S. Flaherty, *Executive Power Essentialism and Foreign Affairs*, 102 MICH. L. REV. 545 (2004) (arguing against more sweeping thesis that Vesting Clause, U.S. Const. art. II, §1, cl. 1, grants President broad residual authority over foreign affairs).

[32] U.S. CONST. art. II, §3.

[33] *Id.*

the President felt it would injure U.S. foreign policy to do so.[34] Third, Hamilton cited the Vesting Clause,[35] which vests executive power in the President. The first two arguments are relatively narrow, providing support for the collaborative view of the President and Congress as working together. The third argument is potentially far broader, but was not necessary for justifying Washington's decision.

On Hamilton's view of the Take Care Clause, the President had to balance treaties, including the treaty with France, statutes, and the Constitution itself—all "laws" that the President must take care to ensure are faithfully executed. To execute a treaty, Hamilton reasoned, a President had to have some discretion in interpreting the treaty's terms. No terms are completely clear, and some U.S. official had to have the power to read the terms and say how they translated into policy. The Senate was too unwieldy a body to accomplish that task, Hamilton implied, while the President could interpret the treaty in an efficient manner that served U.S. foreign policy.[36] Hamilton's Vesting Clause argument could be read broadly as asserting a sweeping presidential power to read laws as the President wished,[37] or could be read more narrowly, as merely reflecting the same measure of discretion discussed above. Hamilton gained additional support for this position from the President's power to receive ambassadors,[38] which implies, but never states directly, that the President can refuse to receive ambassadors to express his opposition to a country's foreign policy. That power, Hamilton suggested, must also include some authority to construe the terms of treaties, and ensure that a treaty interpretation is consistent with U.S. foreign policy. Moreover, as we shall see, Hamilton asserted that Washington's reading of the treaty as not requiring U.S. military help to France also preserved Congress's constitutional prerogative to declare war.[39]

Based on these arguments, Hamilton turned to interpreting the treaty itself. He asserted that the President had the power to interpret the treaty with France to *not* require military help to France in the conflict with Britain. On its face, this interpretation was farfetched. The treaty required that the United States help France militarily upon the latter's request. The ever-creative Hamilton argued that the United States' duty to help varied according to the new republic's military might. Because the U.S. military at that time was weak, Hamilton asserted that the United States could not "assist" France in any real sense.[40] According to

---

[34] President Obama wielded this Article II power in December 2014 in declaring his intention to resume normal diplomatic relations with Cuba, including sending a U.S. ambassador to Havana and receiving a Cuban ambassador to the United States.

[35] U.S. CONST. art. II, §1, cl. 1.

[36] *See* Alexander Hamilton, *Letters of Pacificus No. 1* (June 29, 1793), *in* LETTERS OF PACIFICUS AND HELVIDIUS ON THE PROCLAMATION OF PRESIDENT WASHINGTON 5, 11-12 (1845) (hereinafter *Letters of Pacificus*), *available at* http://ia600208.us.archive.org/11/items/lettersofpacific00hami/lettersofpacific00hami.pdf.

[37] *Id.* at 11.

[38] *Id.* at 13.

[39] *Id.* at 11-12.

[40] *Letters of Pacificus No. 6, supra* note 36, at 43.

Hamilton, the United States' duty to help did not commit it to futile gestures that would embroil the country in European wars.

Hamilton argued that President Washington's treaty interpretation respected Congress's constitutional prerogative to declare war. Congress could still decide to enter the European war, Hamilton conceded. Washington's treaty interpretation permitted Congress to authorize war, if it chose. Reading the treaty to *require* military help to France would have bypassed Congress, Hamilton asserted, pushing the United States into war without congressional authorization.[41] Read in this way, Hamilton's argument for the Neutrality Proclamation actually confirms the collaborative view of congressional and executive power.

The evolution of neutrality policy also demonstrated the importance of collaboration in another way. A number of the Framers of *The Federalist* who favored presidential power, including John Jay and James Wilson, believed that the United States could base criminal prosecutions of Americans who sought to help France solely on violation of the Proclamation or international law,[42] without Congress enacting a statute expressly prohibiting such conduct. This would have posed problems both for the separation of powers and for individual rights, since neither a presidential policy declaration nor international law provide the fair warning that a statute offers. However, after a jury acquitted a defendant who had helped France, the administration quickly pivoted toward a partnership with Congress.[43] Washington worked with Congress to enact a statute that codified the Proclamation's bar on assistance to the warring European powers.[44]

While the Founding Era illustrated the limits of the President's ability to act in defiance of Congress, it also showed the power that the political branches could summon when they collaborated. The Louisiana Purchase, which greatly expanded the area of the United States, was a product of just such a collaboration. The Constitution did not expressly give Congress the power to enlarge the United States. Jefferson observed later that because the French offer was so advantageous to the United States and the time to take advantage of the offer so short, the President and Congress had no alternative but to complete a deal with the French and throw themselves on the people's mercy.[45] However, Jefferson did not suggest that the Louisiana Purchase could have been completed solely on the President's say-so. The episode confirmed the need for an executive-legislative partnership on matters of policy.

---

[41] *Letters of Pacificus No. 1, supra* note 36, at 11-12.

[42] *See* Henfield's Case, 11 F. Cas. 1099, 1103 (C.C.D. Pa. 1793) (Grand Jury Charge of Jay, C.J.); *cf. id.* at 1119-21 (Grand Jury Charge of Wilson, J.) (asserting that common law prosecution was permissible and labeling individuals who defied neutrality policy as short-sighted; by risking war, such individuals would be "destroying not only those with whom we have no hostility, but destroying each other").

[43] *See* Larry D. Kramer, The People Themselves: Popular Constitutionalism and Judicial Review 3 (2004); Robert J. Reinstein, *Executive Power and the Law of Nations in the Washington Administration*, 46 U. Rich. L. Rev. 373, 434 (2012).

[44] *See* Reinstein, *supra* note 43, at 440.

[45] Youngstown Sheet & Tube Co. v. Sawyer, 343 U.S. 579, 638 n. 5 (1952) (Jackson, J., concurring).

VII. INDIVIDUAL RIGHTS

We also know that the Framers conceived of individual rights as a way of keeping any branch of government from becoming too powerful. Individual rights constrain government's ability to silence political opponents. They supplement the restraint that the Framers built into the separation of powers.

Consider the three rights built into the original Constitution, before enactment of the Bill of Rights. The Framers in Article I, §9 of the Constitution, right after the extensive powers granted to Congress in §8, restrained the government in two key respects that we will discuss in greater depth in the chapters on detention and military commissions. First, the Framers protected access to the "Great Writ" of habeas corpus, which since the days of England's Magna Carta of 1215 had allowed individuals to go to court to seek release from unjust confinement.[46] Second, the Framers included the Ex Post Facto Clause,[47] which requires that government provide fair warning of acts that it regards as criminal. Because of the Ex Post Facto Clause, individuals must be placed on notice of conduct that can land them in jail. That clear notice gives people a fair opportunity to stay on the right side of the law. By requiring fair warning, the Framers ensured that the United States would not copy England's practice of targeting unpopular groups by passing laws to punish conduct that had already occurred. Third, the Framers in Article III preserved the right to a jury trial,[48] ensuring that individuals accused of a crime would have access to judgment by their peers, not by government bureaucrats.

The amendments to the Constitution in the Bill of Rights added even more restraints on government. The First Amendment protected speech, giving critics of government a safe haven. The Fourth Amendment barred unreasonable searches and seizures, limiting government's ability to inspect people's homes and private effects. The Fifth Amendment barred the use of coercion in interrogation, requiring the government to find evidence to support a criminal charge. The Sixth Amendment required a fair trial, and was eventually read by the Supreme Court to require access to a lawyer in criminal cases. In short, these rights constrained government, deterring officials who might otherwise have used the law to target political foes. These rights are particularly important in national security cases, where popular support for military efforts might otherwise trample on individual rights.

---

[46] U.S. Const. art. I, §9, cl. 2.
[47] Id. cl. 3.
[48] U.S. Const. art. III, §2, cl. 3.

VIII.   JUDICIAL REVIEW

Individual rights would mean little without judicial enforcement, which is another vital aspect of the separation of powers. Alexander Hamilton, in Federalist No. 78, praised the judiciary as a guardian of individual rights, with the long-term perspective to temper the political branches' tendency to sacrifice enduring values for short-term gain. The Framers took this to heart, and provided for the judicial power of the United States in Article III of the Constitution, which established a Supreme Court and required lifetime tenure for federal judges.[49] According to Article III, §2, cl. 1, federal courts' power reaches "all Cases . . . arising under this Constitution." In the landmark case of *Marbury v. Madison*,[50] the Supreme Court decided that the Constitution granted federal courts the power to determine that an Act of Congress was unconstitutional.

Chief Justice Marshall, writing for the Court in *Marbury*, asserted that judicial review was necessary to ensure that the government envisioned by the Framers remained "a government of laws, and not of men."[51] According to Marshall, the Constitution was a set of "fundamental principles" that would not change with the direction of the political winds of the day.[52] To ensure that the Constitution's principles endured, Chief Justice Marshall proclaimed that it is the "province and duty of the judicial department to say what the law is."[53] The political branches might be tempted, as Hamilton had speculated, to sacrifice constitutional principles. Federal judges, in contrast, were insulated from political pressures because of their lifetime appointments. They were thus situated ideally to engage in the independent review that Hamilton had urged in Federalist No. 78. Both individual rights guaranteed in the Constitution and the entire scheme of separation of powers required the check supplied by the judiciary's independent review. Although, as we shall see, the courts lend a measure of deference to the political branches, and also use various procedural doctrines such as standing to limit their intrusion into the political branches' prerogatives, judicial review is a central aspect in the Framers' plan. As the following chapters reveal, it plays a vital role in national security law.

---

[49] *Id.* §1.
[50] 5 U.S. 137 (1803).
[51] *Id.* at 163.
[52] *Id.* at 177.
[53] *Id.*

CHAPTER 2

Modern Separation of Powers: The Framework Cases

I. INTRODUCTION

The allocation of powers vested by the Constitution in the federal government generally, and the three branches of the government more specifically, established an essential framework for national security decision making. This framework has been substantially influenced by several crucial Supreme Court decisions. Former State Department Legal Adviser and Yale Law School dean Harold Hongju Koh characterized this amalgam of constitutional text and national security jurisprudence as a "national security constitution."[1]

In what is perhaps the Supreme Court's most ubiquitous national security related decision, *Youngstown Sheet & Tube, Co. v. Sawyer*,[2] Justice Jackson (who had served as Attorney General to President Franklin Roosevelt during a time he characterized as "transition and public anxiety") highlighted the paucity of

---

[1] *See* HAROLD HONGJU KOH, THE NATIONAL SECURITY CONSTITUTION (1990).
[2] Youngstown Sheet & Tube Co. v. Sawyer, 343 U.S. 579 (1952).

national security precedents and why national security legal questions are so inherently cryptic:

> A judge, like an executive adviser, may be surprised at the poverty of really useful and unambiguous authority applicable to concrete problems of executive power as they actually present themselves. Just what our forefathers did envision, or would have envisioned had they foreseen modern conditions, must be divined from materials almost as enigmatic as the dreams Joseph was called upon to interpret for Pharaoh. A century and a half of partisan debate and scholarly speculation yields no net result but only supplies more or less apt quotations from respected sources on each side of any question. They largely cancel each other. And court decisions are indecisive because of the judicial practice of dealing with the largest questions in the most narrow way.[3]

This paucity likely explains why the Court's infrequent decisions addressing national security related issues have assumed such profound significance in this field of government practice. However, as Justice Jackson emphasized, this influence transcends the precedential impact these decisions have on lower courts, as these decisions significantly influence legal advisors charged with advising policy makers through the complex process of national security decision making.[4]

II.   THE *STEEL SEIZURE CASE*

Of all the Court's forays into national security territory, none has been more influential than *Youngstown Sheet & Tube Co. v. Sawyer*. Known as the *Steel Seizure Case, Youngstown* arose in the context of the Korean War and in response to President Truman's executive order to seize private steel manufacturing companies in the United States. Truman's executive order directing the seizure stated that the production paralysis resulting from a labor dispute between the steel mills and their employees had caused a national emergency because of its impact on war production. Because Congress had refused to authorize industry seizure as a measure in response to such labor disputes, the President could not assert statutory authority to support the seizure. Instead, he emphasized the necessity of uninterrupted steel production to support the ongoing hostilities in Korea. He then invoked the aggregate powers inherent in his vested power as Chief Executive and Commander in Chief as the legal basis for the seizure. According to his executive order:

---

[3] *Id.* at 634-35.

[4] Koh, however, argues that in the years following *Youngstown*, courts have been remarkably tolerant of executive actions and have ruled in favor of the President excessively. Koh, *supra* note 1, at 134-49.

II. The *Steel Seizure Case*

> WHEREAS the weapons and other materials needed by our armed forces and by those joined with us in the defense of the free world are produced to a great extent in this country, and steel is an indispensable component of substantially all of such weapons and materials; and
>
> . . .
>
> WHEREAS a continuing and uninterrupted supply of steel is also indispensable to the maintenance of the economy of the United States, upon which our military strength depends; and
>
> . . .
>
> WHEREAS a work stoppage would immediately jeopardize and imperil our national defense and the defense of those joined with us in resisting aggression, and would add to the continuing danger of our soldiers, sailors, and airmen engaged in combat in the field; and
>
> WHEREAS in order to assure the continued availability of steel and steel products during the existing emergency, it is necessary that the United States take possession of and operate the plants, facilities, and other property of the said companies as hereinafter provided:
>
> NOW, THEREFORE, by virtue of the authority vested in me by the Constitution and laws of the United States, and as President of the United States and Commander in Chief of the armed forces of the United States, it is hereby ordered as follows:
>
> 1. The Secretary of Commerce is hereby authorized and directed to take possession of all or such of the plants, facilities, and other property of the companies named in the list attached hereto, or any part thereof, as he may deem necessary in the interests of national defense; and to operate or to arrange for the operation thereof and to do all things necessary for, or incidental to, such operation. . . . [5]

Thus, the precise question addressed by the Court in *Youngstown* was whether the President could, by executive order, authorize the government seizure of steel production facilities, placing them under the control of the Secretary of Commerce.

From the President's perspective, the need to ensure the continued provision of essential war materials to U.S. armed forces engaged in intense hostilities rendered the seizure both justified and necessary, even though Congress had considered granting a statutory seizure authority but had rejected doing so. For the property owners, Truman lacked legal authority to order the seizure, resulting in a deprivation of property without due process of law. Because the government could not cite any statutory authority as its legal basis for the seizure, it asked the Court to validate the seizure based on the inherent power of the President,

---

[5] 17 Fed. Reg. 3139 (Apr. 10, 1952).

derived from the aggregate of his vested constitutional authority as Chief Executive and Commander in Chief.

The narrow issue of the case—whether the President is vested with inherent constitutional authority to order the seizure of private industry to ensure continued production of a commodity necessary for satisfying government procurement needs—was obviously the central concern for the property owners. However, this issue has become somewhat of a footnote to the wider significance of the decision. It was instead the much broader constitutional analysis necessary to resolve this issue that has taken on much greater significance as a template for assessing presidential powers in the realm of national security.

Deciphering the opinion is not, however, a simple task. *Youngstown* was a multi-faceted decision, with six separate opinions. Each of these opinions approached the presidential power question at the core of the case differently. Over time, two concurring opinions, those of Justices Jackson and Frankfurter, have overshadowed the other opinions in terms of the impact on national security practice. There are, however, several threads that run through the various opinions, and these threads weave together to provide important insight into the constitutional boundaries of national security powers. It is therefore useful to consider these common connections first, and then turn to the seminal Jackson and Frankfurter concurrences.

Justice Black authored the opinion of the Court, rejecting President Truman's assertion of inherent constitutional power and striking down his seizure order. Although five other Justices joined in the judgment, none of them embraced Black's strict textualist analysis. For Black, the challenge was easily resolved by application of a simple premise: Congress, and not the President, makes law. Because the seizure order had the effect of lawmaking, the seizure order violated this constitutional allocation of power. After noting that not only was there no statute authorizing the seizure by the President—either expressly or by implication—Black then emphasized that Congress had actually rejected a proposal to provide for such authorization when it enacted the 1947 Taft-Hartley Act.[6] Black then concluded:

> Nor can the seizure order be sustained because of the several constitutional provisions that grant executive power to the President. In the framework of our Constitution, the President's power to see that the laws are faithfully executed refutes the idea that he is to be a lawmaker. The Constitution limits his functions in the lawmaking process to the recommending of laws he thinks wise and the vetoing of laws he thinks bad. And the Constitution is neither silent nor equivocal about who shall make laws which the President is to execute. The first section of the first article says that "All legislative Powers herein granted shall be vested in a Congress of the United States. . . ." After granting many powers to the Congress, Article I goes on to provide that Congress may "make all Laws which shall be necessary and proper for carrying into Execution the foregoing

[6] Labor Management Relations Act of 1947, 29 U.S.C. §§401-531 (2012).

II. The *Steel Seizure Case*

Powers, and all other Powers vested by this Constitution in the Government of the United States, or in any Department or Officer thereof."[7]

For Black, the Necessary and Proper Clause foreclosed any argument that the seizure was necessary to avert a national emergency. Congress, and not the President, is vested with the authority to make this judgment and enact law "necessary and proper" in response.

None of the five Justices who joined Black's opinion shared his strict textualist rejection of inherent presidential emergency response authority, although they all concluded that the labor dispute that triggered the seizure was insufficient to trigger this authority. Perhaps more importantly, they all seemed to agree that by rejecting the inclusion of seizure authority in the Taft-Hartley Act, Congress had by implication prohibited the President's action. Indeed, this common thread—that once Congress had exercised its constitutional lawmaking authority it had in essence "occupied the field" and foreclosed presidential action overriding Congress's judgment—is the most apparent and significant link between all the concurring opinions. However, several Justices arguably qualified even this aspect of the decision. Justice Frankfurter's opinion, for example, suggests that he might have sided with the President had the seizure been limited to a brief period of time, with an automatic expiration should Congress fail to endorse the action by statute.

The three dissenting Justices viewed the case quite differently than the majority, concluding that the seizure was actually authorized by Congress. For the dissent, the combined effect of several statutes provided the President with sufficient statutory authority to support the seizure order. Specifically, the Taft-Hartley Act, although not expressly authorizing the seizure, did direct the President to make efforts to resolve labor disputes. More importantly, other statutes required the President to provide ammunition and equipment to the armed forces. As the dissent noted, the only way the President could "take care" that these procurement laws were executed was to order seizure of the steel mills in order to resolve the labor dispute.

There is, therefore, a common thread that connects all the opinions: Had the President's order been based on a grant of statutory authority, the seizure would have been sustained. Ultimately, however, the majority of Justices concluded it was not. This reflects two important lessons of the *Youngstown* decision. First, presidential authority to respond to what he concludes is a threat to national security is always enhanced when the response is based on a valid assertion of statutory authority. Second, when Congress has asserted its authority, either expressly or by implication, characterizing an issue as one involving national security will rarely permit the President to substitute his judgment for that of Congress.

Concluding there was no statutory authority for the seizure did not, however, completely resolve the question before the Court. Instead, resolution necessitated

---

[7] *Youngstown*, 343 U.S. at 587-88.

consideration of a secondary and equally significant question: Is the President vested with inherent authority to order what would normally require some form of lawmaking, and if so what triggers that authority? Accordingly, several of the opinions provide insight into when, if ever, the President may exercise what is in essence lawmaking power to respond to a national security crisis.

Although a majority of Justices rejected the assertion of such power in this instance, skepticism over the gravity of the asserted emergency significantly influenced this aspect of the various opinions. All five Justices who joined in the Court's judgment concluded that when Congress clearly chose *not* to grant the asserted authority to the President, the Constitution did not allow for the presidential action. Furthermore, several of the Justices agreed with Justice Black that a presidential assertion of imperative necessity could not, by itself, create an implied power to respond to emergency. As Justice Jackson noted:

> The appeal, however, that we declare the existence of inherent powers *ex necessitate* to meet an emergency asks us to do what many think would be wise, although it is something the forefathers omitted. They knew what emergencies were, knew the pressures they engender for authoritative action, knew, too, how they afford a ready pretext for usurpation. We may also suspect that they suspected that emergency powers would tend to kindle emergencies . . . they made no express provision for exercise of extraordinary authority because of a crisis. I do not think we rightfully may so amend their work. . . . Their experience with emergency powers may not be irrelevant to the argument here that we should say that the Executive, of his own volition, can invest himself with undefined emergency powers.[8]

As emphasized by Justice Jackson, only Congress is vested with the authority to enact law that is "necessary and proper" to enable the nation to respond to emergency. However, with the exception of Justice Black, all of the Justices indicated that the President is constitutionally vested with some inherent emergency response authority, so long as the emergency is genuine and Congress has not foreclosed executive action by statute. Thus, for the concurring Justices, it was the exercise of lawmaking power prohibiting the President's action, coupled with skepticism about the nature of the asserted national security emergency, that was decisive. For example, Justice Clark noted:

> that where Congress has laid down specific procedures to deal with the type of crisis confronting the President, he must follow those procedures in meeting the crisis; but that in the absence of such action by Congress, the President's independent power to act depends upon the gravity of the situation confronting the nation. I cannot sustain the seizure in question because here, as in *Little v. Barreme* [concluding that a presidential order to seize enemy ships leaving French ports during the quasi war with France exceeded the seizure authority

---

[8] *Id*. at 650-51.

II. The *Steel Seizure Case*

provided by statute], Congress had prescribed methods to be followed by the President in meeting the emergency at hand.[9]

And according to Justice Burton:

> The foregoing circumstances distinguish this emergency from one in which Congress takes no action and outlines no governmental policy. In the case before us, Congress authorized a procedure which the President declined to follow . . . he issued an executive order to seize the steel properties in the face of the reserved right of Congress to adopt or reject that course as a matter of legislative policy.[10]

The nature of the asserted national security emergency seemed to be even more significant for several other Justices, who qualified their concurrences by emphasizing that if the national emergency had been of a different nature, the President may have been authorized to order the seizure. As noted above, Justice Frankfurter indicated that even in the face of a statutory restriction, had the seizure order been limited in duration, automatically expiring in the absence of congressional endorsement, he might have sided with the dissent. Similarly, Justice Burton noted that:

> This brings us to a further crucial question. Does the President, in such a situation, have inherent constitutional power to seize private property which makes congressional action in relation thereto unnecessary? We find no such power available to him *under the present circumstances*. The present situation is not comparable to that of an imminent invasion or threatened attack. We do not face the issue of what might be the President's constitutional power to meet such catastrophic situations.[11]

Like Justice Burton, context also seemed decisive for Justice Jackson, and both Justices indicated that the seizure may have been constitutionally valid had it occurred in a genuine "theater of war" (although neither sought to define this term).

Thus, taken as a whole, *Youngstown* cannot be (and has not been) understood to stand for Justice Black's restrictive textualist assessment of presidential power. Instead, the meaning is far more nuanced. First, in the absence of controlling legislation, most of the Justices indicated that the President's inherent powers do provide some authority to engage in what might best be characterized as "quasi-lawmaking." Second, while under these circumstances congressional action trumped this inherent presidential authority, it is not clear that this would always be the case. For example, a presidential exercise of authority may be constitutional, even if contrary to a statutory limitation, if genuinely linked to his vested power as Commander in Chief—an action related to the successful prosecution of a conflict and not so attenuated from prosecution of an ongoing conflict

---

[9] *Id*. at 662.
[10] *Id*. at 659.
[11] *Id*.

to render it indistinguishable from domestic lawmaking. Furthermore, presidential action in response to a genuine national emergency—as determined by a reviewing court—might withstand constitutional challenge, especially if temporary in nature, thereby demonstrating respect for Congress's lawmaking function (the conclusion derived from combining the opinions of the dissenting Justices with those of Justices Frankfurter and Burton, and Justice Jackson's cryptic reference to martial law).

Thus, there is another critical thread that runs through the entire decision: The Constitution not only limits the President's authority to contradict congressional will, but also Congress's authority to restrict presidential action. Just as the President may not usurp Congress's lawmaking function, Congress may not exercise that function to intrude upon the President's constitutional authority. This thread is reflected in the opinions critiquing the President's assertion of inherent power to seize the steel mills derived from the aggregate of his vested Article II powers. Although all but the three Justices in the dissent rejected this assertion, only Justice Black did so without qualification. Thus, assessing the scope of inherent Article II power became critical to the decision, and by implication for assessing the validity of future assertions of presidential power.

Indeed, several Justices emphasized their rejection of a narrow reading of constitutional powers vested in the President. Perhaps most notably, Justice Frankfurter emphasized that, "[t]o be sure, the content of the three authorities of government is not to be derived from an abstract analysis. The areas are partly interacting, not wholly disjointed. The Constitution is a framework for government."[12] Justice Jackson opined that, "[t]he actual art of governing under our Constitution does not and cannot conform to judicial definitions of the power of any of its branches based on isolated clauses or even single Articles torn from context."[13] Justice Clark noted, "[i]n describing this authority I care not whether one calls it 'residual,' 'inherent,' 'moral,' 'implied,' 'aggregate,' 'emergency,' or otherwise. I am of the conviction that those who have had the gratifying experience of being the President's lawyer have used one or more of these adjectives only with the utmost of sincerity and the highest of purpose."[14]

This necessarily led each of these Justices to consider whether this inherent power extended to the President's seizure order. On this question, the concurring opinions by Justices Jackson and Frankfurter have had the most significant impact on subsequent national security practice.

Justice Frankfurter began his opinion by emphasizing how a central feature of our constitutional government, the existence of checks and balances, creates complexity in resolving issues of overlapping powers:

> Before the cares of the White House were his own, President Harding is reported to have said that government after all is a very simple thing. He must have said

---

[12] *Id*. at 610.
[13] *Id*. at 635.
[14] *Id*. at 662.

that, if he said it, as a fleeting inhabitant of fairyland. The opposite is the truth. A constitutional democracy like ours is perhaps the most difficult of man's social arrangements to manage successfully. Our scheme of society is more dependent than any other form of government on knowledge and wisdom and self-discipline for the achievement of its aims. For our democracy implies the reign of reason on the most extensive scale. . . .

To that end [the Founders of our Nation] rested the structure of our central government on the system of checks and balances. For them the doctrine of separation of powers was not mere theory; it was a felt necessity.[15]

Justice Frankfurter then rejected Justice Black's textual approach to such questions. Instead, he emphasized the importance of viewing the Constitution as a framework for the exercise of government power, particularly when the power under scrutiny is not textually and exclusively committed to a specific branch of the government. Frankfurter then emphasized what he considered the critical interpretive value of past governing practice to guide the resolution of such questions. For him, the long-standing practice of inter-branch accommodation of government powers provides evidence of how the drafters of the Constitution intended those powers to be exercised. Accordingly, he indicated that:

Deeply embedded traditional ways of conducting government cannot supplant the Constitution or legislation, but they give meaning to the words of a text or supply them. . . . In short, a systematic, unbroken, executive practice, long pursued to the knowledge of the Congress and never before questioned, engaged in by Presidents who have also sworn to uphold the Constitution, making it as it were such exercise of power part of the structure of our government, may be treated as a gloss on "executive Power" vested in the President by §1 of Art. II.[16]

This theory that longstanding inter-branch practice may illuminate the true meaning of the Constitution was based on two critical considerations. First, past practice is relevant not just because it occurred, but because the political branches of the government initiating or acquiescing to the exercise of such power both shared the obligation to interpret the Constitution. Accordingly, their actions and accommodations reflect the constitutional meaning as assessed by co-equal branches. Second, assessing when historical practice provides this "gloss" on the Constitution's text necessitates exacting critique of such practice, because the issue at stake will be the meaning of the Constitution itself.[17]

Accordingly, Justice Frankfurter's "historical gloss" test contained several critical elements. First, the practice had to be "systematic, unbroken . . . [and]

---

[15] *Id.* at 593.

[16] *Id.* at 610-11.

[17] WILLIAM C. BANKS & PETER RAVEN-HANSEN, NATIONAL SECURITY LAW AND THE POWER OF THE PURSE 121-29 (1994) (describing what authors call "customary national security law"); Curtis A. Bradley & Trevor W. Morrison, *Historical Gloss and the Separation of Powers*, 126 HARV. L. REV. 411, 415 (2012) (discussing test of acquiescence).

long pursued" by the executive. Thus, isolated incidents or recent trends are insufficient to support the conclusion that a President is exercising inherent constitutional power. Review of the 13-page Appendix to Frankfurter's opinion, detailing every prior government property seizure, to include duration and source of authority, illustrates the type of demanding scrutiny Justice Frankfurter indicated was necessary when making this assessment. Second, executive practice is relevant only if Congress had notice of the practice. Absent such notice, congressional "acquiescence"[18] to the practices loses all probative value as an indication of congressional endorsement. Thus, past executive practice must establish not only that Presidents believed they were vested with certain constitutional powers, but also that Congress shared in that belief, which may be inferred only when Congress had notice of the practice. The final requirement, linked to this "notice" consideration, is absence of any indication that Congress has in the past questioned or challenged the President's exercise of the power at issue. Obviously, evidence that Congress has challenged the constitutionality of a prior presidential assertion of such authority undermines the conclusion that historical practice reflects a consensus between the political branches that the power is indeed inherent in Article II.

In *Youngstown*, Frankfurter concluded that historical practice did not support the conclusion that the President's seizure order was based on inherent constitutional authority. However, his opinion also indicates that a presidential assertion of inherent authority consistent with historical practice would make, "as it were such exercise of power part of the structure of our government, [and] may be treated as a gloss on 'executive Power' vested in the President by §1 of Art. II."

This "historic gloss" aspect of Frankfurter's concurrence holds obvious significance for both the President and Congress. From the President's perspective, a record of prior exercises of a given power, especially in the realm of national security, may be invoked to assert inherent executive authority for future action. From Congress's perspective, acquiescence to such assertions of presidential power will almost certainly increase the risk of a President repeating such assertions in the future. It will also increase the probability that a reviewing court will look to prior congressional acquiescence as evidence to support the conclusion that the power asserted is within the President's inherent Article II powers.

Like Justice Frankfurter, Justice Jackson sought to reconcile the powers of the two political branches. To achieve this goal, he divided presidential actions into three categories, based on the degree of collaboration between the President and Congress. The extent of collaboration determines the deference that a court will accord to presidential action. The President receives greatest deference for acts consistent with Congress's will, some deference for acts that occur when Congress is silent, and little or no deference for acts that clash with legislative intent.[19]

---

[18] Such acquiescence may result from legislative myopia—the fact that Congress legislates to deal with events of the immediate past, rather than the future, because that is how voters vote—bad drafting of laws, ineffective tools, or a lack of political will. KOH, *supra* note 1, at 123-33.

[19] *Youngstown*, 343 U.S. at 637.

II. The *Steel Seizure Case*

In Jackson's first category, the President acts in conjunction with an express or implied expression of legislative support. Courts will typically defer to presidential acts in this category. That deference flows from the combined democratic legitimacy and expertise signaled by collaboration between the political branches. Collaboration combines the vital ways in which the political branches are accountable to the electorate. The President has been elected by all the voters in the nation to a four-year term, prevailing over opponents in enough states to gain a majority of the votes in the Electoral College. Members of the people's house, the House of Representatives, are closest to the voters, standing for election in their districts every two years. Members of the Senate—two in each state—have the luxury of a six-year term that enables them to deliberate over the long-term risks and benefits of legislation. When public officials accountable to the voters in these three separate, constitutionally mandated ways are on the same page, a presidential act embodying this collaboration attains the maximum democratic legitimacy possible. Courts consisting of unelected judges cannot match that legitimacy.

Moreover, collaboration between the political branches signals that the President and Congress have pooled their expertise. Collaboration combines the judgment of trusted advisors and staff members, access to information from the intelligence community and the diplomatic corps, and the ability to call on outside experts in hearings and informal consultations. Courts that rely on briefs submitted by adversaries in litigation cannot match that combined expertise.

There are limits to the judicial deference triggered by democratic legitimacy and expertise in Jackson's first category. Combined action by the political branches will not pass muster if it violates individual rights guaranteed by the Constitution. For example, an attempt by the President to punish the speech of political opponents would violate the First Amendment, even if Congress approved of the President's acts. In contexts where presidential action did not threaten individual rights, however, courts will typically defer to collaboration between the President and Congress.

Jackson's second category entails presidential action taken when Congress is silent. This second category is the least definite in Jackson's analysis: He himself referred to it as a "zone of twilight." In the second category, the President cannot point to specific legislation for support. As a result, courts will not accord presidential acts in the second category the same heightened deference received by executive action in the first tier. However, as Justice Frankfurter noted, the President can gain support by pointing to a sustained pattern of congressional acquiescence in presidential action. Where Congress has notice of a presidential assertion of power, and does not object, Justice Jackson indicated a President will act to fill the void, especially in an emergency. For example, in *United States v. Midwest Oil Co.*,[20] a case cited by Justice Frankfurter, the President asserted control over federal land to shield it from exploitation by corporations seeking to drill for oil. Congress had not specifically authorized the President to protect

---

[20] 236 U.S. 459 (1915).

federal land in this way. However, Congress had been aware for some time that presidents had taken such steps. Congress had done nothing to impede such presidential action. Indeed, presidential action in this context actually helped Congress, by preserving federal land while Congress deliberated about how to balance environmental conservation and orderly development. By acting quickly, the President used the executive virtue of decisive action to preserve Congress's ability to legislate in the future. Presidential action thus contributed to a tacit collaboration with Congress that served democratic goals.

Jackson's discussion of this second category of legislative silence also reminds Congress about the importance of taking responsibility for public policy. Jackson warned Congress of the risks of inertia in times of crisis, when the President's speed and decisiveness will fill the void. According to Jackson, in such instances, "congressional inertia, indifference or quiescence may sometimes, at least as a practical matter, enable, if not invite, measures on independent presidential responsibility."[21] As Jackson noted further:

> But I have no illusion that any decision by this Court can keep power in the hands of Congress if it is not wise and timely in meeting its problems. A crisis that challenges the President equally, or perhaps primarily, challenges Congress. If not good law, there was worldly wisdom in the maxim attributed to Napoleon that "The tools belong to the man who can use them." We may say that power to legislate for emergencies belongs in the hands of Congress, but only Congress itself can prevent power from slipping through its fingers.[22]

Jackson's third category consisted of situations where the President acts contrary to the express or implied will of Congress. In these situations, the action is constitutional only when the President is able to invoke an exclusively vested Article II authority. If the action is based on such exclusive constitutional authority, separation of powers prohibits Congress from impeding the President's power. For example, imagine Congress enacts, over presidential veto, a statute dictating the use or disuse of a certain tactical measure in the course of military efforts to repel a foreign invasion. The President would be in Jackson's third category if he were to ignore the statute, as he would be acting contrary to the express will of Congress. Nonetheless, he would almost certainly assert that the statute intrudes upon his exclusive constitutional authority as Commander in Chief, and is therefore an unconstitutional assertion of congressional power.

In such situations, it will therefore be necessary to determine the express and inherent authority vested in the President by Article II. Without such a determination, it would be impossible to analyze the constitutionality of a presidential order that is inconsistent with the express or implied legislative will. This necessity is reflected in Justice Jackson's concurrence, which analyzed and rejected the President's claim of inherent authority to seize domestic industry to ensure continued

---

[21] *Youngstown*, 343 U.S. at 637.
[22] *Id.* at 654.

procurement of ammunition and supplies for the armed forces during hostilities. Once Jackson (along with the six other Justices in the plurality) concluded that Article II did not vest the President with this broad inherent authority, Truman's order could not trump a statute implicitly denying him seizure authority.

The interaction of Jackson's second and third categories can raise a question regarding the President's war powers. Suppose that past inter-branch practice, such as legislative acquiescence, is itself a form of constitutional lawmaking. If that is true, legislative acquiescence in presidential military action might *permanently* augment the President's inherent Article II power. Fortified by legislative acquiescence, a President could prevail even if Congress changed its mind; after all, a statute cannot alter the Constitution. If, however, past practice merely functions as a gap filler in the absence of contrary congressional action, then Congress should be able to alter a longstanding practice by statute, so long as it does not intrude upon an exclusive Article II presidential authority (as discussed in a subsequent chapter, this question is particularly significant in relation to war powers and the constitutionality of the War Powers Resolution).

Summing up, Justice Jackson's three-tiered executive power model turns on the degree of collaboration between the two political branches concerning issues of shared or uncertain constitutional authority. Although it emerged from a case that involved a domestic taking, this model has proved to be well suited to assessing the scope of presidential powers in the much broader national security decision-making context. It recognizes and accounts for the reality that the text of the Constitution is insufficient to resolve many questions related to presidential powers in this realm, as so many national security issues implicate powers shared by the two political branches. Perhaps more importantly, it emphasizes the immense national benefit of cooperative national security decision making while acknowledging the substantial role of Congress in limiting presidential authority.

III.   CONJUNCTION OR DISJUNCTION WITH FOREIGN AFFAIRS INTERESTS

Another important aspect of assessing the scope of presidential national security authority is the locus of the specific issue along a theoretical spectrum ranging from predominantly domestic issues to predominantly foreign affairs issues. Indeed, in *Youngstown* it was the framing of the issue—for the majority a domestic taking; for the dissent an action necessitated by a foreign affairs crisis—that contributed to the divide between the majority and dissent.

Assessing assertions of executive power that implicate inherent presidential foreign affairs authority differently than assertions of such power that implicate domestic affairs is consistent with the Constitution's allocation of powers, as indicated by several other Supreme Court decisions. Like *Youngstown*, two of these opinions are considered especially instructive when assessing the scope of presidential powers: *Curtiss-Wright Export Corporation,*[23] and *Dames & Moore v. Regan.*[24]

A.   Curtiss-Wright

In *Curtiss-Wright,* a corporation criminally prosecuted for violating a federal statute challenged the constitutionality of the delegation of lawmaking authority to the President. The law, in the form of a joint resolution, was enacted to enable the President to restrict the sale of armaments to belligerents engaged in a civil war in the Chaco region of Bolivia, and provided that:

> *Resolved by the Senate and House of Representatives of the United States of America in Congress assembled,* That if the President finds that the prohibition of the sale of arms and munitions of war in the United States to those countries now engaged in armed conflict in the Chaco may contribute to the reestablishment of peace between those countries, and if after consultation with the governments of other American Republics and with their cooperation, as well as that of such other governments as he may deem necessary, he makes proclamation to that effect, it shall be unlawful to sell, except under such limitations and exceptions as the President prescribes, any arms or munitions of war in any place in the United States to the countries now engaged in that armed conflict, or to any person, company, or association acting in the interest of either country, until otherwise ordered by the President or by Congress.
>
> Sec. 2. Whoever sells any arms or munitions of war in violation of section 1 shall, on conviction, be punished by a fine not exceeding $10,000 or by imprisonment not exceeding two years, or both.[25]

The President subsequently issued a proclamation invoking the criminal provision of the Joint Resolution.

Curtiss-Wright did not dispute Congress's authority to criminalize the sale of armaments to the belligerents. Instead, the corporation argued that the Joint Resolution unconstitutionally delegated lawmaking authority to the President by granting him the authority to decide when it was necessary to prohibit and criminally sanction such sales. Thus, much like *Youngstown,* this case involved a corporation that believed it had been deprived of the constitutionally required "process due" before the government could deprive it of a protected interest.

The Supreme Court rejected the challenge and upheld the conviction. In so doing, the Court, in an opinion authored by Justice Sutherland, indicated the significance of the foreign affairs nature of the activity Congress sought to regulate. First, the Court suggested that it would have likely agreed with Curtiss-Wright had Congress, by the Joint Resolution, proscribed conduct that primarily

---

[23] United States v. Curtiss-Wright Export Corp., 299 U.S. 304 (1936).

[24] Dames & Moore v. Regan, 453 U.S. 654 (1981).

[25] H.R.J. Res. 347, 73d Cong. (1934).

implicated a domestic issue. In such a context, the delegation may have indeed been unconstitutionally overbroad. However, as Justice Sutherland noted, the external focus of the law necessitated a fundamentally different assessment of the delegation. According to the Court:

> Whether, if the Joint Resolution had related solely to internal affairs, it would be open to the challenge that it constituted an unlawful delegation of legislative power to the Executive we find it unnecessary to determine. The whole aim of the resolution is to affect a situation entirely external to the United States and falling within the category of foreign affairs. The determination which we are called to make, therefore, is whether the Joint Resolution, as applied to that situation, is vulnerable to attack under the rule that forbids a delegation of the lawmaking power. In other words, assuming (but not deciding) that the challenged delegation, if it were confined to internal affairs, would be invalid, may it nevertheless be sustained on the ground that its exclusive aim is to afford a remedy for a hurtful condition within foreign territory?[26]

The significance of this distinction would be fully developed by the opinion, and emerge as a valuable precedent in the arsenal of inherent executive power. Adding to this value, the Court's analysis extended beyond the conclusion that the President had been authorized by statute to issue the challenged proclamation, and addressed the broader issue of the source and extent of the President's foreign affairs powers.

To support the conclusion that delegations related to foreign affairs issues should be assessed differently than those related to domestic affairs issues, the Court drew a distinction between the source and nature of executive power under Article II in these two areas. According to the Court, federal powers in the domestic realm were strictly limited to those granted to the federal government by the sovereign states. Accordingly, in this context, delegations of the lawmaking function necessitated a strict critique, for where the delegation becomes overbroad, it essentially grants the President an authority (to in effect make law) beyond that granted by the states.

In contrast, the Court noted that the President's foreign affairs powers were not limited to those granted by the states. Instead, these powers derived from the status of the nation as a sovereign member of the international community. As such, the Chief Executive, by virtue of the fact that he is the external manifestation of the nation's sovereignty, was never truly dependent on a grant from the several states that, by the Constitution, formed the "more perfect union." Instead, the foreign affairs powers of the nation and the Chief Executive devolved from the British Crown to the Colonies in their collective capacity, and subsequently to the federal government established by the Constitution. According to the Court:

> The two classes of powers are different both in respect of their origin and their nature. The broad statement that the federal government can exercise no powers except those specifically enumerated in the Constitution, and such

---

[26] *Curtiss-Wright*, 299 U.S. at 315.

implied powers as are necessary and proper to carry into effect the enumerated powers, is categorically true only in respect of our internal affairs . . . since the states severally never possessed international powers, such powers could not have been carved from the mass of state powers, but obviously were transmitted to the United States from some other source. . . .

As a result of the separation from Great Britain by the colonies, acting as a unit, the powers of external sovereignty passed from the Crown not to the colonies severally, but to the colonies in their collective and corporate capacity as the United States of America. . . . Sovereignty is never held in suspense. When, therefore, the external sovereignty of Great Britain in respect of the colonies ceased, it immediately passed to the Union.[27]

Based on this distinction, the Court then explained that sovereignty itself gave the federal government control over foreign affairs, unless the Constitution limited the extent of that control. For example, the Court explained that the federal government, by virtue of its sovereign character, possessed the inherent authority to engage in diplomatic relations, to make treaties, and to wage war. However, the Constitution placed limitations or conditions on the exercise of these powers: Treaties may be ratified only with the advice and consent of two-thirds of the Senate; Ambassadors had to be approved by the Senate; only Congress possessed the authority to declare war on behalf of the nation.

Nonetheless, the Court emphasized that in the foreign affairs realm, it is the President, as the Chief Executive of the nation, who played the predominant role in exercising national power:

Not only, as we have shown, is the federal power over external affairs . . . different from that over internal affairs, but participation in the exercise of the power is significantly limited. In this vast external realm, with its important, complicated, delicate and manifold problems, the President alone has the power to speak or listen as a representative of the nation.[28]

The inference derived from the Court's analysis is clear: Domestically, the President may exercise only powers granted in the Constitution and those additional powers provided by statutes. However, in the realm of foreign affairs—what the Court characterized as the "external" realm—the President's inherent power is much more expansive, and includes those powers necessary to protect and advance the sovereign interests of the nation within the broader international community. While the Constitution imposes some limits on these powers, the interpretive presumption is that absent an express or implied constitutional limitation on a foreign affairs power, the power is vested in the Executive. To characterize the nature of this executive power, the Court quoted a speech delivered by John Marshall while he was a congressman and prior to becoming

---

[27] *Id.* at 315-17.
[28] *Id.* at 319.

III. Conjunction or Disjunction with Foreign Affairs Interests

Chief Justice, in which Marshall noted that, "The President is the sole organ of the nation in its external relations, and its sole representative with foreign nations."[29]

This "sole organ" quotation has become perhaps the most oft cited aspect of the decision. Whether then Congressman Marshall intended the expansive meaning ascribed to his quote by the Court is debatable, as he was merely referring to the President's authority to negotiate treaties. But it seems clear that Justice Sutherland considered characterization to intend a much broader conception of inherent executive power. Proponents of expansive executive foreign affairs and national security powers routinely invoke both *Curtiss-Wright* and this reference to Marshall's speech.

Of course, for Curtiss-Wright, even this conceptual divide between domestic and external powers of the federal government did not resolve the precise issue at hand: Had Congress enacted an unconstitutionally broad delegation? But the Court's analysis set the conditions for resolution, allowing the Court to answer that question with little difficulty by emphasizing that the exercise of government authority required consideration of both the nature of the delegation and the President's inherent foreign affairs authority:

> It is important to bear in mind that we are here dealing not alone with an authority vested in the President by an exertion of legislative power, but with such an authority plus the very delicate, plenary and exclusive power of the President as the sole organ of the federal government in the field of international relations—a power which does not require as a basis for its exercise an act of Congress but which, of course, like every other governmental power, must be exercised in subordination to the applicable provisions of the Constitution. It is quite apparent that if, in the maintenance of our international relations, embarrassment—perhaps serious embarrassment—is to be avoided and success for our aims achieved, congressional legislation which is to be made effective through negotiation and inquiry within the international field must often accord to the President a degree of discretion and freedom from statutory restriction which would not be admissible were domestic affairs alone involved.[30]

This combination of congressional action with inherent executive foreign affairs authority led the Court to sustain a delegation ostensibly broader than what the Court would tolerate in relation to a purely domestic issue. The Court then bolstered its decision by emphasizing the logic for such an approach to assessing the permissible scope of legislation intended to arm the President with tools needed to deal with foreign affairs issues:

> Moreover, he [the President], not Congress, has the better opportunity of knowing the conditions which prevail in foreign countries, and especially is this true in time of war. He has his confidential sources of information. He has his agents in the form of diplomatic, consular and other officials. Secrecy in respect

---

[29] *Id.* at 319.
[30] *Id.* at 319-20.

of information gathered by them may be highly necessary, and the premature disclosure of it productive of harmful results.

Thus, the Court was influenced by an important assumption: In the realm of foreign affairs, the nature of the problems, intelligence, and diplomacy, all suggest that Congress will often find it necessary to legislate in very general terms in order to enable the President to fill gaps as situations evolve.

Congress will frequently perceive a practical benefit to granting the President relatively broad statutory authority over foreign affairs issues, providing legal and policy flexibility frequently demanded to effectively respond to such issues. Doing so does result in a certain degree of institutional risk, as it may be difficult to subsequently limit presidential action where Congress is concerned that the delegation is being stretched too far. What *Curtiss-Wright* stands for, however, is that courts will tend to defer to broad legislative delegations in the foreign affairs realm.

Curtiss-Wright, of course, raises a critical question: What distinguishes an exercise of executive (and perhaps legislative) power in the foreign affairs realm from the domestic realm? While the Court concluded that the Joint Resolution at issue in that case fell into the foreign affairs category, it provided little guidance on how to make such an assessment. Not all issues that touch on foreign affairs automatically fall into the *Curtiss-Wright* zone of executive authority. A prime example of the fallacy of such an assumption is provided by *Youngstown*, which is a reminder that an exercise of presidential power may be motivated by a foreign affairs interest, but nonetheless produce a primary domestic effect.

Indeed, *Youngstown* warrants a more restrictive reading of *Curtiss-Wright*. First, at its core, *Curtiss-Wright* merely reflects the logic of Justice Jackson's highest tier of executive power: The President acted with the express support of Congress in the form of the Joint Resolution. Second, the opinion also invoked a methodology similar to Justice Frankfurter's historic gloss, noting towards its conclusion that,

> [i]n the light of the foregoing observations, it is evident that this court should not be in haste to apply a general rule which will have the effect of condemning legislation like that under review as constituting an unlawful delegation of legislative power. The principles which justify such legislation find overwhelming support in the unbroken legislative practice which has prevailed almost from the inception of the national government to the present day.[31]

After reviewing the history of similar delegations, the Court concluded that, "[T]he uniform, long-continued and undisputed legislative practice just disclosed rests upon an admissible view of the Constitution which, even if the practice found far less support in principle than we think it does, we should not feel at liberty at this late day to disturb."[32]

---

[31] *Id.* at 322.
[32] *Id.* at 329.

III. Conjunction or Disjunction with Foreign Affairs Interests

Accordingly, *Curtiss-Wright* would not seem to support an assertion of executive authority *contrary to* the express or implied will of Congress. While this case certainly does indicate that the President is the nation's primary actor in the foreign affairs arena, it seems to provide little support for such an expansive assertion of executive authority. Indeed, Justice Jackson emphasized the limits of *Curtiss-Wright* in his *Youngstown* concurrence:

> It is in this class of cases that we find the broadest recent statements of presidential power, including those relied on here. *United States v. Curtiss-Wright Corp.*, 299 U.S. 304, involved not the question of the President's power to act without congressional authority, but the question of his right to act under and in accord with an Act of Congress. . . .
>   That case . . . recognized internal and external affairs as being in separate categories, and held that the strict limitations upon congressional delegations of power to the President over internal affairs does not apply with respect to delegations of power in external affairs. It was intimated that the President might act in external affairs without congressional authority, *but not that he might act contrary to an Act of Congress.* . . .[33]

Ultimately, the extent of executive authority derived from this important decision will turn on a range of factors, including the locus of the issue along the domestic/foreign affairs spectrum, the relationship between the presidential action and Article II authority, relative conjunction or disjunction with legislative support, and past executive practice.

B. Dames & Moore

The Supreme Court's 1981 decision in *Dames & Moore v. Regan*[34] brought together all the threads that run through both *Youngstown* and *Curtiss-Wright*. This case arose from the intersection of the Iran Hostage Crisis and the efforts of American companies to recover, through lawsuits in U.S. federal courts, losses incurred as the result of the regime change in Iran. Dames & Moore was one of these companies, and the lawsuit it pursued against Iran in the United States would ultimately require the Court to rule upon the extent to which the President's foreign affairs authority extended to nullifying domestic judicial claims.

In response to the unlawful seizure of American diplomats and workers in Iran, President Carter invoked the International Emergency Economic Powers Act (IEEPA)[35] to freeze Iranian assets in the United States. IEEPA was enacted by Congress to provide the President extensive authority to utilize economic measures to respond to international crises. President Carter, acting pursuant to

---

[33] *Youngstown*, 343 U.S. at 635 n.2 (Jackson, J., concurring).
[34] 453 U.S. 654 (1981).
[35] International Emergency Economic Powers Act, 50 U.S.C. §§1701-1707 (2011).

IEEPA, then authorized the issuance of licenses that authorized certain judicial proceedings against Iran, but not final judgments. This was later clarified to authorize pre-judgment attachments of Iranian assets by individuals or corporations seeking judicial resolution of claims against Iran. Pursuant to one such license, Dames & Moore filed a lawsuit and attached Iranian assets.

President Carter subsequently negotiated an agreement with Iran for the release of the U.S. hostages. Key provisions of that agreement required the United States to terminate all pending lawsuits against Iran, and for the two countries to establish a claims commission to adjudicate claims against Iran and Iranian assets by corporations like Dames & Moore. Specifically, the agreement provided that, "[i]t is the purpose of [the United States and Iran] . . . to terminate all litigation as between the Government of each party and the nationals of the other, and to bring about the settlement and termination of all such claims through binding arbitration."[36] President Carter then issued a series of executive orders to implement this agreement, revoking all licenses for pre-judgment attachments, thereby nullifying all previously licensed pre-judgment attachments. Soon after his inauguration, President Reagan then issued a subsequent executive order (after actual release of the hostages) ratifying President Carter's orders and essentially ordering the termination of all judicial claims against Iran in the courts of the United States.

Dames & Moore then challenged the constitutionality of both the nullification of the pre-judgment attachment and the termination of its claim against Iran, asserting the President lacked authority to nullify these property interests. When the challenges reached the Supreme Court, it presented the Court with two questions of presidential authority: Did the President have authority to terminate the attachment, and did the President have authority to terminate the claim? The Court would treat each of these exercises of executive authority as distinct, and analyze them pursuant to the *Youngstown* framework.

The Court first considered the President's authority to order nullification of the pre-judgment attachments. Concluding that IEEPA expressly authorized such actions, the Court essentially invoked Justice Jackson's highest tier of executive authority, noting that:

> Because the President's action in nullifying the attachments and ordering the transfer of the assets was taken pursuant to specific congressional authorization, it is "supported by the strongest of presumptions and the widest latitude of judicial interpretation, and the burden of persuasion would rest heavily upon any who might attack it." *Youngstown*, 343 U.S. 637 (Jackson, J., concurring). Under the circumstances of this case, we cannot say that petitioner has sustained that heavy burden. A contrary ruling would mean that the Federal Government as a whole lacked the power exercised by the President, *see id.* at 636-637, and that we are not prepared to say.[37]

[36] *Dames & Moore*, 453 U.S. 654, 665 (1981).
[37] *Id.* at 656.

III. Conjunction or Disjunction with Foreign Affairs Interests

This did not, however, resolve the question of whether the President could unilaterally settle Dames & Moore's claim against Iran, unquestionably a deprivation of a property interest.

The Court first determined that the President's claim settlement did not belong in Justice Jackson's first category, since no statute expressly or impliedly approved this practice. The Court first considered whether either IEEPA or the Hostage Act, a law enacted in 1868 to empower the President to order measures short of war to secure the release of certain U.S. citizens, authorized the nullification.[38] The Court concluded neither statute could be read as granting the President authority to nullify a court judgment. IEEPA did authorize ordering dissolution of the pre-judgment attachments in the case, but not the termination of the actual summary judgment in favor of Dames & Moore. The Hostage Act seemed a more appealing source of statutory authority, as it provided that:

> Whenever it is made known to the President that any citizen of the United States has been unjustly deprived of his liberty by or under the authority of any foreign government, it shall be the duty of the President forthwith to demand of that government the reasons of such imprisonment; and if it appears to be wrongful and in violation of the rights of American citizenship, the President shall forthwith demand the release of such citizen, and if the release so demanded is unreasonably delayed or refused, the President shall use such means, not amounting to acts of war, as he may think necessary and proper to obtain or effectuate the release; and all the facts and proceedings relative thereto shall as soon as practicable be communicated by the President to Congress.[39]

However, based on the Act's legislative history, the Court rejected an interpretation of the Act as authority for the President's Order. Instead, the Court concluded that the Congress enacted the law to address situations where foreign nations refused to recognize an assertion of U.S. citizenship. As the Court noted, "[A]lthough the Iranian hostage-taking violated international law and common decency, the hostages were not seized out of any refusal to recognize their American citizenship—they were seized precisely *because of* their American citizenship."[40] Thus, unlike the dissolution of the pre-judgment attachment, which had been authorized by IEEPA and, as a result, fell within the zone of maximum executive authority—Justice Jackson's first category—the President's settlement of private claims against Iran did not warrant the fullest measure of judicial deference.

However, the Court found that some deference was due, because the President's claims settlement fell into Justice Jackson's second category of executive action when Congress is silent. Here, *Dames & Moore* complements *Youngstown*. Unlike *Youngstown*—a case also involving a due process based challenge to a property taking—there was no indication that IEEPA or the Hostage Act impliedly

---

[38] 22 U.S.C. §1732 (2012).
[39] *Id.*
[40] *Dames & Moore*, 453 U.S. at 676-77.

prohibited the President's action. Nothing suggested Congress had considered granting the President this authority and then chosen not to do so, as was the case in *Youngstown*. Nonetheless, neither statute granted the judgment nullification authority, therefore placing the President's order in Justice Jackson's "twilight zone" of executive power—somewhere between express or implied congressional authorization or disapproval.

Three factors bolstered the finding that the President's claims settlement belonged in Justice Jackson's second category. First, the presidential action implicated a genuine foreign affairs interest. Second, the Court regarded the *absence* of an express statutory prohibition as particularly significant in the context of a foreign affairs delegation, since the Congress in cases like *Curtiss-Wright* has repeatedly given the President open-ended authority. Third, the Court cited Congress's historic acquiescence in presidential claims settlement.

On the first consideration, the Court emphasized the relationship between the executive order and the effective resolution of the international crisis created by the hostage situation. As a result, while the executive order certainly produced a "domestic" consequence for plaintiffs like Dames & Moore, it was directed primarily towards a foreign affairs interest. This seemed to be the exact opposite conclusion reflected in *Youngstown*, where every Justice in the majority considered the taking focused primarily on a domestic affairs interest, having only a secondary or peripheral foreign affairs impact. Of course, the *Youngstown* dissenters viewed the issue differently, but their view only bolsters the conclusion that this consideration may be decisive when assessing assertions of presidential power. *Dames & Moore* certainly supports this conclusion, especially when the assertion of presidential power falls within the "twilight zone."

In *Dames & Moore*, the Court concluded that the

> [f]ailure of Congress specifically to delegate authority does not, "especially . . . in the areas of foreign policy and national security," imply "congressional disapproval" of action taken by the Executive. On the contrary, the enactment of legislation closely related to the question of the President's authority in a particular case which evinces legislative intent to accord the President broad discretion may be considered to "invite" "measures on independent presidential responsibility,"[41]

Thus, the fact that Congress had provided closely related claims termination or limitation authority in IEEPA led to an inference that Congress *did not* intend to foreclose other measures to resolve claims related disputes, even though those measures were not expressly provided for in the statute. Of course, unlike *Youngstown*, IEEPA's legislative history did not indicate Congress had considered and then rejected granting the President this authority, a point emphasized in the same portion of the opinion where the Court qualified its conclusion by noting, "[t]here is no contrary indication of legislative intent."[42]

---

[41] *Id.* at 678.
[42] *Id.*

IV. Putting It All Together

Having concluded the issue was related primarily to foreign affairs and that IEEPA did not expressly or implicitly prohibit the action, the Court then applied a Frankfurter type "historic gloss" analysis to assess the extent of congressional acquiescence to this type of presidential claims termination action. This assessment resulted in the conclusion that there was indeed a longstanding practice of presidential claims settlements through executive agreements and executive orders, dating back to the presidency of John Adams. This history of presidential initiative and congressional acquiescence confirmed the existence of constitutional authority to settle claims to fulfill an important foreign affairs objective.

While this approach appears more flexible than Justice Jackson's model, the Court emphasized that when a case involves an issue of uncertain constitutional authority, implied or express congressional approval of presidential conduct remains a critical constitutional consideration. Perhaps more importantly, the Court, by emphasizing the absence of congressional opposition to the executive order, reaffirmed Justice Jackson's conclusion that the President's constitutional authority is at its lowest point where the action is contrary to the express or implied will of Congress. As the Court noted, "just as importantly, Congress has not disapproved of the action taken here. Though Congress has held hearings on the Iranian Agreement itself, Congress has not enacted legislation, or even passed a resolution, indicating its displeasure with the Agreement."

IV.   PUTTING IT ALL TOGETHER

One of the most important aspects of understanding national security law is recognizing how the analytical methodology reflected in the *Curtiss-Wright/ Youngstown/Dames & Moore* trilogy of decisions permeates national security practice. These key decisions will be referenced repeatedly throughout the remaining chapters of the text. This will reinforce the understanding of both the substance and influence of these decisions, as both these aspects will be illustrated through their contextual application. There are, however, several principles derived from these decisions.

First, although national security involves vital national interests, the exercise of government power in pursuit of national security will frequently implicate core constitutional rights of individuals, organizations, commercial entities, or sometimes even foreign interests entitled to claim some protection from the Constitution. As a result, the pursuit of national security objectives will frequently trigger constitutional friction, not only between the political branches but also between the government and the aggrieved individual or entity.

Second, the start point for assessing the legality of government national security actions must begin with an assessment of vested and implied constitutional powers. As Justice Jackson noted in *Youngstown*, and the Court affirmed in *Dames & Moore*, even where the President acts pursuant to express or implied statutory authority, the presumptive legality of his action is substantially enhanced when the action also reflects an exercise of Article II power.

Third, the presumption of constitutionality, even based on the most extensive cooperation between the political branches of government, is never conclusive. Even where Congress expressly grants the President authority to act in the realm of national security, the protections and limitations included in the Constitution remain supreme, and if government action runs afoul of these, it is unlawful. This, however, is an unusual situation for one primary reason: The increasingly significant role of national security lawyers in the policy development process mitigates (although does not eliminate) the risk that policies will progress to the point of execution when they present a serious likelihood of violating a core constitutional right.[43]

Fourth, although the President is undoubtedly the dominant actor in the field of national security, Congress is in many ways the "super-branch" of the government. Congress may empower the President to achieve objectives he would otherwise lack authority to pursue; Congress may impose limits on national security policy, or even foreclose avenues altogether, and by so doing circumscribe the President's powers to those tethered to an exclusive grant of Article II authority; Congress may leverage its mighty power of the purse to impede even the exercise of core Article II foreign affairs powers; and Congress could, in the extreme, remove the President from office. While it is rare for a division between Congress and the President to trigger such congressional action, *Youngstown* is a powerful reminder that when Congress chooses to express its will, the extent of the President's powers, even when invoked to advance a national security or foreign affairs interest, will in large measure turn on that expression.

Fifth, both Congress and the President must be acutely sensitive to the significance of historic practice. These practices, especially in the realm of foreign affairs and national security, will be relied on by future legal advisors and considered by courts as evidence of the true meaning of the distribution of constitutional authorities. However, Justice Frankfurter also reminds those engaged in this process that historical trends cannot be casually assessed. Instead, an exacting analysis is required to ensure that the contemplated exercise of power is indeed a reflection of past practice, and not merely an action sharing past motivations. The consequence of claiming authority derived from "constitutional custom" demands nothing less.

---

[43] Late Chief Justice Rehnquist commented on the *trend* towards increased scrutiny of the "least justified curtailments of civil libert[ies] in wartime," but believed that the maxim *inter arma enim silent leges* (Latin, which roughly translates to: in times of war, the laws fall silent) remains descriptive if not completely accurate. Rehnquist instead concluded that the "laws will not be silent in time of war, but they will speak with a somewhat different voice." WILLIAM H. REHNQUIST, ALL THE LAWS BUT ONE 224 (1998). *But cf.* Hamdi v. Rumsfeld, 542 U.S. 507, 579 (2004) (Justice Scalia dissenting, concludes that "[T]he view that war silences law or modulates its voice, . . . has no place in the interpretation and application of a Constitution designed precisely to confront war and, in a manner that accords with democratic principles, to accommodate it.")

IV. Putting It All Together

Sixth, national security challenges, especially in the realm of foreign affairs, are difficult to predict and even more difficult to address through precise "anticipatory" legislation. Accordingly, Congress will have more flexibility in framing national security delegations than it will when dealing with purely domestic issues.

Seventh, the nature of national security and foreign affairs challenges will often demand presidential initiative, in situations where the will of Congress is frequently unclear or unexpressed. As Justice Jackson noted, it is the inevitable function of the Chief Executive to fill the power vacuum. When so doing, his powers will be bolstered by several factors: first, past practice of a similar nature; second, closely related legislation "inviting" him to fill the void; and third, the locus of the issue along the domestic/foreign affairs interest spectrum. While uncertainty is inherent in this "twilight zone" of presidential initiative, it seems clear that, especially in relation to foreign affairs issues, congressional silence or acquiescence will indeed "invite" presidential initiatives.

Finally, perhaps the most important principle to take from this trilogy of decisions is that our government, and by implication our national security, is always strongest when the two political branches manifest their close cooperation. The intersecting powers vested in each branch by the Constitution certainly create a risk of inter-branch friction, but they also create the opportunity for the nation to wield a powerful proverbial fist. The tighter the fist, the stronger the punch.

CHAPTER 3

War Powers in U.S. History and Practice

There is perhaps no aspect of national security where the Framers' vision of constitutional checks and balances is better manifested than over questions of war. Every aspect of war-making decisions—why, when, where, how, for how long, and with what means the nation utilizes its military power—implicates vested and inherent powers of the two political branches of government, and may lead to involvement of the judicial branch. Over time, a complex mosaic of textual authority, longstanding practice, inter-branch assertions of power, and judicial opinions have provided a practical, if not legal, framework for assessing the constitutionality of war powers. Looming above all these authorities is the War Powers Resolution: a statutory effort to clarify how these questions must be resolved in the modern era.[1] In spite of the best intentions of the Congress that enacted the War Powers Resolution over President Nixon's veto, it has not resolved these questions, and arguably has produced even more confusion.

I. OVERLAPPING POWERS OF CONGRESS AND THE PRESIDENT

As discussed in Chapter 1, the war powers of Congress and the President overlap. Article I of the U.S. Constitution vests Congress with an array of powers that have both direct and peripheral effects on war authorization, making, and sustainment. These include the power to declare war; control over, raise, and support armies;[2] provide for a navy;[3] make laws for calling forth the state militia to federal service;[4] make rules for the land and naval forces;[5] and make rules for captures on the land and sea.[6] In addition, Article I grants Congress power to raise money for the federal government[7] and decide how that money should be appropriated in support of different federal and state functions,[8] and make all laws that are necessary and proper for executing the powers of the government (to include those of the two coordinate branches).[9]

The war related powers vested in the President by Article II are less comprehensive than those in Article I, but also significant. The President is the Commander in Chief of the national armed forces, and of the militia when called into service of the nation.[10] In addition, the President is the

---

[1] War Powers Resolution, Pub. L. No. 93-148, 87 Stat. 555 (1973) (codified at 50 U.S.C. §§1541-1548 (2000)).

[2] U.S. Const. art. I, §8, cl. 12.

[3] U.S. Const. art. I, §8, cl. 13.

[4] U.S. Const. art. I, §8, cl. 15.

[5] U.S. Const. art. I, §8, cl. 14.

[6] U.S. Const. art. I, §8, cl. 11.

[7] U.S. Const. art. I, §8, cl. 1.

[8] U.S. Const. art. I, §8, cl. 7.

[9] U.S. Const. art. I, §8, cl. 18.

[10] U.S. Const. art. II, §2, cl. 1. ("The President shall be Commander in Chief of the Army and Navy of the United States, and of the Militia of the several States, when called into the actual Service of the United States; he may require the Opinion, in writing, of the principal Officer in each of the

I. Overlapping Powers of Congress and the President

Chief Executive,[11] bears an obligation to "take care that the laws be faithfully executed,"[12] appoints ambassadors and makes treaties, and appoints officers of the nation (to include officers of the armed forces).[13]

From the inception of the nation the two political branches have struggled to define their respective powers over war.[14] Assessing the interaction of these interrelated authorities is the great challenge of war powers analysis.[15] Surveying the boundaries of each branch's constitutional authority has never been as simple as adding up the respected war power related provisions on a ledger sheet, or engaging in a strict textualist analysis. Instead, Justice Jackson insightfully noted in his *Youngstown* concurrence the extent that presidential national security powers—which by implication includes war powers—fluctuate depending on the degree of conjunction or disjunction with congressional action.[16] In practice, from the Founding Era to the present, the paradigm has been functional rather than textual, stressing the institutional strengths of each branch.

The complexity of determining the limits of constitutional war powers is exacerbated by the fact that both the contemporary nature of military operations and the legal concept of "war" are radically different from those the Framers were

---

executive Departments, upon any Subject relating to the Duties of their respective Offices, and he shall have Power to grant Reprieves and Pardons for Offences against the United States, except in Cases of Impeachment.").

[11] U.S. CONST. art. II, §1, cl. 1.

[12] U.S. CONST. art. II, §3, cl. 5.

[13] U.S. CONST. art. I, §1, cl. 8.

[14]

> The open, politically contestable allocation of war powers under the Constitution not only permits differing and perhaps conflicting interpretations of the legal demarcations of branch authority but also accommodates differing normative preferences for determining which values and which branches are best-suited for war-making. Furthermore, this system adapts over time in response to inter-branch dynamics and shifting value judgments that are themselves politically contingent. Thus, the American war powers model is an intrinsically political—not legal—process for adjusting and managing the different institutional capabilities of the legislative and executive branches to substantiate and reconcile accountability and efficiency concerns.

David Jenkins, *Judicial Review Under British War Powers Act*, 45 VAND. J. TRANSNAT'L L. 611, 617-18 (May 2010); *see also* David Jenkins, *Efficiency and Accountability in War Powers Reform*, 14 J. CONFLICT & SECURITY L. 145, 150-53 (2009) (discussing different interpretative approaches to the Constitution's distribution of war powers); *see, e.g.*, EDWARD CORWIN, THE PRESIDENT: OFFICE AND POWERS, 1787-1984, 201 (1984) (describing authority under the constitution as a struggle between the President and Congress); David Barron & Martin Lederman, *The Commander in Chief at the Lowest Ebb—Framing the Problem, Doctrine and Original Understanding*, 121 HARV. L. REV. 689 (2008) (discussing the congressionalist approach); Jide Nzelibe & John Yoo, *Rational War and Constitutional Design*, 115 YALE L.J. 2512 (2006) (discussing the presidentialist approach).

[15] Saikrishna Prakash, *The Separation and Overlap of War and Military Powers*, 87 TEX. L. REV. 299, 306-08 (2008).

[16] Youngstown Sheet & Tube Co. v. Sawyer, 343 U.S. 579, 635-38 (1952).

familiar with and ostensibly contemplated. Starting with the Pact of Paris in 1928[17] (which prohibited states from using war as a means to resolve disputes) and culminating with the Charter of the United Nations (UN) in 1945[18] (which prohibited aggression by one state against the sovereignty or political independence of any other states and limits use of military force to situations of self-defense, collective self-defense, or actions authorized by the Security Council to enforce international law), war has become an obsolete legal concept. Unfortunately, armed hostilities between states or between states and organized non-state belligerent groups have not. As a practical matter, the United States since 1945 has used, and will almost certainly continue to use, its military power to conduct operations involving armed hostilities—what most laymen would call "wars." The fact that such operations are no longer characterized formally as "wars" within the meaning of international law calls into question the relevancy of the Constitution's vesting of the authority to declare war in Congress.

The evolution of armed conflict has also had an effect on the third branch of government: the courts. Because judicial decisions, or in some cases judicial abstention based on justiciability concerns, affect the exercise of war powers, it is useful to first consider the judicial role in war powers decisions.

II. ROLE OF THE JUDICIARY

Federal courts are reluctant to intervene in constitutional war powers conflicts. That reluctance, however, is not absolute. While it is true that courts have routinely invoked doctrines of judicial restraint to dismiss such cases,[19] they have also indicated that, if presented with the right set of facts, they would reach the merits of a war powers dispute.[20] Doctrines of judicial restraint influence both the

---

[17] General Treaty for Renunciation of War as an Instrument of National Policy, Aug. 27, 1928, 46 Stat. 2343 (commonly known as the Kellogg-Briand Pact, named after its two main authors, United States Secretary of State Frank B. Kellogg and French foreign minister Aristide Briand).

[18] This is the foundational treaty of the United Nations. As a charter, it binds all United Nations members by its articles.

[19] *See, e.g.,* Luftig v. McNamara, 373 F.2d 664 (D.C. Cir.) (dismissing suit by soldier who refused to obey orders on political question grounds), *cert. denied*, 387 U.S. 945 (1967); Davi v. Laird, 318 F. Supp. 478 (W.D. Va. 1970) (holding that determination of validity of Vietnam War was political question); United States v. Sisson, 294 F. Supp. 511 (D. Mass. 1968) (ruling that, although government did not formally declare war, draft notice must be honored); Velvel v. Johnson, 287 F. Supp. 846 (D. Kan. 1968) (dismissing suit against President for entering undeclared war), *aff'd sub nom.* Velvel v. Nixon, 415 F.2d 236 (10th Cir. 1969), *cert. denied*, 396 U.S. 1042 (1970).

[20] One case in particular suggests that the courts will be far more likely to intervene to resolve a fully ripe dispute between the Congress and the President on the issue of war power than they are to issue a ruling that crystallizes such a dispute. In *Crockett v. Reagan*, a federal court was again asked by members of Congress to determine whether the War Powers Resolution was

II. Role of the Judiciary

President and Congress when they assess the scope of authority in relation to war powers decisions. Furthermore, cases addressing war powers challenges during the Vietnam conflict provide essential background to understanding the goals and content of the 1973 War Powers Resolution.

In assessing the justiciability of a case involving war powers, it is essential to consider the different contexts in which this issue might be presented to a court. As a general proposition, these challenges will usually involve a separation of powers argument contesting the constitutionality of a presidential decision to initiate hostilities or prolong ongoing hostilities.[21] While there are exceptions to this general rule (for example, where a litigant might invoke international law to challenge the legality of a congressional war authorization), this is the most likely scenario a court will face. What becomes far more significant than the challenging subject matter is *who* is presenting the challenge. Again, as a general rule, these challenges will most likely originate from one of three groups asserting harm resulting from the exercise of war powers. First, a member or members of Congress may seek declaratory or injunctive relief to prevent the President from exercising war powers based on an asserted deviation from constitutional or statutory authorization requirements.[22] Second, a service member may challenge the

---

triggered by a relatively minor United States military operation that involved the dispatch of 56 military advisors to El Salvador. *Crockett v. Reagan*, 558 F. Supp. 893 (D.D.C. 1982) per curiam, *Crockett v. Reagan*, 720 F.2d 1355 (D.C. Cir. 1983), *cert. denied*, 467 U.S. 1251 (1984). The court concluded "that the fact-finding that would be necessary to determine whether U.S. forces have been introduced into hostilities or imminent hostilities in El Salvador renders this case in its current posture non-justiciable." *Id.* at 898. The court held that this issue was more appropriate for congressional, not judicial, investigation and determination. *Id.* The court did, however, distinguish two other situations where it suggested that a similar case would be justiciable. First, it indicated that if asked to determine whether a commitment of forces on a scale similar to that in Vietnam triggered the War Powers Resolution, "it would be absurd for [the court] to decline to find that U.S. forces had been introduced into hostilities after 50,000 American lives had been lost." *Id.* Second, and perhaps more significantly for the proposition that a clear and ripe dispute between the branches would be justiciable, the court stated that: If Congress doubts or disagrees with the Executive's determination that U.S. forces in El Salvador have not been introduced into hostilities or imminent hostilities, it has the resources to investigate the matter and assert its wishes. . . .

Geoffrey S. Corn, *Presidential War Power: Do the Courts Offer Any Answers?*, 157 MIL. L. REV. 180, 255 n.51 (1998).

[21] *See, e.g.*, Holtzman v. Schlesinger, 484 F.2d 1307 (2d Cir. 1973); Olrand v. Laird, 443 F.2d 1039 (1971); Berk v. Laird, 429 F.2d 302 (1970); Dellums v. Bush, 752 F. Supp. 1141 (1990); Campbell v. Clinton, 203 F.3d 19 (2000); Kucinich v. Obama, 821 F. Supp. 2d 110 (2011).

[22]
When a member of Congress is a plaintiff in a lawsuit, concern about separation of powers counsels judicial restraint even where a private plaintiff may be entitled to relief. Where the plaintiff's dispute appears to be primarily with his fellow legislators, judges are presented not with a chance to mediate between two political branches but rather with the possibility of thwarting Congress's will by allowing a plaintiff to circumvent the process of democratic decisionmaking.

Holtzman v. Schlesinger, 484 F.2d 1307 (2d Cir. 1973); *see also Crockett*, 558 F. Supp. at 902 (citing Riegle v. Fed. Open Mkt. Comm., 656 F.2d 873 (D.C. Cir. 1981)).

legality of military orders to deploy to an area of hostilities based on the same asserted violation of constitutional or statutory war authorization requirements.[23] Finally, an individual with an interest in property negatively impacted by ongoing or anticipated hostilities may seek a judicial order prohibiting the exercise of war powers in order to prevent an arbitrary deprivation of that property.[24]

Each of these hypothetical challenges implicates doctrines of judicial restraint: those of political question, standing, and ripeness. Because courts have routinely invoked these doctrines in war powers related litigation, these challenges rarely proceed to a merits-based decision. However, it is error to assume that this type of challenge could never be decided based on the merits. Ultimately, the form in which the case is presented will dictate justiciability. While it may be unlikely for a case to arise with a factual situation sufficient to overcome each of these justiciability barriers, it is not inconceivable, as has been emphasized in dicta by the Supreme Court and lower courts in dismissed cases where these barriers were insurmountable.

A. Political Question

The first justiciability doctrine, almost automatically, implicated by a war powers–related challenge is the political question doctrine. This doctrine is based on separation of powers and judicial respect for the vested authority of the coordinate political branches of the government. Where a case requires courts to interfere in an inherently political issue—understood as an issue whose resolution is, by function of the Constitution, properly left to the political branches—judicial restraint demands that courts leave the issue to the political branches for resolution.

In its groundbreaking political question opinion *Baker v. Carr*,[25] the Supreme Court articulated a number of situations that fall within the scope of the political question doctrine. The two most relevant in the context of war powers litigation are:

1. Where an issue is textually and exclusively vested in a coordinate branch of government[26] (for example, the authority to appoint Ambassadors, vested by Article II in the Executive, would be immune from judicial scrutiny based on this prong of the doctrine[27]).

---

[23] Orlando v. Laird, 443 F.2d 1039 (2d Cir. 1971).

[24] El-Shifa Pharm. Indus. v. United States, 378 F.3d 1346 (Fed. Cir. 2004).

[25] 369 U.S. 186 (1962).

[26] "Prominent on the surface of any case held to involve a political question is found a textually demonstrable constitutional commitment of the issue to a coordinate political department." *Id.* at 217.

[27] U.S. Const. art. II, §2, cl. 2.

II. Role of the Judiciary

    2. Where an issue involves a lack of judicially discoverable and manageable standards[28] (for example, whether President Bush's decision to order a "surge" of military forces in Iraq qualified as a tactical reinforcement of ongoing hostilities or the first step towards expanding the conflict into Iran would likely be immune from judicial scrutiny because a court would be unable to discover standards to make this determination).

In the past, courts have invoked both of these categories of political question to dismiss war powers–related litigation. However, each of these categories requires very precise analysis.

    In seeking dismissal, the government will almost always assert that the decision to engage in hostilities is textually committed to the President as Commander in Chief.[29] During the Vietnam Conflict and the first Gulf War, courts explained that this assertion is constitutionally overbroad. Nonetheless, this "textual commitment" prong was routinely invoked to dismiss such challenges. This was not, however, based on the conclusion that the President is vested with unilateral authority to initiate hostilities. Instead, courts that addressed this question emphasized that the Constitution demands some evidence of cooperation between the two political branches in relation to such decisions.[30] It was evidence of such cooperation, however, that produced the political question dismissal.[31] Thus, these courts applied the "textual commitment" prong of the doctrine to questions textually committed to the *mutual* judgment of the two political branches—the sine qua non of war questions.

    To understand this permutation of the political question doctrine, it is essential to recognize that assessing whether such inter-branch cooperation has in fact occurred is not a political question, but one subject to judicial analysis. This is based on the textual allocation of constitutional war powers to *both* political branches, indicating that the Constitution requires cooperation between the

---

[28] "Prominent on the surface of any case held to involve a political question is . . . a lack of judicially discoverable and manageable standards for resolving it." *Baker*, 369 U.S. at 217.

[29] This assertion was made primarily during the Vietnam Conflict. *See, e.g., Holtzman*, 484 F.2d at 1308-09; DaCosta v. Laird, 471 F.2d 1146, 1147 (2d Cir. 1973); Massachusetts v. Laird, 451 F.2d 26, 28-29 (1st Cir. 1971); *Orlando*, 443 F.2d at 1041; Berk v. Laird, 429 F.2d 302, 304-05 (2d Cir. 1970); Atlee v. Laird, 347 F. Supp. 689, 691 (E.D. Pa. 1972), *aff'd sub nom.* Atlee v. Richardson, 411 U.S. 911 (1973); Mottola v. Nixon, 318 F. Supp. 538, 539-40 (N.D. Cal. 1970), *rev'd on other grounds*, Mottola v. Nixon, 464 F.2d 178 (9th Cir. 1972); Michael Ratner & David Cole, *The Force of Law: Judicial Enforcement of the War Powers Resolution*, 17 Loy. L.A. L. Rev. 715, 727 (1984).

[30] Geoffrey S. Corn, *Clinton, Kosovo, and the Final Destruction of the War Powers Resolution*, 42 Wm. & Mary L. Rev. 1149, 1168-69 (2001).

[31] *Orlando*, 443 F.2d 1039. ("We held in the first *Berk* opinion that the constitutional delegation of the war-declaring power to the Congress contains a discoverable and manageable standard imposing on the Congress a duty of mutual participation in the prosecution of war. Judicial scrutiny of that duty, therefore, is not foreclosed by the political question doctrine.").

President and Congress in relation to the decision to initiate and wage war. As one Vietnam era decision explained:

> As to the power to conduct undeclared hostilities beyond emergency defense, then, we are inclined to believe that the Constitution, in giving some essential powers to Congress and others to the executive, committed the matter to both branches, whose joint concord precludes the judiciary from measuring a specific executive action against any specific clause in isolation. . . . In arriving at this conclusion we are aware that while we have addressed the problem of justiciability in the light of textual commitment criterion, we have also addressed the merits of the constitutional issue.

Massachusetts v. Laird, 451 F.2d at 33.

Once evidence of this cooperation is presented, however, the judicial inquiry terminates, and the *manner* of mutual cooperation between the two political branches to authorize or support hostilities is the non-justiciable political question,[32] barring litigants from demanding—and the court from requiring—any particular modality to satisfy this constitutional mutual cooperation requirement (for example, a judicial decision requiring Congress to authorize hostilities by declaring war).

It must be noted that there could be other types of war powers issues falling within the exclusive power of the President, and therefore falling into the textual commitment prong of the political question doctrine. These would include almost all tactical decisions related to ongoing or anticipated hostilities since such decisions are quintessentially within the Commander in Chief power. The President's decision to respond to an actual or imminent threat of aggression against the United States or citizens abroad would also likely fall into this category based on a legitimate claim of inherent executive "defensive" war power (discussed in detail below). Closely related to this power would be a presidential decision to initiate a military operation to rescue U.S. nationals abroad. Because all of these issues fall within the exclusive authority of the President, they would likely be immune from judicial scrutiny pursuant to the political question doctrine.

---

[32]
"Beyond determining that there has been *some* mutual participation between the Congress and the President, which unquestionably exists here, with action by the Congress sufficient to authorize or ratify the military activity at issue, it is clear that the constitutional propriety of the means by which Congress has chosen to ratify and approve the protracted military operations in Southeast Asia is a political question. The form which congressional authorization should take is one of policy, committed to the discretion of the Congress and outside the power and competency of the judiciary, because there are no intelligible and objectively manageable standards by which to judge such actions."

Id. at 1043.

II. Role of the Judiciary

B. *Ripeness*

The ripeness doctrine was established early in our nation's history by the Supreme Court to enforce the constitutional "case or controversy" requirement as a precondition for an exercise of federal court jurisdiction.[33] Federal courts will not provide advisory opinions,[34] and as a result issues presented to them must involve a ripe dispute and not one that is still hypothetical.[35] This will not normally be an impediment to a service member or aggrieved property owner seeking judicial intervention in relation to ongoing hostilities, or even imminent hostilities. However, when members of Congress, or the public in general, seek to challenge the anticipated action by the President to initiate hostilities, ripeness may be a major obstacle to justiciability.

Legislative plaintiffs bear the burden of establishing that the President and Congress have reached what some courts have labeled a "constitutional loggerhead."[36] Unless and until a situation reaches this point of political impasse, courts will be extremely reluctant to intervene, but instead will allow the political process to continue.[37] As a practical matter, this will almost always necessitate an affirmative legislative vote to authorize or prohibit the anticipated military action. Absent such a vote, it is difficult to establish the requisite constitutional loggerhead. The War Powers Resolution (discussed in detail below) may provide an alternate statutory basis for establishing a ripe dispute, as it prohibits initiation of hostilities (or even introduction of U.S. forces into a situation of imminent hostilities) absent express statutory authority or in response to an attack on the United States or our armed forces.[38] To date, however, no court has seemed willing to treat this provision of the WPR as providing a sufficient basis for

---

[33] The Supreme Court established four criteria for determining if a claim satisfies the case or controversy requirement: (1) the dispute must be " 'definite and concrete' "; (2) the dispute must touch " 'the legal relations of parties having adverse legal interests' "; (3) the dispute must "be 'real and substantial,' " which in the declaratory judgment context would mean the controversy was " 'of sufficient immediacy and reality to warrant the issuance of a declaratory judgment' "; and (4) the dispute must " 'admi[t] of specific relief through a decree of a conclusive character, as distinguished from an opinion advising what the law would be upon a hypothetical set of facts.' " *See generally* MedImmune, Inc. v. Genentech, Inc., 549 U.S. 118 (2007).

[34] *See* Vt. Agency of Natural Res. v. United States ex rel. Stevens, 529 U.S. 765, 774 (2000) (quoting Steel Co. v. Citizens for Better Env't, 523 U.S. 83, 102 (1998)).

[35] *MedImmune,* 549 U.S. at 127.

[36] Resolution of this loggerhead would require the judiciary to decide a constitutional interpretation. Dellums v. Bush, 752 F. Supp. 1141 (D.D.C. 1990). *See* Marbury v. Madison, 5 U.S. (1 Cranch) 137, 177 (1803) (holding that it is "emphatically the province and the duty of the judicial department to say what the law is").

[37] The inference drawn from this opinion is that, when the conduct of the President contradicts the express will of Congress on a war power issue, it is the proper role of the judiciary to "mediate between the two political branches." *Crockett,* 558 F. Supp. at 902 (citing *Riegle,* 656 F.2d at 881).

[38] Standing questions "whether the litigant is entitled to have the court decide the merits of the dispute or of particular issues." Warth v. Seldin, 422 U.S. 490, 498 (1975)

satisfying the ripeness requirement in relation to a legislative lawsuit against the President.

Ripeness also requires that the challenged military action be either ongoing or imminent.[39] Speculating as to what the President might do in the future is unlikely to overcome a ripeness challenge.[40] However, this does not necessarily mean that the military action must have already been initiated. If the objective facts, including the statements of the President and other executive branch officials, indicate a high probability that military action will be ordered, the courts will likely consider the action imminent, therefore presenting a ripe issue. Ultimately, however, this will be a fact-intensive inquiry.

C.   Standing

Standing is another element of the case and controversy requirement, and requires the party seeking judicial relief to establish that he or she has suffered an injury in fact, traceable to the conduct of the defendant, subject to judicial remedy.[41] A lack of standing requires dismissal of a lawsuit,[42] and when the issue is the legality of a presidential war-making initiative, the plaintiff must meet this test. This will normally not be difficult for a service member plaintiff, as the source of potential injury in fact are the orders issued by the President through the chain of command directing the service member to deploy to combat.

Standing is, however, a major obstacle for legislators who seek a judicial remedy to what they assert is an unconstitutional exercise of presidential war powers. These litigants must establish legislative standing, which requires much more than an assertion of *ultra vires* executive action. In *Raines v. Byrd*, the Supreme Court established the test for legislative standing: The legislative plaintiff must establish that the challenged executive action "completely nullified" their vote in Congress.[43] This is a daunting test, and is intended to prevent courts from interfering in political battles between Congress and the President before Congress has taken a firm position on the issue and the President has in fact ignored, or has indicated an intent to ignore, this position.

In the context of war powers, legislative standing appears to require enactment of a statute prohibiting military action, or perhaps an affirmative vote against authorizing such action, followed by a presidential decision to ignore

---

[39] *Dellums*, 752 F. Supp. at 1151-52. The court found that the claim brought by the plaintiffs lacked ripeness and judicial interference was not necessary because the President had not yet committed to imminent military action.

[40] "[A] claim is not ripe for adjudication if it rests upon contingent future events that may not occur as anticipated, or indeed may not occur at all." *See* Texas v. United States, 523 U.S. 296, 300 (1998) (citing Thomas v. Union Carbide Agric. Prods. Co., 473 U.S. 568, 581 (1985)).

[41] Lujan v. Defenders of Wildlife, 504 U.S. 555, 560-61 (1992).

[42] U.S. Const. art III, §2.

[43] 521 U.S. 811, 823 (1997). This is known as a "*Coleman* exception." *See* Coleman v. Miller, 307 U.S. 433, 438 (1939).

the express will of Congress.[44] Unless such clearly crystalized positions exist, it is unlikely a legislative plaintiff can establish the President has completely nullified her vote. In this regard, it is important to note that this "complete nullification" test will not be satisfied when the legislative plaintiff loses a vote to prohibit presidential action.[45] In such a situation, the standing doctrine prevents a court from in effect awarding a victory to a legislator who was unable to secure the necessary votes to prevent presidential action.

Because of this complete nullification requirement, legislative standing is closely related to the ripeness doctrine. Pursuant to either principle of judicial restraint, an affirmative vote against the challenged presidential initiative is a necessary predicate to jurisdiction, either to establish the requisite constitutional loggerhead to create a ripe dispute, or to meet the "complete nullification" requirement of legislative standing. Furthermore, because (as is explained below) courts may treat Congress's decision to refrain from voting to authorize or prohibit a presidential war powers action as a type of congressional "silence," this exercise of legislative war authorization prerogative also implicates the political question doctrine. This is because the manner in which Congress chooses to manifest its support for the President—whether through express statutory authorization or alternatively by implication (from funding coupled with the decision not to challenge the initiative)—will likely be treated as a decision textually committed to Congress. In short, absent express congressional action to prohibit or halt a presidential war powers action, a legislator challenge will likely fail to overcome any of these three doctrines of judicial restraint.

III. AUTHORIZING WAR

What the Constitution requires for war to be properly authorized has been a recurring question since the inception of the nation, and it is a question further complicated by the changing international legal environment on war itself.[46] It is unlikely that the uncertainty of this question will be categorically resolved in the future. However, certain touchstones of constitutionality have emerged over time.

---

[44] "Certainly, were Congress to pass a resolution to the effect that a report was required under the [War Powers Resolution], or to the effect that the forces should be withdrawn, and the President disregarded it, a constitutional impasse appropriate for judicial resolution would be presented." *See* Goldwater v. Carter, 444 U.S. 996 (1979) (Powell, J., concurring).

[45] *See Raines*, 521 U.S. at 825 (the Court states that legislative standing requires "vote nullification," which is greater than an "abstract dilution of institutional legislative power").

[46] *See* Prakash, *supra* note 15, at 386 n.1.

A.   Perfect and Imperfect War

Early in the nation's history, the Supreme Court addressed Congress's power to both authorize and limit hostilities. In several cases challenging the allocation of prize awards resulting from the seizure of commercial shipping during hostilities with France, plaintiffs alleged that France could not be the enemy of the nation because Congress had not declared war.

In *Bas v. Tingy*,[47] the Supreme Court disagreed with this assertion. To determine whether France qualified as an "enemy" for purposes of statutes authorizing prize awards, the Court noted that Congress had authorized limited hostilities against France by statute.[48] The Court distinguished what it characterized as "perfect" from "imperfect" war. To legally "perfect" a state of hostilities—create a "perfect" war—required a declaration of war, which would place the entire nation on a full-scale war footing against the enemy nation.[49] However, the war authorization power vested in Congress was interpreted to include the power to authorize more limited, or "imperfect," war.[50] The Court noted that Congress has an obvious interest in tailoring the scope of war authorization to meet the necessities of the situation, and that this included the authority to limit war in terms of objectives, location, and duration.[51]

Bas v. Tingy, and the Court's subsequent decision related to the quasi-war with France in *Talbot v. Seeman*,[52] are important foundational decisions, for they

---

[47] Bas v. Tingy, 4 U.S. (4 Dall.) 37 (1800).

[48]

> In March 1799, congress had raised an army; stopped all intercourse with France; dissolved our treaty; built and equipt ships of war; and commissioned private armed ships; enjoining the former, and authorising the latter, to defend themselves against the armed ships of France, to attack them on the high seas, to subdue and take them as prize, and to re-capture armed vessels found in their possession.

Id. at 41.

[49] "If it (war) be declared in form, it is called solemn, and is of the perfect kind; because one whole nation is at war with another whole nation." *Id.* at 40.

[50] "[H]ostilities may subsist between two nations more confined in its nature and extent; being limited as to places, persons, and things; and this is more properly termed imperfect war." *Id.*

[51]

> "Congress is empowered to declare a general war, or congress may wage a limited war; limited in place, in objects and in time. If a general war is declared, its extent and operations are only restricted and regulated by the jus belli, forming a part of the law of nations; but if a partial war is waged, its extent and operation depend on our municipal laws."

Id. at 43.

[52]

> "The whole powers of war being, by the constitution of the United States, vested in congress, the acts of that body can alone be resorted to as our guides in this enquiry. It is not denied, nor in the course of the argument has it been denied, that congress may authorize general hostilities, in which case the general laws of war apply to our situation; or partial hostilities, in which case the laws of war, so far as they actually apply to our situation, must be noticed."

5 U.S. (1 Cranch) 1, 28 (1801).

50

III. Authorizing War

indicate that Congress has almost plenary authority to define the scope and objectives of war. Furthermore, Congress is not obliged to provide such authorization in the form of a declaration of war, but may instead utilize a statute or joint resolution to do so. Both of these conclusions have been confirmed by practice since that time. Indeed, most express war authorizations have taken the form of joint resolutions authorizing the use of military force, not formal declarations of war.

Another early case added an important component to this war authorization equation: Once Congress sets an express statutory limit on the scope of hostilities, that limit binds the President, even if it is operationally illogical.[53] In *Little v. Barreme*,[54] the Court again addressed a case involving a prize award. The owner of the ship *Flying Fish* sued the U.S. Navy Captain who seized his ship on the high seas. The captain, in turn, invoked an order issued by the Secretary of the Navy, pursuant to directives issued by President Jefferson, as the legal authority for the seizure.[55] That order clearly authorized the challenged seizure. However, the Court concluded that the President's order (which directed seizure of ships sailing *to* French ports) exceeded the limits on seizures established by the statute enacted by Congress to authorize limited hostilities against France (which authorized seizure of ships sailing *from* French ports).[56]

These early cases indicate that Congress is vested with broad war authorization powers, and may tailor an authorization to meet the necessities of a given situation. They also indicate that this power includes the authority to impose binding limits on the scope, duration, and manner of hostilities.[57] While such limitations have not been common features of express war authorizations, these cases nonetheless lay an important foundation for any future congressional action to limit the discretion of a President in engaging in a conflict they choose to authorize. For example, it is increasingly common for Congress to consider granting authority to engage in hostilities while imposing a prohibition on introducing ground forces into the conflict. Or Congress may place a temporal limitation on an authorized conflict, such as it did when it reached a compromise with

---

[53] JOHN H. ELY, WAR AND RESPONSIBILITY: CONSTITUTIONAL LESSONS OF VIETNAM AND ITS AFTERMATH 55 (1993) (opponents of presidential war power interpret this case to mean that courts can hear war powers cases and that Congress can regulate the conduct of war, even if it conflicts with presidential orders).

[54] 6 U.S. (2 Cranch) 170 (1804).

[55] *Id.* at 177.

[56] At least one scholar has argued that *Little v. Barreme* has no relevance on the question of war authorization, but was instead a case based exclusively on Article I authority to make rules for captures on the land and water. This scholar also dismisses the significance of other early era cases, and asserts that the declaration clause provides Congress with the limited authority to formalize by law situations of de facto war initiated by the President. This view seems inconsistent with those of nearly every court that has addressed the scope of Congress's war powers.

[57] "Those cases do not imply that once Congress authorizes war, the President is at liberty to choose the time, location and scope of military activities. In authorizing war, Congress may place limits on what Presidents may and may not do." LOUIS FISHER, PRESIDENTIAL WAR POWERS 25 (2d ed., rev. 2004).

President Reagan to authorize the continuation of the U.S. contribution to a peacekeeping mission in Lebanon.[58]

It is important to note that Congress exercises its "power of the purse" to impose such restrictions or limitations on participation in hostilities. Such a restriction may be attached to any appropriation bill, which may present the President with a dilemma of having to veto a bill funding other government activities or accept a limitation on military operations (an example of this method of restricting hostilities occurred at the end of the conflict in Vietnam).[59] However, no matter what statutory mechanism Congress chooses to use to impose such limitations upon the President, it seems relatively clear it must do so explicitly and in the form of a statute.[60]

B.   Defensive or Responsive War

Not all conflicts are initiated by the United States. Throughout our history, the nation has periodically been the victim of acts of aggression committed by both states and nonstate groups (such as Al Qaeda).[61] When this occurs—when war is "thrust upon the nation"—the inherent authority derived from Article II permits the President to use the nation's military to respond to an attack thrust upon the nation.

This inherent defensive or responsive war authority is derived from the Supreme Court's seminal decision in *The Prize Cases*.[62] At the initiation of the American Civil War, President Lincoln ordered the U.S. Navy to lay blockade to southern ports. In accordance with established naval warfare custom, merchant ships captured while attempting to run the blockade were subject to condemnation as prizes, and the crew of the capturing ship would share the proceeds of the prize condemnation and award.

A number of U.S. citizens whose property was condemned pursuant to this process challenged the constitutionality of the action. They argued that disposition of seized shipping by prize proceedings could only be justified pursuant to the *jus belli*, or laws and customs of naval warfare. Because Congress had not declared war against the rebellious southern states, or even provided statutory authorization to wage the war, the situation, they asserted, was not a war. Accordingly, the invocation of prize rules was invalid, and the deprivation of property violated due process.

---

[58] Multinational Force in Lebanon Resolution, Oct. 12, 1983, P.L. 98-119, 97 Stat. 805 (Congress allowed troops to remain in Lebanon for an 18-month period beginning on the Resolution's date of enactment).

[59] *See* Peter Raven-Hansen & William C. Banks, *Pulling the Purpose Strings of the Commander in Chief*, 80 Va. L. Rev. 833 (May 1994).

[60] When there is a conflict between a presidential order and a congressional statute relating to war powers, the statute will take precedence. Prakash, *supra* note 15, at 304.

[61] UN Charter art. 51.

[62] *The Brig Amy Warwick ("The Prize Cases")*, 67 U.S. (2 Black) 635 (1863).

III. Authorizing War

In a divided opinion, the Supreme Court disagreed and upheld the invocation of the *jus belli* to justify the prize proceedings.[63] The division of the Court did not turn on whether the use of the U.S. armed forces to repress the rebellion was authorized. All Justices concurred on that point. For the dissenters, however, the authority for the military response to the rebellion was traced back to the Militia Clause of the Constitution, and the Insurrection Act—the law Congress enacted that authorized the President to call forth the militia to suppress rebellion.[64] However, they agreed with the ship owners that absent an express statutory authorization, the situation could not properly be considered a "war," and therefore there was no legal basis for invoking prize rules derived from the *jus belli*.[65]

The majority disagreed. While the Court noted that Congress had in fact enacted retroactive statutory authorizations for all of the actions taken by President Lincoln in response to the rebellion, this authority was functionally superfluous with the President's inherent authority to respond to the attack. The Court held that no such authorization is required when war is "thrust upon the nation," whether by a foreign foe or states in rebellion.[66] When such challenges are presented to the nation, it is not only the right but the duty of the President to meet the challenge in the form it is presented—in other words, to choose the most effective and appropriate military response to defend the nation.[67] As a result, invocation of prize authority was justified as the rebellion initiated a state of war, thereby triggering all the rights and obligations derived from the *jus belli*.[68]

This defensive or responsive war became increasingly significant in the post–World War II era. During the Cold War, the United States relied (and to a large

---

[63] "The right of prize and capture has its origin in the "jus belli," and is governed and adjudged under the law of nations." 67 U.S. (2 Black) at 666.

[64] *Id.* at 690-91.

[65]

Congress alone can determine whether war exists or should be declared; and until they have acted, no citizen of the State can be punished in his person or property, unless he had committed some offence against a law of Congress passed before the act was committed, which made it a crime, and defined the punishment.

Id. at 693.

[66]

If a war be made by invasion of a foreign nation, the President is not only authorized but bound to resist force by force. He does not initiate the war, but is bound to accept the challenge without waiting for any special legislative authority. And whether the hostile party be a foreign invader, or States organized in rebellion, it is none the less a war, although the declaration of it be "unilateral."

Id. at 668.

[67] "He (the president) must determine what degree of force the crisis demands." *Id.* at 670.

[68] "The proclamation of blockade is itself official and conclusive evidence to the Court that a state of war existed which demanded and authorized a recourse to such a measure, under the circumstances peculiar to the case." *Id.*

extent continues to rely) on the forward deployment of U.S. armed forces to deter aggression against allies and to ensure prompt and effective response to any such attack.[69] These forward deployed forces served as proverbial "trip wires," sending a clear and unambiguous message to adversaries that any attack on an ally would immediately trigger conflict with the United States.[70] From a constitutional perspective, they also ensured that any such attack would immediately trigger the President's inherent constitutional authority to respond with the full might of the U.S. military.[71] This authority is even reflected in the War Powers Resolution, without question the high water mark of congressional efforts to limit presidential war powers. According to §1541 of this law, the only situation justifying the introduction of U.S. armed forces into hostilities *without* express statutory authorization is an attack upon the United States *or* its armed forces.[72]

---

[69] KEITH SLEDD, U.S. ARMY WAR COLLEGE, STRATEGIC RESPONSIVENESS—DOES JOINT FORCE CAPABILITY SUPPORT NATIONAL SECURITY STRATEGY? 4-5 (2009), *available at* handle.dtic.mil/100.2/ADA498276.

[70] Richard Spencer, *50 Years of Trip-Wire Weirdness End as U.S. Leaves Korean Border*, THE TELEGRAPH (Nov. 2, 2004), http://www.telegraph.co.uk/news/worldnews/asia/southkorea/1475665/50-years-of-trip-wire-weirdness-end-as-US-leaves-Korean-border.html.

> We are led in this way to a new interpretation of the 'trip-wire' [of US troops in Europe]. The analogy for our limited war forces in Europe is not, according to this argument, a trip wire that certainly detonates all-out war if it is in working order and fails altogether if it is not. What we have a graduated series of trip wires, each attached to a chance mechanism, with the daily probability of detonation increasing as the enemy moves from wire to wire. The critical feature of the analogy, it should be emphasized, is that whether or not the trip wire detonates general war is—at least to some extent—outside our control. . . .

THOMAS SCHELLING, THE STRATEGY OF CONFLICT 120 (1980).

[71] "The President's role under our Constitution as Commander in Chief and Chief Executive vests him with the constitutional authority to order United States troops abroad to further national interests such as protecting the lives of Americans overseas." *Authority to Use United States Military Forces in Somalia*, 16 Op. O.L.C. 1, 8 (Dec. 4, 1992) [hereinafter *Authority to Use Forces in Somalia*].

> Our history is replete with instances of presidential uses of military force abroad in the absence of prior congressional approval. This pattern of presidential initiative and congressional acquiescence may be said to reflect the implicit advantage held by the executive over the legislature under our constitutional scheme in situations calling for immediate action. Thus, constitutional practice over two centuries, supported by the nature of the functions exercised and by the few legal benchmarks that exist, evidences the existence of broad constitutional power.

Presidential Power to Use the Armed Forces Abroad Without Statutory Authorization, 4A Op. O.L.C. 185, 187 (1980) [hereinafter *Presidential Power*].

"It is well established that the President has the constitutional power as Chief Executive and Commander-in-Chief to protect the lives and property of Americans abroad. This understanding is reflected in judicial decisions . . . and recurring historic practice which goes back to the time of Jefferson." *Presidential Powers Relating to the Situation in Iran*, 4A Op. O.L.C. 115, 121 (1979) [hereinafter *Situation in Iran*].

[72] 50 U.S.C.S. §1541(c).

III. Authorizing War

C. *September 11 and Congress's Authorization of Military Force*

After September 11, 2001, Congress enacted an Authorization for the Use of Military Force (AUMF) that authorized the President to take all action that was "necessary and appropriate" to prevent further attacks by those responsible. Both the Bush and Obama administrations have construed the AUMF to permit action against Al Qaeda and "associated forces." The AUMF clearly authorized the initial U.S. intervention in Afghanistan in 2001 that resulted in the deposal of the Taliban. In 2002, Congress passed another AUMF specifically authorizing military force in Iraq (the 2002 AUMF). Questions have arisen about the 2001 AUMF's coverage of subsequent executive actions, including drone strikes in Pakistan or other countries, such as Yemen and Somalia. In 2014, questions also arose about whether the 2001 or 2002 AUMFs covered U.S. military action in Syria against the Islamic State of Iraq and Syria (ISIS).

Drone strikes in Pakistan are the easiest case. Since Pakistan shares a border with Afghanistan and forces attacking U.S. troops in Afghanistan have sought a safe harbor across the border, a consensus has emerged that the 2001 AUMF covers drone strikes in Pakistan.

Drone strikes in Yemen and Somalia have been more controversial. The Obama administration has argued that its targets in Yemen belong to Al Qaeda in the Arabian Peninsula (AQAP), which the administration regards as a group affiliated with "core" Al Qaeda, the group formerly led by Osama bin Laden and now led by bin Laden's old second-in-command, Dr. Ayman al-Zahawiri. Support for the administration's view stems from AQAP's public announcements of loyalty to core Al Qaeda, as well as some evidence of collaboration on broad strategy. Based on this position that AQAP is a force associated with core Al Qaeda, the Obama administration launched a substantial number of drone strikes targeting alleged AQAP operatives, including the U.S. citizen Anwar al-Awlaki, who was killed in 2011. Some members of Congress, including members of the U.S. Senate Foreign Relations Committee, have pressed the administration for more precision on its position and recommended that the administration propose an updated AUMF that could provide more specific authorization for strikes beyond Afghanistan and Pakistan. As of October 2014, the administration has not put forward a new legislative initiative and no legislative initiative has gained significant traction.

The U.S. position on Somalia is more nuanced. The United States does not argue that Al Shabab, the major Somali violent extremist group, is associated with Al Qaeda. However, the United States has stated that certain *members* of Al Shabab are associated with Al Qaeda, because of those individuals' contacts. Citing that position, the United States has targeted members of Al Shabab, including the group's leader, who was killed in 2014.

The Obama administration has also indicated that even if the 2001 and 2002 AUMFs were repealed and no further legislative authorization was forthcoming, the President would have authority under Article II of the Constitution to target violent extremist groups if those groups posed an imminent threat to the United States. However, the Obama administration has always indicated that it would prefer to operate pursuant to legislative authorization.

The interaction of the AUMFs and the President's Article II authority has also been important in analyzing the drone strike that killed Anwar al-Awlaki. A U.S. statute bars killing a U.S. national abroad.[73] A literal reading of the statute would suggest that the President acted illegally in ordering al-Awlaki's killing. In addition, a series of executive orders (EOs), including EO 11905, 12036, and 12333 (issued during the Ford, Carter, and Reagan administrations, respectively) bar "assassination" of heads of state or other individuals abroad. The U.S. response has been that the statute that prohibits killing must be read together with another provision[74] that defines "murder" as an "unlawful killing." According to the administration, since al-Awlaki was part of a group (AQAP) associated with Al Qaeda and was planning imminent attacks on the United States, the AUMF and the President's Article II authority provide "public authority" for his killing. Under this "public authority" doctrine, the U.S. use of lethal force abroad in the course of an armed conflict or to defend against an imminent threat is authorized by both domestic and international law.[75]

In broad terms, the "public authority" doctrine is clearly correct. The U.S. military must be able to use lethal force against an adversary in an armed conflict, even if that individual is a U.S. citizen. However, some continue to question whether al-Awlaki was actually a direct participant in an armed conflict. A finding that al-Awlaki was not a participant in an armed conflict with the United States might compel the conclusion that the strike on him did violate federal law. However, courts considering the issue have cited procedural grounds, including standing and the political question doctrine, in rejecting a challenge to the strike against al-Awlaki.[76]

The legal authorization for U.S. attacks on ISIS in both Iraq and Syria is perhaps the most difficult issue of all. ISIS is a descendant of an earlier group, Al Qaeda in Iraq (AQI), that was allied with "core" Al Qaeda and fought against U.S. forces in the period following the U.S. military intervention in Iraq in 2003. While the collaboration with core Al Qaeda was in effect, the 2001 AUMF appeared to cover strikes on the Iraq group. Moreover, the 2002 AUMF authorizing military intervention in Iraq clearly covered initial U.S. strikes on the group. However, as AQI transformed itself into ISIS, it became increasingly estranged from core Al Qaeda. That estrangement has made reliance on the 2001 AUMF increasingly problematic.[77] The 2002 AUMF does not clearly cover current attacks on ISIS, because the withdrawal of U.S. forces from Iraq in 2011 has made the 2002 AUMF a more tenuous basis for U.S. military action.

---

[73] 18 U.S.C. §1119(b).

[74] 18 U.S.C. §1111(a).

[75] *See* Department of Justice White Paper, *Lawfulness of a Lethal Operation Directed Against a U.S. Citizen Who Is a Senior Operational Leader of Al-Qa'ida or An Associated Force*, available at http://msnbcmedia.msn.com/i/msnbc/sections/news/020413_DOJ_White_Paper.pdf.

[76] *See, e.g.*, Al-Aulaqi v. Obama, 727 F. Supp. 2d 1 (D.D.C. 2010).

[77] Robert M. Chesney, *Beyond the Battlefield, Beyond Al Qaeda: The Destabilizing Legal Architecture of Counterterrorism*, 112 MICH. L. REV. 163 (2013).

III. Authorizing War

As of October 2014, the Obama administration has argued that both the 2001 and 2002 AUMFs provide a sufficient legal basis for moves against ISIS. The administration has argued that the history of ISIS's involvement with core Al Qaeda provides a basis under the 2001 AUMF. It has also argued that since ISIS includes many individuals allied with the regime of former Iraqi dictator Saddam Hussein who participated in attacks on U.S. forces in Iraq prior to the U.S. withdrawal, the 2002 AUMF also authorizes U.S. attacks on ISIS. Some members of Congress, including Virginia Democratic senator Tim Kaine, have disagreed, asserting that new legislative authorization is needed. Congress has authorized assistance to Syrian rebels, but has not, as of October 2014, authorized the direct use of force against ISIS by the United States. Congress may take up this issue again after the 2014 mid-term elections.

D. Rescue

Closely related to defensive war power is what is commonly referred to as the rescue power: the authority to use military force to rescue U.S. nationals abroad. Unlike defensive war power, there is no clear Supreme Court precedent indicating whether the use of military force in such situations falls within the President's inherent Article II authority. However, courts have decided several cases that implied such a power. Presidential legal advisers routinely cite two of these cases to support this authority: *In re Neagle*[78] and *Durand v. Hollins*.[79] Ironically, neither of these cases involved rescuing Americans abroad. Nonetheless, both indicated in dicta that it is the President whom U.S. nationals rely on for such rescue when endangered abroad.

In re Neagle involved the inherent authority of the President to authorize a U.S. Marshall to protect a Supreme Court justice. Neagle, in execution of that duty, shot and killed an assailant who made an assassination attempt against the Justice. California charged Neagle with criminal homicide, and he then petitioned a federal court for habeas corpus based on a federal habeas corpus statute that prohibited detention of any person for executing federal law. The Supreme Court confronted the issue of whether an order from the President to protect the Justice qualified as "law" within the meaning of the statute.[80] A majority of the Court answered that question in the affirmative, relying on the inherent authority

---

[78] 135 U.S. 1 (1890).

[79] 8 F. Cas. 111 (C.C.S.D.N.Y. 1860).

[80]

It is urged, however, that there exists no statute authorizing any such protection as that which Neagle was instructed to give Judge Field in the present case (by the President), and indeed no protection whatever against a vindictive or malicious assault growing out of the faithful discharge of his official duties.

Neagle, 135 U.S. at 58.

of the President to take measures to protect vital federal functions.[81] The dissent rejected this conclusion, noting that the President's authority as Chief Executive did not extend to "making" law.[82]

Both the majority and dissent, however, cited what was known as the Koszta incident.[83] That "incident" involved the "rescue" of a naturalized U.S. citizen. In response to Koszta being held against his will on a Hungarian naval ship in Smyrna, the captain of a U.S. Navy ship "trained his guns" on the Hungarian ship and secured Koszta's release. Although Congress had in no way authorized the captain to threaten the use of force against the Hungarian ship, Congress celebrated his action by awarding him a special citation. For the *Neagle* majority, this incident provided evidence of the President's inherent authority (acting through subordinate officers) to protect and rescue Americans.[84] The dissent, in contrast, simply emphasized that this authority applied only when the American was in jeopardy abroad.[85] What is clear, however, is that both the majority and dissent agreed that the President is vested with inherent authority to order the use of military force to rescue Americans *abroad*. *Durand v. Hollins* reinforces this conclusion, although like *Neagle* did not involve the rescue of Americans.[86] In *Durand*,

---

[81] *Id.* at 67.

> In the view we take of the Constitution of the United States, any obligation fairly and properly inferrible from that instrument, or any duty of the marshal to be derived from the general scope of his duties under the laws of the United States, is "a law" within the meaning of this phrase. The Court coupled this constitutional interpretation with the President's power under the Constitution, section 3, article 2, to take care that the laws be faithfully executed.

Id. at 59.

> Chapter fourteen of the Revised Statutes of the United States, section 788 declares: "The marshals and their deputies shall have, in each State, the same powers, in executing the laws of the United States, as the sheriffs and their deputies in such State may have, by law, in executing the laws thereof."

Id. at 68.

[82]

> Again, while it is the President's duty to take care that the laws be faithfully executed, it is not his duty to make laws or a law of the United States. The laws he is to see executed are manifestly those contained in the Constitution, and those enacted by Congress, whose duty it is to make all laws necessary and proper for carrying into execution the powers of those tribunals.

Id. at 83.

[83] *Id.* at 64, 84.

[84] *Id.* at 64.

[85] "We answer, that such action of the government was justified because it pertained to the foreign relations of the United States, in respect to which the federal government is the exclusive representative and embodiment of the entire sovereignty of the nation, in its united character." *Id.* at 84-85.

[86] Durand v. Hollins, 8 F. Cas. 111. at 112. "It is to [the President], also, the citizens abroad must look for protection of person and of property, and for the faithful execution of the laws existing and intended for their protection."

III. Authorizing War

a U.S. citizen sued a U.S. Navy ship commander who shelled Greytown, Nicaragua, in retaliation for the Nicaraguan government's refusal to make reparations for attacks against U.S. citizens and property. The shelling was conducted pursuant to orders issued by the President and Secretary of the Navy. In his capacity as a circuit judge, Justice Nelson concluded the shelling was conducted pursuant to constitutional authority, even though Congress had in no way authorized the action. According to the opinion: "Acts of lawless violence, or of threatened violence to the citizen or his property, cannot be anticipated and provided for; and the protection, to be effectual or of any avail, may, not unfrequently, require the most prompt and decided action."[87] Perhaps more importantly, Justice Nelson noted that whether the President had a duty to act to protect the citizens involved "was a public political question . . . which belonged to the executive to determine."[88]

This inherent executive rescue power is also supported by decades of practice. U.S. history is replete with examples of forcible military actions for the purpose of rescuing or protecting American nationals and property abroad. Military doctrine characterizes these missions as noncombatant evacuation operations (NEO), and this same doctrine recognizes that a NEO may be either permissive (with the consent of the host nation) or non-permissive (without such consent and requiring forcible entry and extraction).[89] There are numerous U.S. Attorney General opinions related to these missions, all of which rely on these two seminal decisions (as well as longstanding practice) to conclude the President is vested with the inherent authority to order the use of military force for this purpose.[90] Prominent examples of non-permissible rescue or protection missions include the rescue of the U.S. merchant vessel *Mayaguez* from Cambodian forces

---

[87] *Id.*

[88] *Id.*

[89]

Noncombatant evacuation operations (NEOs) are conducted to assist the Department of State (DOS) in evacuating noncombatants, nonessential military personnel, selected host-nation citizens, and third country nationals whose lives are in danger from locations in a host foreign nation to an appropriate safe haven and/or the United States. NEOs usually involve swift insertions of a force, temporary occupation of an objective, and a planned withdrawal upon completion of the mission. During NEOs, the US Ambassador is the senior authority for the evacuation and is ultimately responsible for the successful completion of the NEO and the safety of the evacuees. The Ambassador speaks with the authority of the President and serves as direct representative on site.

Joint Chiefs of Staff, United States Military Joint Publication 3-68 I-1 (Jan. 22, 2007), *available at* http://www.fas.org/irp/doddir/dod/jp3-68.pdf.

[90] *Authority to Use Forces in Somalia, supra* note 71, at 8 (finding that President Clinton has authority to commit troops to protect American citizens providing humanitarian aid in Somalia based on *Durand*). *See also* 40 Op. Att'y Gen. 58, 62 (1941) (Jackson, A.G.) ("the President's authority has long been recognized as extending to the dispatch of armed forces outside of the United States, either on missions of good will or rescue, or for the purpose of protecting American lives or property or American interests").

in 1975,[91] the 1980 attempt to rescue U.S. hostages held in Iran,[92] the 1983 invasion of Grenada,[93] and the 1989 invasion of Panama to protect the tens of thousands of U.S. nationals from the Panamanian Defense Forces under the command of General Manuel Noriega.[94]

Congress has never raised any significant objection to the execution of these type of rescue missions. However, the War Powers Resolution (WPR) *did not* include rescue or protection of U.S. nationals abroad within its enumeration of situations justifying a President's introduction of U.S. armed forces into hostilities or situations of imminent hostilities.[95] This omission was cited by President Nixon as a principal reason for his decision to veto the WPR.[96] No President has since that time acknowledged the constitutionality of the WPR, and each of the rescue missions mentioned in the prior paragraph were ordered subsequent to the enactment of the law. Because Presidents continue to assert inherent constitutional authority to order these missions, and because no Congress has challenged these assertions of authority even following enactment of the WPR, the Resolution's omission of rescue authority must be considered to have minimal probative value when assessing the constitutional authority of future Presidents to order similar missions.

E. *"Twilight Zone" War*

The tautology of war powers leads inevitably to an authority twilight zone: a military action initiated by the President, in the absence of either congressional

---

[91] "According to a special study issued by the House Committee on Foreign Affairs, the majority of Members of Congress after the Mayaguez incident supported the concept that the President had constitutional authority to use armed forces for a rescue operation of the type involved in that incident." *Overview of the War Powers Resolution*, 8 Op. O.L.C. 271 (Oct. 30, 1984) [hereinafter *Overview of the WPR*] (quoting *War Powers Resolution: A Special Study of the Committee on Foreign Affairs* 211, 216 (House Comm. on Foreign Affairs 1982)).

[92] *Situation in Iran*, *supra* note 71 (issued immediately after the Iranian Embassy was seized).

[93] *See* Robert J. Beck, *International Law and the Decision to Invade Grenada: A Ten-Year Retrospective*, 33 VA. J. INT'L L. 765 (Summer 1993).

[94] *See* Ved P. Nanda, *U.S. Forces in Panama: Defenders, Aggressors or Human Rights Activists?: The Validity of United States Intervention in Panama Under International Law*, 84 AM. J. INT'L L. 494 (Apr. 1990).

[95]

The constitutional powers of the President as Commander-in-Chief to introduce United States Armed Forces into hostilities, or into situations where imminent involvement in hostilities is clearly indicated by the circumstances, are exercised only pursuant to (1) a declaration of war, (2) specific statutory authorization, or (3) a national emergency created by attack upon the United States, its territories or possessions, or its armed forces.

50 U.S.C.S. §1541(c).

[96] *Veto of the War Powers Resolution*, PUB. PAPERS 893, 893 (Oct. 24, 1973) [hereinafter *President's Veto*]. The War Powers Resolution "would seriously undermine this Nation's ability to act decisively and convincingly in times of international crisis."

III. Authorizing War

approval or prohibition, that is not conducted in response to an imminent attack against the nation, its armed forces, or to rescue Americans abroad. Or, perhaps the President continues hostilities in a conflict that Congress had initially authorized by joint resolution that it later revoked. These are not far-fetched hypotheticals, but in fact periodically arise in the exercise of U.S. war powers. What is the basis and scope of presidential war powers in these situations?

No war powers question generates more scholarly and political debate than this issue. As a generalization, responsive theories fall into three general categories. On one extreme is the strict textualist view that the Declaration Clause indicates an absolute requirement for affirmative congressional authorization for anything other than defensive or rescue hostilities.[97] Thus, Presidents lack constitutional authority to initiate or continue hostilities in the absence of such affirmative authorization. On the other extreme is the unilateral Commander in Chief theory, which posits that Congress's power is limited to "perfecting" de facto wars initiated pursuant to the inherent power of the President as Commander in Chief.[98] Under this theory, congressional ambivalence or silence in response to a presidential war making initiative is virtually irrelevant, especially if Congress provides the fiscal means to execute the operation. At most, the declaration power permits Congress to prohibit initiation of hostilities, but only by enacting a law to that effect.

Between these two extremes lies a more pragmatic theory of presidential war powers, one that seems to accord with actual practice. This theory is in large measure consistent with Justice Jackson's *Youngstown* three-tier framework for assessing presidential power: Where Congress has failed to expressly authorize military action, but has nonetheless provided support for such action through its fiscal power (and perhaps also its power to raise armies in the form of authorizing conscription), the President will assert his initiative is backed by the implied support of Congress.[99] Even if congressional action in response to the imminent or initiated hostilities is ambivalent, the President will assert that the lack of express opposition to his action justifies the conclusion that it is constitutionally

---

[97]
Arguing that the Framers intended Congress to have exclusive control over the decision to go to war, they interpret the Declare War Clause as a separation of powers provision that not only empowers Congress, but also limits executive abilities to make war. Under this approach, in order to wage war, the President must receive a declaration of war or its "functional equivalent" from Congress. Should the President overstep these constitutional boundaries, the federal courts must intervene to right the balance by declaring the war unconstitutional or even by enjoining the President's actions.

John Yoo, *The Continuation of Politic by Other Means: The Original Understanding of War Powers*, 84 Calif. L. Rev. 167, 171 (1996).

[98] *Id.* 174-75; *see also* Arthur H. Garrison, *The History of Executive Branch Legal Opinions on the Power of the President as Commander-in-Chief from Washington to Obama*, 43 Cumb. L. Rev. 375 (2012-2013) (discussing the views of each administration related to plenary commander-in-chief power).

[99] Charles Tiefer, *War Decisions in the Late 1990s by Partial Congressional Declaration*, 36 San Diego L. Rev. 1, 18-21 (1999).

permissible. If, however, Congress were to expressly oppose military action by enacting law to that effect (to include restricting the expenditure of funds to conduct the action), the President would be bound to yield to congressional will.[100]

Whether this tautology reflects established constitutional custom or merely the exercise of power of dubious constitutional validity is a constant question related to military action conducted within this framework. However, it does seem relatively clear that many Presidents have relied on this type of "implied support" theory to justify their military initiatives.[101] Several prominent examples are worth noting. These include the latter phase of the Vietnam conflict,[102] the 1999 air and missile attack against Serbia,[103] and several large scale missions conducted under the auspices of a UN peacekeeping authorization that involved a high probability of (if not actual) hostilities, such as the military deployments in Lebanon,[104] Bosnia,[105] Kosovo,[106] and Somalia.[107] In each of these situations, President's confronted congressional reactions that were ambivalent at best and confused at worst.

Perhaps the first incident of a major and long-term "non-defensive" conflict conducted without express congressional authorization was the Korean War. This war, which is legally still ongoing (hostilities ended on July 27, 1953 when an armistice was signed), was "hot" for nearly three years. During that time, the United States provided nearly 90 percent of the allied military force, suffered approximately 36,000 killed in action, and spent more than $69 billion in support of the war.[108] President Truman initially ordered the U.S. military action as an exercise of collective self-defense pursuant to Article 51 of the Charter of the United Nations, and subsequently pursuant to a use of force authorization enacted by the UN Security Council.[109] Congress never declared war, nor did it enact a specific statutory authorization. It did, however, support the war by resurrecting conscription, authorizing activation of reserve forces, and funding the war. President Truman relied on these indications of implied support, coupled with

---

[100] U.S. Const. art. II, §3, cl. 5. *Cf.* Barron & Lederman, *supra* note 14 (discussing the President's ability to act in contravention to congressional will).

[101] *See* Corn, *supra* note 20, at 212-15 (discussing the President's authority in military actions that cannot be classified as "responsive" or "defensive" war).

[102] Norman A. Graebner, *The President as Commander in Chief: A Study in Power, in* Commander in Chief: Presidential Leadership in Modern Wars 42 (Joseph G. Dawson, III ed., 1993). "A congressional majority underwrote the war in Vietnam from 1961 until 1973 through its power of the purse; that war always belonged to Congress as much as to the presidents. They fought it together."

[103] Exec. Order No. 13,119, 64 Fed. Reg. 18,797 (Apr. 13, 1999).

[104] *Multinational Force in Lebanon Resolution*, Oct. 12, 1983, P.L. 98-119, 97 Stat. 805.

[105] *Proposed Deployment of United States Armed Forces in Bosnia and Herzegovina*, 19 Op. O.L.C. 327, 327 (Nov. 30 1995) [hereinafter *Bosnia and Herzegovina*].

[106] *See* Corn, *supra* note 30.

[107] *Authority to Use Forces in Somalia*, *supra* note 71, at 8.

[108] *See* Korean War Facts, CNN Library, *available at* http://www.cnn.com/2013/06/28/world/asia/korean-war-fast-facts/.

[109] *See generally* Robert F. Turner, *Truman, Korea, and the Constitution: Debunking the Imperial President Myth*, 19 Harv. J.L. & Pub. Pol'y 533 (1995-1996).

his authority derived from the Commander in Chief power, the responsibility to act pursuant to the UN Charter, a treaty ratified by the United States.[110]

The war powers precedential significance of the Korean War is the source of substantial debate.[111] The United States has never participated in any other conflict of similar magnitude and duration without express statutory authorization. However, the war does suggest that Congress may choose to manifest support for a conflict with something less than express authorization. As will be explained below, this method of providing "implied" support for a presidential war-making decision became an even more complicated issue following enactment of the War Powers Resolution (WPR) in 1973.

The air war against Serbia is a more contemporary example of a "twilight zone" war, both because of the conflicting nature of the congressional reaction and the fact that the operation ostensibly violated even the most expansive reading of the War Powers Resolution. In 1999, President Clinton led the NATO alliance in a decision to launch a large scale attack against Serbia in order to force Serbian President Slobodan Milosevic to terminate military action in the Serbian province of Kosovo that was, according to the allies, intended to ethnically cleanse Muslims from that province.[112] Because the UN Security Council refused to authorize the attack as a measure of collective security, many experts considered the attack as a blatant violation of international law (see Chapter 5 for a discussion of the relationship between international law and U.S. legal authority). Nonetheless, President Clinton and his NATO allies were determined to prevent a repeat of the genocide that occurred in Bosnia, and launched the operation.[113]

President Clinton did not seek express statutory authority for the U.S. participation in the air war, nor could he (or did he) plausibly assert inherent authority to defend the nation or to rescue U.S. nationals.[114] Instead, he relied on an amalgam of authorities to justify his decision to commit the nation to hostilities against another nation. These included his inherent power as Commander in Chief, his inherent foreign affairs powers and the accordant need to support the NATO alliance, and an assertion that the War Powers Resolution acknowledged the authority of the President to commit U.S. armed forces to hostilities

---

[110] *Id.*

[111] *See, e.g.,* LOUIS F. FISHER, PRESIDENTIAL WAR POWER (3d ed. 2013); *see also* LOUIS F. FISHER, THE LAW OF THE EXECUTIVE BRANCH: PRESIDENTIAL POWER (2014), 332-34.

[112] *Address to Nation on Airstrikes Against Serbian Targets in the Federal Republic of Yugoslavia (Serbia and Montenegro)*, 1 PUB. PAPERS 450, 451 (Mar. 24, 1999).

[113] Rick Rowden, *Clinton to Bomb Again—Now Serbia/Is the U.S. Interest to "Stop the Killing" or to Expand the Police Power of NATO?*, S.F. GATE (Mar. 24, 1999), http://www.sfgate.com/opinion/openforum/article/Clinton-to-Bomb-Again-Now-Serbia-Is-the-U-S-2940173.php.

[114] The Clinton administration argued that the President could, "acting without specific statutory authorization, lawfully [] introduce United States ground troops into Bosnia and Herzegovina . . . to help the North Atlantic Treaty Organization . . . ensure compliance with the recently negotiated peace agreement." *Bosnia and Herzegovina, supra* note 105, at 327. The WPR was interpreted to "lend[] support to the . . . conclusion that the President has authority, without specific statutory authorization, to introduce troops into hostilities in a substantial range of circumstances." *Id.* at 335.

for up to 60 days (as will be explained below, this is a dubious interpretation of the WPR).[115]

The congressional reaction to the initiation of hostilities was mixed. Unsurprisingly, some members of Congress supported the President, while others asserted that the absence of express congressional authorization for the conflict rendered his action unconstitutional. This mixed reaction came to a head in a series of votes in the House of Representatives in 1999. On April 28, the House of Representatives voted on four related legislative proposals: first, against a declaration of war,[116] and second, against two concurrent resolutions: one to authorize continued military force in Kosovo,[117] and the other directing the President to remove the Armed Forces from Serbia within 30 days.[118] Third, Congress voted to prohibit the use of any appropriated funds to support the introduction of ground troops in Kosovo without specific congressional authorization.[119] Finally, in early May, Congress enacted a supplemental funding bill to support the continuation of the air war against Serbia.[120]

The net result of this legislative record was that Congress neither expressly approved nor disapproved of the air conflict against Serbia, but did implicitly endorse the conflict by appropriating funds for its continuation.[121] This record did not support the conclusion that the President was acting *contrary* to the express or implied will of Congress. Instead, it supported the opposite conclusion: that the President was acting consistently with the *implied* support of Congress.[122] Even if the probative value of the enactment of funding to support an operation already initiated by the President is dismissed on the theory that Congress had no other viable alternative at that point, the congressional failure to expressly oppose the conflict would still leave the President in a strong constitutional position for two reasons. First, it would place his initiative into Justice Jackson's "twilight zone" of power, suggesting that his assertion of initiative would be rewarded because of an inability of Congress to coalesce in opposition to his action. Second, as a practical matter, this same lack of coalescence in opposition to the President would, as noted above, prevent any member of Congress from meeting the requirements of legislative standing. Because there would be no vote—much less law—in opposition to the President that could be considered "totally nullified" by continued prosecution of the war, an opposing legislator would lack standing to contest the action judicially.[123]

---

[115] *See* Clinton v. Campbell, 52 F. Supp. 2d 34, 37 (D.C.C. 1999) (citing Pls.' Mot. Summ. J., Ex. 19).

[116] H.R.J. Res. 44, 106th Cong. (1999).

[117] S. Con. Res. 21, 106th Cong. (1999).

[118] H.R. Con. Res. 82, 106th Cong. (1999).

[119] H.R. 1569, 106th Cong. (1999).

[120] 1999 Emergency Supplemental Appropriations Act, Pub. L. No. 106-31, 113 Stat. 57.

[121] *Id.*

[122] *Authorization for Continuing Hostilities in Kosovo*, 2000 OLC LEXIS 16, at *26-28 (Dec. 19, 2000).

[123] *See* 521 U.S. at 823.

III. Authorizing War

This approach to assessing the constitutionality of presidential war-making initiatives might be best understood as "support by implication." It is distinct from the broad theory of unilateral inherent war-making authority pressed by the most ardent supporters of presidential power because it relies on indications—albeit not express—of inter-branch consensus in support of such initiatives (or at least a failure of congressional consensus in opposition). Because such evidence of implied support for such initiatives will almost always exist, it is understandable how this theory might be viewed as pragmatically indistinguishable from a pure unilateral theory of presidential war powers. However, this approach is distinct from a unilateral theory of presidential war power precisely because it is based on an assertion of cooperation between the two political branches. The implication of this is critical: a recognition that Congress retains the ability to prevent initiation or continuation of a conflict by withdrawing all indicia of implied support and/or expressly opposing the conflict.

This approach to assessing the constitutionality of presidential war powers played a major role in the numerous cases that arose out of challenges to the legality of the Vietnam conflict. Almost all of these cases were resolved based on justiciability grounds. However, it was the conclusion that Congress supported the President, either expressly or by implication, that created the decisive political question: *How* Congress chooses to support a war is beyond judicial scrutiny. What is critical to understand the significance of the analytical approach used by these courts was that they first demanded evidence of *some* significant mutual cooperation in the war-making policies. That cooperation was found in the form of express statutory authorization (the Gulf of Tonkin Resolution), appropriations, and authorization for conscription. Once this was established, the courts addressing these challenges then concluded that whether this type of support was constitutionally sufficient was a political question. Ultimately, Congress and the President must cooperate, but how they cooperate is up to them. The following quote from the district court decision in one of these cases exemplifies the judicial rationale that resulted in these dismissals:

> It is passionately argued that none of the acts of the Congress which have furnished forth the sinew of war in levying taxes, appropriating the nation's treasure and conscripting its manpower in order to continue the Vietnam conflict can amount to authorizing the combat activities because the Constitution contemplates express authorization taken without the coercions exerted by illicit seizures of the initiative by the presidency. But it is idle to suggest that the Congress is so little ingenious or so inappreciative of its powers, including the power of impeachment, that it cannot seize policy and action initiatives at will, and halt course of action from which it wishes the national power to be withdrawn. Political expediency may have counseled the Congress's choice of the particular forms and modes by which it has united with the presidency in prosecuting the Vietnam combat activities, but the reality of the collaborative action of the executive and the legislative required by the Constitution has been present from the earliest stages.[124]

---

[124] Orlando v. Laird, 317 F. Supp. 1013, 1019 (E.D.N.Y. 1970).

As will be explained later in this chapter, the War Powers Resolution calls into question the validity of this "implied support" analysis. However, because the binding effect of the WPR remains uncertain, this method of assessing constitutional war powers remains vitally important. Indeed, at least one judge assessing a post-WPR war powers challenge specifically noted the continuing validity of this analytical approach.[125]

F.   The War Powers Resolution

By 1973, a war-weary nation finally saw the end of U.S. involvement in the Vietnam conflict.[126] That end had been sought by congressional opponents of the conflict for several years, opponents who had consistently gained legislative momentum for their objective of forcing the President to extricate the nation from the conflict. It was not, however, until Congress and the President reached agreement on terminating all appropriations for the conflict that their goal was achieved. In the interim, every legislative measure they took to halt the conflict fell short of producing that effect. Even after Congress repealed the Tonkin Gulf Resolution[127]—the express statutory authority relied on by several courts as the principal source of authorization for the conflict—U.S. involvement continued. Judicial challenges to this continued involvement failed, as courts looked to other sources of less explicit authority to conclude that Congress was not in opposition to efforts to "wind down" U.S. involvement, rather than end it precipitously.

The President's continuation of the conflict even following the repeal of the Resolution, and the cases that concluded his actions were constitutional, indicated the impact of a "support by implication" theory of presidential war powers. This impact was most dramatically manifested in the final judicial challenge to the conflict in *Holtzman v. Schlesinger*.[128] In that case, a group of Air Force pilots, joined by Representative Elizabeth Holtzman (an ardent critic of both the war and President Nixon), sought an injunction to prevent enforcement of military orders to conduct bombing missions against communist forces challenging the Cambodian Lon Nol regime allied with the United States. The plaintiffs argued the President lacked any constitutional authority to commit U.S. armed forces into this conflict, and therefore their orders to fly the missions exposed them to the risk of losing their lives in violation of due process of law.[129]

---

[125] In a footnote, Judge Greene stated that "if the Congress decides that United States forces should not be employed in foreign hostilities, and if the executive does not of its own volition abandon participation in such hostilities, actions by the courts would appear to be the only available means to break the deadlock in favor of the constitutional provision." *Dellums*, 752 F. Supp. at 1144 n.5.

[126] *See* Agreement on Ending the War and Restoring Peace in Viet-Nam, U.S.-Vietnam, Jan. 27, 1973, 24 U.S.T. 4.

[127] Pub. L. 88-408, 78 Stat. 384 (1964), *repealed by* Pub. L. 91-672, 12, 84 Stat. 2055 (1971).

[128] 484 F.2d 1307.

[129] *Id.* at 1308.

III. Authorizing War

The District Court for the Eastern District of New York agreed with the plaintiffs, and in July 1973 issued a permanent injunction prohibiting respondent Department of Defense officials from "participating in any way in military activities in or over Cambodia or releasing any bombs which may fall in Cambodia."[130] The court noted that the entire legislative record up to that point indicated congressional determination to terminate U.S. involvement in the conflict in Southeast Asia. This record included not only the repeal of the Gulf of Tonkin Resolution, but a June 1973 bill to cut off all funding for any military operations in that region. Although the law that was finally enacted extended funding for operations through mid-August, this was only the result of a threat by President Nixon to veto the bill with the original June cut-off date. In response, the mid-August date was settled as a compromise between the President and Congress. The district court concluded that the majority vote by both houses of Congress reflected evidence of binding congressional intent to terminate all support for the conflict.[131]

The Second Circuit Court of Appeals disagreed and stayed the injunction. The court rejected reliance on the original defunding bill to justify issuance of the injunction. Instead, it noted that the bill ultimately enacted into law authorized funding of the challenged military operations and therefore contradicted any inference that Congress was collectively opposed to the bombing missions.[132] The court specifically rejected the plaintiffs' argument that the veto threat placed Congress in a political and practical "straightjacket," compelling them to authorize a more extensive duration of hostilities than the legislative majority truly supported.[133] For the court of appeals, this was nothing more than our political system at work, and Congress's inability to muster the super-majority needed to override a veto of its original bill coupled with its decision to compromise on the bill ultimately enacted into law rendered the law, and not the original bill, decisive in assessing the scope of the President's authority to order continued hostilities.

Cases like *Holtzman*, and the overall difficulty Congress faced in the effort to force an end to the Vietnam conflict, led Congress to enact the War Powers Resolution.[134] This law (joint resolution) was clearly intended to prevent future Presidents from placing Congress in the same type of practical "straightjacket" Congress confronted when it sought to end the conflict in Vietnam—the untenable position of having to cut off support for an ongoing conflict. The WPR sought to mitigate the risk that future Presidents could present Congress with a war powers *fait accompli* by initiating a conflict Congress would then be bound to

---

[130] *Id.*

[131] *See* Holtzman v. Schlesinger, 361 F. Supp. 553, 565 (E.D.N.Y. 1973) (detailed description of the district court's reasoning).

[132] *Holtzman*, 484 F.2d *at* 1313-14.

[133] *Id.* at 1314 (The court held that the President did not "coerce" congressional consent by threat of exercising his veto power because there was "unquestionably a Congressional impasse" and there is no constitutional authority indicating that the President cannot exercise his veto power with respect to an authority vested solely in Congress).

[134] Corn, *supra* note 30, at 1173-74.

support (lest it risk "abandoning" the troops in the field or giving the enemy a *de facto* victory by demanding an immediate end to hostilities). According to §1541 of the WPR:

> It is the purpose of this chapter to fulfill the intent of the framers of the Constitution of the United States and insure that the collective judgment of both the Congress and the President will apply to the introduction of United States Armed Forces into hostilities, or into situations where imminent involvement in hostilities is clearly indicated by the circumstances, and to the continued use of such forces in hostilities or in such situations.[135]

The WPR cites the Necessary and Proper Clause of Article I to justify enacting a law that restricts the exercise of presidential war powers, noting that this clause vests Congress with the "power to make all laws necessary and proper for carrying into execution, not only its own powers but also all other powers vested by the Constitution in the Government of the United States, or in any department or officer hereof."[136]

The WPR seeks to accomplish the objective noted above through several provisions. First, the WPR requires the President to provide timely notice of any anticipated initiation of hostilities or introduction of forces into situations where hostilities were imminent.[137] Second, it enumerates the three exclusive situations in which the President is constitutionally authorized to commit U.S. armed forces to hostilities: where Congress has declared war; where Congress has provided some other form of *express* statutory authority for the hostilities; or where the President is responding to attack on the United States or its armed forces.[138] Third, it prohibits presidential reliance on anything other than *express* statutory authority to justify initiation or continuation of hostilities.[139] Fourth, it allows Congress to order the immediate termination of *any* U.S. involvement in hostilities at *any* time by concurrent resolution—a majority vote by both houses of Congress that does not require presentment and therefore cannot be nullified by presidential veto.[140]

Unsurprisingly, President Nixon considered the joint resolution that Congress enacted as the War Powers Resolution unconstitutional.[141] Nonetheless, Congress enacted the WPR when it overrode his veto. No President since Nixon has acquiesced to the constitutionality of the WPR.[142] Even when

---

[135] 50 U.S.C.S. §1541(a).

[136] U.S. CONST. art. I, §8, cl. 18.

[137] 50 U.S.C.S. §1543(a)(1).

[138] *Id.* §1541(c).

[139] *Id.* §1547.

[140] *Id.* §1544(c).

[141] "While I am in accord with the desire of the Congress to assert its proper role in the conduct of our foreign affairs, the restrictions which this resolution would impose upon the authority of the President are both unconstitutional and dangerous to the best interests of our Nation." *President's Veto, supra* note 96.

[142] *War Powers*, LIBRARY OF CONG., http://loc.gov/law/help/war-powers.php (last visited Nov. 6, 2013). "Since 1973, every president, from Nixon to Barack Obama, has voiced skepticism, either

submitting reports that appear to comply with the Resolution's reporting requirements, Presidents have always indicated they are acting "consistent with" versus "in compliance with" the law.[143] Nonetheless, the WPR is law, and inevitably influences the inter-branch dialogue on war powers initiatives. Each provision, therefore, must be considered both in terms of its relative constitutional validity or invalidity, and in terms of how it actually influences this policy interaction.

1. The Authority Provisions: What Does and Does Not Qualify as War Powers Authorization

Section 1541 of the WPR provides that the President may introduce U.S. armed forces into hostilities or situations of imminent hostilities only pursuant to a declaration of war, a specific statutory authorization, or a national emergency created by attack upon the United States, its territories or possessions, or its armed forces.[144] This provision reflects a rejection of the support by implication approach that dominated war powers analysis during the Vietnam Conflict.[145] By its terms, the WPR prohibits reliance on anything short of "specific" statutory authorization to commit the nation to hostilities.[146] Any doubt as to the type of statutory authorization that qualifies as "specific" within the meaning of the provision is resolved by reference to §1547, which provides that authority to introduce U.S. armed forces into hostilities or situations of imminent hostilities shall not be inferred from any statute or treaty, and specifically prohibits reliance on

---

privately or in public, over the constitutionality of the War Powers Resolution." *See also* Andrew Glass, *Nixon Vetos [sic] the War Powers Resolution, Oct. 24, 1973*, THE POLITICO, Oct. 24, 2011. http://www.politico.com/news/stories/1011/66654.html.

[143] RICHARD F. GRIMMETT, CONG. RESEARCH SERV., R42699, WAR POWERS RESOLUTION: AFTER THIRTY-EIGHT YEARS 17 (Sept. 24, 2012), *available at* https://www.fas.org/sgp/crs/natsec/R42699.pdf. *See also id.* at 52 app. (a complete listing of all 136 instances reported under the War Powers Resolution). The only incident to specifically cite §4(a)(1) was Mayaguez seizure in 1975. *Id.* at 48.

[144] 50 U.S.C.S. §1541. The actual text reads:

> The constitutional powers of the President as Commander-in-Chief to introduce United States Armed Forces into hostilities, or into situations where imminent involvement in hostilities is clearly indicated by the circumstances, are exercised only pursuant to
>
> (1) a declaration of war,
> (2) specific statutory authorization, or
> (3) a national emergency created by attack upon the United States, its territories or possessions, or its armed forces.

Id.

[145] Geoffrey S. Corn, *Triggering Congressional War Powers Notification: A Proposal to Reconcile Constitutional Practice with Operational Reality*, 14 LEWIS & CLARK L. REV. 687, 690 (Summer 2010).

[146] Corn, *supra* note 30, at 1174. ("The War Powers Resolution is clear: Only express legislative support for combat operations may be regarded as constitutionally sufficient.")

appropriation acts as a source of implied war powers authority.[147] Accordingly, specific statutory authorization within the meaning of the WPR means explicit authorization, such as an Authorization for the Use of Military Force.[148]

When considered against the backdrop of Justice Jackson's three-tier model for assessing presidential powers, it seems apparent that Congress sought to eliminate Jackson's second tier of power (the twilight zone) from the war powers equation.[149] The specific statutory authorization requirement prohibits presidential assertions of congressional cooperation or acquiescence in situations of ambivalence or uncertainty, such as in the Kosovo example. Perhaps more significantly, it also nullifies the notion of "implied" congressional support, which would otherwise place an assertion of presidential power into Jackson's first tier. In essence, Congress, through these provisions, barred reliance on anything short of express statutory authorization as evidence of inter-branch war powers cooperation. Accordingly, the WPR transforms congressional uncertainty into opposition to presidential action, transforming a "twilight zone" situation to a tier three "opposition" situation.[150]

It is therefore unsurprising that no President has acknowledged the validity of this WPR provision. Instead, it was at the time and has been since criticized as inconsistent with constitutional custom.[151] Interestingly, Kosovo and other

---

[147] 50 U.S.C.S. §1547. The actual text expressly indicates authority may not be inferred from:

> (1) from any provision of law (whether or not in effect before November 7, 1973), including any provision contained in any appropriation Act, unless such provision specifically authorizes the introduction of United States Armed Forces into hostilities or into such situations and states that it is intended to constitute specific statutory authorization within the meaning of this chapter; or
> (2) from any treaty heretofore or hereafter ratified unless such treaty is implemented by legislation specifically authorizing the introduction of United States Armed Forces into hostilities or into such situations and stating that it is intended to constitute specific statutory authorization within the meaning of this chapter.

Id.

[148] Harold Hongju Koh, *The Coase Theorem and the War Power: A Response*, 41 Duke L.J. 122, 126 (1991) ("an authorization to use force is an adequate mechanism for Congress to 'constitutionally manifest its understanding and approval for a presidential determination to make war'"). *See* Authorization for Use of Military Force, Pub. L. No. 107-40, 115 Stat. 224 (Sept. 18, 2001).

[149]

> Particularly in the post-Watergate era, Congress filled nearly every shadowy corner of the zone of twilight with its own imprimatur. That is not to say that Congress placed a relentless series of checks on the executive. Rather, Congress strove to establish ground rules, providing a limiting framework such as the War Powers Resolution for each effusive authorization. . . . This leaves Jackson's second category essentially a dead letter.

Daniel J. Freeman, *The Canons of War*, 117 Yale L.J. 280, 283-84 (Nov. 2007).

[150] Corn, *supra* note 145, at 691.

[151] *See* John W. Rolph, *The Decline and Fall of the War Powers Resolution: Waging War Under the Constitution After Desert Storm*, 40 Naval L. Rev. 85, 91-93 (1992); Robert F. Turner, *The War Powers Resolution: Unconstitutional, Unnecessary, and Unhelpful*, 17 Loy. L.A. L. Rev. 683, 683-85 (1984). ("The idea that Congress can by silence or inaction deprive the President of a fundamental

post-1973 military actions indicate that this custom continued even after enact-ment of the WPR. The fact that not even subsequent Congresses have seemed particularly interested in seeking to enforce this provision also undermines its validity. This itself raises an interesting question: Can one Congress dictate to future Congresses the mode of expressing their support or cooperation with a President on the issue of war powers initiatives? In this regard, it is equally inter-esting to consider the effect this provision should have on future Congresses. By its terms, it creates a serious consequence for congressional failure to take an affirmative position on a war powers initiative. Unlike the Vietnam era, a congres-sional failure to take such an express position on a presidential war powers initiative must, according to this provision, be interpreted as opposition to the President. Congress may no longer hesitate in reaction to such an initiative without creating the risk that their hesitation must be interpreted as opposition. Thus, the effect of this "express authorization" aspect of the WPR seems to not only place limits on future Presidents, but also place demands of affirmative action on future Congresses.

Even if this provision is constitutional, however, its impact cannot be fully assessed without also considering the impact of the legislative standing doctrine. When, in *Campbell v. Clinton*, legislators opposed to the continued execution of the air war against Serbia sought injunctive and declaratory relief in federal court, relying in part on a violation of this provision of the WPR, the court dismissed the lawsuit for lack of standing.[152] The asserted violation of a statute enacted in 1973 by a prior Congress was insufficient to satisfy the "total nullification" require-ment of *Raines v. Byrd*.[153] Instead, because the sitting Congress had failed to vote to prohibit further military action, the court concluded that the opposition legis-lators had not met this standing requirement. The court, therefore, rendered this WPR provision legally superfluous in legislator initiated court challenges, for only an affirmative vote in opposition to the President would provide both standing and a constitutionally ripe dispute.[154] Of course, this provision might prove valuable to a service member seeking to challenge deployment, as standing in such a case would not necessitate an affirmative vote in opposition to the chal-lenged hostilities.

None of this is to suggest that this WPR provision is irrelevant. Because it will always create "authorization uncertainty" in the absence of express congressional support for a presidential war powers initiative, it has significantly influenced the inter-branch dialogue on such initiatives. Presidents assume added risk when they assert constitutional war powers in the absence of such express statutory support, and the provision also arms legislative opponents with a significant weapon in the debate over whether such authorization is required. The influence of this provision is arguably manifested by the record of inter-branch cooperation on

---

expressed constitutional power—in a time of national emergency, no less—is incompatible with our system of separation of powers.")

[152] 203 F.3d 19 (2000).

[153] *See* 521 U.S. at 823.

[154] *Id.* at 824.

almost all major commitments of U.S. armed forces into hostilities since enactment of the WPR. In almost all of these cases, Presidents have sought (and
received) the type of express statutory authorization demanded by the WPR
(this excludes military actions based on inherent presidential rescue or self-
defense authority). While Presidents who sought this support always insist that
it is not constitutionally required, it seems undeniable that the provision has
produced the type of cooperation the WPR sought to ensure.

2.   The Consultation Provision

Congress established §1542 of the War Powers Resolution, known as the consultation provision, to increase communication between Congress and the
executive branch.[155] This communication aimed at making a joint decision,
and is consistent with the constitutional check and balance system because it guarantees that the decision to enter into war is weighed and scrutinized by both political branches.[156] The section provides that:

> The President in every possible instance shall consult with Congress before
> introducing United States Armed Forces into hostilities or into situations where
> imminent involvement in hostilities is clearly indicated by the circumstances,
> and after every such introduction shall consult regularly with the Congress until
> United States Armed Forces are no longer engaged in hostilities or have been
> removed from such situations.

Section 1542 requires that the President consult with Congress before introducing U.S. armed forces into hostilities or situations where hostilities are imminent, and to continue such consultations as long as U.S. armed forces remain in
such situations.[157] The State and Defense Departments have defined hostilities as
"a situation in which American forces are actively exchanging fire with opposing
units." Imminent hostilities means "a situation where there is a serious risk from

---

[155] *See* Turner, *supra* note 151, at 693-94 (suggesting that regular communication between the
executive and legislative branches raises the Executive's awareness of probable congressional
attitudes when confronted with an emergency requiring immediate action and alleviates Congress's
fear of being ignored and will raise awareness regarding administration policy and programs).
See also RICHARD F. GRIMMETT, CONG. RESEARCH. SERV., RL 33532, WAR POWERS RESOLUTION:
PRESIDENTIAL COMPLIANCE 1 (2009), *available at* http://www.fas.org/sgp/crs/natsec/RL33532.pdf. "The
purpose of the [War Powers Resolution] is to ensure that Congress and the President share in
making decisions that may get the United States involved in hostilities."

[156] Julia L. Chen, Note, *Restoring Constitutional Balance: Accommodating the Evolution of War*, 53
B.C. L. REV. 1767, 1796 (citing Joseph R. Biden, Jr. & John B. Ritch III, Commentary, *The War
Power at a Constitutional Impasse: A "Joint Decision" Solution*, 77 GEO. L.J. 367, 371-72 (1988)). *See also*
THE CONSTITUTION PROJECT, DECIDING TO USE FORCE ABROAD: WAR POWERS IN A SYSTEM OF CHECKS AND
BALANCES 101 (2005), *available at* http://www.constitutionproject.org/pdf/28.pdf.

[157] 50 U.S.C.S. §1542.

III. Authorizing War

hostile fire to the safety of U.S. forces."[158] Congress required that the consultation take place "in every possible instance" in order to take a firm stance that allowed for flexibility.[159] The Senate Committee on Foreign Relations stated that determining whether consultation is necessary is a decision to be made by Congress and the President.[160] This consultation can end when the armed forces are no longer engaged or have been removed from the theater of operations. There is also indication that the President no longer needs to consult with Congress if there has been a declaration of war or other specific congressional authorization.[161] The WPR does not create any exceptions based on the size of the intervention or chances of escalation.[162]

Nonetheless, there appear to be a few exceptions to the consultation provision. First, there may be a temporary exception created for threats to national security that require the President to act swiftly and "repel sudden attacks" when there is no time to consult Congress.[163] This is bolstered by the legislative use of the word "possible" in the consultation clause, which accounts for situations that require instantaneous responses.[164] However, when this potential exception occurs the President should consult as soon as possible with Congress since consultation is required in "every" situation, which appears to encompass "extraordinary and emergency situations."[165] Second, the Obama administration declared that the use of technology, such as UAVs and cyber-warfare fall outside the War Powers Resolution since troops are not being introduced into hostilities and their use can therefore be implemented without consultation.[166] Finally, the wartime involvement of government civilians and contractors

---

[158] *Presidential Power, supra* note 71, at 185 (citing *War Powers: A Test of Compliance Relative to the Danang Sealift, the Evacuation of Phnom Penh, the Evacuation of Saigon, and the Mayaguez Incident, Hearings before the Subcommittee on Int'l Security and Scientific Affairs of the House Comm. on Int'l Relations,* 94th Cong., 1st Sess. 75 at 38-40 (Mayaguez) (1975) [hereinafter *War Powers: A Test of Compliance*]).

[159] 1979 OLC Lexis 94 *12 (Nov. 11, 1979) (citing H. Rep. No. 287, 93d Cong., 1st Sess. 6 (1973)).

[160] "After the hostage rescue mission in Iran, the Senate Committee on Foreign Relations asserted that . . . the judgment about whether consultation is required in a particular situation 'must be made jointly by the President and Congress.'" *Overview of the WPR, supra* note 91, at 275-76.

[161] The War Powers Resolution "requires the President in every possible instance to consult with Congress before introducing American armed forces into hostilities or imminent hostilities unless there has been a declaration of war or other specific congressional authorization." *See* GRIMMETT, *supra* note 155, at 2.

[162] Jeremy Telman, *A Truism That Isn't True? The Tenth Amendment and Executive War Power*, 51 CATH. U. L. REV. 135, 168 (Fall 2001).

[163] John H. Ely, *Suppose Congress Wanted a War Powers Act that Worked*, 88 COLUM. L. REV. 1379, 1388 (Nov. 1988).

[164] 1979 OLC Lexis 94 (Nov. 11, 1979) (citing H. Rep. No. 287, 93d Cong., 1st Sess. 6 (1973)).

[165] *Id.*

[166] Chen, *supra* note 156, at 1798 (citing Matthew C. Waxman, *Cyber Attacks as "Force" Under UN Charter Article 2(4), in* INTERNATIONAL LAW AND THE CHANGING CHARACTER OF WAR 43, 48 (Raul A. Pedrozo & Daria P. Wollschlaeger eds., 2011)). Secretary of State Hillary Clinton announced in a 2010 address: "In an internet-connected world, an attack on one nation's networks can be an attack

does not require consultation since, again, United States Armed Forces are not involved.[167]

As with the reporting requirement, almost all Presidents have endeavored to act "consistently with" instead of "in accordance with" the consultation requirement.[168] Despite the fact that compliance with this section has been higher than with other sections of the War Powers Resolution,[169] there is still disparity between the presidential and congressional interpretation of what constitutes compliance.[170] The Senate Committee on Foreign Relations has stated that consultation involves "permitting Congress to participate in the decision-making."[171] It is unclear how that participation takes shape, specifically regarding who needs to be involved, the timing of the consultation, and how much information the President needs to disclose.[172] Congress argues that the President needs to consult before introducing troops into hostilities, per the statutory language. However, Presidents typically do not define consultation as meaning "seeking advice prior to a decision to introduce troops."[173] Additionally, the WPR fails to indicate who specifically the President must consult with in Congress in order to comply with this requirement.[174] In order to avoid practical difficulties that would arise if the consultation requirement included the entire Congress, the term has been interpreted to include only the "relevant congressional leadership."[175]

---

on all." Hillary Rodham Clinton, U.S. Sec'y of State, Remarks on Internet Freedom (Jan. 21, 2010), http://www.state.gov/secretary/rm/2010/01/135519.htm.

[167] Id. (citing Scott M. Sullivan, *Private Force/Public Goods*, 42 Conn. L. Rev. 853, 859 (2010)).

[168] This "consistent with" language has been used by many Presidents since Nixon in letters to Congress regarding the War Powers Resolution. *See Letter to Congressional Leaders Reporting on the Deployment of United States Military Personnel as Part of the Kosovo International Security Force*, 2 Pub. Papers 1544, 1544 (Nov. 14, 2003); *Letter to Congressional Leaders on the Situation in Somalia*, 1 Pub. Papers 836, 836 (June 10, 1993); *Letter to Congressional Leaders on the Persian Gulf Conflict*, 1 Pub. Papers 52, 52 (Jan. 18, 1991); *Letter to the Speaker of the House of Representatives and the President Pro Tempore of the Senate on the United States Reprisal Against Iran*, 2 Pub. Papers 1212, 1212 (Oct. 20, 1987).

[169] Ely, *supra* note 163, at 1401.

[170] 8 Op. O.L.C. 271 *275-76 (Oct. 30, 1984). "Based upon the reactions by Members of Congress to the "Mayaguez" consultations by President Ford, it seems likely that virtually any level or degree of consultation will leave some Members unsatisfied."

[171] Id.

[172] Id. (Congressional members have complained about the "level, extent, or timeliness" of the consultation after almost every incident invoking the War Powers Resolution. Additionally, "members of Congress have generally been unsatisfied if the 'consultation' has not occurred prior to the decisionmaking, has not included participation by the President himself as well as his staff, or because a perceived insubstantial number of Members have been involved in the consultations").

[173] Grimmett, *supra* note 155.

[174] *See* Turner, *supra* note 151, at 693-94. "Certainly the President cannot be expected to talk individually with all 535 members of Congress, and at times events move so quickly that even the best-intentioned Commander-in-Chief can do little more than instruct his staff to keep congressional leaders informed."

[175] Ely, *supra* note 163, at 1400-01. *See* Grimmett, *supra* note 155. (Legislation containing a clearly defined consultative group has been proposed a number of times, but none has succeeded. In 1988, S.J. Res. 323 proposed establishing a "permanent consultation group of 18 Members consisting of the leadership and the ranking and minority members of the Committee on Foreign

III. Authorizing War

Those opposed to the consultation provision disagree for political, constitutional, and informational reasons. In each case, the proponents of the consultation provision provide counterpoints. Politically, the more risk-adverse congressional members prefer not to be consulted. Staying out of the decision-making process allows them the "flexibility to jump on the . . . bandwagon if things go well, or to sharpen their swords and distances themselves politically from the President if things go badly."[176] Consultation limits the opposition's potential political gains since "flip-flopping on support for a war tends to be politically costly."[177] Constitutionally, consultation may pose an issue under *INS v. Chadha*[178] since it is unclear how there can be "real involvement" of Congress in "such typically fast-breaking decision-making" without the use of formal legislative action taken by both Houses and submitted to the President.[179] Proponents argue that the WPR allows the President to determine the form of consultation, and therefore does not interfere with his constitutional powers. The Executive has argued that a President may proceed without consulting Congress for security reasons if he determines that it would contradict his constitutional rights.[180] From an informational stance, it is argued that the President has superior knowledge to Congress.[181] Therefore, he should be permitted to assess the information and reach a conclusion on his own. On the other hand, allowing Congress to assess the information would obviously enable Congress to fulfill its constitutional war authorization role.

As with the entire WPR, the consultation provision is viewed by the executive and legislative branches in light of its role in the process. Regardless, the WPR does seem to accomplish its goal of facilitating communication between the branches in relation to the war powers decision-making process.

3. The Notification Provision

One of the objectives of the WPR was to mitigate the risk that Congress would not have an opportunity to consider the wisdom of a presidential decision to commit U.S. armed forces to hostilities until after the fact.[182] The obvious reason for

---

Relations, Armed Services, and Intelligence." In 1993 and in 1994, a group similar to the National Security Council was proposed.)

[176] Jide Nzelibe, *A Positive Theory of the* War-Powers *Constitution*, 91 Iowa L. Rev. 993, 1014 (2006).

[177] Matthew Fleischman, Note, *A Functional Distribution of War Powers*, 13 N.Y.U. J. Legis. & Pub. Pol'y 137, 151 (2010).

[178] 462 U.S. 919 (1983).

[179] 1984 OLC Lexis 48 *10-11 (Oct. 30, 1984).

[180] 1980 OLC Lexis *26-27 (Feb. 12, 1980) (citing *War Powers: A Test of Compliance*, *supra* note 156, at 100).

[181] *See* Nzelibe & Yoo, *supra* note 14, at 2523.

[182] *Cf.* Grimmett, *supra* note 155, at 2. "Many Members of Congress became concerned with the erosion of congressional authority to decide when the United States should become involved in a war or the use of armed forces that might lead to war."

this was the fact that, as a practical matter, it is far more difficult for Congress to demand termination of hostilities once commenced than to prohibit them prior to their commencement.[183] This has been a painful lesson of the Vietnam conflict: Although public and congressional support for the conflict declined significantly following the Tet Offensive of 1968,[184] it took nearly four more years to finally reach the point where Congress could totally terminate support for the conflict. The cost in national resources during this time period was substantial. Subsequently, Congress sought to ensure it was notified of anticipated military actions before initiation. When this requirement is coupled with the prohibitory effect of a congressional decision not to specifically authorize such anticipated military actions, Congress would be empowered to more effectively control the initiation of hostilities.

Section 1543 of the WPR therefore imposed a reporting requirement upon the President.[185] The trigger for this reporting requirement includes both

---

[183] *Id.* "Compliance [with the War Powers Resolution] becomes an issue whenever the President introduces U.S. forces abroad in situations that might be construed as hostilities or imminent hostilities." *See also* Corn, *supra* note 145, at 691.

[184] Edwin E. Moise, *The Vietnam Wars, Section 8, The Tet Offensive and its Aftermath*, CLEMSON UNIVERSITY, (Nov. 6, 1998), http://www.clemson.edu/caah/history/facultypages/edmoise/viet8.html.

[185] *See* 50 U.S.C. §1543(a)(1), which provides that:

In the absence of a declaration of war, in any case in which United States Armed Forces are introduced:

    (1) into hostilities or into situations where imminent involvement in hostilities is clearly indicated by the circumstances;

    (2) into the territory, airspace or waters of a foreign nation, while equipped for combat, except for deployments which relate solely to supply, replacement, repair, or training of such forces; or

    (3) in numbers which substantially enlarge United States Armed Forces equipped for combat already located in a foreign nation;

the President shall submit within 48 hours to the Speaker of the House of Representatives and to the President pro tempore of the Senate a report, in writing, setting forth—

    (A) the circumstances necessitating the introduction of United States Armed Forces;

    (B) the constitutional and legislative authority under which such introduction took place; and

    (C) the estimated scope and duration of the hostilities or involvement.

(b) Other information reported. The President shall provide such other information as the Congress may request in the fulfillment of its constitutional responsibilities with respect to committing the Nation to war and to the use of United States Armed Forces abroad.

(c) Periodic reports; semiannual requirement. Whenever United States Armed Forces are introduced into hostilities or into any situation described in subsection (a) of this section, the President shall, so long as such armed forces continue to be engaged in such hostilities or situation, report to the Congress periodically on the status of such hostilities or situation as well as on the scope and duration of such hostilities or situation, but in no event shall he report to the Congress less often than once every six months.

Id.

III. Authorizing War

hostilities and situations where, "involvement in hostilities is clearly indicated by the circumstances."[186] This has unsurprisingly led to conflicting presidential/congressional interpretations of the trigger for this reporting requirement.[187] Does an unplanned engagement with border security forces of another nation qualify as hostilities? For example, in 1998 three U.S. Army soldiers patrolling the border between Macedonia and Serbia as part of a UN peacekeeping mission came under fire from Serbian border forces and were subsequently captured. Was this a reportable incident? Even more susceptible to divergent interpretations is what circumstances "clearly" indicate hostilities are imminent? For example, during the 1980s, U.S. Special Forces advisers were routinely deployed to provide training and advice to U.S. allies in Central America, most notably the El Salvadoran armed forces. These advisers would accompany El Salvadoran combat forces during military operations against the FMLN communist insurgents, although they were permitted to use force only in self-defense. Their numbers never exceeded 150 troops. President Reagan did not consider this a deployment triggering the WPR reporting requirement, a conclusion that frustrated some members of Congress.[188] In *Lowry v. Reagan*, a federal court concluded that deciding whether such a deployment qualified as one involving "imminent hostilities" lacked judicially manageable and discoverable standards, and therefore was a non-justiciable political question.[189]

---

[186] 50 U.S.C.S. §1543(a)(1).

[187] Assistant Attorney General John Harmon is of the opinion that "the term 'hostilities' should not be read necessarily to include sporadic military or paramilitary attacks on our armed forces stationed abroad. Such situations do not generally involve the full military engagements with which the Resolution is primarily concerned. For the same reason, we also believe that as a general matter the presence of our armed forces in a foreign country whose government comes under attack by "guerrilla" operations would not trigger the reporting provisions of the War Powers Resolution unless our armed forces were assigned to 'command, coordinate, participate in the movement of, or accompany' the forces of the host government in operations against such guerrilla operations." 4A Op. O.L.C. 185, 194 (Feb. 12, 1980).

[188] *See Overview of the WPR, supra* note 91 (referencing Foreign Affairs Special Study at 249-52). *See also Crockett*, 558 F. Supp. 893 (court held that the President's decision to deploy troops was non-justiciable, but states that in certain situations a court may be able to require compliance with the reporting requirement of the War Powers Resolution).

[189]

> If the Court were to grant or deny declaratory relief, and decide whether United States Armed Forces stationed in the Persian Gulf are engaged in "hostilities or . . . [in] situations where imminent involvement in hostilities is clearly indicated by the circumstances," the Court would risk "the potentiality of embarrassment [that would result] from multifarious pronouncements by various departments on one question." Indeed, such a declaration necessarily would contradict legislative pronouncements on one side or the other of this issue. Moreover, a declaration of "hostilities" by this Court could impact on statements by the Executive that the United States is neutral in the Iran-Iraq war and, moreover, might create doubts in the international community regarding the resolve of the United States to adhere to this position. Because this Court concludes that the volatile situation in the Persian Gulf demands, in the words of *Baker v. Carr*, a "single-voiced statement of the Government's views," the Court refrains from joining the debate on the question of whether "hostilities" exist in that region.

676 F. Supp. 333, 340-41 (1987).

Congress did attempt to provide general guidance for assessing what triggers this hostilities reporting requirement. Section 1543 provides that a report is required whenever U.S. armed forces are introduced:

> (2) into the territory, airspace or waters of a foreign nation, while equipped for combat, except for deployments which relate solely to supply, replacement, repair, or training of such forces; or
> (3) in numbers which substantially enlarge United States Armed Forces equipped for combat already located in a foreign nation;

These two touchstones raise their own set of complex questions. First, U.S. forces rarely deploy anywhere without the capability to defend themselves from attack—what the military calls "force protection." Such deployments are frequently ordered as "show of force" missions intended to deter aggressors from acting against U.S. or allied interests. Do these deployments justifiably fall within a war powers reporting obligation? Or are they exercises of the President's inherent foreign affairs authority—what might be best understood as military diplomacy? This is a critical question, for if they fall into the latter category, it is difficult to justify the imposition of a reporting obligation on the President. For example, from 1988 to 1989, U.S. armed forces were deployed in substantial numbers to Panama, almost doubling the pre-crisis U.S. military presence.[190] These deployments served two objectives: first, to exercise U.S. rights pursuant to the Panama Canal treaties; and second, to pressure General Noriega, Panama's rogue military leader, to leave the country and turn power over to a democratically elected government. Was this an exercise of the President's inherent foreign affairs power, or a prelude to imminent war? The United States did not attack the Panamanian Defense Forces until December 1989.[191] What was the nature of the U.S. troop increase for the 18 months prior to that date?

The exemption for training deployments also raises uncertainty. The line between a deployment for purposes of training, deterrence, or pre-positioning in anticipation of combat is frequently quite blurry. This is because deployment for any of these purposes would be relatively ineffective if the forces are not equipped with the resources necessary to engage in combat, which means they are deployed equipped "for combat." How are these types of deployments to be distinguished from those that trigger the reporting requirement? It seems the answer must turn on the *purpose* of the deployment, and not on some objective indicator of *capability* of the forces. This, however, is an inherently subjective touchstone, and one a President could conveniently manipulate to avoid

---

[190] Nicholas E. Reynolds, Just Cause: Marine Operations in Panama 1988-1990, Dep't of the Navy (1996), *available at* http://community.marines.mil/news/publications/Documents/Just%20Cause%20Marine%20Operations%20in%20Panama%201988-1990%20PCN%2019000313400_1.pdf.

[191] *Authority of the President Under Domestic and International Law to Use Military Force Against Iraq*, 26 Op. O.L.C. 1, 189-90 (Oct. 23, 2002). *See also Address to the Nation Announcing United States Military Action in Panama*, 2 Pub. Papers 1733, 1723 (Dec. 20, 1989) (Bush committed troops after consulting with Congress, but without congressional approval).

reporting. Panama provides another example. During the build up for the U.S. invasion of Panama, large numbers of U.S. forces were deployed to Panama to conduct combat training at the Jungle Operations Training Center.[192] Did these deployments trigger the reporting requirement? No report was submitted by President Bush, although within a matter of weeks of their arrival they were involved in combat operations.

It must be noted, that Presidents have in fact provided reports that satisfy this provision of the WPR on numerous occasions, always characterized as reports "consistent with," and not "in compliance with," the WPR. It seems that reporting the obvious has not been considered particularly problematic by these administrations.[193] Submitting such reports to Congress may actually accrue to the benefit of the President. This is because administrations will almost certainly consider the effect of congressional acquiescence to the reported military action a sign of implicit support.[194] The significance of this acquiescence is obviously enhanced by the notification of the action provided by the report.

It must also be noted that there is a significant collateral effect to submitting a report within the meaning of §1543: It triggers the 60-day clock provision of §1544. As explained below, this means that the 60-day "grace period" for the conduct of hostilities in the absence of specific statutory authority begins to run when the report is submitted.[195] Submitting such a report will therefore place pressure on Congress to take specific action either in support or opposition to the military action. It will also increase the risk of a challenge to the continuation of the operation beyond 60 days in the event Congress does not do so.

This relationship between the WPRs reporting provision and the 60-day clock led Congress to include within the WPR a provision intended to prevent a President from avoiding the 60-day clock by simply refusing to submit a required report.[196] Thus, in the absence of a report, the clock begins to run on the date a report *was required*—the date armed forces were committed to hostilities or to a situation of imminent hostilities.[197] Of course, how this "fail safe" provision will function is unclear. It is almost certain that a President who does not feel obligated

---

[192] Ronald H. Cole, Joint History Office, Office of the Chairman of the Joint Chiefs of Staff, Operation Just Cause: The Planning and Execution of Joint Operations in Panama, February 1988-January 1990, 7-10 (1995), *available at* http://www.dtic.mil/doctrine/doctrine/history/justcaus.pdf.

[193] Grimmett, *supra* note 143, at 17.

[194] Corn, *supra* note 145, at 702.

[195] *Id.*; *cf.* Nat'l War Powers Cmm'n, Miller Ctr. of Pub. Affairs, Nat'l War Powers Cmm'n Report 24 (2008), http://millercenter.org/policy/commissions/warpowers/report (indicating that Presidents believe acting consistently with this provision does not start the 60-day clock but is sufficient to impart notice to Congress under the War Powers Resolution, whereas acting pursuant to would start the clock and implicate §5(b)).

[196] When Presidents have made reports pursuant to the Resolution, they do so only after the military operations have been completed. Ellen Collier, *Statutory Constraints: The War Powers Resolution, in* The U.S. Constitution and the Power to Go to War: Historical and Current Perspectives 55, 61 (Gary M. Stern & Morton H. Halperin eds., 1994).

[197] 50 U.S.C.S. §1544.

to report a military deployment will then impose upon themself an obligation to terminate the operation in 60 days.[198] Even if Congress were to pass a concurrent resolution indicating they believe a report was required at a prior date, it will still be unlikely the non-reporting President will consider this in any way binding on her.[199] Congress could, of course, enact a law prohibiting the continuation of the military action, but if they can accomplish this, the reporting/60-day clock provision will be functionally superfluous. Requesting declaratory relief from a court indicating the date the report was required may be another option for frustrated legislators, although it seems it would have to be relatively obvious that the deployment qualified within the meaning of the reporting provision in order to overcome the political question barrier.

The Resolution's reporting requirement has proved to have mixed results. Like the rest of the WPR, it has probably contributed to enhancing the dialogue between Presidents and Congress; which may be its ultimate value.

4.   The Sixty-Day Clock

Without question, the most controversial provision of the WPR was what is commonly referred to as the "sixty-day clock."[200] Section 1544 provides that:

> Within sixty calendar days after a report is submitted or is required to be submitted pursuant to section 1543 (a)(1) of this title, whichever is earlier, the President shall terminate any use of United States Armed Forces with respect to which such report was submitted (or required to be submitted), unless the Congress
>
> (1) has declared war or has enacted a specific authorization for such use of United States Armed Forces,
> (2) has extended by law such sixty-day period, or

---

[198] "The executive branch no longer seems restricted to any time limit in using military force." Louis Fisher & David Gray Adler, *The War Powers Resolution: Time To Say Goodbye*, Pol. Sci. Q. 1, 17 (1998).

> During earlier administrations, such as President Reagan's action in Grenada and President Bush's invasion of Panama, executive officials occasionally behaved as though the sixty-day clock was running, even if it had not been legally triggered by a report under Section 4(a)(1). Under those conditions it could be argued that the War Powers Resolution did have a constraining effect on presidential initiatives.

Fisher, *supra* note 57, at 142.

[199] Congress has a weaker argument for trying to use a concurrent resolution to veto a presidential exercise of executive power. Robert F. Turner, *The War Powers Resolution: An Unnecessary, Unconstitutional Source of "Friendly Fire" in the War Against International Terrorism?*, The Federalist Society (Feb. 15, 2005), http://www.fed-soc.org/publications/detail/the-war-powers-resolution-an-unnecessary-unconstitutional-source-of-friendly-fire-in-the-war-against-international-terrorism.

[200] Grimmett, *supra* note 143, at 9.

    (3) is physically unable to meet as a result of an armed attack upon the United States. Such sixty-day period shall be extended for not more than an additional thirty days if the President determines and certifies to the Congress in writing that unavoidable military necessity respecting the safety of United States Armed Forces requires the continued use of such armed forces in the course of bringing about a prompt removal of such forces.

By plain meaning, the President is obligated to terminate any deployment involving hostilities or into situations where hostilities are likely unless Congress specifically authorizes continued operations within 60 days. As President Nixon noted in his veto message, this provision provides an illogical windfall to any U.S. opponent because the opponent will know at the initiation of hostilities that victory will be assured on day 61 so long as Congress is incapable of enacting specific statutory support.[201] Nixon, like Congress, must have been equally influenced by his own experience during the Vietnam conflict. For several years he dealt with a Congress incapable of taking a firm and explicit position either in support of or in opposition to the war. Had this provision been binding at that time, his efforts to meet the strategic objectives of the nation would have been totally undermined.

    This practical strategic impact of §1544 is not, however, the only source of objection. Legally, the provision seems facially incoherent. This is because it presupposes initiation of hostilities in the absence of specific statutory authority. In such situations, the WPR renders the military action illegal. As a result, how can it be "legal" for 60 days, but become "illegal" on day 61? If, in contrast, the initial commitment of U.S. armed forces to a situation triggering the notification requirement by the President was lawful, how can Congress alter that legal basis by taking no action simply by allowing 60 days to transpire? Either the President possesses constitutional authority on day 1 and day 61, or he does not. And if he does not, then how can Congress sanction 60 days of ongoing operations?[202]

    There is, however, a logical response to this question. Section 1544 is a recognition that there may be situations where the President either believes he is acting pursuant to inherent Article II authority (for example, to defend the nation from an imminent attack), or that the nature of the deployment does not trigger the notification provision of the WPR. In either case, §1544 provides a buffer period during which Congress will assess the claim of presidential authority. If, at the end of this period, Congress does not specifically endorse the claim by authorizing continued operations, it indicates a rejection of the asserted legal authority and requires immediate termination of the mission (unless Congress authorizes a 30-day extension in accordance with §1544(b)[203]).

---

[201] *President's Veto, supra* note 96.

[202] THE CONSTITUTION, THAT DELICATE BALANCE (Columbia University Seminars on Media and Society 1984).

[203] 50 U.S.C.S. §1544(b).

Because §1544 by its terms acknowledges the possibility that U.S. armed forces will be committed into hostilities *without* prior specific authorization, it has created tremendous uncertainty. Although reference to §1544[204] makes it clear that Congress did not intend this 60-day grace period to provide any authority for such introduction of armed forces, this is exactly the effect it has had. Indeed, the most common misrepresentation about the WPR is almost certainly the assertion that it authorized the President to commit forces into hostilities or situations of imminent hostilities for up to 60 days. This is simply not accurate. Nonetheless, even executive branch legal advisers have invoked §1544 as a source of authority for conducting military operations of limited duration, an interpretation that seems truly disingenuous as the WPR itself prohibits such invocation.[205]

Ultimately, §1544 can only be understood by distinguishing authorization from toleration. This provision of the WPR was not, and should not be, invoked as providing authority for any military action, even of very short duration. However, it certainly indicates tolerance for such initiatives by the President, but places a 60-day limit on that tolerance. This might reflect a certain degree of political pragmatism—Congress may need to tolerate presidential war powers initiatives simply as a result of the rapid pace of developments and uncertain nature of situations necessitating such initiatives. The 60-day tolerance period gives the President and Congress adequate time to reach agreement on specifically authorizing such initiatives, and if such support is not forthcoming protects congressional war powers by mandating termination of the operation. However, this tolerance provision is as illogical strategically as it may be logical politically. No President can predict with certainty how a military action will unfold once initiated. Indeed, it is unlikely President Johnson ever anticipated the level of commitment that evolved out of the Gulf of Tonkin incident, or President Clinton anticipated the air war against Serbia would drag on more than 60 days. By imposing this automatic termination date for the tolerance provided by §1544, the nature of U.S. resolve is arbitrarily undermined for ongoing military actions.

Like the rest of the WPR, perhaps the most significant impact of §1544 is the risk it creates for a President who chooses to initiate and continue a military action beyond 60 days. It is unlikely any President would want to be perceived as blatantly violating the WPR, even if they consider the law unconstitutional. Acting without specific statutory authority for up to 60 days may be inconsistent with the plain meaning of the WPR, but at least it is consistent with the de facto tolerance period built into §1544. Continuing the operation beyond that period of time cannot plausibly be characterized as consistent with the WPR. This may be why the air war against Serbia is the only combat operation initiated by a President since 1973,

---

[204] 50 U.S.C.S. §1544.

[205] Richard H. Fallon, *Interpreting Presidential War Powers*, 63 DUKE L.J. 347, 388 (Nov. 2008) (citing FISHER, *supra* note 57, at 145 (describing the War Powers Resolution as "recognizing that the President may use armed forces for up to 90 days without seeking or obtaining legislative authority")).

without specific statutory authorization or within the scope of defensive or rescue powers, that continued beyond 60 days. And it is unlikely President Clinton either anticipated or wanted the operation to last that long.

The WPR generally, and §1544 specifically, increases the political and strategic value of the President seeking, and Congress granting, specific statutory authority for military actions involving hostilities or even a substantial likelihood of hostilities prior to initiation or within this 60-day period.

5. The Concurrent Resolution Termination Provision

As noted above, the overall effect of the WPR is to transform anything less than specific and express statutory authority for a military action involving hostilities or a high probability of hostilities into congressional opposition. Congress must have also recognized that the 60-day tolerance period for action in the absence of such authorization created a risk that Presidents would initiate military action without such authority. Section 1544 also created risk that a President might initiate operations based on an asserted attack on the United States or its armed forces, and that Congress might not share this interpretation of the situation and therefore consider the action constitutionally unjustified. Accordingly, Congress included what might be understood as a failsafe provision, allowing Congress to demand termination of a military action at *any* time by concurrent resolution. Section 1544 provides:

> Notwithstanding subsection (b) of this section [the 60-day clock provision], at any time that United States Armed Forces are engaged in hostilities outside the territory of the United States, its possessions and territories without a declaration of war or specific statutory authorization, such forces shall be removed by the President if the Congress so directs by concurrent resolution.

This WPR provision reflects a simple logic: Because a presidential request for authorization to engage in hostilities could be defeated by a simple majority vote by only one house of Congress, a majority vote by both houses to terminate an operation must be constitutionally binding on the President. It also represents an attempt to forgo the barrier the plaintiff's confronted in *Holtzman v. Schlesinger*: the necessity of a super-majority to overcome a presidential veto of a bill passed by a majority of both houses of Congress to terminate funding for continued operations in Southeast Asia.[206] This provision gives binding effect to the concurrent majority, and because the concurrent resolution does not require presentment,

---

[206] Plaintiffs argued that Congress only acted "because it was coerced by the President who had vetoed Congressional Bills which would have immediately cut off Cambodian funds. Not being able to muster sufficient strength to overcome the veto, the argument runs, the Congress was forced willy nilly to enact the appropriation legislation." 484 F.2d at 1313.

there is no risk that a veto will necessitate a super-majority to impose congressional will to terminate a conflict.[207]

In theory, this WPR provision seems logical: If a majority of either house of Congress can vote down a request to authorize hostilities, why shouldn't a majority of both houses be sufficient to require termination of hostilities? The answer to this question comes from a case unrelated to war powers: *INS v. Chadha*.[208] In that case, the Supreme Court considered whether Congress could, by concurrent resolution, "veto" a decision made by an executive agency pursuant to a statutory grant of authority. The Court held this "legislative veto" violated the Constitution because it enabled Congress to repeal authority granted with a legislative measure short of a statute.[209] According to the Court, Congress may override a decision made pursuant to a grant of statutory authority only by enacting a subsequent statute, which would require presentment and, if vetoed, a veto override.[210] In essence, *Chadha* stands for the premise that "what Congress giveth by law, Congress must taketh away with law."

Chadha is widely regarded as nullifying §1544. In fact, this was precisely the effect of the decision highlighted by Justice White in his dissent. In criticizing the breadth of the holding, White noted that:

> During the 1970's, the legislative veto was important in resolving a series of major constitutional disputes between the President and Congress over claims of the President to broad impoundment, war, and national emergency powers. The key provision of the War Powers Resolution, 50 U.S.C. §1544(c), authorizes the termination by concurrent resolution of the use of armed forces in hostilities.[211]

Later in his dissent, he included §1544 in an appendix of statutory provisions ostensibly invalidated by the *Chadha* holding.[212]

Congress has never attempted to utilize a concurrent resolution to demand termination of ongoing military hostilities, and as a result of *Chadha* it is unlikely

---

[207]

A concurrent resolution is adopted by both chambers, but it does not require presentment to the President for signature or veto. Some legal analysts contend, nevertheless, that the War Powers Resolution is in a unique category which differs from statutes containing a legislative veto over delegated authorities. Perhaps more important, some observers contend, if a majority of both Houses ever voted to withdraw U.S. forces, the President would be unlikely to continue the action for long, and Congress could withhold appropriations to finance further action.

GRIMMETT, *supra* note 143, at 8.

[208] 462 U.S. 919 (1983). The case addressed whether the Immigration and Nationality Act could constitutionally authorize only the House of Representatives to veto the Attorney General's determination to deport Chadha, who over stayed his student visa.

[209] *Id.* at 952-56. The legislative veto was "essentially legislative in purpose and effect" and failed to fall within a discretely defined exception from the bicameralism and presentment requirements of Article I. Therefore, it was not constitutional.

[210] *Id.* at 956-58.

[211] *Id.* at 970-71.

[212] *Id.* at 1003.

they will do so in the future. However, it is interesting to question whether the invalidating effect on §1544 Justice White noted is in fact produced by *Chadha*. It seems significant that unlike the statute at issue in *Chadha*, the WPR did not purport to grant or delegate any war powers to the President. Indeed, §1547 indicates that nothing in the WPR may be interpreted as such a grant of authority. Accordingly, §1544 does not technically allow the revocation of any granted statutory authority by concurrent resolution. Instead, it merely reflects the majority will of Congress in opposition to a military action. Nonetheless, the overall weight of the *Chadha* holding very likely renders §1544 a dead letter.

6. "No Boots on the Ground": War Powers Resolution Gamesmanship?

The most recent illustration of the complexity associated with War Powers Resolution compliance was the "no boots on the ground" theory of inapplicability advanced by President Obama's administration during the air campaign against Libya in 2011. The UN Security Council authorized limited military action against Libyan armed forces in order to protect civilians and to facilitate provision of humanitarian aid. NATO then took the lead in conducting the operation, with the United States playing a prominent—although according to President Obama not dominant—role. This included large-scale sea-launched missile attacks, and manned and unmanned aerial reconnaissance and combat strikes in Libya.

Although authorized by the Security Council, President Obama neither sought nor received express congressional authorization for this military operation. Based on what it concluded was the "limited nature" of the operation, the Attorney General's Office of Legal Counsel concluded that the President possessed inherent constitutional authority to order the operation without implicating Congress's constitutional war declaration authority, concluding that, "President Obama could rely on his constitutional power to safeguard the national interest by directing the anticipated military operations in Libya—which were limited in their nature, scope, and duration—without prior congressional authorization."

What OLC concluded would be a short-duration operation stretched out longer than probably expected by President Obama at inception. On the 60th day of the operation President Obama sent a letter to Congress to explain why he believed the operation fell outside the scope of the War Powers Resolution. That letter highlighted the administration's theory that the strategic significance of U.S. support to the NATO effort justified continued action. Although the letter acknowledged that bipartisan support for the operation in the form of some congressional authorization would demonstrate U.S. commitment and unity, the President did not indicate he considered such action as necessary to continue operations.

Any doubt about the President's conclusion that congressional authorization was not required and that the operation did not violate the War Powers Resolution was resolved approximately one month later. On June 15, 2011, the administration released a document that included the rationale for the President's conclusion that the operation fell outside the scope of the War Powers Resolution:

> The President is of the view that the current U.S. military operations in Libya are consistent with the War Powers Resolution and do not under that law require further congressional authorization, because U.S. military operations are distinct from the kind of "hostilities" contemplated by the Resolution's 60 day termination provision. U.S. forces are playing a constrained and supporting role in a multinational coalition, whose operations are both legitimized by and limited to the terms of a United Nations Security Council Resolution that authorizes the use of force solely to protect civilians and civilian populated areas under attack or threat of attack and to enforce a no-fly zone and an arms embargo. U.S. operations do not involve sustained fighting or active exchanges of fire with hostile forces, nor do they involve the presence of U.S. ground troops, U.S. casualties or a serious threat thereof, or any significant chance of escalation into a conflict characterized by these factors.

Of course, the War Powers Resolution draws no distinction between combat action by air and naval forces versus ground forces. Nor does the statute indicate that the motive for, or duration of, an operation should influence assessment of when compliance is required. Nonetheless, this "no boots on the ground" theory was obviously central to the Obama administration's conclusion that the statute did not restrict either initiation of the operation, or continuing the operation beyond 60 days.

How the Libyan action will influence future interpretation of the War Powers Resolution is unclear. It does, however, represent the first assertion that the conduct of combat operations without commitment of ground forces somehow exempts an action from the scope of the WPR. This theory could certainly become increasingly significant as military technology provides presidents with more robust and effective engagement options that do not require commitment of ground assets.[213]

7.   The Future

The WPR remains a source of confusion and uncertainty to this day: a statute never acknowledged as binding by any President, often ignored by Congress, relatively unenforceable by the courts, and partially nullified by subsequent Supreme Court precedent.[214] Nonetheless, no introduction of U.S. armed forces into hostilities or situations of imminent hostilities has or will occur without some

---

[213] *See* Eric Talbot Jensen, *The Future of the Law of Armed Conflict: Ostriches, Butterflies, and Nanobots*, 35 MICH. J. INT'L L. 253-317 (2014).

[214] GRIMMETT, *supra* note 155, at 6.

consideration of, and in many cases action consistent with, the WPR. What then is the future of this congressional effort to mandate a robust legislative role in war powers decision making?

The most obvious answer is that the WPR will continue to function as it has since its enactment: Presidents will disavow any compliance obligation, but will nonetheless endeavor to act "consistently" with its terms to avoid arming opponents with added ammunition to attack their initiatives; Congress will selectively invoke it to pressure Presidents to be more "respectful" of its role in war powers decisions; the pre-WPR model of "support by implication" will continue to provide presidential legal advisers (and perhaps courts asked to review the constitutionality of war powers initiatives) with evidence of adequate constitutional cooperation to justify presidential actions in the absence of specific and express statutory authorization. Thus, like the history of the WPR, the future impact of this law will most likely be a mixed bag.

It is, however, difficult to dispute the fact that the WPR has produced a more robust war powers interaction between the two political branches. If nothing else, the routine executive practice of providing notice to Congress consistent with §1543 whenever armed forces are committed to situations the President determines fall within the scope of the WPR notification provisions has enhanced the vitality of this cooperation. Indeed, this notice bolsters executive reliance on subsequent congressional inaction, as it at least indicates a lack of express congressional opposition *by the then-sitting Congress* to the notices of military action. And, of equal importance, it provides Congress an early opportunity to demand more information, and if necessary muster the type of specific and express opposition to the military action that will almost certainly restrain the President. Thus, perhaps the WPR, while never implemented according to the vision of those who enacted it, has in large measure produced a positive effect.

8. Ending War

One of the most complex issues related to inter-branch authorities and war powers is the process for ending or terminating war. This is because the process of extricating the nation from an ongoing, and ostensibly authorized conflict implicates core responsibilities of both the President and Congress. Furthermore, the fact that hostilities are ongoing creates immense practical challenges to the manner in which the conflict is terminated.

The Vietnam conflict provides a compelling illustration of this complex challenge. By 1968, the war had become increasingly unpopular, and both Democratic and Republican politicians were seeking an exit strategy for the United States. Indeed, Richard Nixon emphasized his determination to end the war during his 1968 presidential campaign. During this time, Congress became increasingly assertive in its efforts to force an end to U.S. involvement in hostilities in Southeast Asia. Nonetheless, it took five more years to achieve this objective, during which time more Americans died in Southeast Asia than did prior to Richard Nixon becoming President.

It is overly simplistic to assume that terminating war requires nothing more than cutting off funding or repealing a prior statutory authorization. While this may be an appealing solution in the abstract, the Vietnam experience indicates that these are not always feasible solutions to a congressionally perceived problem of forcing a termination of hostilities. For example, even after Congress repealed the Gulf of Tonkin Resolution, federal courts rejected arguments that continued hostilities were no longer constitutionally authorized.

DaCosta v. Laird[215] provides an excellent example of why repeal of such an authorization will not normally indicate a requirement to immediately terminate hostilities. In that case, the Second Circuit considered a constitutional challenge to the war when a draftee sought to prevent enforcement of deployment orders to Vietnam.[216] By the time of this challenge, Congress had repealed the Tonkin Gulf Resolution.[217] Emphasizing the Second Circuit's prior holding in *Orlando v. Laird*[218] that the Tonkin Gulf Resolution served as substantial evidence of congressional authorization for the war, the plaintiff argued that this requisite congressional support no longer existed, thereby rendering continued prosecution of the war by the President unconstitutional.

The court, however, refused to treat the Tonkin Gulf Resolution's repeal as sufficient evidence that Congress no longer supported the war.[219] Instead, it found requisite evidence of support in defense appropriations and selective service authorizations that continued in effect after the repeal.[220] Characterizing the repeal of the Tonkin Gulf Resolution as a means of influencing a "winding down" the war, the court held that how the President and Congress chose to bring a conflict to an end was as much a political question as how they chose to authorize a conflict.[221] Based on this asserted continued cooperation between the two political branches, the court dismissed the challenge as non-justiciable.[222] The court indicated, however that, "if the executive were now escalating the prolonged struggle instead of decreasing it, additional supporting action by the legislative branch over what is presently afforded, might well be required."[223]

This "winding down" response to the plaintiff's assertion that *Orlando* required the court to conclude that Congress no longer supported the war soon presented an even more difficult dilemma for the court. On May 8, 1972, President Nixon announced his decision to mine the ports of North Vietnam and to step up the bombing campaign. In response to the breakdown of peace negotiations, Nixon indicated that denying the enemy the capability to continue to wage war was necessary to force a negotiated end of hostilities. Subsequent to this

---

[215] 448 F.2d 1368 (2d Cir. 1971).

[216] *Id.* at 1368-69.

[217] *See* Pub. L. No. 91-672, ß 12, 84 Stat. 2055 (1971).

[218] 443 F.2d 1039 (2d Cir. 1971), *cert. denied*, 404 U.S. 869 (1971).

[219] *DaCosta*, 448 F.2d at 1369.

[220] *Id.* at 1369-70.

[221] *Id.* at 1370.

[222] *Id.* at 1368.

[223] *Id.* at 1370.

announcement, DaCosta once again sought an injunction preventing his deployment to Southeast Asia.[224] Armed with these new facts, and relying on the "now escalating" qualification in the court's denial of his first effort to block his deployment, he asserted that the President unilaterally and unconstitutionally decided to escalate the war and that military leaders were therefore not authorized to carry out the President's orders.[225]

The Second Circuit once again dismissed the action as a political question,[226] framing the issue in the following terms,

> We are called upon to decide the very specific question whether the Secretary of Defense, the Secretaries of the Army, Navy, and Air Force, and the Commander of American military forces in Vietnam, may implement the directive of the President of the United States, announced on May 8, 1972, ordering the mining of the ports and harbors of North Vietnam and the continuation of air and naval strikes against military targets located in that battle-scarred land. The appellant seeks a declaratory judgment that the military operations undertaken pursuant to that directive are unlawful in the absence of explicit Congressional authorization, and asks for what he terms "appropriate equitable relief."[227]

Thus framed, the court focused on whether "the President's conduct has so altered the course of hostilities in Vietnam as to make the war as it is currently pursued different from the war which we held in *Orlando* and *DaCosta* to have been constitutionally ratified and authorized."[228] The court then clarified the meaning of the "now escalating" language, upon which the appellant relied. According to the court, this language "implied, of course, that litigants raising such a claim had a responsibility to present to the court a manageable standard which would allow for proper judicial resolution of the issue."[229] Failure to do so resulted in dismissal based on the political question doctrine, because the judiciary lacks the ability to resolve such an issue absent such standards. According to the court,

> The difficulty we face in attempting to decide this case is compounded by a lack of discoverable and manageable judicial standards. Judge Dooling [who decided the case for the District Court] believed that the case could be resolved by simply inquiring whether the actions taken by the President were a foreseeable part of the continued prosecution of the war. That test, it seems to us, is superficially appealing but overly simplistic. Judges, deficient in military knowledge, lacking

---

[224] DaCosta v. Laird, 471 F.2d 1146 (2d Cir. 1973).

[225] *Id.* at 1146. This case highlighted the difficulty in trying to draw a line between the commander in chief, as the "top general," properly directing the execution of a constitutionally authorized war, and the President unconstitutionally altering the very nature of a previously authorized commitment.

[226] *Id.*

[227] *Id.* With the issue framed this narrowly, the court held that the "lack of judicially manageable standards" prong of the political question doctrine mandated dismissal. *Id.* at 1155.

[228] *Id.* at 1154.

[229] *Id.* at 1156.

vital information upon which to assess the nature of battlefield decisions, and sitting thousands of miles from the field of action, cannot reasonably or appropriately determine whether a specific military operation constitutes an "escalation" of the war or is merely a new tactical approach within a continuing strategic plan.[230]

Although it dismissed DaCosta's second challenge, the court refused to abandon the proposition that a large-scale escalation of the war might require additional congressional support. Rather, it chose to place the burden on the litigant to provide standards by which a court could determine whether the action was in fact an unauthorized escalation. The court also re-emphasized the significance of what it concluded was continued congressional support for the war in the form of funding and conscription.[231]

Coupling the repeal of a war authorization with a termination of funding would, arguably, create the type of impasse between the President and Congress that should compel termination of hostilities. Pragmatically, however, this solution is not particularly feasible. First, Congress would ostensibly need to muster the super-majority necessary to override a presidential veto of a bill cutting off funding. Even assuming such a majority was available, Congress would be in the difficult position of cutting off funds to troops engaged in ongoing hostilities, an action obviously fraught with immense political risk. In short, once a conflict is ongoing, Congress will often feel compelled to provide the means to execute the conflict lest they be perceived as "abandoning" the forces in the field.

As the final blows of the war in Southeast Asia were being thrown, Congress sought to accommodate the competing goals of cutting off funding while allowing for an orderly withdrawal of forces by enacting legislation with a future funding termination date. By this time, the United States had largely withdrawn forces from South Vietnam, but substantially increased bombing missions in Cambodia in a futile attempt to prevent a Khmer Rouge victory against the regime supported by the United States and led by General Lon Nol. President Nixon resisted efforts to impede these operations, and threatened to veto the fiscal restriction passed by Congress. This led to a compromise between the two branches, with Nixon ultimately agreeing to a later funding cutoff date.

This failed effort to force an end to U.S. air operations over Cambodia led to the final war powers challenge of the war, *Holtzman v. Schlesinger*.[232] As noted earlier in this chapter, the plaintiffs in this case (Air Force pilots joined by Congresswoman Elizabeth Holtzman) argued that President Nixon's threat to veto the bill cutting off all funds for continued Cambodian operations placed Congress in a constitutional "straightjacket" because it necessitated a super-majority to restrict war where only a simple majority is needed to authorize war. Accordingly, they argued that the original funding termination legislation reflected the true will of Congress, and not the ultimate compromise legislation procured by the President's veto threat.[233]

---

[230] *Id.* at 1155-56.
[231] *Id.* at 1157.
[232] 484 F.2d 1307 (2d Cir. 1973), *cert. denied*, 416 U.S. 936 (1974).
[233] *Id.* at 1313.

IV. Conclusion

Although this argument proved successful at the district court, it was quickly rejected by the court of appeals, which concluded that the political compromise generated by the veto threat was a reflection of the type of lawmaking envisioned by the Constitution.[234] This decision, in effect, confirmed that it is indeed much more difficult for Congress to force an end to a war than to authorize a war advocated by the President at inception. For the court of appeals, there was nothing problematic about this reality. Instead, it was merely a consequence of the checks and balances woven into the Constitution. Ultimately, cases like *Orlando* and *Holtzman* affirm that Congress does in fact have the power to demand an end to war, but also indicate that doing so against the will of the President is an extremely difficult undertaking.

IV. CONCLUSION

Perhaps no area of national security decision making presents more potential for both inter-branch cooperation and conflict than war powers. The Vietnam conflict was a watershed event in this area of interwoven constitutional powers, resulting in a number of judicial decisions providing important insight into how this power is best exercised. The conflict, and these decisions, also led Congress to enact the War Powers Resolution in an effort to prevent war-making power grabs by future Presidents, and more subtly to prevent politically motivated ambivalence by future Congresses. While the constitutionality of this law may have been dubious from enactment, it has been the pattern of post-WPR interaction between the political branches that suggests the futility of this congressional effort to alter the traditional modes of inter-branch war-making cooperation.

War powers decisions, while implicating vital national policy interests, are inevitably framed by law. Assessing the legality of such decisions requires consideration of a number of factors. First, is the action offensive, defensive, or rescue in nature? Second, the extent of inter-branch cooperation and how that cooperation is manifested is a critical question. Third, what are the limits on the authority of each branch of government to intrude into areas of authority vested by the Constitution in their counterparts. Finally, looming in the background of all war powers decisions is the War Powers Resolution, and the potential that law might have on legal interpretations both within the executive branch and potentially by a court called upon to assess the legality of a conflict. While Congress possesses vast powers to both authorize and restrain presidential war-making initiatives, history indicates that presidential initiative will often put Congress in the difficult position of needing to support the nation's strategic goals while seeking to play a role in determining the appropriate scope of military action to achieve those goals.

---

[234] *Id.* at 1308.

CHAPTER 4

National Security Law and the Use of Military Force

The use of military force is the ultimate expression of national security power. The decision to use military force by one nation against another and the decisions concerning how to use that force once it is employed are highly regulated by both international and domestic law. These decisions can cause enormous friction within the U.S. national security structure, as well as between the federal government and the various states and between the federal government and individuals. This chapter discusses the framework for the decisions to use military force and the frictions it can cause.

I. THE USE OF MILITARY FORCE PARADIGM

As long as there has been conflict between humans, there have been rules intended to limit both the conduct of hostilities and the decision to resort to hostilities. The rules governing the legality of going to war are known as the *jus ad bellum*. The rules that apply once war has commenced are known as the *jus in bello*. This chapter examines both sets of regulations and their impact on national security law in the United States.

A. *The* Jus ad Bellum

A complete history of the *jus ad bellum* is much too long to be detailed in this chapter. However, a brief historical introduction is useful. One of the most prominent early historical theories on the law governing the resort to war was the "Just War" Theory. This theory, practiced particularly throughout Europe between 335 B.C. and 1800 A.D., allowed a resort to force only if the cause was "just." According to St. Thomas Aquinas in his *Summa Theologica*, three specific factors needed to be

I. The Use of Military Force Paradigm

present for a "just war": 1) The authority of the sovereign had to be present; 2) The cause had to be just—namely those who were attacked had to deserve it on account of some fault; and 3) The attacker had to have a right motive—the goal had to be to advance some good, not personal gain or for the purpose of inflicting cruelty. Later explanations of just cause enlarged Aquinas's three factors to include additional requirements: 1) The action had to be a last resort—after other peaceful means had failed; 2) The war had to be conducted in accordance with the rules of general proportionality; 3) There had to be a reasonable chance of success; and 4) The military action should be preceded by a formal declaration of war.

With the rise of the nation-state in the eighteenth and nineteenth centuries, governments began to take a more legalist/positivist approach to war making. The idea of a "just" war gave way to war as an instrument of national policy. Reliance on the practice of states for understanding rules of warfare, the notion of "realpolitik" as guiding the exercise of sovereignty, and the use of war as a method of implementing state policy all began to shift the justifications for war and the application of the rules governing its conduct. Sovereigns felt free to use force as one of a number of options in carrying out foreign relations. During this period, the first codifications of rules began to develop, including the 1899 and 1907 Hague Conventions, which required an official declaration of war before hostilities could commence.[1]

After World War I, many of the world powers joined together to form the League of Nations—an organization created with the goal to outlaw war through a "collective security" system where each member would guarantee the protection of the other from aggression by coming to the victim's aid.[2] At its peak (1934-1935) the League had 58 members, including many of the nations involved in World War I, though the United States never joined.

Most of these same nations also signed the Kellogg-Briand Pact, which renounced the recourse to war.[3] When initially signed in 1928, only France, the United States, and Germany were parties, but now a total of 63 nations have signed or acceded to the treaty and it remains in effect. Unfortunately, it has not had the intended effect of preventing hostilities, though it has been instrumental in changing the lexicon of international law from the word "war" to "armed conflict" and other similar terms in order for states to not be in violation of the treaty's legal obligations.

---

[1] Convention for the Pacific Settlement of International Disputes, July 29, 1899, 32 Stat. 1779, T.S. 392, 1 Bevans 230; Convention Respecting the Laws and Customs of War on Land, with Annex of Regulations, Oct. 18, 1907, 36 Stat. 2277, 1 Bevans 631.

[2] League of Nations Covenant, June 28, 1919, 225 Consol. T.S. 188, *available at* http://avalon.law.yale.edu/20th_century/leagcov.asp.

[3] Treaty Providing for the Renunciation of War as an Instrument of National Policy art. I, Aug. 27, 1928, 46 Stat. 2343, 94 L.N.T.S. 57. ("Art. I. The High Contracting Parties solemnly declare in the names of their respective peoples that they condemn recourse to war for the solution of international controversies, and renounce it, as an instrument of national policy in their relations with one another.").

Chapter 4.   National Security Law and the Use of Military Force

In the aftermath of World War II, the world powers once again convened, this time committed to attempting a more effective regime to control the resort to force. These meetings led to the formation of the United Nations. The Charter of the United Nations was signed on June 26,1945 and the United Nations officially came into existence on October 24, 1945. The Charter is the current legal paradigm for regulating the use of force.

1.   Prohibition

One of the key goals of the Charter was to establish a presumptive prohibition on the use of force by states. Previous efforts had shown that a complete prohibition on the use of force was unrealistic, but a presumption against the use of force, with specific exceptions, was thought to be more practical. The Charter set out to accomplish this by prohibiting the use of force and then granting the responsibility for the maintenance of international peace and security to the Security Council (UNSC).

a.   Article 2

Article 2 of the UN Charter contains the general rules on threatening or using force to resolve international disputes. Article 2.3 requires nations to seek peaceful settlement of conflict and Article 2.4 states that "All Members shall refrain in their international relations from the threat or use of force against the territorial integrity or political independence of any state, or in any other manner inconsistent with the Purposes of the United Nations."[4] This presumptive prohibition has become the binding legal paradigm regulating force internationally.

The operative language in Article 2.4 is "use of force," which is not defined in the Charter and has been a matter of much discussion since the Charter's inception. In the famous "Paramilitary Activities" case,[5] the International Court of Justice found that if a state merely funds guerrillas who are engaged in insurgency operations against another state, that funding did not equate to a use of force. In contrast, if a state arms and trains those guerrillas, those actions may rise to the level of a use of force and are illegal under international law.[6] These examples leave much room for discussion. In determining what other actions qualify as a use of force, many scholars and government officials have taken notice of the following criteria: severity, immediacy, directness, invasiveness, measurability

---

[4] UN Charter, art. 2.4.

[5] Military and Paramilitary Activities in and Against Nicaragua (Nicar. v. U.S.), 1986 I.C.J. 14 (June 27).

[6] *Id.* at 228.

of effects, military character of the actions, amount of state involvement, and the presumption of legality under international law.[7]

b.   Security Council Role

The prohibition in Article 2.4 is coupled with the grant of responsibility to the UNSC to maintain international peace and security.[8] Then, in Article 25, "The Members of the United Nations agree to accept and carry out the decisions of the UNSC in accordance with the present Charter." In doing this, the nations of the world embraced the collective security idea of the League of Nations, but created an enforcement mechanism through the UNSC.

2.   Exceptions

The prohibition on the use of force is not absolute. There are three exceptions to that prohibition: 1) authorization from the UNSC; 2) consent by the state where the use of force will take place; and 3) self-defense. These exceptions are discussed individually below.

a.   UNSC Authorization

Because Articles 24 and 25 of the UN Charter give the UNSC the responsibility for maintaining international peace and security and commit member states to accept and carry out their decisions, any use of force or authorization to use force by the UNSC does not fall within the prohibition of Article 2.4. The UNSC is precluded from "interven[ing] in matters which are essentially within the domestic jurisdiction of any state"[9] but can otherwise take whatever action it deems necessary to maintain peace. The primary mechanisms for accomplishing this are found in chapters VI and VII of the Charter. Chapter VI outlines non-forceful measures and chapter VII outlines forceful measures that the UNSC might use. These measures are generally considered illustrative, and not limiting.

Though Article 43 contemplates member nations providing forces for the UNSC to use directly in situations which require military force, the historic pattern that has developed is more one of the UNSC authorizing member nations who want to use force, to do so. For example, in 1990, in response to the invasion of Kuwait by Iraq, the UNSC passed Resolution 678, which "[a]uthorize[d] Member States co-operating with the Government of Kuwait, unless Iraq on or before

---

[7] Michael N. Schmitt, *Computer Network Attack and the Use of Force in International Law: Thoughts on a Normative Framework*, 37 COLUM. J. TRANSNAT'L L. 885 (1999). For an example, see the discussion on "use of force" in the Tallinn Manual. THE TALLINN MANUAL ON THE INTERNATIONAL LAW APPLICABLE TO CYBER WARFARE 48-51 (Michael N. Schmitt ed., 2013).

[8] UN Charter, art. 24.

[9] UN Charter, art. 2.7.

15 January 1991 fully implements, as set forth in paragraph 1 above, the forego-
ing resolutions, to use all necessary means to uphold and implement resolution
660 (1990) and all subsequent relevant resolutions and to restore international
peace and security in the area." After the Resolution, a coalition of more than
30 nations provided personnel and/or equipment for the military action that
evicted Iraqi forces from Kuwait and reestablished the sovereignty of Kuwait.

b.   Consent

The second exception to the use of force prohibition under Article 2.4 is
consent of the state where the military action will take place. Historically, consent
has been used often by nations to justify their military actions. Two recent examples suffice. In 1989, when the United States invaded Panama, as forces were
landing and engaging in combat operations, the U.S. forces brought Guillermo
Endara, the recently elected President of Panama who had been denied office by
General Noriega, to the airport, along with a justice of the Panamanian Supreme
Court. The Justice administered the oath of office to President Endara who
immediately requested the military aid of the United States to evict General
Noriega and allow President Endara to take his rightful role as President.
The United States justified its action in part by arguing the legitimate govern-
ment of Panama had requested, or consented to, the U.S. military action. Other
members of the international community looked skeptically at this use of
consent.

Similarly, after the non-consensual invasion of Afghanistan by U.S. forces in
2001, following the 9/11 attacks, an International Conference on Afghanistan was
held in Germany, where Hamid Karzai was selected by prominent Afghan political
figures to serve a six-month term as Chairman of the Interim Administration.
Upon taking office, he requested the United States and allies to use military
force within Afghanistan to fight the remnants of the Taliban and Al Qaeda.

Another example is the use of force in Yemen against Al Qaeda of the Arabian
Peninsula (AQAP). The government of Yemen requested the use of armed drones
by the U.S. military in support of its fight against AQAP and the United States has
done so.

There is an argument that this is really not an exception to Article 2.4 because
the consensual use of force is not against the territorial integrity or political independence of the requesting nation. However one resolves this definitional claim,
consent is worth noting as it is an oft-used basis for one state to use force in the
territory of another.

c.   Self-Defense

Self-defense is the most controversial exception to Article 2.4's prohibition
on the use of force. The scope of actions that have been justified as fitting into this
exception leaves many viewing it as the proverbial "exception that swallows
the rule."

I. The Use of Military Force Paradigm

i. Article 51

In its purest form, the self-defense exception is stated in Article 51, the first sentence of which says: "Nothing in the present Charter shall impair the inherent right of individual or collective self-defense if an armed attack occurs against a Member of the United Nations, until the Security Council has taken measures necessary to maintain international peace and security."

The triggering language in Article 51 is that a nation can act in self-defense "if an armed attack occurs." The definition of armed attack is controversial and some argue, including many of the U.S. allies in Europe, that the use of the word "if" means that, in the post-Charter world, a nation can only respond in self-defense once the attack has occurred. They argue that it is the UNSC's job to maintain international peace and security and allowing nations to act in advance of an actual attack is really just a justification for aggression. Therefore, a nation cannot attack another nation in self-defense until it has been the object of an actual armed attack, i.e., tanks rolling across the border and engaging targets, and then it can do so only until the Security Council takes some action.

Others, including the United States, disagree with this interpretation and look to the word "inherent" as a descriptor to this right of self-defense. They argue that the "inherent right" incorporates the traditional customary rights to respond in self-defense. These are discussed below.

ii. Anticipatory

Of the customary understandings of the "inherent" right of self-defense, the most well accepted is "anticipatory" self-defense. Some states argue that there is no requirement to stand idly by until the actual attack has occurred. Instead, if the attack is imminent, the soon-to-be victim can act in self-defense by "anticipating" that attack and taking defensive military action before the attack actually begins. The actual requirements of anticipatory self-defense come from a letter written by U.S. Secretary of State Daniel Webster relating to the *Caroline* affair where British troops crossed into the United States and seized the *Caroline*, a vessel suspected of being used in attacks into Canada. Webster's famous formulation of anticipatory self-defense is limited to cases that "show a necessity of self-defence, instant, over-whelming, leaving no choice of means, and no moment for deliberation."[10]

The use of unmanned aerial vehicles ("drones") by the United States abroad has raised related issues on the scope of permissible self-defense. In some situations, the United States has used drones to stop imminent threats by terrorist groups. However, the definition of imminence here has not necessarily entailed attacks that would occur in the near future—i.e., tomorrow, next week, or even next month. The United States has relied on a broader definition of imminence in

---

[10] *Letter from Daniel Webster, U.S. Secretary of State, to Henry Fox, British Minister in Washington* (Apr. 24, 1841), *in* 29 BRITISH AND FOREIGN STATE PAPERS 1138 (1857).

cases such as the drone attack that killed U.S. citizen Anwar al-Awlaki, a U.S. citizen living in Yemen whom the United States believed had become an operational leader of the group, Al Qaeda in the Arabian Peninsula (AQAP). In such cases, the United States has argued that the attack came at the last "window of opportunity" before a plot became fully operational.[11] Beyond the last window of opportunity, individuals involved in the plot might go "underground," making self-defense efforts far more difficult. In addition, after the window of opportunity closed, an attack might be reasonably certain to occur, even if it occurred at a later point. The United States has pointed to the long period taken to execute the 9/11 plot, which Al Qaeda had initiated well over a year before the date of the attacks. Using lethal force to stop such attacks earlier may be consistent with the imminence requirement, if one accepts the "last window of opportunity" theory. A number of states, including the United States and the United Kingdom, clearly accept this proposition, although its adoption is not yet universal.

Of the theories of self-defense that allow a potential victim to respond before the actual attack occurs, this is the most accepted. However, in the cases where states have explicitly relied on this theory, there is far from universal acceptance of the decision.

iii.   Interceptive

Another theory of self-defense, originating with prominent Israeli scholar Yoram Dinstein, is "interceptive" self-defense. Under this theory, once an adversary has "committed itself to an armed attack in an ostensibly irrevocable way,"[12] the potential victim of the attack has the right to use force in self-defense. This theory is even less well accepted than "anticipatory" self-defense.

Interceptive self-defense can be illustrated by two historical examples. First assume that prior to the Japanese attack on Pearl Harbor in 1941, the United States discovered the plans for the attack. The United States could have conducted an "interceptive" attack on the Japanese fleet prior to the actual attack on Pearl Harbor.

Similarly, consider a situation between the Soviet Union and the United States during the Cold War. Assume that a fleet of U.S. strategic bombers, carrying nuclear warheads, had crossed the line of no return—the point where they could safely return to friendly territory. Under this theory of interceptive self-defense, the Soviet Union would not need to wait for the aircraft to actually launch their missiles before taking self-defense actions.

---

[11] *See* Samuel Issacharoff & Richard H. Pildes, *Targeted Warfare: Individuating Enemy Responsibility*, 88 N.Y.U. L. REV. 1521, 1580 n. 199 (2013); Michael N. Schmitt, *Extraterritorial Lethal Targeting: Deconstructing the Logic of International Law*, 52 COLUM. J. TRANSNAT'L L. 77, 89 (2013).

[12] YORAM DINSTEIN, WAR, AGGRESSION AND SELF-DEFENSE 191 (4th ed. 2005).

I. The Use of Military Force Paradigm

iv. Preemptive/Preventive

Preventive self-defense is highly controversial as it is perceived by many to push the limits of state action beyond even customary norms. Preventive self-defense allows action to prevent a potential attack before it is imminent or even capable of being launched. This theory of self-defense was used by Israel in 1981 when it launched an attack against the Osirak nuclear facility south of Baghdad, Iraq. At the time, many nations condemned Israel for taking such actions, including the UNSC.[13]

Twenty years later, the U.S. 2002 National Security Strategy embraced a similar approach with respect to terrorist actions. The Strategy states:

> We must be prepared to stop rogue states and their terrorist clients before they are able to threaten or use weapons of mass destruction against the United States and our allies and friends. . . .
>
> We must adapt the concept of imminent threat to the capabilities and objectives of today's adversaries. . . .
>
> The United States has long maintained the option of preemptive actions to counter a sufficient threat to our national security. The greater the threat, the greater is the risk of inaction—and the more compelling the case for taking anticipatory action to defend ourselves, even if uncertainty remains as to the time and place of the enemy's attack. To forestall or prevent such hostile acts by our adversaries, the United States will, if necessary, act preemptively.[14]

Some have discussed this theory as applying at the last point at which a state can successfully intervene. There is no consensus in the international community on this notion of self-defense. In fact, it is likely one of the most contested current issues in the *jus ad bellum*. However, as some states continue to justify their actions using this theory, it at least adds support to its continued viability through state practice.

d. Protection of Nationals

Another basis for the use of force abroad that is considered by some states as an exception to the Article 2.4 prohibitions is when a state uses force to protect its nationals abroad. As with some forms of self-defense, this is considered part of the "inherent" right of self-defense and is rejected by some states in the post–UN Charter era, but there are many examples of states relying on this theory for using force.

In its simplest form, the doctrine allows a state to intervene, even militarily, in another state if it feels the host state is unable to protect the nationals of the first

---

[13] Security Council Resolution 487 (1981).

[14] U.S. National Security Council, National Security Strategy (Sept. 2002), *available at* http://georgewbush-whitehouse.archives.gov/nsc/nss/2002/nss5.html (last visited Apr. 25, 2011).

state. Before intervening, the first state is generally required to ascertain that the host state is unable or unwilling to provide the necessary protections and then put the host state on notice of the use of force.[15]

Modern examples of this justification for exercising self-defense to protect nationals include the Israeli raid at Entebbe, Uganda on July 4, 1976 to rescue 94 Israeli passengers and the plane's crew (the rest of the non-Israeli passengers had been released) from an Air France plane that had been hijacked by the Popular Front for the Liberation of Palestine. Protection of nationals was also one of the justifications used in the U.S. invasion of Panama discussed above as well as the U.S. military action in Grenada in 1983.

e. Humanitarian Intervention/Responsibility to Protect

Another potential exception to Article 2.4 is the authorization or duty to intervene when a humanitarian disaster is imminent or underway. States have relied on humanitarian intervention to authorize the use of force and the emerging concept of the responsibility to protect (R2P) has also been discussed in recent military actions.

Humanitarian intervention is broadly defined as "the threat or use of force by a state, group of states, or international organization primarily for the purpose of protecting the nationals of the target state from widespread deprivations of internationally recognized human rights."[16] Though few countries actual use the term to describe their use of military force, humanitarian intervention has been mentioned in connection with recent military operations in Kosovo, Libya and as a justification for further action in Syria.

In 2001, the International Commission on Intervention and State Sovereignty (ICISS) issued its report on the Responsibility to Protect.[17] The Report's "central theme" is that sovereign states have a responsibility to protect their own citizens from avoidable catastrophe—from mass murder and rape, and starvation—but that when they are unwilling or unable to do so, that responsibility must be borne by the "broader community of states." In other words, once the humanitarian need is established, the Responsibility to Protect is seen as an obligation rather than an authorization as in the case of humanitarian intervention.

The ICISS Report was favorably received by the UN General Assembly and has been embraced in numerous United Nations resolutions and other fora.

---

[15] Sir Humphrey Waldock, *The Regulation of the Use of Force by Individual States in International Law*, 81 RECEUIL DES COURS 455, 467 (1952); Ashley S. Deeks, *"Unwilling or Unable": Toward a Normative Framework for Extraterritorial Self-Defense*, 52 VA. J. INT'L L. 483, 499-503 (2012) (analyzing "unwilling or unable" test based on law of neutrality).

[16] SEAN D. MURPHY, HUMANITARIAN INTERVENTION: THE UNITED NATIONS IN AN EVOLVING WORLD ORDER 11-12 (1996).

[17] *See* http://responsibilitytoprotect.org/ICISS%20Report.pdf.

I.   The Use of Military Force Paradigm

There is a "Special Advisor on the Responsibility to Protect." The three accepted pillars of the Responsibility to Protect include:

1. The State carries the primary responsibility for protecting populations from genocide, war crimes, crimes against humanity and ethnic cleansing, and their incitement;
2. The international community has a responsibility to encourage and assist States in fulfilling this responsibility;
3. The international community has a responsibility to use appropriate diplomatic, humanitarian and other means to protect populations from these crimes. If a State is manifestly failing to protect its populations, the international community must be prepared to take collective action to protect populations, in accordance with the Charter of the United Nations.[18]

While the Responsibility to Protect has been almost universally accepted as a theoretical notion, the practical application of military force in support of the notion is less well developed. Time will provide increased examples of state practice and, important for this chapter, the role it will play in U.S. national security law as a theory for the use of force.

B.   *The* Jus in Bello

In contrast to the *jus ad bellum*, which deals with the law of going to war, the *jus in bello* governs conflict once it has started. One of the key reasons for differentiating between the two and confirming they are separate paradigms is to ensure that the law is applied during hostilities, even if there was no legal basis for the initiation of the conflict. In other words, even if a country violates the law by initiating an armed conflict, each party to that conflict must conduct hostilities in compliance with the law regulating armed conflict. These laws have traditionally been known as the laws of war, but more recently called the law of armed conflict (LOAC) and even more recently termed international humanitarian law or IHL. Though not completely synonymous, for this chapter, the term LOAC will be used throughout.

From the beginning of regulation of conflict, the major provisions regulating war have been made by the warriors, for the warriors.[19] These rules have been characterized by their distinctive utilitarian nature and their basis in reciprocity. For example, Article 87 of the 1863 Lieber Code stated "Ambassadors, and all other diplomatic agents of neutral powers, accredited to the enemy, may receive

---

[18] *See* http://www.un.org/en/preventgenocide/adviser/responsibility.shtml.
[19] Eric S. Krauss & Mike O. Lacey, *Utilitarian vs. Humanitarian: The Battle over the Law of War*, 32 PARAMETERS 73 (Summer 2002).

safe-conducts through the territories occupied by the belligerents, unless there are military reasons to the contrary, and unless they may reach the place of their destination conveniently by another route. It implies no international affront if the safe-conduct is declined. Such passes are usually given by the supreme authority of the State, and not by subordinate officers."[20] It was both in the best interest of warring parties, and especially so if reciprocally honored, to allow the transit of foreign neutral agents.

Similarly, Article 114 of the same Code prohibits a variant of the age-old war crime of perfidy, or "false flag," which bars the deceptive practice of feigning surrender to lure in an adversary and then using lethal force against that adversary once its guard is down. Article 114 states that "If it be discovered, and fairly proved, that a flag of truce has been abused for surreptitiously obtaining military knowledge, the bearer of the flag thus abusing his sacred character is deemed a spy. So sacred is the character of a flag of truce, and so necessary is its sacredness, that while its abuse is an especially heinous offense, great caution is requisite, on the other hand, in convicting the bearer of a flag of truce as a spy."[21]

1.   General Principles

Article 51 of Additional Protocol I (AP I) of the Geneva accords[22] sets out the two central principles of the LOAC. These principles are distinction and proportionality. While the United States has not ratified AP I, it accepts these two principles as elements of customary international law (CIL) that bind all nations. (CIL derives from a consensus concerning state practice and state acknowledgment (*opinio juris*) that practice is legally binding on states.)

The principle of distinction bars targeting civilians.[23] Each party to an armed conflict can target the armed forces of the other side and other "military objectives," including factories that produce armaments or other material necessary for war-fighting. LOAC does not categorically prohibit harm to civilians (sometimes called "collateral damage"). However, it imposes limits on such harm.

---

[20] Francis Lieber, Instructions for the Government of Armies of the United States in the Field; Guerilla Parties Considered with Reference to the Laws and Usages of War, art. 87 (1863), *available at* http://www.icrc.org/applic/ihl/ihl.nsf/Treaty.xsp?documentId=A25AA5871A04919BC12563 CD002D65C5&action=openDocument.

[21] Francis Lieber, Instructions for the Government of Armies of the United States in the Field; Guerilla Parties Considered with Reference to the Laws and Usages of War, art. 114 (1863), *available at* http://www.icrc.org/applic/ihl/ihl.nsf/Treaty.xsp?documentId=A25AA5871A04919BC12563CD00 2D65C5&action=openDocument.

[22] *See* Protocol Additional to the Geneva Conventions of 12 August 1949, and Relating to the Protection of Victims of International Armed Conflicts (Protocol I), art. 1(4), adopted June 8, 1977, 1125 U.N.T.S. 3, *available at* http://www.icrc.org/ihl.nsf/7c4d08d9b287a42141256739003e636b/ f6c8b9fee14a77fdc125641e0052b079.

[23] *Id.*, art. 51(2).

I. The Use of Military Force Paradigm

The principle of proportionality bars collateral damage that is "excessive in relation to the concrete and direct military advantage anticipated."[24] There is no hard and fast rule for determining the level of damage that is "excessive." Acceptable harm will vary with the military worth of the selected target. For example, it would be disproportionate to take action that resulted in the deaths of ten civilians, if the military advantage sought was merely the death of one foot soldier. However, if commanders ordering an attack intended to kill Osama bin Laden, killing ten civilians would not be disproportionate, given the importance of the target.

An additional duty entails the obligation to use "precautions" in an attack. An attacker must take all "feasible" precautions to avoid or minimize harm to civilians.[25] The duty to take precautions does not require an attacker to take all *possible* precautions. It merely requires "feasible" precautions. For example, suppose a state has a prototype weapon that will increase the precision of its bombs. The state that has not completed testing on the weapon does not have to outfit all of its units with the prototype. Moreover, since sophisticated weapons are often also costly, a state need not outfit all of its units with the most advanced weaponry if the cost would be prohibitive. Instead, it need only deploy precise weapons when the cost of deployment will not unduly affect other aspects of the war effort, including providing logistical support such as food, clothing, and weapons maintenance to its ground troops. Similarly, a state need not provide specific warnings to civilian areas of the precise location of attacks on military targets. If the target was mobile (such as a mortar battery), a specific warning of this kind would encourage the state's adversary to move the target. A state can comply with the duty to provide precautions in attack by supplying general warnings to the civilian population that may be affected.

The principle of distinction has an important corollary: Because the forces of a party to an armed conflict *can* be targeted, while civilians cannot be targeted, the protection of civilians requires that those participating in hostilities "distinguish themselves from the civilian population."[26] Traditionally, combatants have worn uniforms (think the "blue" and "gray" of the U.S. Civil War.) However, AP I relaxed the requirement that combatants distinguish themselves. The drafters believed that certain kinds of armed forces, such as "peoples fighting against colonial domination and alien occupation and against racist regimes in the exercise of their right of self-determination,"[27] could not as a practical matter distinguish themselves by wearing conventional uniforms. Therefore, AP I allows such combatants to forgo wearing conventional uniforms, as long as they carry arms openly in a "military deployment preceding the launching of an attack."[28] According to AP I, combatants who carry arms in a deployment preceding an

---

[24] *Id.*, art. 51(5)(b).
[25] *Id.*, art. 57(2)(a)(ii).
[26] *Id.*, art. 44(3).
[27] *Id.*, art. 1(4).
[28] *Id.*, art. 44(3).

attack, even without wearing a uniform or any other distinctive signs of combat status, will *not* have committed the age-old war crime of perfidy, which entails "feigning civilian . . . status" in order to facilitate the use of lethal force against an adversary.[29]

The United States believes that Article 44(3) does not adequately ensure that nontraditional combatants, such as terrorist groups, will distinguish themselves from civilians and refrain from perfidy. Largely for this reason, the United States has declined to ratify AP I.

2.   History and Evolution of the LOAC

During the nineteenth century, two somewhat parallel traditions developed in the LOAC. One was the Hague tradition, centered mostly on means and methods of warfare, and the second was the Geneva tradition, centered mostly on protections of victims of armed conflict. As will be explained below, the two traditions have mostly merged at this point, but it is still worth considering them separately to highlight different perspectives on the LOAC and why the law developed the way it has.

3.   Hague

The codification efforts of the nineteenth century culminated in two international conferences held in 1899 and 1907, which resulted in the adoption of a comprehensive set of rules to regulate the conduct of hostilities. The conferences were held in The Hague, Netherlands, and became the namesake of the utilitarian/warrior tradition of the law of war.

a.   1899/1907 Hague Rules

At the behest of the Tzar of Russia, the great powers of the day met in The Hague in 1899 to discuss the rules of land warfare. The meeting resulted in the Regulations appended to the Convention (II) with Respect to the Laws and Customs of War on Land of July 29, 1899.[30] A similar subsequent meeting in 1907 led to Convention (IV) respecting the Laws and Customs of War on Land of October 18, 1907.[31] Combined, these two international treaties established foundational LOAC rules concerning 1) the qualifications of lawful combatants; 2) prisoners of

---

[29] *Id.*, citing art. 37(1)(c).

[30] Convention (II) with Certain Powers Respecting the Laws and Customs of War on Land, July 29, 1899, 32 Stat. 1803, T.S. No. 403.

[31] Convention No. IV Respecting the Laws and Customs of War on Land and Its Annex, Regulation Concerning the Laws and Customs of War on Land, Oct. 18, 1907, 36 Stat. 2277, 205 Consol. T.S. 277.

I. The Use of Military Force Paradigm

war; 3) lawful and unlawful means and methods of warfare; 4) the status and treatment of spies in wartime; 5) flags of truce, capitulations, and armistices; and 6) military occupation of enemy territory. The two sets of regulations are identical in almost all respects. There are currently 49 States Party to the 1899 Convention and 35 States Party to the 1907 Convention, and the 1907 Convention, at least, is considered to reflect customary international law and therefore is binding on all states regardless whether they have ratified it.[32]

The preamble, which has come to be known as the Marten Clause (named after the Russian delegate to the conference) states that

> Until a more complete code of the laws of war has been issued, the High Contracting Parties deem it expedient to declare that, in cases not included in the Regulations adopted by them, the inhabitants and the belligerents remain under the protection and the rule of the principles of the law of nations, as they result from the usages established among civilized peoples, from the laws of humanity, and the dictates of the public conscience.[33]

This "overarching principle" of humanity undergirds the principles of the LOAC.

Two other key provisions of the Conventions are worth detailing. Articles 22 and 23 are indicative of the focus of the rules and the reasons they were drafted. Their content has been foundational to all subsequent law of armed conflict treaties.

> Art. 22. The right of belligerents to adopt means of injuring the enemy is not unlimited.
> Art. 23. In addition to the prohibitions provided by special Conventions, it is especially forbidden:
>
> (a) To employ poison or poisoned weapons;
> (b) To kill or wound treacherously individuals belonging to the hostile nation or army;
> (c) To kill or wound an enemy who, having laid down his arms, or having no longer means of defence, has surrendered at discretion;
> (d) To declare that no quarter will be given;
> (e) To employ arms, projectiles, or material calculated to cause unnecessary suffering;
> (f) To make improper use of a flag of truce, of the national flag or of the military insignia and uniform of the enemy, as well as the distinctive badges of the Geneva Convention;

---

[32] *See, e.g.*, DEPARTMENT OF THE ARMY, FIELD MANUAL 27-10: THE LAW OF LAND WARFARE, para. 6, July 18, 1956 (revised July 15, 1976), *available at* http://armypubs.army.mil/doctrine/DR_pubs/dr_a/pdf/fm27_10.pdf (last visited Dec. 17, 2014) (noting that the regulations appended to 1907 Hague IV "have been held to be declaratory of the customary law of war, to which all States are subject").

[33] Convention No. IV Respecting the Laws and Customs of War on Land and Its Annex, Regulation Concerning the Laws and Customs of War on Land, Preamble, Oct. 18, 1907, 36 Stat. 2277, 205 Consol. T.S. 277.

(g) To destroy or seize the enemy's property, unless such destruction or seizure be imperatively demanded by the necessities of war;

(h) To declare abolished, suspended, or inadmissible in a court of law the rights and actions of the nationals of the hostile party. A belligerent is likewise forbidden to compel the nationals of the hostile party to take part in the operations of war directed against their own country, even if they were in the belligerent's service before the commencement of the war.[34]

This same conference also produced Convention (VIII) Relative to the Laying of Automatic Submarine Contact Mines;[35] the Convention (IX) Respecting Bombardment by Naval Forces in Time of War;[36] the Convention (V) Respecting the Rights and Duties of Neutral Powers and Persons in Case of War on Land;[37] the Convention (VI) Relative to the Status of Enemy Merchant Ships at the Outbreak of Hostilities;[38] and the Convention (XIII) Concerning the Rights and Duties of Neutral Powers in Naval War.[39]

These utilitarian restrictions on the conduct of warfare enshrined a process whereby states would assemble and discuss the conduct of war and decide, by consensus, to place voluntary limitations that would provide benefits to the warfighters and the state. Since the Hague Conventions, there has been a fairly continuous stream of similar type agreements, most of them targeting either a limitation on the use of particular weapons (i.e., weapons control agreements) or on the limitation of specific methods of warfare.

b.   Weapons Control Agreements

Though some limitations on the use of weapons in warfare have taken place throughout history, the twentieth century brought an exponentially increased movement in that area. Beginning with the 1899/1907 Hague Conventions and continuing to the present day, there is a long line of such agreements. These agreements vary in scope and in how long they actually survived the onslaught of warfare. Many were made in reaction to excesses during war, such as the 1925

---

[34] Convention No. IV Respecting the Laws and Customs of War on Land and Its Annex, Regulation Concerning the Laws and Customs of War on Land, arts. 22, 23, Oct. 18, 1907, 36 Stat. 2277, 205 Consol. T.S. 277.

[35] Convention Relative to the Laying of Automatic Submarine Contact Mines, Oct. 18, 1907, 36 Stat. 2332, 1 Bevans 669.

[36] Convention Concerning Bombardment by Naval Forces in Time of War, Oct. 18, 1907, 36 Stat. 2351, 1 Bevans 681.

[37] Convention Respecting the Rights and Duties of Neutral Powers and Persons in Case of War on Land, Oct. 18, 1907, 36 Stat. 2310, 1 Bevans 654.

[38] Convention Relating to the Status of Enemy Merchant Ships at the Outbreak of Hostilities, Oct. 18, 1907, 205 Consol. T.S. 305, 3 Martens Nouveau Recueil (ser. 3).

[39] Convention Concerning the Rights and Duties of Neutral Powers in Naval War, Oct. 18, 1907, 205 Consol. T.S. 395, 1 Bevans 723.

Gas Protocol,[40] which came in response to the horrific use of various weapons such as mustard gas during the trench warfare of World War I. Some represent a long progression of constraining a particular form of weapon, such as nuclear weapons.[41] Others represent continuing forums for discussion of weapons issued as they develop.[42]

Whatever form these agreements take, weapons control agreements come mostly from within the Hague tradition and are based on the idea of states agreeing to limit their otherwise lawful options in order to accomplish specific political goals. These agreements reflect the utilitarian and reciprocal ideas of the Hague tradition.

c.   Limitation on Methods of Warfare

In addition to weapons control agreements, the Hague tradition also includes constraints on methods of warfare. For example, the 1899/1907 Hague Conventions contained restraints on declaring no quarter would be given, wounding treacherously, and the use of the flag of truce. The 1899 Hague Declaration (IV,1), prohibiting projectiles from balloons,[43] placed limits on a potential new method of warfare. In 1922, the victorious World War I powers created the Treaty relating to the Use of Submarines and Noxious Gases in Warfare.[44] Though unratified, it demonstrates nations' attempts to limit a method of warfare for utilitarian purposes.

Voluntary limitations on potentially effective methods of warfare demonstrate clearly the utilitarian approach that underlies the Hague tradition. This tradition continues today, as will be discussed below.

4.   Geneva

As a complement to the utilitarian Hague tradition, the Geneva tradition reflects a strong desire to protect the victims of armed conflict. The Geneva tradition began in 1859 when Henri Dunant traveled to see the Emperor of France

---

[40] Protocol for the Prohibition of the Use of Asphyxiating, Poisonous or Other Gases, and of Bacteriological Methods of Warfare. Geneva, 17 June 1925, *available at* http://www.icrc.org/applic/ihl/ihl.nsf/Treaty.xsp?documentId=921B4414B13E58B8C12563CD002D693B&action=openDocument.

[41] For example, see Treaty on Further Reduction and Limitation of Strategic Offensive Arms, Jan. 3, 1993, U.S.-Russ., S. Treaty Doc. No. 103-1 (1993).

[42] Convention on Prohibitions or Restrictions on the Use of Certain Conventional Weapons Which May be Deemed to be Excessively Injurious or to have Indiscriminate Effects, with annexed Protocols, opened for signature April 10, 1981, U.N. Doc. A/CONF.95/15, Annex I, at 20 (1980), *reprinted in* 19 INT'L LEG. MAT. 1524 (1980).

[43] Declaration (IV,1), to Prohibit, for the Term of Five Years, the Launching of Projectiles and Explosives from Balloons, and Other Methods of Similar Nature, The Hague, 29 July 1899, *available at* http://www.icrc.org/ihl/INTRO/160?OpenDocument.

[44] Treaty relating to the Use of Submarines and Noxious Gases in Warfare. Washington, 6 February 1922, *available at* http://www.icrc.org/ihl/INTRO/270?OpenDocument.

and arrived at the aftermath of a battle between French and Austrian forces near the village of Solferino. He was overcome by the death and carnage and the lack of care for the sick and wounded as they lay on the battlefield. In response, he wrote *A Memory of Solferino*, which acted as a call to action for the major powers. Led by the Swiss government, a conference was called in 1864 that resulted in the first Geneva Convention to protect the wounded in war.[45] The 1864 Convention was updated in 1906 to, inter alia, protect the battlefield sick, which was subsequently updated in 1929 and a new treaty dealing with the treatment of prisoners of war was also adopted. These treaties became the foundation of the Geneva tradition which seeks to protect those who are not actively engaged hostilities, due to shipwreck, injuries, illness, or capture.

In the wake of World War II, it was clear that there were significant gaps in intended areas of coverage. For example, many of the treaties only applied in cases where the parties acknowledged that they were at war. Further, because "war" was considered to be a conflict among states, none of the protections applied to internal conflicts such as the Spanish Civil War of the 1930s. Finally, and perhaps most significantly in the context of World War II, none of the treaties dealt with the treatment of the civilian population. In an effort to fix some of these issues, the nations of the world gathered again in Geneva to update the existing Geneva Conventions.

a. 1949 Conventions

The States Party who met in Geneva produced four new conventions built on the preexisting Geneva conventions: Convention (I) for the Amelioration of the Condition of the Wounded and Sick in Armed Forces in the Field (GWS);[46] Convention (II) for the Amelioration of the Condition of Wounded, Sick and Shipwrecked Members of Armed Forces at Sea (GWS Sea);[47] Convention (III) Relative to the Treatment of Prisoners of War (GPW);[48] and Convention (IV) Relative to the Protection of Civilian Persons in Time of War (GCC).[49]

---

[45] Convention for the Amelioration of the Condition of the Wounded in Armies in the Field. Geneva, 22 August 1864; *available at* http://www.icrc.org/applic/ihl/ihl.nsf/Treaty.xsp?documentId=477CEA122D7B7B3DC12563CD002D6603&action=openDocument.

[46] Geneva Convention for the Amelioration of the Condition of the Wounded and Sick in Armed Forces in the Field, Aug. 12, 1949, 6 U.S.T. 3114, 75 U.N.T.S. 970, *available at* http://www.icrc.org/ihl.nsf/FULL/365?OpenDocument.

[47] Geneva Convention for the Amelioration of the Condition of Wounded, Sick and Shipwrecked Members of the Armed Forces at Sea, Aug. 12, 1949, 6 U.S.T. 3217, 75 U.N.T.S. 971, *available at* http://www.icrc.org/ihl.nsf/FULL/370?OpenDocument.

[48] Geneva Convention Relative to the Treatment of Prisoners of War, Aug. 12, 1949, 6 U.S.T. 3316, 75 U.N.T.S. 972, *available at* http:// www.icrc.org/ihl.nsf/FULL/375?OpenDocument.

[49] Geneva Convention Relative to the Protection of Civilian Persons in Time of War, Aug. 12, 1949, 6 U.S.T. 3516, 75 U.N.T.S. 973, *available at* http://www.icrc.org/ihl.nsf/FULL/380?OpenDocument.

I. The Use of Military Force Paradigm

These Conventions accomplished a number of important advances in the LOAC. The first few important advances are contained in the first three articles common to all four conventions. Article 1 requires states to respect the provisions of the conventions, regardless of the principle of reciprocity. Article 2 provides a clear statement on the applicability of the LOAC as applying to conflicts between two States, known as international armed conflicts, or IACs. Article 3, in contrast, applies to conflicts not of an international character occurring in the territory of one of the High Contracting Parties, known as non-international armed conflicts, or NIACs. NIACs, which we will discuss in detail shortly, may be conflicts between a state and rebels within that state, or between a state and a transnational terrorist groups, such as Al Qaeda. Common Article 3 extends to NIACs protections for captives that are also applicable to conflicts between nations. The theory underlying these protections is that captives are defenseless and at their captor's mercy, so that any mistreatment is inconsistent with the principle of humanity. In addition, as a policy matter, mistreatment of captives undermines a party's incentive to surrender, since one of the virtues of surrender is that a party that surrenders will receive humane treatment. Accordingly, Common Article 3, prohibits "violence to life and person, including . . . mutilation, cruel treatment, and torture."[50] It also prohibits "outrages upon personal dignity, in particular humiliating and degrading treatment."[51]

In addition to requiring each State Party to implement means of compliance, each Convention also established certain violations of its provisions that were so grave as to be considered a crime for which there was universal jurisdiction. States Party also agreed to provide new protections for civilians, an extension that had not been codified until that time.

Every country has ratified the 1949 Geneva Conventions and thus they represent the minimum obligations of states in any international armed conflict, as a matter of treaty law. However, they have also been recognized as customary international law and would be binding even in the face of a denunciation.

b. 1977 Protocols

In the decades after World War II, it became clear that the Geneva Conventions of 1949 still left gaps in the LOAC. One glaring example was Article 3 and its minimal legal rules applicable to non-international armed conflicts. To remedy this situation, the nations of the world promulgated two additional agreements in 1977: 1) The Protocol Additional to the Geneva Conventions of 12 August 1949, and Relating to the Protection of Victims of International Armed Conflicts (AP I);[52] and 2) The Protocol Additional to the Geneva Conventions of 12 August

---

[50] Art. 3(1)(a).

[51] *Id.*, art. 3(1)(c).

[52] Protocol Additional to the Geneva Conventions of 12 August 1949, and Relating to the Protection of Victims of International Armed Conflicts, June 8, 1977, 1125 U.N.T.S. 17512, *available at* http://www.icrc.org/ihl.nsf/FULL/470?OpenDocument.

1949, and relating to the Protection of Victims of Non-International Armed Conflicts (AP II).[53]

Though the United States was actively engaged in the formulation of both Protocols and signed both, neither has received the advice and consent from the Senate and the United States is therefore not a party to either. However, the United States does treat both as mostly reflective of customary international law.

AP I applies to international armed conflict and represents the merger of the Hague and Geneva traditions. It contains not only many provisions concerning the victims of armed conflict that characterize the Geneva tradition, but also contains rules on targeting and methods of warfare normally associated with the Hague tradition. AP II is a much shorter version of AP I and is intended to apply certain key provisions of AP I to non-international armed conflict, including the protections afforded to detained persons under Article 75 of AP I, which are found in Article 6 of APII.

As of the 2014, 171 states are party to AP I and 166 states are party to AP II.[54] The wide acceptance and general adherence to both treaties by nations around the world make them an important military legal consideration for the United States. Though not legally binding on the United States, these provisions clearly impact the decisions that the United States makes concerning its potential use of force.

Recent conflicts, including the conflict with Al Qaeda, have caused states and other organizations to seek greater clarity on the targeting of particular individuals and groups of civilians. The ICRC has issued what has come to be known as the "ICRC's Interpretive guidance."[55] In this document, the ICRC (through its author Nils Melzer) grapples with the modern realities of armed conflict where fighters intentionally don't mark or distinguish themselves while fighting. A state can target individuals who directly participate in hostilities (DPH). Direct participation includes using weapons against an opposing force, or against civilians under the protection of that opposing force. Civilians who refrain from DPH cannot be targeted.

Civilians who do engage in DPH come in two categories. The ICRC recognizes that members of organized armed groups who serve a "continuous combat function" (CCF) within these groups should be targetable constantly.[56] A leader of

---

[53] Protocol Additional to the Geneva Conventions of 12 August 1949, and Relating to the Protection of Victims of Non-International Armed Conflicts, June 8, 1977, 1125 U.N.T.S. 17513, *available at* http://www.icrc.org/ihl.nsf/FULL/475?OpenDocument.

[54] The United States has ratified a third additional protocol that establishes the red crystal as a protective symbol on equal footing with the red cross and the red crescent. Protocol Additional to the Geneva Conventions of 12 August 1949, and Relating to the Adoption of an Additional Distinctive Emblem, Dec. 8, 2005, 2404 U.N.T.S. 1.

[55] *See* NILS MELZER, INTERPRETIVE GUIDANCE ON THE NOTION OF DIRECT PARTICIPATION IN HOSTILITIES UNDER INTERNATIONAL HUMANITARIAN LAW 27 (2009), *available at* http://www.icrc.org/eng/assets/files/other/icrc-002-0990.pdf.

[56] *See* NILS MELZER, INTERPRETIVE GUIDANCE ON THE NOTION OF DIRECT PARTICIPATION IN HOSTILITIES UNDER INTERNATIONAL HUMANITARIAN LAW 27 (2009), *available at* http://www.icrc.org/eng/assets/files/other/icrc-002-0990.pdf.

a terrorist group who makes decisions about mounting new attacks would clearly be CCF.

On the other hand, a vigorous debate has emerged between the ICRC and states like the United States on whether civilians in non-leadership positions who DPH are *also* CCF. The ICRC suggests that foot soldiers who fight for part of the year and then return home to harvest crops are targetable for only as long as they are fighting. They are not targetable while they are at home. The ICRC would also maintain that terrorist bomb makers are targetable as DPH only when they are making bombs. Once the bomb maker returns home, he or she is similarly off-limits. Similarly, according to the ICRC, individuals not serving combat functions, such as cooks or maintenance personnel, are not targetable unless they take some specific action that qualifies as individual direct participation. For example, the ICRC would agree that a truck driver who transports explosives to the planned site of a terrorist attack is targetable. However, according to the ICRC, a truck driver who merely transported the explosives from their point of manufacture to a middle point would not be targetable, even if the driver knew his cargo. In contrast, the United States and other states argue that the ICRC's interpretation creates a "revolving door" that enables members of terrorist groups to engage in DPH and then escape being targeted.[57]

To block this revolving door, the United States interprets both DPH and CCF more broadly. The United States would argue that any individual who is part of Al Qaeda or associated forces may be targeted. Individuals who provide support to Al Qaeda that is reasonably related to Al Qaeda's ability to engage in violence would fall into this category. Cooks or maintenance personnel would be targetable; cooks provide food that is necessary for keeping an armed force ready for fighting, while maintenance workers ensure that transportation is available to move fighters toward the action. Moreover, in a traditional state-run army, many cooks and maintenance workers will be in uniform, targetable like all other uniformed personnel. In addition, the United States would view many individuals as engaging in a CCF, even though the ICRC's narrower definition would grant such individuals respite. The United States would view any active fighter as liable to return to the battlefield and hence as presenting a threat, even if the individual in question had temporarily left the fray.[58]

One additional recent discussion relative to the use of force in armed conflict deserves mention here. With respect to Article 41 of the Geneva Convention

[57] Michael N. Schmitt, *Deconstructing Direct Participation in Hostilities: The Constitutive Elements*, 42 N.Y.U. J. INT'L L. & POL. 697, 719-20 (2010) (criticizing narrow view of causation in ICRC Guidance).

[58] *Cf.* Kenneth Watkin, *Opportunity Lost: Organized Armed Groups and the ICRC "Direct Participation in Hostilities" Interpretive Guidance*, 42 N.Y.U. J. INT'L L. & POL. 641, 656-57 (2010) (critiquing narrowness of ICRC definitions as promoting asymmetry between uniformed forces and nonstate actors)

dealing with Prisoners of War,[59] some have argued that the law requires soldiers to use the least harmful means possible to effect the submission of the enemy, meaning that there is a legal obligation for a combatant to offer surrender to another combatant prior to using lethal force in certain circumstances.[60] This assertion has been appropriately countered by others who argue that the LOAC imposes no such obligation.[61]

The general rules on application of international law will be discussed in Chapter 5, and apply equally to the international law pertaining to the use of force. While these laws certainly bind the United States as a matter of international law, their implementation as a matter of U.S. national security law leads to many frictions within the federal government, between the federal government and state governments, and between the federal government and individuals.

5.   Classifying an Armed Conflict as a NIAC

The LOAC is a specialized body of law (*lex specialis*) that governs only for the duration of war. During hostilities, the law of armed conflict displaces human rights law, which provides greater procedural safeguards.[62] If there is no

---

[59] *See* Geneva Convention Relative to the Treatment of Prisoners of War, art. 41, Aug. 12, 1949, 6 U.S.T. 3316, 75 U.N.T.S. 972, *available at* http:// www.icrc.org/ihl.nsf/FULL/375?Open-Document which states:

2. A person is "hors de combat" if:

(a) he is in the power of an adverse Party;
(b) he clearly expresses an intention to surrender; or
(c) he has been rendered unconscious or is otherwise incapacitated by wounds or sickness, and therefore is incapable of defending himself;

provided that in any of these cases he abstains from any hostile act and does not attempt to escape.

[60] Ryan Goodman, *The Power to Kill or Capture Enemy Combatants*, 24 Eur. J. Int'l L. 819 (2013).

[61] Geoffrey S. Corn et al., *Belligerent Targeting and the Invalidity of a Least Harmful Means Rule*, 89 Int'l L. Stud. 536 (2013).

[62] One can argue that the fundamental human rights duty to refrain from arbitrary deprivations of life applies even in situations of armed conflict. The United States and many scholars of LOAC assert that by following LOAC, including the principles of distinction and proportionality, a state has also complied with the human rights duty to refrain from arbitrary deprivations of life. European courts have recently questioned this view, asserting that human rights principles may prevail over LOAC norms, even during an armed conflict. For example, courts have held that detention of participants in an armed conflict without independent review violates the European Convention on Human Rights, at least absent a United Nations Security Council resolution that expressly permits such detention. *See* Al-Jedda v. United Kingdom, App. No. 27021/08, 2011 Eur. Ct. H.R. 1092; *cf.* James Farrant, *Is the Extra-Territorial Application of the Human Rights Act Legally Justified?*, 9 Int'l Crim. L. Rev. 833, 833-54 (2009) (critiquing House of Lords opinion). Comprehensive discussion of the relationship of LOAC and human rights law is beyond the scope of this book.

I. The Use of Military Force Paradigm

armed conflict, human rights law will govern how a state treats civilians within its borders and other individuals outside its borders but subject to its control.

Under international law, the existence of a non-international armed conflict hinges on the intensity and duration of violence and the existence of an organized armed group (OAG) responsible for the violence.[63] Those criteria are less important in a traditional international armed conflict, such as World War II. We can more readily discern the existence of international armed conflicts, because states often publicly declare that they are engaging in hostilities. Furthermore, the strategy and tactics of the nonstate party may often result in military action very different in nature than those associated with more traditional conflicts between states. Nonstate actors may resort to terrorism, feigning an innocent status in order to facilitate the use of lethal force against civilians—think of a suicide bomber who conceals explosives under an ordinary overcoat. States, in contrast, depend on uniformed personnel, who are readily identifiable. In a non-international armed conflict, such readily identifiable signs of conflict are often not present, at least for the nonstate party to the conflict. Courts have therefore looked to factors like intensity and duration as well as whether the nonstate actor is an organized armed group (OAG) to determine when the law of armed conflict displaces human rights law.

The criteria for determining the existence of a NIAC should be applied pragmatically. Intensity and duration, on this view, are not separate criteria.[64] Rather, they exist on a sliding scale. Attacks that are more intense will tend to show the existence of a NIAC, even if those attacks are more intermittent. For example, a single attack on an army base by a group of rebels may be sufficient to show the existence of a NIAC.[65] Even intermittent attacks by terrorist groups are evidence of a NIAC when those attacks occur in areas without functioning government institutions. In regions where civilian institutions are weak, it is reasonable to permit military institutions to take up the slack, as long as military institutions follow the laws of armed conflict.

Policy reasons support this more flexible view. Suppose attacks of an intermittent nature by violent nonstate actors did not provide sufficient evidence for labeling violence a NIAC. A state would be less able to hold members of violent nonstate groups accountable for attacks that targeted civilians or otherwise violated international law, because the state would have to rely solely on the civilian criminal justice system, instead of also having the option of military commission prosecution. Terrorists would be free to plan and execute attacks, especially in areas where the government lacked the ability to impose its authority. Since terrorists often target civilians in violation of LOAC, allowing military commissions

---

[63] *Cf.* TALLINN MANUAL ON THE INTERNATIONAL LAW APPLICABLE TO CYBER WARFARE 87 (Michael N. Schmitt ed., 2013) (suggesting that duration tends to fold into intensity).

[64] *Id.*

[65] Abella v. Argentina (Tablada Case), IACHR No. 11.137, Rep. 55/97, Para. 152 (Nov. 18, 1997).

to try charges arising from such attacks promotes accountability for violations and prevents a vacuum of state authority that terrorist groups could exploit.

As we shall see, this sliding scale view of intensity and duration has drawn critics; critics have similarly attacked the U.S. view of what counts as an organized armed group (OAG). Courts have sometimes included language suggesting that an OAG must be rigidly defined, with state-like characteristics. This language suggests that an OAG must have a headquarters in a fixed physical location, an elaborate chain of command, and a formal system of internal discipline. A more careful look at the cases, however, indicates that courts have recognized that such tests need to be flexibly applied. Accordingly, courts have found that violent non-state groups are OAGs when they have a rough chain of command and some ability to speak with one voice to the outside world.[66] For at least one court, the ability to engage in a pattern of violence traceable to the group is itself strong evidence of the organization that international law requires.[67]

II.   THE FEDERAL GOVERNMENT

With this background in place, let us consider domestic law governing U.S. involvement in armed conflicts abroad. Congress has passed laws that enable U.S. compliance with UN Security Council resolutions on multinational uses of force. In response to the UN Charter duty to participate in use of force authorized by the Security Council, Congress passed the UN Participation Act,[68] which required further approval for the commitment of U.S. forces under Article 43, but exempted the President from needing this specific approval for the use of U.S. forces under Article 42 where the Security Council has specifically called for military action to "restore international peace and security."

Assume a situation where the Security Council authorizes the use of force against a certain nation or organized armed group such as a terrorist organization. The President, in turn, commits military forces to action in compliance with the UNSCR. In the conflict with Iraq in 1991, Congress chose to issue an AUMF. Even more difficult would be a situation where the Security Council *mandates* specific military action. Though there is no precedent for this, there is certainly textual authority to do so in the UN Charter.

---

[66] *See* Prosecutor v. Limaj, Judgment, ICTY Trial Chamber, Case No. IT-03-66-T, Paras. 113-17, 131-32 (Nov. 30, 2005); *cf.* Peter Margulies, *Networks in Noninternational Armed Conflicts: Crossing Borders and Defining "Organized Armed Group"*, 89 Int'l L. Stud. 54 (2013), *available at* http://ssrn.com/abstract=2142851 (arguing for flexibility in OAG factors); Jelena Pejic, *The Protective Scope of Common Article 3: More than Meets the Eye*, 93(881) Int'l Rev. Red Cross 189, 191-92 (2011) (analyzing factors).

[67] Prosecutor v. Boskoski & Tarculovski, Case No. IT-04-82-T, Judgment (Trial Chamber), Para. 204, July 10, 2008.

[68] 22 U.S.C. §§287 to 287e-2 (2006), as amended.

III. The Federal and State Governments

It is unclear whether the President would choose to rely on this international law obligation as a domestic law authorization. Based on the OLC memo mentioned earlier, there is at least some indication that the President does not believe he is obligated to do so. Historically, Presidents have taken both views, and commentators disagree on the extent to which the UN Participation Act affects this. It seems likely that the President would be hesitant to rely on the UN Participation Act as his basis for action because Congress could repeal the Act and thus repeal the President's authority.

A similar concern is evidenced with respect to the North Atlantic Treaty Organization (NATO). As part of the founding Treaty of the Organization, article 5 states:

> The Parties agree that an armed attack against one or more of them in Europe or North America shall be considered an attack against them all and consequently they agree that, if such an armed attack occurs, each of them, in exercise of the right of individual or collective self-defence recognised by Article 51 of the Charter of the United Nations, will assist the Party or Parties so attacked by taking forthwith, individually and in concert with the other Parties, such action as it deems necessary, including the use of armed force, to restore and maintain the security of the North Atlantic area.[69]

This language commits the United States to respond to an armed attack against any other NATO member. The only time this article has been invoked was in response to the attacks of 9/11.

Since the Senate provided its advice and consent to this provision of the treaty, the question remains as to whether that authorizes the President to take action without consulting Congress any further. Clearly during the days of the Cold War with the Soviet Union, when U.S. forces were stationed across the border from Soviet forces and an attack by the Soviets would have required an immediate response, this question may have been easier to answer. But in light of Article 5's application to the 9/11 attacks, which left time for deliberation and consultation of Congress, the President might understand this provision to allow response only in emergent circumstances and require congressional approval otherwise. Again, there is disagreement on the answer to this question. Since there is no historical gloss upon which to judge, this question remains one that will be worked out in the future.

III. THE FEDERAL AND STATE GOVERNMENTS

Most people think of the use of military force as being in the sole province of the federal government, but that was not always the case. In fact, in the early days

---

[69] North Atlantic Treaty, art. 15, Apr. 4, 1949, 63 Stat. 2241, 34 U.N.T.S. 243, *available at* http://www.nato.int/docu/basictxt/treaty.htm#Art5.

of the United States, before the Constitution, there was no standing army and the states played a significant role in providing forces to fight the British soldiers during the Revolutionary War. Much has changed since then, including specific provisions of the Constitution that allow for a federal Army and Navy. However, vestiges of the prior paradigm remain and can lead to great cooperation, but also frictions between the states and the federal government.

There are generally three main divisions of military forces within the United States: 1) the active duty armed forces, which are composed of the Army, Navy, Air Force, Marine Corps, and Coast Guard;[70] 2) the National Guard, which is composed of the Army National Guard and the Air National Guard;[71] and 3) the "Reserve," which is composed of the Army Reserve, Air Force Reserve, Marine Corps Forces Reserve, Navy Reserve, and Coast Guard Reserve.[72]

As discussed in Chapter 13, each of these broad divisions has different roles, though they may often work side by side. The following subsections will explain the roles of each of these three main divisions and also some general guiding principles that can lead to frictions between states and the federal government.

A.   Armed Forces

The armed forces are the full-time, active duty forces whose main mission is to fight and win the nation's wars. They are often stationed within the United States, but traditionally their attention is generally focused outside the borders of the United States. That has changed somewhat since the events of 9/11 and the subsequent formation of the Department of Homeland Security with its cabinet status, and the creation of Northern Command, which is one of six geographic commands and includes the defense of the United States with active duty military forces.

The armed forces generally do not do much within the United States, though there are some specific exceptions. As outlined in Chapter 13, these forces may provide assistance to civil support in cases of natural disaster, such as Hurricane Katrina in 2005. They have also routinely provided support to state and territorial governors when requested and approved by the President. When serving in this capacity, there are a number of limitations on their activities, such as *posse comitatus*, which will be discussed below.[73]

---

[70] 10 U.S.C. 101(a)(4).

[71] 10 U.S.C. 101(c)(1).

[72] 10 U.S.C. 101(c)(6). Definitionally, the "reserve component" consists of both the National Guard and the Reserves as broken out here. However, in an effort to distinguish their functions, the current breakdown is more helpful.

[73] See CTR. FOR LAW & MILITARY OPERATIONS, THE JUDGE ADVOCATE GEN.'S LEGAL CTR. & SCH., DOMESTIC OPERATIONAL LAW HANDBOOK FOR JUDGE ADVOCATES (2011), for detailed explanation of the concepts in this section.

III. The Federal and State Governments

B. *National Guard*

The National Guard is the modern equivalent to the militias discussed in Article 1, §8, cl. 15 and 16 of the U.S. Constitution.[74] Congress has the authority to organize, arm, discipline, and call them forth to federal service, but the various states have the authority to appoint members of the National Guard and to train them. These clauses must be balanced by Article 1, §10, cl. 3, which states "No State shall, without the Consent of Congress, lay any Duty of Tonnage, keep Troops, or Ships of War in time of Peace, enter into any Agreement or Compact with another State, or with a foreign Power, or engage in War, unless actually invaded, or in such imminent Danger as will not admit of delay."

The Constitution establishes a necessary relationship between the federal government and the states in the management of the National Guard.[75] Traditionally, the National Guard units have been the primary responders during emergencies within a state and have operated under the control of the state governor and the state adjutant general. The use of federal forces to assist in these cases is generally only done after state resources are exhausted or overwhelmed and the federal assistance has been asked for by the governor.

As contemplated in Article 1, §8, cl. 15, the National Guard can also be called forth to serve in a federal status under the direction of the federal government.

C. *Reserves*

The Reserves generally support the armed forces and often conduct overseas military operations in conjunction with the regular armed forces. They can also play roles within the United States as needed and as instructed by the President. In fact, some important military missions that apply specifically to the defense of the United States are predominately located in the Reserves.

D. *Limitations*

There are a number of limitations that affect the application of military forces to activities within the United States. These are dealt with in detail in Chapter 13.

---

[74] Clauses 15 and 16 of Section 8 read:

> To provide for calling forth the Militia to execute the Laws of the Union, suppress Insurrections and repel Invasions;
> To provide for organizing, arming, and disciplining the Militia, and for governing such Part of them as may be employed in the Service of the United States, reserving to the States respectively, the Appointment of the Officers, and the Authority of training the Militia according to the discipline prescribed by Congress.

[75] Michael Bahar, *The Presidential Intervention Principle: The Domestic Use of the Military and the Power of the Several States*, 5 HARV. NAT'L SECURITY J. 537 (2014).

The limitations apply differently to each of the three categories of forces described above. The application of these limitations often carries the potential for frictions between the state and federal governments.

For example, one of the most significant limitations on federal armed forces is the Posse Comitatus Act (PCA), which state "Whoever, except in cases and under circumstances expressly authorized by the Constitution or Act of Congress, willfully uses any part of the Army or the Air Force as a posse comitatus or otherwise to execute the laws shall be fined under this title or imprisoned not more than two years, or both."[76] The PCA has the effect of prohibiting federal armed forces from acting in a law enforcement role. In other words, when any of the three categories of forces listed above are serving as federal armed forces, they cannot carry out law enforcement functions such as arresting individuals.

Contrast that limitation with many state statutes that provide that non-federalized National Guard units are specifically authorized to exercise law enforcement duties. For example, Arkansas law provides that when the National Guard are not in federal service "they shall have all powers, duties, and immunities of peace officers of the State of Arkansas in addition to all powers, duties and immunities now otherwise provided by law."[77]

Various presidential directives, executive orders, and executive branch regulations also provide limitations (and some authorities) that apply to the use of military force within the United States. Over time, state governors and federal officials have come to work very well together, but there are always continuing frictions, often caused by these limitations, such as was demonstrated in the aftermath of Hurricane Katrina.

E. Conclusion

The use of military force seldom happens within the United States, though the military forces are organized in order to respond should such a situation arise. The creation of the Department of Homeland Security and of Northern Command demonstrate that the military is becoming much more focused on defense of the United States. This refocus affects both the National Guard and the Reserves as well. The use of these resources within states during civil emergencies or natural disasters is almost certainly a good thing, but also a source of potential friction between the state and federal governments that will continue to demonstrate itself.

[76] 18 U.S.C. §1385 (2006).
[77] AR Code §12-61-112a (2012).

IV.   THE FEDERAL GOVERNMENT AND INDIVIDUALS

Finally, the use of military force for national security also creates tension between individuals and the federal government. The subsections below will highlight several of the areas where these frictions exist.

A.   Intelligence Collection

Intelligence collection is not normally considered a use of military force but absolutely uses military assets. The use of military resources to collect intelligence has been a well-covered topic both in the media and in other chapters of this book. Revisiting this topic in any detail is unnecessary here. However, it is worth making a few points with specific relation to the use of military force in gathering intelligence.

The NSA, as a part of the Department of Defense (DoD), is heavily engaged in intelligence collection and this collection has supported the use of military force against individuals, particularly in the case of targeted strikes with unmanned aerial vehicles, or drones. Recent disclosures by the Department of Justice have also made it clear that certain prosecutions have been based on intelligence collection targeted at specific individuals. Both of these examples demonstrate situations where the U.S. military might be used in connection with specific individuals. Several court cases are developing in this area and will undoubtedly provide greater clarity as time progresses.

B.   Capture/Rendition

Many believe that at least 136 individuals have been captured and then been subject to extraordinary rendition by the CIA since 9/11.[78] As discussed above with respect to the frictions between the judiciary and the Executive, the ability for someone to challenge their capture and subsequent rendition is extremely limited. In fact, despite several notorious rendition cases, such as that of Abu Omar,[79] there is yet to be a successful action in the United States by an individual with respect to an illegal rendition.

These alleged illegal renditions were carried out by the CIA, rather than the DoD, but it is clear that in most of these cases, force was used as an instrument of the capture and that force was directed by the U.S. government. So, in a larger

---

[78] *See* http://www.opensocietyfoundations.org/voices/20-extraordinary-facts-about-cia-extraordinary-rendition-and-secret-detention.

[79] Francesco Messineo, *The Abu Omar Case in Italy: "Extraordinary Renditions" and State Obligations to Criminalize and Prosecute Torture under the UN Torture Convention*, 7 J. Int'l Crim. Just. 1023, 1023-24 (2009).

sense, this action still implicates the military force of the U.S. government. Regardless of how this question is resolved, from the perspective of the person who is captured and rendered, there is little effective ability to fight such actions, leaving great frictions between the individual and the federal government.

C. Use of Deadly Force

There is no greater friction between individuals and the U.S. government than with respect to the decisions to take the life of an individual. The earlier discussion of al-Awlaki and his targeting and subsequent death adequately highlight this friction. According the U.S. Supreme Court, one of the requirements for al-Awlaki to exercise his rights would have been for him to appear in the U.S. courts and make his claim. Clearly, al-Awlaki did not feel disposed to do so, knowing he would be immediately detained with little chance of being able to fight his detention.

While al-Awlaki was a U.S. citizen abroad, some have argued that similar government decisions could apply to citizens within the United States who may be associated with Al Qaeda or other similar groups.[80] In a recent speech, President Obama said, "For the record, I do not believe it would be constitutional for the government to target and kill any U.S. citizen—with a drone or with a shotgun—without due process. Nor should any president deploy armed drones over U.S. soil."[81] Of course, that process does not mean judicial process, as Attorney General Eric Holder has made clear.[82]

Again, this is likely an unresolved issue that will continue to be litigated in U.S. courts. However, the potential use of military force against individuals, including U.S. citizens, by the U.S. government will only become a more intense debate.

D. Conclusion

In addition to the many other frictions with respect to military force and national security, those between individuals and the U.S. government are some with the highest stakes, as the very lives of individuals hang in the balance. While litigation may eventually resolve this friction, it will likely prove difficult to adjudicate given the current judicial stance on these issues.

---

[80] Marshall Thompson, *The Legality of Armed Drone Strikes Against U.S. Citizens Within the United States*, 2013 BYU L. Rev. 153 (2013).

[81] Remarks at National Defense University, 2013 Daily Comp. Pres. Doc. (May 23, 2013), *available at* http://www.gpo.gov/fdsys/pkg/FR-2009-01-27/pdf/E9-1885.pdf.

[82] *Contemporary Practice of the United States Relating to International Law, Use of Force and Arms Control: Attorney General Discusses Targeting of U.S. Persons*, 106 Am. J. Int'l L. 673, 674 (2012).

V. CONCLUSION

This chapter has highlighted frictions with respect to the use of military force to accomplish national security objectives. These frictions demonstrate themselves in numerous situations, both within and without the government. The inter-branch frictions are pervasive and have proven to be especially difficult in the wake of the 9/11 attacks. The President, Congress, and the courts will likely continue to debate how to exercise the constitutional authorities in a manner to effectively provide for the safety of the United States and its citizens, while still maintaining the individual and collective rights equally important under a constitutional analysis.

As this debate continues, the necessary balancing between national security and individual rights will continually be revisited, especially in the light of the use of force. Since few expressions of national power have more far-reaching effects, these discussions will play an important role in the continuing evolution of national security law.

CHAPTER 5

National Security Law and International Law

International law, at its most basic level, is the law that governs the interaction of nations,[1] though its competence is gradually growing to include many nonstate entities including individuals. International law's implications on the various roles of the government branches as well as the substantive law and procedural methodologies of applying the law creates another friction point in national security law. This was vividly demonstrated in the recent judicial case of *Hamdan v. Rumsfeld*[2] (which will be discussed in detail below) where the U.S. Supreme Court told the President how to apply international law to an armed conflict happening almost completely outside the United States. *Hamdan* was just one more incident in a long line of interactions between the three branches of the federal government as they push and pull to understand their proper and evolving role in governance. This chapter will analyze how international law has impacted and continues to impact U.S. national security law and lay out some trends to watch

---

[1] *See* RESTATEMENT (THIRD) ON FOREIGN RELATIONS §101 (1987), which describes international law as the "rules and principles of general application dealing with the conduct of States and of international organizations and with their relations *inter se*, as well as with some of their relations with persons, whether natural or juridical."

[2] Hamdan v. Rumsfeld, 548 U.S. 557 (2006).

in analyzing continuing frictions within the federal government, between the federal and state governments, and between these governments and their citizens.

I. INTERNATIONAL LAW

It is appropriate to start this chapter with a brief explanation of international law. The origins of international law are historically important and involved some of the greatest thinkers in history. With the rise of the nation-state after the Treaty of Westphalia, the law governing nations and their interactions began to take a prominent role across Europe. Writings by Grotius,[3] Gentili,[4] Vattel,[5] and others[6] set the stage for contemporary rules.

Modern international law can generally be divided into two broad categories: treaty law and custom (or customary international law).[7] Each of these has its unique aspects and a full discussion is beyond the space (or need) in this chapter. However, some foundational information in each of these two categories is useful.

A. Treaties

A treaty is an "international agreement concluded between States (meaning nations) in written form and governed by international law."[8] Treaties can be between two nations or between many nations. In one sense, they are like a contract on an international scale. Many of the same ideas behind the validity of contracts also apply to treaties. Treaties are formed in many different ways, one of which is that some group of nations that is interested in a particular topic will call

---

[3] Hugo Grotius, Law of War and Peace (1625).

[4] Alberico Gentili, De Jure Belli Libri Tres (1589).

[5] Emer de Vattel, The Law of Nations (1758) (2008 Liberty).

[6] See, e.g., Samuel Pufendorf, De Jure Naturae et Gentium, Libri Octo (1672).

[7] Restatement (Third) of Foreign Relations §102 (1987). See also Statute of the International Court of Justice art. 38(1), June 26, 1945, 59 Stat. 1055, 3 Bevans 1179, which states:

1. The Court, whose function is to decide in accordance with international law such disputes as are submitted to it, shall apply:

a. international conventions, whether general or particular, establishing rules expressly recognized by the contesting states;
b. international custom, as evidence of a general practice accepted as law;
c. the general principles of law recognized by civilized nations;
d. subject to the provisions of Article 59, judicial decisions and the teachings of the most highly qualified publicists of the various nations, as subsidiary means for the determination of rules of law.

[8] Vienna Convention on the Law of Treaties art. 1(a), May 23, 1969, 1155 U.N.T.S. 331 (entered into force Jan. 27, 1980).

for a meeting more generally of all nations and then discuss the topic and attempt to seek agreement. If agreement is reached, that agreement will be written down and the terms specifically included.

Treaties can also be thought of instructively as statutes in that the same interpretative techniques often apply to treaties as generally apply to statutes. For example, the Vienna Convention on the Law of Treaties devotes several articles specifically to the interpretation of treaties, including many principles that mirror similar principles of statutory interpretation.[9] Other principles such as a non-retroactivity, scope of application, and conflict resolution also apply to treaties.[10]

Once treaty negotiations are completed, those nations who agree with the current text will then sign the treaty and take it back to their own nations to comply with whatever domestic process is required to make a treaty come into force for that nation. In the United States, this process requires the President to present the signed treaty to the Senate who then provide their advice and consent by a two-thirds vote and return it to the President who signs it, affixes the Seal of the United States, and deposits it with the group or nation that is the official depository for ratified documents. At that point, the United States is a "party" to the treaty and is bound, as a matter of international law, to comply with the treaty's provisions and would be in violation of international law if it did not.

Treaties become binding on all parties. Most treaties have provisions for settlement of disputes and a stated method to withdraw from the treaty obligation, even after a nation has ratified. Treaties may not be called a treaty but may go by the name of convention, protocol, or some other similar designation.

B. Custom

Custom, or customary international law, is different in some very important ways. First of all, it has two elements: 1) state practice; and 2) *opinio juris*. State practice is the widespread and representative practice, including a virtually uniform practice among states that are specially affected, of states as to a certain action or principle. In other words, most states do it. But, having most states comply with or follow a certain practice is insufficient to establish custom. That practice has to be accompanied by *opinio juris*, which is the requirement that the states that are complying are doing so because they believe they have a legal obligation to do so. This element of *opinio juris* is often difficult to establish.

In fact, whether a principle of norm is customary international law is hard to establish. There are lots of examples where nations or others have argued that a specific principle is customary but others disagree. This discussion is very important because one of the other differences between custom and treaties is that

---

[9] Vienna Convention on the Law of Treaties arts. 31-33, May 23, 1969, 1155 U.N.T.S. 331 (entered into force Jan. 27, 1980).

[10] Vienna Convention on the Law of Treaties arts. 28-30, May 23, 1969, 1155 U.N.T.S. 331 (entered into force Jan. 27, 1980).

customary international law is generally binding on all states, not just those who are willing to accede to it, such as those who sign a treaty. Because of this universally obligating nature of custom, the standard for its establishment is recognized as a very high one.

Customary international law is only "generally" binding on all nations because each nation has the option to be a persistent objector, meaning that they persistently object to that customary principle being considered custom or at least being considered binding on the objecting nation. If a nation is a persistent objector, that principle of international law is not binding on the objecting nation unless the principle being objected to is considered to be *jus cogens*, meaning that it is of such a fundamental nature to the international legal system that no state can object to its application. There are very few principles that have been universally accepted as *jus cogens*, including the illegality of slavery, piracy, and genocide. Other principles that are debated as *jus cogens*, but suffer from definitional difficulties, include the prohibition on terrorism and torture.

Two prominent examples of the United States as a persistent objector to principles of international law that some nations raise as customary include the death penalty and the extraterritorial application of human rights. In both cases, the United States has objected to the accretion of these principles into customary law and has made its persistent objection well known through continuing official statements of U.S. government officials.

Further complicating the issue, the divide between these two categories is not always clear. In many cases, sufficient states will sign onto a treaty and that will be the evidence that it is accepted as customary international law. Additionally, some principles of customary international law subsequently become the subject of treaties.

In addition to treaty and custom, there are other potential sources of international law. These other sources would include the decisions of international, regional, and domestic courts, the writings of known and respected jurists, the actions of the United Nations Security Council (UNSC), and, to a lesser extent, the official actions of the General Assembly (GA).

C. U.S. Approach

The Constitution places the primary responsibility for foreign relations on the Executive, and the Department of State (DoS) has taken the leading role among government agencies. In fact, with respect to treaties, the Vienna Convention on the Law of Treaties recognizes only certain members of a nation as having "full powers" to obligate the United States under international law simply by their position. In the United States, all of these positions are in the executive branch.[11]

---

[11] Vienna Convention on the Law of Treaties art. 7, May 23, 1969, 1155 U.N.T.S. 331 (entered into force Jan. 27, 1980), include the President, the Secretary of State, and ambassadors or heads of delegation to a specific treaty conference.

The DoS establishes guidelines for the negotiating and signing of treaties.[12] They adjudge what principles of international law are accepted as customarily binding on the United States. They advise the President on establishing the Treaty Priority List, which tells the Senate which proposed treaties should be addressed first for advice and consent.

In recent years, the United States has come under international pressure for its national security decisions, which some have argued have violated international law; one such decision was the treatment of detainees in Guantanamo Bay. Though President Bush argued that the treatment was in compliance with domestic and international law obligations, many nations around the world criticized the United States as violating international law. It is to topics such as these that the chapter will now turn.

II.   INTERNATIONAL LAW IS PART OF OUR LAW

The perspective of the Framers on international law is a topic of continuous debate, but it seems fairly clear that they viewed international law as a key concern in creating the new nation and certainly recognized its potential impact on the fledgling United States. There are numerous references to international law in both the Declaration of Independence[13] and the Constitution.[14] *The Federalist* is full of discussion about international law and its potential role in domestic governance.[15] And the United States, even before its official genesis, had already started engaging in international law by signing treaties and sending ambassadors.

Perhaps the quintessential statement about international law as it is/should be applied in U.S. domestic applications is found in the famous U.S. Supreme Court case of *The Paquete Habana*. The incident took place during the Spanish-American War and involved two Cuban vessels that had been seized and brought to the

---

[12] *Circular 175 Procedure*, U.S. Dep't of State, http://www.state.gov/s/l/treaty/faqs/70132.htm (last visited Mar. 22, 2014).

[13] The Declaration of Independence (U.S. 1776) ("That these United Colonies . . . as Free and Independent States . . . have full Power to levy War, conclude Peace, contract Alliances, establish Commerce, and to do all other Acts and Things which Independent States may of right do.").

[14] U.S. Const. art. I, §8, cl. 10-11 (discussing Congress's power concerning the "law of nations" and to "grant Letters of Marque and Reprisal"); *Id.* at art. 2, §2, cl. 2 (discussing the President's power to make treaties—with the advice and consent of the senate—and to appoint ambassadors).

[15] *See, e.g.*, The Federalist No. 3 (John Jay) ("It is of high importance to the peace of America that she observe the laws of nations . . . "), No. 42 (James Madison) ("if we are to be one nation in any respect, it clearly ought to be in respect to other nations").

III.   The Federal Government

United States for condemnation as prizes of war. In deciding the case, Justice Gray wrote that

> International law is part of our law, and must be ascertained and administered by the courts of justice of appropriate jurisdiction, as often as questions of right depending upon it are duly presented for their determination. For this purpose, where there is no treaty and no controlling executive or legislative act or judicial decision, resort must be had to the customs and usages of civilized nations, and, as evidence of these, to the works of jurists and commentators who by years of labor, research, and experience, have made themselves peculiarly well acquainted with the subjects of which they treat.[16]

This dictum from the Supreme Court has resulted in an ongoing debate that has filled the pages of law reviews.[17] Stating that international law is part of our law does not answer the question of *how* it is our law, and how it is to be applied, particularly in the face of other competing national interests and constitutional principles. Subsequent court decisions, such as *Filartiga v. Pena-Irala*,[18] *Sosa v. Alvarez-Machain*,[19] and *Medellin v. Texas*[20] have not resolved the debate. Questions such as the extent to which customary international law is part of the federal common law, and the extent to which it binds the President continue to be debated. The lack of clarity on this issue will be revisited below in the discussion of international law's impact on national security law.

III.   THE FEDERAL GOVERNMENT

As the above sections have introduced, international law has a significant impact on national security. Responding to foreign affairs situations within the paradigm of international law often creates significant frictions both between the three branches of the federal government and within the branches of the federal government, including between their agencies or subdivisions.

---

[16] 175 U.S. 677, 700 (1900).
[17] Curtis A. Bradley & Jack L. Goldsmith, *Customary International Law as Federal Common Law: A Critique of the Modern Position*, 110 HARV. L. REV. 815 (1997); William S. Dodge, *Customary International Law and the Question of Legitimacy*, 120 HARV. L. REV. F.19 (2007).
[18] 630 F.2d 876 (2d Cir. 1980).
[19] 542 U.S. 692 (2004).
[20] 552 U.S. 491 (2008).

A.   Friction over Recognizing Foreign Governments

The President's role, as opposed to that of Congress, with respect to foreign relations was the topic of a recent court case dealing with the recognition of states and governments.[21] International law establishes criteria for the recognition of states, including a defined territory. While it is clear that the United States recognizes Israel as a nation, the territorial dispute between Israel and the potential nation of Palestine is at the very core of the on-going peace negotiations between the two entities.

This background brings us to the interesting case of *Zivotofsky v. Clinton*.[22] The DoS had a policy that only the city of birth would be used in areas where there were disputed borders. In 2002, Congress passed a law that stated "[f]or the purposes of the registration of birth, certification of nationality, or issuance of a passport of a United States citizen born in the city of Jerusalem, the Secretary shall, upon the request of the citizen or the citizen's legal guardian, record the place of birth as Israel."[23] At the time President Bush signed the bill, he included a signing statement that stated the specific provision would "interfere with the President's constitutional authority to . . . determine the terms on which recognition is given to foreign states."[24]

Zivotofsky was born after the congressional statute and his parents wanted his passport to list his place of birth as "Israel" rather than Jerusalem, which was his actual place of birth. The DoS considered the request and, despite the statute, denied the request. The case went all the way to the Supreme Court on the issue of whether such a question was a political question that the courts could resolve, and the Supreme Court determined that it was and then remanded it back to the court of appeals for final resolution.

In deciding the case, the court of appeals looked at both the text and originalist theories of the Constitution as well as the post-ratification history. Relying at least in part on the prior holding in *Curtiss-Wright*, the appeals court held that the President "exclusively holds the power to determine whether to recognize a foreign sovereign"[25] and that the congressional statute "impermissibly intrudes on the President's recognition power and is therefore unconstitutional."[26]

---

[21] Interestingly, before resolution, the case reached the Supreme Court on the issue of whether the case presented a political question that the judiciary should not decide. The Supreme Court ruled that the courts were "fully capable of determining whether this statute may be given effect, or instead must be struck down in light of authority conferred on the Executive by the Constitution." Zivotofsky v. Clinton, 132 S. Ct. 1421, 1425 (2012).

[22] Zivotofsky v. Sec'y of State, 725 F.3d 197 (D.C. Cir. 2013), *cert. granted*, 134 S. Ct. 1873 (2014).

[23] Foreign Relations Authorization Act, Fiscal Year 2003, 116 Stat. 1350, Section 214.

[24] Statement on Signing the Foreign Relations Authorization Act, Fiscal Year 2003, Public Papers of the Presidents, George W. Bush, Vol. 2, Sept. 30, 2002, p. 1698 (2005).

[25] Zivotofsky v. Sec'y of State, 725 F.3d 197, 214 (D.C. Cir. 2013).

[26] Zivotofsky v. Sec'y of State, 725 F.3d 197, 220 (D.C. Cir. 2013).

III. The Federal Government

This case, and others that are similarly decided, seems to support Executive claims at the expense of Congress.

B. *International Agreements*

Another area where there is national security tension between the Congress and the President is in the area of international agreements. As discussed above, both Congress and the President clearly have roles to play in the formation of treaties, but those constitutionally mandated roles do not resolve every question that arises. Further, Presidents routinely conclude a multitude of other international agreements that are not considered treaties, at least not by the executive branch, which implicate national security concerns and in which Congress either takes a limited part or no part at all. These will be discussed below.

1. Treaties

Recalling that a treaty is an "international agreement concluded between States (meaning nations) in written form and governed by international law,"[27] it is easy to see the connection with international law in the case of treaties. And there are certainly many treaties that have profound impacts on national security, including weapons control treaties such as the Chemical Weapons Convention,[28] Status of Forces Agreements like the North Atlantic Treaty Organization (NATO) Status of Forces Agreement (SOFA),[29] and international crime and process agreements such as the Cybercrime Convention.[30]

a. Treaty Priority List

Each new Congress, the President sends to the Senate a Treaty Priority List. This list ranks in order of preference the specific international agreements on which the Executive is most interested in getting the Senate's advice and consent. Many of these international agreements have significant national security implications and present important issues that the President is anxious to become a party to under international law. The Senate certainly considers the Treaty Priority List, but is not necessarily responsive to the President's desires.

---

[27] Vienna Convention on the Law of Treaties art. 1(a), May 23, 1969, 1155 U.N.T.S. 331 (entered into force Jan. 27, 1980).

[28] Convention on the Prohibition of the Development, Production, Stockpiling and Use of Chemical Weapons and on their Destruction, Jan. 13, 1993, 32 I.L.M. 800.

[29] North Atlantic Treaty Organization Status of Forces Agreement, Apr. 4, 1949, 63 Stat. 2241, 34 U.N.T.S. 243.

[30] Convention on Cybercrime, opened for signature Nov. 23, 2001, Europ. T.S. No. 185.

One of the most notorious examples of the Senate not heeding the President's call for action is the United Nations Convention on the Law of the Sea (UNCLOS).[31] Since its formulation in 1982, Presidents have consistently sought the advice and consent for this convention. The Senate has responded that ratifying the convention is not in the best interests of the military and national security. The President has responded by having the heads of the military services and the Chairman of the Joint Chiefs of Staff all sign a letter stating how important it is for the United States to become a party to UNCLOS and the strategic importance of the provisions of the convention. The Senate has remained unmoved.

This leaves the President in a difficult position. He feels strongly that it is important for the United States to demonstrate its support and compliance with the provisions of UNCLOS (except the provisions on the seabed which have become moribund at this point). And yet, he cannot become a party to the convention because of the uncooperative Senate. In response to this situation with UNCLOS, the President has made a statement that most of the provisions are reflective of customary international law and directed all executive agencies to comply with the provisions of the convention.[32]

The example of UNCLOS is instructive. A similar situation has arisen with Additional Protocol II to the Geneva Conventions of 1949.[33] The President has sought the advice and consent of the Senate, the Senate has refused to provide its advice and consent, and the President has declared the protocol reflective of customary international law and directed executive agencies to comply with its provisions.[34]

In both cases listed above, the President's declaration results in the United States being bound, as a matter of international law, to apply the provisions of those two international agreements. Any noncompliance would be a violation of international law, even though not a violation of domestic U.S. law.

---

[31] United Nations Convention on the Law of the Sea, Dec. 10, 1982, 1833 U.N.T.S. 397.

[32] Senate Hearing, 110th Cong., 1st Sess. (Sept. 27 & Oct. 4, 2007) ("The [UNCLOS] completed in 1982, was a victory for the U.S. negotiators on almost every front. The only exception was deep seabed mining. Due to flaws in that chapter, President Reagan decided not to sign it. However, he considered the Convention's other aspects so favorable, that in 1983 he directed that the United States Government abide by these provisions and to encourage other countries to do likewise.").

[33] Additional Protocol II to the Geneva Conventions of 12 August 1949, and Relating to the Protection of Victims of Non-International Armed Conflicts, *adopted* 8 June 1977, *entered into force* 7 Dec. 1978, U.N. Doc. A/32/144 Annex II, 1125 U.N.T.S. 609.

[34] Press Release, The White House, Fact Sheet: New Actions on Guantanamo and Detainee Policy (Mar. 7, 2011), *available at* http://www.lawfareblog.com/wp-content/uploads/2011/03/Fact_Sheet_-_Guantanamo_and_Detainee_Policy.pdf ("Additional Protocol II, which contains detailed humane treatment standards and fair trial guarantees that apply in the context of non-international armed conflicts, was originally submitted to the Senate for approval by President Reagan in 1987. The Administration urges the Senate to act as soon as practicable on this Protocol, to which 165 States are a party. An extensive interagency review concluded that United States military practice is already consistent with the Protocol's provisions.").

III.   The Federal Government

It is doubtful this is how the Framers of the Constitution intended the process to work, but the frictions caused by international law in the area of national security between the President and Congress force adaptation. The President, in order to accomplish his foreign affairs priorities, has elected to accomplish his intended tasks despite Congress's lack of support.

b.   Self-Execution

Another area of tension that has arisen concerning the application of international law in U.S. law is the doctrine of self-execution of treaties. The issue here is whether a treaty, once it has been through the domestic U.S. ratification process discussed in section I.A above, now has binding legal authority in U.S. courts. Some treaties are said to be self-executing, meaning they need nothing more than the above process and they immediately provide a rule of decision in U.S. courts. These treaties normally contain language that indicates the Treaty is intended to be self-executing. Other treaties are non–self-executing, meaning that the Congress must take additional steps to implement the provisions of the treaty before the courts can apply the treaty. Though not universally agreed, after the case of *Medellin v. Texas*,[35] the majority approach seems to be that in the absence of some clear indication of self-execution, a treaty is assumed to be non–self-executing and that some statement of Congress is necessary in order for a treaty to be considered self-executing.

This approach by the courts has again created friction between the President and Congress on national security issues. The President may assume a treaty is self-executing and send it to Congress, only to have Congress not add any language signaling its acceptance of the President's approach. The President may make a commitment to the other nations who are parties to the treaty that the United States will consider a treaty to be self-executing and then have a non-responsive Congress take a different approach.

Similarly, but not tied specifically to self-execution, the President may sign a treaty that requires specific implementing legislation and then Congress may refuse or simply not get around to implementing the treaty. In both cases, the friction prevents the President from realizing his national security goals.

2.   Executive and Other Agreements

At least partially in response to the frictions with Congress on treaties and getting the Senate's cooperation, the President has begun to rely less on formal treaties and more on "other" international agreements—agreements that don't require the Senate's two-third's advice and consent. These "other" agreements, known generally as executive agreements, have become an increasingly effective

---

[35] 552 U.S. 491 (2008).

tool for the President as he works to accomplish his foreign affairs responsibilities. These agreements allow the President to avoid the required support from two-thirds of the Senate, which is often difficult to attain. The chart below, published in a 2001 Congressional Research Study, illustrates the rise in executive agreements, particularly in recent decades.

Period	Treaties	Executive Agreements
1789-1839	60	27
1839-1889	215	238
1889-1939	524	917
1939-1989	702	11,698
Total	1,501	12,880[36]

Executive and other agreements come in three basic types: 1) executive agreements; 2) congressional-executive agreements; and 3) sole executive agreements. Each of these are discussed below.

a.   Executive Agreements

These agreements are generated as a result of an approved treaty for which the Congress has provided its advice and consent. The theory for these agreements is that since Congress already provided advice and consent for the broader treaty, it impliedly (if not explicitly) authorized the President to make subsequent agreements in order to carry out the provisions of the treaty. Although there is no constitutional, statutory, or direct judicial authority for these agreements, the U.S. Supreme Court seemed to imply that they were constitutionally sound.[37]

For example, a weapons control treaty might require inspections by members of an international monitoring committee. In that case, the President would likely have to make additional agreements to allow for the entrance, exit, and work of the monitoring committee. It would be implied from Congress's advice and consent that the President had the authority to make such international agreements without having to return to Congress for its further advice and consent.

b.   Congressional-Executive Agreements

Congressional-executive agreements come in two basic types: 1) an agreement where both houses of Congress delegate authority in advance for the

---

[36] CONGRESSIONAL RESEARCH SERVICE, 106TH CONG., TREATIES AND OTHER INTERNATIONAL AGREEMENTS: THE ROLE OF THE UNITED STATES SENATE, 39 (Comm. Print 2001). The same study also has a chart depicting the number of treaties and executive agreements by year from 1930 to 1999.

[37] Wilson v. Girard, 354 U.S. 524, 528-29 (1957).

President to conduct negotiations and sign an international agreement prior to the President beginning the negotiations, or at least prior to his signing; and 2) agreements that have already been negotiated and signed by the President, which are then enacted into law by both houses of Congress without being treated as a treaty. These types of agreements are often used with respect to trade agreements, and many important recent agreements have occurred through one of these two methods. For example, the 1992 North American Free Trade Agreement (NAFTA) was a congressional-executive agreement.

These agreements are not without constitutional controversy. It is unclear what makes any specific international agreement a treaty and what agreements can be handled in other ways. Important agreements such as NAFTA and the 1994 General Agreement on Tariffs and Trade raise serious constitutional questions because of their significant impact on the United States generally. Many members of Congress have expressed concerns over agreements that were concluded as congressional-executive agreements rather that as treaties.

c. Sole Executive Agreements

Even more controversial are sole executive agreements. These are international agreements where the President does not seek any congressional approval at all. Though there are fewer of these in quantity, they often cause quite a bit of concern when they are made. However, the U.S. Supreme Court has upheld such agreements on several occasions.[38]

The recent experience of the Status of Forces agreement with Iraq illustrates the point. After the end of World War II, the President negotiated the NATO SOFA with the other NATO nations and then presented it to the Senate for advice and consent, which was given on July 15, 1953. At that time, the President obviously thought that a SOFA was an international agreement that required Senate approval. In 2008, however, President Bush determined that the U.S.–Iraq SOFA[39] did not require Senate advice and consent, despite the Senate's objections and belief that it did.[40]

---

[38] American Insurance Association v. Garamendi, 539 U.S. 396 (2003); Dames & Moore v. Regan, 453 U.S. 654 (1981); United States v. Belmont, 301 U.S. 324 (1937).

[39] Agreement Between the United States of America and the Republic of Iraq on the Withdrawal of United States Forces from Iraq and the Organization of Their Activities During Their Temporary Presence in Iraq, U.S.–Iraq, Nov. 17, 2008.

[40] Karen DeYoung, *U.S., Iraq Negotiating Security Agreements*, WASH. POST (Apr. 11, 2008), http://www.washingtonpost.com/wp-dyn/content/article/2008/04/10/AR2008041004073.html ("Congressional Democrats have said that the agreement, as outlined by the administration, constitutes a defense treaty commitment requiring Senate ratification.").

3. Last-in-Time Rule

Another principle that significantly affects the impact of international law on domestic national security is the "last-in-time" rule. In the domestic sense, the last-in-time rule states that a later statute will take precedence over an earlier one, meaning the statute that is passed later in time governs the legal dispute. But how does this principle apply to international law?

a. Treaties

As mentioned above, treaties become the governing law of the land, just as statutes do, giving each equal weight in the U.S. legal system. But what happens when a statute and treaty conflict. The general rule is that, assuming the treaty is self-executing, the latest in time has precedence. So, if the President has previously ratified a self-executing treaty, after receiving the advice and consent from the Senate, the Congress is still free to pass a subsequent statute that will overrule provisions of that treaty.[41] Similarly, if the Congress provides its advice and consent and the President ratifies a treaty that then conflicts with an earlier statute, the treaty takes precedence because it came into effect later in time.[42] However, in the case of a last-in-time treaty, it would only overrule the congressional action with respect to international law, and not domestic law. In other words, the treaty would have the legal effect of changing the United States' international obligations, but the congressional statute would still govern any application of domestic law.

b. Customary International Law

Customary international law is not quite as clear on the last-in-time rule. For the circumstances where Congress overrides a customary international law norm, the last-in-time congressional action takes precedence. So, if a court is faced with a conflict between a previously recognized principle of customary international law and a subsequently passed congressional statute, the statute governs.

However, in the case where a principle of international law gains customary status in contravention of a previously passed statute, U.S. practice is not quite as clear. There is some evidence that the last-in-time rule applies to this situation as well,[43] but the U.S. Restatement on Foreign Relations says that "[i]t has not been authoritatively determined whether a rule of customary international law that developed after, and is inconsistent with, an earlier statute or international agreement of the United States should be given effect as the law of the United States."[44]

---

[41] Whitney v. Robertson, 124 U.S. 190 (1888).

[42] Cook v. United States, 288 U.S. 102 (1933).

[43] For example, law of the sea principles that developed into customary international law norms had the effect of overriding previously passed contrary statutes.

[44] RESTATEMENT (THIRD) OF FOREIGN RELATIONS §115 cmt. d (1987).

III. The Federal Government

4. *Charming Betsy* Canon

A canon is a rule for use by courts that guides them in applying the law. The *Charming Betsy* Canon comes from the case of *Murray v. Charming Betsy*,[45] and is well accepted. The canon holds that statutes enacted by Congress "ought never to be construed to violate the law of nations if any other possible construction remains."[46] This is an important principle of domestic law, particularly in light of national security concerns.

In a case where there appears to be a principle of international law that is binding on the United States that conflicts with a congressional statute, the courts will apply the *Charming Betsy* Canon and try to resolve the case in a way that does not put the two legal norms in direct confrontation. Several cases involving national security issues have discussed the *Charming Betsy* Canon[47] and more are likely to do so as national security issues continue their prominence in U.S. politics.

5. Espionage

Recent events in the war against terrorism have highlighted some of the frictions that can occur with regard to espionage and covert action between the President and Congress with respect to international law. International law provides no proscription on spying. In fact, state practice shows a clear and uninterrupted pattern of spying by nations, even on their allies.[48] And in the wake of such scandals, it has never been alleged that the espionage was illegal, just that it was bad form, especially amongst allies. This seems to establish the *opinio juris* to make the norm customary.

The national security law of espionage is discussed elsewhere in this book, but it is important to note here that the restrictions placed on spying as a matter of domestic law are completely unnecessary under international law. Congress has established constraints on the Executive[49] and the Executive has self-imposed constraints,[50] but neither of these are required under international law. So, in the wake of the terrorist attacks of September 11, when President Bush wanted to increase global espionage capabilities, frictions were created. For example, the NSA's online and other signal's intelligence collection methods have raised the

---

[45] 6 U.S. (2 Cranch) 64.

[46] 6 U.S. (2 Cranch) 64, 118 (1804).

[47] Ghaleb Nassar Al-Bihani v. Obama, 619 F.3d 1 (D.C. Cir. 2010).

[48] *Edward Snowden: Leaks That Exposed US Spy Programme*, BBC NEWS (Jan. 17, 2004, 09:56 ET), http://www.bbc.co.uk/news/world-us-canada-23123964; Dave Boyer, *NSA Spying Sours Relations with Germany, Brazil*, WASH. TIMES (Oct. 24, 2013), http://www.washingtontimes.com/news/2013/oct/24/nsa-spying-sours-relations-with-germany-brazil/?page=all.

[49] *See, e.g.*, 50 U.S.C. §§1801-1885 (2006).

[50] *See, e.g.*, Exec. Order No. 12,333, 3 C.F.R. 200 (1981).

concern of the American people and the ire of Congress.[51] As the debate continues about how far to go with surveillance, both past and present executives continue to use the NSA extensively in both foreign and domestic circumstances.

6.   Covert Action

International law treats covert actions[52] almost exactly opposite to how it treats espionage. Whereas in espionage international law was permissive and domestic law usually acts as the constraining force, with respect to covert action almost the exact opposite is true. By definition, and as shown by state practice, covert action will almost always amount to an intervention that violates sovereignty and/or a use of force that violates the UN Charter.[53] In these cases, international law precludes such actions unless through consent, Security Council action, or in self-defense to an armed attack. The vast majority of covert actions are not carried out this way, or there would be no need for them to be covert.

In the United States, and in many other countries, domestic law specifically allows for covert actions, despite the international law proscription. The President and Congress have often disagreed on the use of covert action, including claims that the President was acting beyond his statutory authority.[54] There are claims that the President has stepped outside his authority, as granted by Congress, and

---

[51] James Risen & Eric Lichtblau, *Bush Lets U.S. Spy on Callers Without Courts*, N.Y. TIMES (Dec. 16, 2005), http://www.nytimes.com/2005/12/16/politics/16program.html?pagewanted=all&_r=0; John R. Quain, *"Gaming" the System: NSA Sucking Data from Apps Like "Angry Birds,"* FOXNEWS.COM (Jan. 28, 2014), http://www.foxnews.com/tech/2014/01/28/gaming-system-nsa-sucking-data-from-apps-like-angry-birds/; Tom Cohen, Jim Acosta & Mariano Castillo, *Despite Obama's NSA Changes, Phone Records Still Collected*, CNN (Jan. 17, 2004, 4:01 PM EST), http://www.cnn.com/2014/01/17/politics/obama-nsa-changes/.

[52] 50 U.S.C. §413b(e) defines covert actions:

As used in this subchapter, the term "covert action" means an activity or activities of the United States Government to influence political, economic, or military conditions abroad, where it is intended that the role of the United States Government will not be apparent or acknowledged publicly, but does not include—

(1) activities the primary purpose of which is to acquire intelligence, traditional counterintelligence activities, traditional activities to improve or maintain the operational security of United States Government programs, or administrative activities;
(2) traditional diplomatic or military activities or routine support to such activities;
(3) traditional law enforcement activities conducted by United States Government law enforcement agencies or routine support to such activities; or
(4) activities to provide routine support to the overt activities (other than activities described in paragraph (1), (2), or (3)) of other United States Government agencies abroad.

[53] Dana Priest, *Covert Action in Colombia*, WASH. POST (Dec. 21, 2013), http://www.washingtonpost.com/sf/investigative/2013/12/21/covert-action-in-colombia/ (describing how the CIA helped Columbia kill several rebel leaders).

[54] One of the most notorious of these cases was the Iran-Contra affair in the early 1980s. *See* http://www.pbs.org/wgbh/americanexperience/features/general-article/reagan-iran/.

that the President isn't keeping Congress appropriately informed, as required. There are counterclaims of information leaks from Congress when protected information is shared. Of course, any publicized news about covert operations not only puts the specific operation at risk, but also makes public any violations of international law.

7.   Foreign Sovereign Immunity

Perhaps one of the most long-standing doctrines of public international law is sovereign immunity. In its most simple form, the doctrine is that each sovereign nation is equal in its power and authority and that no one sovereign should exercise its power over another. This doctrine was recognized by the Supreme Court early in the nation's history in *Schooner Exchange v. McFadden*.[55] In this case, two American citizens tried to take title to a ship that was known to belong to the Emperor of France. In deciding that the ship enjoyed sovereign immunity from seizure, the Court stated: "One sovereign being in no respect amenable to another; and being bound by obligations of the highest character not to degrade the dignity of his nation, by placing himself or its sovereign rights within the jurisdiction of another, can be supposed to enter a foreign territory only under an express license, or in the confidence that the immunities belonging to his independent sovereign station, though not expressly stipulated, are reserved by implication, and will be extended to him."

The treatment of sovereign immunity has evolved over the years, moving from an absolute rule of sovereign immunity as announced in *Schooner Exchange*, to a modified rule where the Department of State would assert sovereign immunity in cases where it thought it was important, to a restricted rule of immunity under the current Foreign Sovereign Immunity Act (FSIA).[56] Under the current Act, visiting "nations" still enjoy absolute immunity in many of their actions, but the statute also carves out specific areas, such as commercial activities, where the foreign nation enters the marketplace as a player and not a regulator, where the foreign state loses its immunity within U.S. courts.

The recent case of *Permanent Mission of India v. City of New York*[57] is a good example of this restricted sovereign immunity. The case involved a building belonging to the Indian mission to the UN. The building was used not only to house the official business of India, but also provided accommodations for many of the employees of the Indian mission. New York City wanted to tax the building because it was not being exclusively used for UN business, but was prevented from doing so under the international law doctrine of sovereign immunity. In a rather

---

[55] 11 U.S. (7 Cranch) 116.
[56] Honorable Marianne D. Short & Charles H. Brower, II, *The Taming of the Shrew: May the Act of State Doctrine and Foreign Sovereign Immunity Eat and Drink as Friends*, 20 HAMLINE L. REV. 723 (1997) (discussing briefly the evolution of the treatment of foreign sovereign immunity).
[57] 551 U.S. 193 (2007).

creative move, New York City allowed the unpaid tax bill to become a tax lien and then sued under the real property exception in the FSIA. This decision by the Court clearly illustrates the potential for the courts and the executive branch to have different conclusions about the foreign affairs powers.

8.   Act of State Doctrine

The Act of State doctrine is not a principle of international law but grows out of the domestic recognition of international law principles and doctrines, such as foreign sovereign immunity. It holds that U.S. courts will exercise review of foreign government acts only in limited circumstances. In one of the landmark cases concerning the doctrine, *Banco de Nacional de Cuba v. Sabbatino*,[58] Fidel Castro's recently formed revolutionary government began expropriating the property of foreign citizens and corporations, including sugar owned by a company called C.A.V. Farr, Whitlock & Co. had contracted to buy the sugar from C.A.V. but after the seizure bought it directly from the government of Cuba. However, instead of paying Cuba, Farr, Whitlock & Co. paid the representative of C.A.V. The National Bank of Cuba then sued the representative of C.A.V. for the proceeds.

In deciding for the National Bank of Cuba, the Court stated: "However offensive to the public policy of this country and its constituent States an expropriation of his kind may be, we conclude that both the national interest and progress toward the goal of establishing the rule of law among nations are best served by maintaining intact the act of state doctrine in this realm of its application." The case was then remanded to the district court for rehearing, but before it could rehear the case, Congress passed a law that allowed courts to proceed in similar cases unless the President makes a proffer that adjudicating the case will be detrimental to foreign affairs. Despite this congressional action, courts have applied the law very narrowly and continued to uphold the act of state doctrine.

9.   Conclusion

Though less frequent than those between Congress and the President, differing opinions and approaches also exist between the President and the courts concerning the application of international law to national security matters. In response to these frictions, the courts will often consider the issue a political question and not become involved in the case. However, courts will also apply international law doctrines such as foreign sovereign immunity and act of state to adjudicate cases in which they may or may not follow the desires of the Executive.

---

[58] 376 U.S. 398 (1964).

C. *The Congress and the Courts*

Frictions between Congress and the courts are also less frequent than between the President and Congress, though recently there is an increasing potential for such intra-governmental issues. The courts and Congress often resolve these conflicts through a continuing exchange between the two through passage of law and ruling on the constitutionality of the law. The courts have also developed doctrines, including standing and ripeness, that become methods of resolving these national security disputes. These issues will be discussed below.

1. Invalidating Statutes

After *Marbury v. Madison*, courts have accepted the role of interpreting the law and ensuring its constitutionality. This includes invalidating congressional statutes. Recent national security issues have provided several examples of this with respect to international law and the detention and trial of those being held at Guantanamo Bay.

One example includes the 2006 Military Commissions Act, which contained a habeas corpus stripping provision. The Act stated that "[n]o court, justice, or judge shall have jurisdiction to hear or consider an application for a writ of habeas corpus filed by or on behalf of an alien detained by the United States who has been determined by the United States to have been properly detained as an enemy combatant or is awaiting such determination."[59] For example, in *Boumediene v. Bush*,[60] this habeas provision was held to be unconstitutional, sending Congress back to redraft the Act.[61] This is just one example, but the Court has felt free to invalidate other congressional action with respect to international law and national security, and will likely continue to do so.

2. Standing and Ripeness

The doctrines of standing and ripeness are discussed elsewhere in this book so there is no need to go into much depth here. However, those doctrines have caused friction between the court and Congress on several occasions with respect to international law.

---

[59] Pub. L. No. 109-366, §7, 120 Stat. 2600, 2636 (2006).
[60] 553 U.S. 723 (2008).
[61] The 2006 MCA was followed subsequently with a newer version in 2009.

a.   Standing

Courts have ruled against congressional plaintiffs on several occasions with respect to standing. *Campbell v. Clinton*[62] involved 31 members of the House of Representatives who sued President Clinton in order to get a declaration that his actions with respect to the air campaign against Kosovo were both unconstitutional and a violation of the War Powers Resolution. In a similar case, *Kucinich v. Obama*,[63] ten members of the House of Representatives alleged President Obama's actions with respect to Libya in 2011 were also a violation of the War Powers Clause of the Constitution and a violation of the War Powers Resolution. In both cases, the courts have relied on prior precedent, including *Raines v. Byrd*,[64] and held that members of Congress do not have standing unless their votes have been "completely nullified" by the President's action.

b.   Ripeness

The doctrine of ripeness is another source of tension between Congress and the courts. The doctrine of ripeness has also been covered elsewhere in this book and also has application to national security and international law. One example will suffice here. In *Dellums v. Bush*,[65] 53 members of the House of Representatives and one Senator sued President George H.W. Bush to enjoin the use of military forces against the Iraqi military who had invaded Kuwait. Relying on the ripeness standard from *Goldwater v. Carter*, the court held that an "impasse" did not yet exist so the issue was not ripe for decision.

3.   Conclusion

Though differences of approach between Congress and the courts are less frequent with respect to national security and international law, they certainly happen and the courts have established doctrines such as ripeness and standing to help avoid confrontations, but are also willing to openly invalidate a statute when the Constitution requires it.

D.   The Executive Branch

Inter-branch interactions are not the only significant source of tension that international law brings to national security issues. There are also intra-branch

---

[62] 52 F. Supp. 2d 34 (D.D.C. 1999).
[63] 821 F. Supp. 2d 110 (D.D.C. 2011).
[64] 521 U.S. 811, 829 (1997).
[65] 752 F. Supp. 1141 (D.D.C. 1990).

III. The Federal Government

difficulties, particularly within the various agencies of the executive branch. One particularly important area of potential intra-branch conflict is international agreements.

International agreements have already been discussed above. However, in the context of intra-branch frictions, international agreements again take a prominent place. Among the executive agencies, the Department of State (DoS) is clearly the agency designated with responsibility for international agreements, but other agencies are also engaged in making and keeping such agreements.

1. Case-Zablocki Act[66]

The Case-Zablocki Act requires the Secretary of State to transmit to Congress the text of any international agreement, other than a treaty, within 60 days of the United States becoming a party. The DoS has then promulgated guidance to the executive branch as a whole concerning compliance with the Act. For example, the DoS Foreign Affairs Manual (FAM) has a section on how to determine which process should be used for an international agreement.[67] All executive agencies are required to comply with the FAM and its outlined procedures.

2. Army Regulation 550-51[68]

Though DoS is responsible for international agreements, the Department of Defense (DoD), for example, conducts a great many transactions with foreign governments, many of which DoD is not interested in getting DoS involved in. The DoD has promulgated a directive[69] that provides guidance to the Armed Services, and the Army has in turn produced a regulation that implements the Directive. To illustrate the frictions within the executive branch, it is interesting to note that the Army Regulation defines not only international agreements that must be coordinated with the DoS, but also "other international arrangements" that do not require DoS involvement.[70] The Directive and Regulation also allow some measure of discretion to the member of the military involved in making the international agreement to determine what is "policy significant" and would require DoS involvement, even if not otherwise needed.

---

[66] 1 U.S.C. §112b.
[67] 11 Foreign Affairs Manual 723.3.
[68] U.S. DEP'T OF ARMY, REG. 550-51, INTERNATIONAL AGREEMENTS (15 Apr. 1998).
[69] Department of Defense Directive 5530.3.
[70] AR 550-51 3b, 3c.

E. Conclusion

The federal government is a huge institution and any attempts to make it run smoothly are inherently difficult due to the size and diversity of the operation. National security issues are no different. As the federal government tries to allocate and administer power in accordance with the Constitution, many frictions arise, both between and within branches of government. This section has discussed some of those. The next section will look at the relationship between the federal and state governments and analyze what frictions exist there.

IV. THE FEDERAL AND STATE GOVERNMENTS

Two areas in particular adequately illustrate the difficulties international law creates with respect to national security issues between the federal and state governments: international agreements and foreign policy. This section will discuss these two areas of the law.

A. International Agreements

Two aspects of international agreements under international law create the potential for significant tensions under domestic law. These two areas are supremacy and exclusivity.

1. Exclusivity

When the Constitution was written, it was the intent of the Framers to center most international relations at the federal government. Hence, Article I restricts the ability of states (meaning members of the United States) to make international agreements with foreign nations. Paragraph 3 of section 10 states: "No State shall, without the Consent of Congress, . . . enter into any Agreement or Compact with another State, or with a foreign Power. . . ."

This language has not resulted in a complete preclusion of international agreements between states and other nations, but it has severely limited that ability, particularly when the agreement has any effect on foreign affairs. For example, states and even cities can sign economic agreements with foreign nations and their entities. They can sign "sister city" agreements and arrange various exchanges in connection with those agreements. However, the federal government holds exclusively the power to make international agreements that affect the foreign affairs and national security of the United States. As stated by the Supreme Court, "Our system of government is such that the interest of cities, counties and states, no less than the interest of the people of the whole nation, imperatively requires that federal power in the field affecting foreign relations be left entirely free from local interference."[71]

The treaty power is broad, but it is not unlimited. When Congress passes legislation to implement a treaty, courts will defer to Congress if the implementing statute is reasonably related to a foreign affairs purpose, such as ensuring the international protection of human rights. However, the Supreme Court will not defer to treaties that curtail U.S. civil liberties. In *Reid v. Covert*,[72] the Court declined to enforce an agreement that would have deprived a jury trial to a U.S. spouse of a member of the U.S. armed forces stationed abroad. In *Boos v. Barry*,[73] the Court on First Amendment grounds struck down a statute enacted by Congress that barred signs critical of a foreign government within 500 feet of any foreign embassy or consulate within the District of Columbia.

Moreover, the Supreme Court has recently indicated that it will assume that Congress in implementing a treaty did not wish to interfere with traditional areas of state concern. In *Bond v. United States*,[74] the Court invalidated a federal criminal conviction based on a statute Congress had passed implementing the Chemical Weapons Convention. The conviction arose from conduct by a jealous spouse who had sought to poison a rival by repeatedly spreading toxic chemicals on the rival's car door, mailbox, and doorknob. A creative federal prosecutor secured a conviction in federal court under the federal Chemical Weapons Convention Implementation Act. The *Bond* majority, in an opinion by Chief Justice Roberts, said that Congress could not possibly have wished to cover criminal conduct normally punishable under state law. Chief Justice Roberts invoked a clear statement rule that would require Congress to clearly express its intent to "override[]" the "usual constitutional balance of federal and state powers." Absent such a clear expression of Congress's wishes, the Court would read a statute to preserve the usual federal–state balance. Congress, the majority found, had not clearly stated its wish to punish criminal conduct, like the jealous spouse's efforts, with purely "local" implications. The Court, applying this clear statement rule, interpreted the statute as dealing only with core foreign affairs concerns, such as trafficking in weapons of mass destruction. Because the criminal conviction at issue dealt with purely local conduct, the Court vacated the conviction as exceeding the federal statute's scope.

In a concurrence in *Bond*, Justice Scalia declared that he would have gone further in curtailing Congress's power under the Treaty Clause. Scalia contended, with some support in the wording of the federal statute, that the plain meaning of the statute identified a chemical weapon as any chemical used to inflict harm, as opposed to a chemical used in a purely lawful, peaceful application, such as agriculture. Citing this language, Scalia would have struck down the federal statute as

---

[71] Hines v. Davidowitz, 312 U.S. 52, 63 (1941).
[72] 353 U.S. 1 (1957).
[73] 485 U.S. 312 (1988).
[74] 2014 U.S. Dist. LEXIS 3988 (June 2, 2014).

an unconstitutional intrusion on power reserved to the states by the Tenth Amendment to the Constitution, which leaves with the states any power not expressly or impliedly granted to the federal government.

2. Supremacy

Another aspect of international agreements that the Constitution clarified was the relationship between international agreements and state law. Within the Constitution itself, Article VI states that "all Treaties made, or which shall be made, under the Authority of the United States, shall be the supreme Law of the Land. . . ." This is a clear statement of the supremacy of international agreements over non-conforming state law.

Preemption can come either explicitly by a specific provision of an international agreement, or more subtly, such as the federal government simply taking actions that preempt state law. Either way, the result is the same—federal law in the form of the international agreement is supreme and state law is preempted.

The doctrine of treaty preemption began early in the life of the new nation. In the Treaty of Paris, which ended the Revolutionary War, the United States and Great Britain agreed that creditors on both sides should be able to recover legitimate debts. Virginia passed a conflicting law, restricting the ability of British creditors to collect on debts in Virginia. A British creditor sued and the Supreme Court, in *Ware v. Hylton*,[75] held the Virginia statute invalid. In the more recent case of *Arizona v. United States*,[76] the Court applied the preemption doctrine to strike down portions of an Arizona statute that appeared to conflict with federal discretion to enforce immigration laws. The Court also read another portion of the Arizona law narrowly, to severely limit the time that Arizona state or local law enforcement officers could detain an individual for suspected violations of federal immigration law.

Similarly, in *Missouri v. Holland*,[77] Missouri brought a bill in equity to prevent the enforcement of a Congressional statute implementing the Migratory Bird Treaty between the United States and Canada. Missouri alleged that the implementing Act was an "unconstitutional interference with the rights reserved to the States by the Tenth Amendment."[78] In upholding the statute, the Supreme Court decided that "a national interest of very nearly the first magnitude is involved" and that "[i]t is not sufficient to rely upon the States."[79]

In *Crosby v. National Foreign Trade Council*,[80] the Supreme Court struck down a Massachusetts statute that "restricted the authority of its agencies to purchase

---

[75] 3 U.S. (3 Dall.) 199 (1796).
[76] 132 S. Ct. 2492, 2498 (2012).
[77] 252 U.S. 416 (1920).
[78] 252 U.S. 416, 431 (1920).
[79] 252 U.S. 416, 435 (1920).
[80] 530 U.S. 363 (2000).

goods or services from companies doing business with Burma."[81] Relying on the Supremacy Clause, the Court held that "Because the state Act's provisions conflict with Congress's specific delegation to the President of flexible discretion, with limitation of sanctions to a limited scope of actions and actors, and with direction to develop a comprehensive, multilateral strategy under the federal Act, it is preempted, and its application is unconstitutional, under the Supremacy Clause."[82]

B. Foreign Policy

Similar to international agreements, federal foreign policy also preempts state law. In situations where there is a clear federal policy on an issue, whether expressed in some formal manner or merely a clearly stated policy, the courts will preempt state law that does not conform.

For example, in *United States v. Belmont*[83] and *United States v. Pink*,[84] the federal government had established relations with the newly created Soviet Union and, as part of that recognition, agreed to certain financial considerations with respect to prior debts. The Supreme Court held that this agreement, even though not a formal treaty, preempted conflicting state laws. In the more recent case of *American Insurance Association v. Garamendi*,[85] California passed the Holocaust Victim Insurance Relief Act that required all insurance companies doing business in California that sold insurance policies in Europe between 1920 and 1945 to make those policies public, including the names of the policy owners and the status of the policies. The Court held that the state law was in "clear conflict" with "express federal policy" and recent international agreements between the United States and Germany.

In a somewhat different application of federal supremacy with respect to foreign policy, the federal government may also attempt to remove friction between state and federal law, based on foreign policy concerns. The Sudan Accountability and Divestment Act of 2007 is such a case. The Act was passed to put into effect certain foreign policy goals of the President. The Act authorizes "State and local governments to divest assets in companies that conduct business operations in Sudan," even when such divestment might conflict with other pre-existing law.

C. Conclusion

International law and foreign affairs have resulted in, and will continue to cause, frictions between the federal government and the states. The Constitution clearly

---

[81] 530 U.S. 363, 366 (2000).
[82] 530 U.S. 363, 388 (2000).
[83] 301 U.S. 324 (1937).
[84] 315 U.S. 203 (1942).
[85] 539 U.S. 396 (2003).

makes foreign policy and national security a federal concern. This has been reinforced with respect to states and state law. The exclusivity and supremacy doctrines of federal law with respect to international law and foreign affairs help resolve most of these frictions in favor of the federal government.

V.   THE FEDERAL GOVERNMENT AND INDIVIDUALS

Frictions between national security and individual rights are significant and have been addressed more fully in Chapter 4. However, international law and its interaction with national security also produce tensions between the federal government and its citizens. The following subsections highlight some of these principles and the potential conflicts they can cause.

A.   Sovereignty

The international law principle of sovereignty, and its implications for national security, has already been discussed above. However, it deserves attention here also because the application of the doctrines of sovereignty can create tensions between the federal government and individuals.

1.   Sovereign Immunity

Remember that sovereign immunity has been codified in the FSIA, which generally accepts the idea of absolute sovereign immunity and then carves out exceptions to that immunity based on the sovereign's actions. Some of those exceptions have been discussed above with respect to allocation of power between the President and the courts, but there are also important exceptions that are based on international law and directly affect individuals. For example, the commercial activities[86] exception might allow recovery from a foreign state regardless of whether it was in the national best interest as determined by the President. Similarly, the exception to sovereign immunity for tortious actions or omissions of foreign states or officials or employees while acting within the scope of employment[87] might work against particular foreign policy interests of the federal government.

---

[86] 28 U.S.C §1605(a)(2).
[87] 28 U.S.C §1605(a)(5).

V. The Federal Government and Individuals

Perhaps the exception to sovereign immunity that has the most potential for interference with foreign policy goals is the "Terrorist State" exception.[88] This exception states that "[a] foreign state shall not be immune from the jurisdiction of courts of the United States or of the States in any case . . . in which money damages are sought against a foreign state for personal injury or death that was caused by an act of torture, extrajudicial killing, aircraft sabotage, hostage taking, or the provision of material support or resources for such act. . . ." Family members of Jack Armstrong and Jack Hensley used this exception to recover money damages from Syria in the case of *Gates v. Syrian Arab Republic*,[89] where they were awarded more than $400 million in damages. Because the court found that Syria had supported the terrorist organization that killed Armstrong and Hensley, it allocated liability to the state under the statute, despite the sovereign status of Syria.

Regardless of the exception to foreign sovereign immunity relied on, it seems likely that the congressionally allowed actions by individuals could certainly work in contravention to the foreign policy goals of the Executive. Such a situation recently arose when individuals served process on Robert Gabriel Mugabe, the sitting head of state of Zimbabwe, and Stan Mudenge, the Minister of Foreign Affairs, while they visited the United Nations in New York City. The Department of Justice had to enter a memorandum asserting immunity of foreign officials in the Southern District of New York in order to resolve the case.[90]

2. Act of State Doctrine

This doctrine has already been discussed above, but it is important to note here that the act of state doctrine also creates friction between the government and individuals. Inevitably, acts of states affect individuals and to the extent that a state can claim immunity for that act, it will leave the individual without redress.

B. *Human Rights*

The area of international law known as human rights has been very busy growing lately. What started as a simple non-binding statement of fundamental rights of individuals has grown to be a whole separate discipline within international law. The subsections below only highlight three examples of the frictions caused by human rights with respect to national security, but they are very important frictions that deserve close attention.

---

[88] 28 U.S.C. §1605A.

[89] 580 F. Supp. 2d 53 (D.D.C. 2008).

[90] Government's Memorandum of Law in Reply to Plaintiffs' Answering Brief Concerning Defendants' Immunity, Tachiona v. Mugabe, 234 F. Supp. 2d 401 (S.D.N.Y. 2002) (No. 00 Civ. 6666), *available at* http://www.state.gov/documents/organization/16626.pdf.

1. Alien Tort Statute[91]

The Alien Tort Statute (ATS) stood basically unused from the creation of the Constitution until the case of *Filartiga v. Pena-Irala*.[92] In that case, Joel Filartiga and his daughter, Dolly, sued Pena-Irala for torturing and killing Joelito, their son and brother, respectively. At the time of the torture and killing, Pena-Irala was the Inspector General of Police in Asuncion, Paraguay. The question in the case revolved around whether human rights violations, based mainly in customary international law, were part of the "law of nations" under the ATS. The court held that clear and well-accepted violations of customary international law, such as the proscription against torture, can be heard under the ATS, even when the violator may have been acting in his official capacity.[93] While it is likely that in the vast majority of similar cases the President would have no reason to object to rulings in line with the above cases, it is not difficult to imagine a sensitive situation concerning ongoing negotiations of national importance where a current prosecution of a foreign national would prove an impediment to the President's foreign policy goals.

2. Torture Victims Protection Act[94]

Several years after *Filartiga*, in *Tel-Oren v. Libyan Arab Republic*,[95] a severely divided court unanimously determined that aliens who were injured in Israel by the Palestine Liberation Organization could not recover under the ATS. Judge Bork, in his opinion, called on Congress to take action affirmatively allowing the ATS to be used for suits alleging violations of international human rights.

The Torture Victims Protection Act (TVPA) was passed specifically as implementing legislation of international human rights obligations. It also provides a cause of action for torture and extrajudicial killings specifically, but requires that the perpetrator be acting "under actual or apparent authority, or color of law, or any foreign nation." Numerous cases have been heard under the TVPA, including *Ford v. Garcia*[96] where the Court held that the international law doctrine of command responsibility creates liability for violations of the law.

The passage of the TVPA has raised a number of issues with relation to the ATS. One of those was whether the TVPA precluded a claim for torture or extrajudicial killing. In *Enahoro v. Abubakar*,[97] the court was faced with that exact issue

---

[91] 28 U.S.C. §1350. The statute reads: "The district courts shall have original jurisdiction of any civil action by an alien for a tort only, committed in violation of the law of nations or a treaty of the United States."

[92] 630 F.2d 876 (2d Cir. 1980).

[93] Samantar v. Yousuf, 560 U.S. 305 (2010).

[94] Pub. L. No. 102-256, 106 Stat. 73 (1991).

[95] 726 F.2d 774 (D.C. Cir. 1984)

[96] 289 F.3d 1283 (11th Cir. 2002).

[97] 408 F.3d 877 (7th Cir. 2005).

and determined that the TVPA "does, in fact, occupy the field."[98] Many other questions about the application of these two statutes and their intersection still remain, and will most likely be the source of future litigation.

3.   Extraterritoriality

Another prominent human rights issue is the potential extraterritoriality of individual human rights. In other words, when do nations owe human rights protections to individuals outside their geographic borders? Currently, in the United States, there is a presumption against extraterritorial application of human rights.[99] Kiobel v. Royal Dutch Petroleum Co., 133 S. Ct. 1659 (2013), reinforced that presumption in the context of an ATS suit. The United States has consistently maintained its position on non-extraterritorial application of human rights.

Emerging international law norms, particularly in human rights bodies, are urging for an expanded understanding of a nation's responsibility in this area. As one human rights expert has recently written, "a longitudinal review of the cases reveals a distinct trend toward an understanding that States' human rights obligations follow their agents and instrumentalities offshore whenever they are in a position to respect—or to violate—the rights of individuals they confront abroad."[100] Recent cases from the European Court of Human Rights, such as *Case of Al-Skeini and Others v. The United Kingdom*[101] and *Case of Al-Jedda v. The United Kingdom,*[102] illustrate this point. Both reflect an expansion of human rights obligations to areas beyond territory, even in times of armed conflict. It now seems that except for the persistent objection of the United States, it is generally accepted that "human rights obligations exist wherever a State exercises de facto authority or control over territory, individuals, or a transaction and has the power to respect and ensure the enjoyment of rights and freedoms."[103]

As this international law doctrine continues to expand, despite the objection of the U.S. government, national security law and policy will feel continuing pressure to conform to what allies and others have accepted as binding customary law.

---

[98] *Id.* at 884-85.

[99] One of the first cases to presume against extraterritorial application of US law was United States v. Palmer, 16 U.S. 610 (1818).

[100] Beth Van Schaack, *The United States' Position on the Extraterritorial Application of Human Rights Obligations: Now Is the Time for Change*, 90 INT'L L. STUD. 20, 32 (2014).

[101] Al-Skeini v. The United Kingdom, 53 Eur. Ct. H.R. 18, ¶ 149 (2011), *available at* http://hudoc.echr.coe.int/sites/eng/pages/search.aspx?i=001-105606.

[102] Al-Jedda v. The United Kingdom, 53 Eur. Ct. H. R. 789 (2011), *available at* http://hudoc.echr.coe.int/sites/eng/pages/search.aspx?i=001-105612.

[103] Beth Van Schaack, *The United States' Position on the Extraterritorial Application of Human Rights Obligations: Now Is the Time for Change*, 90 INT'L L. STUD. 20, 52 (2014).

4. Rendition

Another human rights issue that has impacted national security during the war against terrorism is the use of rendition in violation of the *non-refoulement* provision of the Convention Against Torture, which states, "No State Party shall expel, return ("refouler") or extradite a person to another State where there are substantial grounds for believing that he would be in danger of being subjected to torture."[104] Rendition, or the act of removing an individual from one jurisdiction to another, is not illegal under international law. In fact, such actions occur between states as a matter of course. However, it is a violation of individual human rights to do so when the individual being returned is likely to be tortured.

The United States is alleged to have used illegal rendition in at least one acknowledged case[105] and is accused of having done so in multiple other cases. It is not a defense to the international law violation to argue that the illegal rendition was done with the consent of the host state or that the person being rendered was a terrorist. Individuals who have alleged rendition by U.S. authorities have already sought redress in U.S. courts[106] but have generally been unsuccessful, based on a claim of state secrets privilege.

C. Conclusion

International law, which was originally understood as the law governing the interaction of nations, is clearly allowing for more and more cognizance of individuals. As the inclusion of individual issues, such as human rights, increases, the impact on national security will also increase.

VI. CONCLUSION

There is no doubt that international law is part of our law. And its impact is particularly significant in the area of national security. Applying and complying with international law often causes tensions both between the different branches of government and within the branches of government. Some of those tensions have been highlighted above. Similarly, international law produces frictions between the state and federal governments and between the government and individuals. Managing these frictions is a key aspect of national security law and the practice of law with respect to national security.

---

[104] Convention Against Torture and Other Cruel, Inhuman or Degrading Treatment or Punishment, art. 3, *available at* http://www.hrweb.org/legal/cat.html.

[105] Rachel Donadio, *Italy Convicts 23 Americans for C.I.A. Renditions*, N.Y. TIMES (Nov. 4, 2009), http://www.nytimes.com/2009/11/05/world/europe/05italy.html?_r=0 (describing the Abu Omar rendition from Italy).

[106] *See, e.g.*, Mohamed v. Jeppesen Dataplan, Inc., 614 F.3d 1070 (9th Cir. 2010).

CHAPTER 6

Criminal Process
and National Security

I. INTRODUCTION

The use of criminal sanction is a vital tool in the national security arsenal. Successful prosecution of crimes that implicate national security concerns incapacitates wrongdoers, disrupts efforts to harm U.S. and at times international interests, and ideally deters future threats and contributes to the rehabilitation of individual wrongdoers. Federal and state prosecutors today are armed with an increasingly robust arsenal of criminal statutes that have been enacted to protect national security, and many other statutory provisions that, while perhaps not originally motivated by national security concerns, are nonetheless used to advance national security interests. Perhaps the most significant of these—the federal Material Support to Terrorism Statute—is addressed first in this chapter. The chapter then considers how national security considerations affect other procedural and evidentiary aspects of the criminal sanction process.

II. THE FEDERAL MATERIAL SUPPORT STATUTE

Laws that bar material support of terrorism have become the primary weapon for the government in holding terrorists accountable in the civilian criminal justice system. Two statutes passed during the Clinton administration prohibit material support.[1] The first provision, 18 U.S.C. §2339A, passed in 1994, bars material support of terrorist activity.[2] Section 2339B bars material support of designated terrorist groups, such as Hamas. Material support covers a broad range of activity, including tangible items, such as explosives and weapons, and intangible items, including financial services, personnel, and training. Section 2339A also requires proof that a defendant specifically intended to promote attacks on persons or property. After the Oklahoma City bombing, Congress came to believe that this specific intent requirement unduly limited terrorism prosecutions. Accordingly, it passed §2339B, which banned *any* contribution of material support to groups like Hamas that the Secretary of State designated as foreign terrorist organizations (DFTOs).

Congress's use of the criminal law to shape conduct of our foreign relations, including relationships with rogue states and nonstate actors, is not new. Since the Founding Era, Congress has enacted laws that criminalized trade and other activity with certain states regarded as causing problems for the United States on the

---

[1] Portions of this subsection originally appeared in AMERICAN BAR ASSOCIATION STANDING COMMITTEE ON LAW AND NATIONAL SECURITY & MEDILL SCHOOL OF JOURNALISM, NORTHWESTERN UNIVERSITY, NATIONAL SECURITY LAW IN THE NEWS (Paul Rosenzweig, Tim McNulty & Ellen Shearer eds., 2012).

[2] Robert M. Chesney, *The Sleeper Scenario: Terrorism-Support Laws and the Demands of Prevention,* 42 HARV. J. LEGIS. 1, 12-18 (2005).

II. The Federal Material Support Statute

world stage. To avoid entanglement in the conflict between Britain and France in the 1790s, Congress enacted legislation that imposed penalties on trade of U.S. citizens with France. More recent laws have criminalized unauthorized travel to Cuba or to states that support terrorism, such as Iran. Courts have regularly upheld such bans as neutral measures with merely incidental effects on free speech.[3] Since the McCarthy Era in the early 1950s, courts have also cited First Amendment grounds to distinguish such laws from measures that directly regulated the expression of ideas.

After September 11, the government decided that the material support laws were a useful building block in efforts to stop terrorist attacks before they reached a critical stage. Prosecutors brought dozens of cases under each statute.[4] In addition, as part of the PATRIOT Act, Congress added to the conduct criminalized by the statutes, including the broad term "services" as well as "expert advice or assistance."

Congress amended the statute in 2004 to provide, as the First Amendment requires, that the term "personnel" exempted any individual expressing an *independent* opinion that just happened to coincide with views expressed by Hamas or another DFTO.[5] In other words, an individual who stands up in the public square and praises Hamas would not violate the statute, as long as Hamas exercises no control over his activities. A sensible reading of the statute also exempts scholarship, journalism, human rights monitoring, legal advocacy, and mediation à la the Carter Center.[6] Moreover, the statute does not cover domestic organizations such as militia groups.[7] Congress also added other clarifications, which the Supreme Court addressed in a 2010 case, *Holder v. Humanitarian Law Project*,[8] discussed later in this section.

A. Prosecutions for Aiding Terrorist Activity Under §2339A

The government used §2339A to prosecute Jose Padilla, a U.S. citizen arrested in Chicago whom it had detained for three and a half years without charges because of the government's concerns that Padilla was seeking to build a "dirty bomb" that would spew radiation along with explosive debris.[9] The dirty bomb

---

[3] Regan v. Wald, 468 U.S. 222 (1984).

[4] Richard B. Zabel & James J. Benjamin, Jr., *In Pursuit of Justice: Prosecuting Terrorism Cases in the Federal Courts—2009 Update and Recent Developments* (2009) (discussing prosecutions and noting that prosecutors have been successful in obtaining convictions).

[5] Holder v. Humanitarian Law Project, 561 U.S. 1, 23 (2010).

[6] Peter Margulies, *Advising Terrorism: Material Support, Safe Harbors, and Freedom of Speech*, 63 Hastings L.J. 455, 506-12 (2012) (arguing that this reading of the statute is consistent with constitutional precedent).

[7] *See Humanitarian Law Project*, 561 U.S. at 39.

[8] 561 U.S. 1 (2010).

[9] *See* Peter Margulies, Law's Detour: Politics, Ideology, and Justice in the Bush Administration 112-13 (NYU Press 2010).

scenario could not be proven in court because it would have required the use of evidence obtained through coercion. In 2006, when the courts' pushback against unreviewable detention suggested that the government would eventually have to release Padilla, the Justice Department charged Padilla with violations of §2339A.

The government's charges against Padilla illustrate the value of §2339A as a counterterrorism tool. The charges did not mention the dirty bomb plot, or indeed any post-9/11 conduct. Instead, they focused on allegations that Padilla had traveled abroad with the intention of aiding violent jihad in the Balkans, the Middle East, and South Asia. The government did not prove that Padilla had participated in any specific attack. Rather, under the statute, the government needed only to prove that Padilla and his co-defendants had 1) conspired to provide material support to 2) a *broader* conspiracy that violated §956 of the criminal code, which bans conspiracies to "murder, kidnap, or maim overseas."

The combination of §2339A's counterterrorism provisions and §956's broad conspiracy language is particularly powerful. Participation in a terrorist training camp overseas, for example, constitutes a §956 violation, even without proof that a defendant has planned to participate in any specific terrorist plot. Rather, courts have treated a terrorist training camp as one big terrorist enterprise, on the theory that aspiring participants know they are not attending a Michael Jordan basketball camp. Once courts make this legal link between §2339A and §956, conspiracy law permits a conviction based on relatively modest evidence. In Padilla's case, for example, the government introduced a completed application for attendance at a camp with Padilla's fingerprints, a few phone conversations including Padilla, and a substantial number of phone conversations between Padilla's co-defendants discussing his activities. The latter would ordinarily be considered hearsay, and would be inadmissible, but courts have held that the government can use hearsay evidence in conspiracy cases to prove the existence and scope of a conspiracy. The prosecution of Padilla was successful; Padilla was convicted and a federal appeals court affirmed the conviction.[10]

The cases also offer wide latitude on evidence in other respects. For example, suppose that an aspiring terrorist camp attendee has expressed opinions hostile to the United States and generally favorable to violent jihad. Under the First Amendment, the government in the purely domestic context cannot ban expression of such opinions unless they rise to the level of incitement to violence. To meet this test, the opinions have to be reasonably likely to spur imminent violence, and the speaker has to intend for them to have this effect.[11] The material support laws do not challenge this bedrock "content-neutrality" of modern free speech doctrine in the purely domestic realm, although, as we shall see, they depart from content-neutrality in governing relationships with DFTOs. In any case, in a material support prosecution, the government may introduce the speaker's opinions as *evidence* of the speaker's *intention* to provide material support.

---

[10] *See* United States v. Jayyousi, 657 F.3d 1085, 1105-06 (11th Cir. 2011).
[11] Brandenburg v. Ohio, 395 U.S. 444 (1969).

II. The Federal Material Support Statute

Since the speaker's state of mind is an essential element in such prosecutions, precluding the government from introducing evidence of the speaker's opinion would put the government at an unfair disadvantage.[12] As an example, suppose that the defendant has purchased a plane ticket to Pakistan and claims that he merely planned to see relatives or visit tourist destinations. The government may use the defendant's expressed beliefs to show that his actual intent was to participate in a terrorist training camp.

Sometimes the government's efforts to introduce such evidence will require a trial court to weigh the prejudice created by such material in the minds of the jury against the material's relevance and probative value to the government's case. For example, suppose that the government wants to submit other evidence of the defendant's state of mind, such as photographs or videos of Osama bin Laden or of terrorist attacks in the defendant's possession. The trial court must determine whether less inflammatory ways of presenting such evidence, such as describing the material instead of actually showing it to the jury, will minimize prejudice to the defendant while still allowing the government to prove its case.[13] An appellate court will typically defer to the trial court's resolution of these issues, given the trial judge's unique perspective on the context of the proceeding.

B. Prosecutions for Aiding a Designated Foreign Terrorist Organization

Section 2339B criminalizes not only material support to illegal activity, but *any* aid that is coordinated with, or under the direction and control of, a designated foreign terrorist group. Most of the activity prohibited by this section involves cash contributions or similar aid, which courts have uniformly viewed as imposing merely incidental restrictions on speech.[14] In one decision, however, *Holder v. Humanitarian Law Project (HLP)*,[15] the Supreme Court in a 6–3 vote held that Congress could limit the *content* of speech.[16] To avoid ceding too much power to Congress, the Court's decision in *HLP* suggested that the constitutional power to regulate such speech was narrow and that individuals and groups had a number of safe harbors available.

---

[12] United States v. Mehanna, 735 F.3d 32, 60-61 (1st Cir. 2013), *cert. denied*, 2014 U.S. Dist. LEXIS 5478 (Oct. 6, 2014).

[13] *Id.* at 62-63.

[14] Humanitarian Law Project v. Reno, 205 F.3d 1130, 1136 (9th Cir. 2000), *cert. denied*, 532 U.S. 904 (2001) (holding that Congress could prohibit financial contributions to foreign terrorist groups).

[15] 561 U.S. 1, 23 (2010); *cf.* Margulies, *Advising Terrorism, supra* note 6 (analyzing decision).

[16] Chief Justice Roberts wrote the majority opinion in *HLP*. Justices Alito, Kennedy, Scalia, Stevens, and Thomas joined that opinion. Justice Breyer dissented, joined by Justices Ginsburg and Sotomayor.

The comprehensive framework set out in §2339B starts with designation of a foreign terrorist organization. Under the designation process, the Secretary of State determines there is evidence indicating that particular organizations, such as Al Qaeda, Hamas, or the LTTE (the now-defunct Tamil Tigers from Sri Lanka), have a track record of violence, particularly violence against innocents. The government then informs the organization's representatives, who have a chance to review unclassified evidence and rebut the government's claims.[17] If the government designates the group as a foreign terrorist organization, the group can appeal to a federal court. Courts will reject a designation that is arbitrary, not based on substantial support, or inconsistent with procedural safeguards.[18]

While critics of the designation process charge that courts merely rubber-stamp the government's determination,[19] judicial review is more robust than many critics acknowledge. In one case, *Holy Land Foundation v. Ashcroft*,[20] a court considered the organization's evidence that its aid to families of "martyrs" was not assistance for relatives of suicide bombers, but merely aid to families of anyone killed by the government. Upon closer examination, the court discovered that the organization used a different term to describe families in the latter context, suggesting that its use of the term "martyrs" in fact referred to suicide bombers. After this inquiry, the court sustained the designation.

Once courts uphold a designation, the government can prohibit the provision of any and all financial support to the group.[21] Courts take this view because groups like Hamas reject traditional accounting principles.[22] Once a donor contributes money to a group such as Hamas, he or she has no way to ascertain where the money is actually going. DFTOs can shift a contribution intended for a non-violent activity to programs supporting violence. Moreover, money is fungible, so cash contributed to one aspect of a group's operations frees up money that the group can use for violent activities. Finally, a DFTO uses social services not merely for help for the needy, but for recruitment and maintenance of operatives whose families have become dependent on the DFTO.[23]

---

[17] 8 U.S.C. §1189(c)(3); *cf.* People's Mojahedin Org. of Iran v. United States Dep't of State, 613 F.3d 22 (D.C. Cir. 2010) (discussing process and holding that the government had violated due process by failing to give DFTO an opportunity to view unclassified evidence prior to making a final decision denying petition to revoke designation).

[18] *See* United States v. Afshari, 426 F.3d 1150, 1160 (9th Cir. 2005) (upholding process and barring collateral review of designation in subsequent criminal cases).

[19] *See* SUSAN N. HERMAN, TAKING LIBERTIES: THE WAR ON TERROR AND THE EROSION OF AMERICAN DEMOCRACY 41-43 (Oxford U. Press 2011).

[20] 219 F. Supp. 2d 57, 71-73 (D.D.C. 2002), *aff'd*, 333 F.3d 156, 164 (D.C. Cir. 2003).

[21] *See* David Cole, *Hanging with the Wrong Crowd: Of Gangs, Terrorism, and the Right of Association*, 1999 SUP. CT. REV. 203.

[22] *See* Kilburn v. Socialist People's Libyan Arab Jamahiriya, 376 F.3d 1123, 1130 (D.C. Cir. 2004) (commenting that "terrorist organizations can hardly be counted on to keep careful bookkeeping records").

[23] Boim v. Holy Land Found. for Relief & Dev., 549 F.3d 685, 698 (7th Cir. 2008); Margulies, *Advising Terrorism, supra* note 6, at 484; *cf.* Weiss v. Nat'l Westminster Bank PLC, 2014 U.S. App.

II. The Federal Material Support Statute

Courts have uniformly held that restrictions on financial or other tangible aid are merely incidental restrictions on speech.[24] Incidental restrictions are content-neutral, involve important governmental interests, and are appropriately tailored to serve those interests. Section 2339B's ban on cash assistance is content-neutral; an individual who wishes to express his or her support for the DFTO is still free to shout that sentiment from the rooftops.[25] It serves an important governmental interest: limiting DFTOs' access to funds. Finally, it is tailored to achieve that purpose, because the United States would otherwise have to depend on foreign governments to arrest and prosecute individuals abroad with direct ties to violence. Foreign governments may be unwilling or unable to perform this task.

Instruction provided to a DFTO on fundraising is just as criminal as providing cash. Supposed that an individual has offered to train Hamas to seek financial aid from humanitarian organizations. The Supreme Court found in *HLP* that the terrorist groups have exploited United Nations refugee facilities to gain cover for training in violence.[26] The LTTE, or Tamil Tigers of Sri Lanka, used humanitarian assistance to needy Tamil families to acquire child soldiers for LTTE.[27] Providing instruction to a DFTO on raising money is just as dangerous as contributing money directly.

C. Material Support and Speech

A recent case, *United States v. Mehanna*,[28] took §2339B beyond the realm of cash help into the provision of propaganda to Al Qaeda. Tarek Mehanna was convicted in December 2011 in federal court in Massachusetts of conspiring to commit violence in this country, go to an Al Qaeda training camp abroad, and furnish Al Qaeda with propaganda.[29] This last charge has First Amendment implications, since propaganda is speech. For DFTOs, however, propaganda is inextricably linked to operations; terrorist plots are not random, but are carefully planned to maximize propaganda value.

LEXIS 18061, at 15-16 (2d Cir. Sept. 22, 2014) (holding that plaintiffs arguing that bank had financed a terrorist organization and was therefore liable for harm caused by terrorist attacks under Antiterrorism Act, 18 U.S.C. §§2331(1)(A), 2333(a), and 2339B(a)(1) had shown genuine issue of material fact that was sufficient to defeat summary judgment motion).

[24] *See* Humanitarian Law Project v. Reno, 205 F.3d 1130, 1136 (9th Cir. 2000).

[25] Of course, the Supreme Court has also recently equated money with speech in the context of campaign contributions. *See* Citizens United v. FEC, 130 S. Ct. 876 (2010). However, the *Citizens United* Court did not suggest that its decision would affect the many areas, such as commercial finance and foreign relations, in which government has traditionally regulated money.

[26] *See HLP*, 130 S. Ct. at 2729-30.

[27] Peter Popham, *Tamil Tigers Break UN Pledge on Child Soldiers*, THE INDEPENDENT (London), Feb. 4, 2000, at 18.

[28] 735 F.3d 32 (1st Cir. 2013).

[29] *See* Abby Goodnough, *U.S. Citizen Is Convicted in Plot to Support Al Qaeda*, N.Y. TIMES, Dec. 21, 2011, at A26.

Mehanna made two claims at trial to counter the government's claims. First, he claimed the material he provided consisted of translations into English of prominent texts justifying violent jihad by religious and political thinkers. Mehanna said that these texts were of scholarly value, and had a merely abstract relationship to any particular acts of violence. Second, Mehanna said that he had posted these texts to an online chat room visited by others with a purely intellectual interest in these texts. Members or organizers of the chat room who had requested that Mehanna translate the documents were, according to Mehanna, acting independently of Al Qaeda. The expression of abstract support for violence by someone acting independently of a DFTO is protected by the First Amendment, even when those views happen to coincide with those of DFTO leaders. Such views do not constitute illegal incitement to violence, which entails the intent to cause imminent violence and the reasonable likelihood that violence will result.

The government saw the case differently. It argued that Mehanna knew that the chat room, sponsored by an entity called Tibyan Publications, was in fact run by persons who were part of Al Qaeda's network. Assistance to a known intermediary for Al Qaeda is just as criminal as assistance to Al Qaeda itself. The government also introduced evidence, culled from Mehanna's own emails, that he had knowingly provided specific individuals with religious authorizations for going abroad to kill U.S. personnel.[30] The government took the position that terrorist networks are not hierarchical but instead are widely dispersed. Security concerns mean that Al Qaeda's former leader, Osama bin Laden, or current leader, Dr. Ayman al-Zawahiri, rarely offer specific operational advice. Instead, most orders and advice come from a broad group of people around the world. Courts have never required the government to prove that conspirators in ordinary cases involving drugs or organized crime had contact with the kingpins of the organization. The government can prevail in such cases by simply showing that defendants were "spokes in a wheel" who had agreed with other conspirators to

---

[30] *See* United States v. Mehanna, No. 09-10017-GAO, Trial Transcript, Nov. 23, 2011, at 98-101 (available on PACER) (testimony of Daniel Genck, Special Agent, FBI). The emails recount Mehanna's conversations with three individuals who attempted to go abroad to fight U.S. forces after requesting material from the defendant. One, Ehsanul Sadequee, was subsequently convicted in federal court. Discussing another individual, referred to as Aboo K, an administrator at Tibyan told Mehanna, "[Aboo] told me that he would be going soon. So maybe he made it." Mehanna replied, "I just hope he isn't translating books while he is there. . . . It would be funny in the middle of a battle he remembers that he translated a word wrong." "LOL," the administrator replied. *Id.* at 98. For a summary of related testimony, see Milton J. Valencia, *British Investigator Tells Court of Contact with Terrorists; Still No Evidence Presented to Show Mehanna Acted*, Boston Globe, Nov. 11, 2011, Metro section, p. 3; for a more skeptical view of the danger posed by internet speech relating to terrorism, see Steven R. Morrison, *Terrorism On-Line: Is Speech the Same As It Ever Was?*, 44 Creighton L. Rev. 963 (2011) (concluding that online recruitment does not pose distinctive threat, and may be smaller security risk than face-to-face recruitment or other traditional methods). An online debate about the *Mehanna* case between Peter Margulies and David Cole, a critic of the material support statute, is available at http://www.lawfareblog.com/2012/04/peter-margulies-responds-to-david-cole/, with follow-up at http://www.lawfareblog.com/2012/04/david-cole-and-peter-margulies-an-exchange-on-tarek-mehanna/.

II. The Federal Material Support Statute

further the conspiracy's objectives. Proving conspiracy under §2339B should be no different, the government contended.[31]

HLP itself addressed an issue that was closer than *Mehanna* to protected political speech. The *HLP* Court, in an opinion by Chief Justice Roberts, held that Congress could prohibit speech by those who coordinated their activity with a DFTO or acted under the DFTO's direction or control. This activity is more dangerous than independent speech, the Court said, because it allows the DFTO to tailor its interactions to maximize its tactical advantage. Recall that courts have said that DFTOs are poor accountants.[32] In *HLP*, the Court extended this concern from the context of financial contributions to the realm of speech coordinated with a DFTO, such as instructions on international law or nonviolence or negotiating on a DFTO's behalf with a state. This narrow band of speech, the Court asserted, entailed a relationship with a terrorist organization and was therefore more dangerous than speech outside the DFTO's ambit.

At first blush, regulating instruction in nonviolence or international law may seem counterintuitive.[33] Nonetheless, Chief Justice Roberts had a point. As an analogy, consider an author who wants to sell a manuscript to a publisher. Independent praise for the manuscript on a book-lovers' web site could be useful; however, it cannot substitute for the efforts of a literary agent who can tailor her campaign to the author's likes and dislikes. In the DFTO setting, this tailored relationship gives the organization an advantage not merely in ideas, but also in operational tactics. That is the kind of relationship-based speech that the Court ruled that Congress could prohibit.

---

[31] Ultimately, courts upheld Mehanna's conviction, ruling that the trial court had accurately stated the law by instructing the jury that Mehanna was guilty if he coordinated his speech with Al Qaeda, and that the jury could in any case have reasonably found that Mehanna was guilty of material support because he visited Yemen with the intent of securing terrorist training. *Mehanna*, 735 F.3d at 43-51.

[32] *See* Kilburn v. Socialist People's Libyan Arab Jamahiriya, 376 F.3d 1123, 1130 (D.C. Cir. 2004).

[33] *HLP*, incidentally, did not involve an actual prosecution. The plaintiffs in the case never submitted evidence that the government had investigated their activities. Rather, they claimed that §2339B would chill their lawful speech. While plaintiffs have brought such "preenforcement" challenges previously, these challenges have usually involved statutes that clearly prohibited the plaintiffs' conduct. In those situations, the court has a sufficient record to assess the parties' claims. Justice Stevens at the oral argument in *HLP* said that the *HLP* plaintiffs' efforts were more amorphous and abstract, amounting to an effort to stop "a potential prosecution against somebody for making a potential speech." Courts tend to be more wary of granting claims pervaded by such uncertainty, which may help account for the *HLP* plaintiffs' defeat. By the way, Prof. Margulies, one of the co-authors of this volume, was co-counsel on an *amicus curiae* brief filed on behalf of Scholars, Attorneys, and Former Public Officials with Experience in Terrorism-Related Issues that asked the Supreme Court to uphold the constitutionality of the federal material support statute and carve out safe harbors for journalists, scholars, human rights groups, and attorneys. *See* http://www.americanbar.org/content/dam/aba/publishing/preview/publiced_preview_briefs_pdfs_09_10_08_1498_PetitionerAmCuTerrorismExperts.authcheckdam.pdf.

To understand why the Court ruled the way it did, consider a hypothetical suggested by the examples given in the *HLP* decision. Suppose a DFTO such as Hamas decided to invite in a speaker on nonviolent techniques. In the past, the Court noted, DFTOs had repeatedly sought to convey a "kinder, gentler" face to the world in order to elicit cash contributions from gullible donors and conceal a renewed military build-up.[34] Such groups have repeatedly broken truces, the Court observed, under circumstances showing that they had agreed to the truce only to buy time for rearmament. For example, the Lebanese group Hezbollah has acquired thousands of rockets from Iran after an attack it launched on Israeli border forces led to a 2006 conflict. Hamas has also rearmed after rocket attacks on Israel led to a 2008-2009 confrontation. That rearmament sparked renewed confrontations in 2012 and 2014.

The *HLP* Court ruled that even a speaker who did not intend to aid such ruses could still be deceived by a DFTO into providing cover for the DFTO's rearmament. The difficulty of acquiring information about conduct overseas compounded this problem, according to Chief Justice Roberts. In the domestic sphere, the government can obtain a warrant authorizing surveillance when it has probable cause to believe that the target of an investigation is breaking the law. Overseas, however, the government's ability to engage in surveillance is far more limited, and the United States must rely on other nations that may lack either the ability or the inclination to cooperate. As a result, the Court said that the government had advanced a compelling interest in regulating this particular kind of speech.

The Court's decision in *HLP* left many safe harbors for speakers who wished to offer information about topics such as nonviolence or international law. A speaker who acted independently of the DFTO in posting material on a publicly accessible web site would be engaged in protected speech.[35] So would a speaker independent of the DFTO who praised the organization's apparent commitment to nonviolence, or offered abstract praise of the group's violent activities. Moreover, a range of other activities, such as scholarship, journalism, human rights monitoring, legal advocacy, and mediation à la the Carter Center would not be subject to restrictions.

In sum, the material support statute is a powerful tool for prosecutors. It can play a useful role in disrupting terrorist financing, as well as the relationships with agents on whom terrorist organizations rely. While the statute can impinge on the content of speech, the need for the government to show "coordination" with a terrorist group leaves plenty of safe harbors that protect First Amendment rights.

---

[34] *Humanitarian Law Project*, 56 U.S. at 36-37.
[35] *Id.* at 39.

III.   EXTENDING U.S. CRIMINAL JURISDICTION BEYOND U.S. BORDERS

Use of criminal prosecution and sanction to protect national security will create an almost self-evident need to project federal criminal law beyond U.S. borders. It is therefore unsurprising that the federal criminal code includes a number of "long-arm" criminal statutes: Laws that apply outside the territory of the United States.[36] These statutes provide federal prosecutors with the jurisdiction needed to leverage the nation's criminal sanction power to protect a wide range of national security interests, including among others the protection of sensitive information, deterrence of acts of terrorism directed against U.S. nationals and interests, limiting the proliferation of weapons of mass destruction, and enhancing the efficacy of U.S. trade restrictions.

Projecting U.S. criminal laws beyond national borders also implicates international relations, as it will always create a risk that other nations may consider the application of U.S. criminal law to activities that occur in their territory or to their nationals an intrusion into or interference with their sovereignty. Of course, this concern does not only arise in relation to U.S. long-arm statutes, but instead whenever any state enacts criminal laws with analogous jurisdictional reach. Indeed, there may be situations where it is the United States that considers the invocation of long-arm jurisdiction by another state to be unjustified.

In order to mitigate the friction that may arise when states do extend their laws beyond their borders, principles of international criminal jurisdiction evolved over time and are today considered part of customary international law. These principles provide a framework for assessing the international legal legitimacy of state assertion of domestic criminal jurisdiction to activities or individuals beyond its borders. As such, these principles serve the interests of the international community by mitigating the risk that such extensions will produce disputes between states, by establishing the conditions or situations that justify, from an international law perspective, these invocations of national criminal jurisdiction.

For some nations, these customary international law principles dictate the permissible scope of their extraterritorial jurisdiction; not the United States. This is because the positive enactments of Congress—U.S. statutes—will always trump any customary international legal limits on U.S. national power. This is simply a manifestation of the "law prioritization" established in Article VI of the U.S. Constitution, which establishes the "supremacy" of U.S. law, or more specifically that statutes and treaties ratified by the United States are supreme over all other sources of law.[37] As a result, these international principles of

---

[36] 18 U.S.C. §2332a (use of weapons of mass destruction); 18 U.S.C. §2332f (making it a crime to bomb public places where the victim is a United States national); 18 U.S.C. §2339C (making it a crime to finance terrorism outside of the United States).

[37] CHARLES DOYLE, CONG. RESEARCH SERV., RS22497, EXTRATERRITORIAL APPLICATION OF AMERICAN CRIMINAL LAW # 20 (2012) [hereinafter CHARLES DOYLE].

jurisdiction are not binding on the nation: If Congress enacts criminal laws that do not comport with these principles, U.S. courts must give full force and effect to these laws.[38]

This does not, however, mean that these principles have no significance in U.S. practice; far from it. Instead, these principles of jurisdiction are best understood as highly persuasive authority to guide judicial interpretation of the jurisdictional scope of domestic criminal law. Accordingly, when a defendant charged with violating a federal criminal statute based on conduct that occurs outside U.S. territory challenges the validity of the asserted criminal jurisdiction extension, it is very likely the court ruling on the challenge will turn to these principles to guide ruling on the challenge.

As noted above, these principles do not bind or restrict Congress if it chooses to extend U.S. criminal jurisdiction beyond the scope of what these principles seem to permit.[39] However, it is a principle of statutory construction for U.S. courts to presume U.S. criminal law applies only domestically.[40] This presumption, while rebuttable, is given greater weight when extraterritorial application of the law would conflict with customary international law principles of jurisdiction. Accordingly, U.S. courts will look for either a clear indication that Congress intended the law to apply extraterritorially, or to the nature of the criminal prohibition itself to assess whether Congress must have anticipated extraterritorial application. According to a Congressional Research Service Report addressing extraterritorial criminal jurisdiction:

> [T]he question of the extent to which a particular statute applies outside the United States has generally been considered a matter of statutory, rather than constitutional, construction. General rules of statutory construction have emerged which can explain, if not presage, the result in a given case. The first of these holds that a statute that is silent on the question of overseas application will be construed to have only territorial application unless there is a clear indication of some broader intent.
>
> A second rule of construction states that the nature and purpose of a statute may provide an indication of whether Congress intended a statute to apply beyond the confines of the United States. . . .
>
> The final rule declares that unless a contrary intent is clear, Congress is assumed to have acted so as not to invite action inconsistent with international law.[41]

Customary international law principles of extraterritorial jurisdiction provide, therefore, a source of persuasive authority when interpreting the scope of federal criminal law. According to the Restatement (Third) of Foreign Relations

[38] *Id.*
[39] *Id.* at 10.
[40] *Id.*
[41] *Id.* at 8-10.

III. Extending U.S. Criminal Jurisdiction Beyond U.S. Borders

Law,[42] the following categories of extraterritorial criminal jurisdiction are recognized as consistent with international law:

1. The territorial principle: punishing conduct that occurs outside national borders when the impact of the offense occurs within national borders (for example, a conspiracy to engage in a terrorist attack against a target in the United States).[43]
2. The nationality principle: punishing nationals who commit offenses outside the territory of their nation (for example, a statute prohibiting any U.S. national from soliciting child prostitutes abroad).[44]
3. The passive personality principle: punishing individuals for crimes committed outside national territory when the victim of the crime is a national of the punishing state (for example, prosecuting a foreign national who kills a U.S. national abroad by an act of terrorism).[45]
4. The protective principle: punishing individuals whose crimes impact the vital national interests of the state (for example, prosecuting a defendant who produced and introduced counterfeit U.S. currency into circulation).[46]
5. The universal principle: punishing individuals for violating rules of international law that are universally recognized and condemned (for example, prosecuting a defendant for piracy committed abroad).[47]

It is important to note that these principles merely indicate contexts in which international law acknowledges the legitimacy of a state extending its criminal law beyond its national borders; they do not have any independent proscriptive effect.[48] In other words, conduct falling into one of these categories is not automatically a crime, and a federal prosecutor could not indict an individual based on an assertion that the conduct fits within one of these categories. Instead, the state—for purposes of this discussion the United States—must enact a criminal law prohibiting conduct, but should be guided by these principles when defining the jurisdictional scope of such statutory prohibitions.

When a criminal statute, by its terms, indicates extraterritorial applicability, resolving a challenge to its application presents little difficulty. Even if a court were to conclude that the nature of the proscribed conduct does not fall within one of the international law categories outlined above, the primacy of the statute requires the court to apply it pursuant to congressional intent.

Most federal criminal statutes do not, however, include an explicit indication of congressionally intended scope. It is therefore common for defendants to be

---

[42] *Id.* at 11.
[43] *Id.* at 12.
[44] *Id.* at 13.
[45] *Id.* at 14.
[46] United States v. Rezaq, 134 F.3d 1121, 1133 (D.C. Cir. 1998).
[47] CHARLES DOYLE, *supra* note 37, at 14.
[48] *Id.* at 20.

charged with violating federal criminal law that does not clearly indicate its scope of application. In these cases, the reviewing court will consider the relative consistency or inconsistency with these international law principles. This is based on the assumption that Congress normally seeks to reconcile the scope of the criminal laws it enacts with international legal limits on the scope of national jurisdiction. Accordingly, courts will presume a statute that does not include an explicit indication of jurisdiction scope was intended to comport with these principles, at least without a clear indication of a contrary congressional intent.[49]

In contrast, where extraterritorial application of a federal criminal statute fits within one of these international jurisdiction categories, validity of the application will be substantially bolstered. In such cases, a court will then look to other indicators of the statute's intended scope of applicability. These include the legislative record—the general objective of the criminal proscription. When that objective logically includes extraterritorial conduct, the court is likely to endorse extraterritorial application.

A useful illustration of this interpretive process is the case of *United States v. Yousef*.[50] In that case, the defendant, an alien, was indicted for violations of federal criminal law for his complicity in a plot to blow up commercial airliners flying out of Manila.[51] Yousef and his co-conspirators planned to destroy 12 aircraft flying various routes in Southeast Asia by boarding the planes, assembling the bombs while in flight, and then exiting the planes at the first layover.[52] Yousef argued that subjecting him to federal criminal jurisdiction violated international law and that Congress exceeded its authority when it criminalized conduct of an alien outside the United States.[53]

The trial court rejected Yousef's motion to dismiss the indictment.[54] The Second Circuit Court of Appeals affirmed, concluding that each count was based on a legitimate extraterritorial extension of U.S. criminal law.[55] The court analyzed a number of counts because the targets of the bombing plot were not all of the same character.[56] However, the court first noted that although the federal statute criminalizing the destruction of commercial airliners did not explicitly indicate that Congress intended the law to apply to extraterritorial conduct, the objective of the proscription—to punish and thereby deter individuals from directing acts of terrorism against commercial airliners—indicated that such application was logical.[57]

---

[49] *Id.* at 10.
[50] *Yousef*, 327 F.3d 56 (2d Cir. 2003).
[51] *Id.* at 83.
[52] *Id.* at 79.
[53] *Id.* at 97.
[54] *Id.* at 97-98.
[55] *Id.* at 92-99.
[56] *Id.* at 95.
[57] *Id.* at 108-10.

III. Extending U.S. Criminal Jurisdiction Beyond U.S. Borders

The court then had little difficulty dealing with the counts of the indictment alleging the targeting of U.S. flagged aircraft.[58] Extending U.S. criminal law to prohibit bombing U.S. aircraft fell within the passive personality concept of international criminal jurisdiction, as the victim of the misconduct would be U.S. flagged aircraft.[59] One count of the indictment, however, alleged that the target aircraft was not U.S., but Japanese. This proved more problematic for the court, as extending the law to that offense could not be justified based on the passive personality principle. The government asserted that this count fell within the scope of the universal principle of international jurisdiction.[60] Yousef contested this assertion, arguing that because there was no universal international legal consensus on the definition of terrorism, terrorism was not a crime subject to the universal jurisdiction principle.[61]

The court rejected Yousef's argument. While acknowledging that there is indeed no international consensus on the definition of terrorism, the court noted that there is universal state condemnation of terrorism (however defined).[62] The court then noted that while the definition of terrorism may be uncertain at the periphery, international treaties, most notably the Tokyo Convention on Offences and Certain Other Acts Committed on Board Aircraft, indicate that bombing commercial aircraft is a universally condemned act. The court then bolstered its conclusion by citing the protective principle, noting that Congress and the nation have a legitimate and logical interest in demonstrating U.S. commitment to protecting *all* commercial airliners from acts of terrorism, and therefore extending U.S. criminal law to such acts, even when targeting aircraft of another nation, contributes to a vital U.S. foreign policy objective.[63]

Other courts have applied similar reasoning to validate the extension of federal criminal law to aliens abroad, especially for conduct related to terrorist activities.[64] Indeed, as terrorism knows no borders, and threats to the United States and its national security interests posed by terrorists is often initiated if not consummated abroad, it is logical that courts would assume Congress intended criminal laws targeting such activities to apply outside the United States, even when the defendant is not a U.S. national.

---

[58] *Id.* at 111.

[59] *Id.* at 96.

[60] *Id.* at 111.

[61] *Id.* at 106-08.

[62] *Id.* at 106.

[63] *Id.* at 110.

[64] United States v. Vasquez-Velasco, 15 F.3d 833, 841 (9th Cir. 1994); United States v. Felix-Gutierrez, 940 F.2d 1200, 1206 (9th Cir. 1991); United States v. Benitez, 741 F.2d 1312, 1316 (11th Cir. 1984).

IV. CONSTITUTIONAL LIMITS ON INVESTIGATORY POWERS

Application of criminal laws to protect national security interests will almost always be preceded by an investigation process. Unlike what might be loosely called the "normal" criminal investigative process, investigations that implicate national security interests may not initially—or even primarily—be focused on criminal prosecution. Indeed, national security risk identification and mitigation will often be central to investigations that evolve into criminal prosecutions. Furthermore, a wide range of government investigatory agencies and assets—federal, state, and even local—will often play a role in the conduct of such investigations.

While the motives, scope, and participants in national security related investigations may be significantly different from more common criminal investigations, they will not be exempted from constitutional constraints on government power, but must instead comply with the fundamental constitutional rules related to surveillance, interrogation, and ultimately trial of those falling within the crosshairs of government suspicion. The national security aspect of such investigations may, however, trigger certain exceptions to the normal law enforcement related application of these rules. Accordingly, understanding when and how the Fourth, Fifth, and Sixth Amendments of the Constitution apply to government efforts to protect national security is essential to understand how the criminal power of the nation may be properly leveraged to achieve this vital goal.

A. Overview of the Fourth Amendment

Because assessment and investigation of national security threats often begin with surveillance, determining if and when such surveillance is subject to the requirements of the Fourth Amendment is essential. Furthermore, once that determination is made, it becomes necessary to assess how those requirements are satisfied.

The Fourth Amendment[65] provides that:

> The right of the people to be secure in their persons, houses, papers, and effects, against unreasonable searches and seizures, shall not be violated, and no Warrants shall issue, but upon probable cause, supported by Oath or affirmation, and particularly describing the place to be searched, and the persons or things to be seized.

However, it is important to note that not all government surveillance triggers the Fourth Amendment. Instead, three "triggering" conditions must be met. First, the

---

[65] U.S. CONST. amend. IV.

target of the surveillance must qualify as an individual within the meaning of the term "people" as used in the Amendment; second, the surveillance must be conducted by or at the direction of a U.S. government agent; and third, the surveillance must intrude upon a protected Fourth Amendment interest (is a search or seizure within the meaning of the Amendment). If these requirements are not met, neither the surveillance nor the subsequent use of any information obtained as evidence in a criminal trial will implicate the Fourth Amendment.

B. *Who Does the Fourth Amendment Protect?*

In *United States v. Verdugo-Urquidez*,[66] the Supreme Court considered whether a non-resident alien brought into the United States involuntarily could invoke the protections of the Fourth Amendment. Verdugo-Urquidez, who was apprehended in Mexico and brought to the United States to stand trial for complicity in the murder of a DEA agent, sought to challenge the admissibility of evidence seized in a joint FBI/Mexican search of his home in Mexico. In an opinion written by Chief Justice Rehnquist the Court held that the Fourth Amendment's protection against unreasonable search and seizure did not extend to Verdugo-Urquidez. According to the Court, the term "people" in the amendment was not without substance, and indicated an individual with some connection to the political community of the United States. The Court contrasted the term "people" in the Fourth Amendment with the term "person" in the Fifth Amendment, and noted that "people" was linked to the Preamble of the Constitution, and therefore indicated a more narrow category of "beneficiary" than the Fifth Amendment.[67] As a non-resident alien in the United States involuntarily, Verdugo-Urquidez was not within that more restricted class of beneficiaries.

Verdugo-Urquidez has not been applied broadly by lower courts, and aliens in the United States voluntarily—ostensibly even undocumented aliens—are generally considered to fall within the protections of the Fourth Amendment. However, national security surveillance will frequently be conducted abroad to target aliens with no connection to the United States. In such situations, *Verdugo-Urquidez* establishes that U.S. government agents need not consider application of, or compliance with, the Fourth Amendment as a condition to their surveillance efforts. Even if the surveillance techniques would trigger the Fourth Amendment if directed against a U.S. person (citizen or resident alien)—in other words it is a technique that intrudes upon what would qualify as a protected interest for a U.S. national—they may be utilized without implicating the Fourth Amendment.

---

[66] United States v. Verdugo-Urquidez, 494 U.S. 259 (1990).
[67] *Id.* at 265.

C.   Who Does the Fourth Amendment Restrict?

Based on *Verdugo-Urquidez*, the Fourth Amendment protects individuals who do have a meaningful connection to the United States—which includes any U.S. national or aliens with a voluntary presence in the United States—whether in the United States or abroad. When these individuals are targeted for surveillance, the next question will be whether the surveillance is the result of U.S. government action. In 1914, in *Weeks v. United States*,[68] the Supreme Court held that evidence obtained by a U.S. Marshal in violation of the Fourth Amendment was subject to suppression. However, the Court also held that evidence *provided to* the Marshal by state officials—who at that time were not subject to the Fourth Amendment—related to the same offense was not subject to suppression. This outcome would, of course, be different today, as the Fourth Amendment has applied to the states since 1949, when the Supreme Court decided *Wolf v. Colorado*.[69] However, the *Weeks* holding remains the foundation for what is sometimes called the "Silver Platter" doctrine: When U.S. government agents receive evidence obtained by individuals (or even governments) that fall beyond the scope of the Fourth Amendment, that evidence may be used with no Fourth Amendment implication. In short, the government is permitted to use evidence that is handed to it on a "silver platter."

Because the Fourth Amendment has applied to the states through the Due Process Clause of the Fourteenth Amendment since 1949, the Silver Platter doctrine would no longer apply in a case like *Weeks*. However, it will apply when there is no U.S. or state government action associated with the search or seizure. Thus, if a private party acquires evidence subsequently turned over to the government, use of that evidence does not implicate the Fourth Amendment. This same rationale extends to evidence collected by foreign government agents, no matter how beneficial to U.S. interests that evidence may be.

There is one significant limitation to the Silver Platter doctrine: When an agency relationship exists between the private or foreign actor and U.S. officials, the search or seizure will trigger the Fourth Amendment.[70] This exception requires analysis of whether the private or foreign agent was acting at the direction or control of U.S. officials. Direction and control need not be express, and may be

---

[68] Weeks v. United States, 232 U.S. 383 (1914).

[69] Wolf v. Colorado, 338 U.S. 25 (1949). (Holding that the privacy protections of the Fourth Amendment were enforceable against the states through the Due Process Clause of the Fourteenth Amendment. It is worth noting that the Court considered the remedy of exclusion of evidence obtained in violation of the Fourth Amendment a distinct issue from the applicability of the right itself. At this time, the Court held that suppression was not mandatory.

[70] This exception to the doctrine exists to ensure that Fourth Amendment protections cannot be circumvented by having a foreign party commit the illegal search, but balances the issue so as to only be restrictive if the U.S. government is involved in the violation of the Fourth Amendment, hence the agency/joint venture requirement. *See* Byars v. United States, 273 U.S. 28 (1927); Stonehill v. United States, 405 F.2d 738, 743 (9th Cir. 1968); United States v. Behety, 32 F.3d 503, 510 (11th Cir. 1994).

implied from indications of a joint venture between U.S. and private/foreign agents. However, mere awareness, presence, or observation of the activities of private/foreign actors by U.S. officials will not trigger this exception.

D. What Type of Surveillance Falls Within the Scope of the Fourth Amendment?

If U.S. government agents direct surveillance against someone falling within the protective meaning of the Fourth Amendment, it is then necessary to determine whether the surveillance qualifies as a search or seizure. If so, the Fourth Amendment is triggered, and the government conduct must be "reasonable" within the meaning of the Amendment. If the government conduct does not qualify as a search or seizure, it will not implicate the Amendment. Therefore, identifying what qualifies as a search or seizure is essential to determining whether the government action is subject to the reasonableness requirement of the Fourth.

To qualify as a seizure, government agents must interfere with property within an individual's possessory interest (although not necessarily property owned by the target), and that interference must be meaningful. This rule is based on *United States v. Karo*,[71] where the Supreme Court defined a seizure of property as any "meaningful interference of a possessory interest." *Karo* involved the placement of a beeper in a chemical drum prior to the target taking possession of the drum. Once in his possession, government agents used the beeper to track his public movements. The Court held that because Karo did not even know the beeper was placed on the drum, and because it in no way interfered with his use of the drum or its contents, the drum had not been seized within the meaning of the Fourth Amendment. Accordingly, taking some action towards a target's property that does not interfere with the use of the property would not qualify as a seizure. However, it is equally clear that taking physical custody of property in a manner that deprives the target of use of the property is a seizure.

It is important to note, however, that government conduct that does not qualify as a seizure may nonetheless trigger the Fourth Amendment if it qualifies as a search. The Supreme Court's decision in *Jones v. United States* made this clear.[72] *Jones* involved the placement of a GPS tracking device on the undercarriage of a car within the suspect's possession, followed by a month of almost constant monitoring. As will be explained in more detail below, the Court held that while considered only for the question of whether the emplacement was a seizure, *Karo* dictated a negative answer because Jones never knew the GPS was on the car. However, the Court then analyzed whether the placement of the GPS on the car *for the purpose of gathering evidence* qualified as a *search* within the meaning of the Fourth Amendment. The Court answered that question in the affirmative.

---

[71] United States v. Karo, 468 U.S. 705 (1984).
[72] Jones v. United States, 356 U.S. 257 (1960).

Accordingly, while a *Karo*-type intrusion onto a target's possession might not qualify as a seizure, following *Jones* it may very well qualify as a search. The Court did, however, highlight the fact that in *Karo*, the beeper was placed on the drum *prior* to Karo taking possession, which indicated it was neither a seizure nor a search.

When will surveillance qualify as a search within the meaning of the Fourth Amendment? This is obviously a vital question in relation to government activities motivated by a national security interest, as those activities will frequently involve both electronic and physical surveillance, both within and outside the United States. While procedures necessary to comply with the Fourth Amendment's reasonableness requirement may turn on the purpose of the surveillance, whether such surveillance is even subject to this requirement will be dictated by whether the activity qualifies as a Fourth Amendment search.

Looking for something is not enough to qualify as a search. Instead, it is where and how the government "looks" that distinguishes "looking" from "searching." Based on the Supreme Court's most recent decisions on this question, in *United States v. Jones*[73] and *Florida v. Jardines*,[74] determining when surveillance qualifies as a search requires a two-part analysis. First, did government agents physically trespass against the target's home or effects for the purpose of gathering information? If so, the government conduct qualifies as a search, as it is directed against an area or item explicitly protected by the text of the Fourth Amendment. However, government surveillance will routinely extend to areas that fall outside the scope of this textual protection. In such situations, a search will occur if the surveillance intrudes into the target's reasonable expectation of privacy.

Prior to *Jones* and *Jardines*, a physical trespass against an individual's home or effects was generally not considered a search if the object of surveillance had been "held out to the public." Thus, in *Jones*, the government argued that it had not engaged in a search because the GPS tracking device had been placed on the undercarriage of the automobile, and the automobile had been tracked only while travelling on public roads, with neither activity intruding into an area Jones had made an effort to shield from public view. And in *Jardines*, the government argued that because any person could go up to the front porch of Jardines's home, they had not intruded into an area Jardines sought to keep private.

These arguments reflected the widely accepted understanding that only an intrusion into a reasonable expectation of privacy qualified as a search. That understanding derived from the Court's seminal decisions in *Katz v. United States*[75] and *Smith v. Maryland*.[76] The reasonable expectation of privacy test was first established in *Katz*, when the Court held that using a listening device placed on the exterior of a public telephone booth to record the suspect's conversation was a Fourth Amendment search, even though there was no trespass against the

---

[73] United States v. Jones, 132 S. Ct. 954 (2012).
[74] Florida v. Jardines, 133 S. Ct. 1409 (2013).
[75] Katz v. United States, 389 U.S. 347 (1967).
[76] Smith v. Maryland, 442 U.S. 735 (1979).

suspect's property interest. In his seminal concurring opinion, Justice Harlan enunciated a two-part test for assessing when an expectation of privacy is reasonable: 1) Did the target of the surveillance manifest a subjective expectation of privacy by shielding the activity from the public?; and 2) If so, is it an expectation of privacy that society is willing to recognize as reasonable? Answering both of those questions affirmatively indicates an actual (subjective) and reasonable (objective) expectation of privacy, protected from unreasonable government search by the Fourth Amendment.

In *Smith v. Maryland*, the Supreme Court incorporated Justice Harlan's two-part test into its holding.[77] That case involved use of a pen register (a trap and trace device) placed on a telephone exchange to record the numbers dialed from the suspect's telephone. That information was then used to obtain a warrant that led to the seizure of incriminating evidence. Smith argued that the surveillance method allowed the government to look into his apartment to see the numbers he was dialing, and was therefore a search.

The Court rejected this argument, holding that Smith had no reasonable expectation of privacy in the numbers he conveyed to the telephone company.[78] The Court rejected Smith's claim of a subjective expectation of privacy, because Smith had voluntarily conveyed the numbers to the telephone company and had to have been aware that he was doing so because those numbers are then listed on his monthly bill.[79] However, even assuming Smith harbored some subjective expectation of privacy in the numbers dialed, the Court held this was not a reasonable expectation, because no reasonable person would consider information voluntarily exposed to the public to be private.

Based on these decisions, the Fourth Amendment protects any place where an individual could claim a reasonable expectation of privacy, which required some effort to shield the thing from public view, and an objective determination that the subjective expectation of privacy such an effort produces is one society is prepared to recognize as reasonable. Key to this assessment was whether the individual held the area or thing out to public observation. If so, there was no claim to Fourth Amendment protection, as the individual could have no expectation of privacy. Until recently, this test was widely understood as the exclusive measure for what qualified as a search within the meaning of the Fourth Amendment. This understanding, however, is no longer valid.

The Supreme Court's most recent analysis of the scope of Fourth Amendment protection in *Jones* and *Jardines* fundamentally altered this assumption that the *Katz* reasonable expectation of privacy standard was the exclusive measure for assessing what qualifies as a search. Rejecting this assumption, the Court held in both cases that the *Katz/Smith* reasonable expectation of privacy test was not the exclusive measure for assessing what constitutes a search, but instead supplemented the textual definition of a search. In neither case did the government intrude

[77] *Id.* at 740.
[78] *Id.* at 745.
[79] *Id.* at 742.

upon the suspect's reasonable expectation of privacy. However, by reframing this test as a supplement to the textual protections of the Fourth Amendment, this fact did not exclude the surveillance from the scope of the Fourth Amendment. In *Jardines*, that textual definition was interpreted to mean any physical trespass against a target's home (to include the curtilage) for the purpose of gathering evidence (in *Jardines*, the Court held that bringing a drug detection dog to the front porch of the suspect's home and allowing the dog to dart back and forth near the front door in order to detect the odor of narcotics qualified as a search). In *Jones*, the Court held that the textual definition also included the physical trespass on an item, or "effect" (a car), within the suspect's possession for the purpose of gathering evidence.

Neither of these cases, however, altered the existing reasonable expectation of privacy test for assessing when surveillance that extends beyond an individual's home or effect qualifies as a search. Thus, for any surveillance that does not implicate a textual object of Fourth Amendment protection, the reasonable expectation of privacy measure remains controlling. In such situations, the government will rely on the established test for assessing what is and what is not within a target's reasonable expectation of privacy: whether or not the target exposed the words, item, activity, smell, sound, etc. to the public. If so, "looking" for or at it *is not* a search. If not, it is. This rule has been extended to disclosure of conversations to the government by so-called "false friends," bank records, telephone and email records (although the content of calls and emails does fall within a reasonable expectation of privacy), mail covers (where postal inspectors record date from the outside of an envelope or package), and looking through abandoned property.[80] Because none of these situations involve intrusion into a reasonable expectation of privacy, none qualify as searches within the meaning of the Fourth Amendment (unless they trigger the *Jones/Jardines* definition of search).

E.   Complying with the Fourth Amendment

If government action qualifies as a search or seizure, thereby triggering the Fourth Amendment, the government action must be "reasonable" within the meaning of the Amendment. While the Fourth Amendment includes a Warrant Clause, a warrant is not always required to satisfy this reasonableness touchstone. Instead, a warrant based on probable cause will trigger a presumption that the search or seizure was reasonable, requiring the defendant challenging the government action to rebut this presumption (by showing the warrant lacked requisite specificity, or the issuing magistrate was not neutral and detached, or probable cause was insufficient, or the method of execution shocked the conscience).

---

[80] *See* United States v. Choate, 576 F.2d 165 (1978) (mail cover does not encroach upon the privacy of an individual); United States v. Dzialak, 441 F.2d 212 (1971) (search of abandoned property is not a violation of the Fourth Amendment); On Lee v. United States, 343 U.S. 747 (1952) (the use of false friends does not violate the Fourth Amendment).

In contrast, all warrantless searches and seizures are presumptively unreasonable, requiring the government to prove the applicability of an established exception to the warrant and/or probable cause requirement.

In reality, most searches and seizures occur without a warrant. In such cases, one of any number of exceptions may apply to render the action reasonable. Commonly invoked exceptions include consent, search incident to arrest, exigent circumstances, and plain view. In the context of national security surveillance, two exceptions are particularly significant: the foreign intelligence exception to the warrant requirement, and the special needs exception to both the warrant and probable cause requirements.

V. NATIONAL SECURITY SURVEILLANCE AND THE WARRANT REQUIREMENT

In *United States v. District Court* (known as the *Keith* case),[81] the Supreme Court considered whether national security related surveillance justified a broad exception to the warrant requirement, permitting the President to authorize such surveillance. In that case, the defendant sought to suppress evidence obtained by the government during surveillance targeted against members of a domestic dissident group responsible for bombing a CIA facility in Ann Arbor, Michigan. The surveillance had been conducted without a warrant, and no other established exception to the warrant requirement applied. The government argued that the Warrant Clause was inapplicable because the objective of the surveillance was to protect the federal function against a threat to national security:

> The Government argues that the special circumstances applicable to domestic security surveillances necessitate a further exception to the warrant requirement. It is urged that the requirement of prior judicial review would obstruct the President in the discharge of his constitutional duty to protect domestic security.[82]

The Court rejected this broadly asserted national security exception. The Court noted that the history of and motivation for the Fourth Amendment necessitated the exact opposite conclusion—that interposing a neutral magistrate between the government and such surveillance protected the people from the risk the government would use its powers to target and chill legitimate political dissent. According to the Court:

---

[81] United States v. U.S. Dist. Court, 407 U.S. 297 (1972).
[82] *Id.* at 318.

History abundantly documents the tendency of Government—however benevolent and benign its motives—to view with suspicion those who most fervently dispute its policies. Fourth Amendment protections become the more necessary when the targets of official surveillance may be those suspected of unorthodoxy in their political beliefs. The danger to political dissent is acute where the Government attempts to act under so vague a concept as the power to protect "domestic security." Given the difficulty of defining the domestic security interest, the danger of abuse in acting to protect that interest becomes apparent.[83]

The *Keith* Court, however, included two critical qualifiers in the opinion. First, it noted that normal criminal warrant and probable cause requirements may not be well suited for surveillance motivated by national security concerns—like the surveillance that led to the evidence at issue. As a result, the Court essentially invited Congress to consider adopting a modified warrant process when the surveillance is not conducted in support of criminal prosecution, but instead domestic national security. As is noted in greater detail below, Congress subsequently acted on this invitation. However, Congress did not go nearly as far as the Court suggested it might. Instead, it enacted the Foreign Intelligence Surveillance Act (FISA), which limited the modified search authorization process to surveillance directed against a foreign intelligence threat, and did not extend to general national security threats with no connection to a foreign power.

Second, the Court emphasized that it was not dealing with surveillance directed against a foreign intelligence threat, but instead a broad assertion of national security surveillance that included targeting domestic dissident groups:

> Further, the instant case requires no judgment on the scope of the President's surveillance power with respect to the activities of foreign powers, within or without this country. The Attorney General's affidavit in this case states that the surveillances were "deemed necessary to protect the nation from attempts of *domestic organizations* to attack and subvert the existing structure of Government" (emphasis supplied). There is no evidence of any involvement, directly or indirectly, of a foreign power.[84] We are told further that these surveillances are directed primarily to the collecting and maintaining of intelligence with respect to subversive forces, and are not an attempt to gather evidence for specific criminal prosecutions. It is said that this type of surveillance should not be subject to traditional warrant requirements which were established to govern investigation of criminal activity, not ongoing intelligence gathering.[85]

Later in the opinion, the Court explained why this distinction was so important: The holding had no impact on surveillance for the purpose of detection and

---

[83] *Id.* at 314.
[84] *Id.* at 308-09.
[85] *Id.* at 318-19.

V. National Security Surveillance and the Warrant Requirement

defeat of foreign intelligence threats—so-called foreign intelligence surveillance—suggesting that a warrant exception may actually apply to such surveillance.

> We emphasize, before concluding this opinion, the scope of our decision. As stated at the outset, this case involves only the domestic aspects of national security. We have not addressed, and express no opinion as to, the issues which may be involved with respect to activities of foreign powers or their agents.[86]

As explained below, the Court's invitation to Congress to adopt a modified warrant and probable cause standard applicable to national security surveillance did not produce the broad legislative response the Court hinted might be permissible. Instead, Congress limited FISA to situations of foreign intelligence surveillance, *not* domestic national security surveillance writ large. As a result, *Keith* stands for the clear proposition that there is no general national security exception to the normal warrant and probable cause requirements of the Fourth Amendment, either as a matter of constitutional interpretation or statutory modification. But *Keith* did set the conditions for what would become FISA, a statute that alters the normal criminal investigation warrant and probable cause requirements when, and only when, a significant purpose of the surveillance is counterintelligence (which includes counterterrorism) and the target of the surveillance is an agent of a foreign power (which may include a U.S. person, so long as the person is an agent of a foreign power or foreign terrorist organization).

FISA, however, did not resolve all issues related to the applicability of the warrant requirement, even in relation to foreign intelligence surveillance. In its original form, FISA applied only to surveillance targeting U.S. persons (citizens, resident aliens, and U.S. majority share corporations) *within* the United States. What if the intelligence-related surveillance targets an alien within the United States, or a U.S. person outside the United States?

Foreign intelligence surveillance of aliens both outside and within the United States is generally understood to fall within the inherent power of the President as Commander in Chief. Gathering foreign intelligence and thwarting the efforts of foreign agents to gather intelligence against the United States (counterintelligence) is directly linked to protecting the nation from external threats. Although the Supreme Court has never ruled directly on the source of constitutional authority for engaging in such intelligence surveillance, the *Keith* decision distinguished surveillance of alien targets from surveillance of U.S. persons. This distinction is reflected in executive branch policies and directives related to the intelligence activities of numerous government agencies and departments, including the Department of Defense, FBI, and CIA.[87] Furthermore, executive branch

---

[86] *Id.* at 321-22.
[87] DOD 5240.1-R, Procedure 5; *See* FISA §102, 50 U.S.C. §1802; *See* FISA §105, 50 U.S.C. §1805.

authorization for such surveillance dates back to the very inception of the nation.[88] This longstanding practice bolsters the conclusion that even when occurring within the United States and directed against an alien agent with some meaningful connection to the nation, such surveillance is reasonable within the meaning of the Fourth Amendment when properly authorized pursuant to Executive policies and directives.

When surveillance targets U.S. persons—even when located outside the United States—because they are considered agents of a foreign power (to include international terrorist organizations), the Fourth Amendment is applicable. In *Reid v. Covert*,[89] a plurality of the Supreme Court concluded that the protections of the Bill of Rights, including the protection against unreasonable search and seizure, apply extraterritorially. While the majority of Justices reached a slightly more restrictive conclusion—that only the fundamental guarantees of the Bill of Rights apply extraterritorially—the protection against unreasonable search and seizure is arguably within even that more restrictive category of protections. Accordingly, even when targeting a U.S. person abroad, the government must comply with the Fourth Amendment's reasonableness requirement.

While the Supreme Court has never ruled on what type of substantive justification and oversight procedures satisfy this reasonableness requirement in relation to foreign intelligence surveillance abroad, lower courts have. *United States v. Bin Laden*[90] is instructive. In that case, al Hage, a U.S. citizen, sought to suppress evidence seized by FBI agents in a joint operation with Kenyan officials involving electronic surveillance and a physical search of his residence in Nairobi, Kenya. Hage argued that the failure of the FBI to obtain a warrant rendered the search unreasonable.

The District Court for the Southern District of New York disagreed. According to the district court, Fourth Amendment protection did extend to Hage while in Kenya. The court rejected, however, the assertion that failure to comply with the Warrant Clause of the Amendment rendered the search unreasonable. Instead, the court endorsed an exception to the Warrant Clause for the conduct of surveillance abroad. This was based on the court's conclusion that the benefit of applying the warrant requirement to such surveillance was outweighed by a number of prudential and practical considerations. First, unlike domestic surveillance, U.S. courts would be asked to authorize searches or seizures in the sovereign territory of another nation, which could raise significant foreign policy implications. Because such implications might interfere with the conduct of foreign affairs, this would represent an unjustified intrusion into the inherent authority of the

---

[88] United States House of Representatives Comm. on Foreign Affairs: History of the Comm., http://democrats.foreignaffairs.house.gov/about.asp?sec=history.

[89] Reid v. Covert, 354 U.S. 1 (1957) (the Court held that the use of a military tribunal to try the spouse of a U.S. military personnel accused of murder while in England, in peacetime, was in violation of the due process rights guaranteed by the Fifth Amendment, which extend to U.S. citizens even when they are outside of the territorial limits of the nation).

[90] United States v. Bin Laden, 126 F. Supp. 2d 264 (S.D.N.Y. 2000).

President. Second, the warrant application process might chill the willingness of foreign nations to cooperate in such surveillance operations due to a concern the process might compromise secrecy and lead to embarrassment. Finally, unlike reviewing warrant applications in the domestic context, federal magistrates would be generally unfamiliar with the intricacies of foreign intelligence surveillance operations conducted on foreign territory.

Taken together, these considerations led the court to endorse a foreign intelligence warrant exception. According to the court, such surveillance is reasonable so long as it is authorized by the President or the Attorney General, and is conducted for a "primary" foreign intelligence purpose. It must be noted, however, that this "primary purpose" component of the exception predated the opinion of the Foreign Intelligence Surveillance Court in *In re Sealed Case*[91] concluding that neither FISA nor the Fourth Amendment ever require a "primary purpose" test for foreign intelligence surveillance. Instead, based on a variety of sources, including the PATRIOT Act amendment to FISA, surveillance falls within the category of foreign intelligence collection so long as it is conducted for a "significant" intelligence or counterintelligence purpose.

This foreign surveillance warrant exception was also impacted significantly by subsequent amendments to FISA. As noted below, FISA now applies to certain foreign surveillance of U.S. persons. Accordingly, even assuming a warrant is not required to comply with the Fourth Amendment when conducting such surveillance, FISA provides a statutory requirement to obtain such a warrant.

VI.   BORDER SEARCHES AND SPECIAL NEEDS CHECKPOINTS

Searching individuals and their property when entering through the borders of the United States is obviously an important method of protecting the nation from national security threats. The Supreme Court has long held that such searches are reasonable in the absence of individualized suspicion or cause as an incident of national sovereignty. These border searches may be conducted at any international port of entry, to include international airports within the United States, and fixed interior border search checkpoints. No distinction is made between U.S. persons and aliens in relation to border search authority.

The one exception to this general rule applies when the method of search is unusually intrusive. In such cases, reasonable suspicion (a level of cause below probable cause but greater than a purely subjection hunch) is required to render

---

[91] In re Sealed Case, 310 F.3d 717 (FISA Ct. Rev. 2002) (this case abrogated the FISA Review Court's previous ruling in In re All Matters Submitted to Foreign Intelligence Surveillance Court, 218 F. Supp. 2d 611 (Foreign Intell. Surveillance Ct. 2002)).

the search reasonable within the meaning of the Fourth Amendment. This would include body cavity searches of an individual and searches of property that result in destruction of the property.[92] As such, this is a very narrow exception to the broad border search authority. It should be noted, however, that the Ninth Circuit has extended this exception and reasonable suspicion requirement to the search of an individual's personal computer.[93]

Closely related to the border search exception to the warrant and probable cause requirement of the Fourth Amendment is the special needs exception. This exception allows the government to engage in narrowly tailored seizures and searches without individualized suspicion or cause when the primary purpose is not to discover evidence, but to protect that public from an imminent danger that cannot be addressed by following the normal individualized suspicion requirement.

In *Michigan v. Sitz*,[94] the Supreme Court held that use of sobriety checkpoints was reasonable within the meaning of the Fourth Amendment as a special needs seizure. The Court noted that the primary purpose of the stops was to detect and deter intoxicated drivers, thereby reducing a public safety risk. Other factors supporting the Court's determination of reasonableness included the narrowly tailored nature of the stops, conducting them in a location and manner that minimized citizen anxiety, and selecting subjects for the stop based on a pre-established fixed formula that deprives individual officers of the discretion to select subjects on their own initiative. The Court also held that the method used need not be the most effective in achieving the public safety objective; the test is not whether it is the best method, but whether it is reasonably effective.

In the subsequent case of *Indianapolis v. Edmond*,[95] the Court rejected application of the special needs exception to justify drug detection highway checkpoints. The Court held that the interest associated with discovery of drugs was indistinguishable from crime prevention, and therefore the checkpoint program failed the primary purpose test. However, the Court also noted that counterterrorism checkpoints fell within the range of ostensibly legitimate application of the exception.

In *MacWade v. Kelly*,[96] the District Court for the Southern District of New York considered application of the special needs doctrine to a counterterrorism

---

[92] Unusually intrusive allows wide latitude to officials conducting border searches. The Supreme Court has held that the disassembly of a vehicle's gas tank as part of a search was not unusually intrusive. U.S. v. Flores-Montano, 541 U.S. 149 (2004).

[93] In an *en banc* rehearing of U.S. v. Cotterman, 709 F.3d 952 (9th Cir. 2013), the Ninth Circuit held that a comprehensive forensic search of a defendant's laptop required reasonable suspicion. This holding limited the Ninth Circuit's earlier ruling in U.S. v. Arnold, 553 F.3d 1003 (9th Cir. 2008), to now stand for the proposition that a cursory search, such as asking that a laptop be booted up and logged into, does not require reasonable suspicion because such a search is less intrusive than a comprehensive forensic analysis of a computer's hard drive, and thus falls along a different point on the reasonableness spectrum.

[94] Michigan Dep't of State Police v. Sitz, 496 U.S. 444 (1990).

[95] Indianapolis v. Edmond, 531 U.S. 32 (2000).

[96] MacWade v. Kelly, 460 F.3d 260 (2d Cir. 2006).

checkpoint and search. The case arose out of a challenge to the New York City subway bag check program, which involved established stations on subway platforms where uniformed police officers would check passenger bags capable of concealing an explosive device. The bag checks were based on a fixed formula, and were narrowly tailored to search only for indicia of explosives. To minimize intrusiveness, passengers were requested to open their own bags and expose the contents to the officer. Only when a passenger refused to do so would an officer physically search the bag. Finally, the checkpoints were identified with signs and passengers were free to decline to enter the subway.

Relying on *Sitz* and *Edmond*, the court held that the program fell within the special needs exception. In support of this ruling, the court emphasized the gravity of the contemporary terrorist threat and the inability to effectively protect the public from that threat without deviating from the normal individualized suspicion requirement of the Fourth Amendment. Thus, a genuine special need.

It is likely that this exception will become an increasingly prominent aspect of counterterrorism efforts. As the *MacWade* court recognized, the nature of this threat necessitates deviation from normal Fourth Amendment requirements. It is important to note, however, that *any* contraband discovered while acting within the scope of the exception may be seized based on the plain view doctrine and will be admissible against the defendant at trial. There is no requirement that the contraband be related to the threat that triggered the special need. Thus, the special needs exception produces an ironic anomaly: When the primary purpose of the search or seizure is discovery of evidence, any evidence discovered will be inadmissible. However, when the primary purpose *is not* discovery of evidence (but protection of public safety), any evidence discovered will be admissible.

VII.   FISA

Whenever foreign intelligence surveillance targets a U.S. person, the Fourth Amendment is only the starting point for legality analysis. The enactment of FISA subsequent to the *Keith* decision substantially impacted this legality analysis. Accordingly, no understanding of national security surveillance authority is complete without an understanding of FISA. For discussion of FISA, please read Chapter 7 (intelligence-gathering).

VIII.   CONSTITUTIONAL LIMITS ON INTERROGATIONS

In addition to physical and electronic surveillance, national security related investigations frequently involve interrogations by government agents. When conducted by U.S. agents, compliance with the Fifth Amendment's due process prohibition against actual coercion, and the *Miranda* rule protecting suspects from the effects of inherent coercion, will ensure any statements obtained during such interrogations may be used as evidence at trial, and protect the government from accusations of civil rights violations.

A. Due Process

The Due Process Clause of the Fifth Amendment prohibits government agents from using actually coercive interrogation methods, and prohibits the use of such statements in criminal trials against the suspect.[97] A statement is considered involuntary and therefore coerced if, as the result of government action, it is not the product of the suspect's free will. Coercion may take the form of physical or psychological pressure, and is measured based on a totality of the circumstances analysis. The defendant bears the burden of proving a statement was coerced, which is often a difficult burden to satisfy. Factors such as the physical and mental condition of the suspect, conditions of interrogation, duration and location of interrogation, threats of harm for failing to cooperate, fatigue, hunger, isolation, and trickery are all relevant factors in this analysis.[98] If a statement is considered coerced, it is inadmissible for any purpose, including impeachment.[99]

There is no national security exception to this prohibition against actually coerced involuntary confessions. Establishing such coercion, however, is a difficult burden to satisfy. This is especially true when government agents obtain a valid *Miranda* waiver from a suspect,[100] which will often be the case even when the interrogation relates to a national security investigation. Nonetheless, use of actually coercive interrogation techniques will violate due process, even if the government agents perceive an extremely compelling need for information that only the suspect might provide.

B. Miranda *and the Public Safety Exception*

Even if government interrogation techniques do not amount to actual coercion, use of a statement as evidence in a subsequent criminal trial will depend on compliance with the *Miranda* rule. In *Miranda v. Arizona*,[101] the Supreme Court held that statements obtained from a suspect subjected to custodial

---

[97] *See* Spano v. New York, 360 U.S. 315 (1959); Arizona v. Fulminante, 499 U.S. 279 (1991).

[98] *Spano*, 360 U.S. at 323 (the Court found that the petitioner's will was overborne as a result of the totality of these factors).

[99] Mincey v. Arizona, 437 U.S. 385, 398-402 (1978) (the Court determined that statements made by a person in a hospital, in great pain, and near a coma were involuntary and could not be used against him, even for impeachment purposes).

[100] Missouri v. Seibert, 542 U.S. 600 (2004).

[101] Miranda v. Arizona, 384 U.S. 436 (1936).

interrogation are inadmissible unless the government proves the suspect was advised of his "*Miranda* rights" and executed a knowing and voluntary waiver. The Court did not limit the applicability of *Miranda* to only criminal investigations. As a result, *Miranda* applies to all questioning of suspects by government agents when the suspect is in custody. Nor is custody limited to situations of formal arrest. Based on the Court's decision in *Berkemer v. McCarty*,[102] custody must be assessed functionally, and includes any situation where a reasonable person in the suspect's position would feel restrained to a degree tantamount to formal arrest. Accordingly, even when the detention is not necessarily the result of a prosecutorial motive, an individual may be in custody for *Miranda* purposes. This obviously implicates the detention and questioning of individuals for purposes of obtaining intelligence or other national security–related information.

Nor is the *Miranda* rule limited to U.S. persons. Because Miranda was established to safeguard the Fifth Amendment privilege against compelled self-incrimination—a protection that unlike the Fourth Amendment applies to any "person"—*Miranda* applies to any individual subjected to U.S. custodial interrogation, including aliens. Furthermore, although never addressed directly by the Supreme Court, government practice has been to apply *Miranda* to custodial interrogations that occur both within and outside the United States, and several federal circuits have held that *Miranda* applies extraterritorially.[103]

If the *Miranda* requirement is triggered by custodial interrogation, there is no recognized national security or foreign intelligence exception. This does not, however, indicate that questioning is impermissible. Instead, unlike actually coercive interrogation techniques—techniques that violate due process and may result in civil liability distinct from any evidentiary consequence—the consequence of a *Miranda* violation is purely evidentiary, and far narrower than the blanket inadmissibility that results from actual coercion. The exclusive remedy for a *Miranda* violation is inadmissibility of the statement in the prosecution's case in chief.

This means that if a *Miranda* violation occurs, a statement may still be used to obtain an indictment, a warrant, and for impeachment of the accused at trial.[104] In addition, a *Miranda* violation will not taint evidence derived from the confession, as the Court has held that such a violation is not *ipso facto* a violation of the

---

[102] Berkemer v. McCarty, 468 U.S. 420 (1984).

[103] United States v. Yunis, 859 F.2d 953 (D.C. Cir. 1988) (the Court held that, even though the circumstances of the arrest were uncomfortable, Yunis made a valid *Miranda* waiver); United States v. Bourdet, 477 F. Supp. 2d 164 (D.C. Cir. 2007) (defendants knowingly and voluntarily made *Miranda* waivers after being arrested in El Salvador and placed on a plane taking them back to the United States).

[104] Harris v. New York, 401 U.S. 222 (1971) (a defendant's credibility can be impeached using prior statements obtained in violation of *Miranda*); Oregon v. Hass, 420 U.S. 714 (1975) (citing *Harris v. New York* that previously inadmissible statements in violation of *Miranda* can be admissible against a defendant when impeaching his credibility).

Fifth Amendment itself.[105] Instead, a *Miranda* violation triggers only a presumption of involuntariness, and rarely indicates actual coercion. This means that evidence derived from the statement made in violation of *Miranda*, to include a subsequent statement that complies with *Miranda* and repeats the content of the inadmissible statement, may be introduced into evidence.

There is one exception to the *Miranda* warning and waiver requirement that is especially relevant in the national security context: the so-called public safety exception. In *New York v. Quarles*,[106] the Supreme Court considered the admissibility of a statement by a suspect made in response to a police question immediately following his apprehension and arrest. Quarles was suspected of having just raped a woman, and discovered by a uniformed officer in a bodega. When the officer placed him under arrest, he noticed Quarles was wearing a pistol holster but that the holster was empty. The officer immediately asked him where the pistol was located, and Quarles responded by signaling towards an aisle. The pistol was then discovered.

Because the officer had not first obtained a *Miranda* waiver, Quarles argued that *Miranda* mandated suppression. The Court, however, noted that the circumstances surrounding the questioning did not create a serious risk of the type of inherent coercion that led the *Miranda* Court to impose the warning and waiver requirement. Instead, the spontaneous nature of the question and the primary motive of protecting the officer and others in the vicinity from the risk associated with an unsecured firearm indicated that Quarles was not subjected to the type of interrogation necessitating a warning in order to ensure his statement was not the product of presumptive coercion.

Quarles, therefore, appears to have been based on a two-part rational: First, the primary motivation of the questioning was not to obtain a confession for use as evidence, but instead to protect the public from an imminent danger. Second, Quarles was not subject to the type of incommunicado interrogation environment where police are able to use calculated interrogation methods to wear down a suspect. What was not clear was whether the exception should apply outside the context of the type of spontaneous questioning that occurred in *Quarles* so long as the primary motivation for the questioning is public safety.

This is obviously a critical question in the context of national security investigations, especially those involving counter-terrorism. If law enforcement agents apprehend a suspect they believe has information related to an imminent terrorist attack, may they question the suspect to obtain such information in a location and for a duration that exceeds the type of spontaneous, on the scene questioning that occurred in *Quarles*?

The Supreme Court has never elaborated on *Quarles*, and therefore there is no clear answer to this question. However, in one prominent case, a district court confronted this question and extended *Quarles* to an interrogation that lasted 45

---

[105] Oregon v. Elstad, 470 U.S. 298, 306-07 (1985); United States v. Patane, 542 U.S. 630, 636-37 (2004).

[106] New York v. Quarles, 467 U.S. 649 (1984).

minutes, well after the suspect had been apprehended while he was located in a hospital in police custody. That case arose out of the so-called underwear bomber incident, where Faruk Abdulmutallab attempted to detonate his bomb-laden underwear on a transatlantic flight from London to Detroit.[107] Fortunately, the bomb did not operate properly, and Abdulmutallab was apprehended and taken into custody when the flight landed safely in Detroit. Because he was burned from the failed attempt, he was transported under police custody to a hospital for treatment.

A joint FBI/Customs and Border Protection interrogation team then questioned him without *Miranda* warnings for approximately 45 minutes. The focus of the questioning was to determine whether other flights were at risk of imminent terrorist attack. Abdulmutallab made incriminating statements in response to the questioning. Once the interrogation team was satisfied that it had the necessary information to eliminate the concern of a coordinated attack on other aircraft, it terminated that questioning. At that point, a new interrogation team took over and advised Abdulmutallab of his *Miranda* rights. Abdulmutallab then invoked his right to silence and the interrogation terminated.[108]

Prior to trial, Abdulmutallab moved to suppress the statement, arguing that the location and duration of the questioning distinguished his situation from that of Quarles. The government responded by emphasizing that the purpose of the questioning was not to obtain a confession for use against Abdulmutallab at trial, but to protect airline passengers from a possible imminent threat of other suicide bombers prepared to initiate a catastrophic terrorist attack. The court ruled that the *Quarles* exception applied to the questioning.[109] Emphasizing the grave nature of the potential terrorist threat, and the primary focus of the questioning, the court concluded that the difference from *Quarles* in terms of location and duration of the questioning did not justify rejecting application of the exception.[110]

The Abdulmutallab incident also triggered a significant dialogue between the Executive and Congress on the applicability of the public safety exception to terrorist suspects.[111] Testifying before the Senate, the Attorney General proposed that Congress enact a law authorizing public safety questioning of such suspects for a 48-hour period.[112] Although Congress did not act on the proposal, the

---

[107] U.S. v. Adbulmutallab. Not reported. Westlaw citation: 2011 WL 4345243.

[108] *Id.* at 5.

[109] *Id.*

[110] *Id.*

[111] Senate Select Committee On Intelligence: *Unclassified Executive Summary of the Committee Report on the Attempted Terrorist Attack On Northwest Airlines Flight 253* (May 18, 2010), *available at* http://www.intelligence.senate.gov/100518/1225report.pdf.

[112] Eric Holder, Attorney Gen., *Attorney Gen. Eric Holder Testifies Before the Senate Committee on Appropriations Subcommittee on Commerce, Justice, Science, and Related Agencies* (May 6, 2010), *available at* http://www.justice.gov/opa/speech/attorney-general-eric-holder-testifies-senate-committee-appropriations-subcommittee.

Department of Justice again asserted its belief that the exception applied to such questioning for 48 hours after it apprehended the surviving Boston Marathon bombing suspect, Dzhokhar Tsarnaev.[113] Of course, should Congress enact such a law in the future, it could not override a more limited, judicially imposed scope for the exception. Such legislation, however, would likely influence any future Supreme Court assessment of what actually triggers the exception. These cases do indicate that the Executive will likely continue to assert an expansive interpretation of the exception when questioning terrorist suspects on the theory that the public safety motivation is the controlling aspect of a legitimate application of the exception.

C.   Interrogation by Foreign Agents

Questions about admissibility of a confession may also arise when a statement is obtained by foreign agents and subsequently provided to the U.S. government. Federal courts that have addressed efforts to suppress such confessions have generally applied a two-prong analysis of admissibility. First, they have rejected the argument that foreign interrogation triggers a *Miranda* warning and waiver requirement, at least where there is no evidence that the interrogation was a joint venture with U.S. agents. If, in contrast, the foreign interrogation was part of a joint venture with U.S. agents, or if the foreign interrogators were acting at the direction and control of U.S. agents, *Miranda* would be applicable. However, even assuming the foreign agents acted completely independently, the resulting confessions may be subject to due process coercion analysis.[114]

In United States v. Abu Ali,[115] both the federal district court and the Fourth Circuit Court of Appeals indicated that a confession procured by foreign agents is subject to due process coercion scrutiny. However, to date there has been no case where this issue has been successfully asserted. Whether the Supreme Court would agree with this extension of due process protection to the conduct of foreign government agents is unclear, although it does seem inconsistent with the Court's continued emphasis that U.S. government is necessary to trigger due process scrutiny of both confessions and identifications.[116] It is therefore unclear how a motion to suppress such a confession provided to the United States on a proverbial silver platter would in fact be decided. While the suggestion that a confession actually coerced by foreign agents should be unavailable for use against a

---

[113] *See* Joanna Wright, *Applying* Miranda's *Public Safety Exception to Dzhokhar Tsarnaev: Restricting Criminal Procedure Rights by Expanding Judicial Exceptions*, 113 COLUM. L. REV. Sidebar 136 (2013).

[114] *See, e.g.,* United States v. Abu Ali, 528 F.3d 210 (4th Cir. 2008) (assessing the merits of a due process based coercion challenge to the admissibility of a confession obtained by Saudi government agents in Saudi Arabia).

[115] *Id.*

[116] *See* Perry v. New Hampshire, 132 S. Ct. 716, 721 (2012).

defendant in U.S. court certainly has humanitarian appeal, it suffers from a serious analytical flaw. In *Colorado v. Connelly*,[117] the Supreme Court rejected the applicability of due process coercion analysis where the coercion was not the product of government action, holding that this causal relationship is an essential element of due process scrutiny. It is difficult to reconcile *Connelly* with the suggestion that coercion in no way involving U.S. government agents could trigger due process suppression. Nonetheless, this remains an area of some uncertainty.

IX. JURISDICTION AND PUBLIC TRIAL

National security related criminal trials often implicate constitutional rights related to a fair trial and extending beyond evidentiary rules. Any criminal defendant brought to trial in the United States will be entitled to assert all fundamental trial rights, to include the right to counsel, confrontation, compulsory process, and speedy trial. However, two issues related to ensuring a fair trial may be especially significant in cases involving national security considerations: whether the international abduction of a suspect impacts the jurisdiction to try the case, and whether the right to public trial may be limited.

Bringing suspects before U.S. courts for trial at times necessitates apprehending them abroad and transporting them to the United States. In most cases, this will be done in cooperation with the state where the suspect is located, frequently pursuant to an extradition treaty. There are, however, times when this cooperative process is unavailable or deemed non-feasible. In such situations, the United States may abduct the suspect abroad and transport him against his will to the United States.

When this occurs, the suspect may seek to challenge the jurisdiction of the court by asserting that the method of being brought within that jurisdiction violates both international law and due process. Such challenges are rarely, if ever, effective. First, there is no clear international legal prohibition to such conduct by states. Instead, the international legal concept of *male captus, bene detentus*[118] suggests that the manner of bringing an individual within the jurisdiction of the state has no bearing on the authority of the state to assert that jurisdiction.

Due process jurisprudence includes an analogous doctrine, known as the *Ker-Frisbee* doctrine.[119] Based on two cases involving international abductions and subsequent trial in the United States, the general rule is that jurisdiction of a court is in no way limited by the manner in which the defendant is brought within

---

[117] Colorado v. Connelly, 479 U.S. 157 (1986).

[118] Roughly translates to: wrongly captured, properly detained.

[119] The doctrine's name derives from two key cases: Ker v. Illinois, 119 U.S. 436 (1886), and Frisbee v. Collins, 342 U.S. 519 (1952).

the jurisdiction. Thus, even if the method is illegal, jurisdiction may still be asserted.

The one limited exception to this rule is known as the *Toscanino* exception, and is based on a case involving Toscanino's international abduction.[120] In that case, the court held that the methods used by government to secure Toscannino's presence before the court "shocked the conscience." As a result, the government was prohibited from asserting jurisdiction, and the case against Toscanino was dismissed.

It is a rare case where a defendant subjected to international abduction successfully invokes this exception to the *Ker-Frisbee* doctrine. Abduction alone will not qualify as "conscience shocking" treatment.[121] In one of the more interesting rejections of the exception, the U.S. District Court for the Southern District of Florida rejected General Manuel Noriega's assertion that invading his country in order to capture him and transport him to the United States to stand trial on an outstanding indictment shocked the conscience. Absent blatant physical abuse of a suspect, the method of securing his presence before a court for trial will rarely nullify the court's jurisdiction.

X. LIMITING THE RIGHT TO PUBLIC TRIAL

Among the package of rights provided to a criminal defendant by the Sixth Amendment is the right to a speedy and *public* trial. The tradition of public trials dates back to English common law[122] and continues to this day. Public trials serve at least two important functions. First, the transparency of public trials ensures the integrity of the judicial system and guards against its abuse. "The knowledge that every criminal trial is subject to contemporaneous review in the forum of public opinion is an effective restraint on possible abuse of judicial power."[123] Public trials also serve to enhance the quality of testimony by subjecting witnesses to the scrutiny of their peers.[124] Second, public confidence in the justice system is possibly as important as an impartial judiciary itself, and open courts help maintain that trust.[125] As the Third Circuit

---

[120] United States v. Toscanino, 500 F.2d 267 (2nd Cir. 1974).

[121] Toscanino's case is distinguished from cases to which *Ker-Frisbee* applies because along with his abduction from Uruguay, Toscanino was allegedly tortured and interrogated in Brazil prior to being brought to the United States to stand trial while U.S. officials prosecuting the case were aware of his torture and interrogation.

[122] In re Oliver, 333 U.S. 257, 266 (1948).

[123] *Id.* at 270.

[124] William K. Meyer, *Evaluating Court Closures After Richmond Newspapers: Using Sixth Amendment Rights to Enforce A First Amendment Right*, 50 Geo. Wash. L. Rev. 304, 304-05 (1982).

[125] United States v. Cianfrani, 573 F.2d 835, 851 (3d Cir. 1978).

X. Limiting the Right to Public Trial

Court of Appeals noted in *Cianfrani*, "secret hearings though they be scrupulously fair in reality are suspect by nature."[126]

National security related cases can, of course, raise the competing government interest of secrecy and protection of national security information that might otherwise be exposed as the result of a public trial. This friction between transparency and security in the context of criminal trial was central to the illustrative case of *United States v. Rosen*.[127] Rosen was charged with violating the Espionage Act,[128] specifically conspiring to communicate national defense information (NDI) to unauthorized recipients. A member of the American Israel Public Affairs Committee, Rosen had been the subject of an FBI investigation for some time prior to his trial.

Because Rosen's trial involved classified material, the trial court utilized the Classified Information Procedures Act[129] (CIPA) to deal with admissibility and defense access to this information. CIPA attempts to "harmonize" the competing government interest of protecting classified information with the defendant's interest in obtaining and presenting exculpatory evidence. To achieve this end, CIPA allows the government to declassify material, or to submit substitutions "admitting relevant facts that the classified information would tend to prove," or a "summary of the specific classified information."[130] The suitability of the proposed substitutions is determined by the court, and the dispositive question is "whether the proposed substitutions afford the defendant substantially the same ability to make his defense as the specific classified information."[131]

Should the court rule against the use of the proposed substitutions, the government may object to disclosure of the classified material, at which point the material may not be disclosed. However, the court may then: dismiss the indictment in whole or part; find against the government on any issue related to the classified information; or preclude a witness's testimony. This recognizes the government's right to protect sensitive and properly classified national security information, but also that such a right may not be used to prejudice a defendant's ability to present evidence in his defense or confront witnesses and/or evidence against him.

In *Rosen*, the government proposed an elaborate procedure where the defense, jurors, and court would have access to the confidential materials, but it would be referenced in code in open court so that the public would not know the details of the information being discussed. The use of coded substitutions in open court was not a novel proposal; in fact, such a procedure was termed the "silent witness rule."[132] The use of this rule had, however, been extremely limited, and

---

[126] *Id.*

[127] U.S. v. Rosen. 487 F. Supp. 2d 703 (E.D. Va. 2007).

[128] 18 U.S.C. §793 (2012).

[129] 18 U.S.C. App. 3 (2012).

[130] 18 U.S.C. App. 3 §4 (2012).

[131] *Rosen*, 487 F. Supp. 2d at 707.

[132] It is important to note that the procedures authorized by CIPA and those proposed by the government differ in that under the government's proposal, the public is presented with less than

the government's proposal in this case would call for the expansive use of the rule as had never been previously done. This would prove to be highly problematic, as such extensive use of the rule would, as presiding judge Ellis concluded, "exclude the public from substantial and critical parts of the trial."[133]

Rosen and his co-defendant challenged the government's proposed procedures on statutory grounds relating to CIPA, as well as on the constitutional grounds that such procedures violated the Sixth Amendment right to a public trial. Although considered a fundamental right and an element of due process applicable to both the federal government and to the states via the Fourteenth Amendment, the right to a public trial is not absolute. Instead, it is qualified, and may yield when public access to the trial would compromise a compelling government interest. However, the standard to override the right and rebut the powerful presumption in public trial is extremely demanding. Accordingly, the *Rosen* court applied a four-part test first laid out by the Supreme Court in *Press-Enterprise v. Superior Court of California*. Pursuant to this test, the facts must indicate that:[134]

1. There is an overriding government interest in the closed trial;
2. The closure must be no broader than necessary;
3. The court must consider reasonable alternatives to closure; and
4. The court makes specific findings on the record concerning the existence of the overriding interest, the breadth of the closure, and the unavailability of alternatives to facilitate appellate review.

Importantly, when moving to close a court to the public, the burden rests on the government to make a specific showing of harm to national security, and the judiciary is tasked with making the inquiry into the legitimacy of the asserted national security interest. In *Rosen*, the court found that while the protection of national security is an important overriding concern in the abstract, the government had failed to show that any harm would result in refusing closure. The court therefore concluded that the government had failed to do anything more "than to invoke 'national security' broadly and in a conclusory fashion, as to all the classified information in the case."[135]

As for the scope of the closure, the court concluded that because the government had failed to identify with specificity the harm to national security that would result, it would not be possible to determine if the requested breadth of the closure was no more broad than necessary. Furthermore, the court held that the procedures authorized by CIPA would be satisfactory for the case, and, as such, provided an adequate alternative to closing the court. The motion to close the court was therefore rejected.

---

what the jurors, defense, and judge see. The CIPA substitutions would be disclosed to all in the same format.

[133] *Id.*

[134] Press-Enterprise v. Superior Court of California, 464 U.S. 501 (1984).

[135] *Rosen*, 487 F. Supp. 2d at 717.

XI. Conclusion

The last element of the test is largely for appellate purposes and is not itself a substantive test regarding the closure of a court. It is implemented as a requirement so that should a proceeding be closed, the record will afford sufficient information on review as to the trial court's application of the *Press-Enterprise* test.

XI.   CONCLUSION

Using criminal laws to deter threats to national security, and when those threats manifest themselves as crimes, to punish those responsible, is a critical tool in the arsenal of national power. The investigation and prosecution of national security threats will, however, almost inevitably implicate fundamental criminal procedure rights. Understanding how these rights apply to the context of national security threats is essential to ensure the government complies with the Constitution it seeks to protect against these threats.

CHAPTER 7

Intelligence Exploitation

I.   FOREIGN INTELLIGENCE SURVEILLANCE ACT, 50 U.S.C. §§1801 *ET SEQ.*

A.   *Statutory Framework*

1.   General Overview

Since the 9/11 terrorist attacks the U.S. government has invested enormous resources to collect foreign intelligence information to prevent acts of terrorism and protect national security. The government's efforts have been successful in preventing large-scale terrorist attacks on the homeland. However, they have been less effective in thwarting attacks by "lone wolf" terrorists, such as the Boston Marathon bombing, and preventing small-scale terrorist attacks, such as the Al Qaeda–related attack on the U.S. embassy facility in Benghazi, Libya, that claimed the lives of U.S. Ambassador Christopher Stevens and three other Americans.[1] At the same time, serious concerns have been raised about the National Security Agency's (NSA) intelligence collection programs and whether the collection of phone record metadata of U.S. citizens is an unconstitutional violation of civil liberties.[2]

---

[1] Terrorist Attack in Benghazi: The Secretary of State's View: Hearing Before the H. Comm. on Foreign Affairs, 113th Cong. 1-2 (2013) (statement of Ed Royce, Chairman).

[2] *See generally Administration White Paper, Bulk Collection of Telephony Metadata Under Section 215 of the USA PATRIOT Act* (Aug. 9, 2013) [hereinafter *White Paper on Bulk Collection of Telephony Metadata*] (discussing the scope and legal justification for the telephone metadata program under which the NSA collects information such as what phone numbers were used to make and receive calls, when the calls took place, and how long the calls lasted, but does not collect the actual content of those telephone communications). *See also* In re Application of the Federal Bureau of Investigation for an Order Requiring the Production of Tangible Things from [Redacted], Amended Memorandum Opinion, No. BR 13-109 at 4-8 (FISC, Aug. 29, 2013) [hereinafter *In re Application of the Federal Bureau of Investigation*]; Potential Changes to the Foreign Intelligence Surveillance Act (FISA): Hearing Before the H. Select Comm. on Intelligence, 11th Cong. 2-4 (2013) (joint statement for the record of James R. Clapper, Dir. of Nat'l Intelligence, et al.).

I. Foreign Intelligence Surveillance Act, 50 U.S.C. §§1801 *et seq.*

The Foreign Intelligence Surveillance Act (FISA), 50 U.S.C. §§1801 *et seq.*, is the legal authority for the collection of foreign intelligence information.[3] In 1978, Congress enacted FISA "to authorize and regulate certain government electronic surveillance of communications for foreign intelligence purposes."[4] FISA was a response to three concerns: "(1) the judicial confusion over the existence, nature and scope of a foreign intelligence exception to the Fourth Amendment's warrant requirement that arose in the wake of the Supreme Court's 1972 decision in *United States v. United States District Court*, 407 U.S. 297 (1972);[5] (2) the congressional concern over perceived Executive Branch abuses [of electronic surveillance];[6] and (3) the felt need to provide the Executive Branch with an appropriate means to investigate and counter foreign intelligence threats."[7] Congress sought to address these concerns by establishing detailed procedures for the executive branch to follow when obtaining court orders to collect foreign intelligence information "without violating the rights of citizens of the United States."[8] Following the terrorist attacks of September 11, 2001, FISA has become a prominent and important tool for the government to detect and prevent terrorist attacks.[9]

FISA authorizes members of the secret Foreign Intelligence Surveillance Court to order electronic surveillance for foreign intelligence purposes if there is "probable cause" to believe that 1) the target is a "foreign power" or an "agent of a foreign power," and 2) each of the specific "facilities or places at which the electronic surveillance is directed is being used . . . by a foreign power or an agent of a

---

[3] Foreign Intelligence Surveillance Act of 1978, Pub. L. 95-511, 92 Stat. 1783 (Oct. 25, 1978), 50 U.S.C. §§1801 *et seq.*

[4] Clapper v. Amnesty Int'l USA, 133 S. Ct. 1138, 1143 (2013).

[5] In United States v. United States Dist. Court, 407 U.S. 297 (1972) [hereinafter "*Keith*"], the Supreme Court held that the legal standards and procedures that law enforcement officials must follow when conducting "surveillance of 'ordinary crime'" might not be required in the context of surveillance conducted for domestic national security purposes. *Id.* at 322-23. Moreover, the Court implicitly suggested that a special legal framework for electronic surveillance of foreign intelligence information might be constitutionally permissible. *Id.*

[6] FISA was enacted in response to the findings of the Senate Select Committee to Study Government Operations with Respect to Intelligence Activities (the "Church Committee") that the executive branch had engaged in warrantless domestic intelligence-gathering activities in the name of national security in violation of the Fourth Amendment right against unreasonable search and seizure. S. Rep. No. 95-604, at 7. In the view of the Senate Judiciary Committee, the Act went "a long way in striking a fair and just balance between protection of national security and protection of personal liberties." *Id.*

[7] United States v. Rosen, 447 F. Supp. 2d 538, 542-43 (E.D. Va. 2006). *See also* William C. Banks & M.E. Bowman, *Executive Authority for National Security Surveillance*, 50 Am. U. L. Rev. 1, 75-76 (2000) (describing the reasons motivating FISA).

[8] United States v. Hammoud, 381 F.3d 316, 332 (4th Cir. 2004) (en banc), *vacated on other grounds*, 543 U.S. 1097, *reinstated in pertinent part*, 405 F.3d 1034 (2005).

[9] In 2012 alone, the government applied for 1,856 warrants from the FISA Court, of which 1,789 pertained to authorization for electronic surveillance. One application was withdrawn by the government, but the remaining 1,855 warrants were granted. Peter J. Kadzik, Dep't of Justice, Annual FISA Report to Cong. 1 (2013), *available at* http://www.fas.org/irp/agency/doj/fisa/2012rept.pdf.

foreign power."[10] FISA was subsequently amended to authorize physical searches,[11] the use of pen registers and trap and trace devices,[12] and the seizure of business records and other "tangible things" for the purpose of gathering "foreign intelligence information."[13]

The purpose of obtaining a FISA warrant substantially differs from that required for a Title III wiretap or traditional search warrant. Title III allows a court to enter an *ex parte* order authorizing electronic surveillance if it determines on the basis of facts submitted in the government's application that "there is probable cause to believe that an individual is committing, has committed, or is about to commit" a specified criminal offense.[14] FISA by contrast requires a showing of probable cause to believe that the intended target is a "foreign power" or "agent of a foreign power" and that each of the facilities or places at which the electronic surveillance is directed is being used, or about to be used, by a "foreign power" or "agent of a foreign power."[15] Further, a "significant purpose" of the FISA order must be to obtain "foreign intelligence information."[16] There is no requirement that the information sought is evidence of a crime or connected to criminal activity. Moreover, under FISA the term "foreign intelligence information" is broadly defined and includes evidence of crimes such as espionage, sabotage, and international terrorism.[17] Finally, the term "agent of a foreign power" is not limited to foreign nationals, but includes U.S. persons suspected of being involved in espionage, sabotage, or international terrorism.[18] Thus, U.S. persons may be the target of a FISA court order.

---

[10] 50 U.S.C. §1805(a)(2)(B).

[11] *See* Intelligence Authorization Act for Fiscal Year 1995, Pub. L. No. 103-359, §807, 108 Stat. 3423, 3443 (1994) (codified as amended 50 U.S.C. §§1821-29 (2008)).

[12] *See* Intelligence Authorization Act for Fiscal Year 1999, Pub. L. No. 105-271, §601(2), 112 Stat. 2396, 2405 (codified as amended at 50 U.S.C. §§1841-46 (2008)). Pen registers capture the numbers dialed on a targeted phone line (only the outgoing calls placed from the targeted phone), while trap and trace devices identify the originating number of a call on a targeted telephone line (who called the targeted number). *See* 18 U.S.C. §§3127(3)-(4) (2008). Such information does not include the contents of any communication.

[13] *See* USA PATRIOT Act, Pub. L. No. 107-56, 115 Stat. 272 (2001) (codified at 50 U.S.C. §1861). The term "foreign intelligence information" is defined by 50 U.S.C. §1891(e).

[14] 18 U.S.C. §2518(3)(a).

[15] 50 U.S.C. §1805(a)(2).

[16] *Id.* 1804(a)(6)(B).

[17] *Id.* §1801(e)(1). "International terrorism" refers to activities that "involve violent acts or acts dangerous to human life that are a violation of the criminal laws of the United States or of any State, or that would be a criminal violation if committed within the jurisdiction of the United States or any State." *Id.* §1801(c)(1). "Sabotage means activities that involve a violation of chapter 105 of [the criminal code], or that would involve such a violation if committed against the United States." *Id.* §1801(d).

[18] *Id.* §§1801(b)(2)(A), (C).

I. Foreign Intelligence Surveillance Act, 50 U.S.C. §§1801 *et seq.*

2. The FISA Court

In enacting FISA, Congress created two new Article III courts—the Foreign Intelligence Surveillance Court (FISC or FISA Court) and the Foreign Intelligence Surveillance Court of Review (FISCR or FISA Review Court). FISA authorizes the Chief Justice of the U.S. Supreme Court to designate 11 federal district court judges as members of the FISC, "which shall have jurisdiction to hear applications for and grant orders approving electronic surveillance anywhere in the United States" and, in certain cases, in foreign countries.[19] While the FISA statute requires the Chief Justice to designate the 11 district court judges from at least 7 of the U.S. judicial circuits, there are no other requirements for selection to the FISC.[20] The Chief Justice is afforded plenary power in making these selections; neither Congress nor the President plays any role in the selection or approval of FISA judges. The FISA judges sit on a rotating basis holding classified, *ex parte* proceedings in a secure facility located in the federal courthouse in Washington, D.C. Further, the FISC only hears from one side—the government. Department of Justice attorneys from the Office of Intelligence and Policy Review appear before the Court to present applications for FISA warrants.[21] Private lawyers are not permitted to appear before the FISC to represent the interests of FISA targets or to challenge the legal sufficiency or credibility of the evidence presented to the FISC. The FISA applications and court orders are classified and rarely declassified or disclosed to the public. The FISC has been accused of "rubber stamping" the government's FISA applications because government requests for FISA warrants are rarely denied by the FISC.[22]

Rulings of the FISC are subject to review by the FISCR, which consists of three federal district court or circuit court judges also designated by the Chief Justice.[23] Once again, the Chief Justice is afforded unfettered discretion in appointing the members of the FISC. The FISCR has convened only twice since the statute's enactment: 1) when it rejected a constitutional challenge to FISA;[24] and 2) when it dismissed an as-applied constitutional challenge to certain provisions of the Protect America Act of 2007, which permits the government to conduct

---

[19] *Id.* §§1803(a)(1), 1881a. The FISC may also consider *ex parte* applications for the government to conduct physical searches, use pen registers or trap and trace devices, or seize business records and other "tangible things" for the purpose of obtaining "foreign intelligence information." *See id.* §1842.

[20] *Id.* §1803(a). At least three of the judges must "reside within 20 miles" of Washington, D.C. *Id.* Each judge serves for seven years and is not eligible for reappointment to the FISC. *See id.* §1803(d).

[21] *See id.* §§1803(a)(1), 1804(a).

[22] *See* Kadzik, *supra* note 9.

[23] 50 U.S.C. §1803(b).

[24] *See* In re Sealed Case, 310 F.3d 717 (FISCR 2002).

warrantless foreign intelligence surveillance on targets reasonably believed to be located outside the United States.[25]

3.   FISA's Scope and Application

a.   A "Significant Purpose" to Obtain "Foreign Intelligence Information"

The definitions of "foreign intelligence information," "foreign power," and "agent of a foreign power" are crucial to understanding the FISA statutory scheme. The term "foreign intelligence information" is broadly defined to cover two categories of information. The first category is found in §1801(e)(1) and includes "counterintelligence" or "protective" foreign intelligence information. Such information must relate to, and if concerning a U.S. person is necessary to, the ability of the United States to *protect* against:

1. actual or potential attack or other grave hostile acts of a foreign power or an agent of a foreign power;
2. sabotage, international terrorism, or the international proliferation of weapons of mass destruction by a foreign power or an agent of a foreign power; or
3. clandestine intelligence activities by an intelligence service or network of a foreign power or by an agent of a foreign power.[26]

Thus, the definition of foreign intelligence information includes sabotage, international terrorism, the international proliferation of weapons of mass destruction, and espionage. However, while "foreign intelligence information" includes information to protect against "international" terrorism, FISA does not apply to threatened acts of domestic terrorism. The term "international terrorism" has three essential components. First, the activities are limited to violent acts or acts dangerous to human life that are a violation of the criminal laws of the United States or would constitute a crime if committed within the jurisdiction of the United States.[27] Second, such activities "must appear to be intended (A) to intimidate or coerce a civilian population; (B) to influence the policy of a government by intimidation or coercion; or (C) to affect the conduct of a government by assassination or kidnapping."[28] Third, the acts must "occur totally outside the United States, or transcend national boundaries in terms of the means by

---

[25] *See* In re Directives Pursuant to Section 105B of the Foreign Intelligence Surveillance Act, 551 F.3d 1004 (FISCR 2008).
[26] 50 U.S.C. §1801(e)(1).
[27] *Id.* §1801(c)(1).
[28] *Id.* §1801(c)(2).

I. Foreign Intelligence Surveillance Act, 50 U.S.C. §§1801 *et seq.*

which they are accomplished, the persons they appear intended to coerce or intimidate, or the locale in which their perpetrators operate or seek asylum."[29] Further, the government does not need to prove that the intelligence information sought to be captured is critical or essential to protecting the United States against a terrorist attack. Instead, the information need only "relate" to such terrorist threats.[30]

The second category of foreign intelligence information is found in §1801(e)(2) and includes information necessary to "the national defense or the security of the United States," or "the conduct of the foreign affairs of the United States."[31] This definition involves information referred to as *affirmative* or "positive" foreign intelligence information rather than *protective* or "counterintelligence" information in the first category.[32]

A "significant purpose" of a FISA application must be to gather "foreign intelligence information."[33] Thus, obtaining a FISA warrant to collect domestic intelligence information or solely for the purpose of gathering evidence of a crime falls outside the scope of FISA. As originally enacted, FISA required a high-ranking executive officer to certify that "the purpose" for which a FISA warrant was being sought was to obtain "foreign intelligence information."[34] Several circuits acknowledged that while Congress viewed arrest and prosecution as one of the possible outcomes of a FISA investigation, surveillance under FISA would be "appropriate only if foreign intelligence surveillance is the government's *primary* purpose."[35] The First Circuit explicitly interpreted FISA's purpose wording in §1804(a)(7)(B) to mean that "[a]lthough evidence obtained under FISA subsequently may be used in criminal prosecutions, the investigation of criminal activity cannot be the primary purpose of the surveillance."[36] Further, in 1995, the Justice Department not only adopted the primary purpose requirement, but "[a]pparently to avoid running afoul" of that restriction it adopted procedures prohibiting the sharing foreign intelligence information between law enforcement and intelligence officials.[37] The procedures "eventually came to be narrowly interpreted

---

[29] *Id.* §1801(c)(3).

[30] *Id.* §1801(e)(1).

[31] *Id.* §1801(e)(2).

[32] *See* In re Sealed Case, 310 F.3d at 723 n.9.

[33] 50 U.S.C. §1804(a)(6)(B). *See also* United States v. Abu-Jihaad, 630 F.3d 102, 119 (2d Cir. 2010) ("[U]pon satisfaction of all other FISA requirements, Congress authorized FISA Court judges to issue warrants upon executive certification that acquisition of foreign intelligence information is 'a *significant* purpose' of the requested surveillance.") (citation omitted) (emphasis added).

[34] 50 U.S.C. §1804(a)(7)(B) (Supp. V 1981).

[35] United States v. Megahey, 553 F. Supp. 1180, 1189-90 (E.D.N.Y. 1982) (emphasis added), *aff'd sub nom.* United States v. Duggan, 743 F.2d 59, 77 (2d Cir. 1984) (stating that "[t]he requirement that foreign intelligence information be the *primary* objective of the surveillance is plain not only from the language of §1802(b) but also from the requirements in §1804 as to what the application must contain") (emphasis added).

[36] United States v. Johnson, 952 F.2d 565, 572 (1st Cir. 1991) (citations omitted), *cert. denied,* 506 U.S. 816 (1992).

[37] In re Sealed Case, 310 F.3d at 727-28.

within the Department of Justice" so as to erect "a 'wall' to prevent the FBI intelligence officials from communicating with the Criminal Division regarding ongoing [intelligence] investigations."[38]

In the aftermath of September 11, 2001, President Bush asked Congress to substitute "a purpose" for "the purpose" requirement of FISA in order to dismantle the wall that had been erected between intelligence and law enforcement personnel to ensure that the "primary purpose" of any FISA order was to obtain foreign intelligence information and not evidence of a crime.[39] While Congress did not accept the Executive's proposed language, it did agree that certification of a primary purpose to obtain foreign intelligence information should not be required to obtain a FISA warrant.

In 2001, Congress amended FISA as part of the Uniting and Strengthening America by Providing Appropriate Tools Required to Intercept and Obstruct Terrorism Act (PATRIOT Act).[40] Among other things, Congress amended FISA to change "the purpose" language in §1804(a)(7)(B) to a "*significant* purpose" of the requested surveillance.[41] Thus, if gathering foreign intelligence information is a "significant purpose," another purpose, such as criminal prosecution, could be primary.[42] It also added a provision allowing "Federal officers who conduct electronic surveillance to acquire foreign intelligence" to "consult with Federal law enforcement officers . . . to coordinate efforts to investigate or protect against" attack or other grave hostile acts, sabotage, international terrorism, or clandestine activities, by foreign powers or their agents.[43]

While it is unclear at what point the foreign intelligence purpose advanced by the government might be so trivial as to preclude it from being properly pursued under FISA, the FISCR has construed the "significant purpose" standard to require "that the government have a measurable foreign intelligence purpose other than just criminal prosecution of even foreign intelligence crimes."[44] The

---

[38] *Id.* at 728; *see also* NAT'L COMM. ON TERRORIST ATTACKS UPON THE U.S., THE 9/11 COMMISSION REPORT 78-80 (2004) [hereinafter 9/11 COMMISSION REPORT] (discussing constraints imposed by the "primary purpose" requirement on sharing of intelligence information between federal prosecutors and intelligence agents).

[39] In re Sealed Case, 310 F.3d at 732.

[40] Uniting and Strengthening America by Providing Appropriate Tools Required to Intercept and Obstruct Terrorism Act, Pub. L. No. 107-56, 14 Stat. 271 (2001) [hereinafter PATRIOT Act].

[41] *See id.* §218, 114 Stat. at 291 (codified as amended at 50 U.S.C. §1804(a)(6)(B)) (emphasis added). *See also* United States v. Abu-Jihaad, 630 F.3d at 121 (affirming the constitutionality of the FISA statute, holding that "we identify no constitutional defects in FISA's certification requirement of a 'significant' rather than a primary 'purpose . . . to obtain foreign intelligence information'").

[42] *See* In re Sealed Case, 310 F.3d at 734. According to Senator Feinstein, one of the PATRIOT Act's strong supporters, "[t]he effect of this provision will be to make it easier for law enforcement to obtain a FISA search or surveillance warrant for those cases where the subject of the surveillance is both a potential source of valuable intelligence and the potential target of a criminal prosecution." 147 Cong. Rec. S10591 (Oct. 11, 2001) (quoted in In re Sealed Case, 310 F.3d at 732-33).

[43] 50 U.S.C. §1806(k)(1).

[44] In re Sealed Case, 310 F.3d at 735.

FISCR has also ruled that the significant purpose requirement specifically "excludes from the purpose of gaining foreign intelligence information a sole objective of criminal prosecution" even for foreign intelligence crimes.[45]

Finally, the government's certified purpose in seeking a FISA warrant is subject to judicial review. Thus, if the FISA court determines that the government's sole objective is "merely to gain evidence of past criminal conduct—even foreign intelligence crimes—to punish the agent rather than halt ongoing espionage or terrorist activity, the application should be denied."[46] Further, the FISCR has ruled that to satisfy the significant purpose test, it must appear that "the government entertains a realistic option of dealing" with the target of the FISA surveillance "other than through criminal prosecution."[47]

b. Foreign Power or Agent of a Foreign Power

The FISA court may grant an order to obtain foreign intelligence information if "there is probable cause to believe that . . . the target of the electronic surveillance is a foreign power or an agent of a foreign power," and that "each of the facilities or places at which the electronic surveillance is directed is being used, or is about to be used, by a foreign power or an agent of a foreign power."[48] The term "foreign power" includes traditional state or state-related entities such as a foreign government or any component thereof, a faction of a foreign nation, or an entity that is directed and controlled by a foreign government.[49] The term "foreign power" also includes nonstate entities, such as a group engaged in international terrorism, as well as an entity engaged in international proliferation of weapons of mass destruction.[50] Thus, FISA authorizes the use of electronic surveillance, physical searches, pen registers and trap and trace devices, and the seizure of business records and other tangible things against a foreign terrorist organization (FTO), such as Al Qaeda, Hamas, and Hezbollah, for the purpose of gathering foreign intelligence information.[51] Since these FTOs are groups engaged in international terrorism, they fall within the FISA definition of "foreign power." Further, the FISA target need not be involved in actually perpetrating acts of terrorism. It is enough for a target to simply be "engaged" in such activities, including preparatory acts and acts of facilitation.[52]

---

[45] *Id.*

[46] *Id.*

[47] *Id.*

[48] 50 U.S.C. §1805(a)(2).

[49] *Id.* §§1801(a)(1)-(2), (6).

[50] *Id.* §§1801(a)(4), (7).

[51] Pursuant to 8 U.S.C. §1189, the Secretary of State, in consultation with the Secretary of Treasury and Attorney General, may designate a foreign organization as an FTO upon finding that "(A) the organization is a foreign organization; (B) the organization engages in terrorist activity . . . ; and (C) the terrorist activity . . . threatens the security of United States nationals or the national security of the United States." *Id.* §§1189(a)(1)(A)-(C).

[52] *See* 50 U.S.C. §§1801(b)(2)(A)-(E).

The term "agent of a foreign power" differs depending on whether the FISA target is a foreign national or U.S. person. If the target is a foreign national, "agent of a foreign power" means a person who: 1) acts as an officer, employee, or member of a foreign power; 2) acts for or on behalf of a foreign power engaged in clandestine activities in the United States, aids and abets any such person, or conspires with another person to engage in such activities; 3) engages in international terrorism or related preparatory acts; 4) engages in the international proliferation of weapons of mass destruction or activities in preparation thereof; or 5) engages in the international proliferation of weapons of mass destruction for or on behalf of a foreign power.[53]

In the case of a person suspected of engaging in international terrorism there is no requirement that such person act for or on behalf of a foreign power. In 2004, Congress amended FISA to expand the government's authority to target suspected international terrorists. Commonly referred to as the "lone wolf" amendment, §6001(a) of the Intelligence Reform and Terrorism Prevention Act broadened the definition of an "agent of a foreign power" to include any non-U.S. person who "engages in international terrorism or activities in preparation therefor."[54] The "lone wolf" provision was prompted by an investigation of Zacarias Moussaoui, who was believed to be responsible for the 9/11 terrorist attacks.[55] On August 16, 2001, FBI agents arrested Moussaoui after being tipped off by a flight school who was concerned by his suspicious behavior.[56] FBI agents suspected that Moussaoui had planned a terrorist attack and detained him on an immigration violation. The FBI agents then sought a FISA order to examine the contents of Moussaoui's laptop computer and other possessions.[57] However, prior to the "lone wolf" amendment, FISA required proof that the premises to be searched were owned or controlled by a foreign power or its agent. The definition of "foreign power" included FTOs and individuals involved in international terrorism on behalf of such terrorist organizations were considered "agents of a foreign power."[58] Because the FBI was unable to prove that Moussaoui was acting for or on behalf of a FTO, it was unable to prove that he was an agent of a foreign power and therefore unable to obtain a FISA order to search his belongings. The 2004 "lone wolf" amendment to FISA eliminated the foreign power nexus when an individual is suspected of engaging in international terrorism, authorizing electronic surveillance of a suspected foreign terrorist operating as a "lone wolf."[59]

---

[53] *Id.* §§1801(b)(1)(A)-(E).

[54] *Id.* §1801(b)(1)(C).

[55] 9/11 COMMISSION REPORT, *supra* note 38, at 273-74; *see also* EDWARD C. LIU, CONG. RESEARCH SERV., R40138, AMENDMENTS TO FOREIGN INTELLIGENCE SURVEILLANCE ACT (FISA) EXTENDED UNTIL JUNE 1, 2015 4-5 (2011) (providing historical context for the "lone wolf" provision).

[56] 9/11 COMMISSION REPORT, *supra* note 38, at 274. Moussaoui was taking flying lessons on a Boeing 747 jumbo jet despite having no experience on smaller planes and only wanted to learn how to steer the jet in the air—not take off or land.

[57] 9/11 COMMISSION REPORT, *supra* note 38, at 274.

[58] *Id.*

[59] *See* LIU, *supra* note 55, at 5.

I. Foreign Intelligence Surveillance Act, 50 U.S.C. §§1801 *et seq.*

The definition of an agent of a foreign power also includes a U.S. person who "knowingly engages in clandestine intelligence gathering activities . . . which activities involve or may involve a violation of the criminal statutes of the United States," or "knowingly engages in sabotage or international terrorism, or activities that are in preparation therefor[.]"[60] However, the U.S. person must be acting on behalf of a foreign power. The "lone wolf" provision does not extend to U.S. persons suspected of engaging in international terrorism. Such persons must be acting as agents of a foreign power.

4. Application for Court Orders, 50 U.S.C. §1804

The FISA procedures for obtaining a court order authorizing electronic surveillance or physical searches are generally parallel in nature. A FISA electronic surveillance or physical search application must be made by a senior federal intelligence official "in writing upon oath or affirmation" to a FISA judge.[61] The FISC only hears from one side of the case—the government—and its findings are almost never made public. A single judge signs most surveillance orders. In 2012, there were nearly 1,800 surveillance orders issued by the FISC.[62] Each application must include the identity of the federal officer making the application,[63] and the identity, if known, or a description of the person whose communications are to be intercepted.[64] The application must also include a statement of the facts relied upon by the applicant to justify the belief that the target is a foreign power or an agent of a foreign power, and that the targeted facilities or places are used by such a foreign power or its agent.[65] The FISA application must also contain a statement of proposed "minimization procedures" to be followed,[66] and a description of the communications to be intercepted and the information sought.[67] The "minimization procedures" are specific procedures adopted by the Attorney General that are reasonably designed to protect "against the acquisition, retention, and dissemination of nonpublic information which is not foreign intelligence information."[68] According to the FISA Review Court:

> By minimizing the *acquisition*, Congress envisioned that, for example, "where a switchboard line is tapped but only one person in the organization is the target,

---

[60] 50 U.S.C. §§1801(b)(2)(A), (C).

[61] *Id.* §1804(a).

[62] *See* Evan Perez, *Secret Court's Oversight Gets Scrutiny*, WALL ST. J. (online), June 9, 2013, http://online.wsj.com/news/articles/SB10001424127887324904004578535670310514616 (of the 33,900 warrant applications received by the FISA court from 1979 to 2012, only 11 have been rejected).

[63] 50 U.S.C. §1804(a)(1).

[64] *Id.* §1804(a)(2).

[65] *Id.* §§1804(a)(3)(A)-(B).

[66] *Id.* §1804(a)(4).

[67] *Id.* §1804(a)(5).

[68] In re Sealed Case, 310 F.3d at 731.

the interception should probably be discontinued where the target is not a party" to the communication. H. Rep. at 55-56. By minimizing *retention*, Congress intended that "information acquired, which is not necessary for obtaining[,] producing, or disseminating foreign intelligence information, be destroyed where feasible." H. Rep. at 56. Furthermore, "[e]ven with respect to information needed for an approved purpose, *dissemination* should be restricted to those officials with a need for such information. . . .

If the data is not foreign intelligence information as defined by statute, the procedures are to ensure that the government does not use the information to identify the target or third party, unless such identification is necessary to properly understand or assess the foreign intelligence information that is collected."[69]

The minimization procedures allow, however, the retention and dissemination of non-foreign intelligence information that is evidence of "ordinary crimes" for purposes of prosecution.[70] Thus, if evidence of "a serious crime totally unrelated to intelligence matters" is incidentally acquired through FISA electronic surveillance or searches, the evidence is "not . . . required to be destroyed."[71]

An application for electronic surveillance must also contain a "certification" by the Assistant to the President for National Security Affairs or a designated executive branch official, such as the Director of the FBI.[72] Such an official must certify that: 1) the information sought is foreign intelligence information; 2) a "significant purpose" of the surveillance is to obtain foreign intelligence information;[73] and 3) such information cannot "reasonably be obtained by normal investigative techniques."[74] The certification must also designate the type of foreign intelligence information being sought using the categories described in §1801(e)'s definition of "foreign intelligence information."[75] Further, the certifying official must include a statement of the *basis* for the certification that "(i) the information sought is the type of foreign intelligence information designated; and (ii) such information cannot be obtained by normal investigative techniques."[76]

Each application must also contain a statement of the means by which the surveillance will be conducted,[77] the period of time for which the electronic surveillance is required,[78] and whether any previous applications have been made to

---

[69] *Id.* (emphasis added).

[70] 50 U.S.C. §1801(h)(3).

[71] In re Sealed Case, 310 F.3d at 731 (citations omitted).

[72] 50 U.S.C. §1804(a)(6). The executive branch official must be designated by the President from among those executive officers employed in the area of national security or defense and appointed by the President with the advice and consent of the Senate, or the Deputy Director of the FBI. *Id.*

[73] *Id.* §1804(6)(B).

[74] *Id.* §1804(6)(C).

[75] *Id.* §1804(6)(D).

[76] *Id.* §§1804(6)(E)(i)-(ii).

[77] *Id.* §1804(7).

[78] *Id.* §1804(9).

any judges involving any of the persons, facilities, or places specified in the application as well as the action taken on each previous application.[79] Finally, such application must be approved by the Attorney General, the Deputy Attorney General, or, upon the designation of the Attorney General, the Assistant Attorney General for National Security.[80]

5.   Issuance of FISA Electronic Surveillance and Physical Search Orders

The FISC may issue an order approving electronic surveillance or physical searches upon a finding that the application requirements have been met and there is probable cause to believe that the target is a foreign power or the agent of a foreign power and the targeted facilities are used, or about to be used, by foreign powers or their agents.[81] Orders approving electronic surveillance must identify or describe: 1) the person whose communications are to be intercepted; 2) the nature and location of the targeted facilities or places, if known; 3) the type of communications or activities targeted and the kind of information sought; 4) the means by which interception is to be accomplished and whether physical entry is authorized; and 5) set forth the period of time during which electronic surveillance is approved.[82] For both electronic surveillance and physical searches, an order may be granted for a period of 90 days, though extensions may be granted if the government submits another application to the FISC.[83] However, if the target is a foreign power as defined in §1801(a)(1), (2), or (3) (foreign government, faction of a foreign nation, or entity that is acknowledged by a foreign government to be directed and controlled by that foreign government), the order may extend for up to one year.[84] Further, if the target is an agent of a foreign power who is not a U.S. person as defined in §1801(b)(1), the order may be approved for a period not to exceed 120 days.[85]

The court order must also include a provision directing the government to follow the specified minimization procedures. Furthermore, there must also be a provision stating that upon request, electronic communication service providers and others must: 1) provide assistance; 2) observe certain security precautions in providing such assistance; and 3) be compensated for that assistance.[86] Finally, the order must specify that the electronic surveillance must expire when its purpose is accomplished, but not later than the authorized time period, unless extended.[87]

---

[79] *Id.* §1804(8).
[80] *Id.* §1801(g).
[81] *Id.* §§1805(a)(2)(A)-(B); 1824(a)(1)-(4).
[82] *Id.* §§1805(c)(1)(A)-(E).
[83] *Id.* §§1805(d)(1), (2); 1824(d)(1), (2).
[84] *Id.*
[85] *Id.*
[86] *Id.* §1805(c)(2)(D).
[87] *Id.* §1805(c)(1)(E).

The requirements for an order authorizing physical searches for foreign intelligence information generally parallel those procedures applicable to electronic surveillance. However, the procedures to obtain a court order to install a pen register or trap and trace device, as well as to obtain business records or other tangible things, do not require that the foreign intelligence information be connected to a foreign power or agent of a foreign power. The PATRIOT Act eliminated the foreign power or agent of a foreign power nexus for these types of orders.[88] Each type of order may now be granted upon a showing that the information sought is relevant to an authorized investigation to obtain foreign intelligence information not concerning a U.S. person, or to protect against international terrorism or clandestine activities.

Section 206 of the PATRIOT Act amended FISA to permit "roving" wiretaps, which target persons rather than places.[89] Prior to the enactment of §206, a FISA court order authorizing electronic surveillance needed to identify the location or facility subject to that court order.[90] Also, only identifiable third parties could be directed by the government to furnish the information, facilities, or technical assistance necessary to accomplish the electronic surveillance.[91] In cases where the location or facility was unknown, the identity of the persons needed to assist the government with electronic surveillance could not be specified in the order.[92] This inability to identify the persons that could be directed to assist the government effectively limited the reach of electronic surveillance to "known and identifiable locations."[93] Section 206 of the PATRIOT Act amended §1805(c)(2)(B), authorizing FISA orders to direct "other persons" to assist with electronic surveillance if "the Court finds, based on the specific facts provided in the application, that the actions of the target of the application may have the effect of thwarting the identification of a specified person."[94]

---

[88] *See* USA PATRIOT Act §214(a)(2), 115 Stat. at 286 (codified at 50 U.S.C. §§1842(c)(2), 1861(b)(2) (2008)).

[89] *See* USA PATRIOT Act of 2001, P.L. 107-56, §206 (codified at 50 U.S.C. §1805(c)(2)(B) (2008)). The discussion of the "roving" wiretap provision is taken, in large part, from JIMMY GURULÉ & GEOFFREY CORN, PRINCIPLES OF COUNTER-TERRORISM LAW (West 2010).

[90] *See* 50 U.S.C. §1805(c)(1)(B) (2001) (requiring FISA warrants to identify the "nature and location of each of the facilities or places at which electronic surveillance will be directed").

[91] *See id.* §1805(c)(2) (2001). Section 1805(c)(2) then provided:

> . . . that, upon the request of the applicant, a *specified* communication or other common carrier, landlord, custodian, or other *specified person* furnish the application forthwith all information, facilities, or technical assistance necessary to accomplish the electronic surveillance in such a manner as will protect its secrecy and produce a minimum of interference with the services that such carrier, landlord, custodian, or other person is providing that target of electronic surveillance.

Id. (emphasis added).

[92] *See* ANNA C. HENNING & EDWARD C. LIU, CONG. RESEARCH SERV., R40138, AMENDMENTS TO THE FOREIGN SURVEILLANCE INTELLIGENCE ACT (FISA) SET TO EXPIRE FEBRUARY 28, 2010, at 7 (2010) (discussing the "roving" wiretap amendment to FISA) [hereinafter AMENDMENTS TO THE FOREIGN INTELLIGENCE SURVEILLANCE ACT].

[93] *Id.*

[94] 50 U.S.C. §1805(c)(2)(B) (2008).

I. Foreign Intelligence Surveillance Act, 50 U.S.C. §§1801 *et seq.*

Congress provided the following explanation for these statutory changes:

> The multipoint wiretap amendment to FISA in the USA PATRIOT Act (section 206) allows the FISA court to issue generic orders of assistance to any communications provider. This change permits the Government to implement new surveillance immediately if the FISA target changes providers in an effort to thwart surveillance. The amendment was directed at persons who, for example, attempt to defeat surveillance by changing wireless telephone providers or using pay phones.
> Currently, FISA requires the court to "specify" the "nature and location of each of the facilities or places at which the electronic surveillance will be directed." 50 U.S.C. §1805(c)(1)(B). Obviously, in certain situations under current law, such a specification is limited. For example, a wireless phone has no fixed location and electronic mail may be accessed from any number of locations.
> To avoid ambiguity and clarify Congress' intent, the conferees agreed to a provision which adds the phrase, "if known," to the end of 50 U.S.C. §1805(c)(1)(B). The "if known" language ... is designed to avoid any uncertainty about the kind of specification required in a multipoint wiretap case, where the facility to be monitored is typically not known in advance.[95]

Further, in an amendment to the statute that followed, the requirement that the order specify the location of the facilities or places at which the electronic surveillance is to be directed was also changed. This requirement now applies only if such facilities or places are known.[96] These amendments permit FISA orders to direct unspecified individuals ("other persons") to assist the government in performing electronic surveillance of places and locations that are unknown at the time an order is issued, or in situations where the target changes communications providers to thwart surveillance.[97]

The USA PATRIOT Act Improvement and Reauthorization Act of 2005 amended §1805(c) to require that the FISC be notified within ten days after "surveillance begins to be directed at any new facility or place."[98] In addition, the government is required to notify the FISC of 1) the nature and location of each new facility or place at which the electronic surveillance is directed, 2) the facts and circumstances relied upon to justify the new surveillance, 3) a statement of any proposed minimization procedures, and 4) the total number of locations and facilities subject to electronic surveillance under the present order.[99]

---

[95] Conference Report on H.R. 2338, Intelligence Authorization Act for Fiscal Year 2002 (which became P.L. 107-108), H. Rept. 107-328, at 24.

[96] P.L. 107-108, §314(a)(2)(A) (codified at 50 U.S.C. §1805(c)(1)(B)). *See also* AMENDMENTS TO THE FOREIGN INTELLIGENCE SURVEILLANCE ACT, *supra* note 92.

[97] *See* 50 U.S.C. §§1805(c)(1)(B), 1805(c)(2)(B).

[98] P.L. 109-177, §108(b)(4) (codified at 50 U.S.C. §1805(c)(3) (2008)). Upon a finding of good cause, notice to the FISC may be delayed up to 60 days. 50 U.S.C. §1805(c)(3).

[99] 50 U.S.C. §§1805(c)(3)(A)-(D).

While the critics of FISA roving wiretaps might argue that orders authorizing such surveillance do not comport with the requirement contained in the Fourth Amendment that warrants shall "particularly describ[e] the place to be searched,"[100] similar roving wiretaps have been permitted under Title III of the Omnibus Crime Control and Safe Streets Act. In *United States v. Petti*, the Ninth Circuit rejected a legal challenge to a roving wiretap under Title III. In responding to the challenge that such wiretaps do not satisfy the Fourth Amendment particularity requirement,[101] the court commented:

> [T]he test for determining the sufficiency of the warrant description is whether the place to be searched is described with sufficient particularity to enable the executing officer to locate and identify the premises with reasonable effort, and whether there is any reasonable probability that another premise might be mistakenly searched.[102]

Applying this test, the Ninth Circuit upheld the constitutionality of roving wiretaps under Title III.[103] The court reasoned that the particularity requirement of the Fourth Amendment was satisfied because the targets of roving wiretaps had to be identified.[104] Further, the court found that the use of roving wiretaps was limited under Title III and only permitted where the target's actions indicated intent to thwart electronic surveillance. The reasoning in *Petti* would appear to apply with equal force in the case of roving wiretaps under §1805(c)(2)(b). The target of a FISA electronic surveillance order must be identified and the authority to have the FISA order follow the target applies only if the FISA target changes electronic communications service providers in an effort to thwart surveillance.[105]

Finally, FISA makes it a federal crime for federal officials to abuse their authority under either the FISA electronic surveillance or physical search provisions. The prohibitions cover illicit surveillance and searches as well as the use or disclosure of such unlawfully obtained information.[106] Civil liability is also authorized where an aggrieved person has been subjected to electronic surveillance or whose property has been searched, or where information was lawfully gathered but disclosed in violation of FISA.[107] However, those persons directed to assist

---

[100] U.S. Const. amend. IV.

[101] United States v. Petti, 973 F.2d 1441 (9th Cir. 1992); *see also* Amendments to the Foreign Intelligence Surveillance Act, *supra* note 92, at 9 (discussing *Petti*).

[102] *Petti*, 973 F.2d, at 1444 (internal quotations omitted).

[103] *Id. See also* United States v. Bianco, 998 F.2d 1112, 1124 (2d Cir. 1993) (upholding the constitutionality of roving wiretaps under Title III).

[104] *Petti*, 973 F.2d, at 1445.

[105] 50 U.S.C. §1805(c)(2)(B).

[106] *See id.* §§1809, 1827. Such violation is punishable by imprisonment or not more than five years or a maximum fine of $10,000, or both.

[107] *Id.* §§1810, 1828. A person who commits such violation may be ordered to pay actual damages, punitive damages, and reasonable attorneys' fees and court costs. However, both §1810 and §1828 expressly exclude foreign powers or agents of foreign powers from seeking these remedies.

authorities in execution of an electronic surveillance or physical search are immune from civil suit.[108]

The 2008 FISA Amendments Act bars the initiation or continuation of civil suits in either state or federal court based on charges that the defendant assisted any of the U.S. intelligence agencies. Dismissal is required upon the certification of the Attorney General that the person either:

> (1) did not provide the assistance charged; (2) provided the assistance under order of the FISA court; (3) provided the assistance pursuant to a national security letter issued under 18 U.S.C. 2709; (4) provided the assistance pursuant to 18 U.S.C. 2522(a)(ii)(B) and 2518(7) under assurances from the Attorney General or a senior Justice Department official, empowered to approve emergency law enforcement wiretaps, that no court approval was required; (5) provided the assistance in response to a directive from the President through the Attorney General and Director of National Intelligence relating to the acquisition of foreign intelligence information targeting non-U.S. persons thought to be overseas pursuant to 50 U.S.C. 1881a(h); . . . or (7) provided the assistance in connection with intelligence activities authorized by the President between September 11, 2001, and January 17, 2007, relating to terrorist attacks against the United States.[109]

6. Access to "Tangible Things," 50 U.S.C. §§1861-62

Section 215 of the PATRIOT Act, codified at 50 U.S.C. §1861, authorizes the production of any "tangible things" for an investigation to obtain foreign intelligence information not concerning U.S. persons, or to protect against international terrorism or clandestine intelligence activities.[110] Prior to the enactment of §215, FISA authorized orders directing common carriers, public accommodation facilities, storage facilities, and vehicle rental facilities to provide business records to the FBI.[111] To issue an order, the government needed to show "specific and articulable facts giving reason to believe that the person to whom the records pertain is a foreign power or an agent of a foreign power."[112]

After the September 11 attacks, Congress expanded the government's authority to obtain records from additional businesses. Section 215 allows the government to obtain an order "requiring the production of any tangible things (including books, records, papers, documents, and other items)," eliminating the

---

[108] *Id.* §1881a(h)(3).

[109] Gina Fisher & Charles Doyle, Cong. Research Serv. 98-327, Privacy: An Abbreviated Outline of Federal Statutes Governing Wiretapping and Electronic Eavesdropping, at 10 (2012); *see also* 50 U.S.C. §1881a(h)(3).

[110] USA PATRIOT Act of 2001, P.L. 107-55 (2001), §215 (codified at 50 U.S.C. §1861(a)(2) (2008)).

[111] *See* Intelligence Authorization Act for Fiscal Year 1999, Pub. L. 105-272, §602, 112 Stat. 2396, 2410 (1998).

[112] *Id.* §602.

restriction on the types of businesses that can be served with such orders, as well as the requirement that the target be a foreign power or agent of a foreign power.[113] Under §215, the applicant need only "specify that the records concerned are sought for a [foreign intelligence, international terrorism, or espionage investigation.]"[114]

In 2005, Congress amended the statute to require that the FBI's application include "a statement of facts showing that there are reasonable grounds to believe that the tangible things sought are *relevant* to a [foreign intelligence, international terrorism, or espionage investigation]."[115] Such records are presumptively relevant to an authorized investigation if they pertain to 1) a foreign power or agent of a foreign power, 2) the activities of a suspected agent of a foreign power who is the subject of such authorized investigation, or 3) an individual in contact with, or known to, a suspected agent of a foreign power who is the subject of such authorized investigation.[116]

Section 215 is the authority relied on by the FBI and NSA to compel the production of "call detail records" and "telephony metadata" of over 300 million Americans since 2006.[117] Under the NSA's telephony metadata program, telecommunication providers are directed to turn over such data created by their subscribers "on an ongoing daily basis."[118] The NSA collects telephony metadata as business records of these telecommunication providers, compiles the requested metadata into a massive database, stores it for five years, and analyzes it. The purpose of this program is to detect whether known or suspected terrorists are engaged in contact with persons inside the United States.

"Telephony metadata" is defined as "comprehensive communications routing information, including . . . session identifying information (e.g., originating and terminating telephone number, International Mobile station Equipment Identify (IMEI) number, International Mobile Subscriber Identity (IMSI) number) trunk identifier, telephone calling card numbers, and [the] time and duration of [the] call[s]."[119] "Call detail information" is defined as "any information that pertains to the transmission of specific telephone calls, including . . . the number called . . . the number from which [a] call was placed and the time,

---

[113] 50 U.S.C. §1861 (as amended 2008). The only limitation on the types of records that may be obtained with a §215 order is that they be obtainable with a grand jury subpoena. *See id.* §1861(c)(2)(D). "Tangible things" under §215 must be the type of records that could be obtained with either a "subpoena duces tecum issued by a court of the United States in aid of a grand jury investigation or with any other order issued by a court of the United States directing the production of tangible things." *Id.* §1861 (c)(2)(D). The government does not limit its definition of "tangible things" to tactile objects, but understands the term to include "things that are capable of being perceived by the senses," like electronically stored information. *See* H.R. Rep. No. 109-174(I), at 17-18 (2005).

[114] Pub. L. 107-56, §215.

[115] USA PATRIOT Act Improvement and Reauthorization Act of 2005, Pub. L. 109-177, §106(b), 120 Stat. 192 (codified at 50 U.S.C. §1861(b)(2)(A) (2008)) (emphasis added).

[116] 50 U.S.C. §1861(b)(2)(A)(i)-(iii).

[117] *See In re Application of the Federal Bureau of Investigation, supra* note 2, at 1-2 (holding that the telephone metadata program does not violate the Fourth Amendment and further complies with §215 of the USA PATRIOT Act).

[118] *Id.* at 1.

[119] *Id.* at 2.

location, or duration of any call."[120] The requested telephone metadata does not include any information about the content of those calls.[121]

The government maintains that the bulk collection of telephone metadata is necessary to identify individuals who suspected terrorists might be communicating with in the United States. The database is queried using identifiers associated with identified FTOs.[122] Identifiers are "specifically known telephone identifiers," like telephone numbers, or other unique electronic identifiers.[123] If a telephone number identifier is associated with a suspected terrorist or terrorist organization, that number is run through the telephone metadata base to see whether the terrorist-related number has called or received calls from any of the telephone numbers in the database.[124]

In collecting telephony metadata, both the government and the FISC have broadly construed the statutory requirement that the production of tangible things be "relevant" to a terrorism investigation. The government takes the position that tangible items are "relevant" under §215 if they bear on or could reasonably lead to other information that could bear on a terrorism investigation.[125] Thus, the requested records or documents need not be directly connected to a specific ongoing counterterrorism investigation. If the requested information could at some point conceivably lead to other information that directly bears on a counterterrorism investigation such information is "relevant" for purposes of §215. Therefore, according to the government, because the bulk collection of telephone metadata could potentially lead to identifying persons calling or receiving calls from suspected terrorists, all such metadata is "relevant" to a terrorism investigation.[126]

In *In re Application of the Federal Bureau of Investigation*, the FISC held that the telephony metadata program was lawful because "[t]he fact that international terrorist operatives are using telephone communications, and that it is *necessary* to obtain the bulk collection of a telephone company's metadata to determine those connections between known and unknown international terrorist operatives as part of authorized investigations, is sufficient to meet the low statutory hurdle set out in section 215 to obtain a production of records."[127] In essence, the

---

[120] 47 C.F.R. §64.2003(d) (2012).

[121] *Id.*

[122] *See* Klayman v. Obama, 957 F. Supp. 2d 1, 16 (D.D.C. 2013).

[123] *Memorandum for the Deputy Program Manager for Counterterrorism Special Projects, Analysis and Production: Assessments of Reasonable Articulable Suspicion Pursuant to Orders of the [FISC]*, Aug. 29, 2008, at 2 ("the term electronic identifier is intended to include not only email addresses, but also similar routing and addressing information that effects delivery of electronic communications").

[124] *Id.* at 16.

[125] *See White Paper on Bulk Collection of Telephony Metadata*, *supra* note 2, at 9; *see also* American Civil Liberties Union v. Clapper, 959 F. Supp. 2d 724, 746-49 (S.D.N.Y. 2013).

[126] *See Clapper*, 959 F. Supp. 2d at 747-48 (upholding legality of program).

[127] *In re Application of the Federal Bureau of Investigation*, *supra* note 2, at 22-23 (emphasis added). *See Clapper*, 959 F. Supp. 2d at 746 ("[T]he collection of virtually all telephony metadata is 'necessary' to permit the NSA . . . to do the algorithmic data analysis that allow the NSA to determine 'connections between known and unknown international terrorist operatives.'") (internal citations omitted).

FISC equates "relevance" with necessity, and so long as the requested information is necessary to assist the government in identifying suspected terrorists, it is relevant under §215.

The Privacy and Civil Liberties Oversight Board has been critical of this interpretation of the statute, arguing that it "is circular and deprives the word 'relevant' of any interpretive value."[128] According to the Board:

> All records become relevant to an investigation, under this reasoning, because the government has developed an investigative tool that functions by collecting all records to enable later searching. The implication of this reasoning is that if the government develops an effective means of searching through *everything* in order to find *something*, then *everything* becomes relevant to its investigation.[129]

According to the FISC, §215 does not require specific and articulable facts or materiality. The government satisfies the standard under §215 "if it can demonstrate reasonable grounds to believe that the information sought to be produced has *some bearing* on its investigations of the identified international terrorist organizations."[130] The FISC's view that information is "relevant" if it could possibly lead to other information that has *some bearing* on a terrorism investigation imposes an exceedingly low legal threshold for issuing a FISA warrant. It is certainly conceivable that the bulk production of telephone metadata could lead to information that directly bears on an authorized investigation. Thus, under the FISC's reasoning, the daily collection of telephony metadata of over 300 million Americans is relevant to an authorized terrorism investigation.

Another issue raised by §215 is the meaning of the term "authorized investigation."[131] Each application for the production of "tangible things" must include a statement that there are reasonable grounds to believe that the tangible things sought are relevant to an "authorized investigation" to protect against international terrorism or clandestine intelligence activities.[132] The issue is whether the requested business records must be relevant to a "specific" ongoing terrorism investigation or merely some future investigation of suspected terrorists. While the FISC has not explicitly ruled on the issue, the telephone records collected under the NSA's metadata program are not collected in furtherance of specific terrorism investigations involving specified individuals believed to be plotting a terrorist attack against an identified target. Instead, the telephone

---

[128] Privacy and Civil Liberties Oversight Board, Report on the Telephone Records Program Conducted under Section 215 of the USA PATRIOT Act and on the Operations of the Foreign Intelligence Surveillance Court, at 62 (Jan. 23, 2014).

[129] *Id.* (emphasis in original).

[130] *In re Application of the Federal Bureau of Investigation, supra* note 2, at 19.

[131] The definition of "authorized investigation" in §215 expressly excludes "threat assessments." 50 U.S.C. §1861(b)(2)(A). "Threat assessments" have an authorized purpose, but need not be based on any particular factual predication, while "authorized investigations" must be predicated on specific facts or circumstances indicative of terrorism. *Id.*

[132] *Id.*

metadata is being collected and stored, then queried in the future for connections to individuals subsequently identified and suspected of engaging in terrorist-related activities. Alternatively, the government and the FISC have broadly construed the term "authorized investigation" to encompass the global conflict against Al Qaeda and related terrorist organizations. In other words, the government is investigating the entirety of Al Qaeda and its affiliate members and the telephony metadata is relevant to that "authorized investigation."

Proposed legislation introduced in the Senate in July 2014 after negotiations between Senator Patrick Leahy of Vermont and government representatives would roll back the metadata program in the wake of Edward Snowden's disclosures.[133] The Leahy bill, even more than the bipartisan bill that passed the House in May 2014,[134] would preclude the NSA's controversial bulk collection of metadata. The Leahy bill would authorize the government to seek a court order requesting data from phone companies and other private entities based on a "specific selection term."[135] It would also authorize the FISC to appoint amici curiae who could oppose the government's surveillance requests when those requests raised novel legal issues. In addition, the Leahy bill would authorize the FISC and the Foreign Intelligence Surveillance Court of Review (FISCR), which reviews FISC decisions, to certify novel questions to the next court on the appellate ladder (for the FISCR, that would be the U.S. Supreme Court).

In sum, the authority afforded to the FBI and NSA under §215 was sweeping. The term "relevant" was construed broadly to connote anything directly bearing upon, or which could come to bear or even lead to information that has some bearing upon an authorized investigation to protect against international terrorism. The term "authorized investigation" includes the investigation of suspected terrorists that may be identified in the future and queried against the telephone metadata base, or could encompass the entirety of the government's global conflict with Al Qaeda and affiliated groups. Thus, section 215 essentially gives the FBI and NSA the authority to seize the telephone records of every American.

---

[133] *See* Sen. Patrick Leahy et al., A Bill to reform the authorities of the Federal Government to require the production of certain business records, conduct electronic surveillance, use pen registers and trap and trace devices, and use other forms of information gathering for foreign intelligence, counterterrorism, and criminal purposes, and for other purposes, 113th Cong., 2d Sess., *available at* https://www.leahy.senate.gov/download/hen14602 [hereinafter Leahy bill].

[134] *See* Amendment in the Nature of a Substitute to H.R. 3361 (as reported by the Comm. on the Judiciary and the Permanent Select Comm. on Intelligence, May 15, 2014). Offered by Mr. Sensenbrenner of Wisconsin, Mr. Goodlatte of Virginia, Mr. Conyers of Michigan, Mr. Nadler of New York, and Mr. Scott of Virginia, 160 Cong. Rec. H4789-4804 (as passed by House, May 22, 2014), *available at* http://fas.org/irp/congress/2014_cr/h052214-usaf.html.

[135] *See* Leahy bill, §103(a). In November 2014, the U.S. Senate declined to approve the Leahy bill. The Congress will likely enact new legislation by June 2015, when the current legislation sunsets. However, as of December 2014, the fate of the Leahy bill reforms is unclear.

7.   Nondisclosure Orders

Orders issued under FISA are accompanied by a nondisclosure order prohibiting the recipients from disclosing that the FBI has sought or obtained tangible things pursuant to a FISA order.[136] However, the recipient may discuss the FISA order with 1) persons to whom disclosure is necessary to comply with the order, 2) an attorney to obtain legal assistance, and 3) other persons as permitted by the FBI.[137]

The USA PATRIOT Act Improvement and Reauthorization Act of 2005 provides a recipient of a production order under 50 U.S.C. §1861 a process for judicial review of such order and related nondisclosure order.[138] However, judicial review only extends to the recipient of the FISA orders, such as the telecommunications service providers, not the intended target of the FISA order, such as telecommunication subscribers.[139] Once a petition for review is submitted under 50 U.S.C. §1861(2)(A)(i), the FISC must conduct an initial review of the petition within 72 hours.[140] If the petition is frivolous, the order must be affirmed.[141] The order may be modified or set aside only if the judge finds that such order does not meet the requirements of the statute or is otherwise unlawful.[142] Either party may appeal the decision of the FISC to modify or set aside the production order to the FISCR and the Supreme Court.[143]

The recipient of a FISA production order may also challenge the nondisclosure order.[144] However, recipients must wait at least one year after the issuance of the order before filing a petition challenging the nondisclosure order.[145] The FISC may modify or set aside the nondisclosure order if the judge finds that "there is no reason to believe that disclosure may endanger the national security of the United States, interfere with a criminal, counterterrorism, or counterintelligence investigation, interfere with diplomatic relations, or endanger the life or physical safety of any person."[146]

A petition to set aside a nondisclosure order may be denied if the Attorney General, Deputy Attorney General, an Assistant Attorney General, or the Director of the FBI certifies that disclosure would endanger national security or interfere with diplomatic relations.[147] Further, absent a finding that the certification was

---

[136] 50 U.S.C. §1861(d)(1).

[137] *Id.* §§1861(d)(1)(A)-(C).

[138] *Id.* §1861(f)(2)(A)(i).

[139] See *Klayman*, 957 F. Supp. 2d at 23 (holding that "Congress did not intend for third parties, such as plaintiff phone subscribers here, to challenge the Government's compliance with the statute"); *Clapper*, 959 F. Supp. 2d at 742 ("[T]he statutory scheme also makes clear that Congress intended to preclude suits by targets even if they discovered section 215 orders implicating them.").

[140] 50 U.S.C. §1861(f)(2)(A)(ii).

[141] *Id.*

[142] *Id.* §1861(f)(2)(B).

[143] *Id.* §1861(f)(3).

[144] *Id.* §1861(f)(2)(A)(i).

[145] *Id.*

[146] *Id.* §1861(f)(2)(C)(i).

[147] *Id.* §1861(f)(2)(C)(ii).

made in bad faith, such certification is to be treated as *conclusive* by the FISC.[148] Finally, if a petition to modify or set aside a nondisclosure is denied, the recipient may not file another such petition for one year.[149]

8. Electronic Surveillance Without a Court Order

Electronic surveillance under FISA requires a court order, unless the surveillance falls under one of three statutory exceptions.[150] Under the first exception, in 50 U.S.C. §1802(a), the President, through the Attorney General, may authorize electronic surveillance to acquire foreign intelligence information for up to one year without a court order if the Attorney General certifies in writing and under oath that three criteria are satisfied.[151] First, the Attorney General must certify that the electronic surveillance is solely directed at—

(i) the acquisition of the contents of communications transmitted by means of communication used exclusively between or among foreign powers as defined in [50 U.S.C. §1801(a)(1), (2), or (3)]; or
(ii) the acquisition of technical intelligence, other than the spoken communications of individuals, from property or premises under the open and exclusive control of a foreign power, as defined in [50 U.S.C. §§1801(a)(1), (2), or (3)].[152]

Second, there must be no "substantial likelihood" that the surveillance will acquire the contents of any communication to which a U.S. person is a party.[153] Third, the Attorney General must certify that minimization procedures with

---

[148] *Id.* However, in Doe v. Mukasey, 549 F.3d 861 (2d Cir. 2008), the Second Circuit considered a similar provision involving judicial review of a national security letter, holding that the nondisclosure provision violated the recipients First Amendment rights. The Court held that there is no meaningful judicial review of the executive branch to prohibit speech if the position of the executive branch that speech would be harmful is "conclusive" on the reviewing court, absent only a demonstration of "bad faith." *Mukasey*, 549 F.3d at 882.

[149] 50 U.S.C. §1861(f)(2)(C)(iii).

[150] The U.S. Supreme Court has not squarely addressed the constitutionality of the use of warrantless electronic surveillance against foreign powers or their agents. In United States v. United States District Court, 407 U.S. 297 (1972), commonly known as the *Keith* case (the name of the district court judge against whom the government sought a writ of mandamus), the Supreme Court addressed the constitutionality of the use of warrantless electronic surveillance against a purely domestic target. The Court held that, in the case of intelligence gathering involving purely domestic surveillance, prior judicial approval was required to satisfy the Fourth Amendment. *Id.* at 321. However, the Court emphasized that its holding was limited to cases involving only the domestic aspects of national security. *Id.* The Court declared: "[w]e have not addressed, and express no opinion as to, the issues which may be involved with respect to activities of foreign powers or their agents." *Id.* at 321-22.

[151] 50 U.S.C. §1802(a)(1). An analogous provision of FISA authorizes physical searches without a court order. *See id.* §1822(a)(1).

[152] *Id.* §§1802(a)(1)(A)(i)-(ii).

[153] *Id.* §1802(a)(1)(B).

respect to such surveillance meet the definition of minimization procedures under 50 U.S.C. §1801(h).[154] The Attorney General must also report such minimization procedures and any changes thereto to the House Permanent Select Committee on Intelligence and the Senate Select Committee on Intelligence at least 30 days prior to their effective date, unless the Attorney General determines that immediate action is required and notifies the committees of such minimization procedures and the reason for their becoming effective immediately.[155]

Under this court order exception, warrantless electronic surveillance is authorized only against three categories of "foreign powers." Those categories include "(1) a foreign government or any component thereof, whether or not recognized by the United States; (2) a faction of a foreign nation or nations, not substantially composed of United States persons; or (3) any entity that is openly acknowledged by a foreign government or governments to be directed or controlled by such foreign government or governments."[156] Thus, the warrantless electronic surveillance provision does not apply to other statutorily enumerated categories of "foreign powers," such as groups engaged in international terrorism or entities engaged in the international proliferation of weapons of mass destruction. A court-ordered FISA warrant is still required to conduct electronic surveillance of these groups.

The second exception to the FISC order requirement is available in emergency situations. Section 1805(e)(1) provides that notwithstanding any other provision of FISA, if the Attorney General "reasonably determines that an emergency situation exists with respect to the employment of electronic surveillance to obtain foreign intelligence information before an order authorizing such surveillance can with due diligence be obtained," he may authorize electronic surveillance to collect foreign intelligence information if the following procedures are followed. First, the Attorney General must reasonably determine a factual basis exists for issuing an order to approve electronic surveillance.[157] Second, at the time of the Attorney General's emergency authorization, he or his designee must inform the FISC that a decision to employ emergency electronic surveillance has been made.[158] Third, the Attorney General must ensure that the minimization procedures required for the issuance of a judicial order are followed.[159] Finally, an application for a court order must be made as soon as practicable, but not later than seven days after the Attorney General authorizes such emergency surveillance.[160] In the absence of a court order, the surveillance must terminate when the information sought is obtained, when the application for the order is denied,

---

[154] *Id.* §1802(a)(1)(C).
[155] *Id.*
[156] *Id.* §§1801(a)(1)-(3).
[157] *Id.* §1805(e)(1)(B).
[158] *Id.* §1805(e)(1)(C).
[159] *Id.* §1805(e)(2).
[160] *Id.* §1805(e)(1)(D).

or after the expiration of seven days from the time of the authorization from the Attorney General, whichever is earliest.[161]

The third statutory exception to the FISA warrant requirement is set forth in 50 U.S.C. §1811, which provides that the President, through the Attorney General, may authorize electronic surveillance without a court order to acquire foreign intelligence information for up to 15 days following a congressional declaration of war.[162]

Warrantless electronic surveillance is also authorized under FISA for non-U.S. persons located outside the United States. Under the FISA Amendments Act of 2008, 50 U.S.C. §1881a(a), upon the issuance of a court order or upon a determination under subsection (c)(2), the Attorney General and the Director of National Intelligence may jointly authorize, for a period up to one year from the effective date of the authorization, "the targeting of persons reasonably believed to be located outside the United States to acquire foreign intelligence information."[163] Electronic surveillance may be authorized without a court order under §1881a(c)(2), which requires a determination by the Attorney General and the Director of National Intelligence that "exigent circumstances" exist and that without immediate implementation of electronic surveillance abroad "intelligence important to national security of the United States may be lost or not timely acquired and time does not permit the issuance of an order . . . prior to the implementation of such authorization."[164]

9. Targeting Non-U.S. Persons Outside the United States

In the wake of the 9/11 attacks, President George W. Bush authorized the NSA to conduct warrantless wiretapping of telephone and email communications where one party to the communication was located outside of the United States and a participant in the call was "reasonably believed to be a member or agent of al Qaeda or an affiliated terrorist organization."[165] However, based on public and media opposition to the telephone surveillance program, President George W. Bush asked Congress to amend FISA to provide the intelligence community with the authority to collect foreign intelligence information from non-U.S. persons located outside the United States. Congress responded by enacting the FISA Amendments Act of 2008 (FAA), 50 U.S.C. §1881a, which amended FISA and created a new framework for the Attorney General and Director of National

---

[161] *Id.* §1805(e)(3).

[162] *Id.* §1811.

[163] P.L. 95-511, Title VII, §702, as added P.L. 110-261, Title I, §101(a)(2), July 10, 2008, 122 Stat. 2438, *codified at* 50 U.S.C. §1881a(a).

[164] *Id.* §1881a(c)(2).

[165] *See* ACLU v. NSA, 493 F.3d 644, 648 (6th Cir. 2007).

Intelligence to seek approval of the FISC to authorize electronic surveillance targeting non-U.S. persons located outside the United States.[166]

Section 1881a authorizes the electronic surveillance of individuals who are not U.S. persons and are "reasonably believed" to be located outside of the United States.[167] Under the statute, "[n]otwithstanding any other provision of law, upon the issuance of an order in accordance with [50 U.S.C. §1881a(i)(3)] or a determination under [50 U.S.C. §1881a(c)(2)], the Attorney General and the Director of National Intelligence may authorize jointly, for a period of up to 1 year from the effective date of the authorization, the targeting of persons reasonably believed to be located outside the United States to acquire foreign intelligence information."[168] Section 1881a authorizes electronic surveillance on non-U.S. persons located outside the United States using either of two procedures. First, electronic surveillance is authorized upon issuance of an order by the FISC.[169] Second, electronic surveillance may be conducted without a court order on a "determination" by the Attorney General and Director of National Intelligence that exigent circumstances exist and "without immediate implementation of an authorization [of electronic surveillance] intelligence important to the national security of the United States may be lost or not timely acquired and time does not permit the issuance of an order . . . prior to the implementation of such authorization."[170]

a. The Application Process

In order to authorize electronic surveillance outside of the United States under the FAA, the Attorney General and the Director of National Intelligence must apply for and obtain a court order from the FISC, unless exigent circumstances exist that require immediate implementation.[171] Unlike §1804, which only requires approval by the Attorney General, an application for a FISA surveillance order under §1881a requires the joint approval of the Attorney General and

---

[166] P.L. 95-511, Title VII, §702, as added P.L. 110-261, Title I, §101(a)(2), July 10, 2008, 122 Stat. 2438. The FAA also added 50 U.S.C. §1881b, approving the targeting of a *U.S. person* reasonably believed to be located outside of the United States to acquire foreign intelligence information, if the acquisition constitutes electronic surveillance, stored electronic communications, or stored electronic data, and such acquisition is conducted within the United States. See 50 U.S.C. §1881b. Further, the FAA added §1881c, authorizing the targeting of a *U.S. person*, where there is probable cause to believe that the person is reasonably believed to be located outside the United States, and such person is a foreign power, or an officer or employee of a foreign power. 50 U.S.C. §1881c.

[167] 50 U.S.C. §1881a(a).

[168] *Id.*

[169] *Id.*

[170] *Id.* §1881a(c)(2).

[171] See *id.* §§1881a(a), (c)(2). The discussion of the application process for obtaining a surveillance order under §1881a is taken in large part from Jimmy Gurulé & Geoffrey Corn, Principles of Counter-Terrorism Law, *supra* note 89, at 221-22.

I. Foreign Intelligence Surveillance Act, 50 U.S.C. §§1801 *et seq.*

Director of National Intelligence.[172] A §1881a application must include a written certification and supporting affidavit under oath to the FISC.[173] The certification must attest, among other things, that there are "targeting procedures" in place that have been approved or submitted for approval by the FISC that are reasonably designed to ensure that the acquisition of foreign intelligence information is limited to persons reasonably believed to be located outside of the United States. These procedures must prevent the intentional acquisition of any communications as to which the sender and intended recipients are known to be located in the United States.[174] The certification must also attest that the government has "minimization procedures" in place that have been approved, have been submitted for approval, or will be submitted with the certification for approval by the FISC.[175] These procedures must follow the minimization procedures required for electronic surveillance set in §1801(h) or 1821(4) of FISA.[176] Further, the certificate must attest that guidelines have been adopted to ensure compliance with the limitations in section 1881a(b).[177]

Subsection 1881a(b) imposes certain limitations on the requested foreign electronic surveillance. The statute provides that the surveillance may not intentionally target: 1) any person known at the time of acquisition to be located in the United States; 2) any person reasonably believed to be located outside the United States if the purpose of such acquisition is to target a particular, known person reasonably believed to be in the United States; or 3) a U.S. person reasonably believed to be located outside the United States.[178] Also, the surveillance may not intentionally acquire any communications as to which the sender and all intended recipients are known to be located in the United States at the time of acquisition. Finally, the surveillance is required to be conducted in a manner consistent with the Fourth Amendment to the U.S. Constitution.[179]

The certification must also attest 1) that a "significant purpose" of the requested surveillance is to obtain foreign intelligence information,[180] 2) that the surveillance involves obtaining foreign intelligence information from or with the assistance of an electronic communications service provider,[181] and 3) that the surveillance complies with the limitations set forth in §1881a(b).[182] Further, the certificate must be supported by an affidavit of a senior national

---

[172] *See* 50 U.S.C. §1804 (only approval of the Attorney General required) and §1881a (approval of both the Attorney General and the Director of National Intelligence required).

[173] *Id.* §1881a(g)(1)(A).

[174] *Id.* §1881a(g)(2)(A)(i).

[175] *Id.* §1881a(g)(2)(A)(ii).

[176] *Id.* §1881a(g)(2)(A)(ii)(I).

[177] *Id.* §1881a(g)(2)(A)(iii).

[178] *Id.* §§1881a(b)(1)-(3).

[179] *Id.* §§1881a(b)(4)-(5).

[180] *Id.* §1881a(g)(2)(A)(v).

[181] *Id.* §1881a(g)(2)(A)(vi).

[182] *Id.* §1881a(g)(2)(A)(vii).

security official who is appointed by the President and confirmed by the Senate, or is the head of an element of the intelligence community.[183]

Finally, the certification required for a FISA application under the FAA is not required to identify the specific facilities, places, premises, or property at which the surveillance will be directed or conducted.[184] The government is also not required to identify the target of the requested surveillance or establish probable cause that the target of the surveillance is a foreign power or agent of a foreign power.[185] This represents a major departure from §1805(a)(2), which requires the FISC to find probable cause to believe that 1) the target of the surveillance is a foreign power or agent of a foreign power and 2) each of the facilities or places at which the electronic surveillance is directed is being used, or is about to be used, by a foreign power or an agent of a foreign power.[186]

b.   Issuance of an Order

To issue an order approving the government's application to conduct electronic surveillance on non-U.S. persons located outside the United States, the FISC must find that the certification complies with the requirements set forth in subsection (g), and that the targeting and minimization procedures are in accordance with subsections (d) and (e) as well as the Fourth Amendment of the U.S. Constitution.[187] The FISC must complete its review and issue an order not later than 30 days after the date on which the application for electronic surveillance is submitted for approval.[188]

The NSA's PRISM program allows the government direct access to the servers of internet communications providers in order to obtain stored internet communications.[189] The program is authorized by §1881a, which allows electronic surveillance of non-U.S. persons reasonably believed to be located outside of the United States.[190] Unlike the telephony metadata program, PRISM seizes the content of internet communications.[191] PRISM can collect, in real time, a wide breadth of data, including email, video and voice chat (i.e. Skype), file

---

[183] *Id.* §1881a(g)(2)(C).

[184] *Id.* §1881a(g)(4).

[185] *See* Amnesty Int'l USA v. McConnell, 646 F. Supp. 2d 633, 641 (S.D.N.Y. 2009).

[186] 50 U.S.C. §§1805(a)(2)(A)-(B). In June 2014, a district court upheld the constitutionality of §702 of FISA. *See* United States v. Mohamud, 2014 U.S. Dist. LEXIS 85452 (D. Or. 2014).

[187] 50 U.S.C. §1881a(i)(3)(A).

[188] *Id.* §1881a(i)(1)(B).

[189] *PRISM/US-984XN Overview*, NSA Training PowerPoint (Apr. 2013) [hereinafter *PRISM Overview*], *available at* https://www.aclu.org/files/natsec/nsa/20130816/PRISM%20Overview%20Powerpoint%20Slides.pdf.

[190] James Clapper, Directors of National Intelligence, Facts on the Collection of Intelligence Pursuant to Section 702 of the Foreign Intelligence Surveillance Act, June 8, 2013 [hereinafter DNI PRISM Statement], *available at* http://www.dni.gov/files/documents/Facts%20on%20the%20Collection%20of%20Intelligence%20Pursuant%20to%20Section%20702.pdf.

[191] *See PRISM Overview, supra* note 189.

transfers, search history, log in notifications, and social networking details.[192] Since the PRISM program gives the government direct access to the servers of these internet service providers, the NSA does not need to obtain individual court orders and request this data from those service providers.[193] Instead, the NSA need only have reasonable articulable suspicion that one of the parties is outside the United States at the time the communication occurs.[194] While PRISM focuses on non-U.S. persons located outside of the United States, there is a substantial risk that the telephone and email communications of U.S. persons will be inadvertently seized and reviewed.

B. *Legal Challenges to FISA*

1. Standing

In order to reach the merits of a constitutional challenge to a FISA surveillance or physical search order, the court must first determine whether the plaintiffs have standing to bring such cause of action.[195] Article III of the Constitution limits the jurisdiction of federal courts to "Cases" and "Controversies."[196] "The law of Article III standing, which is built on separation-of-powers principles, serves to prevent the judicial process from being used to usurp the powers of the political branches."[197] To establish Article III standing, an injury must be "concrete, particularized, and actual or imminent; fairly traceable to the challenged action; and redressable by a favorable ruling."[198] "[T]hreatened injury

---

[192] *Id.*

[193] *PRISM Tasking Process*, NSA Training PowerPoint (Apr. 2013), *available at* https://www.aclu.org/files/natsec/nsa/20130816/PRISM%20Powerpoint%20Slides%20re%20Data%20Acquisition.pdf.

[194] *See* DNI PRISM Statement, *supra* note 190.

[195] The courts draw a distinction between standing to challenge the government's compliance with the FISA statute and standing to challenge the constitutionality of the FISA order. Only the recipients of a FISA order, such as telecommunications service providers, have standing to challenge whether the electronic surveillance was lawful under FISA. The actual target of a FISA order lacks standing. *See Klayman*, 957 F. Supp. 2d at 23 (holding that "Congress did not intend for third parties, such as plaintiff phone subscribers[ ], to challenge the Government's compliance with the statute"); *See Clapper*, 959 F. Supp. 2d at 742 (holding that "the statutory scheme[ ] makes clear that Congress intended to preclude suits by targets even if they discovered section 215 orders implicating them"). However, FISA targets may raise constitutional challenges to the government's conduct if they can satisfy the standing requirements. *See, e.g., Klayman*, 957 F. Supp. 2d at 25 ("Because FISA contains no broad and seemingly comprehensive statutory language expressly barring judicial review of *any* claims under Section 1861, let alone any language directed at *constitutional* claims in particular, Congress has *not* demonstrated an intent to preclude constitutional claims. . . .") (emphasis in original) (internal citations omitted).

[196] U.S. Const. art. III, §3, cl. 1; *see also* Lujan v. Defenders of Wildlife, 504 U.S. 555, 559 (1992).

[197] Clapper v. Amnesty Int'l USA, 133 S. Ct. at 1146.

[198] Monsanto Co. v. Geerston Seed Farms, 561 U.S. 139 (2010).

must be 'certainly impending' to constitute injury in fact," and "[a]llegations of possible injury" are not sufficient.[199] Because the judicial power of federal courts "exists only to redress or otherwise protect against injury to the complaining party," a federal court's jurisdiction "can be invoked only when the plaintiff . . . has suffered 'some threatened or actual injury, resulting from the putatively illegal action. . . .'"[200] The party invoking the jurisdiction of the court bears the burden of establishing standing.[201] Finally, the plaintiff must assert his own rights, and cannot establish standing on the basis of the legal rights or interests of third parties.[202]

Plaintiffs attempting to challenge the constitutionality of FISA surveillance orders have struggled to establish standing.[203] In *Clapper v. Amnesty International USA*, respondents, a group of U.S. attorneys and human rights, labor, legal, and media organizations, challenged the 2008 FISA Amendments, codified at 50 U.S.C. §1881a.[204] The 2008 amendments authorize surveillance of individuals who are not "United States persons" and are reasonably believed to be outside the United States so long as there is reasonably articulable suspicion that such individuals are associated with a terrorist organization.[205] Respondents sought a declaration that the 2008 amendments were unconstitutional as well as an injunction against being surveilled under the provision.[206] However, the Supreme Court disagreed, and rejected respondents' cause of action. The Court held that respondents failed to establish standing "because they cannot demonstrate that the future injury they purportedly fear is certainly impending and because they cannot manufacture standing by incurring costs in anticipation of non-imminent harm."[207]

Respondents advanced two theories in support of their standing claim. First, given the nature of their clients and the communications they participated in, respondents asserted that their injury was fairly traceable to §1881a. Respondents regularly communicated with "people the Government believes or believed to be

---

[199] Whitmore v. Arkansas, 495 U.S. 149, 158 (1990).

[200] Warth v. Seldin, 422 U.S. 490, 499 (1975) (quoting Linda R.S. v. Richard D., 410 U.S. 614, 617 (1973)).

[201] Lujan v. Defenders of Wildlife, 504 U.S. at 561.

[202] *Warth*, 422 U.S. at 561.

[203] *See, e.g.*, ACLU v. NSA, 493 F.3d at 673 (holding that plaintiffs had failed to establish standing because their alleged injury was too speculative; further plaintiffs failed to satisfy the redressability element of proving standing).

[204] Clapper v. Amnesty Int'l USA, 133 S. Ct. at 1138. The United States District Court for the Southern District of New York granted summary judgment in favor of defendants, and plaintiffs appealed. *See* Amnesty Int'l USA v. McConnell, 646 F. Supp. 2d 663 (S.D.N.Y. 2009). The Second Circuit Court of Appeals reversed, 638 F.3d 118, and denied rehearing en banc, 667 F.3d 163. Defendants petitioned for certiorari.

[205] Clapper v. Amnesty Int'l USA, 133 S. Ct. at 1145-46. The 2008 amendments allow the government to conduct surveillance on these individuals without prior identification or a probable cause warrant.

[206] *Id.* at 1145.

[207] *Id.* at 1155.

associated with terrorist organizations, people located in geographic areas that are a special focus of the Government's counterterrorism or diplomatic efforts, and activists who oppose governments ... supported by the U.S. Government."[208] As such, respondents argued there was an objectively reasonable likelihood that surveillance authorized by the 2008 amendments.

Second, respondents argued that they could establish standing based on measures that they had undertaken to avoid §1881a surveillance.[209] More specifically, respondents maintained that they suffered present injury as a result of the risk of surveillance, which caused them to take costly and burdensome measures to protect the confidentiality of their communications.[210] Respondents claimed that conversations that would have previously occurred over the phone or via email with persons abroad now needed to be conducted in person for fear of revealing incriminating information about their clients to government authorities.[211]

The Supreme Court rejected the "objectively reasonable likelihood" standard applied by the Second Circuit in finding that respondents had standing because it was inconsistent with the requirement that a "threatened injury must be certainly impending to constitute injury in fact."[212] Not only did the Court find that any injury suffered by respondents was not certain or imminent, but it also held that respondents could not satisfy the requirement that the injury be fairly traceable to the law being challenged—here §1881a. In response to respondents' first theory that they had standing because of the risk that they would be subject to surveillance, the Court articulated a chain of speculation that would be required to support respondents' claim:

> [R]espondents' argument rests on their highly speculative fear that: (1) the Government will decide to target the communications of non-U.S. persons with whom they communicate; (2) in doing so, the Government will choose to invoke its authority under §1881a rather than utilizing another method of surveillance; (3) the Article III judges who serve on the Foreign Intelligence Surveillance Court will conclude that the Government's proposed surveillance procedures satisfy §1881a's many safeguards and are consistent with the Fourth Amendment; (4) the Government will succeed in intercepting the communications of respondents' contacts; and (5) respondents will be parties to the particular communications that the Government intercepts.[213]

The Court held that respondents' theory of standing, which relied on a highly attenuated chain of possibilities, did not satisfy the requirement that the threatened injury be certainly impending.[214] Further, the Court seems to suggest

---

[208] *Id.* at 1145.
[209] *Id.* at 1150.
[210] *Id.* at 1150-51.
[211] *Id.* at 1151.
[212] *Id.* at 1147 (quoting *Whitmore*, 495 U.S. at 158).
[213] Clapper v. Amnesty Int'l USA, 133 S. Ct. at 1148.
[214] *Id.*

that establishing standing would require proof that the FISC had actually approved a surveillance order against the plaintiff-target. However, because the FISC meets in secret and its orders are classified and not made public, standing could be proven only in a few rare cases.[215] First, if the government were to prosecute a FISA target and introduce evidence obtained pursuant to a FISA order at trial, the defendant would have an evidentiary basis for establishing standing.[216] Alternatively, an "electronic communications service provider" that the government employed to assist in implementing a §1881 surveillance order would have sufficient grounds to establish standing.[217]

Respondents' second argument—namely, that they can establish standing based on the measures that they had taken to avoid §1881a-authorized surveillance—fared no better. According to the Court, respondents' claim that they are suffering ongoing injuries that are fairly traceable to §1881a because the risk of surveillance requires them to take costly and burdensome measures to protect the confidentiality of their communications amounts to manufactured standing. The Court stated that "respondents cannot manufacture standing merely by inflicting harm on themselves based on their fears of hypothetical future harm that is not certainly impending."[218] Because respondents did not face a threat of certainly impending interception under §1881a, the Court found that the costs they incurred to avoid surveillance were simply the product of their fear of surveillance, which is insufficient to create standing.[219] While acknowledging that prior cases had held that constitutional violations may arise from the chilling effect of "regulations that fall short of a direct prohibition against the exercise of First Amendment rights," the Court declared that none of those cases involved a "chilling effect aris[ing] merely from the individual's knowledge that a governmental agency was engaged in certain activities or from the individual's concomitant fear that, armed with the fruits of those activities, the agency might in the future take some *other* and additional action detrimental to that individual."[220] Ultimately, because "[a]llegations of a subjective 'chill' are not an adequate substitute for a claim of specific present objective harm or a threat of specific future harm," the Court held that the respondents lacked standing.[221]

In a dissent joined by three other justices, Justice Breyer argued that the "certainly impending injury" standard was applied by the majority in an

---

[215] *See* Klayman v. Obama, 957 F. Supp. 2d 1, 26 (D.D.C. 2013) (distinguishing *Clapper v. Amnesty Int'l USA* and holding that plaintiffs had standing, reasoning that "whereas the plaintiffs in *Clapper* could only speculate as to whether they would be surveilled at all, plaintiffs in this case can point to strong evidence that, as Verizon customers, their telephony metadata has been collected for the last seven years (and stored for the last five) and will continue to be collected barring judicial or legislative intervention").

[216] Clapper v. Amnesty Int'l USA, 133 S. Ct. at 1154.

[217] *Id.* at 1154-55; *see also* In re Directives Pursuant to Section 105B, 551 F.3d at 1006-16 (holding that the electronic communications service provider had standing).

[218] Clapper v. Amnesty Int'l USA, 113 S. Ct. at 1151.

[219] *Id.* at 1152.

[220] *Id.* (internal citations omitted).

[221] *Id.* (internal citations omitted).

exceedingly stringent manner.[222] According to the dissent, the injury to be suffered by the respondents was so likely to occur that common sense dictated that they should have standing. In particular, the dissent articulated four primary considerations indicative of a "very high likelihood" of surveillance.[223] There was a high likelihood that the government, authority of §1881a, would seek to obtain surveillance of some of respondent's conversations because: 1) The kinds of communications engaged in by respondents were covered by the 2008 amendment, but not the prior Act;[224] 2) Respondents had a strong motive to engage in, and the government has a strong motive to listen to, conversations of the kind described;[225] 3) In the past, the government had sought, and in all likelihood, it will continue to seek, information about alleged terrorists through means that include surveillance of electronic surveillance;[226] and 4) The government had the capacity to conduct electronic surveillance of this kind, and the government's FISA requests are almost always granted by the FISC.[227] Justice Breyer argued that collectively, these considerations created a very strong likelihood that the government would intercept at least some of the respondents' communications, including some that the government was only authorized to obtain by 2008 amendment, §1881a, but not the pre-2008 Act.[228] Finally, the dissent argued that "certainty" of injury is not, and has never been, the touchstone of standing.[229] Instead, the phrase "certainly impending" describes a *"sufficient* rather than a *necessary,* condition for jurisdiction."[230] The dissent pointed to several cases where the Court applied a less demanding standard. For example, in *Pennell v. San Jose,* the Court found that a "realistic danger of sustaining a direct injury" was sufficient to prove standing.[231] Justice Breyer maintained that "certainly impending" has never been used as the standard for determining standing, and that the Constitution only requires something more akin to "reasonable probability" or "high probability."[232]

2. Fourth Amendment Challenges

FISA warrants have been challenged as a violation of the Fourth Amendment. Challengers have argued that FISA procedures 1) lack a particularity requirement, 2) lack reasonable durational limits, and 3) fail to provide adequate notice

---

[222] *Id.* at 1160.
[223] *Id.* at 1157.
[224] *Id.* at 1157-58.
[225] *Id.* at 1158.
[226] *Id.*
[227] *Id.* at 1158-59.
[228] *Id.* at 1159.
[229] *Id.* at 1160.
[230] *Id.*
[231] *Id.*
[232] *Id.* at 1165.

to persons whose communications are intercepted or premises are to be searched. However, every court that has ever considered the issue, except one, has rejected such claims and held that FISA does not violate the Fourth Amendment.[233] While the Supreme Court has not directly decided whether FISA surveillance and physical search warrants violate the Fourth Amendment, the FISC and FISCR have addressed the issue and rejected Fourth Amendment challenges.[234]

In *In re Application of the Federal Bureau of Investigation*, the FISC reviewed the government's application for an order authorizing the bulk collection of telephony metadata and call detail information from specified electronic communications service providers.[235] As previously discussed, pursuant to §215 of the USA PATRIOT Act, the FBI obtains orders from the FISC directing certain telecommunication service providers to produce the bulk telephone metadata of hundreds of millions of Americans. The purpose of the telephony metadata program is to detect whether known or suspected terrorists are engaged in contact with persons inside the United States. According to the government, the whole production of metadata is relevant to an authorized investigation because it is necessary for the effective use and application of the NSA's analytical tools.[236] The government further contends that substantive queries of the bulk records can only be conducted for counterterrorism purposes.[237] Authorized queries must begin with an "identifier," such as a telephone number previously identified and approved by the FISC.[238] Before a seed identifier can be used to query the

---

[233] *See, e.g.*, United States v. Abu-Jihaad, 630 F.3d 102; In re Directives Pursuant to Sec. 105B, 551 F.3d 1004 (United States v. Wen, 477 F.3d 896, 898 (7th Cir. 2007); In re Sealed Case, 310 F.3d at 742-46; United States v. Pelton, 835 F.2d 1067, 1075 (4th Cir. 1987); United States v. Cavanaugh, 807 F.2d 787, 790-91 (9th Cir. 1987); United States v. Duggan, 743 F.2d 59; United States v. Mubayyid, 521 F. Supp. 2d 125, 140-41 (D. Mass. 2007); United States v. Holy Land Found. for Relief & Dev., 2007 WL 2011319, at *5-6 (N.D. Tex. 2007); United States v. Sattar, 2003 WL 22137012, at *3-5 (S.D.N.Y. 2003); ACLU v. United States Dep't of Justice, 265 F. Supp. 2d 20, 32 & n.12 (D.D.C. 2003). *But see* Mayfield v. United States, 504 F. Supp. 2d 1023, 1036-43 (D. Or. 2007).

[234] In *Keith*, the Supreme Court addressed the constitutionality of the use of warrantless electronic surveillance against a purely domestic target. *See generally* Keith, 407 U.S. 297 (1972). The Supreme Court held that, in the case of intelligence gathering involving purely domestic surveillance, prior judicial approval was required to satisfy the Fourth Amendment. *Id.* at 321. However, the Court emphasized that its holding was limited to cases involving the domestic aspects of national security. *Id.* The Court declared: "We have not addressed, and express no opinion as to, the issues which may be involved with respect to activities of foreign powers or their agents." *Id.* at 321-22.

[235] *In re Application of the Federal Bureau of Investigation*, *supra* note 2. Telephone metadata includes comprehensive communication routing information, including the originating and terminating telephone numbers, as well as the date, time, and duration of the call, but not the content of the communications. *Id.* at 2 n.2; *see also White Paper on Bulk Collection of Telephony Metadata*, *supra* note 2, at 3.

[236] *See White Paper on Bulk Collection of Telephony Metadata*, *supra* note 2, at 4. "It would be impossible to conduct these queries effectively without a large pool of telephony metadata to search, as there is no way to know in advance which numbers will be responsive to the authorized queries." *Id.*

[237] *Id.* at 3.

[238] *Id.*

accumulated metadata, there must be reasonably articulable suspicion (RAS), formed on the basis of specific facts, that the seed identifier is "associated with a specific [FTO] previously identified by the Court."[239] The RAS standard arguably prevents the government from indiscriminately searching the collected data. But according to an internal NSA memo, this standard "does not present a particularly high hurdle," and is comparable to the level of suspicion required for a *Terry* Stop—meaning there must be some "minimal level of objective justification," as opposed to an "inchoate and unparticularized suspicion or 'hunch.'"[240]

In reviewing the government's request to renew authorization for the telephony metadata program, the FISC considered whether the seizure of the requested records violates the Fourth Amendment.[241] The Court upheld the constitutionality of the seizure of the telephone metadata, holding that any Fourth Amendment issues raised by the program are "squarely controlled" by *Smith v. Maryland*.[242] The Supreme Court decided *Smith v. Maryland* in 1979, holding that a person does not have a legitimate expectation of privacy in the type of metadata collected by the NSA.[243]

In *Smith*, police were investigating a robbery victim who claimed that she had received threatening phone calls from someone claiming to be the robber.[244] Without obtaining a warrant, police requested the telephone company to install a pen register on the defendant's phone line, which revealed that a telephone in Smith's house had been used to call the victim.[245] The Supreme Court held that Smith had no reasonable expectation of privacy in the numbers dialed from his phone because be voluntarily transmitted them to the phone company. In *Smith*, the Court articulated the Third-Party Doctrine, finding that once a person has transmitted this information to a third party (in this case, a telephone company), the person "has no legitimate expectation of privacy in [the] information. . . ."[246] "Telephone users . . . typically know that they must convey numerical information to the phone company; that the phone company has facilities for recording this information; and that the phone company does in fact record this information for a variety of legitimate business purposes."[247] According to the Court, the

---

[239] Letter from Preet Bharara, United States Attorney, Southern District of New York, to Hon. William H. Pauley, AT 2 (July 18, 2013). Seed identifiers must be approved by one of 22 designated officials in the NSA's Homeland Security Analysis Center. *Id.*

[240] *Memorandum for the Deputy Program Manager for Counterterrorism Special Projects, Analysis and Production: Assessments of Reasonable Articulable Suspicion Pursuant to Orders of the [FISC]*, at 2 (Aug. 29, 2008) (citing to Terry v. Ohio, 392 U.S. 1, 27 (1968)).

[241] In re Application of the Federal Bureau of Investigation, *supra* note 2.

[242] *Id.* at 6.

[243] Smith v. Maryland, 442 U.S. 735 (1979).

[244] *Id.* at 737.

[245] *Id.*

[246] *Id.* The holding in *Smith* built on the ruling in United States v. Miller, 425 U.S. 435 (1976), where the Supreme Court held that a person does not have a legitimate expectation of privacy in their bank records. The bank records are the bank's business records of how the account was used and therefore the customer has no reasonable privacy rights in the information.

[247] *Smith*, 422 U.S. at 743.

telephone user, having conveyed this information to a telephone company that retains the information in the ordinary course of business, assumes the risk that the company will provide that information to the government.[248] Finally, the Court reasoned that once the caller sends the information to the phone company, and the phone company uses it, the information is the phone company's record of what it did, not the user's property.[249]

The FISC applied the reasoning of *Smith* to the bulk collection of telephone metadata, holding that "because the Application at issue here concerns only the production of call detail records or 'telephony metadata' belonging to a telephone company and not the contents of communications, *Smith v. Maryland* compels the conclusion that there is no Fourth Amendment impediment to the collection."[250] Further, while *Smith* involved the collection of telephone records of a single customer, and the NSA metadata program involves obtaining call records of hundreds of millions of Americans and aggregating them in a massive database, the FISC found that the scale of the records obtained did not make a constitutional difference.[251] In other words, if obtaining pen register information on one user is not a search under the Fourth Amendment, obtaining telephony metadata of millions of users is still not a search because there is no legitimate expectation of privacy in the information collected.

It should be noted that the proceedings were conducted *ex parte* under security procedures mandated by 50 U.S.C. §1803(c), and FISC Rules 3, 17(1)-(b). Because of the secretive nature of the proceedings the FISC only heard from one side—the government. The FISC did not have the benefit of considering arguments countering the government's position. The FISC is a secret court that listens to one-sided petitions of intelligence agencies

---

[248] *Id.* at 744.

[249] *Id.* at 745.

[250] *In re Application of the Federal Bureau of Investigation, supra* note 2, at 9. Lower courts have applied the same principles to the collection of Internet metadata. *See* United States v. Forrester, 512 F.3d 500, 510 (9th Cir. 2008) (IP addresses); United States v. Perrine, 518 F.3d 1196, 1204 (10th Cir. 2008) ("Every federal court to address this issue has held that subscriber information provided to an internet provider is not protected by the Fourth Amendment's privacy expectation."). However, courts have been divided on whether the Fourth Amendment applies to cell-site information collection. The majority view is that cell-site location is unprotected under Smith v. Maryland, 425 U.S. 435 (1979), *e.g.,* In re U.S. for Historical Cell Site Data, 724 F.3d 600 (5th Cir. 2013); United States v. Skinner, 690 F.3d 772 (6th Cir. 2012); United States v. Booker, 2013 WL 2903562 (N.D. Ga. 2013); United States v. Graham, 846 F. Supp. 2d 384, 389 (D. Md. 2012); United States v. Benford, 2010 WL 1266507, at *3 (N.D. Ind. 2010). *But see* State v. Earls, 70 A.3d 630 (N.J. 2013) (holding that users of cellular telephones had a legitimate expectation of privacy in information revealing the location of the telephone).

[251] *In re Application of the Federal Bureau of Investigation, supra* note 2, at 9. The FISC's conclusion is based on two premises. First, the Fourth Amendment protects individuals, not places; second, an individual has no reasonable expectation of privacy in his or her metadata. As a result, "where one individual does not have a Fourth Amendment interest, grouping together a large number of similarly-situated individuals cannot result in a Fourth Amendment interest springing into existence *ex nihilo.*" *Id.*

with strong institutional incentives to tip the balance towards national security.[252]

Since the *Guardian*'s June 5, 2013 publication of the FISC order renewing authorization for the telephony metadata program, challenges to the NSA's program have been filed in federal courts across the country.[253] As of the time of the publication of this book, two district courts had ruled on Fourth Amendment challenges to the telephony metadata program. On December 16, 2013, Judge Leon of the U.S. District Court for the District of Columbia became the first federal judge to hold that the NSA program violated the Fourth Amendment. In *Klayman v. Obama,* the district court found that *Smith* does not govern the NSA's bulk collection of telephony metadata and held that the program was unconstitutional.[254] Eleven days later, on December 27, 2013, U.S. District Judge Pauley of the Southern District of New York dismissed a Fourth Amendment challenge to the telephony metadata program in *ACLU v. Clapper*.[255] These conflicting decisions illustrate the difficulty of reconciling existing Fourth Amendment precedent with modern technological advancements. The different outcomes in these two decisions can be mainly attributed to the way in which each court applied the metadata precedent in *Smith v. Maryland.*

In *Klayman v. Obama,* the district court distinguished *Smith* on a number of grounds, and found that *Smith* does not govern the NSA's bulk collection of metadata. The court noted that the pen register in *Smith* was operational for only a matter of days, while the metadata program involves the creation and maintenance of a historical database containing five years' worth of data.[256] Moreover, the court found that due to advances in cell phone technology "people in 2013 have an entirely different relationship with phones than they did thirty-four years ago."[257] This has resulted in a corresponding transformation in the nature and

---

[252] The FISC's small size prohibits the Court from independently verifying the information contained in government surveillance applications. Instead, the FISC "is forced to rely upon the accuracy of the information that is provided" by the intelligence agencies. *See* Carol D. Leonnig, *Court: Ability to Police U.S. Spying Program Limited*, WASH. POST, Aug. 15, 2013 (statement of the Chief Judge of the FISC). The FISC's dependence on the government's one-sided information is in and of itself a cause for constitutional concern; while the FISC technically operates as an Article III court, it does not hear cases or controversies but listens only to the NSA. At the very least, however, it casts serious doubt on the FISC's ability to act as a meaningful, effective, and independent check on executive excess within the FISA framework.

[253] Klayman v. Obama, Civ. No. 1:13-0851 (D.D.C) (complaint filed June 6, 2013); ACLU v. Clapper, Civ. No. 13-3994 (S.D.N.Y) (complaint filed June 11, 2013); In re Electronic Privacy Information Center, No. 13-58 (S. Ct) (Petition for a Writ of Mandamus and Prohibition, or a Writ of Certiorari (filed July 8, 2013; petition denied Nov. 18, 2013); First Unitarian Church of Los Angeles v. NSA, Civ. No. 13-3287 (N.D. Cal.) (complaint filed July 16, 2013).

[254] *See generally Klayman*, 957 F. Supp. 2d 1.

[255] *See generally Clapper*, 959 F. Supp. 2d 724.

[256] *Klayman*, 957 F. Supp. 2d at 32.

[257] *Id.* at 34.

quantity of information contained in telephony metadata.[258] The court in *Klayman* posited: "the *Smith* pen register and the ongoing NSA Bulk Telephony Metadata Program have so many significant distinctions between them that I cannot possibly navigate these uncharted Fourth Amendment waters using as my North Star a case that predates the rise of cell phones."[259]

The decision in *Smith* was largely based on the Third-Party Doctrine, under which individuals have no reasonable expectation of privacy in metadata because they voluntarily convey that information to telephone companies for billing purposes. As such, collection of metadata can never amount to a Fourth Amendment search. The Third-Party Doctrine articulated in *Smith* has come under recent criticism. In *United States v. Jones*, the Supreme Court held that attaching a GPS device to a car for one month constituted a trespass in violation of the owner's Fourth Amendment rights.[260] Justice Sotomayor, concurring in *Jones*, suggested that the Third-Party Doctrine may need to be reconsidered:

> [I]t may be necessary to reconsider the premise that an individual has no reasonable expectation of privacy in information voluntarily disclosed to third parties. This approach is ill suited to the digital age, in which people reveal a great deal of information about themselves to third parties in the course of carrying out mundane tasks. People disclose the phone numbers that they dial or text to their cellular providers; the URLs that they visit and the e-mail addresses with which they correspond to their Internet service providers; and the books, groceries, and medications they purchase from online retailers.[261]

Justice Sotomayor continued by stating that she doubts "people would accept without complaint the warrantless disclosure to the Government of a list of every Web site they have visited in the last week, or month, or year."[262] She further argued that surveillance justified by the Third-Party Doctrine allows the

---

[258] *See generally* Decl. of Prof. Edward W. Felten [hereinafter Felten Decl.] [Dkt. # 22-1], at ¶¶ 16-20. "Modern metadata can reveal intimate details such as "our religion, if a person regularly makes no calls on the Sabbath, or makes a large number of calls on Christmas Day . . . civil and political affiliations . . . the rise and fall of intimate relationships, the diagnosis of a life-threatening disease, [and] the telltale signs of a corporate merger or acquisition."

[259] *Klayman*, 957 F. Supp. 2d at 37; *see also* Privacy and Civil Liberties Oversight Board, Report on the Telephone Records Program Conducted under Section 215 of the USA PATRIOT Act and on the Operations of the Foreign Intelligence Surveillance Act, at 114 (Jan. 23, 2014) (stating that *Smith* "does not provide a good fit for the telephone records program, particularly in light of rapid technological changes and in light of the nationwide, ongoing nature of the program").

[260] United States v. Jones, 565 U.S. ___, 132 S. Ct. 954 (2012). In *Jones*, the majority's reasoning was based on the theory of trespass. Four justices concurred in the majority's result, but based their reasoning solely on the long-term use of the device. *Id.* at 957 (Alito, J., concurring). Justice Sotomayor joined the majority but wrote separately and based her decision on both trespass and the long-term use of the device. *Id.* at 955-57 (Sotomayor, J., concurring). Thus, five of the current nine Justices agree that surveillance that is reasonable in the short-term can rise to the level of a Fourth Amendment search if conducted for longer periods or on a larger scale.

[261] *Id.* at 957.

[262] *Id.*

government to "evade the ordinary checks that constrain abusive law enforcement practices: limited police . . . resources and community hostility."[263] Instead, the approach advocated by Justice Sotomayor in *Jones* would take into account the unique attributes of the type of surveillance conducted or contemplated "when considering the existence of a reasonable societal expectation of privacy in the *sum* of [the information collected]."[264]

Smith was decided in 1979, two years before the first commercial cell phones were even available in North America.[265] Today, over 91 percent of American adults have a cell phone.[266] Creation of metadata is involuntary when using a cell phone, and individuals are forced to rely on service providers in order to transmit calls, text messages, and other sensitive data. The Third-Party Doctrine, based on the premise that individuals *voluntarily* convey metadata to telecommunication providers, is difficult to apply today, where many people are required to use a cell phone in the scope of their employment and the "only reliable way to avoid creating metadata is to avoid telephonic communication altogether."[267] Moreover, the structured nature of metadata makes it easy to collect, aggregate, and analyze, therefore it is particularly susceptible to abuse by law enforcement.

Justice Alito's concurring opinion in *Jones* supports the view that long-term surveillance violates the target's reasonable expectation of privacy. According to Justice Alito, the Fourth Amendment issue should be analyzed by asking "whether the respondent's reasonable expectation of privacy was violated by the long-term monitoring of the movement of the vehicle he drove."[268] Justice Alito maintains that long-term use of GPS monitoring in criminal investigations impinges on a person's reasonable expectation of privacy.[269] While Justice Alito did not state at what point in time GPS surveillance would become an unreasonable search under the Fourth Amendment, he suggested that "where uncertainty exists with respect to whether a certain period of GPS surveillance is long enough to constitute a Fourth Amendment search, the police may always seek a warrant."[270] Justice Alito's view that long-term GPS surveillance constitutes a search under the Fourth Amendment has obvious application to the NSA telephony metadata program. Under Justice Alito's reasoning, *Smith* does not answer whether a reasonable expectation arises when the metadata of 300 million individuals is indefinitely collected in bulk, aggregated, and stored for five years.

---

[263] *Id.* at 955-56 (Sotomayor, J., concurring).

[264] *Id.* at 956 (emphasis added).

[265] Tom Farley, *Mobile Telephone History*, TELEKTRONIKK, Apr. 2005, 28 ("The first North American commercial system began in August, 1981 in Mexico City.").

[266] Joanna Brenner, Pew Internet: Mobile, Sept. 18, 2013, http://pewintemet.org/Intemet-Mobile.aspx.

[267] *See* Felten Decl., *supra* note 258, at 13.

[268] *Jones*, 132 S. Ct. at 958 (Alito, J., concurring). In *Jones*, federal officers attached a GPS tracking device to a suspect's car without a warrant, which was able to pinpoint the car's movements "within 50 to 100 feet for nearly one month." *Id.* at 948.

[269] *Id.* at 962.

[270] *Id.*

In *In re Sealed Case*, the FISCR had the opportunity to consider whether a FISA order authorizing electronic surveillance of the contents of telephone communications violates the Fourth Amendment's reasonableness requirement.[271] Ultimately, the FISCR upheld the FISA surveillance order.[272] It began its analysis by comparing the requirements for obtaining a surveillance order under FISA and Title III, which authorizes surveillance for law enforcement purposes. The court observed that the Warrant Clause of the Fourth Amendment has three essential requirements: 1) prior judicial review by a neutral and disinterested magistrate; 2) probable cause to believe that the evidence sought will aid in apprehension and prosecution for a particular criminal offense; and 3) that the warrant particularly describe the "things to be seized" and the "place to be searched."[273]

Addressing the first requirement, the FISCR held that both FISA and Title III require *ex parte* judicial review of an application for an order authorizing electronic surveillance. The court found that judicial review by the FISC of the surveillance application satisfied the Fourth Amendment's requirement of prior review by a "neutral and detached magistrate."[274] According to the FISCR, the FISC is a "detached and neutral body" for purposes of the Fourth Amendment.[275] Other courts have embraced this view, finding that the FISA court provides "neutral and responsible oversight of the government's activities in intelligence surveillance."[276] Thus, because FISA interposes a neutral and detached judicial officer between the government and the target of the surveillance, FISA satisfies the judicial review requirement.

Next, in *In re Sealed Case*, the FISCR turned to the probable cause requirement, conceding that FISA and Title III differ in their probable cause showings.[277] Title III allows a court to enter a surveillance order if it finds "there is probable cause for belief that an individual is committing, has committed, or is about to commit" a specified crime.[278] FISA, on the other hand, requires a showing of probable cause that the target is a foreign power or agent of a foreign power

---

[271] In re Sealed Case, 310 F.3d at 717.

[272] *Id.* at 746.

[273] *Id.* at 738 (quoting Dalia v. United States, 441 U.S. 238, 255 (1979)).

[274] In re Sealed Case, 310 F.3d at 738.

[275] *Id.*

[276] United States v. Cavanaugh, 807 F.2d at 790; *see also, e.g.,* United States v. Mubayyid, 521 F. Supp. 2d at 136 ("Although judicial review of FISA applications is certainly more circumscribed than that of search warrant applications generally, it is far from a meaningless rubber-stamp."); United States v. Spanjol, 720 F. Supp. 2d 55, 58 (E.D. Pa. 1989) ("FISA's procedure for obtaining judicial authorization of the Government's electronic surveillance for foreign intelligence purposes interposes a neutral and detached judicial officer between the Government and the target of the surveillance. As such it satisfies the warrant requirement of the Fourth Amendment."); United States v. Megahey, 553 F. Supp. at 1190 ("[T]he FISA warrant is a warrant within the meaning of the Fourth Amendment, since it provides for the interposition of independent judicial magistrates between the executive and the subject of the surveillance which the warrant requirement was designed to assure.").

[277] In re Sealed Case, 310 F.3d at 738.

[278] *Id.* (quoting 18 U.S.C. §2518(3)(a)).

I. Foreign Intelligence Surveillance Act, 50 U.S.C. §§1801 *et seq.*

and that each of the facilities or places at which electronic surveillance is to be directed is used by a foreign power or agent of a foreign power.[279] However, the FISCR found that the differences were not constitutionally significant. While the two probable cause standards differ, the court held that those differences appear reasonably adapted to the particular challenges of foreign intelligence gathering. The court stated that FISA is sufficiently limited and applies only "to certain carefully delineated and particularly serious foreign threats to national security."[280] Further, the court noted that in *United States v. United States District Court* (the *Keith* case), the Supreme Court recognized that the focus of security surveillance "may be less precise than that directed against more conventional types of crime" even in the area of domestic threats to national security.[281]

Addressing the first particularity requirement of the Warrant Clause (particularly describing the things to be seized), the FISCR observed that Title III requires probable cause to believe that particular communications about the specified crime will be obtained through electronic surveillance. FISA, on the other hand, requires an official to delineate the type of foreign intelligence information being sought, and to certify that such information is foreign intelligence information.[282] Further, to ensure that only pertinent information is sought, the certification must be made by a national security officer and approved by the Attorney General or Deputy Attorney General.[283] According to the court, this certification assures written accountability within the executive branch and provides "an internal check on Executive Branch arbitrariness."[284]

With respect to the second element of particularity (particularly describing the facilities subject to surveillance), the FISCR recognized that Title III and FISA have different particularity requirements. Title III generally requires probable cause to believe that the facilities subject to surveillance are being used or about to be used in connection with the commission of a crime or are leased to, listed in the name of, or used by the individual committing the crime, 18 U.S.C. §2518(3)(d). FISA, on the other hand, requires probable cause to believe that each of the facilities or places at which the surveillance is directed is being used, or is about to be used, by a foreign power or its agent, 50 U.S.C. §1805(a)(3)(B).[285] While Title III requires the government to show a nexus between the facilities and communications regarding the criminal offense, the government does not have to show any connection to the target of surveillance. Instead, the Title III particularity requirement is satisfied so long as "an individual"—not necessarily

---

[279] In re Sealed Case, 310 F.3d at 738 (citing 50 U.S.C. §1805(a)(3)).

[280] In re Sealed Case, 310 F.3d at 739.

[281] *Id.* at 738 (citing *Keith*, 407 U.S. at 297). In *Keith*, the Supreme Court rejected a claim of inherent executive authority to conduct warrantless *domestic* security surveillance, but failed to decide the scope of executive authority to conduct surveillance "with respect to activities of *foreign* powers or their agents." *Id.* at 321-22 (emphasis added).

[282] In re Sealed Case, 310 F.3d at 739.

[283] *Id.*

[284] *Id.*

[285] *Id.* at 739-40.

the target—is committing a crime.[286] Conversely, FISA requires probable cause to believe the target be the agent of a foreign power who is using or is about to use the targeted facility.[287] Thus, "FISA requires less of a nexus between the facility and the pertinent communications than Title III, but more of a nexus between the target and the pertinent communications."[288] Accordingly, the FISCR held that FISA's particularity requirements, while different from those of Title III, satisfy the Fourth Amendment.[289]

The FISCR considered other elements of Title III that some courts have determined to be constitutionally significant: necessity, duration, and minimization of surveillance.[290] The court concluded that both Title III and FISA have a "necessity" provision, which requires that the information sought be unobtainable through normal investigative procedures.[291] The statutes also have durational provisions; Title III orders may last for 30 days, while FISA orders may last up to 90 days for U.S. persons.[292] However, the FISCR stated that the longer period for FISA orders is justified based on the nature of national security surveillance, which is "often long range and involves the interrelation of various sources and types of information."[293] Further, the FISCR noted that FISA requires minimization procedures governing the acquisition, retention, and dissemination of non-public information.[294]

Finally, the FISCR focused on the differences between FISA and Title III concerning notice. While Title III requires notice to the target once the surveillance order expires, FISA does not require notice to a person whose communications were intercepted unless the government "intends to enter into evidence or otherwise use or disclose" such communications in a trial or other enumerated proceeding against the target.[295] For example, if evidence obtained through a FISA surveillance order is used in a criminal proceeding, notice to the defendant is required. According to the Court, Congress made a deliberate decision that nondisclosure was justified to preserve secrecy for sensitive counterintelligence sources and methods.[296] Given the balance of competing interests, the FISCR found that the FISA notice requirements are not unreasonable and do not violate the Fourth

---

[286] *Id.* at 740.

[287] *Id.*

[288] *Id.*

[289] *Id.*; *see also* United States v. Cavanaugh, 807 F.2d at 791 ("We reject appellant's suggestion that FISA violates the Fourth Amendment's particularity requirement. . . . "); United States v. Mubayyid, 521 F. Supp. 2d at 138 (FISA satisfies the particularity requirement of the Fourth Amendment).

[290] In re Sealed Case, 310 F.3d at 740.

[291] *Id.* (citing 18 U.S.C. §2518(3)(c); 50 U.S.C. §§1804(a)(7)(e)(II), 1805(A)(5)).

[292] In re Sealed Case, 310 F.3d at 740 (citing 18 U.S.C. §2518(5); 50 U.S.C. §1805(e)(a)).

[293] In re Sealed Case, 310 F.3d at 740 (quoting *Keith*, 407 U.S. at 332).

[294] In re Sealed Case, 310 F.3d at 740 Act. Every Title III order must contain a provision stating that the surveillance will be conducted "in such a way as to minimize the interception of communications not otherwise subject to interception under this chapter" and that it will "terminate upon attainment of the authorized objective[.]" 18 U.S.C. §2518(5).

[295] *Id.* at 741 (citing 50 U.S.C. §1806(c)).

[296] *Id.*

I. Foreign Intelligence Surveillance Act, 50 U.S.C. §§1801 *et seq.*

Amendment.[297] The FISCR posited that "the procedures and government showings under FISA, if they do not meet the minimum Fourth Amendment warrant standards, certainly come close."[298] Balancing the competing interests of protecting an individual's privacy interests and national security, the court held that FISA's surveillance provisions satisfy the Fourth Amendment's reasonableness requirement.[299]

Finally, the FISCR maintained that FISA surveillance orders could be upheld under the "special needs" exception to the warrant requirement.[300] The Supreme Court has upheld warrantless searches that are designed to serve the government's "special needs, beyond the normal need for law enforcement."[301] Examples of such "special needs" include apprehending drunk drivers and securing the border.[302] FISA surveillance warrants are issued for the purpose of gathering foreign intelligence information and protecting national security—interests which, according to the FISCR, are beyond the ordinary need of law enforcement.[303]

In *In re Directives Pursuant to Sec. 105B*, the FISCR relied on the special needs doctrine in rejecting a Fourth Amendment challenge to the warrantless surveillance of certain persons reasonably believed to be located outside of the United States.[304] A communications service provider challenged directives issued by the government pursuant to the Protect America Act (PAA) commanding petitioner to assist in conducting the warrantless surveillance of certain customers reasonably believed to be located outside the United States.[305] The FISCR found that the

---

[297] *Id.*; *see also* United States v. Mubayyid, 521 F. Supp. 2d at 139 (FISA's notice provisions do not violate the Fourth Amendment).

[298] In re Sealed Case, 310 F.3d at 746.

[299] *Id.*; *see also* United States v. Abu-Jihaad, 630 F.3d at 102 (holding that "certification of a significant purpose to obtain foreign intelligence information, together with satisfaction of all other FISA requirements, is reasonable and therefore, sufficient to support the issuance of a warrant under the Fourth Amendment").

[300] In re Sealed Case, 310 F.3d at 745-46.

[301] Vernonia School Dist. 47J v. Acton, 515 U.S. 646, 653 (1995) (quoting Griffin v. Wisconsin, 483 U.S. 868, 873 (1987) (internal quotation marks omitted)) (random drug-testing of student athletes).

[302] *Vernonia School Dist. 47J*, 515 U.S. at 654 (citing Michigan Dep't of State Police v. Sitz, 496 U.S. 444 (1990), and United States v. Martinez-Fuerte, 428 U.S. 543 (1976)).

[303] In re Sealed Case, 310 F.3d at 746. *But see Klayman*, 957 F. Supp. 2d at 39 (rejecting application of the special needs exception to the seizure of telephone metadata, stating: "To my knowledge . . . no court has ever recognized a special need sufficient to justify continuous, daily searches of virtually every American citizen without any particularized suspicion.").

[304] In re Directives Pursuant to Sec. 105B, 551 F.3d at 1004. The FISCR held that petitioner had standing to mount a challenge to the legality of the FISA directives based on the Fourth Amendment rights of third-party customers. *Id.* at 1008. The court reasoned that petitioner "faces an injury in the nature of the burden that it must shoulder to facilitate the government's surveillances of its customers; that injury is obviously and indisputably caused by the government through the directives; and the court is capable of redressing the injury." *Id.*

[305] The PAA provisions sunset on February 16, 2008, and were repealed on July 10, 2008. However, provisions authorizing surveillance targeting non-U.S. persons located outside of the United States to acquire foreign intelligence information were enacted as part of the FISA Amendments Act (FAA) of 2008 (codified at 50 U.S.C. §1881a). However, §1881a requires that an application for electronic surveillance abroad be submitted to the FISC for approval. *See* 50 U.S.C. §1881a(i)(1).

warrantless surveillance fell within the "special needs" exception to the Fourth Amendment's Warrant Clause.[306]

To fall within the "special needs" exception to the warrant requirement, the government must prove 1) that the purpose behind the search and seizure is beyond the normal needs of law enforcement, and 2) that insistence upon a warrant would materially interfere with the accomplishment of that purpose.[307] Applying the two-part test, the FISCR concluded that the central purpose of the FISA surveillance order was to collect foreign intelligence information, not information primarily related to ordinary criminal-law enforcement.[308] Thus, the purpose of the government's action was beyond normal law enforcement, satisfying the first prong of the two-part test.[309] Next, the FISCR posited that there was a high degree of probability that requiring a warrant would hinder the government's ability to gather time-sensitive information and undermine vital national security interests.[310] For these reasons, the FISCR held that the FISA-authorized warrantless surveillance did not violate the Fourth Amendment.[311]

The FISC also held that the warrantless surveillance of persons believed to be located abroad constitutes a reasonable exercise of government power under the Fourth Amendment. The FISCR stated that the reasonableness of the government's actions must be considered against the totality of the circumstances.[312] Further, the totality of circumstances analysis requires balancing the competing interests at stake—namely, the privacy rights of targeted persons against the government's interest in protecting national security.[313] The FISCR posited that national security is an interest of the "highest order or magnitude."[314] The FISCR also emphasized the statute's procedural protections, including those mandated under the certification requirement.[315] Those safeguards, the FISCR observed, comprise at least five components: "targeting procedures, minimization procedures, a procedure to ensure that a significant purpose is to obtain

---

[306] In re Directives Pursuant to Sec. 105B, 551 F.3d at 1016.

[307] Id. at 1010; see also Vernonia Sch. Dist. 47J v. Acton, 515 U.S. at 1995 (upholding the warrantless drug testing of high school athletes, explaining that the exception to the warrant requirement applies "when special needs, beyond the normal need for law enforcement, make the warrant and probable cause requirement[s] impracticable") (quoting Griffin, 483 U.S. at 873); Skinner v. Railway Labor Execs. Ass'n, 489 U.S. 602, 620 (1989) (upholding drug and alcohol testing of railroad workers when the testing was implemented because of safety considerations, not law enforcement concerns).

[308] In re Directives Pursuant to Sec. 105B, 551 F.3d at 1011.

[309] Id.

[310] Id.

[311] Id. at 1012. But see Klayman, 957 F. Supp. 2d at 39 (rejecting the application of the special needs exception to the seizure to telephone metadata).

[312] In re Directives Pursuant to Sec. 105B, 551 F.3d at 1012. See also Samson v. California, 547 U.S. 843, 848 (2006); Tennessee v. Garner, 471 U.S. 1, 8-9 (1985).

[313] In re Directives Pursuant to Sec. 105B, 551 F.3d at 1012.

[314] Id.; see also Haig v. Agee, 453 U.S. 280, 307 (1981) (quoting Aptheker v. Secretary of State, 378 U.S. 500, 509 (1964) ("It is 'obvious and unarguable' that no governmental interest is more compelling than the security of the Nation.").

[315] In re Directives Pursuant to Sec. 105B, 551 F.3d at 1013.

foreign intelligence information, procedures incorporated through Executive Order 1233, §2.5, and procedures outlined in an affidavit supporting the certifications."[316] The FISCR found that collectively these procedures require a showing of particularity, a meaningful probable cause determination, a showing of necessity, and a reasonable duration time limit not to exceed 90 days.[317] Thus, the FISCR held that "[b]alancing these findings against the vital nature of the government's national security interest and the manner of the intrusion . . . the surveillances at issue satisfy the Fourth Amendment's reasonableness requirement."[318]

3. Suppression of FISA Evidence in Criminal Prosecutions

Evidence obtained or derived from electronic surveillance, physical search, or the use of pen registers or trap and trace devices authorized under FISA may be used in a subsequent criminal prosecution if the use comports with FISA procedures.[319] FISA evidence can be used in federal or state criminal proceedings only with the prior authorization of the Attorney General.[320] Further, evidentiary use of FISA evidence requires that prior notice is given to the court and each "aggrieved person" against whom the information is to be used.[321] Upon receiving notice from the government, an aggrieved person may seek to suppress the use of the FISA-derived evidence on the grounds that the evidence was unlawfully acquired or the government did not act in conformity with the relevant FISA order.[322] Further, pursuant to 50 U.S.C. §§1806(f), 1825(g), and 1845(f), the defendant may move to compel disclosure of FISA materials, including the FISA applications, affidavits, court orders, and extensions, as well as any other documents related to the FISA surveillance, search, pen register, or trap and

---

[316] *Id.*

[317] *Id.* at 1016.

[318] *Id.*

[319] *See* 50 U.S.C. §§1806(b) (electronic surveillance), 1825(c) (physical search), and 1845(b) (pen register and trap and trace device).

[320] *Id.* §§1806(c), 1825(d), 1845(c).

[321] *Id.* FISA defines "aggrieved person" to mean "a person who is the target of an electronic surveillance or any other person whose communications or activities were subject to electronic surveillance. *Id.* §1801(k). With respect to physical searches, "aggrieved person" means a "person whose premises, property, information, or material is the target of physical search or any other person whose premises, property, information, or material was subject to physical search." *Id.* §1821(2). Finally, for use of FISA evidence derived from a pen register or trap and trace device, "aggrieved person" means any person—"(A) whose telephone line was subject to the installation or use of a pen register or trap and trace device, or (B) whose communication instrument or device was subject to the use of a pen register or trap and trace device." *Id.* §§1841(3)(A)-(B).

[322] *See* United States v. Abu-Jihaad, 531 F. Supp. 2d 299, 303-04 (D. Conn. 2008); United States v. Rosen, 447 F. Supp. 2d 538, 545 (E.D. Va. 2006) (citing 50 U.S.C. §§1806(e) and 1825(f)). Section 1845(e) authorizes an aggrieved person to file a motion to suppress evidence derived from the use of a pen register or trap and trace device. 50 U.S.C. §1845(e).

trace order.[323] These materials may be necessary to support the defendant's motion to suppress the FISA evidence.[324]

If the defendant moves to compel the disclosure of FISA evidence, the Attorney General may oppose such a request by filing an affidavit stating that the disclosure "would harm the national security of the United States."[325] Upon filing such an affidavit, the district court must conduct an *in camera* and *ex parte* review of the FISA warrant application and related materials to determine whether the surveillance was "lawfully authorized and conducted."[326] After an *in camera* review, the district court has discretion to disclose portions of the documents, under appropriate protective procedures, "only where such disclosure is necessary to make an accurate determination of the legality of the surveillance [or physical search or use of the pen register or trap and trace device]."[327] According to the D.C. Circuit in *Belfield*, disclosure should be rare and occur—

> only where the court's initial review of the application, order, and fruits of the surveillance indicates that the question of legality may be complicated by factors such as "indications of possible misrepresentations of fact, vague identification of the persons to be surveilled, or surveillance records which include a significant amount of nonforeign intelligence information," calling into question compliance and minimization standards contained in the order.[328]

To date, no court has found it necessary to disclose FISA materials in order to make a determination of the lawfulness of FISA surveillance or searches.[329] The courts have uniformly held that FISA's *in camera* review procedures afford a defendant adequate due process.[330] While defendants are significantly disadvantaged by not being able to review the FISA materials needed to effectively

---

[323] *See* 50 U.S.C. §§1806(f), 1825(g), 1845(f).

[324] *See* United States v. Mubayyid, 521 F. Supp. 2d at 129-30.

[325] *See* 50 U.S.C. §§1806(f), 1825(g), 1845(f).

[326] *Id.*

[327] *Id.*; *see also* United States v. Damrah, 412 F.3d 618, 624 (6th Cir. 2005); United States v. Duggan, 743 F.2d at 78; United States v. Islamic Am. Relief Agency, 2009 WL 5169536, at *3 (W.D. Mo. 2009); United States v. Abu-Jihaad, 531 F. Supp. 2d at 310; Unites States v. Mubayyid, 521 F. Supp. 2d at 130.

[328] United States v. Belfield, 692 F.2d 141, 147 (D.C. Cir. 1982) (quoting S. Intelligence Rep. at 64); *see also* United States v. Islamic Am. Relief Agency, 2009 WL 5169536, at *3-4; *Rosen*, 447 F. Supp. 2d at 546.

[329] *See, e.g.*, United States v. Squillacote, 221 F.3d 542, 553-54 (4th Cir. 2000); United States v. Islamic American Relief Agency, 2009 WL 5169536, at *4; United v. Warsame, 547 F. Supp. 2d 982, 987 (D. Minn. 2008) ("No United States District Court or Court of Appeals has ever determined that disclosure to the defense of such materials was necessary to determine the lawfulness of surveillance or searches under FISA."); *Rosen*, 447 F. Supp. 2d at 546 (same, listing cases).

[330] *See* United States v. Damrah, 412 F.3d at 624-25; United States v. Ott, 827 F.2d 473, 476 (9th Cir. 1987); United States v. Badia, 827 F.2d 1458, 1464 (11th Cir. 1987); United States v. Duggan, 743 F.2d at 78; United States v. Abu-Jihaad, 531 F. Supp. 2d at 310; United States v. Mubayyid, 521 F. Supp. 2d at 131.

I. Foreign Intelligence Surveillance Act, 50 U.S.C. §§1801 *et seq.*

challenge a FISA warrant, the courts maintain that Congress made a reasonable effort to balance the competing interests in privacy and national security. The D.C. Circuit in *Belfield* observed:

> We appreciate the difficulties of appellants' counsel in this case. They must argue that the determination of legality is so complex that an adversary hearing with full access to relevant materials is necessary. But without access to relevant materials their claim of complexity can be given no concreteness. . . .
>
> Congress was also aware of these difficulties. But it chose to resolve them through means other than mandatory disclosure. . . . [I]t cannot be said that this exclusion rises to the level of a constitutional violation.[331]

If the district court finds that the surveillance or search was not lawfully authorized or conducted, it must suppress the FISA evidence.[332] Further, the district court reviews the FISA materials *de novo*.[333] Accordingly, the FISC's probable cause determination is given no deference. There is, however, a presumption of validity afforded to the certifications contained in the FISA application.[334] Further, when reviewing the denial of a motion to suppress, an appellate court reviews the lower court's findings of fact for clear error and its conclusions of law *de novo*.[335]

Attacks on the lawfulness of FISA surveillance orders generally focus on two issues: 1) whether the FISC had probable cause to believe that the targets of the surveillance were "agents of a foreign power," as required by FISA; and 2) whether there was proper compliance with the minimization procedures subsequent to the surveillance.[336] Under FISA, a FISC judge must determine whether there is probable cause to believe that "the target of the electronic surveillance is a foreign power or agent of a foreign power" and that "each of the facilities or places at which the electronic surveillance is directed is being used, or is about to be used, by a foreign power or agent of a foreign power."[337] However, in making a probable cause determination, the FISC judge may not consider a U.S. person

---

[331] United States v. Belfield, 692 F.3d at 141; *see also* United States v. Abu-Jihaad, 531 F. Supp. 2d at 310; United States v. Mubayyid, 521 F. Supp. 2d at 131.

[332] *See* 50 U.S.C. §§1806(g), 1825(h), 1845(g).

[333] *See* United States v. Hammoud, 381 F.3d at 332 (conducting *de novo* review of FISA materials), *vacated on other grounds*, 543 U.S. 1097 (2005); United States v. Squillacote, 221 F.3d at 554; United States v. Gowadia, 2009 WL 1649709, at *4 (D. Haw.); United States v. Islamic Am. Relief Agency, 2009 WL 5169536, at *4; *Rosen*, 447 F. Supp. 2d at 545.

[334] *See* United States v. Islamic Am. Relief Agency, 2009 WL 5169536, at *4; *see also* United States v. Hammoud, 381 F.3d at 332 (citing *Squillacote*, 221 F.3d at 554); *Rosen*, 447 F. Supp. 2d at 545.

[335] *See* United States v. Damrah, 412 F.3d at 624; United States v. Foster, 376 F.3d 577, 583 (6th Cir. 2004).

[336] *See* United States v. Islamic Am. Relief Agency, 2009 WL 5169536, at *5 (internal citations omitted).

[337] 50 U.S.C. §1804(a)(3). *See* United States v. Hammoud, 381 F.3d at 332 (finding probable cause that Hammoud was an agent of Hezbollah, a foreign power under FISA).

an agent of a foreign power "solely upon the basis of activities protected by the First Amendment."[338] For example, the FISC could not make a finding that a U.S. person is an agent of an FTO, a foreign power under FISA, solely because that person embraces and advocates some of the views of the terrorist group. However, "the probable cause determination may rely in part on activities protected by the First Amendment, provided the determination also relies on activities not prohibited by the First Amendment."[339]

In a motion to suppress FISA evidence, defendants often argue that the government failed to follow the applicable minimization procedures.[340] The minimization procedures are "designed to protect, as far as reasonable, against the acquisition, retention, and dissemination of nonpublic information which is not foreign intelligence information."[341] Minimization procedures serve the following purposes:

> [M]inimization at the acquisition stage is designed to insure that the communications of non-target U.S. persons who happen to be using a FISA target's telephone, or who happen to converse with the target about non-foreign intelligence information, are not improperly disseminated. Similarly, minimization at the retention stage is intended to ensure that "information acquired, which is not necessary for obtaining, producing, or disseminating foreign intelligence information, be destroyed where feasible. Finally, the dissemination of foreign intelligence information, "needed for an approved purpose . . . should be restricted to those officials with a need for such information."[342]

Even if the government stores an overbroad selection of electronic communications in violation of these minimization procedures, suppression of FISA-related evidence is not mandated so long as the government acted in good faith to minimize the acquisition and retention of irrelevant information.[343] In *Mubayyid*, the court posited: "Absent a charge that the minimization procedures have been disregarded *completely*, the test of compliance is 'whether a good faith effort to minimize was attempted.'"[344] The courts have also denied a motion to

---

[338] 50 U.S.C. §1805(a)(2)(A).

[339] United States v. Rosen, 447 F. Supp. 2d at 548 (finding ample probable cause to believe that targets were agents of a foreign power apart from their First Amendment lobbying activities).

[340] *See, e.g.,* United States v. Islamic Am. Relief Agency, 2009 WL 5169536, at *5; United States v. Rosen, 447 F. Supp. 2d at 550.

[341] In re Sealed Case, 310 F.3d at 731; *see also* United States v. Rosen, 447 F. Supp. 2d at 550 ("Congress intended these minimization procedures to act as a safeguard for U.S. persons at the acquisition, retention and dissemination phases of electronic surveillance and searches."). The minimization procedures for electronic surveillance are found at 50 U.S.C. §1801(h). Section 1821(4) governs minimization procedures for physical searches.

[342] United States v. Rosen, 447 F. Supp. 2d at 551 (internal citations omitted).

[343] *See* United States v. Hammoud, 381 F.3d at 334; United States v. Mubayyid, 521 F. Supp. 2d at 134-35.

[344] United States v. Mubayyid, 521 F. Supp. 2d at 135 (quoting United States v. Armocida, 515 F.2d 29, 44 (3d Cir. 1975)) (internal citations omitted) (emphasis added).

suppress where the government violated minimization procedures by retaining FISA evidence for long periods of time. In *Mubayyid*, the district court stated that "a significant degree of latitude [must] be given in counterintelligence and counter-terrorism cases with respect to the retention of information and the dissemination between and among counterintelligence components of the Government."[345] The court held that the retention of electronic intercepts for more than ten years prior to the indictment did not violate FISA minimization procedures.[346] The FISA *ex parte* and *in camera* procedures also have been upheld against a constitutional challenge alleging a violation of the Sixth Amendment right of confrontation.[347]

C. National Security Letters

1. NSL Statutes

Five statutory provisions require businesses to produce specified records to federal officials (principally the FBI) conducting national security investigations.[348] These requests for the production of business records, comparable to administrative subpoenas, are known as National Security Letters (NSLs).[349] Similar to orders issued pursuant to FISA, NSLs are justified by national security concerns. However, NSLs differ from FISA orders in several important respects. First, FISA orders must be issued by a FISA judge. NSLs do not require a court order and are issued by federal government agencies responsible for national security investigations.[350] Second, FISA court orders authorize electronic surveillance, physical searches, the installation of pen registers and trap and trace devices, and access to certain documents, business records, and other tangible things relevant to national security.[351] The scope of documents and information that can be obtained by NSL is more limited. NSLs require the production of financial records, credit history information, telephone records, and certain information relevant to an investigation of improper disclosure of classified information.[352]

---

[345] *Mubayyid*, 521 F. Supp. at 134 (quoting H.R. Rep. No. 95-1283, pt. I, at 59 (1978)).

[346] *Mubayyid*, 521 F. Supp. at 134.

[347] *See* United States v. Isa, 923 F.2d 1300, 1307 (8th Cir. 1991) (Sixth Amendment right of confrontation not violated by FISA's *in camera* review procedures); United States v. Belfield, 692 F.2d at 148 (same).

[348] The five statutory provisions include §114(a)(5) of the Right to Financial Privacy Act (12 U.S.C. §3414(a)(5) (financial records)); §§626 and 627 of the Fair Credit Reporting Act (15 U.S.C. §§1681u (credit history), 1681v (full credit reports)); Electronic Communications Privacy Act (18 U.S.C. §2709) (telephone records); and §802 of the National Security Act (50 U.S.C. §436) (information concerning investigation of improper disclosure of classified information).

[349] *See* CHARLES DOYLE, CONG. RESEARCH SERV., RL33320, NATIONAL SECURITY LETTERS IN FOREIGN INTELLIGENCE INVESTIGATIONS: LEGAL BACKGROUND AND RECENT AMENDMENTS, CRS REPORT FOR CONGRESS 1 (2009) [hereinafter NATIONAL SECURITY LETTERS IN FOREIGN INTELLIGENCE INVESTIGATIONS].

[350] *See* AMENDMENTS TO THE FOREIGN INTELLIGENCE SURVEILLANCE ACT, *supra* note 92, at 4.

[351] *Id.*

[352] *Id.* at 4 n.229.

Finally, NSLs issued under the Electronic Communications Privacy Act, Right to Financial Privacy Act, and Fair Credit Reporting Act do not require a nexus between the requested records and a foreign power or agent of a foreign power.[353]

The first NSL statute was enacted by Congress in 1986 as an amendment to the Right to Financial Privacy Act, authorizing the FBI to access financial institution records in foreign intelligence cases.[354] In 2004, Congress amended the Act by expanding the definition of "financial institution" to include not only banks and credit unions, but also non-traditional financial institutions such as car dealers, jewelers, real estate agencies, and broker-dealers in securities and commodities.[355] Congress passed the second NSL statute, the Electronic Communications Privacy Act, in 1988.[356] This statute gave the FBI access to local and long distance toll billing records as well as related customer information.

In the mid-1990s, Congress enacted two more NSL provisions. The National Security Act, 50 U.S.C. §436, permits the use of NSLs to access financial institution records, credit reports, and travel records of federal employees suspected of leaking classified information.[357] Passed in the wake of the Ames espionage case,[358] the use of NSLs under the Act is limited to investigations involving the disclosure of classified information by federal employees.[359] Finally, the Fair Credit Reporting Act, 15 U.S.C. §1681u(a), grants the FBI access to credit agency records

---

[353] *See* NATIONAL SECURITY LETTERS IN FOREIGN INTELLIGENCE INVESTIGATIONS, *supra* note 349, at 4.

[354] P.L. 99-569, §404, 100 Stat. 3197 (1986), *codified at* 12 U.S.C. §3414(a)(5)(A). Section 3414(a)(5)(A) provides in relevant part:

> Financial institutions, and officers, employees, and agents thereof, shall comply with a request for a customer's or entity's financial records made pursuant to this subsection by the Federal Bureau of Investigation when the Director of the Federal Bureau of Investigation (or the Director's designee in a position not lower than Deputy Assistant Director at Bureau headquarters or a Special Agent in Charge in a Bureau field office designated by the Director) certifies in writing to the financial institution that such records are sought for foreign counter intelligence purposes to protect against international terrorism or clandestine intelligence activities. . . .

[355] P.L. 108-177, §374, 117 Stat. 2628 (2004), *codified at* 12 U.S.C. §3414(d). Section 3414(d) adopted the definition of "financial institution" set forth in 31 U.S.C. 5312(a)(2).

[356] 18 U.S.C. §2709 (1988 ed.). Section 2709(a) requires a wire or electronic communication service provider to comply with a request from the FBI for "subscriber information and toll billing records information, or electronic communications transactional records in its custody or possession. . . ."

[357] 50 U.S.C. §436 (1994 ed.).

[358] This regulation was prompted largely by the investigation and arrest of CIA officer Aldrich Ames. In 1994, Ames was arrested for espionage on evidence that he had delivered the names of U.S. intelligence assets to the KGB—many of whom had been killed. Ames had taken repeated payments from the Russian intelligence body, purchasing a new Jaguar car and a $564,000 home on a $70,000 a year salary. The financial discrepancies were instrumental in the FBI's investigation. Ames pled guilty to espionage and was sentenced to life in prison without possibility of parole. S. SELECT COMM. ON INTELLIGENCE, AN ASSESSMENT OF THE ALDRICH H. AMES ESPIONAGE CASE AND ITS IMPLICATIONS FOR U.S. INTELLIGENCE, S. Rep. No. 103-90, at 4-9 (1994).

[359] 50 U.S.C. §436. Section 436 provides that NSL may request certain records pertaining to a person who is or was a federal employee where "there are reasonable grounds to believe, based on credible information, that the person is, or may be, disclosing classified information in an unauthorized manner to a foreign power or agent of a foreign power." *Id.*

relevant to an authorized investigation to protect against international terrorism or clandestine intelligence activities.[360] Under the FCRA, a credit reporting agency is required to furnish to the FBI the names and addresses of all financial institutions at which a specified consumer maintains or has maintained an account, to the extent that the reporting agency has such information in its files.[361] The FCRA was enacted because Congress was concerned that the FBI's right to access bank records under the Right to Financial Privacy Act could not be effectively used until the FBI discovered which financial institutions were being utilized by the target of the counterintelligence investigation.[362] While consumer reports maintained by credit reporting agencies were a ready source of such information, these records were not available to FBI counterintelligence investigators.[363] The FRCA was intended to correct this problem by enabling FBI counterintelligence investigators to make more effective use of their authority to access financial records.

The USA PATRIOT Act amended the three NSL provisions available exclusively to the FBI—the Electronic Communications Privacy Act (12 U.S.C. §2709), the Right to Financial Privacy Act (12 U.S.C. §3414(a) (5)), and the Fair Credit Reporting Act (15 U.S.C. §1681u). Section 505 of the PATRIOT Act 1) expanded the FBI's issuing authority to include the heads of FBI field offices (i.e., Special Agents in Charge of a bureau field office), 2) eliminated the requirement that the information sought pertain to a foreign power or agent of a foreign power, 3) required instead that the NSL request be relevant to an investigation to protect against international terrorism or foreign spying, and 4) added the caveat that no such investigation of a U.S. person could be predicated exclusively on First Amendment protected activities.[364]

The PATRIOT Act amendments enhanced the use of NSLs in two important ways. First, they allowed NSL authority to be employed more quickly by eliminating the requirement of prior approval from the FBI headquarters. An NSL can now be issued by a Special Agent in Charge of a bureau field office.[365] Second, the use of NSL authority was expanded by eliminating the requirement that the information sought pertain to a foreign power or agent of a foreign power. Instead, the amendments allow NSLs to be issued for documents relevant to an investigation to protect against international terrorism or clandestine intelligence activities.

Section 358(g) of the USA PATRIOT Act, codified at 15 U.S.C. §1681v, amended the Fair Credit Reporting Act by expanding the use of NSLs beyond the FBI. Now, any governmental agency that is authorized to conduct an

---

[360] 15 U.S.C. §1681u.

[361] *Id.*

[362] H.R. 104-427, at 36 (1996); *see also* NATIONAL SECURITY LETTERS IN FOREIGN INTELLIGENCE INVESTIGATIONS, *supra* note 349, at 3.

[363] H.R. 104-427, at 36 (1996).

[364] *See* NATIONAL SECURITY LETTERS IN FOREIGN INTELLIGENCE INVESTIGATIONS, *supra* note 349, at 4 (citing P.L. 107-56, §505, 114 Stat. 365-66 (2001)).

[365] *See* 12 U.S.C. §3414(a)(5)(A); 15 U.S.C. §1681u; 18 U.S.C. §2709(b); *see also* NATIONAL SECURITY LETTERS IN FOREIGN INTELLIGENCE INVESTIGATIONS, *supra* note 349, at 4.

investigation or analyze intelligence information related to international terrorism can issue NSLs under the FCRA. Section 358(g) provides:

> Notwithstanding section 1681b of this title or any other provision of this subchapter, a consumer reporting agency shall furnish a consumer report of a consumer and all other information in a consumer's file to a government agency authorized to conduct investigations of, or intelligence or counterintelligence activities or analysis related to, international terrorism when presented with a written certification by such governmental agency that such information is necessary for the agency's conduct or such investigation, activity or analysis.[366]

In 2006, Congress created a judicial review process that allows NSL recipients to challenge the document requests.[367] Further, the amendments authorized the government to petition the FISC to compel compliance with NSLs.[368] The amendments made any failure to obey a court order punishable by holding the offender in contempt of court.[369] The nondisclosure requirements did not preclude the recipient from consulting an attorney,[370] and provided a process for a recipient to petition the court for an order modifying or setting aside a nondisclosure requirement.[371] Finally, the 2006 amendments expanded congressional oversight and required an Inspector General's audit of the use of NSL authority.[372]

2. Statutory Framework

Under each of the NSL statutes a government official must certify in each NSL issued that the purpose of the NSL is limited to acquiring information related to national security concerns.[373] For example, under the Electronic Communications Privacy Act, 18 U.S.C. §2709(b), the designated senior FBI official must

---

[366] 15 U.S.C. §1681v(a).

[367] 18 U.S.C. §3511.

[368] *Id.* §§3511(c), 1510(e).

[369] *Id.* §§3511(c), 1510(e).

[370] 12 U.S.C. §3414(a)(3)(A); 15 U.S.C. §§1681v(c)(1); 1681u(d)(1); 18 U.S.C. §2709(c)(1); 50 U.S.C. §436(b)(1).

[371] 18 U.S.C. §3511(b).

[372] P.L. 109-177, §§118-19.

[373] NSLs issued under the Electronic Communications Privacy Act, the Right to Financial Privacy Act, and the first Fair Credit Report Act must be certified by either the Director of the FBI, a senior FBI official (no lower than the Deputy Assistant Director), or the Special Agent in Charge of an FBI field office. 18 U.S.C. §2709 (b); 12 U.S.C. §3414(a)(5)(A); 15 U.S.C. §1681u(b). NSLs issued under the National Security Act can also be certified by a certain senior officials of the agency whose employee is the target of the NSL who are at least an Assistant Secretary or Assistant Director of that agency. 50 U.S.C. §3162(a)(3). Finally, NSLs issued under the second Fair Credit Reporting Act can be certified by a "designated supervisory official" of any agency "authorized to conduct investigations of, or intelligence or counterintelligence activities and analysis related to, international terrorism[.]" 15 U.S.C. §1681v(a).

I. Foreign Intelligence Surveillance Act, 50 U.S.C. §§1801 *et seq.*

certify that "[the information] sought [is] relevant to an authorized investigation to protect against international terrorism or clandestine intelligence activities. . . ."[374] The certification required under the Fair Credit Reporting Act, 15 U.S.C. §1681u, the newer provision of the Fair Credit Reporting Act, and the Right of Financial Privacy Act, 21 U.S.C. §3414(a)(5)(A), are quite similar.[375] Finally, the National Security Act requires a certification that the information is sought to conduct "any authorized law enforcement investigation, counterintelligence inquiry, or security determination. . . ."[376]

Each of the NSL statutes contains a nondisclosure or confidentiality requirement. For example, the Electronic Communications Privacy Act, 18 U.S.C. §2709(c)(1), provides that if the Director of the FBI or his designee certifies that "disclosure may result a danger to the national security of the United States, interference with a criminal, counterterrorism, or counterintelligence investigation, interference with diplomatic relations, or danger to the life or physical safety of any person," the recipient of the NSL shall not disclose to any person that the FBI sought or obtained access to the information or records requested in the NSL.[377] The recipient of the NSL can, however, disclose such information to the extent necessary to comply with the request or to an attorney to obtain legal advice or legal assistance with respect to the request as long as the recipient informs such persons of the nondisclosure requirement.[378] In these instances, the persons receiving such information are subject to the same nondisclosure requirement as the recipient.[379] A breach of the confidentiality requirement committed knowingly and with the intent to obstruct justice is punishable by up to five years in prison, a fine of not more than $250,000 (an organization can be fined up to $500,000), or both.

Section 3511 of Title 18 of the United States Code, provides for judicial review of NSLs and nondisclosure orders issued under the NSL statutes. Section 3511(a) allows the recipient of an NSL to petition a district court for an order to modify or set aside the NSL.[380] The court may modify or set aside the NSL only "if compliance would be unreasonable, oppressive, or otherwise unlawful."[381] Under §3511(b)(2), an NSL recipient subject to a nondisclosure order may also petition a district court to modify or set aside the nondisclosure order. If the NSL was issued

---

[374] 18 U.S.C. §2709(b).

[375] *See* 15 U.S.C. §1681u ("information is sought for the conduct of an authorized investigation to protect against international terrorism or clandestine intelligence activities"); 15 U.S.C. §1681u(a); 12 U.S.C. §3414(a)(5)(A) (same). *See also* NATIONAL SECURITY LETTERS IN FOREIGN INTELLIGENCE INVESTIGATIONS, *supra* note 349, at 8.

[376] 50 U.S.C. §436(a)(1).

[377] 18 U.S.C. §2709(c)(1); *see also* 12 U.S.C. §3414(a)(5)(D)(i); 15 U.S.C. §§1681u(d), 1681v(c)(1); 50 U.S.C. §436(b)(1).

[378] *See* 12 U.S.C. §3414(a)(5)(D)(iii); 15 U.S.C. §§1681u(d)(3), 1681v(c)(3); 18 U.S.C. §2709(c)(3); 50 U.S.C. §436(b)(3).

[379] 12 U.S.C. §3414(a)(5)(D)(iii).

[380] 18 U.S.C. §3511(b)(2).

[381] *Id.* §3511(a).

within a year of such a challenge, a court may grant the petition to modify or set aside the nondisclosure order if it finds that "there is no reason to believe that disclosure may endanger the national security of the United States, interfere with a criminal, counterterrorism, or counterintelligence investigation, interfere with diplomatic relations, or endanger the life or physical safety of any person."[382] However, if a specified high-ranking government official (i.e., the Attorney General, Deputy or Assistant Attorneys General, the Director of the FBI, or agency heads) certifies that disclosure "may endanger the national security of the United States or interfere with diplomatic relations, such certification shall be treated as conclusive unless the court finds that such certification was made in bad faith."[383] The bad faith requirement sets an extremely high bar for the recipient to prevail and significantly tips the scale in favor of the government in a petition challenging the NSL nondisclosure requirement.

Finally, the dissemination of information acquired in response to NSLs is restricted in four of the five NSL provisions. Guidelines approved by the Attorney General govern the sharing of information acquired under the Right to Financial Privacy Act and Electronic Communications Act.[384] Under the Fair Credit Reporting Act, the FBI may share NSL information with 1) other Federal agencies for the purpose of conducting a foreign counterintelligence investigation, and 2) military authorities for the purpose of conducting a joint foreign counterintelligence investigation of a member of the Armed Forces.[385] Under the National Security Act, the requesting agency may only disseminate the NSL-obtained information "(1) to the agency employing the employee who is the subject of the records or information; (2) to the Department of Justice for law enforcement or counterintelligence purposes; or (3) with respect to the dissemination to an agency of the United States, if such information is clearly relevant to the authorized responsibilities of such agency."[386] However, the newer provision of the Fair Credit Reporting Act, 15 U.S.C. §1681v, has no explicit provision restricting dissemination. Finally, three of the NSL statutes offer recipients of NSL immunity from civil liability for complying with the NSL.[387]

3. Legal Challenges

The nondisclosure requirement has been the subject of extensive litigation. In *Doe v. Mukasey*, the Second Circuit Court of Appeals struck down the nondisclosure provision of 18 U.S.C. §2709(c).[388] The Second Circuit held that the

---

[382] *Id.* §3511(b)(2).
[383] *Id.* §3511(b)(2).
[384] *See* 12 U.S.C. §3414(a)(5)(B); 18 U.S.C. §2709(d).
[385] 15 U.S.C. §1681u(f).
[386] 50 U.S.C. §§436(e)(1)-(3).
[387] 15 U.S.C. §§1681u(k), 1681v(e); 50 U.S.C. §436(d).
[388] Doe v. Mukasey, 549 F.3d 861 (2d Cir. 2008).

nondisclosure provision violated the First Amendment because the government did not bear the burden to seek prompt judicial review of the nondisclosure order.[389] In *Doe v. Mukasey*, the FBI delivered a NSL on an Internet service provider requesting the production of specified electronic communication transactional records.[390] The request for documents was authorized by 18 U.S.C. §2709, which prohibited any officer, employee, or agent of the company from "disclosing to any person that the FBI sought or obtained access to information or records."[391]

While the case was pending, Congress enacted the USA PATRIOT Improvement and Reauthorization Act of 2005, which amended the nondisclosure provision, requiring nondisclosure of an NSL request for documents only upon certification by a senior FBI official that "otherwise there may result a danger to the national security of the United States, interference with a criminal, counterterrorism, or counterintelligence investigation, interference with diplomatic relations or danger to the life or physical safety of any person."[392]

The Second Circuit found that while the nondisclosure requirement was not a "classic prior restraint" or a "broad" content-based prohibition on speech requiring the "most rigorous First Amendment scrutiny," it was sufficiently analogous to such restrictions to justify the application of the procedural safeguards against censorship articulated in *Freedman v. Maryland*, 380 U.S. 51 (1965).[393] In *Freedman*, the Supreme Court identified three procedural requirements for restraints on speech: "(1) any restraint imposed prior to judicial review must be limited to 'a specified brief period'; (2) any further restraint prior to final judicial determination must be limited to 'the shortest fixed period compatible with sound judicial resolution'; and (3) the burden of going to the court to suppress the speech and the burden of proof in court must be placed on the government."[394]

While the Second Circuit could not agree on whether §2709(c) constituted a prior restraint subject to strict scrutiny analysis or whether it should be judged under a less demanding standard, the lack of consensus proved inconsequential. First, the government conceded that the strict scrutiny standard applied, and second, the court determined that the result would be the same under the factor common to both standards—whether the nondisclosure requirement is as "narrowly tailored" as possible to protect national security.[395] Applying the strict scrutiny standard, the Second Circuit stated that the government must demonstrate that the nondisclosure requirement is "narrowly tailored to promote a compelling

---

[389] *Id.*

[390] *Id.* at 865.

[391] *Id.* (quoting 18 U.S.C. §2709(a)).

[392] USA PATRIOT Improvement and Reauthorization Act of 2005, §115, Pub. L. No. 109-177, 120 Stat. 192, 211-14 (Mar. 9, 2006), amended by the USA Patriot Act Additional Reauthorizing Amendments Act of 2006, §4(b), Pub. L. No. 109-178, 120 Stat. 278, 280 (Mar. 9, 2006), codified at 18 U.S.C. §2709(c) (West Supp. 2008).

[393] *Mukasey*, 549 F.3d at 871.

[394] *Id.* (quoting Freedman v. Maryland, 380 U.S. 51, 58-59 (1965)).

[395] *Mukasey*, 549 F.3d at 878.

government interest," and that there is no "less restrictive alternative [that] would be at least as effective in achieving the legitimate purpose that the statute was enacted to serve."[396] Since no governmental interest is more compelling than U.S. national security, the Second Circuit posited that the principal strict scrutiny issue was whether the narrow tailoring requirement is met.[397] Citing to the third *Freedman* requirement, the Court held that "in the absence of Government-initiated judicial review, subsection 3511(b) is not narrowly tailored to First Amendment procedural safeguards."[398] To withstand a First Amendment challenge, the Second Circuit stated that §3511(b) must be interpreted to place the burden on the government "to show a 'good' reason to believe that disclosure may result in an enumerated harm, i.e., a harm related to 'an authorized investigation to protect against international terrorism or clandestine intelligence activities,' and to place on a district court an obligation to make the 'may result' finding only after consideration, albeit deferential, of the government's explanation concerning the risk of an enumerated harm."[399]

Further, the Second Circuit deemed insufficient to satisfy either standard the provisions of §§3511(b)(2) and (b)(3) specifying that a certification by a senior government official that disclosure may "endanger the national security of the United States or interfere with diplomatic relations . . . shall be treated as *conclusive* unless the court finds that the certification was made in bad faith."[400] The court posited:

> There is no meaningful judicial review of the decision of the Executive Branch to prohibit speech if the position of the Executive Branch that speech would be harmful is "conclusive" on a reviewing court, absent only a determination of bad faith. To accept deference to that extraordinary degree would be to reduce strict scrutiny to no scrutiny, save only in the rarest of situations where bad faith could be shown. Under either traditional strict scrutiny or a less exacting application of that standard, some demonstration from the Executive Branch of the need for secrecy is required in order to conform the nondisclosure requirement to First Amendment standards.[401]

While judicial review may occur *ex parte* and *in camera*, the Second Circuit stated that such review may not be bound by the executive's "conclusive" certification of harm clause set forth in §3511(b).

Finally, while the Second Circuit acknowledged that it lacked the authority to revise the NSL statutes to create the constitutionally required obligation of requiring the government to initiate judicial review, the Court suggested that the government should assume such an obligation.[402] In an effort to salvage the NSL

---

[396] *Id.* (internal quotations and citations omitted).
[397] *Id.*
[398] *Id.* at 881.
[399] *Id.*
[400] *Id.* at 882 (quoting 18 U.S.C. §3511(b)(2)) (emphasis added).
[401] *Mukasey*, 549 F.3d at 882.
[402] *Id.* at 883.

secrecy provisions, the Second Circuit proposed the following procedures for judicial review:

> The Government could inform each NSL recipient that it should give the Government prompt notice, perhaps within ten days, in the event that the recipient wishes to contest the nondisclosure requirement. Upon receipt of such notice, the Government could be accorded a limited time, perhaps 30 days, to initiate a judicial review proceeding to maintain the nondisclosure requirement, and the proceeding would have to be concluded within a prescribed time, perhaps 60 days.[403]

The Second Circuit held that if the government uses the suggested reciprocal notice procedures as a means of initiating judicial review, §2709(c) would conform to First Amendment requirements.[404] In conclusion, the Court severed the conclusive presumption provision of §§3511(b)(2) and (b)(3) and left intact the remainder of §3511(b) and the entirety of §2709 but added proposed limitations as well as government-initiated review procedures.[405]

Finally, in *In re National Sec. Letter,* the U.S. District Court reached the same conclusion holding that the nondisclosure provision of 18 U.S.C. §2709(c) and judicial review procedures of 18 U.S.C. §§3511(b)(2) and (b)(3) violate the First Amendment.[406] However, unlike the Second Circuit in *Mukasey,* the district court was unwilling to modify or amend the statutes by judicial fiat. Instead, the court enjoined the government from issuing NSLs under section 2709 or enforcing the nondisclosure provision.[407]

The rulings in *Mukasey* and *In re National Sec. Letter* have created an untenable situation, resulting in the disparate application of §§2709(c) and 3511(b)(2) and (b)(3). In the Second Circuit, recipients of NSLs may legally challenge the issuance of the NSL or the nondisclosure provisions under the 10-30-60 day government-initiated procedures established by the Second Circuit. However, outside of the Second Circuit, the statutory procedures of §2709(c) and §§3511(b)(2) and (b)(3) remain fully intact. Finally, after *In re National Sec. Letter,* in the Northern District of California the government is enjoined in all cases from issuing NSLs under §2709 or from enforcing the nondisclosure provisions. The Northern District of California decision is likely to have a chilling effect on the FBI's issuance of NSLs, knowing that the recipient is likely to notify the target of the FBI's request for records and pending investigation because the court overturned the nondisclosure provision.

---

[403] *Id.* at 879.
[404] *Id.* at 883-84.
[405] *Id.* at 885.
[406] In re National Sec. Letter, 930 F. Supp. 2d 1064 (N.D. Cal. 2013).
[407] *Id.*

II. THE TERRORIST FINANCING TRACKING PROGRAM

A central component of the U.S. government's counterterrorism strategy is to deprive terrorists and terrorist organizations of funding. Money is critical to financing terrorist operations (operational costs) and sustaining the organizational infrastructure of terrorist organizations (organizational costs).[408] Terrorists "need money to finance their organizational activities, including paying operatives, recruiting and training new members, bribing government officials, forging ties with other [terrorist groups], paying travel and communication expenses, and acquiring military weapons, explosives and radiological materials to construct a nuclear device or 'dirty bomb.'"[409] Simply stated, "terrorists need money to terrorize."[410] The collection and exploitation of financial intelligence information is critical to preventing the financing of terrorism.

Following the September 11, 2001 terrorist attacks, in an effort to enhance the government's ability to monitor wire transfers and the movement of money globally, the Bush administration established the Terrorist Financing Tracking Program (TFTP).[411] The TFTP allows the government to track and map the funds flowing to terrorist organizations by issuing administrative subpoenas for financial records to the Society for Worldwide Interbank Financial Telecommunication (SWIFT).[412]

This financial intelligence-gathering program was confidential until the *New York Times* disclosed its existence in June 23, 2006.[413] In response to the public backlash, the U.S. Treasury Department staunchly defended the TFTP, explaining that SWIFT information "often fill[s] in the missing links in an investigation chain."[414] According to the government, the TFTP was "exactly the kind of program that . . . the 9/11 Commission was critical of the government for its failure to have . . . in place prior to the September 11th attacks."[415]

---

[408] *See* JIMMY GURULÉ, UNFUNDING TERROR: THE LEGAL RESPONSE TO THE FINANCING OF GLOBAL TERRORISM, 21 (Edward Elgar Publ. 2008).

[409] *Id.*

[410] *Id.* at 40; *see also* Financial Action Task Force, Terrorist Financing (Feb. 28, 2008), *available at* http://www.faft-gafi.org/dataoecd/28/43/40285899.pdf.

[411] *See* Dep't of Treasury, Terrorist Finance Tracking Program Fact Sheet (Aug. 2, 2010), http://www.treasury.gov/resource-center/terrorist-illicit-finance/Terrorist-Finance-Tracking/Pages/tftp.aspx (last visited Mar. 13, 2014) [hereinafter TFTP Fact Sheet].

[412] Eric Lichtblau & James Risen, *Bank Data Sifted in Secret by U.S. to Block Terror*, N.Y. TIMES, June 23, 2006, at A1 (government officials saw SWIFT as "the mother lode, the Rosetta stone, for financial data.").

[413] *Id.*

[414] TFTP Fact Sheet, *supra* note 411.

[415] *Id.*

II. The Terrorist Financing Tracking Program

A. *Society for Worldwide Interbank Financial Telecommunication*

1. SWIFT Overview

In its most basic form, SWIFT is an electronic financial messaging service for the global banking community.[416] SWIFT is not itself a financial institution—it does not "provide financial services nor hold client accounts or assets."[417] Rather, SWIFT's role is solely to provide electronic instructions for electronic funds transfers and other transactions among its members and users. The messages are carried on SWIFT's private, secure, and reliable messaging infrastructure, which can be used by banks, other financial institutions, and certain corporations.[418] Private individuals cannot access the network. Today, SWIFT has over 10,000 users from 214 countries.[419] In 2013, SWIFT transmitted over 5 trillion messages, carrying an average of 20 million messages each day.[420] SWIFT is primarily used for international transactions, where the need for a common standardized language is greatest.[421]

SWIFT was created in the 1970s when the complexity of international transactions began to exceed the ability of paper-based banking procedures, and caused financial institutions to look for electronic solutions.[422] At the time, however, there were many competing computer systems using incompatible procedures that made the exchange of messages among financial institutions both complex and inefficient.[423] SWIFT solved those problems by creating a common IT platform for processing messages, which essentially resulted in a "common language for international financial transactions."[424] By standardizing financial messaging and eliminating language barriers, SWIFT quickly became, and remains, "the *de facto* messaging service for the global banking industry."[425]

---

[416] *See* About SWIFT, Company Information, http://www.swift.com/about_swift/company_information/company_information (last visited Mar. 5, 2014). SWIFT is a Belgium cooperative that is member owned and operated. It is headquartered near Brussels with offices in most major cities in the world. *Id.*

[417] Facts About SWIFT for the Media, 3 (July 2010), *available at* http://www.swift.com/assets/swift_com/documents/about_swift/media_fact_sheet.pdf.

[418] *Id.* at 5. SWIFT opened up to non-bank financial institutions in 1987 and to the corporate customers of banks in 2000. *Id.* at 2.

[419] *See* About SWIFT, Company Information, SWIFT in Figures- SWIFTNET Fin Traffic, December 2013 YTD, *available at* http://www.swift.com/assets/swift_com/documents/about_swift/SIF_2013_12.pdf.

[420] *See* About SWIFT, Company Information, SWIFT History, http://www.swift.com/index.cfm?itemid=1243 (last visited Mar. 4, 2014).

[421] *Id.*

[422] Facts About SWIFT for the Media, *supra* note 417, at 2.

[423] *Id.*

[424] *See* About SWIFT, Company Information, SWIFT History, http://www.swift.com/index.cfm?itemid=1243 (last visited Mar. 4, 2014).

[425] Facts About SWIFT for the Media, *supra* note 417, at 2.

"Virtually every major commercial bank, as well as brokerage houses, fund managers, and stock exchanges" uses the SWIFT network and SWIFT message standards.[426] SWIFT message standards are essentially computer readable communications templates with select data fields to be filled out by the communicating parties.[427] Using SWIFT message standards allows SWIFT users to automate their communications processing, thereby increasing efficiency, lowering transaction costs and risks of ambiguity, and, most importantly, eliminating language barriers.[428] In the ordinary course of business, SWIFT only accesses routing information but not the contents of messages it transmits.[429] However, SWIFT has the *ability* to access message contents since all messages transmitted over the SWIFT network are retained at a SWIFT data center for a period of 124 days.[430] When the TFTP was first established in 2001, SWIFT had two data centers—one in the United States and one in the Netherlands.[431] The two operating centers performed identical tasks.[432] As a result, the entirety of SWIFT's messaging data was stored at each data center. In 2009, SWIFT opened a third data center in Switzerland.[433]

2.   TFTP

In order to access SWIFT's records, the Treasury Department issued administrative subpoenas[434] to SWIFT's U.S. operating center.[435] Initially, the Treasury subpoenas were narrowly targeted and sought the records of individuals reasonably suspected of facilitating terrorism.[436] Since SWIFT lacked the technical capability to screen its database of message contents for specific party names, addresses, dates, and bank accounts, the Treasury Department needed to conduct

---

[426] Lichtblau & Risen, *supra* note 412.

[427] Facts About SWIFT for the Media, *supra* note 417, at 7.

[428] *Id.*

[429] SWIFT Data Retrieval Policy, https://www2.swift.com/uhbonline/books/public/en_uk/drp/index.htm (last visited Mar. 5, 2014).

[430] *Id.*

[431] *See* About SWIFT, Company Information, SWIFT History, http://www.swift.com/index.cfm?itemid=1243 (last visited Mar. 4, 2014).

[432] Facts About SWIFT for the Media, *supra* note 417, at 6. SWIFT is used so widely by the financial community because it is very reliable, guaranteeing the delivery of messages 24 hours a day, 365 days a year. *Id.* at 5. There were two data centers mirroring the work of one another because each data center was designed to be capable of managing all of SWIFT's operations should the other fail. *Id.* at 6.

[433] *Id.* at 6.

[434] Unlike criminal subpoenas, administrative subpoenas need only meet a reasonableness standard and do not require prior judicial authorization. However, should the reasonableness of a SWIFT subpoena be contested and subject to judicial review, a reviewing court would likely be quite deferential to the Treasury Department since the subpoenas are issued pursuant to a counter-terrorism investigation.

[435] TFTP Fact Sheet, *supra* note 411. Since SWIFT has a data center in the U.S., the Treasury Department had jurisdiction to subpoena all of SWIFT's records stored at the U.S. location. *Id.*

[436] Lichtblau & Risen, *supra* note 412.

II. The Terrorist Financing Tracking Program

those scans on its own.[437] As such, the subpoenas ultimately issued under the TFTP did not request information about specific terrorist targets, but rather requested subsets of all the SWIFT data stored in the United States for specified time periods (including message contents).[438]

Data subject to the Treasury subpoena was then delivered from SWIFT's U.S. operating center to OFAC and placed in a "black box" isolated from all other intelligence databases and programs.[439] The U.S. government was only able to see information that was responsive to targeted searches.[440] No search could take place without articulating a specific link between the target of the search and a terrorism investigation.[441] Data searches were based only on persons, entities, or related information with an identified connection to an ongoing terrorism investigation or other intelligence that the target is connected to terrorism.[442]

This process allowed the government to retrieve "customers' names, bank account numbers and other identifying information,"[443] as well as the method of transfer and information about the financial institutions involved in the transaction.[444] Retrieved information was securely given to counterterrorism intelligence analysts in order to trace suspicious transactions and "detect patterns, shifts in strategy, specific 'hotspot accounts,' and locations that had become new havens for terrorist activity."[445] This information "greatly enhanced" the government's ability to "identify and locate [terrorist] operatives and their financiers, chart terrorist networks, and help keep money out of [terrorist] hands."[446]

By 2003, SWIFT had become reluctant about blindly continuing to comply with a program that had initially been presented as an emergency measure.[447] It insisted on narrowing the scope of the subpoenas and implementing greater safeguards on the storage, searches, and use of the data. In response to SWIFT's concerns the Treasury Department agreed to narrow its definition of terrorism and permit an independent international consulting firm to oversee the TFTP and report to SWIFT.[448] SWIFT representatives were also allowed to review all searches in real time and object to or block any searches considered

---

[437] *Id.*

[438] *Id.*

[439] *Terror Finance Tracking Program: Hearing Before the Subcomm. on Oversight and Investigations of the H. Comm. on Financial Servs.*, H. Rep. No. 109-105, at 13 (2006) (statement of Stuart Levey, Under Secretary for Terrorism and Financial Intelligence, U.S. Dep't of the Treasury) [hereinafter Levey Hearing].

[440] *Id.*

[441] *Id.*

[442] *Id.*

[443] Lichtblau & Risen, *supra* note 412.

[444] Josh Meyer & Greg Miller, *U.S. Secretly Tracks Global Bank Data*, L.A. Times, June 23, 2006, at A1.

[445] *Id.*

[446] TFTP Fact Sheet, *supra* note 411.

[447] *See* Lichtblau & Risen, *supra* note 412.

[448] *See* Levey Hearing, *supra* note 439.

inappropriate.[449] Finally, the government agreed to keep an electronic record of every SWIFT data search that could be "systematically logged and audit[ed]."[450]

B.   Legality of the TFTP

1.   Legal Challenges in the United States

On June 23, 2006, the *New York Times* published an article disclosing the existence of the TFTP.[451] In response, several legal challenges were brought in federal court.[452] While the challenges were ultimately dismissed for failure to state a claim and lack of Article III standing, the plaintiffs likely would not have prevailed on the merits. In 1976, the U.S. Supreme Court held in *United States v. Miller* that an individual has no reasonable expectation of privacy in financial information voluntarily conveyed to a bank or third party.[453] Since then, it has been well established that an individual's bank records are not protected by the Fourth Amendment. Absent a statutory prohibition, *United States v. Miller* allows the government to obtain such information by issuing a subpoena to the financial institution in possession of those records.[454]

2.   Legal Problems with Europe

The media disclosure of the wholesale production of SWIFT data under the TFTP was greeted with strong legal opposition in Europe. After the U.S. government publicly acknowledged the existence of TFTP, several European countries alleged that SWIFT (headquartered in Belgium) was violating European privacy laws[455] by allowing the U.S. government to access European financial

---

[449] *Id.*

[450] TFTP Fact Sheet, *supra* note 411.

[451] Lichtblau & Risen, *supra* note 412.

[452] *See* Amidax Trading Group v. S.W.I.F.T. SCRL, 671 F.3d 140 (2d. Cir. 2011); Walker v. S.W.I.F.T. SCRL, 491 F. Supp. 2d 781, 792 (E.D. Va. 2007).

[453] United States v. Miller, 425 U.S. 435 (1976).

[454] Congress created just such a statutory prohibition when it passed the Right to Financial Privacy Act of 1978 (RFPA), 12 U.S.C. §§3401-3442 (2000). Now, the government cannot access records kept by financial institutions without 1) giving notice to the individual whose records are sought, and 2) issuing a subpoena that sufficiently describes the records sought as well as their connection to a legitimate law enforcement inquiry. *Id.* §3402. The TFTP did not violate the RFPA, however, because SWIFT is not a financial institution. *See* Walker v. S.W.I.F.T. SCRL, 491 F. Supp. 2d at 792. Furthermore, the RFPA does not apply to information requested pursuant to a counterterrorism investigation. 12 U.S.C. §3414.

[455] *See* Parliament and Council Directive 95/46/EC of 24 October 1995 on the Protection of Individuals with Regard to the Processing of Personal Data and on the Free Movement of Such Data, 1995 O.J. (L281/40).

records.[456] In order to continue accessing the SWIFT database, the United States negotiated a bilateral treaty with the European Union.[457] The European Union and the United States entered into a treaty that went into effect on August 1, 2010 (Agreement).[458]

The Agreement specifically prohibits access to financial data for payments made exclusively within the Single Euro Payment Area (SEPA) or, in other words, solely intra-European messages.[459] As mentioned above, in 2009, SWIFT opened a third data center in Switzerland. Now, the Netherlands location stores only SEPA data, the U.S. location stores all other messaging data, and the Swiss location stores both types of data should the U.S. or Dutch data center fail.[460] However, the Agreement requires that the SEPA data at the Swiss location be stored separately.[461]

Under the Agreement, the United States is able to access SWIFT data stored on European servers (other than SEPA data) but a copy of any requests for such data must be sent to Europol.[462] Europol reviews the request to confirm that the request 1) clearly identifies the requested data, 2) clearly substantiates the necessity of the data, 3) is tailored as narrowly as possible, and 4) does not request SEPA data.[463] SWIFT only responds to these data requests upon receiving such a confirmation from Europol.[464] The Agreement reaffirms that the collected data may only be accessed for purposes of a terrorism investigation and that all searches must be based on preexisting information.[465] The data must be stored in secure isolation and cannot be connected to any other database outside the U.S.

---

[456] Following the release of the *New York Times* article on June 23, 2006, the Belgian Data Privacy Commission and the Article 29 Working Party issued advisory opinions concluding that, by complying with the Treasury Department's subpoenas, SWIFT violated several provisions of the EU Data Protection Directive 95/46/EC. *See* Belgian Data Protection Authority, Opinion on the Transfer of Personal Data by the SCRL SWIFT by Virtue of UST (OFAC) Subpoenas, www.steptoe.com/assets/attachments/2644.pdf (last visited Mar. 13, 2014); Article 29 Data Protection Working Party, Opinion 10/2006: On the Processing of Personal Data by the Society for Worldwide Interbank Financial Telecommunication (SWIFT), Brussels (Nov. 22, 2006), 01935/06/EN WP128, *available at* http://ec.europa.eu/justice/policies/privacy/docs/wpdocs/2006/wp128_en.pdf. However, in 2009, the European Commission concluded its investigation and confirmed that the United States had respected the safeguards of handling personal data retrieved from the SWIFT database from the outset. *See* SWIFT, Legal, Terrorist Finance Tracking Program, http://www.swift.com/about_swift/legal/terrorist_finance_tracking_program (last visited Mar. 5, 2014).

[457] TFTP Fact Sheet, *supra* note 411.

[458] *See* The Agreement between the United States of America and the European Union on the processing and transfer of financial messaging data from the European Union to the United States for the purposes of the terrorist finance tracking program, 2010 O.J. (L195/5) [hereinafter EU-U.S. Agreement or Agreement].

[459] EU-U.S. Agreement, Article 4(2)(d).

[460] Facts About SWIFT for the Media, *supra* note 417, at 6.

[461] EU-U.S. Agreement, Article 5(4).

[462] *Id.* Article 4(3).

[463] *Id.* Article 4(2).

[464] *Id.* Articles 4(4)-(6).

[465] *Id.* Articles 5(2) and 5(5).

Treasury.[466] Any information extracted from the database must have been extracted as a result of an individualized search in order to be shared with law enforcement, public security, or counterterrorism authorities in the United States and Europe.[467]

---

[466] *Id.* Article 5(4).

[467] *See id.* Article 7. Pursuant to Articles 6(6) and 13(2) of the Agreement, there have been joint E.U.-U.S. reviews on the implementation of the Agreement's safeguards and controls. In 2011 and 2012, the joint reviews concluded that the U.S. has been in compliance with data protection provisions. *See* Commission report on the joint review of the implementation of the agreement between the European Union and the United States of America on the processing and transfer of financial messaging data from the European Union to the United States for the purpose of the terrorist finance tracking program, Brussels, SEC (2011) 438 final (Mar. 16, 2011); Commission report on the second joint review of the implementation of the Agreement between the European Union and the United States of America on the processing and transfer of Financial Messaging data from the European Union to the United States for the purposes of the Terrorist Finance Tracking Program, Brussels, SWD (2012) 454 final (Dec. 14, 2012).

CHAPTER 8

The Power to Detain: From the Framers to Guantanamo

Detention during wartime illustrates one of the Framers' core dilemmas: how to preserve liberty while protecting U.S. security. The September 11, 2001 terrorist attacks raised the stakes for answering this loaded question. In American law, detention typically occurs within the criminal justice system, with modest exceptions such as civil commitment of the mentally ill and quarantine of persons with infectious diseases.[1] The criminal justice system provides vital rights, including the right to a jury trial. In contrast, detention during wartime occurs *outside* the criminal justice system. While some sort of wartime detention is necessary to prevent combatants from rejoining the enemy, detention poses tensions with our structure of rights and separation of powers. Wartime detention can also clash with international law. To manage these adverse effects, courts have limited the power to detain during armed conflicts.

This chapter first takes up the Great Writ of habeas corpus, which the Framers inserted into the Constitution to provide a remedy for arbitrary detention, just as habeas corpus had served since the Magna Carta (Great Charter) of 1215 tempered monarchical rule in Britain. After discussing how the Supreme Court in the historic case of *Ex parte Milligan* limited detention in the United States during the Civil War, the chapter discusses the tragic Japanese-American internment of World War II. This part of the chapter describes why the mass internment of American citizens would not be tolerated by courts today. The chapter then discusses detention of suspected terrorists after September 11, addressing both detention at the U.S. naval base at Guantanamo Bay, Cuba and detention within the United States. The chapter next points out that after September 11, the government tried other kinds of detention, including detention of undocumented immigrants and material witnesses to alleged terrorism-related crimes. In addition, the chapter describes the conditions of detention after September 11, noting that coercive interrogation is illegal under both international and

---

[1] *See* Hamdi v. Rumsfeld, 542 U.S. 50, 556-57 (2004) (Scalia, J., dissenting).

domestic law while forced feeding of hunger-striking detainees is usually legal. Finally, the chapter examines remedies for harsh treatment while in detention, including habeas corpus and lawsuits seeking damages.

I. DETENTION IN THE AMERICAN EXPERIENCE

The Framers, fresh from their experience with British overreaching, viewed arbitrary detention as the essence of tyranny.[2] The Constitution's Suspension Clause[3] and the Due Process Clause of the Fifth Amendment[4] protect against arbitrary detention. Separation of powers among the branches of government is also a safeguard, along with the Equal Protection Clause of the Fourteenth Amendment.

II. CELEBRATING THE GREAT WRIT OF HABEAS CORPUS: WHAT DOES HABEAS CORPUS MEAN, ANYWAY?

The Framers included the Suspension Clause in Article I, §9 to preserve access to the "Great Writ" of habeas corpus. Under the Clause, habeas corpus can only be suspended when the emergency circumstances of rebellion or invasion so require. The Framers' eagerness to protect the Great Writ demonstrates its importance in our constitutional scheme.

In Latin, "habeas corpus" is a judicial command to a jailer (literally meaning, "deliver the body"). A petition for habeas corpus states that the jailer has imprisoned the body or "corpus"—i.e., a person—that the writ seeks to free. The jailer must justify in court the person's continued detention. For almost a thousand years, habeas corpus has been central to the struggle for freedom from tyranny. Habeas corpus is essential because it makes the Executive accountable to the courts.[5] For example, English barons demanded that King John sign the Magna Carta in 1215 because that document guaranteed access to habeas corpus and limited the king's power.

While ordinary citizens in the United States do not usually need to petition for habeas corpus, the Great Writ still protects them. If an individual is arrested and

---

[2] *See* FEDERALIST NO. 83 (Alexander Hamilton), at 499 (Clinton Rossiter ed., 1961) (warning against "arbitrary methods" of government that curtailed individuals' freedom).

[3] *See* U.S. CONST. art. I, §9, cl. 2.

[4] *See* U.S. CONST. amend. V.

[5] *See* FEDERALIST NO. 83 (Hamilton), at 499 (acknowledging importance of habeas corpus).

held without criminal charges for more than 72 hours, the person arrested can seek his release through a petition for habeas corpus filed with a court. A court would require that law enforcement officials respond. If prosecutors failed to charge the petitioner, the court would order his release. Since police and prosecutors know this, they either file charges promptly or release the suspect. You may have seen television shows that portray a lawyer barging into an interrogation room and telling the police, "Charge my client or let him go." The lawyer's words have weight because all the participants in this drama know that the lawyer's next stop is the courthouse, where the lawyer will submit a habeas petition.

To be valid under the Constitution, a suspension of the writ must be express—i.e., government must clearly declare in writing that the writ is suspended because the exigencies of rebellion or invasion require granting the government additional power to maintain order. Suspension must be a comprehensive, across-the-board measure that affects all people within the country or at least in a particular region. The requirement that a suspension be comprehensive is also a protection against oppression, since the political branches risk enormous political blowback in taking such a drastic step. That risk keeps the political branches honest, ensuring that only a dire threat to the republic, such as the rebellion or invasion that the Framers envisioned, will trigger a suspension.

Because a suspension is comprehensive, it resembles martial law—the imposition of military law on a war-torn state or region in which military commanders have discretion to protect both their own troops and the general public. Under martial law, ordinary civilian protections such as the right to a grand jury or a jury trial do not apply, because civilian institutions have temporarily lost the ability to function. When, as we shall see, Congress seeks to limit access to habeas corpus for particular individuals (such as detainees at Guantanamo) but does not suspend the writ in a comprehensive way, Congress must provide an adequate substitute for the judicial recourse that it has curbed.

Like so many issues in national security law, the availability of habeas corpus is wrapped up in the separation of powers and the checks and balances that the Framers engineered into the Constitution. Article I, §9 of the Constitution says that the Great Writ "shall not be suspended, unless . . . in Cases of Rebellion or Invasion." However, the Framers did not spell out which branch of government could suspend habeas. That issue was consequential in the United States' first major test of the scope of the Suspension Clause, during the Civil War.

A.   The Civil War and Habeas Corpus

1.   Suspending Habeas in the War's Early Days

Responding to a dire threat to the Union, President Abraham Lincoln unilaterally suspended habeas corpus in Maryland in April 1861, in the early days of

II. Celebrating the Great Writ of Habeas Corpus

the Civil War.[6] Prior to Lincoln's move, Marylanders sympathetic to the Confederacy had attacked Union troops,[7] impeded the movements of state militias coming to the aid of Washington, D.C.,[8] and burned railroad bridges from Baltimore to points north. Cutting off the nation's capital from the loyal northern states was a Confederate goal that appeared within reach.

Since Congress had adjourned and its members did not have today's technology to facilitate their reconvening in this emergency, action from the legislature was not in the cards. Nevertheless, statutes permitted the President to call out the militia to preserve the authority of the federal courts.[9] These statutes arguably contemplated the declaration of martial law. Under martial law, government enjoyed much of the power it possessed after the suspension of habeas corpus. In light of all of these factors, Lincoln took the extraordinary measure of suspending habeas corpus on the route between Philadelphia and Washington, D.C.[10] He stuck to his decision in the face of an opinion by Chief Justice Taney in *Ex parte Merryman*[11] that ruled that Lincoln had acted illegally in unilaterally suspending habeas corpus. Taney had required the government to produce an individual arrested on suspicion of helping to train a unit to fight alongside Confederate forces against the Union.[12] The Chief Justice based his holding on the placement of the Suspension Clause in Article I, which deals with the powers of Congress.[13] For Taney, textual location was everything: Congress could suspend habeas, but the President could not.

Lincoln took a more pragmatic view in his message to Congress in July 1861.[14] For Lincoln, the textual placement of the Suspension Clause was secondary. In fact, the Constitution's text does not rigidly separate the powers of Congress and the President, which the Framers designed to encourage

---

[6] *See* Sanford Levinson, *Constitutional Norms in a State of Permanent Emergency*, 40 GA. L. REV. 699, 718 (2006) (discussing Lincoln's suspension of habeas corpus). The discussion on Lincoln and habeas corpus is based on an earlier article by one of the co-authors of this volume. *See* Peter Margulies, *True Believers at Law: Legal Ethics, National Security Agendas, and the Separation of Powers*, 68 MD. L. REV. 1, 71-73 (2008).

[7] *See* JAMES F. SIMON, LINCOLN AND CHIEF JUSTICE TANEY: SLAVERY, SECESSION, AND THE PRESIDENT'S WAR POWERS 184-85 (2006).

[8] *See* Paul Finkelman, *Limiting Rights in Times of Crisis: Our Civil War Experience—A History Lesson for a Post-9/11 America*, 2 CARDOZO PUB. L. POL'Y & ETHICS 25, 35 (2003).

[9] *See* Ex parte Field, 9 F. Cas. 1, 6-7 (C.C.D. Vt. 1862), citing the militia statute of 1795 (1 Stat. 424); *cf.* Stephen I. Vladeck, Note, *Emergency Power and the Militia Acts*, 114 YALE L.J. 149, 175-77 (2004) (same).

[10] *See* Frank J. Williams, *Abraham Lincoln and Civil Liberties: Then and Now—The Southern Rebellion and September 11*, 60 N.Y.U. ANN. SURV. AM. L. 463, 466 (2004).

[11] 17 F. Cas. 144 (C.C.D. Md. 1861).

[12] *See* MARK NEELY, THE FATE OF LIBERTY: ABRAHAM LINCOLN AND CIVIL LIBERTIES 10 (1991); FRANK J. WILLIAMS, JUDGING LINCOLN 63 (2002) (recounting that Union officials suspected Merryman was recruiting soldiers for the Confederacy).

[13] *See* Ex parte Merryman, 17 F. Cas. 144, 148 (C.C.D. Md. 1861).

[14] *See* July 4 Message to Congress, IV Collected Works of Abraham Lincoln 430, *available at* http://quod.lib.umich.edu/cgi/text/text-idx?page=browse&c=lincoln (last visited Feb. 7, 2008) (hereinafter July 4 Message).

collaboration between the branches. For example, Article I, §7 is about the President's power: It grants the President power to veto legislation, subject to an override from two thirds of both the House and the Senate, respectively. Lincoln contended that the requirement in the Constitution's Take Care Clause[15] that the President "faithfully execute the laws" required a measure of judgment in times of crisis.[16] According to Lincoln, taking care of "laws" required attention to "the whole of the laws," rather than pondering a single law in isolation, even when that provision was as central as the Suspension Clause.[17] Lincoln contended that he had a higher duty: ensuring that constitutional government did not "go to pieces" as it faced the existential threat of insurrection and secession.[18] On this view, the Take Care Clause required a temporary violation of one of the laws, including the Suspension Clause, if the alternative was permitting "all the laws, *but one*, to go unexecuted. . . ."[19]

As we shall see, Lincoln's pragmatic view of the President's power to authorize suspension of habeas corpus was plausible, but only when that power was narrowly tailored to the emergency facing Washington, D.C. and the absence of Congress. Lincoln's unilateral suspension continued with only minor interruption for over 20 months after that emergency faded, and was therefore constitutionally problematic. However, apart from a brief spate of detentions prompted by a soon-revoked order in August 1862,[20] the actual number of detentions of U.S. civilians who lived north of the border states was small.[21] A handful of detentions targeted dissenters such as Ohio politician Clement Vallandigham, who was tried and convicted by a military commission.[22] While Vallandigham's case, in which the Supreme Court declined to intervene, was troubling, vigorous public debate about Lincoln's policies continued largely unabated.[23] In March 1863, Congress passed a statute suspending the writ with important limits on detention.[24]

2. The 1863 Habeas Corpus Act

The conditions Congress imposed in the 1863 Habeas Corpus Act limited the length of detention in states that remained loyal to the Union. Those states were

---

[15] *See* U.S. CONST., art. II, §3.

[16] *See* July 4 Message, *supra* note 14, at 430.

[17] *See* July 4 Message, *supra* note 14; *see also* ARTHUR M. SCHLESINGER, JR., THE IMPERIAL PRESIDENCY 59 (2004) (discussing Lincoln's exercise of power); David J. Barron & Martin S. Lederman, *The Commander in Chief at the Lowest Ebb—A Constitutional History*, 121 HARV. L. REV. 941, 994-1005 (2008) (arguing that Lincoln's actions were limited, and did not rely on absolutist view of presidential power).

[18] See July 4 Message, *supra* note 14.

[19] *Id.*

[20] NEELY, *supra* note 12, at 53-64.

[21] *Id.* at 131-18.

[22] *Id.* at 65-68.

[23] *Id.* at 137-38.

[24] 12 Statutes at Large 755 et seq., 37th Cong., Sess. III, Chap. 81.

not the site of intense, protracted violence between contending organized armed forces (the definition of a noninternational conflict (NIAC) under the law of war). In these loyal states, courts were open and functioning, so martial law was not required to maintain order. Accordingly, the 1863 Act required the Executive to furnish federal judges with a comprehensive list of all civilians held as "state or political prisoners" who were citizens of states loyal to the Union.

Congress exempted Confederate soldiers captured on the battlefield, who were considered prisoners of war detained under the law of armed conflict. It also excluded states like Missouri, where bloody fighting raged through much of the war. Strict rules governed all other detention caused by the conflict. Judges had to order the release of any named prisoner not promptly indicted by a grand jury, as long as that person took an oath of allegiance to the Union. Prisoners who had been indicted were eligible for bail, like any other criminal defendant. Detainees who were *not* named by the Executive and who were not indicted in a timely fashion could seek their release within 20 days of their arrest.

Statistics on detentions suggest that the government's detentions were largely consistent with the limits in the 1863 Act.[25] Most detainees were POWs, suspected Union deserters, and residents of southern or border states.[26] A relatively small group was detained on other grounds. The experience of one individual from this group led to the landmark 1866 decision of the U.S. Supreme Court, *Ex parte Milligan*.[27]

3.   **Explaining** *Ex Parte Milligan*

Lambdin Milligan was a resident of Indiana, a state loyal to the Union. In late 1864, in the closing months of the Civil War, Federal officials acquired evidence that Milligan had recruited and provided military training to individuals with the purpose of subverting Indiana's lawful government. Officials arrested and detained Milligan, without placing him on a list as the 1863 Act required. Approximately two weeks after his arrest, officials charged Milligan with violations of the law of war and tried him in a military commission, where he was convicted and sentenced to death. After his military commission trial, a grand jury met but did not indict Milligan, who subsequently filed a petition for habeas corpus in federal court.

While Justice David Davis's landmark opinion ultimately turned, as we shall see, on the legality of Milligan's military commission trial, Davis's analysis also limited the government's power to detain. Justice Davis distinguished the emergency in the early days of the Civil War from the calm during the rest of the conflict in states that remained loyal to the Union. The Court included language in its opinion that hinted approval for Lincoln's initial decision. In situations of

---

[25] NEELY, *supra* note 12, at 13-38.
[26] *Id.*
[27] 71 U.S. 2 (1866).

grave "exigency," Justice Davis seemed to admit, waiting for Congress to act could be fatal.[28] When civilian authority has largely collapsed, as in the chaos that ruled Maryland in the early days of the Civil War, Justice Davis hinted that the President needs some authority to detain individuals seeking to do imminent and irreparable harm to the nation. The Maryland insurrectionists who sought to isolate Washington, D.C. from the loyal states to the north surely fell within this category.

This limited, provisional authority to act is consistent with the separation of powers. If, as Lincoln stated in his message to Congress in July 1861, the chaos in Maryland had caused the government to "go to pieces," Congress's power would also have collapsed. By acting to ease an emergency that threatened irreparable harm, Lincoln preserved Congress's very ability to legislate. Moreover, earlier legislation indicated that Congress understood the need for expeditious executive action. In an important pre-*Milligan* case authorizing President Lincoln to establish a blockade of Confederate ports, the Court cited federal laws passed during and shortly after the Founding Era (1795 and 1807), permitting the President to call out the militia and declare martial law.[29] These statutes reinforced the argument that Congress had acquiesced in the need for the provisional exercise of power by the President until Congress reconvened.

The *Milligan* Court took a more skeptical view of suspension's validity in a place and time that did not match the exigency of Maryland in the war's early days. The Court interpreted Congress's 1863 legislation as imposing strict limits on the power to detain outside the criminal justice system. Justice Davis noted that Indiana was a state loyal to the Union where civilian courts were functioning. According to Justice Davis, Milligan was not a combatant acting under orders from the Confederacy. Justice Davis readily acknowledged that Milligan could be prosecuted in a civilian court for his subversive acts. However, no grand jury had indicted Milligan. Pursuant to the 1863 Habeas Corpus Act, Justice Davis opined, Milligan had been entitled to release once he had been held for more than 20 days.

Looking at both the Civil War detentions and the Court's response in *Milligan*, we can draw some lessons. First, detention is dangerous because it can allow the government to bypass the robust protections of the criminal justice system, including the right to a grand jury and trial by a jury of one's peers. Granting the government such power is only prudent in emergencies, and even then requires limits. Second, even in emergencies, unilateral exercise of the power to detain is disfavored; participation from Congress and the courts is vital.[30]

[28] *Id.* at 125.

[29] The Prize Cases, 67 U.S. (2 Black) 635 (1863).

[30] The Court applied a similar rationale 80 years later in Duncan v. Kahanamoku, 327 U.S. 304, 313-14 (1946) (holding that government during World War II lacked power to declare martial law and unilaterally suspend the writ of habeas corpus in the territory of Hawaii, whose residents were "loyal to the United States").

B. Detention, Due Process, and Equal Protection: The World War II Experience

In addition to undermining the criminal justice system's procedural protections, detention can also undermine equality. Without careful checks on the government's ability to detain, hatred and fear toward particular groups can take over. This threat to equality figured in a disturbing example of wartime mass detention over 70 years after *Milligan* was decided—the internment of Japanese-Americans during World War II. The Supreme Court unfortunately upheld measures taken jointly by Congress and President Franklin Roosevelt to force the evacuation of Japanese-Americans from their homes.[31] In taking this wrong turn, the Court cited the cooperation between Congress and the Executive on the internment policy.[32] It also read the Suspension Clause very narrowly. The Court's decisions nevertheless contained important checks on the government's ability to detain Americans in the future.

The Japanese-American internment emerged from the climate of fear that gripped the United States after Japanese forces attacked the U.S. naval base at Pearl Harbor, Hawaii on December 7, 1941, triggering America's entry into World War II. Western states such as California felt vulnerable to the risk of a land invasion by Japan—a risk that never materialized and was probably never a serious possibility. Officials also worried—again without a basis in fact—about the loyalty of Japanese-Americans and the possibility of subversion and espionage. This anxiety combined with envy and resentment of Asian-Americans that had long been a staple of politics in California and elsewhere.

Responding to this pressure, Congress expressly authorized the forced evacuation of Japanese-Americans on the West Coast from their homes and made violation of the military's evacuation orders a federal crime. The government then relocated Japanese-Americans into facilities that the government called "assembly and relocation centers." The War Department relied on a report by General John DeWitt that erroneously claimed that Japanese-Americans had attempted to send radio signals to Japanese air and sea forces to guide targeting the West Coast. J. Edgar Hoover's Federal Bureau of Investigation, not known for its leniency toward possible subversion, pronounced the report a willful falsehood.[33] The government conducted no individualized investigation into the activities of the more than 100,000 individuals detained, including thousands of children. The only specific remedy for Japanese-Americans wrongfully detained was an administrative process that allowed a detainee to leave the West Coast and live freely elsewhere in the U.S. if that individual could prove his loyalty. That process was hardly an adequate remedy for the deprivation of liberty entailed

---

[31] *See* Korematsu v. United States, 323 U.S. 214 (1944).

[32] Hirabayashi v. United States, 320 U.S. 81 (1943).

[33] *See* Korematsu v. United States, 584 F. Supp. 1406, 1417-19 (N.D. Cal. 1984) (discussing historical record as basis for vacating Fred Korematsu's conviction for violating evacuation order).

in the internment: Tens of thousands of Japanese-Americans endured almost three years of detention without *any* showing that they were disloyal.

1.   Separation of Powers and the Japanese-American Internment

The Supreme Court's willingness to uphold the unjust forced evacuation of U.S. citizens stemmed in large part from deference to the joint judgment of Congress and the President on matters of national security. In *Hirabayashi v. United States*,[34] the Court noted approvingly that Congress and the President were "acting together . . . in cooperation."[35] It is far less clear that the Court would have upheld *unilateral* presidential action of this size and scope. Deference to joint action by Congress and the President does not justify the Court's decisions, but helps place them in context.

2.   Suspension and Internment

The Court's decisions upholding aspects of the internment policy also hinged on a narrow reading of *Ex parte Milligan* and the Suspension Clause. At first blush, one might think that the detention of 100,000 U.S. citizens outside the criminal justice system would violate the Suspension Clause. However, the Court viewed *Milligan* narrowly, as forbidding only unilateral actions by the President.[36] Here, as noted above, Congress and the President had acted together. The Court viewed this cooperation as lessening the risk that a President would become a dictator, governing arbitrarily with the military's help. Moreover, the Court noted, the petitioner in *Hirabayashi* was not challenging his detention per se. The petitioner had been tried in an ordinary civilian court[37] for violating the federal statute that made disobedience of military orders a federal crime. This was not a detention case at all, the Court reasoned; it was an appeal from a criminal conviction, albeit one with special significance.

In *Korematsu v. United States*, the Court, in an opinion by Justice Hugo Black, similarly upheld Fred Korematsu's conviction for failing to obey the initial military evacuation order. Trying to limit the precedential effect of the decision, Justice Black (usually an outspoken supporter of civil liberties), narrowed the issue in the case to the legality of the *initial military order to Japanese-Americans to evacuate their homes*. The Court did not purport to address in *Korematsu* the lawfulness of the *continued* detention of Japanese-Americans subsequent to that order.

This reading of *Milligan* and the Suspension Clause was far too narrow. The better view would have been that laws enacted by Congress in support of the

---

[34] 320 U.S. 81 (1943).
[35] *Id.* at 91-92.
[36] *Id.* at 92.
[37] *Id.* at 92-93.

internment policy violated the Suspension Clause by permitting the wholesale detention of thousands of U.S. citizens without any particularized showing of wrongdoing. The Court's narrow view is a grave flaw in the decisions upholding aspects of the internment policy.

C. *Equal Protection and Due Process*

The Court's rejection of the Suspension Clause argument against internment left two grounds for challenging the policy: equal protection and due process. The equal protection principle declares that no person within the United States shall be deprived of equal protection of the laws.[38] The Due Process Clause of the Fifth Amendment requires that government provide procedural safeguards to individuals threatened with government deprivation of life, liberty, or property. While the due process and equal protection challenges did not result in a Supreme Court decision striking down the internment policy, these challenges did provide significant future checks on government and paved the way for the policy's end.

1. Equal Protection Did Not Bar the Internment

On Korematsu's Equal Protection challenge to the evacuation statute, Justice Black first observed that the Constitution frowns on government classifications based on race and ethnicity. Foreshadowing the landmark desegregation decision a decade later in *Brown v. Board of Education*, the Court held that a government law or policy based on race was "suspect" and required "strict scrutiny" by the courts.[39] This careful review by courts was necessary, Justice Black explained, because the political process may not work properly to protect the rights of minorities. Fear and hatred may distort politics, so that persecution of minorities becomes a winning strategy for elected officials. The federal courts, whose judges are appointed for life and are therefore independent of the political process, must intervene.

Unfortunately, the *Korematsu* Court failed to provide this robust judicial review. The Court held that uncertainty about Japanese-American loyalties was an adequate basis for the evacuation order, instead of requiring proof of disloyalty in particular cases. The justification that the Court accepted fell far short of the "pressing public necessity"[40] that the Constitution demanded. Indeed, interning

---

[38] The Equal Protection Clause is found in the Fourteenth Amendment, which by its terms applies only to states. However, the Supreme Court has read the Fifth Amendment, which also applies to the federal government, to include the equal protection principle. *Korematsu* proceeded on this assumption, which was made express by the Court in Bolling v. Sharpe, 347 U.S. 497, 499-500 (1954).

[39] *Korematsu*, 323 U.S. at 215.

[40] *Id.*

over 100,000 Japanese-Americans without proof of disloyal conduct surely demonstrated the "racial antagonism" that the Court said could "never" justify such draconian and arbitrary action.[41]

While the Court's holding was deeply problematic, the verdict of history has limited its impact. Congress passed two statutes granting compensation to the victims of the internment,[42] and a federal court in 1984[43] granted a writ of *coram nobis* voiding Fred Korematsu's conviction, in part because the Justice Department did not fully disclose to the Supreme Court during the original internment litigation the inaccurate information in the DeWitt Report. *Korematsu* is now an example of what courts should *not* do in mass detention cases.

2. Due Process Helped Limit the Internment's Duration

The Court's concern about its legacy may have shaped a far better decision on the Japanese-American internment, *Ex parte Endo*.[44] While the *Korematsu* Court had failed to properly apply equal protection, *Endo* suggested that the Due Process Clause of the Fifth Amendment limited mass detention. *Endo* involved a Japanese-American detainee whom the government had conceded was loyal to the United States. Mitsuye Endo did not challenge the initial evacuation orders that had displaced Japanese-Americans. Instead, she challenged the legality of her continued detention. In an opinion by Justice William O. Douglas, the Court linked due process to the rule of law. Justice Douglas asserted that due process would ordinarily prohibit depriving an individual of liberty without a showing of specific facts demonstrating that individual's dangerousness. When the government conceded Endo's loyalty, it signaled that it could not make such a showing in this case.

The *Endo* Court then turned the separation of powers argument against the executive branch, by using what courts call a "clear statement" approach to reading statutes. Justice Douglas did not assert that Congress lacked the power to authorize Endo's detention. However, Justice Douglas mused, if Congress wished to take the drastic step of detaining loyal U.S. citizens, Congress should have clearly stated its intent in the text of the statute authorizing forced evacuation of Japanese-Americans. Congress had not clearly and unambiguously granted the Executive this power in the statute. That triggered a separation of powers concern. Even if such detention was legal under the Due Process Clause—which Douglas doubted—unilateral action by the Executive was unworthy of judicial deference. The Court therefore held that the President had exceeded his authority by

---

[41] *Id.*

[42] *See* PETER IRONS, JUSTICE AT WAR 348 (1983); Julie Johnson, *President Signs Law to Redress Wartime Wrong*, N.Y. TIMES, Aug. 11, 1988, at A16 (reporting that under statute, each survivor of internment would receive $20,000 and an apology).

[43] Korematsu v. United States, 584 F. Supp. 1406 (N.D. Cal. 1984).

[44] 323 U.S. 283, 294 (1944); Patrick O. Gudridge, *Remember* Endo?, 116 HARV. L. REV. 1933 (2003).

continuing to detain Endo.[45] *Endo*'s clear statement rule may seem like a technical approach that does not do full justice to the weighty interests involved in the mass detention of American citizens. However, the clear statement approach serves vital interests. First, it signals to the political branches and the public the importance of values such as due process. Second, it upholds the separation of powers by countering unilateral executive action and giving Congress a chance to amend a statute if it sees fit. The clear statement approach in *Endo* had substantial practical consequences: The Roosevelt administration learned of the decision in advance and announced the program's end. Moreover, *Endo*'s clear statement requirement, together with *Korematsu*'s demanding test of a compelling state interest for mass detention, signaled the Court's reluctance to permit future detention on such a vast scale.

III.   DETENTION AFTER SEPTEMBER 11

Developments after the September 11 terrorist attacks tested the Court's resolve, but also resulted in limits on government power. In a 2004 decision, *Hamdi v. Rumsfeld*,[46] the Supreme Court declared that that the President did not have a "blank check" to unilaterally detain a suspected terrorist without judicial review.[47] In 2008, the Court declared in *Boumediene v. Bush*[48] that when Congress had not suspended habeas corpus across the board, it could not strip the courts of jurisdiction over the habeas petitions of Guantanamo detainees.

A.   *Detaining Suspected Terrorists Arrested in the United States and U.S. Citizens Seized Anywhere*

In *Hamdi v. Rumsfeld*, the Court cited cooperation between Congress and President George W. Bush in recognizing that the President had the power to detain adversaries in the conflict with Al Qaeda, subject to judicial review of detention. United States forces intervening in Afghanistan after September 11, 2001

---

[45] Justice Douglas used a similar approach over a decade after *Endo* to temper executive action against alleged members of the Communist Party during the Cold War. *See* Kent v. Dulles, 357 U.S. 116 (1958) (holding that Congress had not authorized denying passports to American citizens based on their alleged membership in the Communist Party); *cf.* Zemel v. Rusk, 381 U.S. 1, 16-17 (1965) (holding that broad ban on travel to Cuba, where Communist regime had taken control, was constitutional because it did not single out individuals because of their political beliefs, and imposed purely incidental restriction on individuals' travel choices in order to safeguard Americans' safety abroad and facilitate United States foreign policy).

[46] 542 U.S. 507 (2004).

[47] *Id*. at 536.

[48] 553 U.S. 723 (2008).

had captured Yaser Esam Hamdi, who had been born in the United States and was therefore a presumptive U.S. citizen. After U.S. officials discovered that Hamdi was a citizen, they moved him to facilities in Virginia and South Carolina. Following on the heels of precedents like *Milligan*, the case presented two vital questions: 1) Could Hamdi be detained at all?; and 2) If Hamdi could be detained, what procedural safeguards were constitutionally required for his continued detention?

In *Hamdi*, the Court looked to the Authorization for the Use of Military Force (AUMF) that Congress enacted after the September 11 attacks, which granted the President the power to take "necessary and appropriate" action to deter and prevent future attacks by those responsible for September 11—Al Qaeda and associated forces. To define the scope of detention authority, the Court, in an opinion by Justice Sandra Day O'Connor, relied on the law of armed conflict (LOAC). Justice O'Connor viewed detention of combatants as a necessary incident of waging war,[49] which Congress had implicitly authorized by enacting the AUMF. Without the ability to detain combatants, Justice O'Connor reasoned, a party to an armed conflict could not prevent captured combatants from rejoining the fight.

1.   *Hamdi* and the Suspension Clause

However, Justice O'Connor's approval of detention of the U.S. citizen Hamdi faced an obstacle: the Supreme Court's famed 1866 decision, *Ex parte Milligan*. In *Milligan*, the Court severely limited detention of citizens in locations where civilian courts were open and civilian trials were possible. Recall that Justice Davis in *Milligan* strictly enforced the suspension that Congress had enacted in 1863, which required the release of persons who were not prisoners of war and were residents of states where courts were functioning. The AUMF did not purport to suspend habeas corpus and did not expressly permit the detention of prisoners of war. If *Milligan* applied, Hamdi would have been entitled to immediate release. This was the position of Justice Antonin Scalia, who dissented in *Hamdi*.[50] To sidestep this possibility, Justice O'Connor relied on the narrow reading of *Milligan* adopted by the Supreme Court in the 1942 case of *Ex parte Quirin*.[51]

In *Ex parte Quirin*, the Court upheld the detention of Nazi saboteurs captured in the United States, although two of the eight saboteurs were U.S. citizens. According to the *Quirin* Court, *Milligan* turned on the finding that Lambdin Milligan was a civilian, not a combatant. Combatants like the Nazi saboteurs were different, *Quirin* held, because the LOAC permitted their detention, regardless of their citizenship. According to *Quirin*, the Framers, who were influenced by international law, expected that courts would defer to the LOAC. In other words, detention pursuant to LOAC was an implicit exception to the Suspension

---

[49] *Hamdi*, 542 U.S. at 518.
[50] *Id.* at 554.
[51] 317 U.S. 1 (1942).

III.   Detention After September 11

Clause. Justice O'Connor echoed *Quirin*'s rationale, finding that Hamdi's capture in Afghanistan made him a combatant subject to detention.

By finding that the AUMF implicitly incorporated the law of armed conflict, Justice O'Connor was also able to find that Hamdi's detention was consistent with an earlier statute, the Non-Detention Act.[52] That law barred detention of U.S. citizens without congressional authorization. The AUMF's implicit incorporation of the power to detain under the law of armed conflict was sufficient authorization under the Non-Detention Act, Justice O'Connor found.[53]

2.   Due Process and Hamdi's Detention

However, Justice O'Connor observed, the Due Process Clause imposed limits on the power to detain a U.S. citizen—even one captured while allegedly participating in combat with the United States. According to Justice O'Connor, judicial review (at least of the detention of citizens) was necessary because, "an unchecked system of detention carries the potential to become a means for oppression and abuse of others."[54] To carry out this review, Justice O'Connor applied a test from the Court's due process cases that balanced three factors: 1) the interest of the government in ensuring compliance with law; 2) the individual's interest in liberty; and 3) the risk of error.[55] For Justice O'Connor, the risk of error was the decisive factor requiring judicial review. Unchecked detention, Justice O'Connor asserted, could result in the detention of individuals like students, journalists, and aid workers who were not combatants, but were merely in the wrong place at the wrong time.[56] To address the unacceptable risk of error inherent in unchecked power to detain U.S. citizens, the Court required providing U.S. citizen detainees like Hamdi with the opportunity to go to federal court to seek their release.

3.   Subsequent Cases on Due Process and Post-9/11 Detention of U.S. Citizens and Persons Captured in the United States

Courts have also imposed limits on the detention of terrorism suspects captured in the United States. Consider a case such as *Al-Marri v. Pucciarelli*,[57] that challenged the government's position in ways that *Hamdi* did not. In *Hamdi*, the

---

[52] See 18 U.S.C. §4001(a).

[53] *Hamdi*, 542 U.S. at 517-18; *but see* Stephen I. Vladeck, Policy Comment, *A Small Problem of Precedent: 18 U.S.C. 4001(a) and the Detention of United States Citizen "Enemy Combatants,"* 112 YALE L.J. 961 (2003) (arguing that §4001(a) posed a substantial problem for the government's detention of Hamdi).

[54] *Hamdi*, 542 U.S. at 529-30.

[55] *Id.* at 530 (citing Mathews v. Eldridge, 424 U.S. 319 (1976)).

[56] *Id.*

[57] 534 F.3d 213 (4th Cir. 2007) (en banc).

government relied on the detainee's capture in a theater of war, namely Afghanistan. Capture in the United States was different. While the attacks on September 11 constituted acts of war, the United States was not an active theater of war after September 11. Detention outside the criminal justice system for individuals seized in this country therefore presented a greater risk of the kind of overreaching that the Framers feared. Courts will carefully review such detentions to ensure that a detainee is a combatant with Al Qaeda and not a mere civilian engaged in criminal acts that should be addressed within the civilian criminal justice system. Because the issue of detention after arrest in the United States raises such vital issues, the two cases where courts ruled are worth examining in depth.

a.   *Padilla v. Rumsfeld*

In the first case, U.S. citizen Jose Padilla, a Brooklyn native who moved to Chicago as a youth and became involved in gangs, was arrested at O'Hare Airport in Chicago in May 2002 after allegedly returning from Afghanistan and other states in the Middle East and South Asia. Padilla was briefly detained in New York, and then moved to a navy prison in South Carolina. The government claimed that Padilla had sought Al Qaeda's instructions to assemble a "dirty" bomb (a conventional explosive laced with radioactive material, not an actual nuclear weapon) for use in the United States.[58]

While the future path of the case indicated that the government's concerns about Padilla's Al Qaeda ties had some basis in fact,[59] the government refused in the early days of Padilla's detention to provide much in the way of specific evidence. Instead, the government relied on allegations in a hearsay declaration by a government official with no personal knowledge of the events described. Citing this declaration, the government claimed the power to hold Padilla incommunicado, without judicial review or even the ability to see a lawyer. Moreover, credible evidence indicates that the government subjected Padilla to extraordinarily harsh conditions, such as prolonged sensory deprivation, during his detention, in the course of interrogating him about links to Al Qaeda.[60]

Padilla eventually saw a lawyer, who filed a habeas corpus petition on Padilla's behalf in federal court in New York. The liberal Second Circuit Court of Appeals, based in New York, held that the government should either charge Padilla with a federal crime in a civilian court, or release him.[61] The Supreme Court reversed on procedural grounds.[62] Padilla then filed a habeas petition in the conservative

---

[58] PETER MARGULIES, LAW'S DETOUR: POLITICS, IDEOLOGY, AND JUSTICE IN THE BUSH ADMINISTRATION 16-17 (NYU Press 2010).

[59] *Id.* at 113 (citing Padilla's travel to Afghanistan before 9/11 to join Al Qaeda).

[60] Padilla v. Yoo, 678 F.3d 748, 752 (9th Cir. 2012) (reciting allegations).

[61] Padilla v. Rumsfeld, 352 F.3d 695 (2d Cir. 2003).

[62] Rumsfeld v. Padilla, 542 U.S. 426 (2004) (holding that venue (the particular court) for the habeas petition was improper because Padilla should have filed his petition in South Carolina, where he was then being held, rather than in New York, where he had been held earlier).

Fourth Circuit Court of Appeals, which held in 2005 that the government could detain Padilla, based on evidence that Padilla had traveled to Afghanistan to fight alongside Al Qaeda and the Taliban and had been recruited, trained, and equipped by Al Qaeda leaders to engage in violence in the United States.[63] Before the Supreme Court could hear his appeal, the government decided in 2006 to charge Padilla in ordinary civilian court with conspiracy to murder Americans overseas flowing from his pre-9/11 efforts to join Al Qaeda.[64]

b. *Al-Marri v. Pucciarelli*

The second suspected terrorist seized in the United States was Ali Saleh al-Marri. Unlike Padilla, al-Marri was not a U.S. citizen, but a Qatari national admitted to the United States as a graduate student on a significant date: September 10, 2001, one day before the terrorist attacks in New York and Washington.[65] Just weeks after the September 11 attacks, law enforcement officials interviewed al-Marri, apparently based on telephone records indicating that al-Marri had talked repeatedly with a top Al Qaeda financier linked to the 9/11 attacks. Al-Marri was arrested a couple of months later as a material witness in the 9/11 investigation. After FBI agents found hundreds of stolen credit card numbers on al-Marri's laptop, he was charged in federal court with credit card fraud and lying to the FBI. In 2003, federal law enforcement officials dropped the criminal charges against al-Marri and transferred him to the custody of the Defense Department, which detained him as an enemy combatant at the same navy facility in South Carolina that housed Jose Padilla. Al-Marri's conditions of confinement, like Padilla's, were harsh.[66]

After al-Marri petitioned for a writ of habeas corpus, the government filed a hearsay declaration much like the declaration in Padilla's case. The declaration acknowledged that Al-Marri was not in Afghanistan during active hostilities between the United States and Al Qaeda that commenced after September 11,

---

[63] Padilla v. Hanft, 423 F.3d 386, 388 (4th Cir. 2005).

[64] United States v. Jayyousi, 657 F.3d 1085, 1091-92 (11th Cir. 2011). The Supreme Court, based on the government's belated charging of Padilla in civilian court, viewed Padilla's challenge to his detention as moot. Padilla v. Hanft, 547 U.S. 1062 (2006). At Padilla's criminal trial in 2007, the government's evidence included Padilla's fingerprint on an Al Qaeda recruitment application. Padilla was convicted. He is now serving his sentence in federal prison after appellate courts sustained his conviction. *Jayyousi*, 657 F.3d 1085, *cert. denied sub nom.* Padilla v. United States, 133 S. Ct. 29 (2012).

[65] Al-Marri v. Pucciarelli, 534 F.3d 213, 255 (4th Cir. 2008) (en banc); *vacated and remanded,* Al-Marri v. Spagone, 555 U.S. 1220 (2009) (holding that Al-Marri's appeal was moot because government had transferred him to the custody of the Department of Justice and filed charges against him in civilian court); *cf.* MARGULIES, LAW's DETOUR, supra note 58, at 159 (noting Al-Marri's 2009 guilty plea); Josh Meyer, *Suspect Is Declared an Enemy Combatant,* L.A. TIMES, June 24, 2003, Main News 1 (discussing circumstances of Al-Marri's detention).

[66] Al-Marri v. Davis, 2012 U.S. Dist. LEXIS 20558, at 2 (D. Colo. Feb. 17, 2012), *aff'd,* 714 F.3d 1183 (10th Cir. 2013); *cert. denied,* 134 S. Ct. 295 (2013) (discussing reduction of criminal sentence because of harsh confinement that al-Marri experienced during almost six years in detention).

2001. However, according to the declaration, al-Marri had trained at an Al Qaeda training camp, talked about terrorist missions with Osama bin Laden, and volunteered for a "martyr mission" that involved disrupting the U.S. financial system. According to the government's declaration, al-Marri had entered the United States one day before September 11, 2001 to avoid the additional scrutiny that Al Qaeda leaders expected after the attacks.[67]

In a 2008 decision issued after al-Marri had been detained for over five years, the Fourth Circuit addressed the same issues that the Supreme Court had addressed in 2004 in *Hamdi v. Rumsfeld*: 1) Could al-Marri be detained?; and 2) If so, what procedural safeguards were constitutionally required? A majority of the court answered "Yes" to the first question. On the second question, a different majority of judges found that al-Marri was entitled to procedural protections that were greater than those he had received.

The majority of judges on the first question held that the Suspension Clause did not prohibit detention outside the criminal justice system of a suspected Al Qaeda terrorist seized in the United States. This holding followed the narrow view of the Suspension Clause and *Ex parte Milligan* taken by Justice O'Connor in *Hamdi v. Rumsfeld*. According to the *Al-Marri* majority, the Suspension Clause did not bar detention of combatants, even if those combatants were captured on U.S. territory.[68] Congress did not have to enact a general suspension of habeas corpus. The President had authority based on the AUMF to detain in the United States an individual affiliated with Al Qaeda who planned or actually engaged in conduct on Al Qaeda's behalf intended to do harm to U.S. citizens or property.[69]

However, a different majority on the full Fourth Circuit also held that al-Marri's detention did not comply with due process. According to the majority on this issue, the Due Process Clause required more than mere acceptance of a hearsay declaration.[70] Because a hearsay declaration increases the risk of error, a court would have to ask at least the first of two additional questions: 1) whether the provision of more reliable evidence, such as the testimony of government interrogators, would unduly burden the government; and 2) if the answer to question 1 is "Yes," whether the hearsay declaration was sufficiently reliable to support the government's position that the petitioner should be detained.[71] Because the court below had failed to ask even the first question, the Fourth Circuit ordered that the case be sent back to the court below for further proceedings. The government appealed to the Supreme Court, which in 2009 vacated the judgment of the Fourth Circuit and dismissed the appeal as moot after the government transferred

---

[67] Al-Marri v. Wright, 487 F.3d 160, 165-66 (4th Cir. 2007); *Al-Marri*, 534 F.3d at 215.

[68] *Id.* at 259-61 (Traxler, J., concurring). Because of the way in which the judges of the en banc Fourth Circuit split on the two issues in the case, Traxler's was the controlling opinion. Judge Wilkinson wrote a concurring opinion that offered further guidance on detainability. *Id.* at 293.

[69] *Id.*

[70] *Id.* at 259, 273.

[71] *Id.* at 268.

al-Marri *back* to the Justice Department to face criminal charges, which ultimately resulted in a plea agreement.[72]

While the Supreme Court has not opined after September 11 on detention of a person seized on U.S. soil, we can offer an informed guess about the future. It is unlikely that any court would uphold mass detention of the kind that the government imposed on Japanese-Americans during World War II. A court might hold that detention of an individual person was warranted, if the government could demonstrate that the detainee was a member of Al Qaeda and had acted on Al Qaeda's instructions in planning or committing acts entailing harm to U.S. citizens or property. However, the government would probably have to submit concrete and reliable evidence supporting this claim, including testimony subject to cross-examination. Moreover, the government would come under extraordinary pressure to limit the time of detention and pursue charges in either an Article III court or a military commission.

B.   Detentions at Guantanamo

Detentions at Guantanamo Bay present different issues. Guantanamo detainees, unlike Hamdi and Padilla, are not U.S. citizens. Moreover, unlike Padilla and al-Marri, they were captured abroad, usually in or near a theater of war. However, the United States is holding those detainees in a facility that is under exclusive U.S. control. That last fact has led the Supreme Court to ensure that Guantanamo detainees have access to habeas corpus. The Court's focus on preserving checks and balances has influenced its approach. The separation of powers also figures in ongoing debates about how to close the Guantanamo facility, including the controversy in the spring of 2014 about the exchange of five high-ranking Taliban detainees for U.S. Army soldier Bowe Bergdahl.

1.   Establishing Guantanamo Detainees' Access to Habeas: *Boumediene v. Bush*

The Supreme Court held in the 2008 decision of *Boumediene v. Bush*[73] that Guantanamo detainees had access to habeas corpus. However, this decision did not emerge out of the blue. In January 2002, months after the U.S. intervened militarily in Afghanistan, the U.S. government had started moving detainees seized in Afghanistan and Pakistan to a detention facility at the Guantanamo Bay Naval Base in Cuba. Officials in the administration of

---

[72] In April 2009, al-Marri pleaded guilty to conspiring to provide material support to Al Qaeda, and was sentenced to 100 months (slightly over eight years) in prison. *See* Joel Hood & Josh Meyer, *Marri Pleads Guilty to Helping 9/11 Architects: The Plea Agreement Is Seen as Disposing of a Legally Thorny Case*, L.A. Times, May 1, 2009, at A13.

[73] 553 U.S. 723 (2008).

President George W. Bush had selected Guantanamo as a detention site based on advice from administration lawyers that U.S. courts would not have jurisdiction over petitions for habeas corpus from detainees at a base on foreign territory.[74] By 2008, the U.S. government had released hundreds of detainees. Some were high-ranking leaders in Al Qaeda or Afghanistan's Taliban, which had harbored Al Qaeda at the time of the 9/11 attacks. However, the government had also held people for years who had no discernible links to terrorism.[75] In Guantanamo's early years, and for some time after for high-level detainees held elsewhere such as Khalid Shaikh Muhammed, the alleged mastermind of the 9/11 attacks, conditions were often harsh.

Before *Boumediene*, habeas corpus at Guantanamo had involved a dialogue between Congress and the courts about how to read legislation already on the books. In 2004, when the Supreme Court decided *Hamdi v. Rumsfeld*, holding that the Due Process Clause required judicial review of the detention of a U.S. citizen, it also decided *Rasul v. Bush*.[76] *Rasul* interpreted a general law that granted federal courts jurisdiction over habeas corpus petitions. The *Rasul* Court read that general law to include petitions from Guantanamo detainees. In 2006, Congress, at the urging of the administration of President George W. Bush, responded to *Rasul* by stripping federal courts of jurisdiction over Guantanamo habeas petitions. Congress's action squarely raised the issue decided in *Boumediene*: whether the Constitution's Suspension Clause protected detainees' access to the Great Writ.

The U.S. government argued in *Boumediene* that since the Guantanamo naval base was on Cuban territory, the Suspension Clause did not apply. Rejecting this argument, Justice Kennedy, writing for the majority, cited the 1903 lease by Cuba to the United States of the land for the naval base, which granted the United States "complete jurisdiction and control,"[77] and the 1934 treaty that continued the lease at this country's pleasure. Justice Kennedy worried that if the Court accepted the government's argument, the government could simply outsource detention operations, circumventing the protections built into the Constitution. At least where the U.S. role was enduring and unchallenged, Justice Kennedy suggested, the government could not "contract[] away" constitutional protections like access to habeas corpus.[78]

Justice Kennedy suggested that access to habeas corpus preserved checks and balances. Without judicial review of detention via habeas corpus, the political

---

[74] MARGULIES, LAW'S DETOUR, *supra* note 58, at 54-56.

[75] *Id.* at 35-36.

[76] 542 U.S. 466 (2004).

[77] *Boumediene*, 553 U.S. at 765.

[78] *Id.* Courts have declined to extend habeas corpus jurisdiction to U.S. detention facilities in Afghanistan. Those facilities, courts have held, were not on territory over which the United States had exclusive control, as it does at Guantanamo. In addition, those detention facilities were closer to an active theater of war. Moreover, the United States throughout litigation on this matter was handing over virtually all detainees in Afghanistan to the Afghan government. *See* Maqaleh v. Gates, 605 F.3d 84 (D.C. Cir. 2010).

branches would have "the power to switch the Constitution on and off."[79] That concentration of power, Justice Kennedy wrote, was dangerous to both liberty and stability. Monolithic power would encourage overconfidence among the nation's leaders, leading to bad policy choices that conflicted with longer-term values. Moreover, Justice Kennedy suggested, the ascendancy of the political branches would eventually breed instability. Unchecked power would prompt rebellion among the constituents of the republic, as concentrated power had done in Britain in the seventeenth century, when sweeping authority was the hallmark of both King Charles I and the "Long Parliament" that ruled after King Charles's deposal and execution. The Framers, Justice Kennedy wrote, were frightened of these "pendular swings,"[80] and inserted protections like habeas corpus into the Constitution to promote stability as well as rights.[81]

Given the Court's view that the Suspension Clause applied, the next question in *Boumediene* was whether Congress in stripping federal courts of jurisdiction over Guantanamo detainees' habeas petitions had formally enacted a suspension of the Great Writ. To be legally effective, a suspension of habeas corpus would have to be both express and comprehensive. It would have to clearly state an intention to bar *all* access to habeas corpus for *all* individuals (not just those presently detained at Guantanamo) within all or part of U.S. territory. The Court noted in *Boumediene* that the government did not even argue that the Military Commissions Act of 2006 constituted a formal suspension of the writ.[82]

The *Boumediene* Court then stated that Congress could only restrict habeas without a suspension if it provided an *adequate substitute procedure* that would allow those confined to challenge their confinement. Under the Detainee Treatment Act, Congress had recognized that the Bush administration had established Civilian Status Review Tribunals (CSRTs) and a related administrative forum, Annual Review Boards (ARBs). However, the Court said, there were substantial problems with the scheme that Congress had substituted for the Great Writ. First, CSRTs and ARBs did not provide detainees with access to evidence.[83] The CSRTs therefore posed a high risk of factual error: A detainee could not rebut evidence that was never disclosed to him, or prove his innocence without access to evidence that would show he was not part of Al Qaeda.[84] Moreover, the limited judicial review that Congress had provided in place of habeas was insufficient to rectify this problem. That limited form of judicial review did not permit the appellate court to consider new evidence.[85] Without the ability to consider new evidence, the reviewing court lacked the ability to keep administrative officials in check, and the power to do justice to a detainee who was being wrongfully held. Since the

---

[79] *Boumediene*, 553 U.S. at 765.

[80] *Id.* at 742.

[81] *See* Jared A. Goldstein, *Habeas Without Rights*, 2007 Wis. L. Rev. 1165

[82] *Boumediene*, 553 U.S. at 771.

[83] *Id.* at 783-84.

[84] *Id.* at 785.

[85] *Id.* at 786.

procedure Congress had substituted for habeas was inadequate, the Court struck down Congress's habeas-stripping provisions, and held that federal courts henceforth had jurisdiction over requests for the writ from Guantanamo detainees.

2.   Post-*Boumediene* Developments: Substantive Standards for Guantanamo Detention

In holding that Congress could not strip federal courts of the ability to hear Guantanamo detainees' petitions for habeas, the Supreme Court struck a blow for the rule of law. However, the decision left many questions unanswered. For example, the Court did not address what the government had to show to respond to a habeas petition by a detainee. Case law in the federal District of Columbia Circuit has sought to fill that gap. The D.C. Circuit Court of Appeals has adopted a deferential test for detention.

D.C. Circuit case law since *Boumediene* has indicated that the government must prove that a detainee is part of Al Qaeda or associated forces, including Afghanistan's Taliban, which harbored Al Qaeda before 9/11 and fought alongside Al Qaeda once the United States intervened in 9/11's aftermath.[86] The government, like Justice O'Connor in *Hamdi*, has viewed this test as reflecting international law: Detention of combatants is a legal power possessed by a party to an armed conflict to prevent those captured from rejoining the battle.

Habeas corpus petitions from Guantanamo detainees all follow the same procedural path: The detainee, usually with the help of a lawyer, files a petition in the federal district court (the trial-level court) for the District of Columbia, which pursuant to statute has jurisdiction over all such petitions. Congress took this step to promote uniformity in decisions, and ensure that senior federal officials have the clearest possible guidance on detention issues. For this reason, federal district courts elsewhere—say in Florida, New York, or Tennessee—have no role in hearing Guantanamo habeas cases. Trial judges on the D.C. district court may consider written evidence from the government and the detainee, and may also hear testimony (a detainee may testify via a video link from Guantanamo). Once the district court makes a decision on the habeas petition, the losing party may appeal to the D.C. Circuit Court of Appeals. A loser in that forum can seek certiorari from the U.S. Supreme Court, which is theoretically available but rare in practice; as of December 2014, the Supreme Court had not agreed to hear any Guantanamo habeas case since *Boumediene* in 2008.

The D.C. Circuit has outlined a pragmatic test in determining who can be detained. Proving that a detainee was part of Al Qaeda or associated forces at the time of his capture involves the combination of several factors. Those factors include participation in an Al Qaeda training camp, a stay at an Al Qaeda

---

[86] Hussain v. Obama, 718 F.3d 964 (D.C. Cir. 2013).

guest-house, and living with Al Qaeda or Taliban fighters near battle lines while in possession of a military-grade firearm.[87]

The D.C. Circuit has taken this view despite arguments by detainees and some judges. Petitioners have argued that each factor, viewed independently, could have a completely innocent explanation. For example, the detainee could be a harmless student with some militant classmates, or a journalist reporting on violent extremists. The D.C. Circuit's approach, according to critics, replaces "hard proof" with inference from slender or ambiguous evidence.

In response, the D.C. Circuit in effect adopted the detective's credo: "There's no such thing as a coincidence." One data point, such as a stay at an Al Qaeda guest-house, might not conclusively prove membership in Al Qaeda, but the intersection of multiple data points makes an innocent explanation less and less likely. The court has expressed this logical premise in colloquial terms: Suppose we observe something of unknown origin and ask, "What is it?" Our observation reveals that the subject under investigation "looks like a duck . . . walks like a duck, and . . . quacks like a duck."[88] Mystery solved: The subject under investigation really is a duck.[89] As ducks go, so do detainees, the court has held: With coincidence ruled out, membership in Al Qaeda is the most plausible explanation for the convergence of multiple factors, even when a single factor in isolation does not provide conclusive proof.

3.   Detention and the "Forever War"

While the D.C. Circuit's "duck" standard focuses on the detainee's role at the time of his capture, the passage of time since the detainee's capture may undercut the rationale for detention. Most wars that the United States fought before 9/11 were of relatively brief and definite duration: The U.S. intervention in World War II, for example, took less than four years. The armed conflict between the United States and Al Qaeda has lasted more than three times as long. That in itself may require some rethinking of the rationale for detention.

In addition, traditional wars between states usually end with a formal ceremony, such as the Japanese surrender to General Douglas MacArthur on the U.S.S. Missouri that signaled the end of World War II. In contrast, the armed conflict with Al Qaeda may end through the degradation of Al Qaeda into a weakened entity without the ability to engage in armed conflict. At that point, the authorization for the use of military force (AUMF) that Congress passed shortly after 9/11 may no longer be valid, undermining continued detention's rationale.

---

[87] *Id.* at 968.

[88] *Hussain*, 718 F.3d at 968.

[89] *Id.* This view of inferences and evidence is consistent with mainstream legal thought. *See* Roger C. Park & Michael J. Saks, *Evidence Scholarship Reconsidered: Results of the Interdisciplinary Turn*, 46 B.C. L. Rev. 949 (2006).

Finally, prudence and a regard for the United States' global reputation has already pushed the government to initiate case-by-case reviews, called Periodic Review Boards, of the ongoing dangerousness of detainees. Congressional restrictions on release and resettlement of detainees may limit the government's ability or inclination to release nondangerous detainees or trade detainees for U.S. POWs like Bowe Bergdahl. However, those restrictions clash with the separation of powers.

First, Justice O'Connor in *Hamdi* indicated that the detention of combatants might present more challenging issues when "the practical circumstances of a given conflict are entirely unlike those of the conflicts that informed the development of the law of war."[90] In that event, according to Justice O'Connor, the "understanding" that supported detention might "unravel."[91] The mere length of a conflict may not reflect the different circumstances that Justice O'Connor posited. After all, there is no set duration for any war; no stopwatch or cell phone timer can dictate a war's end. However, there may be a point where the duration of an armed conflict with a violent nonstate entity like Al Qaeda becomes a difference of kind rather than merely degree. At that point, the Supreme Court might revisit the basis for detention of suspected members of Al Qaeda's fighting force.

The passage of time also may undermine the validity of the AUMF in two ways. First, the winding down of the role of U.S. ground troops in Afghanistan could cause the AUMF to lapse as a matter of U.S. law or undermine the international law basis for detention. Second, Al Qaeda's degradation into a disorganized armed group could have the same effect.

The end of U.S. ground troops' combat role in Afghanistan is an important milestone, but not one that is necessarily fatal to the continued validity of the AUMF. The AUMF authorized the President to use "necessary and appropriate force" to combat Al Qaeda and associated forces and deter further attacks from these entities. The "necessary and appropriate force" that the AUMF contemplated is not limited to ground troops, but could also include air power. The regular U.S. use of air power, including drones, against Al Qaeda or associated forces would still constitute a use of force authorized by the AUMF. Similarly, under international law a non-international armed conflict between a state like the United States and a nonstate actor such as Al Qaeda requires violence of a certain intensity and duration carried out by organized armed groups.[92] Violence between contending ground forces is *evidence* of an armed conflict; so is the use of drones or other forms of air power. As long as air operations against Al Qaeda meet international law's intensity standard and Al Qaeda itself is an "organized armed group," the international law basis for detention remains in place.

---

[90] *Hamdi*, 542 U.S. at 521.

[91] *Id.*

[92] *See* Laurie R. Blank & Geoffrey S. Corn, *Losing the Forest for the Trees: Syria, Law, and the Pragmatics of Conflict Recognition*, 46 Vand. J. Transnat'l L. 693, 718 (2013).

III.   Detention After September 11

Additional authorization for detention might be required under both domestic and international law if the efforts of the U.S. and its allies degraded Al Qaeda's capabilities to the point that Al Qaeda was no longer an "organized armed group."[93] Suppose that Al Qaeda dissolved in small, uncoordinated bunches of disgruntled individuals only able to engage in small-scale violence on an intermittent basis. In that event, the AUMF might not provide sufficient basis for detention under domestic law. Without a new authorization, the President might have to rely on Article II authority alone. However, that authority has not generally been viewed as sufficient to permit the sustained use of force in the absence of the need for self-defense against an armed attack. The international law justification for the use of force is also far weaker without a self-defense rationale.[94]

To deal with this problem, some scholars have urged that the President and Congress act now to supply a renewed domestic law basis for both detention and the ongoing use of force against terrorist groups. A new AUMF based on these scholars' recommendations would grant the President authority to make findings that groups not covered by the old AUMF were planning violence against the United States requiring a U.S. military response.[95] Critics of this approach object that it would give the President too much authority, and that such an open-ended delegation to the President might be an unwise invitation to unnecessary military interventions.[96] Mounting a sustained military effort without either an ongoing armed conflict or the occasion for self-defense based on an imminent threat would also clash with international law, which the United States should avoid whenever possible. Detention outside the criminal justice system would present similar concerns, if that detention was based solely on an individual's past role with Al Qaeda.

Fortunately, both domestic and international law provide a fix for these problems. Under domestic law, Congress could pass a law that authorized continued detention based on the current dangerousness of an individual originally captured while serving as part of Al Qaeda or associated forces.[97] Under Article 78 of the Fourth Geneva Convention, detention of ongoing security threats is also consistent with international law, as long as the state provides a process for the periodic review of that individual's current dangerousness. Many scholars view an Article 78 process as a sound prudential step, even while the armed conflict with Al Qaeda persists.[98] In 2011, President Barack Obama issued an executive order

---

[93] *Id.*

[94] *See* Michael N. Schmitt, *The Age of Cyber Warfare: Quo Vadis?*, 25 Stan. L. & Pol'y Rev. 269, 279 (2014).

[95] *See* Robert Chesney, Jack Goldsmith, Matthew C. Waxman & Benjamin Wittes, *A Statutory Framework for Next-Generation Terrorist Threats, available at* http://media.hoover.org/sites/default/files/documents/Statutory-Framework-for-Next-Generation-Terrorist-Threats.pdf.

[96] *See* Jennifer A. Daskal & Stephen I. Vladeck, *After the AUMF*, 5 Harv. Nat'l Sec. J. 115, 138 (2014).

[97] *See* Stephen I. Vladeck, *Detention After the AUMF*, 82 Fordham L. Rev. 2189, 2196-98 (2014).

[98] *See* Matthew C. Waxman, *The Law of Armed Conflict and Detention Operations in Afghanistan*, 85 Int'l L. Stud. 343, 350 (2010).

outlining a periodic review mechanism.[99] Since the fall of 2013, the United States has conducted reviews of ongoing dangerousness, which it calls Periodic Review Boards (PRBs). These proceedings have resulted in the release of a number of Guantanamo detainees. That approach would probably pass legal muster even after the conclusion of the armed conflict with Al Qaeda.

4. Congressional Restrictions on Release of Detainees

Another issue is what authority the President has to release Guantanamo detainees. Congress has passed restrictions on transfer that require notice to Congress and a certification from the Secretary of Defense that an individual poses an acceptable risk and is not likely to return to the battlefield, and/or that the United States has taken measures such as arranging for confinement in a third country that will minimize this risk.[100] The President has indicated in a public signing statement that he regards these restrictions as an unconstitutional intrusion on his authority as Commander in Chief.[101]

In many ways the President has the better of the argument. The Framers believed that "clogging" the passage to war[102] was a sound idea, and they accordingly required agreement between Congress and the President. In contrast, the Framers believed that requiring inter-branch cooperation would dangerously hinder the path to peace. George Mason argued for "facilitating" settlements of conflicts.[103] Oliver Ellsworth of Connecticut said, "It should be more easy to get out of war, than into it."[104] Moreover, Ellsworth acknowledged, peace often required "intricate and secret negotiations."[105] The President's ability to speak with one voice made the Chief Executive the logical choice to conduct such dealings. Getting Congress involved would have made negotiations far more cumbersome, and peace harder to attain. Of course, if the parties to a war wished to formally end the war with a peace treaty, ratification by the Senate would be required for the treaty to acquire the force of law and be binding on the executive branch. However, the Constitution nowhere requires that wars end with treaties.

---

[99] Exec. Order No. 13,567, Periodic Review of Individuals Detained at Guantanamo Bay Naval Station Pursuant to the Authorization for Use of Military Force.

[100] *See* Supplemental Appropriations Act, Pub. L. No. 11-32, §14103, 123 Stat. 1859, 1920-21 (2009); *cf.* David J.R. Frakt, *Prisoners of Congress: The Constitutional and Political Clash Over Detainees and the Closure of Guantanamo*, 74 U. PITT. L. REV. 179 (2012) (discussing congressional restrictions).

[101] *See* Statement on Signing the Ike Skelton National Defense Authorization Act for Fiscal Year 2011, Administration of Barack Obama 2011, Daily Comp. Pres. Doc. 10 (Jan. 7, 2011), *available at* http://www.whitehouse.gov/the-press-office/2011/01/07/statement-president-hr-6523.

[102] 2 RECORDS OF THE FEDERAL CONVENTION OF 1787, at 319 (Max Farrand ed., rev. ed. 1966); *see generally* Chapter 1.

[103] *Id.*

[104] *Id.*

[105] *Id.*

IV. Interrogation of Detainees and Other Conditions of Confinement

The Supreme Court has affirmed the power of the President to wind up wars by repatriating prisoners of war.[106] President Lincoln did so summarily in the last days of the Civil War. President Truman did the same after World War II.

Additional support for this conclusion comes from case law that invests the President with the power of settling international claims involving the United States.[107] The Court has viewed the President as having such power with Congress's acquiescence, since Congress recognized that having a singular decision maker for such agreements would facilitate settlement. Requiring congressional approval would hamstring the President and make agreements between the United States and other states more difficult to achieve.

On the other hand, the Constitution does give Congress the power over "captures."[108] If Congress can regulate captures, that might well include power over the timing and substantive test for release of wartime detainees. On this view, Congress's restrictions on release or transfer of detainees would be constitutional.

The Captures Clause argument actually has less validity than appears at first blush.[109] The Clause actually refers only to a limited class of seizures, involving seizures of vessels on the high seas. There is little evidence that the Clause also applies to *persons* who are seized.

This analysis supports President Obama's decision to release five high-ranking Taliban detainees in May 2014 to obtain an American army sergeant, Bowe Bergdahl, who had been held prisoner by the Taliban for five years.[110] The President must have some power to use his discretion, in order to take advantage of fleeting opportunities for settlement. Without that discretion, another party to the negotiation may become impatient or disillusioned, and the opportunity may evaporate. The President may pay a political price, but that does not diminish the President's legal authority to effect such an exchange. Congress can become involved if a peace agreement requires passage of a statute or ratification of a treaty, but those avenues for achieving peace are not mandatory.

IV. INTERROGATION OF DETAINEES AND OTHER CONDITIONS OF CONFINEMENT

In a chapter dealing in large part with detention, one would be remiss in not addressing an issue that, at least in the 18 months after 9/11, was painfully real to

---

[106] *See* Ludecke v. Watkins, 335 U.S. 160 (1948); David A. Simon, *Ending Perpetual War? Constitutional War Termination Powers and the Conflict Against Al Qaeda*, 41 Pepp. L. Rev. 685 (2014).

[107] Dames & Moore v. Regan, 453 U.S. 654 (1981); *see generally* Chapter 2.

[108] *See* Ingrid Wuerth, *The Captures Clause*, 76 U. Chi. L. Rev. 1683 (2009).

[109] *Id.*

[110] *See* Eric Schmitt & Charlie Savage, *American Soldier Freed by Taliban in Prisoner Trade*, N.Y. Times, June 1, 2014, at A1.

some detainees: conditions of confinement, including interrogation. In the civilian criminal justice system, as the chapter in this book on the Criminal Process makes clear, rigorous rules prohibit coercion. While rules from international law also bar coercive techniques or other mistreatment during detention,[111] states can attempt to mask such methods from the public and humanitarian groups. Courts and lawyers in and out of government, including military lawyers, pushed back against the coercive interrogation employed in the aftermath of 9/11. However, judicial remedies against mistreatment are not as clearly established as the post-*Boumediene* availability of habeas corpus to seek release from detention.

A.   Interrogation Practices After 9/11

Some background is helpful: In the 18 months after the 9/11 attacks, the Bush administration took an extraordinarily aggressive approach to interrogation.[112] While the Bush administration's approach was driven by a fear that other mass terrorist attacks would occur imminently unless the U.S. got information to prevent such tragedies, the consequences of this turn toward harsh interrogation were severe.

A number of Guantanamo detainees were subjected to harsh treatment, including stress positions, which force a detainee to endure modes of standing or sitting for prolonged periods of time that impose substantial strain on the musculoskeletal system. For example, a detainee might be forced to stand on tiptoe for over 30 minutes, or lean against a wall braced by his fingertips. Stress positions leave no marks, and may seem harmless compared to techniques known from popular culture and history as torture, such as putting out a lighted cigarette on a prisoner's forearm. Nevertheless, stress positions can be extraordinarily painful when a prisoner must endure them for protracted periods. In some cases, prisoners were also shackled tightly during such sessions; shackling is never comfortable, but can similarly become excruciating to the prisoner when wrists or ankles swell up with excess fluid because of stress positions. High-value detainees held outside Guantanamo during this period, such as Khalid Shaikh Mohammed, the alleged mastermind of 9/11, were subjected to other "enhanced interrogation techniques," such as waterboarding, in which a subject is strapped on his back to a board with a towel covering his nose and mouth, and water is poured over the towel, quickly eliciting the sensation of drowning.[113]

---

[111] *See* Article 3, Geneva Convention Relative to the Treatment of Prisoners of War, Aug. 12, 1949, 6 U.S.T. 3316, 75 U.N.T.S. 135; Convention Against Torture and Other Cruel, Inhuman, or Degrading Treatment or Punishment, arts. 2, 12, Dec. 10, 1984, 1465 U.N.T.S. 85.

[112] MARGULIES, LAW'S DETOUR, *supra* note 58, at 56-57.

[113] Controversy continues over the effectiveness of the interrogation methods. In December 2014, the Senate Select Committee on Intelligence (SSCI) released a report, signed only by the

IV. Interrogation of Detainees and Other Conditions of Confinement

The interrogation of detainees is governed by both domestic and international law. Common Article 3 of the Geneva Convention on the Treatment of Civilians in Noninternational Armed Conflict bars cruel, inhuman, and humiliating treatment, as well as torture. It prohibits any use of coercion, mental or physical, in interrogation.[114] In *Hamdan v. Rumsfeld*, a plurality of the Supreme Court held that the conflict with Al Qaeda was a conflict "not of an international character," thus triggering Common Article 3's protections.[115] The Court's view was simple, although it has been subject to criticism: Al Qaeda is a nonstate actor, not a nation; so any conflict between a recognized state and Al Qaeda cannot be "international," i.e., between nations. Since all conflicts, the Court asserted, must be either international or non-international, "conflict not of an international character" best fit the United States' struggle with Al Qaeda.

Finding that Common Article 3 governed detention served three important values. First, laws regarding treatment of detainees are premised in part on reciprocity: If one side behaves appropriately toward its detainees, the other side will reciprocate. This expectation of reciprocity helped create a culture of respect for the Geneva Conventions within the U.S. military,[116] since legal advisers in the armed forces had to consider the risk that any U.S mistreatment of detainees would then expose captured U.S personnel to equivalent or worse abuse. Of course, some adversaries of the United States, such as Al Qaeda or the Islamic State of Iraq and Syria (ISIS), will likely not comply with the Geneva Conventions. However, even in the absence of reciprocity, Common Article 3 is a "floor" for the treatment of detainees that represents an international consensus. Treating detainees in a fashion inconsistent with Common Article 3 would make the world less decent, and alienate people throughout the world who *would* otherwise be inclined to support the United States' counterterrorism efforts. Third, restrictions on

---

Democratic majority of the SSCI, that asserted that most information obtained merely corroborated information obtained through other sources. *See* Senate Select Committee on Intelligence, *Executive Summary: Study of the Central Intelligence Agency's Detention and Interrogation Program* (Dec. 3, 2014), *available at* http://www.intelligence.senate.gov/study2014/sscistudy1.pdf. However, both the Central Intelligence Agency and the Senate Intelligence Committee minority report by Republican members of the SSCI argued that the information provided actionable intelligence about Al Qaeda and helped officials prioritize the myriad data points they received about Al Qaeda's structure, operations, and personnel. *See* Senate Select Committee on Intelligence, *Minority Views of Vice Chairman Chambliss et al.* (Dec. 5, 2104), *available at* http://www.intelligence.senate.gov/study2014/sscistudy3.pdf; Director, Central Intelligence Agency, to Hon. Dianne Feinstein & Hon. Saxby Chambliss, SSCI, *CIA Comments on the Senate Select Committee on Intelligence Report on the Rendition, Detention, and Interrogation Program* (June 27, 2013), *available at* https://www.cia.gov/library/reports/CIAs_June2013_Response_to_the_SSCI_Study_on_the_Former_Detention_and_Interrogation_Program.pdf.

[114] *See* Geneva Convention Relative to the Protection of Civilian Persons in Time of War, art. 3, Aug. 12, 1949, 6 U.S.T. 3517, 75 U.N.T.S. 287; *cf.* Lindsey O. Graham & Paul R. Connolly, *Waterboarding: Issues and Lessons for Judge Advocates*, 69 A.F. L. Rev. 65 (2013) (analyzing legality of interrogation techniques).

[115] Hamdan v. Rumsfeld, 548 U.S. 557, 630-31 (2006).

[116] *See* Graham & Connolly, *supra* note 114, at 89; Margulies, Law's Detour, *supra* note 58, at 55.

harsh treatment of detainees promote state forces' good order and discipline. Studies have shown that a more permissive attitude toward the treatment of detainees soon spreads, infecting troops' ability to conduct themselves professionally. Sending a clear message on treatment of detainees prevents this breakdown.[117]

In addition to Common Article 3, the United States is bound by the Convention Against Torture (CAT),[118] which Congress implemented in the U.S. torture statute.[119] Under the CAT, a state official cannot intentionally impose severe pain or mental suffering on any individual in the official's custody. The CAT makes clear that severe pain or mental suffering cannot be imposed for any reason. Emergencies allow states to "derogate" from (create exceptions to) some provisions of treaties or rules of customary international law. However, the CAT expressly prohibits any exceptions, including those arising out of a state emergency. While the U.S. torture statute does not include this "no exceptions" language, it carves out no exceptions. It should be read in the same way as the CAT, since any other meaning would create a huge loophole in the statute.

To understand why the duty to refrain from torture is absolute, consider the familiar "ticking bomb" scenario where interrogators believe that a prisoner has information that will lead to the discovery of a device set to explode imminently.[120] At first blush, one might want to permit the use of torture in this exigent situation. A narrow utilitarian analysis that balances immediate harms against immediate benefits would support the use of torture. Under this narrow analysis, harm to one person would be justifiable if many people could be saved. However, this narrow analysis is both shortsighted and misleading. First, the utilitarian analysis might not apply at all—some things are just wrong in and of themselves. International law says that about slavery, and says the same thing about torture. Second, even if a utilitarian analysis is appropriate, torture may fail the test. As we said in discussing Common Article 3 of the Geneva accords, allowing one's own forces to use torture undermines discipline and erodes legal institutions. A utilitarian analysis should consider these long-term consequences.

Moreover, while torture may be effective in getting information in some cases, it is often ineffective or counterproductive. For every case in which a detainee actually has information that could stop a ticking bomb, there may be several cases where the detainee lacks this information. In the latter context, a detainee subjected to torture is likely to say *anything* that will make the torture stop. The detainee may provide information that is inaccurate, just because his interrogators have signaled that they want to hear it. Prior to the U.S. intervention in Iraq, a captive who had been subjected to physical and mental pain, including

---

[117] *Id.*

[118] *See* United Nations Convention Against Torture and Other Cruel, Inhuman or Degrading Treatment or Punishment, G.A. Res. 39/46, art. 2, U.N. Doc. A/RES/39/708 (Dec. 10, 1984).

[119] 18 U.S.C. §2340 (2014).

[120] *Cf.* Michael W. Lewis, *A Dark Descent into Reality: Making the Case for an Objective Definition of Torture*, 67 WASH. & LEE L. REV. 77, 86-87 (2010) (arguing that "ticking bomb" scenario is too rare to provide guidance on law or policy); Kim Lane Scheppele, *Hypothetical Torture in the "War on Terrorism,"* 1 J. NAT'L SECURITY L. & POL'Y 285 (2005) (same).

threats to his family, told interrogators for the Central Intelligence Agency (CIA) that Al Qaeda and Iraqi dictator Saddam Hussein had operational ties.[121] This was blatantly false. However, it fit preconceptions driving the Iraq policy of certain senior officials in the Bush administration, including Vice President Dick Cheney. It is difficult, if not impossible, to limit the use of torture to situations where it might produce useful information. Therefore, a broader utilitarian analysis would bar torture's use across the board. The Obama administration has made clear that enhanced interrogation techniques such as waterboarding should be viewed as torture.[122]

B.   Remedies for Abusive Conditions of Confinement

The next question to be addressed is whether a petition for habeas corpus is available to modify or stop such treatment. This subsection briefly discusses the availability of habeas in two situations: 1) a challenge to forced feeding at Guantanamo; and 2) a challenge to repatriation of detainees at Guantanamo and elsewhere who allege that they would face torture in violation of the CAT if they are returned to their countries or origin.

The D.C. Circuit Court of Appeals has held that federal courts have jurisdiction over petitions for habeas corpus by Guantanamo detainees challenging forced feeding.[123] Those claims arose because detainees had resorted to hunger strikes to bring attention to their continued detention and pressure the government for their release. In response, the government had determined that emergency measures were required to save detainees' lives, and had implemented a procedure called enteral feeding involving insertion of a feeding tube through each hunger striker's nose and subsequent restraint of the subject of the procedure to prevent regurgitation of the nourishment provided.

In *Aamer v. Obama*, the D.C. Circuit noted the three stages in congressional-judicial dialogue on habeas that culminated in *Boumediene v. Bush*. First, in *Rasul v. Bush*,[124] the Supreme Court in 2004 found a *statutory* grant of habeas jurisdiction. Statutory habeas petitions in ordinary civilian cases had long included claims regarding inappropriate conditions of confinement.[125] Second, Congress in the Military Commissions Act of 2006 and related legislation sought to strip federal courts of jurisdiction to hear habeas petitions by Guantanamo detainees. Third, in

---

[121] MARGULIES, LAW'S DETOUR, *supra* note 58, at 38.

[122] *See* Eric Lichtblau, *Nominee Wants Some Detainees Tried in the U.S.*, N.Y. TIMES, Jan. 16, 2009, at A1 (reporting views of then-Attorney General-designate Eric Holder).

[123] *See* Aamer v. Obama, 742 F.3d 1023 (D.C. Cir. 2014).

[124] 542 U.S. 466 (2004).

[125] The Supreme Court has left open the question of whether the Constitution *requires* that habeas be available for such challenges. Boumediene v. Bush, 553 U.S. 723, 792 (2008). In most ordinary civilian prison settings, a prisoner will have other means available for challenges to conditions of confinement, including 42 U.S.C. §1983, the statute that provides a cause of action for challenges to unconstitutional acts by state and local government officials.

Boumediene v. Bush, the Supreme Court struck down Congress's jurisdiction-stripping measure as a violation of the Constitution's Suspension Clause. In *Aamer*, the D.C. Circuit held that *Boumediene* had restored the habeas status quo after *Rasul*. That is, federal courts had the same jurisdiction over habeas claims by Guantanamo detainees that courts had at the time *Rasul* was decided. Since courts had interpreted statutory grants of habeas jurisdiction to include habeas petitions challenging conditions of confinement, after *Boumediene* courts resumed that jurisdiction.

However, while the D.C. Circuit found that federal courts had *jurisdiction* over petitions based on forced feeding, it ruled against petitioners on the *merits* of their claims. The court found that the applicable standard on the merits required deference to the decisions of prison administrators if those decisions were "reasonably related to legitimate penological interests."[126] Writing for the court, a liberal judge, David Tatel, noted that state courts have held that prison administrators had a legitimate interest in curbing hunger strikes.[127] If an ordinary prison inmate could proceed on a hunger strike, prison administrators would face two unacceptable choices: 1) give in to the inmate, which might entail release of an inmate who had committed a serious crime and posed an ongoing threat to society, and allow the inmate to game the system and encourage others to do the same; or 2) watch the inmate die, which would be "a harm in its own right" and could trigger adverse actions by other inmates or condemnation by external audiences.[128] Although some medical bodies and ethics scholars have condemned forced feeding,[129] the court was persuaded by the case law that forced feeding at Guantanamo meshed with legitimate penological interests, so long as it was conducted in the least intrusive manner required to safeguard the detainee's life and health.

The courts have taken a similar path on habeas corpus regarding transfers from U.S. custody to other countries: finding jurisdiction, but ruling against the detainee on the merits. In *Munaf v. Geren*,[130] the Supreme Court, in an opinion by Chief Justice Roberts, found that a federal court had jurisdiction to hear the habeas petition of Mohammad Munaf, a U.S. citizen detained in Iraq for terrorism-related offenses committed after the U.S. invasion of that country. Munaf had asked the court to block his transfer from U.S. custody to the custody of Iraq, which sought to prosecute him for those offenses. According to Munaf, his prosecution by Iraq might entail torture, as well as an absence of procedural protections provided by the Due Process Clause. The Court found that jurisdiction existed over his claim, citing the U.S. government role in his detention and proposed transfer and Munaf's status as a U.S. citizen.[131]

---

[126] Turner v. Safley, 482 U.S. 78, 89 (1987).

[127] *Aamer*, 742 F.3d at 1040.

[128] *Id.* (citing Matter of Bezio v. Dorsey, 21 N.Y.3d 93, 989 N.E.2d 942, 951 (N.Y. 2013)).

[129] *Aamer*, 742 F.3d at 1039.

[130] 553 U.S. 674 (2008).

[131] *Id.* at 687-88.

IV. Interrogation of Detainees and Other Conditions of Confinement

The *Munaf* Court, having found jurisdiction, then found against the petitioner on the merits. According to the Court, a federal court did not have the power to block the United States from transferring a suspect to the government of another country for prosecution when 1) the government of the second country had unquestioned authority to prosecute the suspect, and 2) the suspect was a) in U.S. custody because U.S. forces had apprehended him in that country, or b) part of or voluntarily associated with U.S. forces when he engaged in the offense that led to his proposed prosecution.

According to the *Munaf* Court, a U.S. citizen who travels abroad and commits a crime in a foreign country has the same rights as a national of that country.[132] This principle promotes uniformity and clarity in understandings between countries about criminal jurisdiction. Any other result would undermine the power of a sovereign country to prosecute crimes within its borders, subjecting that country's authority to a bewildering array of conditions that depended on the nationality of the suspect. Chief Justice Roberts observed that uniformity in Munaf's case also strengthened international institutions: The United States had detained Munaf pending Iraqi prosecution efforts pursuant to a mandate from the United Nations governing the U.S-led Multinational Force (MNF) in Iraq, which authorized the MNF to "take all necessary measures to contribute to the maintenance of security and stability in Iraq," including the internment of individuals for security reasons.[133] Allowing Munaf to evade prosecution would have undermined the UN's goals.

According to Chief Justice Roberts, the transferee's claim that he was at risk for torture did not affect this analysis. On this point there were differences between Chief Justice Roberts and Justice Souter, who concurred and was joined by Justices Breyer and Ginsburg. Chief Justice Roberts noted that in proceedings before the Court, the Solicitor General had stated that as a matter of policy the United States did not transfer individuals to countries where those individuals would be at risk for torture.[134] Moreover, Chief Justice Roberts noted, the nuanced character of the U.S. government's analysis of the possibility of torture in this case allayed fears. The U.S. government had expressly noted concern about the risk of torture in some agencies of the Iraqi government. However, the United States had found that the Justice Ministry of Iraq, which would have custody over Munaf during his prosecution as well as sentence if convicted, met international standards.[135] This textured determination may well have convinced Chief Justice Roberts that the U.S. officials were not ignoring the possibility of torture, but were instead conducting a diligent case-by-case inquiry. Under the circumstances, Chief Justice Roberts asserted, the executive branch was entitled to substantial deference from the courts on the risk of torture. However, Chief Justice Roberts conceded that further judicial inquiry would be appropriate if the U.S.

---

[132] *Id*. at 695.
[133] *Id*. at 697-98.
[134] *Id*. at 702.
[135] *Id*.

government acknowledged the risk of torture but chose to transfer a detainee, anyway.[136]

Justice Souter's concurrence avoided sweeping claims about deference to U.S. officials on the issue of torture. Justice Souter acknowledged that deference was appropriate on the facts in *Munaf*. However, Justice Souter asserted that different questions might arise if there was a substantial probability of torture based on a neutral analysis of the evidence, even if the executive branch did not acknowledge this probability.[137]

V.   EXTRAORDINARY RENDITION

While in *Munaf* the Supreme Court found insufficient basis for claims that the petitioner would be tortured if U.S. officials transferred him to Iraqi custody, in other cases officials have transferred individuals to the custody of other nations to facilitate harsh interrogation. This practice, known as extraordinary rendition, occurred during the administration of President George W. Bush. It violates international law, and may be problematic under U.S. law, as well.

In extraordinary rendition, U.S. officials persuaded other countries such as Poland to receive prisoners from U.S. custody and either interrogate the prisoners with harsh techniques or allow U.S. interrogators in to conduct interrogations. Sending an individual to another country with the intention that interrogators in that state use harsh techniques is illegal under international law. Just as *Boumediene* curbed the government's ability to outsource detention by using the sovereign territory of another state, international law holds that a nation cannot outsource abusive interrogation methods to another state, to avoid responsibility for using such methods.

Consider the troubling case of Maher Arar, a Canadian national who claimed that in 2002 U.S. officials shipped him to Syria, where he was held prisoner for almost a year and subjected to brutal treatment, including being beaten repeatedly with electric cables. In this case of extraordinary rendition, it turned out that Arar had no terrorist ties.[138] Recently, the European Court of Human Rights found that a rendition to Poland violated the European Convention on Human Rights and Fundamental Freedoms.[139] While ordinary rendition such as the transfer in Munaf's case may be appropriate because the receiving state has a lawful interest in prosecuting the individual transferred, transferring an individual merely for purposes of coercive interrogation is inappropriate and illegal.

---

[136] *Id.*

[137] *Id.* at 706.

[138] MARGULIES, LAW'S DETOUR, *supra* note 58, at 36.

[139] *See* Al Nashiri v. Poland, No. 28761/11 (Eur. Ct. Hum. Rts. 24 July 2014), *available at* http://hudoc.echr.coe.int/sites/eng/pages/search.aspx?i=001-146044#.

VI. MATERIAL WITNESSES

After 9/11, the government also used its authority to detain material witnesses as a means to hold individuals it suspected of terrorist ties. The statutory authority to detain material witnesses in civilian criminal prosecutions gives the government some leeway, particularly in fast-moving international investigations. However, the administration of President George W. Bush, acting in the anxious aftermath of 9/11, may have pushed the envelope too far.

Historically, law enforcement has detained material witnesses with personal knowledge of criminal activity to secure the testimony by individuals who were unable or unwilling to testify before a grand jury or at trial.[140] Evidence from these individuals is considered "material"—i.e., it may make a difference in a grand jury's decision about whether to indict a suspect, or a jury's decision at trial to convict. Without the ability to detain individuals in this situation, suspects could intimidate witnesses or bribe them to flee. Courts citing law enforcement practice that probably predates the Constitution have held that the Constitution permits the detention of material witnesses to ensure the availability of such evidence.[141] The federal material witness statute allows detention of a material witness on a showing by law enforcement that it "may become impracticable" to obtain the witness's testimony through other less intrusive means, such as a subpoena served on the witness.[142] Once the deposition is taken and transcribed, law enforcement authorities' interest in detention diminishes, since the government can use a transcript of the deposition before a grand jury and at trial, even without the witness being present. If law enforcement officials can conduct a deposition of the witness that includes the witness's responses to questions about the crime being investigated, detention after the deposition must satisfy a demanding standard: It must be "necessary to prevent a failure of justice."[143]

Bush administration officials, such as Attorney General John Ashcroft, used material witness detention aggressively. Critics charged that law enforcement used material witness detention as a mere pretext to lock up persons suspected of terrorism.[144] For critics, this use of material witness detention was inappropriate, since the power to detain a suspect should rest on a showing to a judge of probable cause that the suspect has committed a crime.[145] Critics asserted that using material witness detention in place of such a showing undermined constitutional protections.

---

[140] MARGULIES, LAW'S DETOUR, *supra* note 58, at 42.

[141] Bacon v. United States, 449 F.2d 933 (9th Cir. 1971).

[142] 18 U.S.C. §3144 (2014); Ashcroft v. al-Kidd, 131 S. Ct. 2074, 2085-86 (2011) (Kennedy, J., concurring).

[143] 18 U.S.C. §3144.

[144] *See* Lauryn P. Gouldin, *When Deference Is Dangerous: The Judicial Role in Material-Witness Detentions*, 49 AM. CRIM. L. REV. 1333 (2012).

[145] *Al-Kidd*, 131 S. Ct. at 2086 (Kennedy, J., concurring).

This broad criticism is misplaced. While critics are right that the broad use of material witness detention as a substitute for probable cause would be problematic, a narrower use of material witness detention as a gap-filler may be appropriate, particularly in the fast-moving context of transnational terror investigations. Consider the case of Maher Hawash, who ultimately pleaded guilty to material support of terrorism in a case involving sponsorship of several individuals who wished to go abroad to join a terrorist group. Federal law enforcement officials knew about Hawash's role in the plot, and knew that he had both the ability and the inclination to flee the country if he realized that law enforcement was investigating him.[146] Moreover, as a co-conspirator with the individuals who planned to join up with the terrorist group, Hawash clearly had knowledge of the criminal activity officials were investigating. The material witness statute does not expressly exclude subjects of an investigation from coverage, if they have knowledge of lawbreaking by others. Moreover, many subjects of investigations ultimately provide information to law enforcement, in exchange for leniency in charging or sentencing. Under the circumstances, seeking a material witness warrant to detain Hawash was a reasonable way of ensuring that law enforcement had access to Hawash's testimony and was necessary to prevent a "failure of justice" that would have occurred if Hawash had fled before he could be apprehended on a traditional arrest warrant. Hawash was indicted about a month after his arrest as a material witness. That amount of time also supports the reasonableness of the material witness warrant in Hawash's case.

Ashcroft v. al-Kidd, a decision by the U.S. Supreme Court, shows both the benefits and the risks of material witness detention. The government detained Abdullah al-Kidd, an American citizen whom the government believed had information about a suspect in a terrorism case, Sami al-Hussayen. Al-Kidd had previously accepted $20,000 from al-Hussayen and met with al-Hussayen's associates after returning from a trip to Yemen. The dealings of the two men supported prosecutors' view that al-Kidd might have information important to al-Hussayen's prosecution.[147] Prosecutors seeking a warrant to detain al-Kidd as a material witness told a judge that the subject of the warrant sought was planning to go to Saudi Arabia. However, they did not tell the judge that the subject had been cooperative in previous meetings with the FBI, had family in the United States, and had been scheduled for months to go abroad to study.[148] Ultimately, prosecutors did not call al-Kidd to testify in the federal trial of his acquaintance, which resulted in an acquittal.

Al-Kidd made a sweeping argument against the government. He asserted that even if the government had demonstrated probable cause to detain him as a material witness, that detention violated the Constitution if it was merely a

---

[146] *See* Ricardo J. Bascuas, *The Unconstitutionality of "Hold Until Cleared": Reexamining Material Witness Detentions in the Wake of the September 11th Dragnet*, 58 VAND. L. REV. 677, 699-701 (2005).

[147] *See* Peter Margulies, *Judging Myopia in Hindsight: Bivens Actions, National Security Decisions, and the Rule of Law*, 96 IOWA L. REV. 195, 232 (2010).

[148] *Al-Kidd*, 131 S. Ct. at 2088 (Ginsburg, J., concurring).

pretext to detain him as a suspected terrorist in his own right. The Court rejected al-Kidd's argument, holding that probable cause was the constitutional touchstone, regardless of the government's motives.[149]

Justice Kennedy, the swing vote in so many cases, suggested in a concurrence that a narrower argument by al-Kidd might have succeeded. Kennedy observed that the Constitution might well prohibit detention of a material witness who had cooperated with law enforcement officials, since detention would not be necessary to secure the witness's testimony.[150]

In sum, material witness detention is best confined to core cases involving witnesses who are unable or unwilling to cooperate with law enforcement. It may be appropriate as a stop-gap measure in cases where a co-conspirator would otherwise flee the country. After a spike upward in material witness detentions after 9/11, law enforcement officials have generally narrowed their use of this approach, thus minimizing the risk of undermining the grand jury and jury trial protections in the Constitution.

VII.   IMMIGRATION AFTER SEPTEMBER 11

The government also used immigration law aggressively after September 11. Most of the government's efforts focused on foreign nationals from the Middle East and South Asia without a lawful immigration status, although the government largely failed to show that its targets possessed terrorist ties.[151] Compared with typical immigration cases, detention was longer and less individually tailored. In addition, senior officials did little to alleviate harsh conditions of confinement, including physical abuse of detainees.

Courts have long held that Congress has plenary (complete) power over immigration. The Supreme Court first articulated the plenary power doctrine in the 1889 *Chinese Exclusion Case*.[152] In the *Chinese Exclusion Case*, the Supreme Court upheld a statute that ordered the removal of most Chinese nationals from

---

[149] *Id.* at 2081-83 (majority opinion).

[150] *Id.* at 2086 (Kennedy, J., concurring).

[151] *Compare* Ashcroft v. Iqbal, 556 U.S. 662, 682 (2009) (asserting that investigation of undocumented Muslim noncitizens after September 11th was a "legitimate policy directing law enforcement to arrest and detain individuals because of their suspected link to the attacks"). A Department of Justice report had a different verdict on this episode. *See* Office of the Inspector Gen., U.S. Dep't of Justice, *The September 11 Detainees: A Review of the Treatment of Aliens Held on Immigration Charges in Connection with the Investigation of the September 11 Attacks* 41-42 (2003), *available at* http://www.justice.gov/oig/special/0306/ (concluding that arrests generally occurred because of "chance encounters or tenuous connections" rather than "genuine indications" of terrorist ties); *see also* DAVID COLE & JULES LOBEL, LESS SAFE, LESS FREE: WHY AMERICA IS LOSING THE WAR ON TERROR 30-31 (2007) (discussing the post-9/11 immigration round-up).

[152] *See* Chae Chan Ping v. United States, 130 U.S. 581 (1889).

the United States. The Court conceded that no single provision of the Constitution granted Congress power over immigration. Instead, the Court viewed the power to control immigration as an essential function of U.S. sovereignty and security. The Court then found that several provisions of the Constitution empowered Congress to address national security, foreign affairs, and the nation's economic well-being: These provisions included the power to declare war and the power to regulate commerce with foreign nations.

The broad principle that Congress should have the power to regulate immigration led to harsh results in the *Chinese Exclusion Case* and subsequent cases. The Court in the *Chinese Exclusion Case* agreed that Congress could single out particular foreign nationals, such as the Chinese, for harsher immigration treatment. The courts would not inquire about the motivations for such treatment, even when those motives appeared based on racial or ethnic prejudice. While distinctions based on national origin, race, and ethnicity are suspect in most U.S. law under the Equal Protection Clause, the Court held that the need to preserve Congress's ability to decisively counter foreign threats required substantial leeway if not absolute discretion.

Detention of foreign nationals seeking entrance to the United States also has a long history in immigration law. During the Cold War, the government detained a number of foreign nationals for indefinite periods when those nationals had sought to enter the country. In at least one case, the detainee was a lawful permanent resident (but not a citizen) who had left the country and was denied entry on national security grounds. In that case, *Shaughnessy v. United States ex rel. Mezei*,[153] the government acted on secret evidence that it declined to disclose to the courts. The Supreme Court nonetheless upheld the detention, viewing the President as acting with Congress's blessing.

While the government characterized its post-9/11 immigration investigation as an inquiry into individuals linked to terrorism, in practice the inquiry focused on ordinary immigration violations committed by Muslim immigrants from the Middle East and South Asia. Justice Department officials acted on numerous tips regarding immigration violations offered by neighbors, landlords, and employers settling scores.[154] An even larger percentage came from people who reported the presence of any number of Middle Eastern or South Asian individuals that the tipster deemed to be suspicious. For example, one lead asserted that a grocery store was "operated by numerous Middle Eastern men."[155] Government investigators raided the grocery, checked employees' immigration status, and arrested and eventually deported those without valid immigration documents.

The government detained over a thousand undocumented immigrants in post-9/11 enforcement efforts. Many of the detainees experienced difficulty in contacting attorneys. Moreover, a significant number of the detainees were subjected to physical abuse by federal correction officers or other nonimmigrant

---

[153] 345 U.S. 206 (1953).
[154] MARGULIES, LAW'S DETOUR, *supra* note 58, at 28.
[155] *Id.* at 28-29.

inmates. When detainees sought their release from detention on bond as they awaited their deportation, the government argued that they were being held pursuant to an investigation into the 9/11 attacks. In virtually all of the cases, however, the government failed to show any evidence of terrorist ties.

Although the post-9/11 immigration detentions were problematic in a number of respects, they did not represent a return to the mass detention policy of the Japanese-American internment. First, the detainees were in virtually all cases foreign nationals without a valid immigration status, who were already subject to detention and removal under federal law. Because the post-9/11 detentions did not for the most part affect U.S. citizens or foreign nationals with a valid immigration status, the detentions did not constitute discrimination based on race, religion, or national origin. Even the longest detentions in the post-9/11 group were far shorter than those endured by the World War II internees. Justice Kennedy, writing in *Iqbal*, described the detention policy as a "legitimate policy directing law enforcement to arrest and detain individuals because of their suspected link to the [9/11] attacks."[156] This finding may well have allowed senior officials to evade responsibility for the mistreatment of many detainees, even though senior officials had ample notice that such mistreatment was occurring and did little or nothing to stop it. Moreover, the courts did not adequately address the misleading arguments the government made in individual bond hearings, where the government's vague assertions of detainees' ties to 9/11 had no basis in fact. However, the legal authority for detention and removal under federal immigration law put the post-9/11 detentions into a less troubling legal category than the Japanese-American internment during World War II.

VIII. SUITS FOR DAMAGES BASED ON UNLAWFUL DETENTION

Courts have also tended to be deferential in their approach to suits for damages against government officials in national security matters. In a case from the heyday of the Warren Court, the Supreme Court allowed a suit for damages against federal officials who had allegedly made a wrongful arrest and overreached in searching the home of a suspect and detaining the suspect during the search.[157] However, two important factors have made courts reluctant to encourage suits for damages against public officials in national security cases.

The courts have worried that excessive suits for damages might chill the ability of public officials to do their jobs. As the saying goes, "hindsight is 20/20." Courts believe that officials' concern about lawsuits will lead to paralysis

---

[156] Ashcroft v. Iqbal, 556 U.S. 662, 682 (2009).
[157] Bivens v. Six Unknown Named Agents of Fed. Bureau of Narcotics, 403 U.S. 388 (1971).

when aggressive action is required (as is often the case in national security). Moreover, courts are worried that the discovery process—the endless parade of interrogatories, document requests, and depositions in civil litigation—will immobilize senior officials who need clear heads and schedules to tackle the nation's business.

As a result, courts have imposed four significant limits on suits for damages: First, the courts will categorically preclude suits for damages when "factors counselling (sic) hesitation," including the need for secrecy, are present. Second, even when the court does not categorically preclude lawsuits, it may hold that the "state secrets privilege" either gives the government a complete defense to a particular lawsuit or shields specific evidence from disclosure to the plaintiff. Third, all government officials have qualified immunity from suit; plaintiffs must establish as a threshold matter that the alleged acts of official defendants violated clearly established law. Fourth, the allegations in the plaintiff's initial complaint must be plausible, even *before* discovery has taken place. Each of these limits shrinks the number of lawsuits that make it to the discovery phase, much less go to trial.

Recent lawsuits seeking damages from alleged improper detention or treatment of suspected terrorists have not made it past the "factors counselling hesitation" stage. A federal appeals court citing this ground threw out the lawsuit of Maher Arar, the Canadian national who claimed that the United States had illegally rendered him to Syria.[158] The court found that the discovery process might result in the disclosure of valuable intelligence information, including sources and methods. The court could have allowed the lawsuit to continue, relying on the government to claim that specific information sought by the plaintiff was shielded from disclosure by the state secrets doctrine (discussed below and in Chapter 10). Instead, the court held that harm would flow from continuing the lawsuit and obliging the government to invoke the state secrets doctrine. Forcing the government into that corner could result in disclosure of scraps of data that a terrorist group might be able to fit together into a "mosaic" of information about counterterrorism efforts. Under the circumstances, the safest course would be to simply bar the lawsuit.

In other cases, the court has directly invoked the state secrets privilege, discussed in Chapter 10 on classified information, which allows the government to either assert as a complete defense that the lawsuit will result in the disclosure of government secrets or shield particular evidence from the plaintiffs and the public.[159]

The qualified immunity doctrine is a third way in which courts discourage lawsuits for damages against public officials. Granting officials immunity if they have not violated clearly established law gives officials a clear guidepost as they make difficult national security decisions. Courts expect that government officials will practice due diligence by consulting court decisions before acting. If the

---

[158] Arar v. Ashcroft, 585 F.3d 559, 580 (2d Cir. 2009) (en banc), *cert. denied*, 560 U.S. 978 (2010).

[159] *See* Mohamed v. Jeppesen Dataplan, Inc., 614 F.3d 1070 (9th Cir. 2010) (en banc).

IX. Conclusion

Supreme Court has already set a clear rule on a particular issue, it is reasonable to expect that an official will know the rule and act accordingly. An official who violates that rule will lose his or her immunity from suits for damages. However, an official should have immunity when the case law is unclear and fails to provide sufficient guidance.

Qualified immunity was an alternative rationale for protecting senior officials in the case of Abdullah al-Kidd, the individual discussed earlier in this chapter whom the government had detained as a material witness. In *al-Kidd*, as discussed above, a majority of the Court rejected on the merits the plaintiff's position that pretextual use of material witness detention was illegal. In addition, even if the majority had not taken this position on the merits of the plaintiff's claim, all eight Justices who participated in the case (Justice Kagan recused herself) would have held that senior officials did not violate clearly established law and were therefore entitled to qualified immunity.[160]

The Supreme Court has also discouraged lawsuits against public officials by requiring that initial pleadings contain specific allegations that are plausible. In *Ashcroft v. Iqbal*,[161] the Supreme Court held that plaintiffs had failed to plausibly plead in their initial complaint that Attorney General Ashcroft and other senior officials had *intended* to target post-9/11 immigration Arab Muslim detainees based on their religion and national origin. The Court held that the plaintiffs' initial complaint had to specify facts showing that the Attorney General intended to discriminate. Justice Kennedy, writing for the Court, asserted that the most likely motivation for the detentions was a desire to forestall further terrorist threats, not a desire to discriminate for its own sake. Kennedy described the post-9/11 detentions as a "legitimate" response to that need,[162] despite the detainees' lack of terrorist ties. While Justice Kennedy may well have been correct in his assessment of the Attorney General's intent, the Court did not give the plaintiffs a chance to conduct discovery to bolster their claims. Including specific facts in an initial complaint is always difficult—that is why discovery is so important. Without the opportunity to conduct discovery, plaintiffs are in a no-win situation, with the courts expecting more specific claims but denying plaintiffs the means to obtain more specific information.

IX. CONCLUSION

In sum, detention implicates important constitutional interests. The Suspension Clause, which protects access to the Great Writ of habeas corpus, limits

---

[160] *See Al-Kidd*, 131 S. Ct. at 2080 (majority opinion); *id*. at 2086-87 (Kennedy, J., concurring); *id*. at 2087 (Ginsburg, J., concurring, joined by Breyer); *id*. at 2089 (Sotomayor, J., concurring).

[161] 556 U.S. 662 (2009).

[162] *Id*. at 682.

detention outside the criminal justice system. It also gives detainees at Guantanamo a means to test the legality of their confinement. Due process and equal protection supplement the Suspension Clause in limiting detention within the United States. Mass detention based on national origin or ethnicity, such as the Japanese-American internment, is a tragic chapter in U.S. history. It is worthy of study, but thankfully unlikely to be repeated if both courts and citizens remain vigilant. Remedies for abusive interrogation and harsh conditions of confinement are available, although courts often defer to executive branch decisions. Material witness and immigration detentions are also tools that the government has used after 9/11, although the government's use of these approaches has been more sparing in recent years. While the criminal justice system should not be the only tool that the government can use to detain individuals who pose a threat, courts have been appropriately cautious in upholding detention outside this core context.

CHAPTER 9

Military Commissions and the Constitution: From the Revolutionary War to the Aftermath of September 11

Military commissions, like detention in wartime, embody the challenge the Framers faced in reconciling liberty and security. This dilemma has become even more acute after September 11. The U.S. Supreme Court has repeatedly found implicit authorization for military commissions in Congress's war powers, because commissions hold adversaries accountable for war crimes. However, without proper tailoring, military commissions pose tensions with individual rights, checks and balances, and international law.

In American law, the civilian criminal justice system is the usual forum for charges that can yield punishments such as death or imprisonment. That system provides valuable rights, including a jury of the defendants' peers, a grand jury that acts as an independent check on prosecutors, and (in the federal system) an independent judge with lifetime tenure appointed pursuant to Article III of the Constitution. Military commissions lack the full measure of such protections. Commissions also may clash with the Constitution's Ex Post Facto Clause, which requires fair warning to individuals that their future acts may be judged and punished. In considering whether individual defendants have received this fair warning, courts will often consult international law, which limits the acts defined as war crimes. Finally, the unilateral establishment of military commissions by the President can intrude on Congress's war powers. To manage these tensions, courts have carefully cabined military commission jurisdiction.

This chapter discusses the interaction of military commissions and the separation of powers. It then discusses commissions, individual rights, and the role of international law. The chapter closes with a discussion of the separate sphere of military justice, including courts-martial for members of U.S. armed forces.

I. MILITARY COMMISSIONS AND THE SEPARATION OF POWERS

Courts have identified Congress's war powers under Article I of the Constitution as authority for the creation of military commissions. Congress is authorized to "provide for the common Defence,"[1] "make Rules for the Government and Regulation of the land and naval forces,[2] "declare War . . . and make Rules concerning Captures on Land and Water,"[3] and "define and punish . . . Offences against the Law of Nations."[4] The Congress may also make "all Laws which shall be necessary and proper" for executing these powers.[5] In *Ex parte Quirin*, the Court read these authorities broadly, as conferring upon Congress the ability to authorize military commissions as an incident of the "power to wage war."[6]

In order for the nation to wage war effectively, the government must have a means to adjudicate charges based on three kinds of conduct. First, the government must have the ability to try and punish violations of discipline by its own troops. This is the domain of "military justice," including courts-martial, which we discuss at the conclusion of this chapter. Second, the government must have the

---

[1] U.S. Const. art. I, §8 cl. 1.
[2] *Id.*, cl. 14.
[3] *Id.*, cl. 11.
[4] *Id.*, cl. 10.
[5] *Id.*, cl. 18.
[6] 317 U.S. 1, 26 (1942).

I. Military Commissions and the Separation of Powers

ability to try and punish conduct by members of an adversary's force that violate commonly accepted standards for the conduct of war, such as the duty to refrain from targeting civilians. Third, the government must have the ability to keep order in areas where violence has disabled civil authority. Military commissions have been important in meeting the second and third conditions.

The Framers were aware of military commissions' role. In the Revolutionary War, General George Washington famously used a military commission to try British Major John Andre for spying in connection with General Benedict Arnold's treachery against the United States.[7] Moreover, during the Revolutionary War the Continental Congress had expressly authorized the convening of general courts-martial without civilian juries to adjudicate charges of espionage involving non-U.S. citizens, and the administration of the death penalty to those convicted.[8] An 1806 statute authorized comparable military proceedings without juries "according to the law and usage of nations."[9] Civil War proceedings built on that practice, extending it to U.S. citizens arrayed on opposing sides in that bloody conflict.[10] Because of the functional importance of military commissions in times of war and the history of these tribunals, courts do not view military commission proceedings as courts under Article III of the Constitution and the Fifth and Sixth Amendments, which require a jury of the defendant's peers. However, courts have construed this implicit exception narrowly, to avoid undermining the protections that the Framers attached to civilian criminal justice.[11]

Courts have been more inclined to defer to the use of military commissions when Congress and the President have cooperated in establishing them. Although the President may have authority under Article II to establish military commissions without express congressional approval, courts have generally viewed Congress's war powers as trumping presidential authority. Maintaining checks on the Executive was one strand in the Supreme Court landmark 1866 post-Civil War decision, *Ex parte Milligan*.[12] In failing to find a lawful basis for the commission in *Milligan*, Justice David Davis observed that Congress had not authorized commissions to try individuals like the defendant, who were not combatants in the conflict. The Supreme Court's World War II decision, *Ex parte Quirin*, upholding the military commission trial of eight alleged Nazi saboteurs, found that Congress

---

[7] *Id.* at 42 n. 14.

[8] *Id.* at 41.

[9] *Id.*

[10] *Id.* at 42 n. 14.

[11] For an important analysis that places military commissions in the overall military justice context, see Stephen I. Vladeck, *Military Courts and Article III*, 103 Geo. L.J. __ (forthcoming 2015), *available at* http://ssrn.com/abstract=2419342. For debate on the merits of commissions, compare Kenneth Anderson, *What to Do with Bin Laden and Al Qaeda Terrorists?: A Qualified Defense of Military Commissions and United States Policy on Detainees at Guantanamo Bay Naval Base*, 25 Harv. J.L. & Pub. Pol'y 591, 613-20 (2002) (suggesting that commissions are consistent with both the Constitution and international law), with David Glazier, *Playing By the Rules: Combating Al Qaeda Within the Law of War*, 51 Wm. & Mary L. Rev. 957, 1033 (2009) (critiquing commissions).

[12] 71 U.S. 2 (1866).

had authorized commissions. The support for this finding was questionable: Congress had merely enacted a savings clause stating that legislation did not preclude commissions if they were *otherwise lawful*. Congress had not directed that commissions be created. Nevertheless, the Court's straining to reach this result indicates the importance of congressional consent or acquiescence.

In the post–September 11 case of *Hamdan v. Rumsfeld (Hamdan I),*[13] the clash between the President and Congress ultimately undid commissions unilaterally established by the administration of President George W. Bush. Justice Anthony Kennedy, concurring in the decision, cited the concurrence of Justice Jackson in the *Steel Seizure Case (Youngstown Sheet & Tube Co. v. Sawyer).*[14] As discussed in Chapter 2, Justice Jackson, summarizing the distribution of powers among the political branches, had opined that the President receives greatest deference when he acts consistently with Congress's will, some deference when executive action occurs against the backdrop of legislative silence, and little or no deference for decisions that clash with Congress.[15] In *Hamdan I*, the Court found that President Bush's decision to unilaterally establish military commissions clashed with Congress's mandate to ensure that commission procedures be as close as "practicable" to courts-martial that tried U.S. armed services members.

Justice Stevens, writing for the majority in *Hamdan I*, noted that the military commissions established by President Bush's order lacked protections required by courts-martial. For example, military judges presiding over commissions had virtually unchecked authority to exclude a defendant from his own trial, and could also admit evidence obtained through coercion.[16] A trial that occurs in the defendant's absence would be fundamentally unfair, since it would deprive the defendant of the chance to participate in the questioning of witnesses or inform his lawyer that evidence was biased or inaccurate. Evidence obtained through coercion is unreliable, because the subject of coercion will try to stop the abuse by saying whatever he believes his interrogators wish to hear.

According to Justice Stevens, the government had not made any showing that military necessity or other exigent factors justified such departures from the procedures guaranteed by courts-martial.[17] Uniformity with court-martial procedures thus was not impractical. Therefore, Justice Stevens reasoned, President Bush's order failed to meet Congress's condition for departures from those procedures. Because President Bush's order clashed with Congress's will, the order belonged in *Youngstown*'s third category, where presidential action receives little

---

[13] 548 U.S. 557 (2006).

[14] *Id.* at 638 (citing Youngstown Sheet & Tube Co. v. Sawyer, 343 U.S. 579, 637 (1952) (Jackson, J., concurring)).

[15] *Id.*; *cf.* David J. Barron & Martin S. Lederman, *The Commander in Chief at the Lowest Ebb—Framing the Problem, Doctrine, and Original Understanding*, 121 Harv. L. Rev. 689 (2008) (analyzing *Youngstown*'s implications).

[16] *Hamdan*, 558 U.S. at 614.

[17] *Id.* at 623-24.

or no deference. The Court then struck down the President's order as exceeding his constitutional authority.[18]

II. COMMISSIONS TRYING U.S. CITIZENS: MANAGING THE THREAT TO INDIVIDUAL RIGHTS

In the landmark Civil War decision, *Ex parte Milligan*, the Supreme Court relied not just on preserving checks and balances, but on preserving individual rights. Justice Davis, writing for the Court, noted that military commissions did not provide defendants with a jury trial in the sense that the Constitution used the term in Article III and the Sixth Amendment, with finders of fact chosen from all walks of civilian life. In military commissions, finders of fact were members of the military. Because of their service status, members of military commissions lacked the independence of civilian jurors. Military commissions also do not include provision for a grand jury to serve as an independent check on prosecutors, as the Grand Jury Clause of the Fifth Amendment requires for any matter not "arising in the land or naval forces" of the United States (which courts have interpreted strictly to cover only current service personnel or contractors accompanying armed forces in the field). While the *Milligan* Court did not view military commissions as inherently unconstitutional, it regarded these deficits as demonstrating the need for limits on commission jurisdiction.[19]

Justice Davis opined in *Milligan* that military commissions lacked jurisdiction over charges based on conduct during the Civil War if 1) ordinary civilian courts were open, and 2) the defendant was not a participant in the conflict. The case concerned Lambdin Milligan, who had petitioned for a writ of habeas corpus after his military commission conviction for attempts to subvert Indiana's state government. According to Justice Davis, Milligan was a civilian, despite his attempts at subversion. Moreover, Justice Davis added, in Milligan's home state of Indiana, civilian courts were functioning and federal authority remained intact throughout the Civil War.[20] Permitting a military commission to decide Milligan's fate under these circumstances would, the Court worried, imperil the right to a civilian jury trial throughout the United States. The Court therefore held that a military commission was inappropriate in Milligan's case. In the World War II case, *Ex parte Quirin*, the Court upheld the military commission conviction of two U.S. citizens, but distinguished *Milligan* on the ground that the defendants

---

[18] *Id.* at 625.

[19] *See generally* Michael W. Lewis & Peter Margulies, *Interpretations of IHL in Tribunals of the United States*, in APPLYING INTERNATIONAL HUMANITARIAN LAW IN JUDICIAL AND QUASI JUDICIAL BODIES (T.M.C. Asser Press 2014).

[20] *Milligan*, 71 U.S. at 121-22.

were not civilians but belligerents in the conflict who acted under the direction of the German High Command.

Meeting *Milligan*'s conditions is necessary for a valid military commission proceeding, but not sufficient. The jurisdiction of military commissions entails three further questions that have become central after 9/11: 1) Did an armed conflict exist at the time of the offense charged?; 2) If an armed conflict did exist, did the defendant have fair warning that he could be tried in a military commission for committing that offense?; and 3) Is the offense reasonably related to a) offenses (such as spying) that international law has traditionally permitted states to try in military commissions or b) offenses (such as the murder of civilians) that constitute international war crimes? The next sections discuss these issues in turn.

III. WHEN DOES AN ARMED CONFLICT START?

The existence of an armed conflict is important under both domestic and international law. Under domestic law, *Milligan* makes clear the involvement of the United States in an armed conflict is required for a valid military commission. Only the extraordinary exigency of an armed conflict can justify an extraordinary proceeding like a military commission. Without that extraordinary exigency, the Constitution provides no basis for departing from the jury trial and grand jury guarantees.

As discussed in Chapter 4 on the international law regarding the use of force and conduct of hostilities, the existence of a noninternational armed conflict (NIAC) hinges on two tests: 1) Is the conflict of sufficient duration and intensity to be a NIAC, not just a riot, crime wave, or routine civil disturbance?; and 2) Is the nonstate party to the violence an organized armed group (OAG), rather than a motley crew of criminals or malcontents?

These issues have become vital to the lawfulness of military commissions in the wake of September 11. An armed conflict clearly existed once the United States intervened militarily in Afghanistan a few weeks after the 9/11 attacks. However, debate has been substantial about whether the September 11 attacks themselves, or earlier acts of violence committed by Al Qaeda against U.S. personnel or interests, occurred during an armed conflict or were simply acts of terrorism that must be tried in civilian courts.

The determination of the start of the U.S. armed conflict with Al Qaeda is central in the pending military commission trial of Abd al-Rahim al-Nashiri, the accused planner of the October 2000 Yemen attack on the U.S.S. Cole. According to the U.S. Convening Authority for military commissions, the attack constituted the war crime of perfidy, since the attackers used an unmarked boat laden with explosives. Al-Nashiri and several scholars argue that the attack was a terrorist incident, and not part of a NIAC. If that argument is valid, then the military commission would not have jurisdiction or al-Nashiri would be entitled to an

III. When Does an Armed Conflict Start?

acquittal. If the United States is correct, the trial and conviction of al-Nashiri in a military commission would be consistent with international law.[21]

In support of the U.S. view, one can argue that Congress has already determined that the U.S.S. Cole attacks and other pre-9/11 acts by Al Qaeda may be tried by military commissions. In the Military Commissions Act of 2006, Congress gave military commissions jurisdiction over acts committed before September 11, recognizing that Al Qaeda's military efforts against the United States predated that event. Congress's determination may be entitled to deference under both domestic law and international law, where the principle of complementarity would suggest that determinations by political branches of a state are worthy of some respect. However, when an armed conflict begins is *not* a "political question" (see Chapter 3) or an issue that is otherwise unreviewable in the courts. Courts should review the determination of when an armed conflict begins, applying international law criteria in the absence of direction from Congress to the contrary, even if courts defer to some degree to U.S. government determinations.

To support the U.S. view, one can argue that the attack on the U.S.S. Cole was a link in a chain of attacks by Al Qaeda dating back to at least August 1998, when Al Qaeda bombed U.S. embassies in Kenya and Tanzania, killing over 220 persons. Two weeks later, President Clinton responded to the embassy bombings with cruise missile strikes in Afghanistan and Sudan. President Clinton informed Congress of the strikes using the language of armed conflict: Citing Article 51 of the UN Charter, which permits self-defense against an armed attack, President Clinton described the U.S. strikes as a "necessary and proportionate response to the imminent threat of further terrorist attacks against U.S. personnel and facilities." Subsequently, President Clinton issued a Memorandum of Notification authorizing CIA-affiliated tribal assets in Afghanistan to seek to capture Al Qaeda's leader, Osama bin Laden. Of course, bin Laden was not captured, but the important data point for defining the start of an armed conflict is U.S. efforts, not results. Since the East African embassy bombings involved the substantial loss of life, they meet the intensity criterion. The U.S. cruise missile strikes also meet this definition. The U.S. efforts to apprehend bin Laden after the cruise missile strikes bolster the durational element, particularly since these efforts relied on assistance from paramilitary or military forces, not the police one would expect to see in a traditional human rights/law enforcement model. Moreover, the attack on the Cole was not the first attempt by Al Qaeda to target U.S. naval vessels. Al Qaeda tried in

---

[21] This question was pending as of October 2014 in the U.S. District Court for the District of Columbia, where al-Nashiri has sought a preliminary injunction against his military commission trial. That motion also raised the issue of whether the federal district court should invoke the abstention doctrine to refrain from exercising its jurisdiction. The government argued that abstention was appropriate, since Congress expressly provided in the Military Commissions Act for commissions, and a conviction in the case will be reviewed in due course by an independent civilian tribunal. Al-Nashiri countered that the matter should be decided immediately, rather than obliging him to needlessly endure the rigors of a commission trial. The government may have the better argument on this complex question of federal jurisdiction. *See* Al-Nashiri v. Obama, 2014 U.S. Dist. LEXIS 177736 (D.D.C. Dec. 29, 2014) (holding that abstention was appropriate and declining to enjoin military commission proceeding).

January 2000 to attack a U.S. destroyer, The Sullivans, but failed because the small vessel packed with explosives that Al Qaeda used for the attack ran aground before hitting its target.[22] The gap in time between the U.S. cruise missile strike and the attack on The Sullivans is about 16 months. If one uses a sliding scale to integrate duration and intensity, the U.S.S. Cole attack may well qualify as an act during an armed conflict.

There are legitimate counterarguments on whether the Cole attack meets the intensity and duration requirements. The two-year gap in time between the embassy attacks and cruise missile strikes in 1998 and the Cole attack in 2000 is significant, even if one can bundle a spectrum of U.S. efforts as rising to the level of armed conflict. Moreover, President Clinton largely responded to the Cole attack with law enforcement measures, although his public remarks were ambiguous. President Clinton mentioned that the attack occurred in a "time of peace," but one can read this comment by President Clinton as merely calling attention to the perfidious nature of the attack itself.

Debate about whether the U.S.S. Cole attack was part of violence with the requisite intensity and duration to qualify as a noninternational armed conflict has spilled over into debate about the 9/11 attacks themselves. The United States has relied on the sheer destructive force of the attacks, which killed 3,000 people, destroyed the towering World Trade Center in New York, and damaged the Pentagon near Washington, D.C. The United States can also point to the attack on the U.S.S. Cole as another link in the chain of violence between the United States and Al Qaeda. However, critics can argue that almost a year passed between the attack on the U.S.S. Cole in October 2000 and the 9/11 attacks. The passage of time does not definitively rule out the existence of an armed conflict, and the period at issue is shorter than the more than two years that separated the attack on the U.S.S. Cole and the East Africa embassy bombings. Critics are right, however, that there is some uncertainty about whether the 9/11 attacks themselves occurred during an armed conflict. That uncertainty does not fully dissolve until the U.S. response to 9/11, including the military intervention in Afghanistan, which clearly exhibited the intensity and duration that an armed conflict requires.

On whether the U.S.S. Cole attack was the product of an OAG, there is less disagreement. Most scholars agree that in the period culminating in the 9/11 attacks, core Al Qaeda had a headquarters in Afghanistan courtesy of its Taliban hosts, who controlled Afghanistan's government. Al Qaeda also had a leader, Osama bin Laden, who spoke for the group and determined overall strategy. The attacks on U.S. East African embassies as well as the U.S.S. Cole revealed meticulous planning, which confirms the existence of an OAG.

In sum, military commission jurisdiction over the mastermind of the U.S.S. Cole bombing in 2000 hinges on whether an armed conflict already existed between the United States and Al Qaeda. A broad view of the nature of conflict

---

[22] Steven Lee Myers, *Failed Plan to Bomb a U.S. Ship is Reported*, N.Y. Times, Nov. 10, 2000, at A11.

between a state and violent nonstate actors such as terrorist groups would suggest that an armed conflict did exist.

IV.   WAR CRIMES AND MILITARY COMMISSION JURISDICTION

Once we have concluded that an armed conflict exists, we ask whether the conduct of a defendant constitutes a war crime that is triable before a military commission. Under both domestic and international law, an individual defendant must have fair warning *at the time of his conduct* that his acts could yield military commission charges. To analyze whether a defendant had this fair warning, courts have asked whether the defendant's alleged conduct constituted a war crime. If the defendant's conduct was a war crime, courts have upheld military commission jurisdiction. If the defendant's conduct was *not* a war crime, courts have held that the military commission lacked jurisdiction, even if the defendant's acts could have been prosecuted in an ordinary civilian court.

Courts asking whether particular conduct constituted a war crime have looked to both Congress's war powers under Article I, sec. 8 of the Constitution, including the power to make rules governing the land and naval forces and the power to define and punish violations of international law,[23] and to the Ex Post Facto Clause, found in Article I, sec. 9,[24] which requires the government to provide fair warning to individuals that their conduct is illegal and renders them subject to punishment.

A.   *The Constitutional Objectives and International Law Origins of the Ex Post Facto Clause*

The Ex Post Facto Clause mirrors the fair warning concept built into the international law principle of legality. Under this fair warning principle, the state must tell people in advance that certain acts are prohibited. Once the state has provided this fair warning, the state may prosecute and punish individuals who disregard the warning. It would be unfair to punish people for engaging in conduct that was not clearly illegal at the time the conduct took place. Laws that create this unfairness are called ex post facto laws—laws that only go into effect *after* ("post") conduct they prohibit has occurred. When the state wields the awesome weapon of criminal law to convict an individual and imprison him or even take his life, it is not fair to change the rules in the middle of the game.

---

[23] U.S. Const. art. I, §8, cl. 10.
[24] *Id.*, art. I, §9, cl. 3.

This core principle of international law found its way into the U.S. Constitution not only because the Framers cared about international law, but because they believed that Britain had regularly used ex post facto laws to reinforce tyrannical rule over its colonies in North America. When the colonists engaged in conduct that the British did not like, Britain would make that conduct criminal after the fact. A government that can change the rules in the middle of the game can more readily reward its political friends and punish its political opponents. To guard against such unfairness, the Framers saw to it that the Constitution prohibited ex post facto laws.

The Ex Post Facto Clause's fair warning principle limits the crimes that Congress can designate for trial in military commissions. Bear in mind that military commissions are rare in American history. In the 50 years after the Constitution's enactment, commissions were used only once—by General Andrew Jackson in 1818 in the First Seminole War.[25] In the period from Jackson's resort to commissions to September 11, the United States used commissions only rarely, for example, during or after the Mexican War, the Civil War, and World War II (with the Civil War having by far the majority of commissions). Unlike civilian courts, which regularly provide guidance to the public on legal principles, gaps in time interrupt legal precedents in commissions. The rarity of commissions has impeded the provision of fair warning.

Adding to concerns about fair warning, the U.S. government has often authorized military commissions *during* conflicts, not before. That timing conflicts with the Ex Post Facto Clause, which typically requires that a criminal statute be in place *before* the conduct that triggers charges. Moreover, in ordinary criminal law, the legislatures list specific offenses that are subject to punishment. While a statute establishing military commission jurisdiction over certain conduct may list specific offenses, such statutes also include provisions that authorize trial of offenses that "by the law of war" may be tried in military commissions.[26] Congress, in the Military Commissions Act of 2006 (MCA), included a provision authorizing trial of charges that a defendant violated the "law of war." The definition of the statutory phrase "law of war" therefore is crucial for determining whether particular charges comply with the Ex Post Facto Clause's fair warning principle.

Under the Ex Post Facto Clause, the key inquiry then becomes, what offenses are encompassed by the "law of war" and what constitutes the "law of war." There are three positions. The first position is that the law of war is strictly and categorically limited to international law, and includes only the precise and express offenses that nations have agreed by consensus, case law, or treaty constitute violations of international law. The second concept or definition would require a reasonable nexus to international law, but would allow states some latitude in framing charges before military commissions, as long as the underlying conduct violated international law. The third approach would detach the "law of war" from

---

[25] *See* Peter Margulies, *Defining, Punishing, and Membership in the Community of Nations: Charging Material Support and Conspiracy in Military Commissions*, 36 FORDHAM INT'L L.J. 1, 32-38 (2013).

[26] *See* Article 21 of Military Commissions Act of 2006, 10 U.S.C. §821.

international law, and allow the United States to define the law of war based on U.S. history and practice. As of July 2014, each position can claim some support in the case law.

Let us consider first the narrow view that the "law of war" only permits the trial in a military commission of charges that have been expressly recognized as war crimes under international law. Because there is no world legislature to list international crimes, the international law governing armed conflicts is largely customary in nature. Nations have until recently recognized war crimes gradually in a common law fashion, referring to states' opinions about which offenses they are bound to prosecute and to state practice. Today, that common law process is supplemented by treaties such as the Statute of Rome, which governs the International Criminal Court (ICC), and case law of current tribunals, such as the ICC and the International Criminal Tribunal for the former Yugoslavia (ICTY).

International law recognizes certain charges that a military commission could try, including the targeting of civilians. War crimes are acts that violate the law of armed conflict's (LOAC) guiding principles of necessity and humanity. Conduct that is necessary to serve a legitimate military objective is authorized under LOAC, even if that conduct involves *incidental* harm to civilians, as long as that conduct does not cause *excessive* harm to civilians in light of the military advantage obtained. The principle of humanity requires that a party to an armed conflict avoid excessive harm to civilians, as well as other conduct, such as the intentional harming of captives who are at that party's mercy. In contrast, conduct such as the targeting of civilians does not serve either necessity or humanity. The deliberate murder of civilians is viewed as both inhumane and unnecessary to the achievement of legitimate military objectives.

International law also prohibits certain acts during combat that are not considered fair fighting. It prohibits such acts in part because such acts may have the effect of endangering civilians and captives. Just as a party to an armed conflict must distinguish between military targets and civilians, that party must also distinguish its own forces, ensuring that they cannot be mistaken for civilians. To accomplish that goal, state forces must wear distinctive insignia to inform others of their combatant status. A party who uses civilian garb to gain an advantage in killing enemies has violated the fundamental norm of LOAC and engaged in conduct that is tantamount to the age-old war crime perfidy—the use of a false flag of surrender to draw in opponents for the kill. By prohibiting such tactics and requiring a "fair fight," LOAC also protects civilians and others outside of combat.[27] Perfidy puts those outside of combat at risk, because a party victimized by perfidy in an armed conflict will in the future kill both those outside of combat and

---

[27] *See* Michael A. Newton, *Exceptional Engagement: Protocol I and a World United Against Terrorism*, 45 TEX. INT'L L.J. 323, 344-47 (2009) (discussing political factors that led to enactment of Protocol I to the Geneva Conventions, which the United States has declined to ratify on grounds that certain of its provisions encourage perfidy and terrorism by relaxing requirement that combatants distinguish themselves from civilians).

those still embroiled in it, to avoid again endangering its own personnel. In sum, charges such as the murder of civilians or perfidy are sufficiently well established in international law to support trial in military commissions.

B.   The Ex Post Facto Clause and Material Support of Terrorism

Tensions between U.S. military commissions and international law emerge because certain charges that the MCA authorized military commissions to try are *not* recognized under international law. The MCA supplied the congressional consent that the Supreme Court had required in *Hamdan v. Rumsfeld,* when the Court held that President Bush had exceeded his authority in unilaterally establishing military commissions. In the MCA, Congress empowered military commissions to try charges of conspiracy and material support to terrorism. The prohibition on material support of terrorism has been part of federal criminal law since 1996,[28] although Congress only authorized military commission adjudication of material support charges in 2006.[29] Material support can include a broad range of activity including the provision of financial help, ammunition, communications equipment, or expert advice.

In the MCA, Congress authorized material support charges for conduct that preceded the effective date of the act. That retroactive imposition of guilt clashed with the Ex Post Facto Clause.[30] As noted above, the MCA also provided for military commission trial of charges that a defendant violated the "law of war." To comply with the fair warning principle, a particular charge would have to be an offense recognized as part of the "law of war" at the time of the defendant's act.

Material support is not a charge recognized under the international "law of war." International tribunals, treaties, and scholars have not viewed conduct such as low-level funding of a terrorist group as a war crime. As a result, a commission based on the international law of war would not have jurisdiction over most conduct that constituted material support of terrorist groups.

---

[28] 18 U.S.C. §2339A; Holder v. Humanitarian Law Project, 561 U.S. 1 (2010) (upholding statute); *see also* Chapter 6.

[29] However, Congress did not expand the jurisdictional reach of federal criminal law on material support until after September 11, when it amended the law to include conduct outside the United States by non-U.S. citizens or residents. Most of the conduct that provided the basis for charges in military commissions occurred *before* September 11. Therefore, the Ex Post Facto Clause would also have been a problem for bringing such charges in ordinary criminal courts.

[30] The conventional wisdom has been that the Ex Post Facto Clause is forum-specific, requiring Congress to expressly authorize charges before a particular tribunal, such as an ordinary federal court for standard criminal charges or a military commission for charges in that forum. *But see* Al Bahlul v. United States, 767 F.3d 1, 18-22 (D.C. Cir. 2014) (en banc) (asserting that al Bahlul, at least under a plain error standard of review that was deferential to government, also received fair warning because a federal criminal statute, 18 U.S.C. 2332(b), prohibited conspiracy to kill a U.S. national outside the United States).

IV. War Crimes and Military Commission Jurisdiction

Material support is also not a charge that has been brought under U.S. military commissions. However, a narrower definition of material support that included only conduct relating to an international war crime, such as the murder of civilians, is the functional equivalent of internationally recognized theories of liability, such as aiding and abetting the crime of murder or participating in a Joint Criminal Enterprise (JCE) to murder civilians.

The D.C. Circuit Court of Appeals held in *Hamdan v. United States (Hamdan II)*[31] that a 2008 conviction in a military commission for material support that occurred in 2001, five years before the MCA became effective, violated both the Define and Punish Clause and the Ex Post Facto Clause. Judge Kavanaugh, writing for the court, noted that no treaty prohibited material support, no international tribunal had convicted someone of the offense, and scholars generally acknowledged that material support was not a crime under international law. According to Judge Kavanaugh, the material support provided by the defendant was largely limited to driving Osama bin Laden to meetings. This kind of generic assistance did not constitute an international war crime. As we shall see, U.S. military tribunals before 9/11 also never charged someone with material support. Because charges of material support were not recognized in either international tribunals or U.S. military commissions during the Civil War or World War II, the D.C. Circuit held that such charges are not part of the "law of war" that Congress incorporated into the Military Commissions Act. Since such charges were not part of the "law of war" in effect as of September 11, material support charges in military commissions for conduct *before* September 11 violate the Ex Post Facto Clause.

C. Conspiracy and the Law of War

The D.C. Circuit has treated conspiracy differently than it treated material support. Conspiracy under the MCA can occur in two ways. First, as international tribunals have recognized, conspiracy can be a plot that results in a completed unlawful act of violence, such as the murder of civilians. Here, conspiracy is not a separate charge, but merely a *theory of liability* for charging a defendant with the crime of murder.[32] The prosecutor's theory of the case is that one who plots to murder civilians is just as guilty as the individual who pulls the trigger.

In contrast, conspiracy is *not* recognized as criminal under international law when it is not a theory of liability for a completed war crime, but is instead a separate, stand-alone charge entailing a mere *agreement* between individuals. In this scenario, there is no completed act, such as the murder of civilians. There is only an agreement. Under U.S. law, a mere agreement can trigger prosecution. A defendant can be guilty of conspiracy to rob a bank under U.S. law merely if

---

[31] 696 F.3d 1238 (D.C. Cir. 2012).

[32] Prosecutor v. Brdanin, Case No. IT-99-36-A, Appeals Chamber Judgment, Paras. 393-95 (Int'l Crim. Trib. for the Former Yugoslavia Apr. 3, 2007).

that individual agrees with others to rob a bank and then takes a minor step to achieve that purpose, such as driving to the bank to observe its security.[33] In contrast, international tribunals have refused to find that mere agreement is a war crime, because of fear that such an offense would be too vague. Conspiracy as mere agreement could ensnare too many defendants who had merely *thought* of committing a war crime. An international tribunal like the ICC will not authorize the trial of an individual who merely plots to kill civilians unless others have *actually killed* the civilians in question and the plot has in some fashion facilitated the killing.

1.   International Tribunals on Conspiracy as a Form of Liability

In cases where the killing of civilians *has* occurred, international tribunals will broadly construe the assistance, including conspiracies among individuals, that supports the charge of murder. One of international law's central concerns is the elimination of impunity—a wrongdoer's evasion of punishment. Courts recognize that the murder of civilians often entails assistance in varying forms provided by many individuals, each eager to minimize or deny his or her role. A broad definition of culpable assistance promotes accountability for those who help commit such serious crimes.

For example, treaties and case law indicate that a conviction for murder of civilians could be based on a defendant's aiding and abetting the killing or participation in a Joint Criminal Enterprise (JCE) to commit the killing. To be guilty of the murder of civilians based on a JCE theory, an individual need only serve as a "cog in the wheel" for a common plan.[34] To be guilty of aiding and abetting, a defendant need not have prior knowledge of a specific act of violence. A defendant need only provide help, including moral encouragement, with the knowledge that those receiving the help are targeting civilians.[35]

Plots and agreements between individuals can support advancing conspiracy as a theory of liability for completed war crimes. Suppose an individual recruits others with the intention that the recruits will murder civilians. If the murder actually occurs, the recruiter would be guilty of that murder on either a JCE or aiding and abetting theory. An individual who drives a truck that transports civilians to a killing site with the knowledge that such killing will occur is similarly guilty of murdering civilians.

---

[33] For a landmark federal case on conspiracy doctrine, see Kotteakos v. United States, 328 U.S 750 (1946) (holding that defendants can be guilty of conspiracy if they agreed to commit acts that were unlawful and acted to further that goal, even if each defendant did not know all or even most of the other defendants in the alleged conspiracy).

[34] Prosecutor v. Tadic, Case No. IT-94-1-A, Appeals Chamber Judgment, Para. 199 (Int'l Crim. Trib. for the Former Yugoslavia July 15, 1999); Prosecutor v. Taylor, Case No. 03-01-T, P6910-11 (SCSL 2012).

[35] Prosecutor v. Sainovic, Case No. IT-05-87-A, Appeals Chamber Judgment (Int'l Crim. Trib. for the Former Yugoslavia Jan. 23, 2014).

2. Conspiracy and *al Bahlul v. United States*

As an example of how conspiracy charges play out in military commissions, consider the case of Ali Hamza al Bahlul, a propagandist for bin Laden. In a July 2014 decision, the full (en banc) D.C. Circuit rejected al Bahlul's Ex Post Facto Clause challenge to his 2008 military commission conviction for conspiracy.[36] Al Bahlul was not charged with the murder of civilians, only with conspiring to commit murder. The judge in the military commission informed the members of the commission that it was not necessary to find a completed act to find al Bahlul guilty. If one looks no further, this would seem to be a conviction for conspiracy as mere agreement, which is not a war crime under international law. Therefore, the court had to look elsewhere for authority supporting al Bahlul's conviction.

In *al Bahlul*, the full D.C. Circuit suggested that the phrase "law of war" in the Military Commissions Act could also refer to U.S. decisions on military commissions, even when those decisions went beyond international law.[37] The majority cited two important episodes in U.S. history involving conspiracy. In one, military commissions tried plotters in the Lincoln assassination on conspiracy charges.[38] In the other, the Supreme Court upheld the military commission convictions of Nazi saboteurs during World War II who were charged with a number of offenses, including conspiracy.[39] In each of these examples, the commission heard charges based on defendants' mere agreement, although each also involved completed acts—most obviously in the Lincoln case, where President Lincoln had in fact been assassinated.

The D.C. Circuit did not definitively say that under the "law of war" referred to by Congress in the MCA, the U.S. history of charging conspiracy as mere agreement trumped international refusal to charge conspiracy as a stand-alone offense. The court said only that al Bahlul had forfeited his right to object to this argument by not objecting in lower courts. Therefore, the court held, a plain error standard applied.[40] That standard is very deferential to the holding of the court below. The court below had found that the fair warning required by the Ex Post Facto Clause regarding the "law of war" could be determined by U.S. practice.

The D.C. Circuit applied a deferential plain error standard based on al Bahlul's forfeiture of his rights at trial because trial courts must have an opportunity to consider a party's legal and factual arguments. Giving trial courts that opportunity

---

[36] Al Bahlul v. United States, 767 F.3d 1 (D.C. Cir. 2014). One of the co-authors of this volume, Prof. Peter Margulies, and an editor of the volume, James Schoettler, Esq., appeared in *al Bahlul* as co-counsel for amici curiae former military lawyers and government officials, as well as national security scholars, arguing that the conviction should be upheld. *See* Amicus Brief, No. 11-1324 (D.C. Cir. Sept. 22, 2014), *available at* http://www.lawfareblog.com/wp-content/uploads/2014/09/Bahlul-Govt-Amicus.pdf.

[37] *Id.* at 23-24.

[38] *Id.* at 24-27.

[39] *Ex parte Quirin*, 317 U.S. 1 (1942).

[40] *Al Bahlul*, 767 F.3d at 8-10.

promotes orderly adjudication and the development of an adequate record for appellate review. To encourage parties to give trial courts that opportunity, courts have held that the failure to make those arguments at trial results in their forfeiture on appeal. While the appellate court will still review the conviction, it will use a deferential "plain error" standard. Under the standard, the reviewing court will uphold the conviction, unless the trial court made obvious mistakes of law or egregious unfairness undermined the integrity of the proceedings.

The standard of review on appeal can make a huge difference in a case. Applying a plain error standard, the court in *al Bahlul* stated that it was not "obvious" that the "law of war" incorporated into the Military Commissions Act was limited to international law.[41] Instead, the court found, the "law of war" referred to in the statute *could* refer to U.S. precedents like the Lincoln plotters' trial and the Nazi saboteur case, where stand-alone conspiracy was one of the charges against the defendants. Viewed in this light, the defendant had received the fair warning that the Ex Post Facto Clause requires.

Because the *al Bahlul* court relied on the deferential plain error standard, a future decision might define the "law of war" more narrowly, as including only international law. That narrower definition might govern a case where the court applied a less deferential *de novo* ("like new") standard of review because a defendant had objected below and hence preserved his right to argue against commission jurisdiction. The D.C. Circuit's *al Bahlul* decision is therefore not a blanket endorsement of the position that the "law of war" can rely solely on U.S. practice when this practice clashes with international law.

The result in *al Bahlul* may actually be consistent with international law, if one adopts a functional view that analyzes the underlying conduct of the defendant, not the precise label of the charge under which the defendant was tried.[42] Al Bahlul's conduct arguably violated international law, making his conviction and punishment consistent with the fair warning principle that underlies the Ex Post Facto Clause. Judge Janice Rogers Brown, in an insightful concurrence, outlined this functional perspective. Recall that under international law, conspiracy can be a form of liability for a completed act, such as the murder of civilians. The threshold of guilt is low: An individual who merely serves as a "cog in the wheel" executing a common plan to murder civilians is guilty of those murders.[43] While the initial charge in al Bahlul's case was based on his agreement and did not require a completed act, overt acts cited in the charges "directly relate[d]" to the 9/11 attacks.[44] Undisputed evidence linking al Bahlul to 9/11 proved the one element—relationship to a completed war crime—that separated the stand-alone

---

[41] *Id.* at 27.

[42] *Id.* at 60 n. 3 (Brown, J., concurring).

[43] Prosecutor v. Tadic, Case No. IT-94-1-A, Appeals Chamber Judgment, Para. 199 (Int'l Crim. Trib. for the Former Yugoslavia July 15, 1999); Prosecutor v. Taylor, Case No. 03-01-T, P6910-11 (SCSL 2012).

[44] *Al Bahlul*, 767 F.3d at 21; Margulies, *supra* note 25, at 83-84, 86-87.

conspiracy charge in al Bahlul's case from internationally recognized conspiracy as a theory of liability.[45]

The undisputed evidence includes the following. Although al Bahlul did not have advance knowledge of the attacks, a letter from al Bahlul introduced into evidence admitted that his conduct was related—albeit in a "simple" and "indirect" way—to 9/11. In the letter, al Bahlul admitted one of the overt acts cited in the charges: administering an al Qaeda loyalty oath to two key participants in the 9/11 plot—Mohamed Atta, the plot's ringleader in the United States, and Ziad Jarrah, one of the pilots.[46] Evidence also showed that al Bahlul administered the oath with the intent that Atta and Jarrah would kill American civilians.[47] Moreover, acting as his own attorney during the trial, al Bahlul acknowledged that his administration of the loyalty oath linked him to the 9/11 plot. The members of the military commission specifically found that al Bahlul had administered the loyalty oath. That finding would support JCE and aiding and abetting liability for murder, given the broad definitions used in international tribunals. In this respect, al Bahlul's conduct fit within the acts that international law authorizes for trial in military commissions. On a functional view, his conviction should stand.

D. Conspiracy and Article III

Al Bahlul has also argued that Article III of the Constitution, which ensures a jury of one's peers and an independent, life-tenured judge to preside over trial, bars military commission adjudication of charges that are not recognized under international law. This argument has some basis in the Nazi saboteur case, *Ex parte Quirin*.[48] On balance, however, it misreads the analysis in that case and in the Supreme Court's landmark 1866 decision, *Ex parte Milligan*.[49]

In *Quirin*, the Supreme Court recognized that "military tribunals . . . are not courts" within the meaning of Article III.[50] The Court drew that conclusion because it believed that the Framers were aware of the early precedents involving military commissions, such as the Revolutionary War proceeding involving British Major John Andre.[51] The Framers recognized, the Court inferred, that the need to conduct military commission proceedings expeditiously and under exigent wartime conditions "preclud[ed] resort" to juries and other "familiar parts of the machinery for criminal trials in the state courts."[52] According to *Quirin*, the

---

[45] *Al Bahlul*, 767 F.3d at 21 (citing United States v. Cotton, 535 U.S. 625, 633 (2002) (describing evidence as "essentially uncontroverted")).

[46] *See* Margulies, *supra* note 25, at 86; Petitioner's Appendix I at 148, Al Bahlul v. United States, No. 11-1324 (D.C. Cir.) (panel on remand from en banc decision).

[47] *Id.*

[48] 317 U.S. 1 (1942).

[49] 71 U.S. 2 (1866).

[50] *Id.* at 39.

[51] *Id.* at 31 n. 9.

[52] *Id.* at 39.

Framers intended only to require a jury for cases that required one under the common law or cases of a "like nature."[53] In contrast, military commission proceedings were "cases in which it was then well understood that a jury trial could not be demanded as of right."[54] Subsequent case law on Article III has deferred to Congress's exercise of its powers under Article I, except in cases involving the risk of congressional control over tort, property, and contract claims arising under state law.[55] Military commissions for belligerents in armed conflicts do not present this risk.

The post-9/11 military commissions at Guantanamo fit this analysis. They are being held at Guantanamo, in part because Congress and the President determined that conducting military commissions within sovereign U.S. territory would pose security concerns. All of the current military commission proceedings, including al Bahlul's, involve foreign belligerents with no preexisting ties to the United States, prosecuted for acts connected to an armed conflict.[56] Under those circumstances, it would be "impracticable and anomalous"[57] to apply Article III safeguards to such tribunals. Moreover, although not all of the charges tried in the post-9/11 commissions have been recognized internationally, all of the charges are at least reasonably related to international war crimes such as perfidy or the murder of civilians. This nexus with international law, and hence with Congress's authority under the Define and Punish Clause, harmonizes with the Supreme Court's Article III jurisprudence.

Ex parte Milligan is also consistent with this analysis. In *Milligan*, the Court vacated a military commission conviction because it determined that the defendant, a U.S. citizen and longtime Indiana resident, had not been a belligerent in the U.S. Civil War. *Quirin* ruled that *Milligan* did not preclude commission proceedings for belligerents, even when two of the defendants were U.S. citizens. If, as al Bahlul acknowledged, he was a belligerent in an armed conflict with the United States, and uncontroverted evidence proved

---

[53] *Id.*

[54] *Id.*

[55] *See* Stern v. Marshall, 131 S. Ct. 2594, 2613 (2011) (in holding that Article III barred Congress from authorizing bankruptcy court to rule on tort claim by petitioner in bankruptcy against an individual who was not a claimant in the bankruptcy proceeding, the Court noted that Article III would not bar adjudication by a non–Article III tribunal where "resolution of the claim by an expert government agency is deemed essential to a limited regulatory objective within the agency's authority"); Commodity Futures Trading Comm'n v. Schor, 478 U.S. 833, 851 (1986) (in discussing Congress's power to create non–Article III tribunals, noting importance of link to Congress's Article I powers and absence of traditional state law claims). *But see* Vladeck, *Military Courts and Article III, supra* note 11 (arguing for broader reading of Article III and less deference to Congress on military commission jurisdiction).

[56] *Cf.* United States v. Verdugo-Urquidez, 494 U.S. 259, 266-67 (1990) (holding that Fourth Amendment does not apply to law enforcement activities outside U.S. sovereign territory targeting foreign nationals with no U.S. ties); *id.* at 277-78 (Kennedy, J., concurring) (suggesting that application of constitutional rights overseas hinges on context and practical consequences, not absolutes).

[57] *Verdugo-Urquidez*, 494 U.S. at 278 (Kennedy, J., concurring).

that he had engaged in conduct, such as the indoctrination of terrorists, reasonably related to international war crimes, *Milligan* and Article III do not bar military commission jurisdiction in his case.

E. *Prospective Efforts to Establish Military Commission Jurisdiction*

Congress may have even more latitude in cases involving conduct that occurred *after* passage of the Military Commissions Act. In these cases, the Ex Post Facto Clause is not a problem, since a defendant had fair warning that the conduct was triable in a military commission. However, questions still arise about Congress's authority under its war powers in general and under the Define and Punish Clause in particular, which refers to violations of the law of nations. Congress's power to prospectively designate charges for adjudication in military commissions also stems from the Necessary and Proper Clause. That provision allows Congress to enact legislation that is "useful" to exercise of the war powers specifically enumerated in Article I, such as the power to declare war.[58] If, as the Supreme Court has said, military commissions are an "important incident" of Congress's war powers,[59] the Necessary and Proper Clause gives Congress authority to designate charges before military commissions that are reasonably related to deterrence of internationally recognized war crimes.

Congress's power to prospectively (as opposed to retroactively) designate crimes as triable in military commissions may come to a head in the case of Abd al Hadi al-Iraqi, who allegedly engaged in a range of pre-MCA conduct but also is accused of conspiracy for post-MCA events. In al-Iraqi's case, that alleged post-MCA conduct involved making false statements to Turkish officials and in immigration documents in 2006 to enable the defendant to enter Iraq to plan attacks on U.S. troops there.[60] According to the United States, participants in those attacks would have feigned civilian status, thus violating the international law prohibition on perfidy. The alleged conspiracy involved mere agreement, not a completed act, since al-Iraqi was captured before the plan could be consummated.

While no court has squarely addressed this issue as of October 2014, Judge Kavanaugh asserted in dicta not joined by the other panel members in *Hamdan II* that Congress was not limited to its power under the Define and Punish Clause, but could also rely on other war power clauses.[61] Relying on other war powers is useful because it gives Congress greater flexibility to deal with conduct that it wishes to have tried in military commissions. On the other hand, reliance on the full range of Congress's war powers imposes few limits on the offenses triable

---

[58] *See* United States v. Comstock, 560 U.S. 126, 133-34 (2010).

[59] *Quirin*, 317 U.S. at 28.

[60] *See* Charge Sheet, Abd al Hadi al-Iraqi (June 2, 2014), p. 12, *available at* http://www.mc.mil/Portals/0/pdfs/alIraqi/Hadi%20Al%20Iraqi%20Referred%20Charge%20Sheet.pdf

[61] 696 F.3d at 1246 n. 6.

in military commissions. Suppose a defendant had knowingly provided a small sum of money to Al Qaeda, which would constitute material support under federal criminal law. Could Congress prospectively make such an offense a war crime triable by a military commission? The Framers, who cared deeply about international law, would likely have been troubled by such a result.

In contrast, a narrow view of Congress's power would suggest that even if the defendant had fair warning, Congress can only use military commissions for conduct that violates international law. On this view, even with the Ex Post Facto Clause out of the picture, Congress would lack power to authorize trial of material support cases in military commissions, at least when the conduct at issue was not equivalent to JCE or aiding and abetting. Trying charges based on mere modest financial assistance to Al Qaeda would still be off-limits. The same analysis would preclude stand-alone conspiracy charges involving mere agreement, not planning a completed act. However, this approach may be too narrow.

As a middle course, one can argue that the United States, like any nation, should have a measure of deference in defining international law, at least when that definition is purely forward-looking in nature and the fair warning principle is observed. Madison's view of Congress's power to define felonies on the high seas under the Define and Punish Clause leans in this direction. Recognizing the uncertainty of law's evolution, Madison argued that Congress needed some room to maneuver.[62] The Constitution's Necessary and Proper Clause gives Congress power to legislate on any matter reasonably related to its enumerated powers. The case law also indicates that Congress should receive a measure of deference. In *United States v. Arjona*,[63] the Court cited the policy benefits of a global system of "wise and equitable commercial laws"[64] in upholding Congress's power under the Define and Punish Clause to prohibit the counterfeiting for foreign currencies. The Court asserted that laxity in deterring counterfeiting would have "disturb[ed] . . . harmony between . . . governments."[65] The Court upheld the legislation based on the risk the defendant's *conduct* posed to international cooperation, despite the silence in treaties or state practice on counterfeiting as a violation of international law.[66]

This middle view of Congress's power to prospectively set military commission jurisdiction would require a reasonable relationship between the charges brought and an accepted war crime, whether or not that war crime was actually completed. On this view, the conspiracy charges against al-Iraqi pass muster, because those charges entail a substantial nexus between the acts alleged and acknowledged war crimes (such as perfidy or targeting civilians): Al-Iraqi

---

[62] *See* FEDERALIST No. 42. at 266 (Clinton Rossiter ed., 1961); *cf.* FEDERALIST No. 37 (James Madison), at 228 (noting uncertainty in maritime law).

[63] 120 U.S. 479 (1887).

[64] *Id*. at 484.

[65] *Id*. at 486-87.

[66] *See* Thomas H. Lee & David L. Sloss, *International Law an Interpretive Tool in the Supreme Court, 1861-1900, in* INTERNATIONAL LAW IN THE U.S. SUPREME COURT: CONTINUITY AND CHANGE 124, 147-48 (David L. Sloss, Michael D. Ramsey & William S. Dodge eds., 2011).

wished to position himself to supervise further acts of this nature by entering Iraq, and his false statements would have facilitated that goal. However, Congress would lack power to criminalize acts without such a nexus. Therefore, providing funds could be criminalized only if the defendant 1) was a principal funder of a terrorist group in a NIAC with the United States 2) who had specific knowledge of the group's LOAC violations and 3) intended to further war crimes by the group. That conduct would amount to JCE or aiding and abetting liability for completed war crimes.

This middle approach tethers Congress to international law. It also recognizes that Congress has a legitimate interest in deterring conduct that could aid in commission of a war crime, even when no war crime actually results. Any other outcome sends an ambiguous message to terrorists plotting LOAC violations.

V. MILITARY JUSTICE: COURTS-MARTIAL AND CIVILIAN DEFENDANTS

To supplement the discussion of military commissions, we should focus briefly on the question of the scope of courts-martial, which the United States has used to hold accountable its own service personnel and persons associated with the services. The legal questions here actually track the questions that arise about military commissions: how to administer an armed force effectively while respecting individual rights. Doing the latter has required limits on the jurisdiction of courts-martial.

The need to reconcile maintaining an effective force and preserving the Constitution's framework of individual rights is evident in the Constitution's text. Congress's authority to establish a separate regime for military justice stems from the power of Congress, set out in Clause 14 of Article I, §8, to "make Rules for the Government and Regulation of the land and naval forces." This provision should be read in tandem with the Fifth Amendment's Grand Jury Clause. That provision requires that a grand jury that is independent of prosecutors serve as a gatekeeper by issuing a presentment or indictment prior to a felony trial, except in cases "arising in the land or naval forces."[67]

These provisions reflect the Framers' competing concerns, which have become fleshed out over more than two centuries of experience. The Framers understood that military effectiveness required a system of justice particular to the military that addressed the special needs of the armed forces. For example, a military court can permit a defendant to move with his unit to another deployment, if commanders so request; such consideration for efficient deployment could not be assured in a civilian court fully independent of the military.

---

[67] Dynes v. Hoover, 61 U.S. (20 How.) 65, 78-79 (1858); *Quirin*, 317 U.S. at 43.

However, it is also important to carefully mark the boundaries of the military justice system to preserve individual rights and the jurisdiction of federal courts established under Article III of the Constitution. As the Supreme Court has recognized, a court-martial in which members of the military make findings of fact will not have the breadth of perspective that a jury of laypersons from "different walks of life" can bring to bear.[68] Moreover, civilian courts and grand and petit juries are independent of the executive branch. In contrast, decision makers in courts-martial are part of the Executive. That institutional fact of life may color their decisions, even when steps are taken to insulate them from command influence and a civilian court reviews their decisions.[69] To reconcile these values, courts have sought to promote accountability by service personnel and those functionally affiliated with the armed services. At the same time, courts have rejected an unduly broad reading of court-martial jurisdiction that would undermine the guarantees of a grand jury and petit jury trial that apply in civilian proceedings.

Consider first the issue of U.S. civilian dependents, such as spouses, of service personnel. Spouses and other dependents do not affiliate in any functional way with the armed services. Their bonds to the service are personal. Based on this premise, the Supreme Court held that spouses of service members should receive the full measure of constitutional protection, including a jury trial. Those protections are not compatible with the more limited protections in the military justice system. As a result, the Court held, courts-martial lack jurisdiction over the dependents of service members.[70]

A different rule prevails for current members of the armed services. For this group, the Supreme Court has held, virtually any offense is triable in a court-martial if Congress so provides. According to the Court, Congress can best decide when to subject an offense committed by a service member to trial in a court martial. Courts should generally defer to Congress's findings. Functional factors buttress this position. Consider the case of sexual or drug offenses committed by current service members. The military has a reputational interest in deterring current service members from engaging in drug abuse, even when it occurs during a service member's leave. The military would suffer if the public came to believe that the military was a haven for drug offenders. The same logic holds true for service members who engage in sexual violence or misconduct. Although the Supreme Court experimented briefly with linking court-martial jurisdiction to the degree of service connection in a given offense, the Court soon recognized that distinctions of this kind were unworkable.[71] However, the Court has also recognized a clear limit on court-martial jurisdiction for service members: Only a

---

[68] United States ex rel. Toth v. Quarles, 350 U.S. 11, 18 (1955).

[69] *Id.* at 17; *cf.* Vladeck, *supra* note 11 (discussing *Toth*).

[70] Reid v. Covert, 354 U.S. 1 (1957); Kinsella v. United States ex rel. Singleton, 361 U.S. 234 (1960).

[71] Solorio v. United States, 483 U.S. 435, 448-49 (1987).

civilian court, not a court-martial, can try an individual who left the service *before* he was arrested for an offense he committed in the military.[72]

A gray area is military jurisdiction over military contractors. Contractors, unlike spouses, have purposefully affiliated themselves with the military and obtained benefits from that affiliation. Contractors who provide assistance abroad during a war or occupation also implicate the same reputational interests as actual service members: Populations abroad will expect that the U.S. military deter misconduct by such individuals and hold accountable those who have engaged in misconduct. Indeed, the ability to deter misconduct abroad by individuals who serve alongside the U.S. military is also an indispensable element of the United States' compliance with international law: A nation engaged in armed conflict or occupation abroad must ensure that it avoids purposely inflicting harm on civilian persons or property abroad. It must also punish its agents for infliction of such harm.

History provides support for the proposition that courts-martial can try sutlers and others who accompany and take direction from armed forces in the field. The Continental Congress passed such a law,[73] and subsequent legislatures after the Constitution's enactment did the same.[74] Adhering to this practice in a recent case,[75] the Court of Appeals for the Armed Forces (CAAF) has found that a court-martial could try a contract interpreter who was a dual Canadian and Iraqi citizen for an assault on another Iraqi interpreter committed while both were assisting U.S. forces in Iraq.

To understand the stakes in court-martial jurisdiction over contractors, it is worth noting disagreement among members of the CAAF panel on the rationale for upholding court-martial jurisdiction. The majority of the panel, in an opinion by Judge Erdmann, upheld court-martial jurisdiction on the sweeping ground that Ali was not a U.S. citizen.[76] This justification has spurred controversy. On the one hand, the Supreme Court has declined to grant the protections of the Fourth, Fifth, and Sixth Amendments of the Bill of Rights to foreign nationals who were not on U.S. soil or otherwise lacked any connection to the United States at the time of the violations of the Bill of Rights that those individuals alleged.[77] However, this principle does not fit well with the functional premise behind trying Ali in a court-martial: his purposeful affiliation with U.S. armed forces in the field.

In contrast, Judge Baker's concurrence sidestepped these pitfalls. Judge Baker relied, not on the nationality of the accused, but on a functional factor: a contractor's purposeful affiliation with the U.S. military in service abroad.[78] According to Judge Baker, Congress's war powers were ample to support court-martial jurisdiction, in

---

[72] United States ex rel. Toth v. Quarles, 350 U.S. 11 (1955).

[73] Edmund M. Morgan, *Court-Martial Jurisdiction Over Non-Military Persons Under the Articles of War*, 4 MINN. L. REV. 79, 89 (1920).

[74] *Id.* at 90.

[75] United States v. Ali, 71 M.J. 256 (C.A.A.F. 2012), *cert. denied*, 133 S. Ct. 2338 (2013).

[76] *Id.* at 266-68.

[77] *Verdugo-Urquidez*, 494 U.S. at 269.

[78] *Id.* at 272-75.

light of the importance of maintaining discipline among both members of the armed forces and contractors accompanying them.[79]

Judge Baker opined that Clause 14 of Article I, §8, which empowers Congress to "make Rules for the Government and Regulation of the land and naval forces," was insufficient in and of itself, and required support from other war-related powers, including the powers in Article I, §8 to "provide for the common Defence" and "define and punish . . . [o]ffenses against the Law of Nations."[80] Here, Judge Baker, perhaps overcompensating for his colleagues' sweeping judgment, may have been unduly parsimonious in interpreting constitutional text. One can readily argue that the power under Clause 14 to "make Rules for the Government and Regulation of the land and naval forces" includes the power to make rules for contractors who serve alongside those forces. Otherwise, as Judge Baker recognized in relying on Congress's war powers generally, Congress would lack authority to ensure the discipline that is crucial to military success. Moreover, on the same logic, one can readily view a contractor's misconduct while serving with U.S. forces abroad in a time of war or occupation as "arising in the land or naval forces" under the Fifth Amendment's Grand Jury Clause. This functional argument is the best justification for the exercise of court-martial jurisdiction in cases like Ali's involving military contractors.

VI. CONCLUSION

Military commissions serve a significant purpose in armed conflict, because they provide a means to deter LOAC violations by both state and nonstate adversaries. Commissions also pose tensions with individual rights, separation of powers, and international law. Courts will continue to strive to reconcile military commissions' uses with their risks. That reconciliation requires flexibility in determining the existence of a NIAC and defining war crimes. To ensure that the risks of commissions do not outweigh their benefits, courts should also insist on congressional-executive cooperation and a nexus with LOAC rules.

[79] *Id.* at 276.
[80] *Id.* at 273.

CHAPTER 10

Classification and Protecting Vital National Security Information

I. INTRODUCTION

Open government and transparency are often cited as key elements of democratic governance. A robust democracy requires that the American people be informed of the activities of their government. However, "throughout our history, the national defense has required that certain information be maintained in confidence in order to protect our citizens, our democratic institutions, our homeland security, and our interactions with foreign nations."[1] The purpose in restricting access to classified information is to prevent it from being used by persons, organizations, and nations to inflict harm upon the United States. The importance of protecting classified information has been dramatically highlighted by two recent incidents. The first occurred when Wikileaks.org, an organization that describes itself as a "public service designed to protect whistleblowers, journalists and activists who have sensitive materials to communicate to the public," obtained more than 91,000 secret military reports related to the wars in Afghanistan and Iraq. WikiLeaks first alerted the *New York Times* and two foreign newspapers, the *Guardian* (United Kingdom) and *Der Spiegel* (Germany), then posted the majority of these unredacted documents on its website.[2] United States officials strongly condemned the leaks, claiming that the disclosure could lead to the loss of lives of U.S. soldiers in Afghanistan.[3] Army Private Bradley Manning, who disclosed the classified information to WikiLeaks, maintained that his actions were motivated by a desire to enlighten the public.[4]

The second incident, which involved the disclosure of classified information by Edward Snowden, a former government contractor, has generated a heated debate about the need to strike a proper balance between protecting U.S. national security and protecting the right of privacy.[5] Snowden leaked approximately 58,000 classified files to the *Guardian*, which disclosed the scale of the National Security Agency's (NSA) "metadata program" under which the agency collects the

---

[1] Exec. Order No. 13,526, 75 Fed. Reg. 707 (Jan. 5, 2010) [hereinafter E.O. 13526].

[2] JENNIFER K. ELSEA, CONG. RESEARCH SERV., R41404, CRIMINAL PROHIBITIONS ON THE PUBLICATION OF CLASSIFIED DEFENSE INFORMATION, at 2 (Sept. 19, 2013). Military officials charged Army Private Bradley Manning with offenses related to the transfer of classified information to WikiLeaks. *Id.* He was convicted by court-martial and sentenced to 35 years' imprisonment, reduction in rank, forfeiture of pay, and a dishonorable discharge. *Id.*

[3] *Id.* at 3.

[4] *Id.* WikiLeaks subsequently released approximately 400,000 documents related to the war in Iraq. *See The Iraq Archive: The Strands of a War,* N.Y. TIMES, *available at* http://www.nytimes.com/2010/10/23/world/middleeast/23intro.html?_r=1 (last visited Mar. 26, 2014). Further, in November 2010, WikiLeaks began publishing what the *New York Times* called a "mammoth cache of a quarter-million confidential American diplomatic cables," dated between approximately 2008 and 2010. *See State's Secrets,* N.Y. TIMES (online edition), Nov. 29, 2010, http://www.nytimes.com/interactive/sorld,statesecrets.html (last visited Mar. 26, 2014).

[5] Jill Lawless, *Guardian: We have published 1 pct of Snowden leak,* ASSOCIATED PRESS, Dec. 3, 2013, http://bigstory.ap.org/article/guardian-we-have-published-1-pct-snowden-leak (last visited Mar. 26, 2014).

cell phone records (but not the content of those communications) of hundreds of millions of Americans.[6] Snowden's critics maintain that the disclosure of the NSA surveillance program has severely compromised national security and aided terrorists, and that he should be criminally prosecuted for his actions.[7] Snowden's defenders, on the other hand, praise him for revealing the U.S. government's expansive violations of civil liberties and highlighting the need for legislative reform as well as greater judicial and legislative oversight to limit the government's surveillance authority.

II.   THE U.S. GOVERNMENT CLASSIFICATION SYSTEM

A.   *Executive Order 13526*

The U.S. government's system for classifying, declassifying, and safeguarding national security information generated by its employees and contractors, as well as information received from foreign governments, is established by Executive Order 13526.[8] The degree of secrecy of such information is known as its sensitivity. Sensitivity is based upon an assessment of the damage to national security that the release of the information would cause. The United States has three levels of classification: Top Secret, Secret, and Confidential.[9] If a person holds a Top Secret security clearance, that person is allowed to handle information up to the level of Top Secret, including Secret and Confidential information. If, on the other hand, one holds a Secret clearance, such person may have access to Secret and Confidential classified information, but not information classified as Top Secret. Generally, information is classified as "Top Secret" if unauthorized disclosure would cause "exceptionally grave damage" to national security.[10] The second highest classification is "Secret." Information is classified as Secret when its unauthorized disclosure would cause "serious damage" to national security.[11] "Confidential" is the lowest classification level of information obtained or produced by the government. Information is classified as "Confidential" if unauthorized disclosure would "damage" national security.[12]

---

[6] *Id.*

[7] *Id.*

[8] E.O. 13526, *supra* note 1. E.O. 13526 replaced earlier executive orders on the topic and amended regulations codified at 32 C.F.R. Part 2001.

[9] E.O. 13526, *supra* note 1, §1.2(a).

[10] *Id.* §1.2(a)(1).

[11] *Id.* §1.2(a)(2).

[12] *Id.* §1.2(a)(3).

Chapter 10. Classification and Protecting Vital National Security Information

The authority to classify information may be exercised only by the President, Vice President, or agency heads and officials designated by the President.[13] Executive Order 13526 limits the type of information that may be classified. Pursuant to §1.4 of E.O. 13526, information shall not be classified unless its unauthorized disclosure could reasonably be expected to damage national security and the information pertains to:

1. military plans, weapons, or operations;
2. foreign government information;
3. intelligence activities (including covert action), intelligence sources or methods, or cryptology;
4. foreign relations or foreign activities of the United States, including confidential sources;
5. scientific, technological, or economic matters relating to national security;
6. United States Government programs for safeguarding nuclear materials or facilities;
7. vulnerabilities or capabilities of systems, installations, infrastructures, projects, plans, or protection services relating to national security; or
8. the development, production, or use of weapons of mass destruction.[14]

Information may not remain classified indefinitely. At the time of the original classification, the authority making the classification decision should establish a specific date or event for declassification.[15] Upon reaching the date or event, the information is automatically declassified.[16] If the original classification authority cannot determine a specific date or event for declassification, the document shall be marked for declassification 10 years from the date of the original classification decision, unless the original classification authority determines that the sensitivity of the information requires that it be marked for declassification for up to 25 years from the date of the original classification.[17] Finally, except for information that would "clearly and demonstrably" reveal the identity of a confidential human source or human intelligence source or the key design concepts of weapons of

---

[13] *Id.* §1.3(a). "Top Secret" original classification authority may be delegated only by the President, the Vice President, or agency heads or officials designated by the President. *Id.* §1.3(c)(2). "Secret" or "Confidential" original classification authority may be delegated only by the President, the Vice President, agency heads or officials designated by the President, or senior agency officials designated under §5.4(d) of E.O. 13526.

[14] *Id.* §1.4.

[15] *Id.* §1.5.

[16] *Id.*

[17] *Id.* §1.5(b). Section 1.7 prohibits the classification of information to:

(1) conceal violations of law, inefficiency, or administrative error;
(2) prevent embarrassment to a person, organization, or agency;
(3) restrain competition; or
(4) prevent or delay the release of information that does not require protection in the interest of national security.

mass destruction, the date for declassification should not exceed the 25-year time frame.[18]

B.   *Declassification*

Information should be declassified when the reasons for its classification no longer exist even if this is prior to the date of automatic declassification. Generally, the federal agency that originally classified the information is responsible for deciding whether it should be declassified.[19] Declassification may also occur when an agency challenges the propriety of another agency's classification decision. E.O. 13526 sets forth three additional means of declassification: 1) automatic declassification (as described above); 2) systematic declassification; and 3) mandatory declassification review.

All classified records that are more than 25 years old are subject to automatic declassification.[20] An agency head may exempt a piece of information from automatic declassification and request that it remain classified for any of nine reasons under §3.3 of E.O. 13526.[21]

---

[18] *Id.* §1.5(a).

[19] *Id.* §3.1(b). Pursuant to §3.1(b), information shall be declassified or downgraded by:

(1) the official who authorized the original classification, if that official is still serving in the same position and has original classification authority;

(2) the originator's current successor in function, if that individual has original classification authority;

(3) a supervisory official of either the originator or his or her successor in function, if the supervisory official has original classification authority; or

(4) officials delegated declassification authority in writing by the agency head or the senior agency official of the originating agency.

Further, the Director of National Intelligence, or persons delegated the authority by the Director of National Intelligence or Principal Deputy Director of National Intelligence, may declassify or downgrade information or intelligence relating to intelligence sources, methods, or activities. *Id.* §3.1(c).

[20] *Id.* §3.3(a).

[21] Pursuant to E.O. 13526, §3.3(b)(1)-(9), an agency head may exempt from automatic declassification the release of information which would "clearly and demonstrably" be expected to:

(1) Reveal the identity of a confidential human source, a human intelligence source, a relationship with an intelligence or security service of a foreign government or international organization, or a nonhuman intelligence source; or impair the effectiveness of a an intelligence method currently in use, available for use, or under development; (2) reveal information that would assist in the development, production, or use of weapons of mass destruction; (3) reveal information that would impair U.S. cryptologic systems or activities; (4) reveal information that would impair the application of state-of-the-art technology within a U.S. weapon system; (5) reveal formally named or numbered U.S. military war plans that remain in effect, or reveal operation or tactical elements of prior plans that are contained in such active plans; (6) reveal information, including foreign government information, that would cause serious harm to relations between the United States and a foreign government; (7) reveal information that would impair the current ability of United States Government officials to protect the President,

Records exempt from automatic declassification are subject to systematic declassification review. Section 3.4 of E.O. 13526 provides that each agency that has originated classified information shall establish and conduct a program for systematic declassification review for records of permanent historical value that are exempted from automatic declassification under §3.3. Thus, records that are exempted from automatic declassification are subject to regular review by the classifying agency to determine if continued classification is justified for the reasons set forth in §3.3(b).

C. FOIA and Access to Government Information

Restricting access to government information is, however, inconsistent with the powerful presumption of public access established by the Freedom of Information Act (FOIA).[22] This law, enacted on July 4, 1966, to take effect one year later, established a right to access "agency records" with no requirement to establish any justification for a request.[23] Thus, instead of imposing a burden on the citizen requesting the government information, the burden was imposed on the government to justify nondisclosure. The clear intent of the statute was to increase government accountability by enhancing public access to government information.

Of course, no government could function effectively if public access to government information was unlimited. Accordingly, FOIA established a number of defined "exemptions" from the disclosure obligation.[24] These exemptions provide the exclusive source of statutory authority to deny a FOIA request. Furthermore, FOIA applies only to "agency records," which indicates that not all government information falls within the scope of the Act.[25] Only government entities that qualify as agencies within the meaning of the law fall within the scope of the statute. In *Armstrong v. Executive Office of the President*, the D.C. Circuit Court of Appeals concluded that the National Security Council was not an agency within the meaning of FOIA, as its function was purely advisory and did not include any decision-making authority related to making or implementing

---

Vice President, and other protectees for whom protection services, in the interest of national security, are authorized; (8) reveal information that would seriously impair current national security emergency preparedness plans or reveal current vulnerabilities of systems, installations, or infrastructures relating to national security; or (9) violate a statute, treaty, or international agreement that does not permit the automatic or unilateral declassification of information at 25 years.

[22] Act of Oct. 28, 2009, Pub. L. No. 111-83, Title V, §564(b) (codified at 5 U.S.C. §552).

[23] *Id. What is FOIA?*, U.S. Dep't of Justice, http://www.foia.gov/about.html (last updated Jan. 2011).

[24] 5 U.S.C. §552(b)(1)-(9).

[25] *FOIA Exemptions*, FOIA Advocates, http://www.foiadvocates.com/exemptions.html (last visited Nov. 11, 2014) [hereinafter *FOIA Exemptions*].

II. The U.S. Government Classification System

policy.[26] Thus, to fall within the scope of FOIA, the government entity must be vested with policy making or implementing authority. Furthermore, the requested information must qualify as an "agency record," which, generally means that the agency either created or obtained the requested material, and that the agency is in control of the material at the time of the FOIA request.[27]

Not all agency records fall within FOIA's disclosure obligation. Unsurprisingly, Congress provided exemptions for national security related information.[28] The two most relevant exemptions that cover such information are Exemptions 1 and 3.[29] Exemption 1 permits the government to withhold information that has been "properly classified" pursuant to executive order.[30] Exemption 3 permits the government to withhold information specifically exempted from disclosure by statute.[31] Because the National Security Act of 1947 has been interpreted to authorize the Executive to withhold intelligence "sources and methods" from disclosure, such information falls within the scope of Exemption 3, and if it is also property classified, within the scope of Exemption 1.[32] Exemption 7(A) limits access to "records of information complied for law enforcement purposes . . . to the extent that the production" of such records "could reasonably be expected to interfere with enforcement proceedings."[33]

Courts have interpreted Exemption 7(A) broadly. In *Center for National Security Studies v. Department of Justice*,[34] the D.C. Circuit held that Exemption 7(A) allowed the government to refuse to release information about foreign nationals detained on immigration grounds after September 11 (*see* Chapter 8 for discussion of post-9/11 immigration detention). That information included the names of detainees, the location of their arrest, and the identities of their attorneys. According to the court, while the disclosure of such information might appear harmless, individual data points could yield a "mosaic" portraying U.S. law enforcement agencies sources and methods. Putting together that mosaic could "allow terrorists to better evade . . . investigation."[35] Driven by these concerns, the court construed Exemption 7(A) to permit the government to decline to disclose this information.

Because FOIA creates a presumption of access to agency records, the agency seeking to withhold bears the burden of establishing the validity of a claimed

---

[26] Armstrong v. Exec. Office of the President, 90 F.3d 553, 567 (D.C. Cir. 1996).

[27] Kissinger v. Reporters Comm. for Freedom of the Press, 445 U.S. 136 (1980); Goland v. Cent. Intelligence Agency, 607 F.2d 339 (D.C. Cir. 2003); Grand Cent. P'ship v. Cuomo, 166 F.3d 473 (2d Cir. 1999).

[28] *FOIA Exemptions, supra* note 25.

[29] 5 U.S.C. §552(b)(1), (3).

[30] *Id.* at §552(b)(1).

[31] *Id.* at §552(b)(3).

[32] Am. Civil Liberties Union v. Dep't of Def., 628 F.3d 612, 619 (D.C. Cir. 2011).

[33] 5 U.S.C. §552(b)(7)(A).

[34] 331 F.3d 918 (D.C. Cir. 2003), *cert. denied*, 540 U.S. 1104 (2004).

[35] Id. at 928. For criticism of the *Center for National Security Studies* decision, see David E. Pozen, Note, *The Mosaic Theory, National Security, and the Freedom of Information Act*, 115 YALE L.J. 628 (2005); *see also* David E. Pozen, *Deep Secrecy*, 63 STAN. L. REV. 257, 278, 282-83, 287 (2010) (analyzing secrecy's risks and benefits, and warning about its potential effect on decisionmaking).

exemption. This is normally done by affidavit articulating the applicability of the exemption. Although courts review the claim of exemption *de novo,* they will also accord substantial weight to the agency's asserted justification withholding.[36] As the D.C. Circuit Court of Appeals noted in *American Civil Liberties Union v. Department of Defense,* summary judgment in the agency's favor is appropriate where "the agency's affidavit describes the justifications for withholding the information with specific detail, demonstrating that the information withheld logically falls within the claimed exemption, and is not contradicted by contrary evidence in the record or by evidence of the agency's bad faith. . . ."[37] Specificity is essential, and the agency risks a more probing level of scrutiny if it fails to provide a detailed justification for withholding each specific record (often meaning document), as opposed to just a general assertion that a claimed exemption applies to a broad record.[38] This detailed explanation of exemption is known as a "Vaughn Declaration," based on the 1973 case of *Vaughn v. Rosen.*[39]

Establishing that an agency record is, in fact, classified does not automatically exempt it from disclosure. In 1974, Congress amended FOIA over presidential veto by including the "properly classified" qualifier to Exemption 1.[40] Accordingly, where a plaintiff can show that an agency record has been improperly classified, the exemption will not apply. This same amendment vested federal courts with the express authority to conduct *de novo* review of agency claims of exemption, *in camera,* to assess the propriety of the claim.[41] This includes classified information. Accordingly, a reviewing court may conduct *in camera* review of the classified information to assess whether classification is consistent with controlling executive orders and agency policies.[42] However, as the D.C. Circuit Court of Appeals noted in *Ray v. Turner,* citing the conference report for the 1974 amendment, *in camera* review should not be considered automatically required.[43] Instead, it should be used only when the invocation of the exemption is not logical and plausible.[44] Ultimately, however, the burden is on the government to justify withholding, and if summary judgment is not appropriate, it must do so during this *in camera* review.[45]

Even if an agency record is properly classified or subject to withholding pursuant to statutory authority, disclosure may be appropriate where the government has already officially acknowledged the information in the record. In *American Civil Liberties Union v. Department of Defense,* the D.C. Circuit Court of Appeals

---

[36] *Id.*

[37] *Id.*

[38] *Id.*

[39] Vaughn v. Rosen, 484 F.2d 820 (D.C. Cir. 1973).

[40] *Veto Battle 30 Years Ago Set Freedom of Information Norms,* THE NATIONAL SECURITY ARCHIVES (Nov. 23, 2004), http://www2.gwu.edu/~nsarchiv/NSAEBB/NSAEBB142/index.htm.

[41] *Id.*

[42] *Id.*

[43] Ray v. Turner, 587, F.2d 1187, 1191 (D.C. Cir. 1978).

[44] *Id.*

[45] *Id.*

emphasized that this "official acknowledgment" exception to otherwise authorized withholding required more than a general acknowledgment.[46] Instead, the court noted that:

> If the government has officially acknowledged information, a FOIA plaintiff may compel disclosure of that information even over an agency's otherwise valid exemption claim. For information to qualify as "Officially acknowledged," it must satisfy three criteria: (1) the information requested must be as specific as the information previously released; (2) the information requested must match the information previously disclosed; (3) the information requested must have already have been made public through an official and documented disclosure.[47]
>
> In this case, the court concluded that the photos of detainees sought by the ACLU did not fall within this official disclosure exception because the information requested was far more extensive than the information related to detainees previously disclosed.[48] This indicates that invoking this exception requires a high level of specificity as to the nature of the prior disclosure and the requested information. It is also essential that the prior disclosure be official in nature, which would not include unauthorized disclosures by prior or currently serving government officials.[49]

Other FOIA exemptions that might be relevant in a national security context include Exemption 4, which covers trade secrets;[50] Exemption 5, which covers inter- and intra-agency memoranda that fall within a legal privilege (like attorney work product);[51] and Exemption 7, which covers certain law enforcement records (like information related to confidential informants).[52]

D. Safeguarding Classified Information

Agencies that produce and utilize classified information have a duty to safeguard it, which includes preventing access by unauthorized persons. Each agency head or senior agency official handling classified information is required to "establish controls to ensure that classified information is used, processed, stored, reproduced, transmitted, and destroyed under conditions that provide adequate protection and prevent access by unauthorized persons."[53] Pursuant to §4.1 of E.O. 13526, a person may have access to classified information provided that:

1. a favorable determination of eligibility for access has been made by an agency head or the agency head's designee;

---

[46] *Am. Civil Liberties Union*, 628 F.3d at 621-22.
[47] *Id.*
[48] *Id.* at 622.
[49] *Id.*
[50] 5 U.S.C. §552(b)(4).
[51] *Id.* at §552(b)(5).
[52] *Id.* at §552(b)(7).
[53] *Id.* §4.1(g).

2. the person has signed an approved nondisclosure agreement; and

3. the person has a need-to-know.[54]

Every person who has met the standards for access to classified information is required to receive training on the proper handling and safeguarding of classified information.[55] Further, E.O. 13526 prohibits removing classified information from official premises without proper authorization.[56] Executive Order 13526 also sets forth procedures for disseminating classified information outside of the original classifying agency to ensure the protection of the information.[57] Moreover, an official or employee leaving agency service is prohibited from removing classified information from the agency's control.[58] Finally, U.S. government officers, employees, and contractors are subject to appropriate sanctions if they knowingly, willfully, or negligently disclose classified information to unauthorized persons.[59] The sanctions may include "reprimand, suspension without pay, removal, termination of classification authority, loss or denial of access to classified information, or other sanctions in accordance with applicable law and agency regulation."[60]

1. Oversight of Classified Information Policies

Four entities have been established and assigned responsibility for overseeing classified information policies: 1) Information Security Oversight Office (ISOO); 2) the Public Interest Declassification Board (PIDB); 3) the Interagency Security Classification Appeals Panel (ISCAP); and 4) the National Declassification Center (NDC).

a. Information Security Oversight Office

The ISOO is responsible for issuing directives necessary to implement E.O. 13526. More specifically, the ISOO establishes standards for

1. classification, declassification, and control marking principles;

2. safeguarding classified information;

3. agencies' security education and training programs;

---

[54] *Id.* §§4.1(a)(1)-(3).
[55] *Id.* §4.1(b).
[56] *Id.* §4.1(d).
[57] *Id.* §4.1(e).
[58] *Id.* §4.1(c).
[59] *Id.* §5.5(b).
[60] *Id.* §5.5(c).

4. agencies' self-inspection programs; and
5. agencies' classification and declassification guidelines.[61]

The ISOO is also responsible for conducting on-site evaluations to determine agency compliance with E.O. 13526,[62] acting on complaints with respect to an agency's implementation of E.O. 13526,[63] and submitting an annual report to the President on the implementation of the classified information policy.[64]

b. Interagency Security Classification Appeals Panel

President Clinton established the ISCAP, which is responsible for resolving declassification disputes.[65] The ISCAP's members include the Director of the ISOO, who serves as its executive secretary and senior-level representatives from the Departments of State, Defense, and Justice, as well as the National Archives, the Office of the Director of National Intelligence, and the National Security Advisor.[66] The ISCAP is responsible for 1) resolving disputes over challenges of the proper classification level of information 2) approving, denying, or amending agency requests for exempting information from automatic declassification, and 3) deciding appeals by persons or entities who have filed requests for mandatory declassification review.[67]

c. Public Interest Declassification Board

The PIDB (or the "Board") is an independent executive branch agency consisting of nine members, five of whom are appointed by the President, and four of whom are appointed by Congress.[68] The Director of the ISOO serves as the PIDB's executive secretary.

The statute creating the PIDB requires the PIDB to advise the President, the Assistant to the President for National Security, the Director of the Office of Management and Budget, and other executive branch officials, as the PIDB considers appropriate, on the identification, collection, review for declassification, and release to Congress, interested agencies, and the public of declassified records and materials, including materials of extraordinary public interest.[69] The PIDB

---

[61] Kevin R. Kosar, Cong. Research Serv., R41528, Classified Information Policy and Executive Order 13526, 7 (Dec. 10, 2010) [hereinafter Classified Information Policy and Executive Order 13526].

[62] E.O. 13526, *supra* note 1, §5.2(b)(4).

[63] *Id.* §5.2(b)(6).

[64] *Id.* §5.2(b)(8).

[65] Exec. Order No. 12,958, 60 Fed. Reg. 19,825 (Apr. 20, 1995).

[66] E.O. 13526, *supra* note 1, §5.3(a)(1).

[67] *Id.* §5.3(b).

[68] *See* Public Interest Declassification Act of Dec. 27, 2000, Pub. L. No. 106-567, Title VII, 114 Stat. 2856 §703 (codified under 50 U.S.C.A. §435 note).

[69] *Id.*

also is responsible for promoting public access to records of significant national security decisions and activities in order to "(A) support the oversight and legislative functions of Congress; (B) support the policymaking role of the Executive Branch; (C) respond to the interest of the public in national security measures; and (D) promote reliable historical analysis and new avenues of historical study in national security matters."[70] Further, the PIDB provides recommendations to the President for the identification, collection, and review of declassification of information of extraordinary public interest that does not undermine national security.[71] Finally, the PIDB advises the President, the Assistant to the President for National Security Affairs, the Director of the Office of Management and Budget, and such other executive branch officials as the Board considers appropriate on policies deriving from the issuance by the President of executive orders regarding the classification and declassification of national security information.[72]

d.   National Declassification Center

Section 3.7 of E.O. 13526 established within the National Archives the NDC "to streamline declassification processes . . . and implement standardized training regarding the declassification of records determined to have permanent historical value."[73] The NDC is headed by a director, who is appointed by the Archivist in consultation with secretaries of agencies that classify significant quantities of information, including the Secretaries of State, Defense, Energy, and Homeland Security, the Attorney General, and the Director of National Intelligence.[74] The NDC is charged with expediting automatic and systematic declassification.[75] Additionally, the NDC is responsible for reducing the significant backlog of classified government records that have been released by agencies to the National Archives but not yet declassified.[76]

One of the causes for delay in declassification involves what is referred to as "multiple agency equity" in classified information, which simply means that when an agency seeks to declassify a document, it may contain information that other federal agencies may wish to keep classified.[77] For example, an effort to declassify a particular document by the Department of Justice may be opposed by the Central Intelligence Agency, State Department, or some other federal agency that has a legitimate interest in keeping the document classified. In these instances, the declassifying agency is required to refer the information to these

---

[70] *Id.* §703(b)(2). *See* CLASSIFIED INFORMATION POLICY AND EXECUTIVE ORDER 13526, *supra* note 61, at 8.

[71] Public Interest Declassification Act, *supra* note 68, §703(b)(3).

[72] *Id.* §703(b)(4)

[73] E.O. 13526, *supra* note 1, §3.7.

[74] *Id.*

[75] *See* CLASSIFIED INFORMATION POLICY AND EXECUTIVE ORDER 13526, *supra* note 61, at 15.

[76] *Id.*

[77] *Id.* at 16.

other agencies and obtain their agreement to declassify it. The NDC is responsible for expediting this process for review and approval of the declassification request.

III.   CRIMINAL PROHIBITIONS ON THE DISCLOSURE OF CLASSIFIED INFORMATION

A.   The Espionage Act

The disclosure of national defense information is prohibited by the Espionage Act of 1917, which is codified at 18 U.S.C. §§793-798.[78] The Act prescribes "separate and distinct offenses or crimes, and provid[es] varying punishments for conviction under each section dependent on the seriousness of each of the offenses."[79] The central statutory provision is 18 U.S.C. §793. Section 793 criminalizes "a wide range of activities associated with the gathering, possession, or communication of information relating to the 'national defense' . . . with the intent or reason to believe the information could 'be used to the injury of the United States or to the advantage of any foreign nation.'"[80] Violators of §793 are subject to fines, forfeiture, and imprisonment for up to ten years.[81]

Sections 793(a) and (b) prohibit obtaining information by physical intrusion into military installations, and obtaining information, documents, or other things connected with "national defense." Section 793(a) prohibits entering a U.S.-owned or U.S.-controlled protected place to obtain certain national defense information "with intent or reason to believe that the information is to be used to the injury of the United States, or to the advantage of any foreign nation."[82] Similarly, §793(b) prohibits individuals with "like intent or reason to believe" from copying, taking, making, or obtaining "any sketch, photograph, photographic negative, blueprint, plan, map, model, instrument, appliance, document, writing,

---

[78] Espionage Act of June 15, 1917, ch. 30, 40 Stat. 217 (codified as amended at 18 U.S.C. §§793 *et seq.*). The Espionage Act was enacted by Congress at the outbreak of the World War I and remains largely in its original form.

[79] United States v. Morison, 844 F.2d 1057, 1065 (4th Cir. 1988). For example, a violation of 18 U.S.C. §793(d), which prohibits a person with lawful access to national defense information from disclosing that information to a person not authorized to receive it, is punishable by a fine or imprisonment not to exceed ten years, or both. However, a violation of 18 U.S.C. §794, which prohibits the disclosure of national defense information of an "agent . . . [of a] foreign government," is a far more serious offense, and may be punished by death or by imprisonment for any term of years or for life.

[80] David E. Pozen, *The Leaky Leviathan: Why the Government Condemns and Condones Unlawful Disclosure of Information*, 127 HARV. L. REV. 512, 522 (2013) (quoting 18 U.S.C. §793(a)).

[81] 18 U.S.C. §§793(f), (h).

[82] *Id.* §793(a).

or note of *anything* connected with national defense."[83] Each subsection includes a rather complicated mental state; the government must prove that the defendant acted with "the intent or reason to believe that the information is to be used to the injury of the United States, or to the advantage of any foreign nation."[84]

Challenges asserting that the requirement that the information be "connected to national defense" is unconstitutionally vague have been rejected by the Supreme Court. In *Gorin v. United States*, the Supreme Court read a *scienter* requirement into §793(a) and §793(b), requiring proof that persons prosecuted acted in bad faith, and upheld the constitutionality of the statute.[85] The Court also broadly construed the words "national defense," finding that "national defense" "'is a generic concept of broad connotations, referring to the military and naval establishments and the related activities of national preparedness."[86]

Section 793(c) creates criminal liability for any individual who "receives or obtains or agrees or attempts to receive or obtain from any person, or from any source whatever" various materials related to the national defense, if the individual "know[s] or ha[s] reason to believe, at the time he receives or obtains [the information] . . . that it has been or will be obtained, taken, or disposed of by any person contrary to the provisions of [the Espionage Act]."[87] "Thus, whereas §793(a) and 793(b) prohibit the *collection* of secret information relating to the national defense, §793(c) prohibits the *receipt* of such information, or even attempts at receipt thereof, so long as the recipient does or should have knowledge that the source, in obtaining the information, violated some other provision of the Espionage Act."[88]

Section 793(d) is one of the most important provisions of the Espionage Act, and the statute is often used to prosecute the unauthorized disclosure of national defense information to members of the media.[89] Section 793(d) prohibits someone with lawful access to national defense information from willfully communicating, delivering, or transmitting the information to a person not entitled to receive it.[90] Courts have viewed both the statute and nondisclosure agreements signed by

---

[83] *Id.* §793(b) (emphasis added).

[84] *Id.* §793(a). Section 793(b) requires that the prohibited conduct be committed "with like intent or reason to believe" to convict for a violation of §793(a).

[85] Gorin v. United States, 312 U.S. 19, 28 (1941); *see also* United States v. Truong Dinh Hung, 629 F.2d 908, 918 (4th Cir. 1980) (discussing *Gorin's* scienter requirement); In re Squillacote, 790 A.2d 514, 519 (D.C. 2002) (same).

[86] *Gorin*, 312 U.S. at 28 (internal citations omitted).

[87] 18 U.S.C. §793(c).

[88] Stephen I. Vladeck, *Inchoate Liability and the Espionage Act: The Statutory Framework and the Freedom of the Press*, 1 HARV. L. & POL'Y REV., 219, 223 (2007) (hereinafter Vladeck, *Inchoate Liability and the Espionage Act*).

[89] *See, e.g.*, United States v. Sterling, 724 F.3d 482 (4th Cir. 2013) (involving the prosecution of a former CIA officer for disclosing national defense information to a journalist); United States v. Kiriakou, 898 F. Supp. 2d 921, 922 (E.D. Va. 2012) (same). The indictment against Jeffrey Sterling is available at http://www.fas.org/spg/jud/serling/indt.pdf.

[90] 18 U.S.C. §793(d). Edward Snowden, a former NSA government contractor working as a computer system administrator, who disclosed classified information about the NSA's "telephony metadata" program, was charged with violating §§793(d) and 798(a)(3) of the Espionage Act and

government employees as consistent with the First Amendment.[91] Supporting this view, courts have recognized the government's need for secrecy in sensitive operations such as the collection of foreign intelligence. The government hires individuals for positions related to these sensitive tasks with the express understanding that employees will maintain secrecy while they are in government service, and after they leave (since post-employment disclosure may compromise ongoing operations and chill discussion of sensitive issues). Maintaining secrecy and ensuring the effective operation of government in these sensitive areas would be impossible, courts have reasoned, if a disgruntled or greedy former employee could publicly disclose information gained in the course of government work. Because of these weighty public interests, courts have rejected First Amendment challenges to the enforcement of government employees' secrecy agreements.

Significantly, the statute is not limited to "classic spying" or the disclosure of secret defense material to an agent of a foreign government, but criminalizes the disclosure to *anyone* "not entitled to receive it."[92] Further, §793(d) distinguishes between "tangible" national defense information, described in the "documents" clause ("any document . . . or note relating to the national defense"), and "intangible" secret information, described in the "information" clause ("information relating to national defense").[93] Disclosure of either "tangible" or "intangible" national defense information is criminal only if the defendant acted "willfully."[94] Under the statute, "[a]n act is done willfully if it is done voluntarily and intentionally and with the specific intent to do something that the law forbids," and is done "with a bad purpose either to disobey or to disregard the law."[95] However, §793(d) imposes an additional scienter requirement when *intangible* national defense information is at issue. If the government's theory is that the defendant willfully disclosed "information relating to national defense," the government must prove not only that the defendant acted willfully, but that he had "reason to believe" that the information could be used "to the injury of the United States or to the advantage of any foreign nation."[96] "[T]he 'reason to

---

theft of government property. *See* Peter Finn & Sari Horwitz, *U.S. Files Charges Against Snowden*, WASH. POST, June 22, 2013, at A1; *see also* http://s3.documentcloud.org/documents/716888/u-s-vs-edward-j-snowden-criminal-complaint.pdf.

[91] *See* Snepp v. United States, 444 U.S. 507 (1980) (holding that government can enforce agreement against former CIA employee by judicial imposition of constructive trust that required the former employee to disgorge any money he had received as a result of unauthorized disclosure); *see also* Haig v. Agee, 453 U.S. 280 (1981) (upholding President's power to restrict travel abroad of former CIA employee who intended to disclose government secrets, including identities of covert operatives).

[92] *See* United States v. Morison, 844 F.2d 1057, 1067 (4th Cir. 1988).

[93] 18 U.S.C. §793(d).

[94] *Id.*

[95] *Morison*, 844 F.2d at 1071.

[96] United States v. Kiriakou, 898 F. Supp. 2d 921, 922-23 (E.D. Va. 2012).

believe could' cause injury language applies to intangible communication only, not to documents or other tangibles."[97]

Courts are divided on whether the "reason to believe" requirement imposes an obligation on the government to prove that the defendant acted with the specific intent to injure the United States or aid a foreign government. The Second Circuit does not require evidence that the defendant intended to harm the United States or aid a foreign government. In *United States v. Abu-Jihaad*, the court stated that to convict for a violation of §793(d), the government is required to prove beyond a reasonable doubt that the defendant:

> (1) lawfully had possession of, access to, control over, or was entrusted with information relating to the national defense; (2) had reason to believe that such information could be used to the injury of the United States or the advantage of any foreign nation; (3) willfully communicated, delivered, or transmitted such information; and (4) did so to a person not entitled to receive it.[98]

The Second Circuit's interpretation of the statute was reiterated in its analysis of the evidence supporting the "reason to believe" element. The court observed that based on the "classified nature of the information" and the defendant's "demonstrated understanding . . . of the impact of an attack on a United States warship, a rational juror could certainly conclude that the defendant had reason to believe" that the disclosed information "could be used to injure the United States."[99] The Second Circuit did not require evidence of the defendant's specific purpose to harm the United States or aid a foreign government to sustain a violation of §793(d). Thus, under the Second Circuit's interpretation, the fact that the defendant may have acted with a salutary motive or acted without a subversive motive is irrelevant for conviction.[100]

In *United States v. Rosen*, a district court in the Fourth Circuit reached the opposite conclusion, holding that the "reason to believe" language required

---

[97] *Id.* at 923; *see also* United States v. Hitselberger, 2012 WL 6238863, at *3 (D.D.C. Dec. 20, 2012) ("In essence, the 'information' clause imposes an additional *mens rea* requirement on the defendant, requiring that the defendant know that the information could be used to injure the United States or advantage a foreign nation.").

[98] United States v. Abu-Jihaad, 630 F.3d 102, 135 (2d Cir. 2010); *see also Kiriakou*, 898 F. Supp. 2d at 926 ("[T]here is no direct, binding authority dealing with the 'reason to believe' clause that imposes a burden on the government to prove that the defendant intended to injure the United States or to aid a foreign government, or that allows a defendant to pose a good faith defense."); United States v. Kim, 808 F. Supp. 2d 44, 55 (D.D.C. 2011) (not requiring proof of a bad purpose to injure the United States or aid a foreign government).

[99] United States v. Abu-Jihaad, 630 F.3d at 136.

[100] *See* United States v. Hitselberger, 2012 WL 6238863, at *5 (rejecting the argument that section 793(e) requires proof that the defendant acted with intent to injure the United States or benefit a foreign nation; in cases involving the "documents" clause, a simple "willfulness" standard is sufficient); United States v. Kiriakou, 898 F. Supp. 2d at 926-27. *Cf.* United States v. Morison, 622 F. Supp. 1009, 1011 (D. Md. 1985) ("evidence of the defendant's patriotism is irrelevant to the issues raised in 18 U.S.C. §793(d) and (e)").

the government to "demonstrate the likelihood of the defendant's bad faith purpose either to harm the United States or to aid a foreign government."[101] The *Rosen* court distinguished the two scienter requirements, finding that the willfulness element "concerns only the quality of the information," whereas the "reason to believe" element "relates to the intended (or recklessly disregarded) effect of the disclosure."[102] According to *Rosen*, in cases involving intangible national defense information disclosures, the government must prove that the defendant had "a bad faith purpose to harm the United States or to aid a foreign government."[103]

While §793(d) prohibits someone having "lawful" access to secret information from willfully disclosing it to a person not entitled to receive it, §793(e) punishes the willful disclosure of documents or information relating to the national defense of the United States by an "unauthorized" possessor.[104] Under §793(e), it is unlawful for a person having unauthorized possession of defense information who has reason to believe the information could be used to harm the national security or benefit any foreign nation, to willfully disclose that information to any person not entitled to receive it.[105] Section 793(e) also prohibits the retention of such information and the failure to deliver such information "to the officer or employee of the United States entitled to receive it."[106] The statute is broad, requiring only a showing that the defendant transmitted information to someone not entitled to receive it, not a showing that the defendant intended to injure the United States or benefit a foreign government. Additionally, §793(f) covers any person lawfully in possession of national defense information who either permits the information to be removed from where it belongs "through gross negligence" or, having knowledge that the information has been removed or delivered to any unauthorized person, fails to report the incident to his superior.[107] While §§793(d) and 793(f) prohibit the dissemination of national security information that is in the

---

[101] United States v. Rosen, 445 F. Supp. 2d 602, 626 (E.D. Va. 2006).

[102] *Id.*; *see also id.* at 641 n.56 ("As noted, the additional scienter requirement contained in the 'reason to believe' clause that applies to the transmission of intangible information, is not superfluous because it relates not to the nature of the information, but to the subjective understanding of the defendant as to the possible *effect* of the disclosure." (emphasis in original)). The courts are further divided on the issue even within the Eastern District of Virginia. In *Kiriakou*, 898 F. Supp.2d at 926, the district court rejected the position taken in *Rosen*, holding that the "heightened scienter requirement for disclosure of intangible NDI [national defense information] only requires the government to establish that 'the possessor ha[d] reason to believe [that the information] could be used to the injury of the United States or to the advantage of any foreign nation.'" *Id.* (quoting 18 U.S.C. §793d).

[103] United States v. Rosen, 520 F. Supp. 2d 786, 793 (E.D. Va. 2007).

[104] Section 793(e) also criminalizes the unauthorized possession and willful retention of NDI. *See, e.g.*, United States v. Aquino, 555 F.3d 124 (3d Cir. 2009) (the defendant was indicted and pled guilty to the unauthorized possession and willful retention of two classified documents relating to the national defense pursuant to 18 U.S.C. §793(e)).

[105] 18 U.S.C. §793(e).

[106] *Id.*

[107] *Id.* §793(f).

lawful possession of the individual who disseminates it, §793(d) prohibits *willful* communication and §793(f) prohibits gross negligence.[108] Finally, §793(g) makes it a crime to engage in a conspiracy to violate any of the provisions of §793.[109]

Both §§793(d) and (e) require the government to prove that the national defense information disclosed "relate[s] to the national defense."[110] This language has been construed to mean that it is "closely held" and that its disclosure "would be potentially damaging to the United States or might be useful to an enemy of the United States."[111] Courts have uniformly rejected the argument that the phrase "relate[s] to the national defense" is unconstitutionally vague.[112] "The vagueness doctrine is rooted in due process principles and is basically directed at lack of sufficient clarity, and precision in the statute."[113] It has been repeatedly stated that a statute that "either forbids or requires the doing of an act in terms so vague that men of common intelligence must necessarily guess at its meaning and differ as to its application, violates the first essential of due process of law."[114] In *Morison*, the Fourth Circuit found the phrase "relating to national defense" in §793(d) constitutional in light of the scienter requirement, which requires the prosecution to prove that the defendant acted willfully, knowing that his conduct was unlawful.[115] In *Rosen*, a district court in the Fourth Circuit also rejected defendant's impermissible vagueness claim, focusing on the limiting effect of the statute's "willfulness" and "reason to believe" elements, and found that these two prongs save the

---

[108] *Id.*

[109] *Id.* §793(g).

[110] *Id.* §§793(d)-(e).

[111] United States v. Morison, 844 F.2d 1057, 1071-72 (4th Cir. 1988); *see also* United States v. Kiriakou, 898 F. Supp. 2d 921, 923 (E.D. Va. 2012).

[112] *See generally* United States v. Squillacote, 221 F.3d 542, 580 n.23 (4th Cir. 2000); *Morison*, 844 F.2d at 1075; United States v. Boyce, 594 F.2d 1246, 1252 n.2 (9th Cir. 1979) (upholding the language of 18 U.S.C. §§794 and 794); United States v. Hitselberger, 2012 WL 6238863 (D.D.C. Dec. 20, 2012); United States v. Kiriakou, 2012 WL 3263854, at *6 (E.D. Va. 2012); United States v. Drake, 818 F. Supp. 2d 909 (D. Md. 2011); United States v. Kim, 808 F. Supp. 2d 44 (D.D.C. 2011); United States v. Abu-Jihaad, 600 F. Supp. 2d 362 (D. Conn. 2009); United States v. Rosen, 445 F. Supp. 2d 602, 626 (E.D. Va. 2006).

[113] *Morison*, 844 F.2d at 1070.

[114] Connally v. Gen. Constr. Co., 269 U.S. 385, 391 (1926); *see also* United States v. Williams, 553 U.S. 285, 304 (2008) ("A conviction fails to comport with due process if the statute under which it is obtained fails to provide a person of ordinary intelligence fair notice of what is prohibited, or is so standardless that it authorizes or encourages seriously discriminatory enforcement."); Kolender v. Lawson, 461 U.S. 352, 357 (1983) ("[T]he void-for-vagueness doctrine requires that a penal statute define the criminal offense with sufficient definiteness that ordinary people can understand what conduct is prohibited and in a manner that does not encourage arbitrary and discriminatory enforcement.").

[115] *Morison*, 844 F.2d at 1071-72; *see also* United States v. Dedeyan, 584 F.2d 36, 39 (4th Cir. 1978) (holding that in the context of §793(f)(2) the phrase "relating to national defense" is not constitutionally vague). The *Morison* court also reasoned that the district court's jury instructions defining "willfully" and "national defense" removed any possibility of vagueness in the application of the statutes. *Morison*, 844 F.2d at 1072.

III. Criminal Prohibitions on the Disclosure of Classified Information

phrase "relating to the national defense" from "fatal vagueness" and enable it to "pass[ ] Due Process muster."[116]

In considering the defendant's claim that the clause "relating to the national defense" is impermissibly vague, the content and markings of the documents communicated or retained are highly relevant. In *United States v. Hitselberger*, the district court found the defendant's vagueness challenge particularly unpersuasive because the documents contained highly sensitive information, including information about U.S. troop movements, activities in the region, the availability of improvised explosive devices, and gaps in U.S. intelligence of the political situation in Bahrain.[117] Further, the documents at issue were marked as "SECRET," a classification level that applied to information that "if lost or compromised, would cause serious damage to the security of the United States."[118] The court also found that the defendant's training placed him on notice that the government considered information contained in the classified documents important to national security.[119]

Defendants have fared no better arguing that §793(d) is overbroad in contravention of the First Amendment. The overbreadth doctrine would invalidate a statute when it "infringe[s] on expression to a degree greater than justified by the legitimate governmental need," which is the valid purpose of the statute.[120] The Supreme Court has held that when the First Amendment is implicated, a party may "argue that a statute is overbroad because it is unclear whether it regulates a substantial amount of protected speech."[121] The Fourth Circuit has articulated three circumstances in which the overbreadth doctrine may properly be applied:

(1) when the governmental interest sought to be implemented is too insubstantial, or at least insufficient in relation to the inhibitory effect on [F]irst [A]mendment freedoms;
(2) when the means employed bear little relation to the asserted governmental interest; and
(3) when the means chosen by the legislature do in fact relate to a substantial governmental interest, but that interest could be achieved by a less drastic means—that is, a method less invasive of free speech interests.[122]

The espionage statutes do not fall within the first two categories given that there is a substantial governmental interest in prohibiting the disclosure of classified information that could damage important and vital national security interests, and the relevant statutes are directly related to achieving this end.[123] Thus,

---

[116] United States v. Rosen, 445 F. Supp. 2d at 622.

[117] United States v. Hitselberger, 2012 WL 6238863, at *4.

[118] *Id.*

[119] *Id.*

[120] Martin H. Redish, *The Warren Court, the Burger Court and the First Amendment Overbreadth Doctrine*, 78 N.W. U. L. Rev. 1031, 1034 (1983-84).

[121] United States v. Williams, 553 U.S. 285, 304 (2008) (quoting Hoffman Estates v. Flipside, Hoffman Estates, Inc., 455 U.S. 489, 494-95 & nn.6-7 (1982)).

[122] United States v. Morison, 844 F.2d 1057, 1075 (4th Cir. 1988) (quoting Redish, *supra* note 120, at 1035).

[123] *Id.* at 1076 (discussing 18 U.S.C. §§793(d)-(e)).

the espionage statutes could be voided for overbreadth only if Congress could have used a less drastic means to achieve its legitimate objective.[124] In *Morison*, the Fourth Circuit held that the district court's narrower definition of "national defense information," encompassed matters which 1) "directly or may reasonably be connected with the defense of the United States," 2) the disclosure of which "would be potentially damaging to the United States or might be useful to an enemy of the United States," and 3) which had been "closely held" by the government and was "not available to the general public." The Fourth Circuit found that this narrower definition removed any legitimate overbreadth objection to the term "national defense information."[125]

Finally, courts have dismissed the claim that prosecution under §§793(d) and (e) for disclosure of national defense information to the media violates the First Amendment. In *Morison*, the Fourth Circuit dismissed the defendant's First Amendment defense, holding:

> [I]t seems beyond controversy that a recreant intelligence department employee who had abstracted from the government files secret intelligence information and had willfully transmitted or given it to one "not entitled to receive it" as did the defendant in this case, is not entitled to invoke the First Amendment as a shield to immunize his act of thievery. To permit the thief thus to misuse the Amendment would be to prostitute the salutary purposes of the First Amendment. Section 793(d) and (e) unquestionably criminalize such conduct by a delinquent government employee and, when applied to a defendant in the position of the defendant here, there is no First Amendment right implicated.[126]

Thus, it is no defense to criminal charges under §§793(d) and (e) that the defendant disclosed classified information to a representative of the media.

Other provisions of the Espionage Act are also important to preventing the disclosure of national defense information. Section 794(a) prohibits classic espionage—the communication, delivery, or transmission of national defense information to a foreign government or representative thereof "with the intent or reason to believe that [the information] is to be used to the injury of the United States or to the advantage of a foreign nation."[127] Similarly, §794(b), which is applicable only in "time of war," prohibits collecting, recording, publishing, or communicating information about troop movement or defense plans "with the intent that the same shall be communicated to the enemy."[128] Thus, §§794(a) and 794(b) create offenses punishing the intentional transmission of national defense information to foreign government recipients. However, §794(b) is narrower than §794(a) because §794(b) prohibits communications to "the enemy," whereas §794(a) prohibits transfers intended or likely to advantage "a foreign

---

[124] *Id.* at 1076.
[125] *Id.*
[126] *Id.* at 1069-70.
[127] 18 U.S.C. §794(a).
[128] *Id.* §794(b).

nation." At the same time, §794(b) is broader than §794(a) in expressly making "publishing" criminal. Thus, publication by the media of certain national defense information *could* fall within §794(b). However, publication would be criminal only if done with the "intent that [the information] shall be communicated to the enemy."[129] But proving the requisite intent would be difficult. The purposes underlying publication will almost always be to inform the public and sell newspapers, not to communicate the classified information to the enemy. Both subsections of §794 also criminalize preparatory conduct. Further, §794(c) punishes conspiracy to violate the other subsections of §794.[130] Violations of §§794(a)-(c) may be punished by death or imprisonment for any terms of years, or for life.[131]

Section 797 applies to whoever "reproduces, publishes, sells, or gives away" photographs of specified defense installations or equipment without authorization, unless the photographs were properly censored.[132] Finally, §798 makes it a crime for anyone, government employee or not, to knowingly and willfully communicate, furnish, transmit, or otherwise make available to an unauthorized person, or publish, or use in any manner prejudicial to the safety or interest of the United States, any classified information regarding the codes, cryptography, or concerning the communications intelligence activities utilized by the United States or any foreign government.[133] The disclosure of such classified information to any foreign government to the detriment of the United States is also prohibited.[134]

B.   *Intelligence Identities Protection Act*

The Intelligence Identities Protection Act of 1982 (IIPA), 50 U.S.C. §3121 (formerly codified at 50 U.S.C. §421), prohibits the disclosure of classified information that reveals the identity of a covert agent, when done intentionally by a person with authorized access to such information.[135] The statute punishes—

> [w]hoever, having . . . authorized access to classified information that identifies a covert agent, intentionally discloses any information identifying such covert agent to any individual not authorized to receive classified information, knowing that the information disclosed so identifies such covert agent and the United

---

[129] *Id.*

[130] *Id.* §794(c).

[131] *Id.* §§794(a)-(c).

[132] *Id.* §797.

[133] *Id.* §798. An FBI contract linguist was criminally prosecuted for providing secret documents to a blogger, in violation of 18 U.S.C. §798. *See* Press Release, Dep't of Justice, *Former FBI Contract Linguist Pleads Guilty to Leaking Classified Information to Blogger* (Dec. 17, 2009), *available at* http://www.justice.gov/opa/pr/2009/December/09-nsd-1361.html (last visited Mar. 26, 2014).

[134] 18 U.S.C. §798.

[135] 50 U.S.C. §3121(a). The offense is punishable by imprisonment not exceeding 15 years. *Id.*

States is taking affirmative measures to conceal such covert intelligence relationship to the United States.[136]

Section 3121(b) punishes disclosure of the identity of a covert agent by persons who learn of the identity of a covert agent as a result of having access to classified information.[137] Further, while §§3121(a) and 3121(b) punish the disclosure of such information by individuals authorized to have access to classified information identifying the covert agent, §3121(c) applies to anyone who "discloses any information that identifies an individual as a covert agent to any individual not authorized to receive classified information, knowing that the information disclosed so identifies such individual and that the United States is taking affirmative measures to conceal such individual's classified intelligence relationship to the United States."[138] In the case of a violation of §3121(c), the government must prove that the individual made the disclosure "in the course of a pattern of activities intended to identify and expose covert agents and with reason to believe that such activities would impair or impede the foreign intelligence activities of the United States."[139]

Sections 3121(a) and (b) differ from the espionage statutes and do not require the government to prove that the defendant had reason to believe that disclosing the identity of a covert agent would cause harm to the United States or benefit a foreign government.[140] In *United States v. Kiriakou*, the court stressed the serious nature of the conduct proscribed under the statute, stating that "[t]he identity of a covert agent is information that goes to the heart of the nation's intelligence activities, and its disclosure could very well threaten the personal safety of the agent whose identity is revealed as well as undermine confidence in the Government's ability to protect its covert officers."[141] Thus, it is no defense to a prosecution under §§3121(a) and (b) that the identity of the covert agent was disclosed to a member of the media for a benign purpose, with no reason to believe that the

---

[136] *Id.* Conservative columnist Bob Novak disclosed the identity of CIA operative Valerie Plame in a July 14, 2003 newspaper column. *See* Robert Novak, *The Mission in Niger*, WASH. POST, July 14, 2003, at A21. Novak reported that two senior administration officials had revealed Plame's identity, arguably in violation of 50 U.S.C. §3121(a).

[137] 50 U.S.C. §3121(b). A violation of subsection (b) is punishable by not more than ten years' imprisonment.

[138] *Id.* §3121(c).

[139] *Id.*

[140] Only 50 U.S.C. §3121(c) requires proof of intent to identify and expose the covert agent and "reason to believe that such activities would impair or impeded the foreign intelligence activities of the United States."

[141] United States v. Kiriakou, 2012 WL 3263854, at *8 (E.D. Va. 2012) (Kiriakou, a former CIA officer, was accused of disclosing to a journalist the identity of a covert CIA officer associated with the CIA's Rendition, Detention, and Interrogation Program); *cf.* In re Grand Jury Subpoena, Judith Miller, 438 F.3d 1141, 1173-74 (D.C. Cir. 2005) (Tatel, J., concurring in the judgment) (stating that "[l]eaks similar to the crime suspected here (exposure of a covert agent) apparently caused the deaths of several CIA operatives in the late 1970s and early 1980s, including the agency's Athens station") (internal citations omitted).

information could be used to harm the United States or benefit a foreign government.

Section 3121(a) has been upheld by courts against an attack that the statute is unconstitutionally vague or overbroad. In *Kiriakou*, the defendant argued that §421 (now codified as §3121) is unconstitutionally vague because the statute does not define the "affirmative measures" that the government must take to conceal a covert agent's identity to trigger application of the statute.[142] According to *Kiriakou*, "[t]his limitation narrows the application of the statute to persons who are by definition aware of the extreme sensitive nature of classified information, their responsibilities in handling it, and the 'affirmative measures' the agency takes to protect the secrecy of covert agents."[143] The district court observed that §421(a) applied only to a limited class of persons—those who "had authorized access to classified information that identifies a covert agent."[144] Further, the court stated that the defendant signed numerous secrecy and nondisclosure agreements that clearly articulated his responsibilities regarding the handling of such information.[145] Thus, the court held that Kiriakou had no credible argument that the term "affirmative measures" is so vague that he lacked adequate warning as to the conduct proscribed, such that his due process rights were violated.[146]

The court in *Kiriakou* also dismissed defendant's argument that §421 (now §3121) is unconstitutionally overbroad because the government need not prove that a defendant intended to harm the United States or had reason to believe that disclosing the information would cause harm to the United States or benefit a foreign government.[147] The court stressed that disclosure of the identity of a covert agent could threaten the safety of the agent whose identity is revealed.[148] Thus, protecting the identity of covert agents implicates an important government interest. Because the statute is narrowly drafted to that end, the court held that §421 (now §3121) is not unconstitutionally broad.[149]

C.   *Other Statutes Prohibiting the Disclosure of Classified Information*

50 U.S.C. §783(a), which was enacted as part of the 1950 amendments to the Espionage Act,[150] overlaps with 18 U.S.C. §794(a). Both statutes prohibit the

---

[142] *Kiriakou*, 2012 WL 3263854.

[143] *Id.* at *5.

[144] *Id.*

[145] *Id.*

[146] *Id.*

[147] *Id.* at *8.

[148] *Id.*

[149] *Id.*

[150] *See* Subversive Activities Control Act of 1950, Pub. L. No. 81-831, Title I, §18, 64 Stat. 987, 1033.

communication of classified information by an "officer or employee of the United States" to agents or representatives of foreign governments.[151] Section 783(a) requires proof of four elements: 1) an officer or employee of the United States or any department or agency thereof, 2) without authorization communicates classified information affecting the security of the United States, 3) to any person whom such officer or employee knows or has reason to believe to be an agent or representative of a foreign government, 4) knowing or having reason to know that such information has been classified.[152] A person who violates §783 may be punished by imprisonment for not more than ten years.[153]

Another important statute is 18 U.S.C. §641, which prohibits the conversion of any "thing of value" to the U.S. government, and also prohibits the knowing receipt of the same "with the intent to convert it to [one's] use or gain.[154] Under the statute, the unauthorized disclosure of national intelligence information constitutes the conversion of a "thing of value" to the U.S. government. The statute applies to the theft of classified government documents. Further, the fact that the defendant may have acted with the purpose of informing or educating the public, rather than for financial gain, is not a defense. In *Morison*, the defendant, a military intelligence employee, was convicted for violation of §641 for transmitting photographs of a new Soviet aircraft carrier to *Jane's Defence Weekly*, an English publisher of defense information.[155] In affirming the convictions, the Fourth Circuit declared:

> The defendant would deny application of [§641] to his theft because he says that he did not steal the material "for private, convert use in illegal enterprises" but in order to give it to the press for public dissemination and information. . . . The mere fact that one has stolen a document in order that he may deliver it to the press, whether for money or for other personal gain, will not immunize him from responsibility for his criminal act.[156]

Additionally, Edward Snowden, a former NSA government contractor who disclosed classified information to the *Guardian* revealing the massive scale of the NSA's metadata program, has also been charged with theft of government property under 18 U.S.C. §641.[157]

---

[151] 50 U.S.C. §783.

[152] *Id.*

[153] *Id.* §783(c).

[154] 18 U.S.C. §641.

[155] United States v. Morison, 844 F.2d 1057, 1057 (4th Cir. 1988). The defendant was also convicted of two provisions of the Espionage Act, 18 U.S.C. §§793(d) and (e).

[156] *Morison*, 844 F.2d at 1077.

[157] *See* Peter Finn & Sari Horwitz, *U.S. Files Charges Against Snowden*, Wash. Post, June 22, 2013, at A1; *see also* http://s3.docmentcloud.org/documents/7168888/u-s-vs-edward-j-snowden-criminal-complaint.pdf.

III. Criminal Prohibitions on the Disclosure of Classified Information

Enacted in 1933, 18 U.S.C. §952 applies to government employees who, without authorization, publish or provide to a third-party diplomatic codes or diplomatic correspondence "obtained while in the process of transmission between any foreign government and its diplomatic mission in the United States."[158] Further, 18 U.S.C. §1924(a) prohibits the unauthorized removal or retention of classified documents or material by an officer, employee, contractor, or consultant of the United States.[159] Under these two statutes, a colorable argument could be made that a reporter using a government employee as a source of classified information would be liable if that source, in the process of disclosing information to the reporter, violated either 18 U.S.C. §952 or §1924.[160]

The Atomic Energy Act of 1954, codified at 42 U.S.C. §§2011-2297h-13, is also relevant to the analysis. Sections 2274 and 2277 prohibit the communication, receipt, and disclosure of "restricted data," which is defined as "all data concerning (1) design, manufacture, or utilization of atomic weapons; (2) the production of special nuclear material; or (3) the use of special nuclear material in the production of energy, but shall not include data declassified or removed from the Restricted Data category pursuant to section 2162 of this title."[161] Section 2274 criminalizes the communication or disclosure of "restricted data" with either the intent or reason to believe such data will be utilized to injure the United States or to secure an advantage to any foreign nation.[162] Section 2277 prohibits the knowing disclosure of restricted data to any person not authorized by the Atomic Energy Commission, but applies only to present and former government employees and contractors.[163] Section 2275 makes criminal receipt of restricted data with intent to injure the United States or to secure an advantage of any foreign nation.[164] Finally, §2276 punishes tampering with restricted data with like intent.[165] However, there are few reported court decisions analyzing 18 U.S.C. §952, §1924, or 42 U.S.C. §2274, 2275, 2276, or 2277 of the Atomic Energy Act. Criminal prosecutions under these provisions are rare.

---

[158] 18 U.S.C. §952.

[159] Id. §1924(a). Under the statute, "classified information of the United States" is defined as –

information originated, owned, or possessed by the United States Government concerning the national defense or foreign relations of the United States that has been determined pursuant to the law or Executive order to require protection against unauthorized disclosure in the interest of national security.

Id. §1924(b).

[160] See Vladeck, *Inchoate Liability and the Espionage Act, supra* note 88.

[161] 42 U.S.C. §2014(y).

[162] Id. §2274.

[163] Id. §2277.

[164] Id. §2275.

[165] Id. §2276.

D.   *The First Amendment and Media Disclosure of National Security Information*

There may be times when the government classification and access controls fail to prevent disclosure of classified or sensitive information. If the media obtains this information, the government may seek to prevent further disclosure by threatening prosecution for violation of the Espionage Act,[166] or perhaps by seeking an injunction. In such cases, a clear conflict may arise between the government's interest in protecting national security and freedom of the press.

This conflict was addressed by the Supreme Court in *New York Times v. United States*.[167] In that case, the Court was called upon to decide whether both the *New York Times* and the *Washington Post* could be constitutionally compelled to terminate publication of the Pentagon Papers, a massive classified study of the war in Vietnam.[168] Daniel Ellsberg, an analyst working for the Department of Defense, provided a copy of the study to both papers, in contravention of restrictions imposed on his access pursuant to the classification of the study.[169]

Both papers struggled with the question of whether extracts should be published in light of the fact that they knew their receipt was unauthorized; and both decided that the public interest outweighed any concern over improper disclosure.[170] The government response was swift.

The government applied for an injunction against the *New York Times* in the United States District Court for the Southern District of New York, seeking to prevent it from further publishing any of the materials from the Pentagon Papers.[171] The government argued that in this instance, prior restraint was justified because of the harm the United States would suffer if the Papers were disseminated.[172] Due to the Top Secret classification of the Papers, the court held an

---

[166] Subsection (e) of the Espionage Act states that

> [w]hoever having unauthorized possession of, access to, or control over any document, writing, code book, signal book, sketch, photograph, photographic negative, blueprint, plan, map, model, instrument, appliance, or note relating to the national defense, or information relating to the national defense which information the possessor has reason to believe could be used to the injury of the United States or to the advantage of any foreign nation, willfully communicates, delivers, transmits or causes to be communicated, delivered, or transmitted, or attempts to communicate, deliver, transmit or cause to be communicated, delivered, or transmitted the same to any person not entitled to receive it, or willfully retains the same and fails to deliver it to the officer or employee of the United States entitled to receive it. . . . Shall be fined under this title or imprisoned not more than ten years, or both. 18 U.S.C. §793(e)-(f) (1996).

[167] N.Y. Times Co. v. United States, 403 U.S. 713 (1971).

[168] *Id.* at 714.

[169] *The Battle for the Pentagon Papers*, TOP SECRET, http://topsecretplay.org/timeline/ (last visited Nov. 8, 2014).

[170] *Id.*

[171] United States v. N.Y. Times Co., 328 F. Supp. 324, 326 (S.D.N.Y. 1971).

[172] *Id.*

III. Criminal Prohibitions on the Disclosure of Classified Information

in camera hearing in order to determine whether the potential harm to the United States outweighed the *Times*'s First Amendment right to freedom of the press.[173] At this hearing, the court did not review the Papers themselves, but asked the government to identify what about the Papers would constitute a threat to national security if disseminated to the public.[174] On June 19, 1971, the court denied the government's request for a preliminary injunction.[175] Simultaneously, the government was fighting a parallel battle in Washington, D.C., seeking to enjoin *The Washington Post* from publishing the Papers.[176] The United States District Court for the District of Columbia also denied the government's request.[177] The government appealed both cases.

On appeal, the Second Circuit and the D.C. Circuit disagreed over the merits of the government's case.[178] On June 23, 1971, the Second Circuit reversed and remanded the decision in the *New York Times* case.[179] On the very same day, the D.C. Circuit upheld the lower court's decision in the *Washington Post* case.[180] Two days later, on June 25, the U.S. Supreme Court granted *certiorari*, and consolidated the cases.[181]

The Supreme Court rejected the government's argument, concluding that the government had not met the heavy burden to justify imposition of prior restraint.[182] The Court emphasized that any imposition of prior restraint on the press—even one motivated by concerns related to national security—results in a "heavy presumption against its constitutional validity", imposing on the government a "heavy burden of showing justification. . . ."[183] According to Justice Black, the First Amendment protected the freedom of the press so that the press could "fulfill its essential role in our democracy."[184] This role, according to Black, was to "censure the government," which included the power to "bare the secrets of government and inform the people."[185] Accordingly, Black concluded that "the Government's power to censor the press was abolished so that the press would remain forever free to censure the Government."[186]

Justice Brennan's concurring opinion was slightly less sweeping. He agreed that the First Amendment imposed "an absolute bar" to imposition of the government's requested injunction, but he emphasized that this was a result of the factual

---

[173] *Id.*

[174] *Id.* at 330.

[175] *Id.* at 331.

[176] United States v. Wash. Post Co., 446 F.2d 1327, 1328 (D.C. Cir. 1971).

[177] *Id.*

[178] *Id;* United States v. N.Y. Times Co., 444 F.2d 544 (2d Cir. 1971).

[179] *Id.*

[180] *Wash. Post Co.,* 446 F.2d at 1332.

[181] *N.Y. Times Co.,* 403 U.S. at 714.

[182] *Id.*

[183] *Id.* (Black, J., concurring).

[184] *Id.* at 717.

[185] *Id.*

[186] *Id.*

circumstances related to the issue presented.[187] As he noted, "the First Amendment tolerates absolutely no prior judicial restraints of the press *predicated upon surmise or conjecture that untoward consequences may result.*"[188] Of course, this qualification indicates that had the government provided more concrete evidence of the harm to national security that would result from continued publication, the outcome may very well have been different.

What concrete consequences might meet this standard of justification? Justice Brennan offered, as comparison, the Court's discussion of prior restraint in *Schenck v. United States,* where the Court noted that such restraint could be justified only when the Nation is at war, and when publication would interfere with ongoing efforts to win the war, such as publication of movement timetables for troop transport ships.[189] Accordingly, Justice Brennan indicated that prior restraint could be justified only when the government offered "proof that publication must inevitably, directly, and immediately cause the occurrence of an event kindred to imperiling the safety of a transport already at sea. . . ."[190] Justice Stewart also focused on the speculative nature of the harm the government sought to avert, noting that there was no proof that "disclosure of [the Papers] will surely result in direct, immediate, and irreparable damage to the Nation or its people. . . ."[191]

The Court's rejection of the government's effort to restrain publication of the Pentagon Papers was hailed as a validation of the First Amendment's protection for the "institutional press."[192] However, the qualifications included by several of the Justices, along with the suggestion that the outcome might have been different if Congress had declared war against Vietnam or if Congress had provided statutory authorization for such restraint, indicates the nuanced nature of the decision. It is overbroad to treat the *New York Times* case as a categorical bar to prior restraint against press publication of classified or other national security information. However, it is clear that such restraint will only be viable in the most extreme circumstances, where the government can convincingly establish publication will imperil ongoing or future operations. What does seem unquestionable is that the First Amendment stands as an absolute bar to the imposition of such restraint to prevent disclosure of information exposing decisions related to past actions, no matter how classified the information, or how embarrassing for the government the disclosure will be.

---

[187] *Id.* at 725-27. (Brennan, J., concurring).

[188] *Id.* at 725-26 (emphasis added).

[189] *Id.* at 726.

[190] *Id.* at 726-27.

[191] *Id.* at 730. (Stewart, J., concurring).

[192] DAVID RUDENSTINE, THE DAY THE PRESS STOPPED: A HISTORY OF THE PENTAGON CASE 349-50 (1996); Charles Bierbauer, *When Everything Is Classified, Nothing Is Classified,* 1 WAKE FOREST J.L. & POL'Y 21, 22 (2011).

IV. PREVENTING THE DISCLOSURE OF NATIONAL SECURITY INFORMATION IN LITIGATION

A. *Preventing Disclosure in Civil Litigation*

The State Secrets Privilege (SSP or "privilege") is a common law evidentiary privilege not explicitly set forth in any statute or legislative act.[193] The privilege is based in the law of evidence rather than the Constitution. In simple terms, the SSP permits the government to bar the disclosure of information if there is a "reasonable danger" that such disclosure would "expose military matters which, in the interest of national security, should not be divulged."[194] The privilege is based on the premise that "in exceptional circumstances courts must act in the interest of the country's national security to prevent disclosure of state secrets, even to the point of dismissing a case entirely."[195]

The contemporary state secrets doctrine encompasses three applications. First, the evidentiary privilege ("the *Reynolds* privilege") excludes privileged evidence (military or state secrets) from a case and could require dismissal of a plaintiff's claims.[196] Second, this privilege bars adjudication of claims where the very subject of the action is a matter of state secret (the "*Totten* bar").[197] Finally, application of the state secrets privilege may require dismissal of the civil action where there is no feasible way to litigate the matter "without creating an unjustifiable risk of divulging state secrets."[198]

The Supreme Court first articulated the state secrets privilege in 1953, when it decided *United States v. Reynolds*.[199] In *Reynolds*, the widows of three civilians who

---

[193] Fed. R. Crim. P. 26(b)(5)(A), generally governs the application of privilege in civil trials. Rule 26(b)(5)(A) provides:

> *Information Withheld.* When a party withholds information otherwise discoverable by claiming that the information is privileged or subject to protection as trial-preparation materials, the party must:
>
> (i) Expressly make the claims; and
> (ii) Describe the nature of the documents, communications, or tangible things not produced or disclosed—and do so in a manner that, without revealing information itself privileged or protected, will enable other parties to assess the claim.

Since the Tort Claims Act expressly makes the Federal Rules of Civil Procedure applicable to suits against the United States, the SSP finds statutory support in the fact that the Federal Rules of Civil Procedure compel only the production of matters which are not privileged.

[194] United States v. Reynolds, 345 U.S. 1, 10 (1953).

[195] Mohamed v. Jeppesen Dataplan, Inc., 614 F.3d 1070, 1077 (9th Cir. 2010) (en banc).

[196] *Id.*; *see also Reynolds*, 345 U.S. at 1.

[197] Mohamed v. Jeppesen Dataplan, Inc., 614 F.3d at 1077; *see also* Totten v. United States, 92 U.S. 105 (1876).

[198] *Jeppesen Dataplan, Inc.*, 614 F.3d at 1087.

[199] *Reynolds*, 345 U.S. at 1. The Supreme Court's discussion of *Reynolds* in Tenet v. Doe, 544 U.S. 1, 8-9 (2005), confirms the continued validity of the SSP.

were killed in the crash of a military aircraft that had been testing secret electronic equipment filed a wrongful death action against the United States under the Federal Tort Claims Act, 28 U.S.C. §1346.[200] In the course of discovery, plaintiffs sought production of the Air Force's official accident investigation report and the statements of three surviving crewmembers taken in connection with the official investigation.[201] In response, the Secretary of the Air Force filed a formal "Claim of Privilege" stating that the documents contained "highly secret," privileged military information, the disclosure of which would "seriously hampe[r] national security, flying safety and the development of highly technical and secret military equipment."[202] The claim was rejected by the district court, and production was demanded.[203] When the government refused, the district court sanctioned the government and found in favor of the plaintiffs.[204] The district court's ruling was affirmed on appeal.[205]

The Supreme Court reversed, denying the plaintiffs' discovery request. The Court recognized "the privilege against revealing military secrets, a privilege which is well established in the law of evidence," and set forth the procedures to be applied in resolving government claims of privilege.[206] The Court stated:

> The privilege belongs to the Government and must be asserted by it; it can neither be claimed nor waived by a private party. It is not to be lightly invoked. There must be a formal claim of privilege, lodged by the head of the department which has control over the matter, after actual personal consideration by that officer. The court itself must determine whether the circumstances are appropriate for the claim of privilege, and yet do so without forcing a disclosure of the very thing the privilege is designed to protect.[207]

While judicial involvement in policing the privilege is important, the Court emphasized limitations on a judge's supervisory function. The *Reynolds* Court opined: "Too much judicial inquiry into the claim of privilege would force disclosure of the thing the privilege was meant to protect, while a complete abandonment of judicial control would lead to intolerable abuses."[208] Recognizing that the conflict presents a "real difficulty," the Court sought to resolve the matter the same way it had resolved a similar dilemma in the self-incrimination context.[209] "[T]he court must be satisfied from all the evidence and circumstances, and 'from the implications of the question . . . that a responsive answer might be dangerous

---

[200] *Reynolds*, 345 U.S. at 3.

[201] *Id.* at 3-4.

[202] *Id.* at 4-5 (internal quotations omitted).

[203] *Id.* at 5.

[204] *Id.*

[205] *Id.*

[206] *Id.* at 6-7.

[207] *Id.* at 7-8; *see also* Mohamed v. Jeppesen Dataplan, Inc., 614 F.3d 1070, 1080 (9th Cir. 2010) (en banc) (same).

[208] *Reynolds*, 345 U.S. at 8.

[209] *Id.* at 8-10.

because injurious disclosure could result.'"[210] Further, once the court is "satisfied" that a request for production of evidence might have a deleterious effect on national security, "the claim of the privilege will be accepted without requiring further disclosure."[211] Further, the *Reynolds* Court made clear that the process of "satisfying" a district judge that the privilege has been properly invoked does not necessarily require *in camera* review of all the materials likely to contain state secrets. The Court declared:

> Judicial control over the evidence in a case cannot be abdicated to the caprice of executive officers. Yet we will not go so far as to say that the court may automatically require a complete disclosure to the judge before the claim of privilege will be accepted in any case. It may be possible to satisfy the court, from all the circumstances of the case, that there is a *real danger* that compulsion of the evidence will expose military matters which, in the interest of national security, should not be divulged.[212]

The Court posited that courts "should not jeopardize the security which the privilege is meant to protect by insisting upon an examination of the evidence, even by the judge alone, in chambers."[213] Instead, once a formal and proper claim of privilege has been made, the judge should attempt to determine the sufficiency of that claim through an explanation by the department head who is lodging the privilege claim.[214] Further, such explanation may take the form of an affidavit or declaration made personally by the department head. If the judge finds that there is a "reasonable danger" of state secrets being exposed, "he need not—indeed, should not—probe further."[215]

Finally, while the plaintiff's "showing of necessity" for the privileged evidence "will determine how far the court should probe in satisfying itself that the occasion for invoking the privilege is appropriate," national security concerns remain paramount because "even the most compelling necessity cannot overcome the claim of privilege if the court is ultimately satisfied that military secrets are at stake."[216] In other words, national security concerns always trump the plaintiff's need for the evidence in order to litigate a civil case.

A second category of cases has emerged from the state secrets doctrine. The state secrets privilege has been construed as "a rule of non-justiciability, akin to a political question, and as a privilege that may bar proof of a prima

---

[210] *Id.* at 9 (quoting Hoffman v. United States, 341 U.S. 479, 486-87 (1951)).

[211] *Reynolds*, 345 U.S. at 9.

[212] *Id.* at 9-10 (emphasis added).

[213] *Id.* at 10.

[214] *See* Sterling v. Tenet, 416 F.3d 338, 344 (4th Cir. 2005).

[215] *Id.*

[216] *Id.* at 11; *see also* Mohamed v. Jeppesen Dataplan, Inc., 614 F.3d 1070, 1081-82 (9th Cir. 2010) (en banc) ("In evaluating the need for secrecy, 'we acknowledge the need to defer to the Executive on matters of foreign policy and national security and surely cannot legitimately find ourselves second guessing the Executive in this arena.'").

facie case."[217] The non-justiciability of certain state secret cases has its origins in *Totten v. United States*, where the Supreme Court held that lawsuits premised on alleged espionage agreements are categorically prohibited.[218] *Totten* arose out of an alleged oral agreement between President Abraham Lincoln and a secret agent who was allegedly dispatched to spy on enemy troops.[219] The estate of the former Union spy brought a breach of contract claim seeking compensation owed for secret wartime espionage services.[220] The Supreme Court dismissed the claim noting that as "a general principle[ ] public policy forbids the maintenance of *any suit* in a court of justice, the trial of which would inevitably lead to the disclosure of matters which the law itself regards as confidential."[221] The Court found that "[t]he secrecy which such contracts impose precludes any action for their enforcement," and noted that "the existence of a contract of that kind is itself a fact not to be disclosed."[222] Thus, under *Totten*, civil actions over secret espionage contracts may not be reviewed by federal courts.

In *Tenet v. Doe*, the Supreme Court upheld the continuing validity of *Totten v. United States*, dismissing a civil action brought to enforce a secret espionage agreement.[223] In *Tenet*, respondents brought suit against the United States and the Director of the Central Intelligence Agency (CIA), asserting estoppel and due process claims for the CIA's alleged failure to provide them with the financial assistance it had promised in return for their espionage services during the Cold War.[224] The government moved to dismiss the complaint relying principally on the ground that *Totten* barred respondents' suit.[225] After the Ninth Circuit affirmed the district court's denial of the government's motion, the Supreme Court reversed, reading *Totten* broadly. The Court stated that there was no basis for respondents' and the Court of Appeals's view that "the *Totten* bar has been reduced to an example of the state secrets privilege."[226] The Supreme Court held that "*Totten* precludes judicial review in cases such as respondents' where success depends upon the existence of their state secrets privilege," and that "*Reynolds* therefore cannot be plausibly read to have replaced the categorical *Totten* bar with the balancing of the state secrets evidentiary privilege in the

---

[217] Al-Haramain Islamic Found., Inc. v. Bush, 507 F.3d 1190, 1197 (9th Cir. 2007); *see also* ACLU v. NSA, 493 F.3d 644, 650 n.2 (6th Cir. 2007) ("The State Secrets Doctrine has two applications: a rule of evidentiary privilege and a rule of non-justiciability.") (internal citations omitted); Kasza v. Browner, 133 F.3d 1159 (9th Cir. 1998) (holding that if a plaintiff cannot prove the prima facie elements of one's claim without resort to privileged information, the cause of action may be dismissed).

[218] Totten v. United States, 92 U.S. 105 (1876).

[219] *Id.*

[220] *Id.*

[221] *Id.* at 107 (emphasis added).

[222] *Id.* at 107.

[223] Tenet v. Doe, 544 U.S. 1 (2005).

[224] *Id.* at 3-5.

[225] *Id.* at 5.

[226] *Id.* at 10.

distinct class of cases that depend upon clandestine spy relationships."[227] Thus, lawsuits premised on alleged espionage agreements remain a special category of cases over which the courts lack jurisdiction, and therefore must be "dismissed on the pleadings without ever reaching the question of evidence."[228] Finally, the *Totten* bar is not limited to cases premised on a plaintiff's espionage relationship with the government, but extends to cases where the very subject matter of a lawsuit is a matter of state secret.[229]

A third category of cases has been recognized requiring dismissal under *Reynolds*. This class of cases includes those where the court determines that litigation would potentially result in an "unacceptable risk of disclosing state secrets."[230] Dismissal is warranted "if state secrets are so central to a proceeding that it cannot be litigated without threatening their disclosure."[231]

Analysis of the state secrets privilege generally involves three steps. First, the district court must "ascertain that the procedural requirements for invoking the state secrets privilege have been satisfied."[232] *Reynolds* requires the government to make a "formal claim of privilege, lodged by the head of the department which has control over the matter, after actual personal consideration by that officer."[233] Second, after a court has confirmed that the *Reynolds* procedural requirements are satisfied, it must make an independent determination of whether the information is privileged from disclosure.[234] The court is required to grant the government's assertion of privilege if it is satisfied "from all the circumstances of the case that there is a reasonable danger that compulsion of the evidence will expose military matters which, in the interest of national security, should not be divulged."[235] Further, while the government is required to submit sufficient information for the court to make a meaningful examination, the determination of whether the state secrets privilege is applicable should be proven without forcing a disclosure of the very thing that the privilege is designed to protect.[236]

In assessing the risk that such a disclosure might pose to national security, a court is required to accord the "utmost deference" to the responsibilities of the executive branch.[237] "Such deference is appropriate not only for constitutional reasons, but also practical ones: the Executive and the intelligence agencies under

---

[227] *Id.* at 8.

[228] *Id.*

[229] *See, e.g.,* Weinberger v. Catholic Action of Haw./Peace Educ. Project, 454 U.S. 139, 146-47 (1981); Mohamed v. Jeppesen Dataplan, Inc., 614 F.3d 1070, 1079 (9th Cir. 2010) (en banc).

[230] *See id.* at 1087; El-Masri v. United States, 479 F.3d 296, 308-09 (4th Cir. 2007).

[231] *Id.* at 308.

[232] *Id.* at 304; *see also* United States v. Reynolds, 345 U.S. 1, 7-8 (1953); Al-Haramain Islamic Found., Inc. v. Bush, 507 F.3d 1190, 1202 (9th Cir. 2007).

[233] *Reynolds*, 345 U.S. at 7-8.

[234] *See El-Masri*, 479 F.3d at 304; *Al-Haramain Islamic Found.*, 507 F.3d at 1202.

[235] *Reynolds*, 345 U.S. at 10.

[236] *See id.* at 7-8; *see also El-Masri*, 479 F.3d at 304; *Al-Haramain Islamic Found.*, 507 F.3d at 1202.

[237] United States v. Nixon, 418 U.S. 683, 710 (1974).

his control occupy a position superior to that of the courts in evaluating the consequences of a release of sensitive information."[238] Further, "[w]here there is a strong showing of necessity, the claim of privilege should not be lightly accepted. . . ."[239] However, "even the most compelling necessity cannot overcome the claim of privilege if the court is ultimately satisfied that military secrets are at stake."[240] In fact, under certain circumstances a court may conclude that an explanation by the government on why a question cannot be answered would itself create an unacceptable threat to national security.[241] In such a case, a court is required to accept the government's claim of privilege under the state secrets doctrine without further demand.[242]

Third, and finally, "the ultimate question to be resolved is how the matter should proceed in light of the successful privilege claim."[243] The effect of the government's successful invocation of privilege "is simply that the evidence is unavailable, as though a witness had died, and the case will proceed accordingly, with no consequences save those resulting from the loss of evidence."[244] In other words, plaintiffs are absolutely prohibited from relying on the privileged evidence to support their legal claim. However, if the information is found to be a privileged state secret, the litigation can proceed if the plaintiffs can prove "the essential facts" of their claims "without resort to material touching upon military secrets."[245] If, on the other hand, "the circumstances make clear that sensitive military secrets will be so central to the subject matter of the litigation that any attempt to proceed will threaten disclosure of the privileged matters," dismissal is the proper remedy.[246]

The courts have regularly granted the government's motions to dismiss, finding that the privileged state secrets were so central to the litigation that any attempt to proceed would threaten to disclose the information.[247] Dismissal is warranted where "the very question on which a case turns is itself a state secret,

---

[238] *El-Masri*, 479 F.3d at 305.

[239] *Reynolds*, 345 U.S. at 11.

[240] *Id.*

[241] *Id.* at 9.

[242] *Id.*

[243] *El-Masri*, 479 F.3d at 304; *see also Al-Haramain Islamic Found.*, 507 F.3d at 1202.

[244] *Al-Haramain Islamic Found.*, 507 F.3d. at 1204 (quoting Ellsberg v. Mitchell, 709 F.2d 51, 64 (D.C. Cir. 1983) (internal citation omitted)).

[245] *Reynolds*, 345 U.S. at 11; *see also El-Masri*, 479 F.3d at 307; *Al-Haramain Islamic Found.*, 507 F.3d at 1204.

[246] *El-Masri*, 479 F.3d at 306 (quoting Sterling v. Tenet, 416 F.3d 338, 348 (4th Cir. 2005) (internal citation omitted)).

[247] *See, e.g., Al-Haramain Islamic Found.*, 507 F.3d at 1205 ("Because we affirm the district court's conclusion that the Sealed Document, along with data concerning surveillance, are privileged, and conclude that no testimony attesting to individual's memories of the document may be admitted to establish the contents of the document, Al-Haramain cannot establish that it has standing, and its claims must be dismissed. . . ."); *El-Masri*, 479 F.3d at 311 ("Even marshaling the evidence necessary to make the requisite showings would implicate privileged state secrets, because El-Masri would need to rely on witnesses whose identities, and evidence the very existence of which, must remain confidential in the interest of national security."); *Sterling*, 416 F.3d at 346-48

IV. Preventing the Disclosure of National Security Information in Litigation

or the circumstances make clear that sensitive military secrets will be so central to the subject matter of the litigation that any attempt to proceed will threaten disclosure of the privileged matters."[248] The critical inquiry is whether the action can be litigated without threatening the disclosure of state secrets. If not, the court should dismiss the action. Further, the court must consider not only whether the plaintiff can establish a prima facie case without resort to the privileged evidence, but whether the defendants could properly defend themselves without using privileged state secrets.[249]

In *El-Masri v. United States*, the plaintiff brought an action, pursuant to *Bivens* and the Alien Tort Statute, against the former Director of the CIA and private transportation companies. The plaintiff alleged that he was illegally detained as part of the CIA's "extraordinary rendition" program, tortured, and subjected to cruel, inhuman, and degrading treatment.[250] The Fourth Circuit affirmed the district court's decision to dismiss the action, holding that dismissal was warranted as plaintiff's claims and the government's defenses could not be fairly litigated without disclosure of state secrets.[251] The court stated:

> To establish a prima facie case, he would be obliged to produce admissible evidence not only that he was detained and interrogated, but that the defendants were involved in his detention and interrogation in a manner that renders them personally liable to him. Such a showing could be made only with evidence that exposes how the CIA organizes, staffs, and supervises its most sensitive operations. . . . Even marshaling the evidence necessary to make the requisite showings would implicate privileged state secrets, because El-Masri would need to rely on witnesses whose identities, and evidence the very existence of which, must remain confidential in the interests of national security.[252]

(affirming dismissal on state secret grounds of Title VII action alleging unlawful discriminatory practices by the CIA); Kasza v. Browner, 133 F.3d 1170 (9th Cir. 1998) (affirming dismissal on state secrets grounds of action alleging that Air Force had unlawfully handled hazardous waste in a classified operating area); Black v. United States, 62 F.3d 115, 118-19 (8th Cir. 1995) (affirming dismissal on state secrets grounds of action alleging that the government had engaged in a "campaign of harassment and psychological attacks" against plaintiff); Bareford v. Gen. Dynamics Corp., 973 F.2d 1138, 1140 (5th Cir. 1992) (affirming dismissal on state secrets grounds of action alleging manufacturing and design defects in military weapons system); Fitzgerald v. Penthouse Int'l, Ltd., 776 F.2d 1236, 1237-38 (4th Cir. 1985) (dismissing cause of action on state secrets grounds of action alleging that a magazine article on classified Navy program had libelously accuse plaintiff of espionage); Halkin v. Helms, 690 F.2d 977, 981 (D.C. Cir. 1982) (affirming dismissal on state secrets grounds of action alleging unlawful CIA surveillance); Farnsworth Cannon, Inc. v. Grimes, 635 F.2d 268, 281 (4th Cir. 1980) (dismissing cause of action on state secrets grounds alleging tortious interference with a classified contract to perform services for the Navy).

[248] *Sterling*, 416 F.3d at 348 (internal citations omitted).
[249] *El-Masri*, 479 F.3d at 309-10.
[250] *Id.* at 296.
[251] *Id.* at 313.
[252] *Id.* at 309.

In *El-Masri*, the court also reasoned that dismissal was warranted because the government could not defend against the plaintiff's allegations without disclosing privileged state secrets.[253] The main avenues of defense available to the government would be to show that 1) the plaintiff was not subject to the mistreatment he alleged; 2) if he was subject to such treatment, the defendants were not involved in it; or 3) if they were involved, the nature of defendants' involvement does not give rise to liability.[254] The court held that any of those three showings would require disclosure of information regarding the means and methods by which the CIA gathers intelligence, which amounted to privileged information.[255] The court stated that "virtually any conceivable response to El-Marsi's allegations would disclose privileged information."[256]

In *Mohamed v. Jeppesen Dataplan, Inc.*, foreign nationals who were allegedly transferred in secret to other countries for detention and interrogation pursuant to the CIA's extraordinary rendition program filed action against Jeppesen Dataplan, Inc. under the Alien Tort Statute.[257] Plaintiffs maintained that Jeppesen, a subsidiary of Boeing, "provided flight planning and logistical support services to the aircraft and crew on all of the flights transporting the five plaintiffs among their various locations of detention and torture."[258] In an en banc decision, the full Ninth Circuit held that the government's assertion of the state secrets privilege required dismissal.[259] The government asserted a privilege over four categories of evidence, which neither it nor Jeppesen should be compelled to disclose:

> [1] information that would tend to confirm or deny whether Jeppesen or any other private entity assisted the CIA with clandestine intelligence activities; [2] information about whether any foreign government cooperated with the CIA in clandestine intelligence activities; [3] information about the scope or operation of the CIA terrorist detention and interrogation program; or [4] any other information concerning CIA clandestine intelligence operations that would tend to reveal intelligence activities, sources, or methods.[260]

The en banc court found that at least some of the matters the government sought to protect from disclosure in the litigation were valid state secrets, and "their disclosure could be expected to cause significant harm to national security."[261]

Having confirmed that the privilege applies, the court considered whether the case must be dismissed under the *Reynolds* privilege. The Ninth Circuit

---

[253] *Id.* at 309-10.
[254] *Id.*
[255] *Id.*
[256] *Id.* at 310.
[257] Mohamed v. Jeppesen Dataplan, Inc., 614 F.3d 1070, 1075 (9th Cir. 2010) (en banc).
[258] *Id.*
[259] *Id.*
[260] *Id.* at 1086.
[261] *Id.*

criticized the Fourth Circuit's decision in *El-Masri* as an "erroneous conflation" of the *Totten* bar's "very subject matter" inquiry with the *Reynolds* privilege, and expressly criticized *Totten* as an ambiguous "judge-made doctrine with extremely harsh consequences."[262] Ultimately, however, the Ninth Circuit determined that dismissal was required under *Reynolds*, as there was "no feasible way to litigate Jeppesen's alleged liability without creating an unjustifiable risk of divulging state secrets."[263]

In recognizing the category of cases requiring dismissal under the state secrets privilege, the Ninth Circuit stated that there exists a point in which the "*Reynolds* privilege converges with the *Totten* bar" to form a "continuum analysis."[264] "A case may fall outside the *Totten* bar and yet it may become clear during the *Reynolds* analysis that dismissal is required at the outset."[265] According to the court, *Reynolds* merges with *Totten* in any case in which litigation would result in an "unacceptable risk of disclosing state secrets."[266] Thus, the state secrets privilege may be invoked to 1) prohibit the disclosure of military matters or other state secrets that could jeopardize national security,[267] 2) dismiss a civil action where the very subject matter of the litigation is a state secret,[268] or 3) dismiss a civil action where there is no feasible way to litigate the action without creating an unjustifiable risk of divulging state secrets.[269]

Finally, the Foreign Intelligence Surveillance Act (FISA), unlike the common law state secrets privilege, provides a detailed regime to determine whether classified information may be disclosed to an "aggrieved person" (including the target of a surveillance order) for the purpose of determining whether the surveillance was lawfully authorized and conducted.[270] The issue raised is whether FISA preempts the state secrets privilege, or whether the privilege could be asserted to preclude the disclosure of secret evidence needed to challenge the legality of a

---

[262] *Id.* at 1088 n.12.

[263] *Id.*

[264] *Id.* at 1083, 1089.

[265] *Id.* at 1089.

[266] *Id.* at 1079. The court stated that even if the government's extraordinary rendition program has been acknowledged by government officials, the program may still be protected by the state secrets privilege. The Ninth Circuit stated: "[P]artial disclosure of the existence and even some aspects of the extraordinary rendition program does not preclude other details from remaining state secrets if *their* disclosure would risk grave harm to national security." *Id.* at 1090 (emphasis in original).

[267] *See* United States v. Reynolds, 345 U.S. 1 (1953).

[268] *See* Totten v. United States, 92 U.S. 105 (1876).

[269] *See Jeppesen Dataplan, Inc.,* 614 F.3d at 1087; El-Masri v. United States, 479 F.3d 196, 309-10 (4th Cir. 2007).

[270] 50 U.S.C. §1806(f) provides that, in cases where "the Attorney General files an affidavit under oath that disclosure or an adversary hearing would harm the national security of the United States," a district court shall conduct an *in camera* and *ex parte* review of the application, order, and other materials relating to, or derived from, an electronic surveillance of an aggrieved person that otherwise might be required, proposed or requested to be disclosed, or suppressed, in connection with a proceeding against the aggrieved person. The purpose of the review is to "determine whether the surveillance of the aggrieved person was lawfully authorized and conducted."

FISA surveillance order under 50 U.S.C. §1806(f).[271] Stated another way, in a proceeding to challenge the legality of a FISA surveillance order, the issue is whether the government may assert the state secrets privilege or whether the matter must be resolved according to the procedures set forth under 50 U.S.C. §1806(f). This issue has not yet been resolved by the courts.

B. Preventing Disclosure in Criminal Litigation

1. Classified Information Procedures Act

The Classified Information Procedures Act (CIPA) was enacted in 1980 "to help ensure that the intelligence agencies are subject to the rule of law and to help strengthen the enforcement of laws designed to protect both national security and civil liberties."[272] CIPA "provides a framework for determining how to proceed with discovery and admissibility of classified information in criminal cases,"[273] so that district courts may rule "on questions of admissibility involving classified information before introduction of the evidence in open court."[274] CIPA establishes procedures for discovery of classified information as well as the use of such information during pretrial and trial proceedings. CIPA's "animating purpose is to harmonize a [criminal] defendant's right to obtain and present exculpatory material with the government's need to withhold information from discovery when disclosure would be inimical to national security."[275] With respect to discovery, CIPA procedures are designed "to protect[ ] and restrict[ ] the discovery of classified information in a way that does not impair the defendant's right to a fair trial."[276]

CIPA contains several provisions that are intended to resolve issues related to the disclosure and use of classified information before trial. For example, §2 provides that after the filing of an indictment, any party may move for a pretrial conference to "consider matters relating to classified information that may

---

[271] *See generally* Al-Haramain Islamic Found., Inc. v. Bush, 507 F.3d 1190 (9th Cir. 2007).

[272] Classified Information Procedures Act (CIPA), 18 U.S.C. App. 3 §§1-16; S. Rep. No. 96-823, at 3 (1980), *reprinted in* 1980 U.S.C.C.A.N. 4294, 4296.

[273] United States v. Sterling, 724 F.3d 482, 515 (4th Cir. 2013). CIPA defines "classified information" as "any information or material that has been determined by the United States Government pursuant to an Executive Order, statute, or regulation, to require protection against unauthorized disclosure for reasons of national security." CIPA, *supra* note 272, §1.

[274] United States v. Sedaghaty, 728 F.3d 885, 904 (9th Cir. 2013) (internal citations omitted).

[275] In re Terrorist Bombings of U.S. Embassies in E. Africa, 552 F.3d 93, 115-16 (2d Cir. 2008).

[276] United States v. Aref, 533 F.3d 72, 78 (2d Cir. 2008); *see also Sterling*, 724 F.3d at 515 ("It was designed to balance the defendant's interest in a fair trial and the government's interest in protecting national security information."); United States v. Pappas, 94 F.3d 795, 799 (2d Cir. 1996) (observing that the purpose of CIPA is to "establish procedures to harmonize a defendant's right to obtain and present exculpatory material upon his trial and the government's right to protect classified material in the national interest") (internal quotations omitted).

arise in connection with the prosecution."[277] Among the issues to be considered at such a hearing are schedules for discovery requests and hearings to determine the relevance and admissibility of classified information.[278]

a. Discovery of Classified Information

Section 4 of CIPA sets forth procedures for redacting or otherwise restricting discovery of classified information. This provision clarifies the district court's power under Federal Rule of Criminal Procedure 16(d)(1) to issue protective orders denying or restricting discovery for "good cause," which includes protecting national security.[279] According to the report on CIPA by the Senate Judiciary Committee, Congress perceived such guidance to be "necessary because some judges [were] reluctant to use their authority [to restrict discovery pursuant to Rule 16(d)(1)]" even though the advisory notes to Rule 16(d)(1) clearly state that "in deciding . . . whether to permit discovery to be 'denied, restricted, or deferred,'" a district court should take into account the need to "protect information vital to the national security."[280]

Section 4 states that, if the discovery to be provided to the defense pursuant to the Federal Rules of Criminal Procedure includes classified information, the district court,

> upon a sufficient showing may authorize the United States to delete specified items of classified information from documents to be made available to the defendant through discovery . . . to substitute a summary of the information for such classified documents, or to substitute a statement admitting relevant facts that the classified information would tend to prove."[281]

Thus, §4 authorizes the district court to permit the government to redact or delete classified information.[282] Alternatively, the court may permit the government to summarize the classified information, or submit a statement admitting

---

[277] 18 U.S.C. App. 3 §2.

[278] *Id.*; *see also* Edward C. Liu & Todd Garvey, Cong. Research Serv., R41742, Protecting Classified Information and the Rights of Criminal Defendants: The Classified Information Procedures Act, at 4 (Apr. 2, 2012).

[279] *See* S. Rep. No. 96-823, at 6 (1980), *reprinted in* 1980 U.S.C.C.A.N. 4294, 4299-4300. The Advisory Committee notes to the 1966 amendment to Rule 16 make clear that "good cause" includes "the protection of information vital to national security." Fed. R. Crim. P. 16 advisory comment n to 1966 amendment. "District courts should take into account . . . the need to 'protect . . . information vital to national security.'" S. Rep. 96-823, at 6 (1980), reprinted in 1980 U.S.C.C.A.N. 4294, 4329-30 (quoting Fed. R. Crim. P. 16 advisory comment n to 1966 amendment).

[280] S. Rep. 96-823, at 6 (1980), reprinted in 1980 U.S.C.C.A.N. 4294, 4329-30 (quoting Fed. R. Crim. P. 16 advisory comment n to 1966 amendment); *see also* In re Terrorist Bombings of U.S. Embassies in E. Africa, 552 F.3d at 122.

[281] 18 U.S.C. App. §4.

[282] *Id.*

"relevant" facts in lieu of providing discovery of the protected information.[283] However, "the protection or restriction of classified information must not impair the defendant's right to a fair trial."[284] At the same time, pursuant to §3, upon motion by the government, the court shall issue an order to protect against the disclosure of any classified information disclosed by the government from being disclosed to the defendant.[285] In other words, while defense counsel may have access to classified information, such information may be withheld from the defendant.

While CIPA does not outright grant the government a privilege to refrain from disclosing classified information, it presupposes such a privilege.[286] "The privilege it presupposes has its origins in the common-law privilege against disclosure of state secrets, which allows the government to withhold from discovery or prohibit disclosure at trial information that would threaten national security."[287] The type of classified information at issue in CIPA falls within the state secrets privilege.[288] However, the state secrets privilege, when invoked in the criminal context, is not absolute and, in certain circumstances, must "give way . . . to a criminal defendant's right to present a meaningful defense."[289]

In a criminal prosecution, there are two important classes of information that the government must disclose to the defendant: *Brady* material and Jencks Act material. In the seminal case of *Brady v. Maryland*, the Supreme Court established an affirmative duty on the prosecution to disclose upon request by the defendant evidence that is "material either to guilt of punishment."[290] In *Brady*, the Court held that failure to disclose evidence that is exculpatory and material to the issue of guilt or punishment deprives a defendant of a fair trial and violates his due process rights, "irrespective of the good faith or bad faith of the prosecution."[291] In *Giglio v. United States*, the Supreme Court extended *Brady*'s application to impeachment evidence.[292] The Court held that a finding of materiality is required

---

[283] *Id.*

[284] *See* United States v. Aref, 533 F.3d 72, 78 (2d Cir. 2008); United States v. O'Hara, 301 F.3d 563, 568 (7th Cir. 2002).

[285] 18 U.S.C. App. §3.

[286] *See* United States v. Abu-Jihaad, 630 F.3d 102, 140 (2d Cir. 2010).

[287] *Id.* at 140-41; *see also Aref*, 533 F.3d at 78 ("The most likely source for the protection of classified information lies in the common-law privilege against disclosure of state secrets."). The House of Representatives Select Committee on Intelligence stated categorically in a report on CIPA that "the common law state secrets privilege is not applicable in the criminal arena." However, the courts have uniformly rejected this view. *See, e.g., Aref*, 533 F.3d at 79 (holding that the cases relied upon by the House Select Committee on Intelligence "do not hold that the Government cannot claim the state-secrets privilege in criminal cases"); United States v. Klimavicius-Viloria, 144 F.3d 1249, 1261 (9th Cir. 1998) (holding that the state secrets privilege applies in CIPA cases).

[288] *See Aref*, 533 F.3d at 79.

[289] *Abu-Jihaad*, 630 F.3d at 141.

[290] Brady v. Maryland, 373 U.S. 83, 87 (1963). For a comprehensive discussion of the rule in *Brady*, see JIMMY GURULÉ, COMPLEX CRIMINAL LITIGATION: PROSECUTING DRUG ENTERPRISES AND ORGANIZED CRIME, at 735 (Juris 3d ed., 2013) [hereinafter GURULÉ, COMPLEX CRIMINAL LITIGATION].

[291] *Brady*, 373 U.S. at 87.

[292] Giglio v. United States, 405 U.S. 150 (1972).

under the rule in *Brady* and the nondisclosure of evidence affecting the credibility of a key government witness falls within this general rule.[293] In *United States v. Agurs*, the Supreme Court further expanded the *Brady* rule, holding that a defendant's failure to request exculpatory evidence does not relieve the government of its legal obligation of disclosure.[294] The Court held that a prosecutor has a constitutional duty to *voluntarily* disclose exculpatory evidence material to the defendant.[295] A defense request is not a prerequisite for the disclosure of *Brady* material.

The Jencks Act, 18 U.S.C. §3500, provides that statements or reports in the possession of the government that were made by a government witness to a law enforcement official and that relate to the witness's testimony at trial are discoverable.[296] However, such material is required to be turned over to the defense only after the witness has testified at trial on direct examination.[297] The Jencks Act imposes three limitations on the disclosure of governmental witness statements:

> First, the terms of the Jencks Act impose a temporal limitation on the disclosure of prior statements made by a prosecution witness to a government agent. Under the Jencks Act, the prosecution is not required to disclose a witness' prior statements until *after* the witness has testified on direct examination. Second, disclosure is not mandated unless the prior statement relates to the witness' testimony on direct examination. Finally, the Jencks Act limits disclosure to only those statements that are truly the witness' own statements, as opposed to a written summary of an interviewing agent.[298]

Classified information that constitutes *Brady* or Jencks Act material is subject to CIPA and may be disclosed to the defendant in a redacted or substituted form.[299]

When considering the government's motion to withhold classified information from discovery, the district court must balance the government's need to protect national security with the constitutional right of a defendant to mount a full defense. In *United States v. Aref*, the Second Circuit set forth the test for determining whether the government is obligated to turn over classified information pursuant to a discovery request.[300] First, the district court must decide whether the classified information in the government's possession is discoverable.[301] Second,

---

[293] *Id*. at 154.

[294] United States v. Agurs, 427 U.S. 97 (1976).

[295] *Id*. at 109.

[296] *See* 18 U.S.C. §3500; *see also* Jencks v. United States, 353 U.S. 657 (1957) (holding that, in a criminal prosecution, the government may not withhold documents relied upon by a government witness, even where disclosure of those documents could threaten national security).

[297] *See* 18 U.S.C. §3500.

[298] GURULÉ, COMPLEX CRIMINAL LITIGATION, *supra* note 290, at 777-78.

[299] *See* United States v. O'Hara, 301 F.3d 563, 569 (7th Cir. 2002) (holding that *in camera* examination and redaction of *Brady* material by the trial court was proper).

[300] United States v. Aref, 533 F.3d 79-80 (2d Cir. 2008)

[301] *See* United States v. Sedaghaty, 728 F.3d 885, 904 (9th Cir. 2013); *Aref*, 533 F.3d at 78.

if the material at issue is discoverable, the court must then determine whether the state secrets privilege applies.[302] The state secrets privilege applies when "(1) there is a reasonable danger that compulsion of the evidence will expose . . . matters which, in the interests of national security, should not be divulged, and (2) the privilege is lodged by the head of the department which has control over the matter, after actual personal consideration by that officer. . . ."[303]

The Fourth Circuit has rejected the requirement that the relevant agency head file a written statement with the district court claiming CIPA protection. In *United States v. Rosen*, the court held that while *Reynolds* requires such a showing in the civil context, CIPA does not require a statement from the relevant agency heads asserting the state secrets privilege to invoke CIPA protection.[304] Finally, once a court finds that the material is discoverable and the state secrets privilege applies, it must decide whether the information is "helpful or material to the defense."[305]

The standard articulated in *Aref* is consistent with *Roviaro v. United States*, where the Supreme Court held that in a criminal case, the government's privilege to withhold the identity of a confidential informant "must give way" when the information is "relevant and helpful to the defense of an accused, or is essential to a fair determination of a cause."[306] The *Aref* court has interpreted "relevant and helpful" under *Roviaro* to mean "material to the defense."[307] Other circuits have adopted the *Roviaro* standard for determining when the state secrets privilege must give way in a CIPA case.[308]

Evidence is "helpful or material" to the defense if it is useful "to counter the government's case or to bolster a defense."[309] However, the courts uniformly hold that to be "helpful" to the accused, the evidence need not satisfy the *Brady* standard for disclosure.[310] "While *Brady* information that is plainly subsumed

---

[302] *See Sedaghaty*, 728 F.3d at 904; United States v. Abu-Jihaad, 630 F.3d 102, 141 (2d Cir. 2010).

[303] *Aref*, 533 F.3d at 80; *see also Sedaghaty*, 728 F.3d at 904.

[304] United States v. Rosen, 557 F.3d 192, 198 (4th Cir. 2009).

[305] *Aref*, 533 F.3d at 80.

[306] Roviaro v. United States, 353 U.S. 53, 60-61 (1957).

[307] *Aref*, 533 F.3d at 79.

[308] *See Sedaghaty*, 728 F.3d at 904; United States v. Varca, 89 F.2d 900, 905 (5th Cir. 1990); United States v. Yunis, 867 F.2d 617, 623 (D.C. Cir. 1989); United States v. Smith, 780 F.2d 1102, 1107-10 (4th Cir. 1985) (en banc); United States v. Pringle, 751 F.2d 419, 427-28 (1st Cir. 1984). In United States v. Amawi, 695 F.3d 457, 470 (6th Cir. 2012), the court articulated a slightly different three-part test for determining whether classified information is discoverable. The Sixth Circuit stated:

> First, the court must assess whether the information "cross[es] the low hurdle of relevance." Second, the court must determine whether "the assertion of privilege by the government is at least a colorable one." Third, because "classified information is not discoverable on a mere showing of theoretical relevance . . . [,] the threshold for discovery in this context further requires that [the information] . . . is at least 'helpful to the defense of [the] accused.'"

[309] *Aref*, 533 F.3d at 80 (internal citations omitted).

[310] *Id.*

within the larger category of information that is 'at least helpful' to the defendant, information can be helpful without being 'favorable' in the *Brady* sense."[311] Moreover, even if the information is "helpful or material," if it is cumulative of other information already disclosed to the defendant, the government is not obligated to turn over the classified documents.[312]

The process of determining whether the evidence is discoverable is complicated by the fact that the defendant is not permitted to see the classified information. "[T]he defendants and their counsel, who are in the best position to know whether information would be helpful to their defense, are disadvantaged by not being permitted to see the information—and thus to assist the court in its assessment of the information's helpfulness."[313] Instead, the district court must place itself in the shoes of the defendant, and act with a view to his interests.[314]

The district court may consider the government's arguments for withholding or protecting discovery of classified information *ex parte* and *in camera*.[315] Every court that has considered the issue has held that CIPA §4 permits *ex parte* hearings.[316] While §4 does not expressly provide for *ex parte* hearings, "[i]n a case involving classified documents . . . ex parte, in camera hearings in which government counsel participates to the exclusion of defense counsel are part of the process that the district court may use in order to decide the relevancy of the information."[317] Because the "government is seeking to withhold classified information from the defendant, an adversary hearing with the defense's knowledge would defeat the very purpose of the discovery rules."[318] Ultimately, if the district court rules against the government and permits discovery, upon motion of the government, the court shall issue a protective order prohibiting the disclosure of any classified information disclosed by the United States to a criminal defendant.[319]

---

[311] United States v. Mejia, 448 F.3d 436, 456-57 (D.C. Cir. 2006); *see also Amawi*, 695 F.3d at 471; *Aref*, 533 F.3d at 80.

[312] *See* United States v. Abu-Jihaad, 630 F.3d 102, 141 (2d Cir. 2010) (district court did not abuse its discretion in determining that the government need not disclose classified information that was cumulative of other discovery); *Smith*, 780 F.2d at 1110 ("A district court may order disclosure only when the information is at least 'essential to the defense,' 'necessary to his defense,' and neither merely cumulative nor corroborative.").

[313] *Mejia*, 448 F.3d at 458.

[314] *Id.*

[315] *Id.*

[316] *See Amawi*, 695 F.3d at 472 (citing cases).

[317] United States v. Klimavicius-Viloria, 144 F.3d 1249, 1261 (9th Cir. 1998); *see also Amawi*, 695 F.3d at 472 (CIPA §4 permits *ex parte* proceedings); United States v. Campa, 529 F.3d 980, 995 (11th Cir. 2008) (observing that "[t]he right that section four confers on the government [to seek deletion or substitution] would be illusory if defense counsel were allowed to participate in section four proceedings because defense counsel would be able to see the information that the government asks the district court to keep from defense counsel's view").

[318] United States v. Aref, 533 F.3d 72, 81 (2d Cir. 2008) (quoting H.R. Rep. 96-831, pt. 1, at 27 n.22).

[319] 18 U.S.C. App. 3, §3.

Finally, if the district court rejects the government's arguments and authorizes the disclosure of classified information or refuses a protective order sought by the government, the government may file an interlocutory appeal with the court of appeals challenging such ruling.[320] The district court's decision based on the "relevant and helpful" standard is reviewed for abuse of discretion.[321]

b. Use of Classified Information During Pretrial or Trial Proceedings

If a defendant expects to disclose or cause the disclosure of classified information at trial or in a pretrial proceeding, he is required, pursuant to §5 of CIPA, to notify the district court and the government of the potential disclosure.[322] If a defendant fails to provide such notice, he may be penalized and prohibited from using such evidence at trial.[323] Further, pursuant to CIPA §5(a), a defendant is prohibited from disclosing classified information until 1) proper notice has been given, 2) the government has been afforded "a reasonable opportunity to seek" a CIPA §6 determination from the court (see below), and 3) the government's time to initiate an interlocutory appeal under CIPA §7 has expired.[324]

Under CIPA §6(a), the government may move for a hearing in the district court "to make all determinations concerning the use, relevance, or admissibility of classified information that would otherwise be made during the trial or pretrial proceedings."[325] Such hearing shall be held *in camera* if the Attorney General certifies to the court that a public proceeding may result in the disclosure of classified information.[326] If the court authorizes disclosure of classified information, the government may then move the court, under CIPA §6(c)(1), to order "the substitution for such classified information of a statement admitting relevant facts that the specific classified information would tend to prove" or "the substitution for such classified information of a summary of the specific classified information."[327] The court must conduct a hearing on any §6(c)(1) motion, and it "shall grant such a motion . . . if it finds that the statement or summary will provide the

---

[320] *See* CIPA, *supra* note 272, §7. Section 7(a) provides:

> An interlocutory appeal by the United States . . . shall lie to a court of appeals from a decision or order of a district court in a criminal case authorizing the disclosure of classified information, imposing sanctions for nondisclosure of classified information, or refusing a protective order sought by the United States to prevent the disclosure of classified information.

[321] *See Amawi*, 695 F.3d at 470; *Aref*, 533 F.3d at 80.
[322] 18 U.S.C. App. §5(a).
[323] *Id.* §5(b).
[324] *See* United States v. Rosen, 557 F.3d 192, 195 (4th Cir. 2009).
[325] 18 U.S.C. App. §6.
[326] *Id.*
[327] *Id.* §6(c)(1).

IV. Preventing the Disclosure of National Security Information in Litigation

defendant with substantially the same ability to make his defense as would disclosure of the specific classified information."[328] The substitution need not be of "'precise, concrete equivalence,'" and the "'fact that insignificant tactical advantages could accrue to the defendant by the use of the specified classified information should not preclude the court from ordering alternative disclosure.'"[329] However, the fundamental purpose of a substitution under CIPA is "to place the defendant, as nearly as possible, in position he would be in if the classified information . . . were available to him."[330] Further, "it is a fundamental principle underlying CIPA that the summary should be evenhanded, worded in a neutral fashion and not tilted or shaded to the government's advantage."[331] More specifically, proposed substitutions should be rejected by a court if the substitutions exclude non-cumulative exculpatory information and fail to provide the defendant with substantially the same ability to make his defense as would the disclosure of the specific classified information.[332]

Generally, CIPA is implicated when the defendant seeks to obtain or plans to disclose national security information, and the government opposes disclosure.[333] However, "evidence sought to be admitted at trial by the government, like that proffered by the defense, is subject to the protections afforded by CIPA."[334] In *United States v. Abu Ali*, the Fourth Circuit declared:

> If classified information is to be relied upon as evidence of guilt, the district court may consider steps to protect some or all of the information from unnecessary public disclosure in the interest of national security and in accordance with CIPA, which specifically contemplates such methods as redactions and substitutions so long as these alternatives do not deprive the defendant of a fair trial.[335]

The government is authorized, pursuant to CIPA §7, to file an interlocutory appeal from any ruling of the court "authorizing the disclosure of classified

---

[328] *Id.*

[329] United States v. Sedaghaty, 728 F.3d 885, 905 (9th Cir. 2013) (quoting H.R. Rep. No. 96-1436, at 12-13 (1980) (Conf. Rep.), *reprinted in* 1980 U.S.C.C.A.N. at 4310-11).

[330] United States v. Moussaoui, 382 F.3d 453, 477 (4th Cir. 2004); *see also* United States v. Rezaq, 134 F.3d 1121, 1143 (D.C. Cir. 1998) (approving substitutions where "[n]o information was omitted from [them] that might have been helpful to [the] defense, and the discoverable documents had no unclassified features that might have been disclosed").

[331] *Sedaghaty*, 728 F.3d at 906 (finding that the "summary is inadequate not only because of its slanted wording but more fundamentally because it is incomplete"); *see also Moussaoui*, 382 F.3d at 478-79 (rejecting proposed substitution that failed to include exculpatory information); United States v. Fernandez, 913 F.2d 148 (4th Cir. 1990) (upholding rejection of proposed substitutions that "would have required the jury to judge [the defendant's] role . . . and thus the truth of his statements about it, in a contextual vacuum").

[332] *See Moussaoui*, 382 F.3d at 478-79.

[333] United States v. Sterling, 724 F.3d 482, 515 (4th Cir. 2013).

[334] *Id.*

[335] United States v. Abu Ali, 528 F.3d 210, 255 (4th Cir. 2008).

information."[336] Finally, the district court's determinations regarding the relevance and admissibility of evidence are subject to judicial review for abuse of discretion.[337] Such decisions are accorded great deference, and may be overturned only "under the most extraordinary circumstances."[338]

---

[336] *See* United States v. Rosen, 557 F.3d 192, 195 (4th Cir. 2009); United States v. Fernandez, 887 F.2d 465, 469-70 (4th Cir. 1989) (recognizing that CIPA §7 authorizes interlocutory appeals from adverse §6(a) and §6(c)(1) rulings).

[337] *Rosen*, 557 F.3d at 199 (stating that the reviewing court may not substitute its judgment for that of the trial court, "which has been immersed in these proceedings for many months and has far more familiarity with the matter than we do").

[338] *Id.* (internal citations omitted).

CHAPTER 11

Economic Sanctions and Terrorist Financing

I. INTERNATIONAL EMERGENCY ECONOMIC POWERS ACT

The International Emergency Economic Powers Act (IEEPA)[1] was enacted in 1977 to amend the Trading with the Enemy Act of 1917 (TWEA).[2] The TWEA grants the President the authority to regulate financial transactions involving enemy nations, including their nationals and allies, during a "time of war."[3] The TWEA's purpose is to deprive enemies of economic benefits by restricting their ability to trade in the United States.[4] However, the TWEA has not always been limited to times of war, and was used to regulate international trade during a "national emergency" for many years.[5] The TWEA was first used in peacetime in 1933, during the Great Depression, when President Franklin D. Roosevelt proclaimed a bank holiday. The bank holiday closed all the banks in the United States in response to what was deemed to be a national emergency related to "extensive speculative activity abroad in foreign exchange . . . [resulting] in severe drains on the Nation's stocks of gold."[6] The bank closures interfered with both foreign and domestic financial transactions. Congress immediately ratified the action and amended §5(b) of the TWEA, extending the emergency powers granted to the President under the original legislation to cover both wartime and "any other

---

[1] The International Emergency Economic Powers Act, 50 U.S.C. §§1701 *et seq*. The IEEPA was enacted by Congress in 1977 and amended by the Uniting and Strengthening America by Providing Appropriate Tools Required to Intercept and Obstruct Terrorism Act of 2001, Pub. L. No. 107-56, 115 Stat. 272 [hereinafter USA PATRIOT Act].

[2] *See* Trading with the Enemy Act of 1917, ch. 106, 40 Stat. 411-426 (codified as amended at 50 U.S.C. App. §§1-44 (2007)).

[3] *Id.*, 50 U.S.C. App. § 5(b)(1). TWEA excludes U.S. citizens and corporations incorporated in the United States from its definition of "enemy." *Id.*, §§2(c) & (a).

[4] *See* KindHearts v. Geithner, 647 F. Supp. 2d 857, 875 (N.D. Ohio 2009).

[5] *See* United States v. Amirnazmi, 645 F.3d 564, 572 (3d Cir. 2011).

[6] *See* M. Maureen Murphy, Cong. Research Serv., RL34254, Executive Order 13438: Blocking Property of Certain Persons Who Threaten Stabilization Efforts in Iraq (2011) (quoting Proclamation No. 2039, 48 Stat. 1689 (Mar. 6, 1933)) [hereinafter CRS Report, Executive Order 13438].

I. International Emergency Economic Powers Act

period of national emergency declared by the President."[7] The 1933 amendment essentially provided the President authority to regulate purely domestic transactions.[8]

The TWEA was amended again in 1940, this time authorizing the President to freeze certain assets. The 1940 amendment went beyond financial transactions with enemies or allies of enemies and extended the TWEA to cover transactions in which any *foreign state or foreign national* has any interest.[9] Further, a 1941 amendment to the TWEA gave the Executive the power to seize and vest title of any property subject to the jurisdiction of the United States belonging to a foreign person or nation.[10] In *Silesian-American Corp. v. Clark*, the Supreme Court upheld the seizing and vesting of property belonging to a non-enemy alien in wartime.[11] The Supreme Court in *Propper v. Clark* also upheld the authority of the Treasury Department to vest assets of an enemy (Austrian) entity, making those assets unavailable to U.S. creditors.[12] Moreover, the freezing order at issue in *Propper v. Clark* nullified any subsequent judicial attempt to collect the Austrian entity's assets through a receiver appointed by the court so that the assets could be distributed to U.S. creditors. The Court declared:

> Through the Trading with the Enemy Act, in its various forms, the nation sought to deprive enemies, actual or potential, of the opportunity to secure advantages to themselves or to perpetrate wrongs against the United States or its citizens through the use of assets that happened to be in this country. To do so has necessitated some inconvenience to our citizens and others who, as here, are not involved in any actions adverse to the nation's interest.[13]

In 1977, Congress amended §5(b) of TWEA, essentially repealing the 1933 amendment by restricting the Executive's authority to use the TWEA to times of declared war—as provided in the original Act.[14] Contemporaneously, Congress enacted IEEPA, which authorizes the Executive to impose economic sanctions during national-emergency situations.[15] "The IEEPA limited the TWEA's application to periods of declared wars and to certain existing TWEA programs, while

---

[7] Act of March 9, 1933, ch. 1, §2, 48 Stat. 1.

[8] *Id.* President Roosevelt invoked TWEA again in peacetime, when Hitler was advancing in Europe, to block the assets of Norway and Denmark and their nationals. *See* CRS Report, Executive Order 13438, *supra* note 6, at 4.

[9] Joint Resolution of May 7, 1940, ch. 185, §2, 54 Stat., at 179; *see also* CRS Report, Executive Order 13438, *supra* note 6, at 5.

[10] Act of December 18, 1941, ch. 593, §301, 55 Stat. 838, 839-41, 77th Cong., 1st Sess.

[11] Silesian-Am. Corp. v. Clark, 332 U.S. 469 (1947).

[12] Propper v. Clark, 337 U.S. 472 (1949).

[13] *Id.* at 481-82.

[14] Pub. L. No. 95-223, tit. I, §101, 91 Stat. 1625 (1977) (striking "or during any other period of national emergency declared by the President" from the text of §5(b)).

[15] *See id.* at tit. II, 91 Stat. at 1626 (codified at 50 U.S.C. §§1701 et seq.).

the IEEPA was applicable during other times of declared national emergencies."[16]

The IEEPA grants the President a considerable breadth of authority to impose economic sanctions to deal with peacetime emergencies originating abroad. To use these powers, the President must declare a national emergency with respect to "any unusual and extraordinary threat, which has its source in whole or in substantial part outside of the United States, to the national security, foreign policy or economy of the United States."[17] Once a national emergency is declared, the IEEPA provides the President broad powers to impose controls over economic transactions and property in which a foreign nation or foreign person has any interest.[18]

Under the IEEPA, economic sanctions may be imposed against transactions and property in which a foreign nation or foreign person has an interest. More specifically, the President may block 1) any foreign exchange transaction, 2) any transfer of credit or payments involving any interest of a foreign state or national thereof, and 3) the import or export of currency or securities, subject to the jurisdiction of the United States.[19] For example, U.S. banks, as well as U.S. branches of foreign banks, could be prohibited from conducting a financial transaction exchanging foreign currency for U.S. dollars to the extent that such a transaction involves any interest of a sanctioned foreign country or national thereof.[20] Further, a U.S.-based bank could be prohibited from engaging in any transaction involving any funds in which a foreign country or national thereof has any interest. Also, "during the pendency of an investigation," the President may block any transaction involving any property subject to the jurisdiction of the United States

---

[16] Islamic Am. Relief Agency v. Unidentified FBI Agents, 394 F. Supp. 2d 34, 41 (D.D.C. 2005); *see also* Regan v. Wald, 468 U.S. 222, 227-28 (1984). According to the Senate Report accompanying the legislation, the IEEPA was enacted in direct response to the Executive's expanding use of the TWEA's emergency powers:

> The purpose of the bill is to revise and delimit the President's authority to regulate international economic transactions during wars or national emergencies. The bill is a response to two developments: first: extensive use by Presidents of emergency authority under section 5(b) of the Trading With the Enemy Act of 1917 to regulate both domestic and international economic transactions unrelated to a declared state of emergency and, second, passage of [the National Emergencies Act of 1976], which provides safeguards for the role of Congress in declaring and terminating national emergencies, but exempts section 5(b) of the Trading With the Enemy Act from its coverage.

S. Rep. No. 95-466, 95th Cong., 1st Sess. 2 (1977).

[17] 50 U.S.C. §1701(b). The statute emphasizes that "[t]he authorities granted to the President . . . may only be exercised to deal with an unusual and extraordinary threat with respect to which a national emergency has been declared for purposes of this chapter and may not be exercised for any other purpose. Any exercise of such authorities to deal with any new threat shall be based on a new declaration of national emergency which must be with respect to such threat." *Id.*

[18] *Id.* §1702(a)(1).

[19] *Id.*

[20] *Id.* §1702(a)(1)(A)(i).

in which any foreign country or national thereof has any interest.[21] Simply stated, once the President has declared a national emergency with respect to a particular threat, the IEEPA authorizes the blocking of financial transactions and property to protect against that threat.[22] Finally, the IEEPA was amended by the USA PATRIOT Act in 2001 to permit the vesting of property—in other words, allowing the Executive to take title to blocked or frozen property.[23]

The President exercises the powers authorized under the IEEPA through a three-step process. First, the President issues an executive order declaring a national emergency (or reaffirming a previous declaration) involving the national security, foreign policy, or economy of the United States.[24] The order describes the nature of the national emergency and the foreign country, persons, and

---

[21] *Id.* §1702(a)(1)(A)(ii).

[22] Islamic Am. Relief Agency v. Gonzales, 477 F.3d 728, 735 (D.C. Cir. 2007). IEEPA §1702(a)(1) authorizes the President to:

    (A) Investigate, regulate, or prohibit—
        (i) any transaction in foreign exchange,
        (ii) transfers of credit or payments between, by, or through, or to any banking institution, to the extent that such transfers or payments involve any interest of any foreign country or a national thereof; and
        (iii) the importing or exporting of currency or securities, by any person, or with respect to any property subject to the jurisdiction of the United States;
    (B) investigate, block during pendency of an investigation, regulate, direct and compel, nullify, void, prevent or prohibit, any acquisition, holding, withholding, use, transfer, withdrawal, transportation, importation or exportation of, or dealing in, or exercising any right, power, or privilege with respect to, or transactions involving, any property in which any foreign country or a national thereof has any interest by any person, or with respect to any property, subject to the jurisdiction of the United States.

[23] The IEEPA now provides:

[T]he President may . . . when the United States is engaged in armed hostilities or has been attacked by a foreign country or foreign nationals, confiscate any property, subject to the jurisdiction of the United States, of any foreign person, foreign organization, or foreign country that [the President] determines has planned, authorized, aided, or engaged in such hostilities or attacks against the United States; and all right, title, and interest in any property so confiscated shall vest, when, as and upon the terms directed by the President, in such agency or person as the President may designate from time to time, and upon such terms and conditions as the President may prescribe, such interest or property shall be held, used, administered, liquidated, sold, or otherwise dealt with in the interest of and for the benefit of the United States, and such designated agency or person may perform any and all acts incident to the accomplishment or furtherance of these purposes.

50 U.S.C. §1702(a)(1)(C).

[24] *See, e.g.,* Exec. Order No. 13,224, Blocking Property and Prohibiting Transactions with Persons Who Commit, Threaten to Commit, or Support Terrorism, 66 Fed. Reg. 49,079 (Sept. 23, 2001) (authorizing blocking all property and interests in property of foreign persons determined "to have committed or to pose a significant risk of committing, acts of terrorism that threaten the security of U.S. nationals or the national security, foreign policy, or economy of the United States") [hereinafter E.O. 13224]; Exec. Order No. 12,947, Prohibiting Transactions with Terrorists Who Threaten to Disrupt the Middle East Peace Process, 60 Fed. Reg. 5,079 (Jan. 25, 1995) [hereinafter E.O. 12947].

entities that are covered by the order.[25] The executive order usually includes an initial list of individuals and entities subject to economic sanctions.[26] The order also delegates the task of implementing the economic sanctions to the Secretary of State or Secretary of the Treasury.[27] Second, the cabinet member charged with implementation of the order may designate additional foreign individuals or entities meeting the sanctions criteria in, and so covered by, the executive order.[28] Third, the Treasury Department's Office of Foreign Assets Control (OFAC)—the executive agency charged with enforcement of economic sanctions—orders the blocking of all property of, and transactions involving, the designated individuals and entities.[29] OFAC "administers economic and trade sanctions based on U.S. foreign policy and national security goals against targeted foreign countries, terrorists, international narcotics traffickers, and those engaged in activities related to the proliferation of weapons of mass destruction."[30] OFAC publishes a list of Specially Designated Nationals (SDN List), which contains the names of thousands of individuals and entities whose property is blocked and with which U.S. persons are prohibited from dealing.[31] Ultimately, OFAC is responsible for ensuring compliance with any executive order imposing economic sanctions.

The IEEPA contains several exemptions and constraints. First, the authority granted to the President does not extend to regulating or prohibiting donations of food, clothing, and medicine intended to be used to relieve human suffering unless the President determines that such humanitarian aid "would seriously impair his ability to deal with" the national emergency or would endanger U.S.

---

[25] *See* E.O. 13224, *supra* note 24; E.O. 12947, *supra* note 24.

[26] For example, in an Annex to E.O 13224, President Bush identified 12 individuals and 15 entities whose assets were to be blocked under the order. The annex included "core members of al Qaeda, affiliated terrorist groups, Islamic charities suspected of funding al Qaeda, and other businesses believed to be a front for al Qaeda." JIMMY GURULÉ, UNFUNDING TERROR: THE LEGAL RESPONSE TO THE FINANCING OF GLOBAL TERRORISM 195 (2008) [hereinafter GURULÉ, UNFUNDING TERROR]. Twelve terrorist organizations were named in the Annex to E.O. 12947, *supra* note 24.

[27] *See, e.g.,* E.O. 13224, *supra* note 24, which delegates the authority for implementing the economic sanctions to both the Secretary of the Treasury and the Secretary of State.

[28] *See* U.S. Treasury Dep't, OFAC, Archive of Specially Designated Nationals Changes, http://www.ustreasgov/offices/enforcement/ofac/sdn/archive.shtml; *see also* Eric Sandberg-Zakian, *Counterterrorism, The Constitution, and The Civil-Criminal Divide: Evaluating the Designation of U.S. Persons Under the International Emergency Economic Powers Act*, 48 HARV. J. LEG. 95, 100 (2011).

[29] *See* U.S. Treasury Dep't, OFAC, *Terrorist Assets Report, Twenty-first Annual Report to Congress on Assets in the United States of Terrorist Countries and International Terrorism Program Designees* 1 (2012) [hereinafter *Terrorist Assets Report*].

[30] U.S. Department of the Treasury, Terrorism and Financial Intelligence, OFAC, "Mission," http://www.treasury.gov/about/organizational-structure/offices/Pages/Office-of-Foreign-Assets-Control .aspx (last visited Jan. 30, 2014).

[31] *See* U.S. Treasury Dep't, SDN List, *available at* http://www.treasury.gov/resource-center/ sanctions/SDN-List/Pages/default.aspz (last visited Feb. 25, 2014). The SDN List categorizes the Specially Designated Nationals (SDNs) according to the reason and authority for their listing, *e.g.*, a Specially Designated Global Terrorist (SDGT) is listed pursuant to the Global Terrorism Sanctions Regulations. *See* 31 C.F.R. §594.

armed forces.[32] Consequently, if the order does not specifically state otherwise, humanitarian aid is generally exempted from blocking. Second, the IEEPA provides no explicit authority over purely domestic transactions. Rather, the IEEPA's authority over financial transactions extends only to "such transfers or payments involv[ing] any interest of any foreign country or a national thereof."[33] Third, the IEEPA provides no authority to regulate gold and silver bullion.[34] Fourth, the IEEPA does not authorize the seizure of business records.[35] Fifth, the IEEPA provides no authority to interfere with international communications.[36] Finally, OFAC may grant specific or general licenses allowing certain individuals or entities to engage in transactions otherwise prohibited by an executive order.[37]

Under 50 U.S.C. §1705(a), it is "unlawful for a person to violate, attempt to violate, conspire to violate, or cause a violation of any license, order, regulation or prohibition" issued pursuant to the IEEPA.[38] The IEEPA provides for a civil penalty up to $250,000 or twice the amount of the culpable transaction for each IEEPA violation.[39] A willful violation of IEEPA is a criminal offense. A person who "willfully" violates, attempts, conspires to commit, or aids and abets a violation of any license, order, regulation, or prohibition issued under the IEEPA can be fined up to $1 million or imprisoned for not more than 20 years, or both.[40] In order to sustain a conviction for a willful violation, the government must prove beyond a reasonable doubt that the defendant acted with knowledge "that his conduct was unlawful," but need not prove that the defendant was aware of a specific statutory or regulatory duty.[41]

---

[32] 50 U.S.C. §1702(b)(2).

[33] *Id.* §1702(a)(1)(A)(ii).

[34] Section 5(b) of the TWEA authorizes the President to regulate "the importing, exporting, hoarding, melting, or earmarking of gold or silver coin or bullion." 50 U.S.C. App. §5(b)(1)(A). However, similar language is not contained in the IEEPA.

[35] The TWEA requires "if necessary to the national security or defense, the *seizure,* of any books of account, records, contracts, letters, memoranda, or other papers, in the custody or control of" persons required to keep reports on covered transactions. *Id.* §5(b)(1)(B) (emphasis added). IEEPA only provides the President authority to compel recordkeeping and the production of records. 50 U.S.C. §1702(a)(2).

[36] Section 3 of the TWEA includes authority to censor international communications. 50 U.S.C. App. §3. In contrast, the IEEPA states that "[t]he authority granted to the President by this section does not include the authority to regulate or prohibit, directly or indirectly . . . any postal, telegraphic, telephonic or other personal communication, which does not involve a transfer of anything of value." 50 U.S.C. §1702(b)(1).

[37] *See* 31 C.F.R. §560.501; *see also* United States v. Mousavi, 604 F.3d 1084, 1090 (9th Cir. 2010). Section 1704 of the IEEPA authorizes the President to issue "such regulations, including regulations prescribing definitions, as may be necessary for the exercise of the authorities granted. . . ." 50 U.S.C. §1704.

[38] *Id.* §1705(a).

[39] *Id.* §1705(b).

[40] *Id.* §1705(c).

[41] *See* United States v. Mousavi, 604 F.3d at 1093-94; *see also* United States v. Homa Int'l Trading Corp., 387 F.3d 144, 147 & n. 2 (2d Cir. 2004) (per curiam) (holding that to support a willful violation of IEEPA and the OFAC's Iranian Transaction Regulations (ITR), the government was not required "to prove that [defendant] knew he was not a depository institution entitled to avail

However, proof of "willfulness" is not required for the IEEPA's civil provisions.[42]

The IEEPA authorizes the President to block the transfer of any property in which a foreign national has "any interest."[43] The term "interest" means an "interest of any nature whatsoever, direct or indirect."[44] Further, the terms "property" and "property interest" have been defined to include currency, negotiable instruments, "evidence of title," and "contracts of any nature whatsoever, and any other property, real, personal, or mixed, tangible or intangible, or interest or interests therein, present, future, or contingent."[45] Courts have broadly construed the term "any interest" as used in the IEEPA.[46] The statute does not require that a foreign national have a legally enforceable interest in targeted assets.[47] "A beneficial interest in the entity's assets may suffice."[48] Further, "any interest" includes domestic corporations where foreign nationals occupy key executive positions or sit on the entity's board of directors.[49]

While the IEEPA authorizes the imposition of economic sanctions against any foreign country or a national thereof, the statute "does not require that the foreign

---

itself of an expressed exception to the [Iranian] Embargo" because "the law does not require such a negative finding by the jury to establish willfulness"); United States v. Dien Duc Huynh, 246 F.3d 734, 739, 744 (5th Cir. 2001) (the IEEPA's "willfulness" requirement was met where defendant "knew that there was an embargo in place against Vietnam, [and a witness] testified that [the defendant] told him he was shipping goods to Vietnam by way of Singapore because of the embargo"); United States v. Quinn, 403 F. Supp. 2d 57, 61 (D.D.C. 2005) (proof of "willfulness" under §1705(c) of the IEEPA does not require knowledge of licensing requirement under the ITR). *But see* United States v. Zhi Yong Guo, 634 F.3d 1119, 1123 (9th Cir. 2011) (rejecting defendant's unconstitutional vagueness challenging, arguing that the scienter requirement in §1705(c) of the IEEPA alleviates any constitutional concerns because to convict for willfully violating §1705(a), "the government was required to prove beyond a reasonable doubt that Defendant knew that a license was required for the export of the particular thermal imaging camera he was dealing with, and that Defendant intended to violate the law by exporting or attempting to export such a thermal imaging camera to China without such a license").

[42] *See* Humanitarian Law Project v. U.S. Dep't of Treasury, 578 F.3d 1133 (9th Cir. 2009).

[43] 50 U.S.C. §1702(a)(1)(B); *see also* Holy Land Found. for Relief & Dev. v. Ashcroft, 219 F. Supp. 2d 57, 67 (D.D.C. 2002). The discussion of the meaning of "any interest" in IEEPA is taken in part from JIMMY GURULÉ & GEOFFREY CORN, THE LEGAL PRINCIPLES OF COUNTER-TERRORISM LAW 299-300 (2011) [hereinafter GURULÉ & CORN, PRINCIPLES OF COUNTER-TERRORISM LAW].

[44] 31 C.F.R. §535.312.

[45] *Id.* §535.311.

[46] *See, e.g.,* Regan v. Wald, 468 U.S. 222, 225-26, 233-34 (1984) (the phrase "any interest" must be broadly construed); KindHearts v. Geithner, 647 F. Supp. 2d 857, 887 (N.D. Ohio 2009).

[47] *See* Global Relief Found., Inc. v. O'Neill, 315 F.3d 748, 753 (7th Cir. 2002); *KindHearts,* 647 F. Supp. 2d at 887.

[48] *Id.* (citing *Global Relief Found., Inc. v. O'Neill,* 315 F.3d at 753).

[49] *See KindHearts,* 647 F. Supp. 2d at 887 (holding that having a board position in a domestic corporation "satisfies the requirement . . . that a foreign national have an interest in the organization"); *see also id.* (the President of KindHearts was a foreign national); Global Relief Found., Inc. v. O'Neill, 315 F.3d at 752-53 (two of the board members were foreign nationals); Al Haramain Islamic Found., Inc. v. U.S. Dep't of Treasury, 585 F. Supp. 2d 1233, 1261 (D. Or. 2008) (foreign nationals served as the President and Treasurer).

I. International Emergency Economic Powers Act

nation be sanctioned prior to blocking the assets of a foreign national,"[50] or that the foreign person or entity itself pose an "unusual or extraordinary threat" to national security.[51] Courts have consistently rejected the argument that the IEEPA requires that blocked individuals have a nexus with a sanctioned nation in order to be blocked.[52] Thus, the IEEPA permits sanctions against a national of a foreign country the United States has never sanctioned.

Further, under the IEEPA, the beneficial interest that a foreign national holds in a U.S. corporation may be blocked. In *Global Relief Foundation, Inc. v. O'Neill*, the Seventh Circuit upheld the blocking of an Islamic charity incorporated in the United States.[53] The court rejected plaintiff's argument that the IEEPA does not apply to corporations incorporated in the United States.[54] Instead, the court decided that the "focus must be on how assets could be controlled and used, not on bare legal ownership."[55] In applying that reasoning, the court found that "[Global Relief Foundation] conducts its operations outside the United States; the funds are applied for the benefit of non-citizens and thus are covered by §1702(a)(1)(B)."[56] Also, the government may use classified information in making designation determinations without disclosing such information to the designee.[57]

There are three ways in which persons whose property interests have been blocked may challenge the blocking orders. First, they may claim that their identity was mistaken and seek to have the blocked property released through the procedures specified by OFAC in 31 C.F.R. §501.806. Second, a designated individual may challenge the sufficiency of the evidence supporting the blocking action. Finally, a blocked individual may assert that the circumstances that led to the designation no longer apply.[58] Upon receiving a petition for reconsideration, OFAC will review the written request and arguments submitted, then provide the petitioner with a written response.[59] If the request is denied, the OFAC decision may be further challenged in federal court. OFAC's denial will be upheld as long as the court finds that the blocking action was supported by substantial evidence and not "arbitrary and capricious."[60]

---

[50] *Al Haramain Islamic Found.*, 585 F. Supp. 2d at 1260.

[51] *See* Islamic Am. Relief Agency v. Gonzales, 477 F.3d at 735.

[52] *See Al Haramain Islamic Found.*, 585 F. Supp. 2d at 1260; *KindHearts*, 647 F. Supp. 2d at 886.

[53] *See* Global Relief Found., Inc. v. O'Neill, 315 F.3d at 753.

[54] *Id.* at 752.

[55] *Id.* at 753.

[56] *Id.*

[57] *See* Al Haramain Islamic Found., Inc. v. U.S. Dep't of Treasury, 686 F.3d 965, 982 (9th Cir. 2011); *see also* Holy Land Found. for Relief & Dev. v. Ashcroft, 333 F.3d 156, 164 (D.C. Cir. 2003); Global Relief Found., Inc. v. O'Neill, 315 F.3d at 754; KindHearts v. Geithner, 710 F. Supp. 2d 637, 660 (N.D. Ohio 2010) [hereinafter *KindHearts II*]; Al-Aqeel v. Paulson, 568 F. Supp. 2d 64, 72 (D.D.C. 2008).

[58] 31 C.F.R. §501.807.

[59] *Id.*

[60] *See, e.g., Al Haramain Islamic Found., Inc. v. U.S. Dep't of Treasury*, 585 F. Supp. 2d 1233 (D. Or. 2008).

Once the President exercises his authority under the IEEPA, he must immediately provide a report to Congress identifying the reasons for his emergency declaration and explaining why the circumstances "constitute an unusual and extraordinary threat."[61] Because U.S. law provides for the automatic termination of national emergencies, to continue the imposition of economic sanctions, declarations of national emergencies must be renewed annually.[62] The procedural requirements of IEEPA are summarized as follows:

> IEEPA requires the President to consult with Congress, whenever possible before declaring a national emergency, and while it remains in force. Once a national emergency goes into effect, the President must submit to Congress a detailed report explaining and justifying his actions and listing the countries against which such actions are to be taken, and why. The President is also required to provide Congress periodic follow up reports every six months with respect to actions taken since the last report and any change in information previously reported.[63]

The IEEPA has been used against foreign states, individuals, and entities that threaten U.S. national security by their participation in acts of terrorism, support of foreign terrorist organizations, or the proliferation of weapons of mass destruction ("WMDs").

II.   ECONOMIC SANCTIONS AGAINST NATION STATES

Historically, the United States has used economic sanctions as a tool to pressure and influence the conduct of foreign governments and regimes that

---

[61] 50 U.S.C. §1703(a) (the President must consult Congress "in every possible instance" before exercising his authority). Pursuant to the IEEPA's requirement that the President provide a report to Congress explaining why the circumstances pose an "unusual and extraordinary threat," immediately following the issuance of E.O. 13224, President Bush declared in a message to Congress:

> I have identified in an Annex to this order eleven terrorist organizations, twelve individual terrorist leaders, three charitable or humanitarian organizations that operate as a front for terrorist financing and support. I have determined that each of these organizations and individuals have committed, supported, or threatened acts of terrorism that imperil the security of the U.S. nationals or the national security. . . .

President Declares National Emergency, Sept. 24, 2001, *available at* http://georgewbush-white-house.archives.gov/news/releases/2001/09/20010924.html.
[62] 50 U.S.C. §1622(d) (providing for automatic termination of declaration of national emergency unless President takes certain actions 90 days prior to anniversary date of declaration).
[63] H. Comm. on Ways and Means, Overview and Compilation of U.S. Trade Statutes 209 (Comm. Print 2003 ed.) (summarizing provisions of 50 U.S.C. §1703). *See also Terrorist Assets Report, supra* note 29.

threaten vital U.S. national security interests. Since IEEPA's inception, Presidents have found "unusual and extraordinary" threats emanating from Afghanistan, Angola, Belarus, Burma, Colombia, Cote d'Ivoire (Ivory Coast), Cuba, Democratic Republic of the Congo, Haiti, Iran, Iraq, Liberia, Libya, Nicaragua, North Korea, Panama, Sudan, Sierra Leone, South Africa, Sudan, Syria, the Western Balkans, and Zimbabwe.[64] As described in detail above, U.S. economic sanctions programs block the property and interests in property of designated individuals and entities located in the United States or in the possession or control of a U.S. person or otherwise "subject to the jurisdiction of the United States." United States persons are also prohibited from engaging in certain transactions with sanctioned parties.[65]

A. *Iranian Sanctions*

While the United States has sanctioned numerous countries under IEEPA, the most extensive and comprehensive economic sanctions have been imposed against Iran. As such, the Iranian sanctions regime will be the focus of this discussion on U.S. economic sanctions against nation states.

1. Early Executive Orders

Since the Iranian Revolution and the Hostage Crisis of 1979, the United States has used economic sanctions against Iran to prevent its support of international terrorist organizations and reduce Iran's ability to develop WMDs. In January 1979, anti-government demonstrators in Iran led by Ayatollah Ruhollah Khomeini, an exiled cleric, caused the collapse of the government of the Shah of Iran, Mohammad Reza Pahlavi, a staunch ally of the United States. On November 4, 1979, pro-Khomeini radicals seized the U.S. embassy in Tehran and took 66 Americans hostage.[66] Ten days later, President Carter issued Executive

---

[64] The nature and scope of the economic sanctions programs, legal documents ordering the sanctions, and guidance can be found at OFAC's website: http://www.treasury.gov/about/organizational-structure/offices/Pages/Office-of-Foreign-Assets-Control.aspx (last visited Jan. 30, 2014); *see also* Executive Documents summarized in the annotations to 50 U.S.C. §1701.

[65] The term "interest" is broadly defined in the OFAC's sanctions regulations. An interest in property may be direct or indirect, including property interests short of full ownership, and the interest may be partial or contingent. *See* 31 C.F.R. §544.305. The regulation governing each program should be consulted as definitions can vary between sanctions programs.

[66] *See* KENNETH M. POLLACK, THE PERSIAN PUZZLE: THE CONFLICT BETWEEN IRAN AND AMERICA, 134-35 (2004) [hereinafter POLLACK, THE CONFLICT BETWEEN IRAN AND AMERICA]. After stoking the revolution while in exile, Ayatollah Khomeini returned to Iran in 1979 when the Shah's government collapsed and he declared an Islamic Republic of Iran. *Id.* at 131, 145. Khomeini fiercely opposed the U.S. government's foreign policy in the Middle East. *Id.* at 146, 156.

Order 12170 declaring a national emergency against Iran.[67] The executive order was designed to coerce the new Iranian revolutionary government to release American hostages from the U.S. Embassy in Tehran.[68] Executive Order 12170 blocked "all property and interests in property of the Government of Iran, its instrumentalities and controlled entities and the Central Bank of Iran which are or become subject to the jurisdiction of the United States. . . ."[69] President Carter also issued an executive order instituting a total embargo on U.S. exports to Iran as well as an executive order that banned all imports from Iran and travel to Iran by U.S. citizens.[70] Further, any attempts to violate the sanctions by entering into specified business transactions with Iran were also prohibited.[71]

These sanctions did not achieve their intended purpose, however, and the Iranian Hostage Crisis was still ongoing when President Reagan took office over a year later. Then, on January 19, 1981, the United States and Iran signed a bilateral agreement known as the Algiers Accords, under which Iran agreed to release the American hostages.[72] In return, the United States revoked all previous executive orders sanctioning Iran.[73]

In 1982, diplomatic hostilities between the United States and Iran escalated once again. In August 1982, during the Lebanese civil war, the United States began stationing Marines in Beirut, Lebanon as part of an international peace-keeping force.[74] On April 18, 1983, a suicide-bomber detonated a truck loaded with explosives in front of the American embassy, killing 63 people and wounding dozens more.[75] Six months later, on October 23, 1983, another suicide bomber detonated a truck bomb inside the U.S. Marine Corps barracks in Beirut[76] and killed 241 American servicemen.[77] Hezbollah, a pro-Iranian terrorist group,

---

[67] Exec. Order No. 12,170, 44 Fed. Reg. 65,729 (Nov. 14, 1979) [hereinafter E.O. 12170].

[68] See Dames & Moore v. Regan, 453 U.S. 654, 662-63 (1981); see also Robert Carswell, Economic Sanctions and the Iran Experience, 60 FOREIGN AFF. 247 (1981-82).

[69] E.O. 12170, supra note 67.

[70] Exec. Order No. 12,205, 45 Fed. Reg. 24,099 (Apr. 7, 1980) (imposing a ban on exports to Iran); Exec. Order No. 12,211, 45 Fed. Reg. 26,685 (Apr. 17, 1980) (prohibiting all imports from Iran and imposing a travel ban).

[71] 31 C.F.R. §560.203. Most U.S. sanctions imposed by President Carter were lifted when the Iranian-hostage crisis was resolved in early 1981 under the "Algiers Accords." See KENNETH KATZMAN, CONG. RESEARCH SERV., RS20871, IRAN SANCTIONS, 1 (2014) [hereinafter Iran Sanctions Report].

[72] POLLACK, THE CONFLICT BETWEEN IRAN AND AMERICA, supra note 66, at 172.

[73] See Exec. Order No. 12,282, 46 Fed. Reg. 7,925 (Jan. 19, 1981); see also Dames & Moore v. Regan, 453 U.S. at 686 (holding that it was within the President's authority under Article II of the Constitution to negotiate the terms of the Algiers Accords and dispose of claims against foreign countries without the express authorization of Congress).

[74] PATRICK TYLER, A WORLD OF TROUBLE: THE WHITE HOUSE AND THE MIDDLE EAST—FROM THE COLD WAR TO THE WAR ON TERRORISM, 283-84 (2009) [hereinafter TYLER, FROM THE COLD WAR TO THE WAR ON TERRORISM].

[75] Id. at 290-92.

[76] Id. at 297-98.

[77] Id. at 298.

claimed responsibility for both terrorist attacks, and American intelligence agencies determined that Iranian officials supervised the attacks.[78]

In response to Iran's support for Hezbollah and complicity in the Beirut terrorist bombings, the State Department declared Iran a state sponsor of terrorism (SST) in January 1984.[79] The designation of Iran as an SST resulted in the imposition of various economic sanctions, such as a ban on arms sales and restrictions on exports of U.S. dual-use items to Iran, as well as a ban on direct U.S. financial assistance to Iran.[80] However, despite Iran's belligerence and SST designation, the United States continued to buy petroleum from Iran. By 1987, Iran had become the second largest supplier of oil for the United States.[81] Even the Department of Energy was purchasing oil from Iran to supply its Strategic Petroleum Reserve.[82]

Outraged by the Department of Energy's purchase of Iranian oil, in 1987, Congress passed resolutions calling for a ban on Iranian imports.[83] After finding that Iran was "actively supporting terrorism as an instrument of state policy," President Reagan responded by issuing Executive Order 12613, which banned all imports of goods and services originating in Iran.[84] The Executive Order was intended, among other things, to "ensure that United States imports of Iranian goods and services will not contribute financial support to terrorism."[85]

The period from 1987 until 1992 was relatively calm with respect to the imposition of Iranian sanctions. However, after U.S. efforts to normalize diplomatic relations with Iran proved fruitless, Congress enacted the Iran-Iraq Arms Non-Proliferation Act of 1992, which significantly tightened restrictions on U.S. exports to Iran.[86] When Republicans took control of Congress after the 1994 mid-term elections, they immediately began to press President Clinton to strengthen his policies against Iran.[87] Despite President Reagan's import ban,

---

[78] *See* POLLACK, THE CONFLICT BETWEEN IRAN AND AMERICA, *supra* note 66, at 203. The terrorist attack on the Marine barracks in Beirut caused the greatest loss of American lives in one day since Vietnam, and led to the withdrawal of American forces from Lebanon. *See* TYLER, FROM THE COLD WAR TO THE WAR ON TERRORISM, *supra* note 74, at 298; POLLACK, THE CONFLICT BETWEEN IRAN AND AMERICA, *supra* note 66, at 205.

[79] *See* U.S. Dep't of State, *2012 Country Reports on Terrorism, Office of the Coordinator for Counterterrorism* (May 30, 2013), *available at* http://www.state.gov/documents/organization/210204.pdf.

[80] *See* Iran Sanctions Report, *supra* note 71, at 3.

[81] *See* Quinton Cannon Farrar, *U.S. Energy Sanctions and the Race to Prevent Iran From Acquiring Weapons of Mass Destruction*, 79 FORDHAM L. REV. 2347, 2356 (2011) [hereinafter Farrar, *Race to Prevent Iran from Acquiring WMDs*]; Jonathan Fuerbringer, *Senators, 98 to 0, Back Import Ban against Tehran*, N.Y. TIMES, Sept. 30, 1987, at A1.

[82] *See* HOSSEIN ALIKHANI, SANCTIONING IRAN: ANATOMY OF A FAILED POLICY 156 (2000).

[83] *Id.*, *see also* Farrar, *Race to Prevent Iran from Acquiring WMDs*, *supra* note 81, at 2356; Fuerbringer, *supra* note 81.

[84] Exec. Order No. 12,613, 52 Fed. Reg. 41,940 (Oct. 28, 1987).

[85] *Id.*

[86] Iran-Iraq Arms Non-Proliferation Act of 1992, Pub. L. 102-484, 106 Stat. 2571 (50 U.S.C. §1701 note).

[87] POLLACK, THE CONFLICT BETWEEN IRAN AND AMERICA, *supra* note 66, at 270.

U.S. companies continued purchasing oil from Iran through their foreign subsidiaries, so by 1995 the United States had become Iran's third-largest trading partner and the largest purchaser of its oil.[88] On March 6, 1995, the problem culminated when Conoco, an American oil company, signed a $1 billion contract to develop oil fields in Iranian waters.[89] Shortly thereafter, on March 15, 1995, President Clinton issued Executive Order 12957, prohibiting all U.S. investment in Iran's energy sector.[90] However, E.O. 12957 was criticized for being too weak, because it still allowed U.S. companies to purchase oil from Iran and sell it to other countries, which accounted for a quarter of Iran's oil sales.[91]

As a result, less than two months later, President Clinton issued Executive Order 12959, which banned all trade with Iran, including trade by the foreign subsidiaries of American corporations. Specifically, E.O. 12959 prohibited "importation into the United States, or the financing of such importation, of any goods or services of Iranian origin"[92] as well as "the exportation from the United States to Iran, the Government of Iran, or to any entity owned or controlled by the Government of Iran, or the financing of such exportation, of any goods, technology . . . or services."[93] By broadly prohibiting all imports from and exports to Iran, E.O. 12959 formed the basis of the core Iranian sanctions regime. In 1997, President Clinton also issued Executive Order 13059, which prevented U.S. companies from knowingly exporting goods to a third country for incorporation into products destined for Iran.[94]

To implement the Clinton executive orders, the Treasury Department considerably expanded the scope of Iranian Transactions Regulations (ITRs),[95] 31 C.F.R. Part 560.[96] Subject to limited exemptions and OFAC licenses, the ITRs

---

[88] *See* Meredith Rathbone, Peter Jeydel & Amy Lentz, *Sanctions, Sanctions Everywhere: Forging a Path Through Complex Transnational Sanctions Laws*, 44 GEO. J. INT'L L. 1055, 1083 (2013) [hereinafter *Sanctions, Sanctions Everywhere*].

[89] POLLACK, THE CONFLICT BETWEEN IRAN AND AMERICA, *supra* note 66, at 271.

[90] Exec. Order No. 12,957, 60 Fed. Reg. 14,615 (March 15, 1995) [hereinafter E.O. 12957].

[91] *See Sanctions, Sanctions Everywhere*, *supra* note 88, at 1083.

[92] Exec. Order No. 12,959, §1(a), 60 Fed. Reg. 24,757 (May 6, 1995) [hereinafter E.O. 12959].

[93] *Id.* §1(b). *See Sanctions, Sanctions Everywhere*, *supra* note 88, at 1084.

[94] Exec. Order No. 13,059, 62 Fed. Reg. 44,531 (Aug. 21, 1997) [hereinafter E.O. 13059]; *see also* Iran Sanctions Report, *supra* note 71, at 4. In 2006, Congress passed the Iran Freedom Support Act, Pub. L. No. 109-293, 120 Stat. 1344 (2006), which, among other things, codified the executive sanctions against Iran issued pursuant to E.O. 12957, *supra* note 90, E.O. 12959, *supra* note 92, and E.O. 13059. *See* 50 U.S.C. §1701 (note).

[95] *See* 31 C.F.R. §560, Iranian Transactions Regulations (ITR).

[96] The ITRs were initially issued in 1985 under the authority of the International Security and Development Cooperation Act of 1985 as a result of Iran's designation as an SST in 1984. Originally, the ITRs only restricted certain imports from Iran. The ITRs were not supplemented by IEEPA authority until 1995, when President Clinton issued E.O. 12957 and E.O 12959 declaring a national emergency in response to Iran's attempts to develop WMDs. Subsequently, the ITRs prohibited virtually all trade between the United States and Iran. Ever since E.O. 12957 established the Iranian embargo, successive executive orders have modified the ITRs, gradually expanding U.S. restrictions on trade with Iran. In 2012, the ITRs were further revised and reissued as the

prohibited "the exportation, re-exportation, sale, or supply, directly or indirectly, from the United States, or by a United States person, wherever located, of any goods, technology, or services to Iran or the Government of Iran."[97] Thus, unless "otherwise authorized" in part 560 of Title 31 of the Code of Federal Regulations, a U.S. person, or any person located in the United States, was prohibited from exporting any goods or services to Iran. The ITRs also prohibited "any new investment by a United States person in Iran or in property (including entities) owned or controlled by the Government of Iran."[98] Further, other than a limited list of exempt transactions requiring OFAC approval,[99] the ITRs prohibited U.S. depository institutions from servicing Iranian accounts.[100] Finally, the ITRs banned any transactions by U.S. persons intended to evade or avoid the prohibitions imposed under the ITRs.[101] In 2012, the ITRs were reissued as the Iranian Transactions and Sanctions Regulations (ITSR).[102]

2. Iran and Libya Sanctions Act of 1996

Although the executive orders and implementing regulations imposed a comprehensive ban on U.S. persons dealing with Iran, the sanctions were not effective at preventing Iran from promoting acts of international terrorism or developing its nuclear program.[103] While U.S. trade with Iran significantly diminished after the issuance of E.O. 12959 in 1995, Iran was still able to sell its oil and

---

Iranian Transactions and Sanctions Regulations (ITSR). *See* 77 Fed. Reg. 64,664 (Oct. 22, 2012). The reissued ITSRs include the entirety of the ITRs and implement President Obama's E.O. 13599 and subsections 1245(c) and (d)(1)(B) of the National Defense Authorization Act for Fiscal Year 2012 (NDAA). The ITSRs retained the same section numbering as the ITRs.

[97] 31 C.F.R. §560.204; *see also* United States v. Mousavi, 604 F.3d 1084 (9th Cir. 2010) (evidence that defendant entered into an agreement to provide services to a Kuwaiti company that sought to do business with Iran constituted a violation of the ITR); United States v. Homa Int'l Trading Corp., 387 F.3d 144, 146 (2d Cir. 2004) (holding that "the execution on behalf of others of money transfers from the United States to Iran is a 'service'" under the ITR); United States v. All Funds on Deposit in United Bank of Switzerland, 2003 WL 56999, at *1 (S.D.N.Y. Jan. 7, 2003) (the term "service" is unambiguous and refers to "the performance of something useful for a fee"). *But see* United States v. Banki, 685 F.3d 99, 111-12 (3d Cir. 2011) (holding that family remittances were exempt from the ITR).

[98] 31 C.F.R. §560.207.

[99] *Id.* §560.516.

[100] *Id.* §560.517.

[101] *Id.* §560.203. For a discussion of the major provisions of the Iranian trade and investment ban. *see* Iran Sanctions Report, *supra* note 71.

[102] 77 Fed. Reg. 64,664 (Oct. 22, 2012).

[103] *See* POLLACK, THE CONFLICT BETWEEN IRAN AND AMERICA, *supra* note 66, at 273. The 1996 terrorist bombing of the Khobar Towers in Saudi Arabia created a political atmosphere friendly to passage of the Iranian sanctions legislation. *Sanctions, Sanctions Everywhere, supra* note 88, at 1084 n.232. The Khobar bombing, which killed nineteen Americans, and wounded more than 300 persons, was widely blamed on a proxy of Iran's Islamic Revolutionary Guard Corps (IRGC).

finance the development of its energy sector by increasing business with other foreign countries.[104]

In response, Congress enacted the Iran and Libya Sanctions Act of 1996 (ISA), which imposed sanctions against *foreign* firms that reached threshold levels of involvement in Iran's energy sector.[105] Prior to the enactment of the ISA, the U.S.-Iranian sanctions regime had never directly covered foreign firms operating entirely abroad. "The ISA was the first U.S. law to apply Iran sanctions to any person or any company anywhere in the world."[106] The ISA was intended to force foreign firms to choose between participating in the U.S. commercial market and entering into energy-related transactions with Iran.[107] The legislation amounted to a secondary boycott of Iran and was widely condemned by the international community.[108]

Among other things, the ISA required the President to impose at least two out of six economic sanctions on foreign companies investing more than $20 million that "directly and significantly" contributed to the enhancement of Iran's ability to develop petroleum resources.[109] The six sanctions from which the President could choose to impose on such foreign entities were:

(1) denial of Export-Import Bank assistance for exports;
(2) denial of export licenses or other specific requests under U.S. export control laws;
(3) denial of loans exceeding $10 million from U.S. financial institutions in any twelve month period;
(4) prohibitions on sanctioned financial institutions from designation as a primary dealer in U.S. debt or as a repository or U.S. government funds;
(5) ban on procurement contracts with the U.S. government; and
(6) case-by-case imposition of import restrictions.[110]

However, the ISA also gave the President the discretion to waive sanctions upon certification that a waiver was "important" to the national interest of the United States.[111] The ISA was largely unpopular and strongly criticized by the international community. In order to minimize the furor among U.S. trading

---

[104] *See Sanctions, Sanctions Everywhere, supra* note 88, at 1084. This process was known as "back-filling." *Id.*

[105] Iran and Libya Sanctions Act of 1996, Pub. L. No. 104-172, 110 Stat. 1541 (1996) (codified in part at 50 U.S.C. §1701 note) [hereinafter ISA]. Libya was eventually added to the sanctions for its complicity in the Pan Am Flight 103 bombing, as well as its support for terrorism. *See* Pollack, The Conflict Between Iran and America, *supra* note 66, at 287.

[106] *Sanctions, Sanctions Everywhere, supra* note 88, at 1084.

[107] *See* Iran Sanctions Report, *supra* note 71, at 8.

[108] *See Sanctions, Sanctions Everywhere, supra* note 88, at 1085; Farrar, *Race to Prevent Iran from Acquiring WMDs, supra* note 81, at 2359-60.

[109] ISA, *supra* note 105, §5(a)(1)(A)-(B).

[110] *Id.* §6.

[111] *Id.* §9(c).

partners, successive U.S. administrations have regularly exercised the waiver and failed to enforce the ISA. Thus, the ISA did not have as significant an effect on Iran's petroleum industry as Congress intended.[112]

3. Comprehensive Iran Sanctions, Accountability, and Divestment Act of 2010

In 2010, Congress enacted the Comprehensive Iran Sanctions, Accountability, and Divestment Act (CISADA), which expanded the ISA by placing new restrictions on financial institutions and targeting Iran's ability to import petroleum.[113] The CISADA greatly expands the scope of prohibited activities, and includes efforts by foreign companies to 1) sell, lease, or provide to Iran any goods, services, technology, information, or support that would allow Iran to maintain or expand its petroleum refineries and 2) supply refined petroleum products to Iran.[114] The CISADA also restricts certain international banking relationships in order to protect the U.S. financial system from Iran's illicit activities, which include Iran's provision of material support to terrorist organizations and its efforts to develop WMDs, as well as the Central Bank of Iran's money laundering.[115]

The CISADA sanctions activities that "directly and significantly" assist Iran in either developing its refining capability or obtaining refined petroleum.[116] Further, the CISADA lowered the ISA's monetary threshold for prohibited transactions from $20 million to $1 million.[117] Moreover, under the Act, the prohibited transactions must have been done knowingly or where the party "should have known, of the conduct, circumstances, or the result."[118] By inserting the negligence standard, which extended liability to parties who "should have known," the CISADA significantly expanded corporate liability beyond the ISA, under which parent corporations were liable only if they approved or facilitated the prohibited transactions.[119]

---

[112] According to one source, Iran actually produced more oil in 1997 than it did in 1994. *See Sanctions, Sanctions Everywhere, supra* note 88, at 1085-86.

[113] Comprehensive Iran Sanctions, Accountability, and Divestment Act of 2010, Pub. L. No. 111-195, 124 Stat. 1312 (2010) (codified in part at 50 U.S.C. §1701 note) [hereinafter CISADA]. Section 103(b)(2) of the Act codified the prohibitions on the exportation of goods, services, and technology of U.S. origin to Iran that were then in effect under the executive orders issued under IEEPA. For a full discussion of CISADA and its provisions, see the U.S. Department of Treasury website, *available at* http://www.treasury.gov/resource-center/sanctions/Documents/hr2194.pdf.

[114] CISADA, *supra* note 113, §102.

[115] U.S. Dep't of Treasury, CISADA, The New U.S. Sanctions on Iran, *available at* http://www.treasury.gov/resource-center/sanctions/Programs/Documents/CISADA_english.pdf.

[116] *Id.*

[117] *Id.*

[118] *Id. See* OFAC CISADA regulations, 31 C.F.R. part 561.

[119] 61 Fed. Reg. 66,067, 66,068 (Dec. 16, 1996).

Additionally, the CISADA requires the President to impose at least three different economic sanctions on violating companies, and has added three new sanctions to the previous list of six sanctions authorized under the ISA.[120] The new sanctions are: 1. prohibition on foreign exchange transactions subject to United States' jurisdiction; 2. prohibition on transfers of credit or payment between, by, through, or to financial institutions that are subject to the United States' jurisdiction; and 3. prohibition on transacting or exercising any right, power, or privilege with respect to property subject to the jurisdiction of the United States.[121] Further, to prevent U.S. taxpayers' dollars from enriching companies that violate the Iranian sanctions, the CISADA requires companies seeking U.S. government procurement contracts to conduct an internal evaluation and certify that neither they nor any of their subsidiaries engage in sanctionable activity.[122] It should also be noted that unlike the ISA, the U.S. government has taken a more aggressive posture in enforcing the CISADA sanctions.[123]

The financial provisions of CISADA are implemented through the Iranian Financial Sanctions Regulations (IFSRs), issued by the Treasury Department.[124] The IFSRs prohibit entities owned or controlled by U.S. financial institutions from knowingly engaging in transactions with or for the benefit of the Islamic Revolutionary Guard Corps (IRGC).[125] Under the IFSRs, the Secretary of the Treasury may prohibit or impose strict conditions on the opening or maintaining in the United States of correspondent accounts or payable-through accounts for foreign financial institutions that knowingly engage in sanctionable activities.[126]

---

[120] CISADA, *supra* note 113, §102(b).

[121] *Id.* §102(b)(2).

[122] *Id.* §102(b)(3).

[123] According to members of the Obama administration, as of December 1, 2010, the CISADA sanctions had caused an 85 percent drop in refined petroleum imports into Iran and cost Iran close to $60 billion in foreign energy investments. *See Implementing Tougher Sanctions on Iran: A Progress Report: Hearing Before the H. Comm. on Foreign Affairs*, 111th Cong. 14-15 (2010) (statement of William J. Burns, Undersecretary of State for Political Affairs). Further, Iran has been almost entirely frozen out of the international financial system. *Id.* at 22-24 (statement of Stuart A. Levey, Undersecretary of Treasury for Terrorism and Financial Intelligence).

[124] 31 C.F.R. §561.201.

[125] *Id.* §561.201(a)(1).

[126] As described in the IFSR, sanctionable activities of a foreign financial institution include:

1. Facilitating the efforts of the Government of Iran to acquire or develop weapons of mass destruction or to provide support for terrorist organizations or acts of international terrorism;

2. Facilitating the activities of a person subject to financial sanctions pursuant to [U.N. Security Council Resolutions] 1737, 1747, 1803, or 1929, or any other Security Council resolution that imposes sanctions with respect to Iran;

3. Engaging in money laundering, or facilitating efforts by the Central Bank of Iran or any other Iranian financial institution, to carry out either of the facilitating activities described above;

4. Facilitating a significant transaction or transactions providing significant financial services for: (i) the IRGC or any of its agents or affiliates whose property and interests in property are blocked pursuant to the [IEEPA], or (ii) a financial institution whose property and interests in

II. Economic Sanctions Against Nation States

4. Iran Threat Reduction and Syria Human Rights Act of 2012

In August 2012, President Obama signed into law the Iran Threat Reduction and Syria Human Rights Act of 2012 (ITRSHRA), which amends portions of the ISA, the CISADA, and §1245 of the National Defense Authorization Act for Fiscal Year 2012 (NDAA).[127] The ITRSHRA adds new categories of prohibited commercial activities with Iran, including knowingly:

- Participating in a joint venture . . . with respect to the development of petroleum resources outside of Iran if the Government of Iran is a substantial partner or investor in the joint venture, or if Iran could receive technological knowledge or equipment not previously available to it which could directly and significantly contribute to the enhancement of Iran's ability to develop its petroleum resources.
- Owning, operating, controlling, or insuring a vessel that . . . was used to transport crude oil from Iran to another country (this does not apply to vessels used to transport crude oil from Iran to a country given a "significant reduction" exception under §1245 of the NDAA).
- Owning, operating, or controlling a vessel that . . . is used in a manner that conceals the Iranian origin of crude oil or refined petroleum products transported on the vessel, including by permitting the vessel's operator to suspend the operation of the vessel's satellite tracking device or obscuring the ownership, operation, or control of the vessel.
- Providing underwriting services, insurance, or reinsurance on or after the enactment of the [ITRSHRA] for the National Iranian Oil Company (NIOC), the National Tanker Company (NITC), or a successor entity to either such company.
- Purchasing, subscribing to, or facilitating the issuance of sovereign debt of the Government of Iran or debt of any entity owned or controlled by the Government of Iran, including bonds, issued on or after the [ITRSHRA's] enactment.[128]

---

property are blocked pursuant to IEEPA in connection with Iran's proliferation of WMD, Iran's proliferation of delivery systems for WMD, or Iran's support for international terrorism.

U.S. Dep't of Treasury, CISADA, The New U.S. Sanctions on Iran, *available at* http://www.treasury.gov/resource-center/sanctions/Programs/Documents/CISADA_english.pdf.

[127] Iran Threat Reduction and Syria Human Rights Act of 2012, Pub. L. 112-158 (Aug. 10, 2012) [hereinafter ITRSHRA].

[128] U.S. State Dep't, *Fact Sheet: Iran Sanctions Contained in the Iran Threat Reduction and Syria Human Rights Act (ITRSHRA)* (Sept. 28, 2012), *available at* http://www.state.gov/e/eb/rls/fs/2012/198393.htm (last visited Mar. 17, 2014).

In addition, ITRSHRA imposes penalties on any person who engages in a "sensitive transaction" with the IRGC.[129] The ITRSHRA also prohibits foreign banks from knowingly facilitating significant transactions with a person 1) sanctioned by the United States in connection with Iran's WMD proliferation activities or support for terrorism or 2) who facilitates the activities of persons working for or on behalf of, or owned or controlled by an entity subject to financial sanctions under Iran-related U.N. Security Council Resolutions.[130] The ITRSHRA codified Executive Order 12959, which extended U.S.-Iranian sanctions to foreign subsidiaries of U.S. companies.[131] ITRSHRA prohibits any entity owned or controlled by a U.S. person that is established or maintained outside of the United States from knowingly engaging in any transaction with the Government of Iran or persons subject to the jurisdiction of the Government of Iran that would be prohibited in the United States or for U.S. persons.[132]

The ITRSHRA expands the list of available economic sanctions from 9 to 12, and requires the imposition of at least five sanctions once the Secretary of State has determined an individual or entity has engaged in sanctionable activity.[133] The three sanctions added to the ISA's list are: 1) a ban on investment in equity or debt of sanctioned persons; 2) denial of a visa or exclusion from the United States of a corporate officer, principal, or controlling shareholder of a sanctioned entity; and 3) the imposition of sanctions on principal executive officers of a sanctioned entity.[134]

---

[129] ITRSHRA, *supra* note 127, §3(c). A "sensitive transaction" means:

(1) a financial transaction or series of transactions valued at more than $1,000,000 in the aggregate in any 12-month period involving a non-Iranian financial institution;

(2) a transaction to facilitate the manufacture, importation, exportation, or transfer of items needed for the development by Iran of nuclear, chemical, biological, or advanced conventional weapons, including ballistic missiles;

(3) a transaction relating to the manufacture, procurement, or sale of goods, services, and technology relating to Iran's energy sector . . . ;

(4) a transaction relating to the manufacture, procurement, or sale of goods, services, and technology relating to Iran's petrochemical sectors; or

(5) a transaction relating to the procurement of sensitive technologies. . . .

[130] *Id.* §302.
[131] *Id.* §218.
[132] *Id.*
[133] *Id.*
[134] *Id.* §204. Under §6(a) of the ISA, *supra* note 105, as amended, there are 12 available sanctions from which the Secretary of State or the Treasury can select:

1. Denial of Export-Import Bank loans, credits, or credit guarantees for U.S. exports to the sanctioned entity;
2. Denial of licenses for the U.S. export of military or militarily useful technology to the entity;
3. Denial of U.S bank loans exceeding $10 million in one year to the entity;
4. If the entity is a financial institution, a prohibition on its service as a primary dealer in U.S. government bonds; and/or a prohibition on its serving as a repository for U.S. government funds;
5. Prohibition on U.S. government procurement form the entity;

II. Economic Sanctions Against Nation States

5. Executive Orders Under the Obama Administration

President Obama has issued several executive orders strengthening the sanctions regime against Iran and extending its application to foreign entities doing business with Iran. In November 2011, President Obama issued Executive Order 13590, which imposes penalties on foreign companies with sales to Iran 1) of equipment and services related to Iran's oil industry exceeding $1 million or 2) of goods or services related to Iran's petrochemical products exceeding $250,000.[135] Additionally, in February 2012, President Obama issued Executive Order 13599, imposing sanctions on the Central Bank of Iran and other entities determined to be owned or controlled by the Iranian government.[136] This order was not implemented by the ITRs, but by the newly reissued ITSRs, which increased the punitive nature of the sanctions. Under the ITRs, absent an exemption or an OFAC authorization, U.S. financial institutions processing a transaction with an Iranian entity were required to reject it and return the funds.[137] Executive Order 13599 and the implementing ITSRs, however, require U.S. financial institutions to freeze the funds and block all U.S.-based assets of the sanctioned entities.[138]

Three months later, the President issued Executive Order 13608, which imposes sanctions on foreign persons and entities that have violated, attempted to violate, conspired to violate, or caused a violation of any sanctions against Iran.[139] Individuals and entities violating or attempting to evade Iranian sanctions are placed on an Iran sanctions evader list. United States persons are prohibited from doing business with anyone on the evader list without prior authorization from OFAC.[140] Executive Order 13608 also suspends the entry of such persons into the United States as either immigrants or nonimmigrants.[141]

---

6. Prohibition in transactions in foreign exchange by the entity;

7. Prohibition on any credit or payments between the entity and any U.S. financial institution;

8. Prohibition of the sanctioned entity from acquiring, holding, using, or trading any U.S.-based property which the sanctioned entity has a (financial) interest;

9. Restriction on imports from the sanctioned entity, in accordance with the International Emergency Economic Powers Act (IEEPA; 50 U.S.C. §1701);

10. A ban on a U.S. person from investing in or purchasing significant amounts of equity or debt instruments of a sanctioned person;

11. Exclusion from the United States or corporate officers or controlling shareholders or a sanctioned firm; and

12. Imposition of any of the ISA sanctions on principal offices or a sanctioned firm.

[135] Exec. Order No. 13,590, 76 Fed. Reg. 72,609 (Nov. 20, 2011).

[136] Exec. Order No. 13,599, 77 Fed. Reg. 6,659 (Feb. 5, 2012) [hereinafter E.O. 13599].

[137] Iran Sanctions Report, *supra* note 71, at 29. On June 21, 2013, OFAC designated 38 entities, mostly oil, petrochemical, and investment companies for blocking under E.O. 13599. *Id.*

[138] E.O. 13599, *supra* note 136.

[139] Exec. Order No. 13,608, 77 Fed. Reg. 26,409 (May 1, 2012).

[140] *Id.*

[141] *Id.* §4.

In July 2012, the Obama administration issued Executive Order 13622, which sanctions foreign financial institutions and persons (not limited to U.S. persons) which knowingly 1) conduct or facilitate significant financial transactions with the National Iranian Oil Company (NIOC) or Naftiran Intertrade Company (NICO) or 2) engage in transactions for the purchase or acquisition of petroleum, petroleum products, or petrochemical products from Iran.[142] A foreign financial institution that violates the ban may be prohibited from opening a correspondent or payable-through account in the United States or have strict conditions imposed on the maintenance of such accounts. [143]

Section 2 of E.O. 13622 prohibits any person from knowingly engaging in a significant transaction for the purchase or acquisition of petroleum, petroleum products, or petrochemical products from Iran. Persons who engage in prohibited conduct are subject to a wide array of sanctions, including the denial of U.S. Export-Import bank loans or credits,[144] and of specific licenses for the export or re-export of goods or technology to the sanctioned person.[145] Federal agencies are also prohibited from entering into a contract for the procurement of any goods or services from individuals or entities violating these sanctions.[146] Further, U.S. financial institutions are prohibited from 1) making loans or providing credits over a threshold amount to a sanctioned person[147] and 2) engaging in any transactions in foreign exchange subject to the jurisdiction of the United States in which a sanctioned person has any interest.[148] The executive order also authorizes blocking the property of persons who materially assist, sponsor, or provide financial, material, or technological support for, or goods or services in support of, the NIOO, the NICO, or the Central Bank of Iran.[149]

In June 2013, President Obama issued Executive Order 13645, which imposes sanctions on any foreign financial institutions that have 1) "knowingly conducted or facilitated any significant transaction related to the purchase or sale of Iranian rials" or 2) "maintained significant funds or accounts outside the territory of Iran denominated in the Iranian rials."[150] Foreign financial institutions that engage in such conduct may be prohibited from opening a correspondent or payable-through account in the United States or have strict

---

[142] Exec. Order No. 13,622, §§1(a)(i)-(ii), 77 Fed. Reg. 45,897 (July 30, 2012) [hereinafter E.O. 13622].

[143] *Id.* §1(b). Under U.S. law, a "correspondent account" is an account established at a U.S. bank by a foreign financial institution "to receive deposits from, make payments on behalf of [the] foreign financial institution, or handle other financial transactions related to such institution." 31 U.S.C. §5318A(e)(1)(B) (2006). A "payable-through account" is an account established at a U.S. bank by a foreign financial institution to enable the foreign bank's customers to access the U.S. banking system. *See id.* §5318A(e)(1)(c).

[144] E.O. 13622, *supra* note 142, §3(a).

[145] *Id.* §3(b).

[146] *Id.* §3(d).

[147] *Id.* §4(a)(i).

[148] *Id.* §4(a)(ii).

[149] *Id.* §5(a).

[150] Exec. Order No. 13,645, 78 Fed. Reg. 33,945 (June 3, 2013) [hereinafter E.O. 13645].

conditions imposed on the maintenance of such accounts.[151] The property and interests in property of such foreign financial institutions that are located in the United States or come within the possession or control of any United States person may also be blocked.[152] Under E.O. 13622, only the purchase or acquisition of petroleum and petrochemicals was prohibited. However, E.O. 13645 also sanctions foreign financial institutions and persons for the "sale, transport, or marketing" of petroleum and petrochemicals.[153] The order also targets the automotive sector of Iran. Section 3 sanctions any foreign financial institution that has knowingly conducted or facilitated any significant financial transaction for the sale, supply, or transfer to Iran of significant goods or services used in connection with its auto industry.[154]

B. Sanctions to Prevent the Development of Weapons of Mass Destruction

1. Executive Order 13382

In 2005, President George W. Bush issued Executive Order 13382 imposing economic sanctions against Iran to prevent the development of WMDs, including nuclear, biological, and chemical weapons.[155] The executive order blocks the property of any person who has "provided, or attempted to provide, financial, material, technological or other support for, or goods or services in support of" the proliferation of WMDs.[156] The order specifically lists the Atomic Energy Organization of Iran (AEOI) as a blocked entity.[157] The AEOI is the principal Iranian organization responsible for research and development activities related to nuclear technology, including Iran's uranium enrichment program.[158] Aerospace Industries Organization (AIO) and Shahid Hemat Industrial Group (SHIG), a subsidiary of AIO, were also listed in the Annex to E.O. 13382 because of their

---

[151] *Id.*

[152] *Id.*

[153] E.O. 13622, *supra* note 142.

[154] E.O. 13645, *supra* note 150.

[155] Exec. Order No. 13,382, 70 Fed. Reg. 38,567 (June 28, 2005) [hereinafter E.O. 13382]. E.O. 13382 strengthens E.O. 12938, *infra* note 182, which prohibits the importation into the United States of goods, technology, or services produced or provided by foreign persons who have been sanctioned because of their WMD proliferation activities.

[156] E.O. 13382, *supra* note 155, §1(a)(iii). The accompanying regulations operate broadly to block "all property and interests in property that are in the United States" of the designated entities. *See* 31 C.F.R. §§544.201(a), 544.301 (2013); 74 Fed. Reg. 16771-01 (Apr. 12, 2009).

[157] E.O. 13382, *supra* note 155.

[158] *See* Press Release, U.S. Treasury Dep't, *Treasury Designates Iranian Nuclear and Missile Entities* (Aug. 12, 2008), *available at* http://www.treasury.gov/press-center/press-releases/Pages/hp113.aspx.

ballistic missile research, development, and production activities as well as their role in overseeing Iran's missile industries.[159]

United States persons are prohibited from engaging in any transactions or dealings with any party designated under E.O. 13382.[160] This essentially denies designated parties access to the U.S. financial and commercial systems. Regulations issued by OFAC prevent anyone from engaging in a transaction to transfer, pay, export, withdraw, or otherwise deal with designated individuals or entities. OFAC regulations prohibit: 1) the performance of services including accounting, financial, brokering, freight forwarding, transportation, or public relations;[161] 2) transfers through an offshore transaction;[162] 3) transfers via charge cards, debit cards, or credit agreements;[163] and 4) taking a setoff against blocked property.[164] Each willful violation of E.O. 13382 can result in criminal penalties of up to 20 years in prison, as well as fines up to $500,000 for corporations and $250,000 for individuals.[165] In addition, E.O. 13382 provides for civil penalties of up to $50,000 per violation.[166]

In 2007, the Department of State designated the Iranian Ministry of Defense and Armed Forces Logistics (MODAFL) as a sanctioned entity under E.O. 13382 for its proliferation activities.[167] The IRGC has also been named as a proliferator of WMDs under E.O. 13382.[168] As the result, U.S. persons are prohibited from engaging in any transaction or dealing with the MODAFL or the IRGC.[169]

---

[159] E.O. 13382, *supra* note 155.

[160] U.S. Treasury Dep't, *Fact Sheet: Designation of Iranian Entities and Individuals for Proliferation Activities and Support for Terrorism* (Oct. 25, 2007), *available at* http://www.treasury.gov/press-center/press-releases/Pages/hp644.aspx (last visited Mar. 17, 2014) [hereinafter *Fact Sheet: Designation of Iranian Entities and Individuals*].

[161] 31 C.F.R. §544.405.

[162] *Id.* §544.406.

[163] *Id.* §544.409.

[164] *Id.* §544.410. A defendant in a lawsuit can claim a setoff against the plaintiff by alleging that the plaintiff owes the defendant money. If granted, the amount of money that the plaintiff owes the defendant is "set off," or subtracted, from the amount of damages awarded to the plaintiff.

[165] U.S. Treasury Dep't, OFAC, *Regulations for the Financial Community* 20 (Jan. 24, 2012), *available at* http://www.treasury.gov/resource-center/sanctions/Documents/facbk.pdf.

[166] *Id.*

[167] *Fact Sheet: Designation of Iranian Entities and Individuals, supra* note 160.

[168] *See* Iran Sanctions Report, *supra* note 71, at 26. The Qods Force, the unit of the IRGC that assists pro-Iranian movements and countries abroad, has been designated an SDGT under E.O. 13224. *Id.*

[169] The international community has also imposed economic sanctions against Iran to prevent it from developing or acquiring WMDs. *See* S.C. Res. 1737, U.N. Doc. S/RES/1737 (2006); S.C. Res. 1747, U.N. Doc. S/RES/1747 (2007); S.C. Res. 1803, U.N. Doc. S/RES/1803 (2008); S.C. Res. 1929, U.N. Doc. S/RES/1929 (2010). Among other things, these Security Council Resolutions require states to freeze the funds, other financial assets, and economic resources which are on their territories that are owned or controlled by persons or entities designated by the Security Council as being "engaged in, directly associated with or providing support for Iran's proliferation, sensitive nuclear activities, or the development of nuclear weapons delivery systems. . . ." S.C. Res. 1737 (2006).

II. Economic Sanctions Against Nation States

Multiple Iranian financial institutions have been directly implicated in facilitating Iran's WMD activities. For example, Iranian state-owned Bank Sepah was designated by the Treasury Department under E.O. 13382 for providing financial services to Iranian entities responsible for developing ballistic missiles, including AIO and SHIG.[170] The Treasury also designated Bank Melli as well as its associated subsidiaries and front companies for providing financial support to entities involved in the proliferation of WMD.[171] Bank Mellat, another Iranian state-owned bank, was also designated for supporting Iran's nuclear program after facilitating the transfer of millions of dollars for the AEOI and its main conduit, Norvin Energy Company.[172] In November 2009, First East Export Bank, a subsidiary of Bank Mellat, was also designated.[173] In October 2008, the Treasury Department also designated the Export Development Bank of Iran under E.O. 13382 for providing financial services to MODAFL.[174] Finally, the Treasury Department has targeted Iranian banks that engage in illicit activity on behalf of these designated Iranian state-owned banks. For example, Treasury designated 1) Post Ban for operating on behalf of Bank Sepah,[175] 2) Bank of Industry and Mine for providing financial services to Bank Mellat and EIH,[176] and 3) Ansar Bank and Mehar Bank for providing financial services to the IRGC.[177]

OFAC designated the Islamic Republic of Iran Shipping Service (IRISL), Iran's national maritime carrier, and affiliated entities for providing logistical support to MODAFL.[178] Further, three IRISL-related shipping companies were sanctioned by the U.N. Security Council for facilitating Iran's nuclear proliferation activities.[179]

---

[170] *See* Press Release, U.S. Treasury Dep't, *Iran's Bank Sepah Designated by Treasury Sepah Facilitating Iran's Weapons Program* (Jan. 9, 2007), *available at* http://www.treasury.gov/press-center/press-releases/Pages/hp219.aspx (last visited Mar. 17, 2014).

[171] *Fact Sheet: Designation of Iranian Entities and Individuals, supra* note 160.

[172] *Id.*

[173] *See* Press Release, U.S. Treasury Dep't, *Treasury Designates Bank Mellat Subsidiary and Chairman Under Proliferation Authority* (Nov. 5, 2009), *available at* http://www.treasury.gov/press-cnter/press-releases/Pages/tg355.aspx (last visited Mar. 17, 2014).

[174] *See* Press Release, U.S. Treasury Dep't, *Export Development Bank of Iran Designated as a Proliferator* (Oct. 22, 2008), *available at* http://www.treasury.gov/press-center/press-releases/Pages/hp1231.aspx (last visited Mar. 17, 2014).

[175] *See* Press Release, U.S. Treasury Dep't, *Department Targets Iran's Nuclear and Missile Programs* (June 16, 2010), *available at* http://www.treasury.gov/press-center/press-releases/Pages/tg747.aspx (last visited Mar. 17, 2014).

[176] *See* Press Release, U.S. Treasury Dep't, *Treasury Designates Iranian State-Owned Bank for Facilitating Iran's Proliferation Activities* (May 17, 2011), *available at* http://www.treasury.gov,press-center/press-releases/Pages/tg1178/aspx (last visited Mar. 17, 2014).

[177] *See* Press Release, U.S. Treasury Dep't, *Treasury Designated Iranian Entities Tied to the IRGC and IRISL* (Dec. 21, 2010), *available at* http://www.treasury.gov/press-center/press-releases/pages/tg/1010.aspx (last visited Mar. 17, 2014).

[178] *See* Press Release, U.S. Treasury Dep't, *Major Iranian Shipping Company Designated for Proliferation Activity* (Sept. 10, 2008), *available at* http://www.treasury.gov/press-center/press-releases/Pages/tg1067.aspx (last visited Mar. 17, 2014).

[179] *See* S.C. Res. 1929, U.N. Doc. S/RES/1929 (2010).

2. Legislative Efforts

Congress has also played a prominent role in seeking to prevent Iran from developing a nuclear weapon. In 1992, Congress passed the Iran-Iraq Arms Non-Proliferation Act, which significantly bolstered restrictions on U.S. exports to Iran and imposed mandatory sanctions on any foreign government that aided Iran's acquisition of "chemical, biological, nuclear, or destabilizing numbers and types of advanced conventional weapons."[180] The Iran-Iraq Non-Proliferation Act, now called the Iran-North Korea-Syria Non-Proliferation Act, also authorizes sanctions on foreign persons (individuals or entities) that have assisted Iran's WMD programs.[181] Sanctions include a prohibition on U.S. exports of arms and dual-use items to the sanctioned entity.[182] Section 104 of the CISADA authorizes sanctions against foreign banks that conduct significant transactions with the IRGC or any of its agents or affiliates sanctioned by any executive order.[183]

As discussed above, the ITRSHRA sanctions individuals or entities that knowingly engage in activities related to Iran's proliferation of WMDs.[184] The ITRSHRA sanctions individuals or entities that export, transfer, permit, or otherwise facilitate the transshipment of any goods, services, technology, or other items that the party knew or should have known would materially contribute to Iran's ability to acquire or develop chemical, biological, or nuclear weapons or related technologies.[185] The ITRSHRA also sanctions persons who participate in a joint venture involving any activity related to mining, producing, or transporting uranium to Iran with: 1) the Government of Iran; 2) any entity incorporated in Iran or subject to the jurisdiction of the Government of Iran; 3) any person acting on behalf or at the direction of either the Government of Iran or an entity subject to its jurisdiction; or 4) any entity or person through which a) uranium is transferred directly or indirectly to Iran, b) the Government of Iran receives significant revenue, or c) Iran could receive technological knowledge or equipment not previously available that could contribute materially to Iran's ability to develop nuclear weapons or related technology.[186] Further, the ITRSHRA prohibits transactions in property or interests of entities that provide vessels or any other shipping service to transport goods that could materially contribute to Iran's

---

[180] Iran-Iraq Arms Non-Proliferation Act of 1992, Pub. L. 102-484, 106 Stat. 2571 (1992).

[181] *Id.*

[182] *See also* Exec. Order No. 12,938, 59 Fed. Reg. 50,475 (Nov. 14, 1994) [hereinafter E.O. 12938]. E.O. 12938 also sanctions such entities by banning U.S. governmental procurement as well as imports to the United States from the sanctioned entity. *Id.*

[183] *See* Iran Sanctions Report, *supra* note 71, at 26.

[184] ITRSHRA, *supra* note 127.

[185] *Id.* §203(a)(1).

[186] *Id.* §203(a)(2).

II. Economic Sanctions Against Nation States

proliferation of WMDs or support of international terrorism.[187] The assets of such entities are also frozen under the Act.[188]

Section 311 of the ITRSHRA requires all U.S. government contractors to certify that they are not knowingly engaging in a significant transaction with the IRGC, or any of its agents or affiliates that have been sanctioned under any executive order.[189] Further, §303 imposes sanctions on agencies of foreign governments that provide technical or financial support for, or goods and services to, members or affiliates of the IRGC that have been sanctioned under U.S. executive orders or U.N. Security Council Resolutions.[190] "Sanctions include a ban on U.S. assistance or credits for that foreign government agency, a ban on defense sales to it, a ban on U.S. arms sales to it, and a ban on exports to it of controlled U.S. technology."[191]

3. International Regulations

The U.N. Security Council has adopted several resolutions intended to thwart Iran's nuclear ambitions. The preamble to U.N. Security Council Resolution 1737 states that the Security Council is "*determined* to constrain Iran's development of sensitive technologies in support of its nuclear and missile programmes" and "*[c]oncerned* by the proliferation risks presented by the Iranian nuclear programme."[192] Resolution 1737 freezes the assets of persons and entities supporting Iran's nuclear weapons proliferation as well as individuals and entities "directly associated with or providing support for Iran's proliferation sensitive nuclear activities or the development of nuclear weapons delivery systems."[193] Moreover, Resolution 1737 imposes a travel ban on such persons.[194] Resolution 1803 requires states to take measures to prevent the supply, sale, or transfer of goods related to nuclear weapons or ballistic missiles.[195]

Resolution 1929 substantially expanded the scope of Iranian sanctions, prohibiting nation-states from allowing 1) Iran to acquire an interest in any commercial activity involving uranium mining, nuclear technology, or technology related to ballistic missiles capable of delivering nuclear weapons or 2) Iranian investments related to these activities in their territory.[196] States are also required

---

[187] *Id.* §302. "Providing a vessel" includes selling or leasing and "shipping services" include providing insurance or reinsurance for such shipments. *Id.* §211(a).

[188] *Id.* §302.

[189] *Id.* §311.

[190] *Id.* §303.

[191] Iran Sanctions Report, *supra* note 71, at 26.

[192] S.C. Res. 1737, U.N. Doc. S/RES/1737 (Dec. 23, 2006).

[193] *Id.* §12.

[194] *Id.* §10.

[195] S.C. Res. 1803, §8, U.N. Doc. S/RES/1803 (Mar. 3, 2008).

[196] S.C. Res. 1929, §7, U.N. Doc. S/RES/1929 (June 9, 2010).

to prevent the transfer of technology related to nuclear weapons or ballistic missiles and take measures to block their nationals from providing Iran with any such technical assistance.[197] Resolution 1929 also requires states to prevent their nationals from 1) engaging in the sale or transfer of large weapons systems, such as tanks, warships, attack helicopters, and missiles to Iran, or 2) providing technical training, financial resources, or other services related to those weapons.[198] In addition, Resolution 1929 prohibits states from providing fuel or services to ships that are owned or controlled by Iran "if they have information that provides reasonable grounds to believe" the ships are carrying prohibited goods.[199]

C. Enforcement of Sanctions

1. Financial Institutions

The Department of Justice (DoJ) has a checkered record of enforcing Iranian economic sanctions against financial institutions. Since 2009, seven major global banks have been investigated for engaging in fraudulent schemes to assist their Iranian customers in evading economic sanctions. Despite being aware of the ban on providing financial services to Iran, Lloyds TSB, Credit Suisse, Barclays Bank, ABN AMRO, ING, Standard Chartered, and HSBC Group admitted to willfully violating the IEEPA and the TWEA by facilitating financial transactions on behalf of Iran as well as other sanctioned countries and entities. In the case of the HSBC Group, from at least 2000 to 2006, the bank:

> knowingly and willfully engaged in practices outside the United States that caused HSBC Bank USA and other U.S. financial institutions to process payments on behalf of banks and other entities located in Cuba, Iran, Libya, Sudan, and Burma, in violation of U.S. sanctions. HSBC Group Affiliates ensured that these transactions went undetected in the U.S. by altering and routing payment messages in a manner that hid the identities of these sanctioned entities from HSBC Bank USA and other U.S. financial institutions. The total value of these transactions during this period was approximately $660 million.[200]

The offending banks were permitted to enter into a deferred prosecution agreement in which the DoJ agreed not to pursue criminal prosecution in exchange for the payment of a fine and a promise from the banks to comply

---

[197] *Id.* §9.
[198] *Id.* §8.
[199] *Id.* §18.
[200] Memorandum and Order, United States v. HSBC Bank USA, N.A. et al., 2013 WL 3306161 (E.D.N.Y. July 1, 2013).

with existing federal regulations that prohibit doing business with Iran and other sanctioned countries.[201]

The Treasury Department also assessed a $152 million penalty against Clearstream Banking, a Luxembourg bank, for violating Iranian economic sanctions.[202] However, neither Clearstream, nor any of its employees who devised and implemented the scheme to evade U.S. economic sanctions, have been prosecuted or held personally accountable.

2.   Individuals

The DoJ has been more assertive in pursuing criminal charges for violating IEEPA sanctions against individuals not connected to financial institutions. The DoJ has prosecuted individuals under the IEEPA for 1) transferring money to Iran for a fee,[203] 2) conspiring to export medical equipment to Iran,[204] 3) conspiring to sell a software program to Iranian entities and entering into an agreement to provide those entities with technology to facilitate the construction of multiple chemical plants,[205] and (4) transmitting funds to and from Iran by means of wire transfers through intermediary money exchanges in Dubai.[206]

3.   Legal Challenges

Legal challenges to the economic sanctions against Iran have been routinely rejected by the courts. Courts that have considered the issue have consistently held IEEPA is not an unconstitutional delegation of legislative power because the

---

[201] *See* Deferred Prosecution Agreement, United States v. Lloyds TSB Bank, No. CR-09-007 (D.D.C. Jan. 9, 2009) (agreed to pay a $350 million penalty); Deferred Prosecution Agreement, United States v. Credit Suisse AG, No. CR-09-352 (D.D.C. Dec. 16, 2009) (agreed to pay a $536 million penalty); Deferred Prosecution Agreement, United States v. Barclays Bank PLC, No. CR 10-218 (D.D.C. Aug. 16, 2010) (agreed to pay a $298 million penalty); Deferred Prosecution Agreement, United States v. ABN AMRO Bank, N.V., No. CR 10-124 (D.D.C. May 10, 2010) (agreed to pay a $500 million penalty); Deferred Prosecution Agreement, United States v. ING Bank, N.V., No. CR 12-136 (D.D.C. June 12, 2012) (agreed to pay a $619 million penalty); Deferred Prosecution Agreement, United States v. Standard Chartered Bank, No. CR 12-1467 (D.D.C. Dec. 10, 2012) (agreed to forfeit $227 million to the DOJ as well as a $100 million civil penalty); Deferred Prosecution Agreement, United States v. HSBC Bank USA, No. CR 12-763 (E.D.N.Y. Dec. 12, 2012) (agreed to pay $1.9 billion penalty). The deferred prosecution agreements also alleged that the banks provided banking services to other sanctioned countries, including Cuba, Libya, Sudan, and Burma.

[202] *See* Press Release, U.S. Treasury Dep't, *Treasury Department Reaches Landmark $152 Million Settlement with Clearstream Banking* (Jan. 23, 2014) *available at* http://www.treasury.gov/press-center/press-releases/Pages/jl2264.aspx.

[203] *See* United States v. Homa Int'l Trading Corp., 387 F.3d 144 (2d Cir. 2004).

[204] *See* United States v. Nazemzadeh, 2014 WL 310460 (S.D. Cal. Jan. 28, 2014).

[205] See United States v. Amirnazmi, 645 F.3d 564 (3d Cir. 2011).

[206] *See* United States v. Esfahani, 2006 WL 163025 (N.D. Ill. Jan. 17, 2006).

statute has sufficient guiding principles, congressional reporting requirements, and other limitations on executive power.[207] In *United States v. Amirnazmi*, the Third Circuit held that the statute "meaningfully constrains" presidential discretion because the President must find an "unusual and extraordinary threat to the national security, foreign policy or economy of the United States," originating on foreign soil that has reached "national emergency" proportions, before invoking IEEPA powers.[208] The courts have also rejected claims that IEEPA regulations implementing Iranian sanctions are unconstitutionally vague.[209] In *United States v. Zhi Yong Guo*, the Ninth Circuit held that "[t]he requirement that §1705(c) places on the government to prove Defendant's knowledge of the law 'mitigate[s] a law's vagueness, especially with respect to the adequacy of notice to the complainant that his conduct is proscribed[.]'"

D. State Sponsors of Terrorism

The designation of a state as a state sponsor of terrorism (SST) is another pillar of the U.S. sanctions regime. The three authorities available to the Secretary of State for designating a foreign state as an SST are §6(j) of the Export Administration Act (50 U.S.C. App. §2405),[210] §40(d) of the Arms Export Control Act (22 U.S.C. §2789(d)),[211] and §620A of the Foreign Assistance Act (22 U.S.C. §2372).[212] The Secretary of State may designate a state as an SST for providing repeated support for acts of international terrorism, which typically involves the provision of financial assistance, training, weapons, and logistical support to international terrorists. States currently designated as sponsors of terrorism include: Cuba, Iran, Sudan, and Syria.[213]

---

[207] *See Amirnazmi*, 645 F.3d at 576-77 (finding that the "IEEPA meaningfully constrains the Executive's discretion"); United States v. Dhafir, 461 F.3d 211, 215-17 (2d Cir. 2006) (concluding that "the authorities delegated [under the IEEPA] are defined and limited"); United States v. Arch Trading Corp., 987 F.2d 1087, 1092-94 (4th Cir. 1993) (finding that the President's powers under the IEEPA are "explicitly defined and circumscribed"); United States v. Mirza, 454 Fed. App'x 249, 256 (5th Cir. 2011) (same); *see also Nazemzadeh*, 2014 WL 310460; *Esfahani*, 2006 WL 163025.

[208] *Amirnazmi*, 645 F.3d at 567.

[209] *See id.* at 591; *see also* United States v. Zhi Yong Guo, 634 F.3d 1119, 1123 (9th Cir. 2011) (affirming convictions for conspiring and attempting to export thermal imaging cameras to China without a license).

[210] Export Administration Act of 1979, Pub. L. 96-72 (codified at 50 U.S.C. App. §2405(j)). This Act has expired but continues to be enforced pursuant to a national emergency under the IEEPA declared by President George W. Bush in 2001, Exec. Order No. 13,222, 66 Fed. Reg. 44,025 (Aug. 22, 2001), and renewed annually ever since.

[211] Arms Export Control Act, Pub. L. 94-329, codified at 22 U.S.C. §2789(d).

[212] Foreign Assistance Act, Pub. L. 87-195 (as amended), codified at 22 U.S.C. §2372.

[213] *See* U.S. Dep't of State, *2012, Country Reports on Terrorism, Office of the Coordinator for Counterterrorism* (May 30, 2013), *available at* http://www.state.gov/documents/organization/210204.pdf.

II. Economic Sanctions Against Nation States

Iran was designated as an SST in 1984.[214] The SST designation was sparked primarily by the 1983 terrorist attacks on the U.S. embassy and Marine Corps barracks in Beirut, Lebanon, for which Hezbollah claimed responsibility.[215] The United States determined that Iran was responsible for training Hezbollah terrorists as well as funding and supervising the attack.[216] Over the years, Iran has provided extensive funding, training, and weapons to Palestinian terrorist groups, such as Hezbollah, Hamas, and the Palestinian Islamic Jihad.[217] According to the Treasury Department, Iran has also permitted Al Qaeda to funnel funds and operatives through its territory.[218] Finally, Iran uses state-owned banks to facilitate the financing of terrorist attacks and related activities.[219] The Treasury Department has designated several Iranian state-owned banks under Executive Order 13224 for providing financial support to terrorist organizations.[220]

Designation as an SST has significant economic consequences. In the case of Iran, the Export Administration Act restricts the export of U.S. dual-use goods and technologies that could contribute to the development of WMD.[221] Section 620A of the Foreign Assistance Act bans direct U.S. financial assistance to Iran and requires that the U.S. representative of an international organization vote against multilateral lending to Iran.[222] Further, §§325 and 326 of the Antiterrorism and Effective Death Penalty Act of 1996 require the President to withhold U.S. foreign assistance to any country that provides foreign assistance or arms to a country designated as a SST.[223] Significantly, however, the SST designation does not bar humanitarian aid.[224]

[214] *Id.* at 196.

[215] Farrar, *Race to Prevent Iran from Acquiring WMDs, supra* note 81, at 2354-55.

[216] *Id.* The United States also wanted to restrict Iran's ability to finance the armed conflict with Iraq, which began in 1980 and lasted for almost a decade. *Id.* at 2355.

[217] *See* U.S. Dep't of State, SST List (Aug. 18, 2011), *available at* http://www.state.gov/j/ct/rls/crt/ 2012/209985.htm (last visited Mar. 17, 2014). Iran allegedly provides Hezbollah with as much as $200 million in funding per year. *See* Press Release, U.S. Treasury Dep't, *Finding that the Islamic Republic of Iran is a Jurisdiction of Primary Money Laundering Concern* (Nov. 18, 2011), *available at* http://www.treasury.gov/press-center/press-releases/Documents/Iran311Finding.pdf.

[218] *Id.* at 9.

[219] *Id.*

[220] *See Fact Sheet: Designation of Iranian Entities and Individuals, supra* note 160.

[221] Export Administration Act, *supra* note 210. Dual-use goods and technologies are items with both civilian and military applications, including items that can contribute to the proliferation of nuclear, biological, and chemical weapons. *See* IAN F. FERGUSSON, CONG. RESEARCH SERV., RL31832, THE EXPORT ADMINISTRATION ACT: EVOLUTION, PROVISIONS, AND DEBATE (2009).

[222] Anti-Terrorism and Effective Death Penalty Act of 1996, Pub. L. 104-132, 110 Stat. 1247-1258, codified at 22 U.S.C. §§2377-78.

[223] *Id.* §§325-26.

[224] *See* Iran Sanctions Report, *supra* note 71, at 3.

III. ECONOMIC SANCTIONS AGAINST SUSPECTED TERRORISTS

A. *Specially Designated Global Terrorists*

The imposition of economic sanctions by the United States and the international community against terrorists, terrorist organizations, and their financial sponsors and support structures is a powerful tool. The effects of these sanctions reach far beyond the blocking of terrorist assets. Economic sanctions deny terrorists access to the U.S. financial system and commercial markets, and, in the case of United Nations designation, the global financial system as well. Further, economic sanctions assist and complement the law enforcement actions of the United States and other governments.

1. Executive Order 13224

After the September 11, 2001 terrorist attacks, President George W. Bush issued Executive Order 13224 (E.O. 13224), invoking his authority under the IEEPA, 50 U.S.C. §1701, and the United Nations Participation Act, 22 U.S.C. §287c.[225] Executive Order 13224 declared a "national emergency" with respect to "grave acts of terrorism and threats of terrorism committed by foreign terrorist, including the terrorist attacks . . . committed on September 11, 2001 . . . and the continuing and immediate threat of further attacks on United States nationals or the United States."[226] The order designated 12 individuals and 15 entities as "Specially Designated Global Terrorists" (SDGTs) and identified them in the Annex to E.O. 13224.[227]

E.O. 13224 also authorizes the Secretary of the Treasury, in consultation with the Secretary of State and the Attorney General, to designate and block the property of *additional* persons who 1) "act for or on behalf of" or are "owned or controlled by" designated terrorists, 2) "assist in, sponsor, or provide financial, material, or technological support for" SDGTs, or 3) are "otherwise associated with the SDGTs.[228] Finally, E.O. 13224 authorizes the Secretary of State, in consultation with the Secretary of the Treasury and the Attorney General, to designate

---

[225] E.O. 13224, *supra* note 24.

[226] *Id.*

[227] *Id.* §3; *see also* 31 C.F.R. §594.310. The individuals and entities designated for blocking included core members of Al Qaeda, affiliated terrorist groups, Islamic charities suspected of funding Al Qaeda, and businesses believed to be a front for Al Qaeda. Executive Order 13,268 amended the Annex to E.O. 13,224 by adding two names: the Taliban and Mohammed Mullah Omar, the leader of the Taliban. *See* Exec. Order No. 13,268, 31 C.F.R. 240-41 (2002), *reprinted as amended in* 50 U.S.C. §1701 note (Supp. IV 2004).

[228] E.O. 13224, *supra* note 24, §§1(c)-(d).

as SDGTs additional persons determined "to have committed, or to pose a significant risk of committing, acts of terrorism that threaten he security of U.S. nationals, or the national security, foreign policy, or economy of the United States."[229]

Being designated under E.O. 13224 has important legal consequences. First, all "property and interests in property" of SDGTs located in the United States or that come within the possession or control of U.S. persons are blocked.[230] Second, U.S. persons are prohibited from entering into any transaction or dealing in property or interests in property blocked pursuant to the order.[231] Third, §2(a) of E.O. 13224 prohibits any U.S. person from "making or receiving . . . any contribution of funds, goods, or services to or for the benefit of" persons determined to be subject to the executive order.[232] Fourth, any transaction by a U.S. person that evades, or has the purpose of evading, or attempts to violate, any of the prohibitions of the executive order is prohibited.[233] Finally, severe civil and criminal penalties may be assessed for a violation of any order, regulation, or license issued pursuant to E.O. 13224.[234]

Because the designation of an individual as an SDGT is an administrative rather than a criminal action, there is no requirement that the designated individual be charged with or convicted of committing acts of terrorism. Moreover, the government is not required to satisfy the "beyond a reasonable doubt" criminal standard of proof. Instead, an individual or entity may be designated as an SDGT if there is a "reasonable basis" to believe that they are "owned or controlled by," "act[s] for or on behalf of," "assist[s] in . . . or provide[s] financial, material, or technological support for, or financial or other services to" or is "otherwise associated with" an SDGT.[235] Additionally, a person may be designated as a SDGT if there is a reasonable basis to believe that the individual has "committed, or . . . pose[s] a significant risk of committing, acts of terrorism that threaten . . . the national security, foreign policy, or economy of the United States."[236]

---

[229] *Id.* §1(b).

[230] *Id.* §1.

[231] *Id.* §2(a).

[232] *Id.*

[233] *Id.* §2(b).

[234] A maximum civil penalty of $50,000 may be imposed for each violation of E.O. 13224. 31 C.F.R. §594.701(a)(1) (2007). Further, a person who "willfully" violates the executive order may be assessed a fine of $50,000 and sentenced to a term of imprisonment not exceeding 20 years, or both. *Id.* §594.701(a)(2) (2008).

[235] E.O. 13224, *supra* note 24, §§1(c), (d)(i)-(ii). *But see* Humanitarian Law Project v. U.S. Dep't of Treasury, 463 F. Supp. 2d 1049, 1070 (C.D. Cal. 2006) (holding that the "otherwise associated with" provision is unconstitutionally vague). In response, the Treasury Department amended the provision, and the amended language has been upheld. *See* Humanitarian Law Project v. U.S. Dep't of Treasury, 484 F. Supp. 2d 1099, 1106-07 (C.D. Cal. 2007).

[236] E.O. 13224, *supra* note 24, §1(b); *see also* GURULÉ, UNFUNDING TERROR, *supra* note 26, at 197-98 (discussing the designation process under E.O. 13224).

Notice of the designation and blocking order is issued by OFAC, which publishes the names of the SDGTs in the Federal Register.[237] OFAC also adds the individual or entity to its SDGT list, and posts a notice of these additions on the OFAC website.[238] United States financial institutions are required to regularly check the OFAC list of SDGTs and other sanctioned persons. If the financial institution is administering accounts for any of the designated individuals or entities, it is required to freeze the funds held in those accounts. The blocked funds must be placed in an interest-bearing account located in the United States, earning interest at a "commercially reasonable" rate.[239] Moreover, all transactions involving property in which any of the listed individuals and entities has any interest are prohibited without specific authorization from OFAC. Simply stated, U.S. persons are prohibited from doing business or engaging in any other dealings with SDGTs. Further, as noted earlier, the USA PATRIOT Act amended the IEEPA, 50 U.S.C. §1702, to authorize blocking actions "during the pendency of an investigation."[240] Finally, under E.O. 13224, OFAC has been delegated the authority to promulgate rules and regulations governing blocking actions.[241]

The U.S. government has designated organizations operating inside the United States suspected of providing financial support to terrorists or terrorist organizations under the order. Specifically, the U.S. Treasury Department has designated over 40 Islamic charities as SDGTs,[242] and their property and interests in property have been blocked. These purported charities include, for example, the Holy Land Foundation for Relief and Development (HLF); Benevolence International Foundation; Islamic American Relief Agency; Al Haramain Islamic Foundation (AHIF); and KindHearts for Charitable Humanitarian Development (KindHearts).[243]

2.   Licensing

E.O. 13224 does not ban all transactions with an SDGT. OFAC has issued regulations that authorize it to issue both "general" and "specific" licenses permitting certain types of transactions otherwise prohibited by the executive order.[244]

---

[237] See, e.g., 78 Fed. Reg. 59,751 (Sept. 27, 2013) (publishing notice of the designation of Badruddin Haqqani as an SDGT).

[238] See U.S. Treasury Dep't, SDN List, available at http://www.treasury.gov/ofac/downloads/t11sdn.pdf (last visited Mar. 17, 2014).

[239] 31 C.F.R. §594.203(b)(1)(i) (2007).

[240] See USA PATRIOT ACT, supra note 1.

[241] E.O. 13224, supra note 24, §7.

[242] See U.S. Treasury Dep't, Office of Terrorism and Financial Intelligence, Designated Charities and Potential Fundraising Fronts for FTOs (Jan. 16, 2014), available at http://www.treasury.gov/resource-center/terrorist-illicit-finance/Pages/protecting-fto.aspx (last visited Mar. 17, 2014). See also GURULÉ, UNFUNDING TERROR, supra note 26, at 18 nn.18-20.

[243] See Terrorist Assets Report, supra note 29, at 7.

[244] See 31 C.F.R. §§501.801(a), (b) (2012).

III. Economic Sanctions Against Suspected Terrorists

The purpose of issuing OFAC licenses is to ameliorate the harsh effects of OFAC blocking actions, which freeze assets of, and prohibit transactions with, designated persons.

OFAC has issued several general licenses permitting transactions in property in which Hamas has an interest. In October 2001, Hamas was designated as an SDGT. After parliamentary elections in the West Bank and Gaza, members of Hamas formed the majority party within the Palestinian Legislative Council. As a result of these elections, OFAC determined that Hamas had a property interest in the transactions of the Palestinian Authority. Accordingly, pursuant to E.O. 13224 and related U.S. regulations, U.S. persons are prohibited from engaging in any transaction with the Palestinian Authority unless authorized by OFAC.

Consistent with U.S. foreign policy, OFAC issued seven general licenses authorizing U.S. persons to engage in certain transactions in which the Palestinian Authority has an interest.[245] One of the general licenses authorized in-kind donations of medicine by U.S. non-governmental organizations to the Palestinian Authority Ministry of Health, provided that such donations are distributed in the West Bank or Gaza, and not intended for resale.[246] OFAC expanded this license from in-kind donations of medicine to medical services and medical devices, including medical supplies.[247] Additionally, OFAC has issued general licenses for the provision of legal services,[248] non-scheduled emergency medical services,[249] transactions related to telecommunications,[250] and transactions incident to the receipt or transmission of mail between U.S. persons and persons whose property or interests in property are blocked.[251]

OFAC regulations also permit a "specific license" authorizing U.S. persons to conduct specific transactions with SDGTs.[252] A person seeking a specific license to engage in transactions otherwise prohibited by E.O. 13224 must file an application with OFAC.[253] OFAC may grant an application for a specific license at its discretion. In one reported case, OFAC granted the Global Relief Foundation, Inc., a U.S.-based Islamic charity, licenses to access blocked funds to pay for legal fees, establishment of a legal defense fund, salaries, payroll taxes, health insurance, rent, utilities, and other continuing operational expenses.[254]

---

[245] *See* 31 C.F.R. §§594.510-515; U.S. Dep't of Treasury, OFAC, General License No. 7 (Jan. 9, 2013), *available at* http://www.treasury.gov/resource-center/sanctions/OFAC-Enforcement/Pages/20130109_33.aspx (last visited Mar. 17, 2014). *See also* GURULÉ, UNFUNDING TERROR, *supra* note 26, at 199-200 (discussing the general licenses issued by OFAC which permit certain transactions with Hamas and the Palestinian Authority).

[246] *See* 31 C.F.R. §594.515.

[247] *Id.*

[248] *Id.* §594.506.

[249] *Id.* §594.507.

[250] *Id.* §594.508.

[251] *Id.* §594.509.

[252] *Id.* §501.801(b).

[253] *Id.* §501.801(b)(2).

[254] *See* Global Relief Found., Inc. v. O'Neill, 207 F. Supp. 2d 779, 786, 805 (N.D. Ill. 2002).

3.   Delisting Process

Treasury Department regulations provide that a person or entity that is designated as an SDGT may seek an administrative review of the designation.[255] A person may petition to have their designation reconsidered on three grounds. First, when a party believes that their funds were blocked due to mistaken identity, the party may request the release of those funds.[256] The petitioner must submit a written request to OFAC to release the funds.[257] After a review of the written submission, OFAC determines whether petitioner's claim of mistaken identity is valid, and, if so, whether the funds should be released.[258] However, OFAC's director, the same officer responsible for making the designation, is also responsible for reviewing the challenge to the designation. Second, when a designated person believes that there is an insufficient basis for the designation, he may petition for reconsideration.[259] Third, a person may assert that the circumstances justifying the designation no longer apply and seek to have the designation rescinded.[260] Where the original designation was based on the petitioner's association with another SDGT, the petitioner would have to show a demonstrable break with the designated entity. To that end, the petitioner might offer proof of his resignation from any position with the designated entity or organization. For example, if a person was designated because he served on the board of directors of an Islamic charity that was designated as an SDGT for funneling money to a foreign terrorist organization (FTO), the designee could petition OFAC for delisting claiming that he lacked knowledge that charitable donations were being used to finance terrorist activities. OFAC may rescind the designation if the petitioner can show that upon learning of such activity, he resigned from the board of directors and severed all ties with the designated charity.

After receiving a removal petition, OFAC may request clarifying, corroborating, or other additional information. Petitions for delisting have almost always involved cases where the petitioner claimed to be no longer engaged in the activity justifying the initial designation.[261] An exchange of correspondence, additional

---

[255] *See* 31 C.F.R. §594.201(a) n.3; §501.807.

[256] *Id.* §501.806.

[257] A request for release of funds should include:

"(1) The name of the financial institution in which the funds are blocked; (2) The amount blocked; (3) The date of the blocking; (4) The identity of the original remitter of the funds and any intermediary financial institutions; (5) The intended beneficiary of the blocked transfer; (6) A description of the underlying transaction including copies of related documents (e.g., invoices, bills of lading, promissory notes, etc.); (7) The nature of the applicant's interest in the funds; and (8) A statement of the reasons why the applicant believes the funds were blocked due to mistaken identity." *Id.* §§501.806(d)(1)-(8) (2014).

[258] *Id.*

[259] *Id.* §501.807(a).

[260] *Id.*

[261] For example, OFAC removed the names of two Somali Swedes from its list of SDGTs after they showed they had severed all ties with the designated entity that was the basis for their

fact-finding, and meetings with OFAC officials usually occur before OFAC decides whether there is a sufficient basis for removal. Further, after conducting its review of the petition, the regulations require that OFAC submit a written decision to the blocked person.[262]

B. Legal Challenges to Designation

1. Administrative Procedure Act

Claims that designation under E.O. 13224 violated the Administrative Procedure Act (APA) have routinely been rejected by the courts. Under the APA, a reviewing court may overturn an agency action only if it was "arbitrary, capricious, an abuse of discretion, or otherwise not in accordance with law."[263] In determining whether an agency's action is arbitrary and capricious, courts "consider whether the decision was based on the relevant factors and whether there was a clear error of judgment."[264] The court reviews the administrative record assembled by the agency to determine whether the agency's decision was supported by a rational basis.[265]

Since designation under E.O. 13224 implicates national security, courts have typically been deferential to OFAC's determinations. In *Islamic American Relief Agency v. Gonzales*, the D.C. Circuit declared that "in an area at the intersection of national security, foreign affairs, and administrative law," judicial review for an agency decision is extremely deferential.[266] That court upheld the designation of the Islamic American Relief Agency USA (ISRA-USA) finding that OFAC's determination was not arbitrary and capricious.[267] In fact, the court found there was ample evidence the ISRA-USA was a branch of the Islamic American Relief Agency, a charity previously designated for blocking by OFAC.[268]

In *Al Haramain Islamic Foundation, Inc. v. U.S. Department of Treasury*, the Ninth Circuit held that there was "substantial evidence" to support OFAC's conclusion that Al Haramain Islamic Foundation Oregon (AHIF-Oregon) was a

---

designation as SDGTs. *See* John Roth et al., National Commission on Terrorist Attacks upon the United States, *Monograph on Terrorist Financing, Staff Report to the Commission* 86 (Washington, D.C., Gov't Printing Office 2004), *available at* http://govinfo.library.unt.edu/911/staff_statements/911_TerrFinMonograph.pdf.

[262] *See* 31 C.F.R. §501.807(d) (2011).

[263] Administrative Procedure Act, 5 U.S.C. §706(2)(A); *see also Marsh v. Oregon Natural Resources Council*, 490 U.S. 360, 377 (1989); Gurulé & Corn, Principles of Counter-Terrorism Law, *supra* note 43, at 308-10 (discussing legal challenges to OFAC designations under the APA).

[264] Marsh v. Oregon Natural Resources Council, 490 U.S. at 378.

[265] *See* Camp v. Pitts, 411 U.S. 138, 142 (1973); Holy Land Found. for Relief & Dev. v. Ashcroft, 333 F.3d 156 (D.C. Cir. 2003).

[266] Islamic Am. Relief Agency v. Gonzales, 477 F.3d 728, 732 (D.C. Cir. 2007).

[267] *Id.* at 728.

[268] *Id.* at 734.

branch office of the designated charity in Saudi Arabia.[269] Also, in *Holy Land Foundation for Relief & Development v. Ashcroft*, the D.C. Circuit held that OFAC's designation of HLF as an SDGT was not arbitrary and capricious.[270] Instead, the court found that OFAC's designation was supported by substantial evidence that HLF was providing financial support to Hamas, an FTO.[271]

2.   First Amendment Claims

Federal courts are divided on whether OFAC blocking actions violate the First Amendment rights to freedom of speech and association of designated parties. In determining whether the ban on making financial donations to SDGTs violates the First Amendment right to freedom of speech, courts have consistently applied the intermediate scrutiny standard.[272] Intermediate scrutiny is applied in reviewing First Amendment challenges "when the 'regulation . . . serves purposes unrelated to the content of expression.'"[273] In other words, intermediate scrutiny is the proper test for "content-neutral" regulations. Regulations are considered content-neutral if "regulation of expressive activity is . . . 'justified without reference to the content of the regulated speech.'"[274] Under the test set forth in *United States v. O'Brien*, governmental action passes intermediate scrutiny if 1) "it is within the constitutional power of the Government"; 2) "it furthers an important government interest"; 3) "the government interest is unrelated to the suppression of expression"; and 4) "the incidental restriction on alleged First Amendment rights is not greater than is essential to the furtherance of that interest."[275]

In *Kadi v. Geithner*, the D.C. District Court rejected Kadi's complaint that prohibiting him from making donations to SDGTs violated his right to freedom of speech.[276] Applying the *O'Brien* four-part test, the court found that the government had the authority to designate Kadi as a SDGT and block his assets subject to U.S. jurisdiction.[277] The court concluded that "blocking or freezing assets that may be used to support terrorists and/or terrorist activities furthers

---

[269] Al Haramain Islamic Found., Inc. v. U.S. Dep't of Treasury, 686 F.3d 965, 979 (9th Cir. 2011).

[270] *Holy Land Found. for Relief & Dev.*, 333 F.3d at 156.

[271] *Id.* at 162.

[272] *See, e.g.*, Kadi v. Geithner, 2012 WL 898778, at *28 (D.D.C. 2012); Holy Land Found. for Relief & Dev. v. Ashcroft, 219 F. Supp. 2d 57, 81 (D.D.C. 2002); Islamic Am. Relief Agency v. Unidentified FBI Agents, 394 F. Supp. 2d 34, 52 (D.D.C. 2005).

[273] *Kadi*, 2012 WL 898778, at *26 (citing Ward v. Rock Against Racism, 491 U.S. 781, 791 (1989)).

[274] Emergency Coal. to Defend Educ. Travel v. U.S. Dep't of Treasury, 545 F.3d 4, 12 (D.C. Cir. 2008) (citing *Rock Against Racism*, 491 U.S. at 791)).

[275] United States v. O'Brien, 391 U.S. 367, 377 (1968).

[276] *Kadi*, 2012 WL 898778, at *29.

[277] *Id.* at *28.

an important government interest."[278] The court also found that the blocking action was unrelated to the suppression of free speech, noting that Kadi did not even claim he intended to donate to any SDGTs for political reasons.[279] Moreover, the court stated that designating Kadi as a SDGT and blocking his assets merely restricted his ability to make financial transfers to other SDGTs, not his ability to express his views generally.[280] Finally, the court held that any incidental restriction on alleged First Amendment freedoms is not greater than is essential to further strong governmental interests.[281]

Plaintiffs' freedom of association challenges have fared no better. In *Islamic American Relief Agency*, the D.C. Circuit held that an SDGT blocking order did not violate freedom of association because SDGT blocking orders do not prohibit associational activity, but instead target the financial support of terrorism.[282] The court stated: "[T]here is no First Amendment fight nor any other constitutional right to support terrorists."[283] In *Holy Land Foundation for Relief & Development v. Ashcroft*, the court reached the same conclusion, holding that OFAC's designations do not prohibit membership in Hamas or endorsement of its views, and so, the designation did not implicate the HLF's associational rights.[284] Rather, OFAC's actions prohibited HLF from providing financial support to Hamas, and "there is no constitutional right to facilitate terrorism."[285]

For content-based regulations of speech, courts apply strict scrutiny—a more exacting standard.[286] For a content-based regulation to survive strict scrutiny, a statute must be narrowly tailored to advance a compelling government interest.[287] In *Al Haramain Islamic Foundation, Inc. v. U.S. Department of Treasury*, the Ninth Circuit applied strict scrutiny in considering a challenge under §2(a) of E.O. 13224, which prohibits U.S. persons or persons located in the United States from providing services, goods, or funds to a SDGT.[288] The activities at issue in *Al Haramain Islamic Foundation, Inc.*, were "pure speech" activities that

---

[278] *Id.*

[279] *Id.*

[280] *Id.*

[281] *Id.*

[282] Islamic Am. Relief Agency v. Gonzales, 477 F.3d 728, 736-37 (D.C. Cir. 2007); *see also* Holder v. Humanitarian Law Project, 561 U.S. 1 (2010) (rejecting freedom of association claim because the material support statute did not penalize mere association, but instead prohibited the act of providing material support to an FTO); Holy Land Found. for Relief & Dev. v. Ashcroft, 333 F.3d 156, 165 (D.C. Cir. 2003) (rejecting HLF's First Amendment challenges); Kadi v. Geithner, 2012 WL 898778, at *28 (because Kadi was designated on the basis that he provided funding to terrorist organizations, his First Amendment freedom of association claim was foreclosed).

[283] *Islamic Am. Relief Agency*, 477 F.3d at 735.

[284] Holy Land Found. for Relief & Dev. v. Ashcroft, 219 F. Supp. 2d 57, 80 (D.D.C. 2002).

[285] *Id.* at 81 (quoting Humanitarian Law Project v. Reno, 205 F.3d 1130, 1133 (9th Cir. 2000)).

[286] *See* R.A.V. v. City of St. Paul, 505 U.S. 377, 385-86 (1992).

[287] Fed. Election Comm'n v. Wis. Right to Life, Inc., 551 U.S. 449, 464 (2007).

[288] Al Haramain Islamic Found., Inc. v. U.S. Dep't of Treasury, 686 F.3d 965, 995 (9th Cir. 2011).

a domestic non-profit organization sought to undertake on behalf of AHIF-Oregon, a SDGT. These activities included participating in coordinated press conferences, issuing coordinated press releases, and holding demonstrations.[289] The Ninth Circuit held that OFAC's designation and blocking action violated plaintiffs' First Amendment rights.[290] The court reasoned that AHIF-Oregon was a "domestic branch of an international organization with little evidence that the pure-speech activities proposed . . . on behalf of the domestic branch will aid the larger international organization's sinister purposes."[291] As such, OFAC's designation of AHIF-Oregon as a SDGT prohibited a domestic organization from engaging in speech-related activities, but did not advance a compelling governmental interest, and therefore, it did not survive strict scrutiny.

3.   Fourth Amendment Claims

Courts are divided on whether blocking assets under E.O. 13224 constitutes an unreasonable seizure under the Fourth Amendment. The Fourth Amendment provides that "[t]he right of the people to be secure in their persons, houses, papers, and effects, against unreasonable searches and seizures, shall not be violated."[292] "A 'seizure' of property occurs when there is some meaningful interference with an individual's possessory interests in that property."[293] A "search," on the other hand, "occurs when an expectation of privacy that society is prepared to consider reasonable is infringed."[294]

Courts that have considered the issue have disagreed as to whether freezing assets is a "seizure" for purposes of the Fourth Amendment.[295] In *United States v. El-Mezain*, the Fifth Circuit found that OFAC's blocking order had a "debilitating effect" because it gave the government complete control over the defendants' assets and "reduced defendants' interests to a minimum."[296] As such, the court concluded that the blocking order constituted a meaningful interference with a

---

[289] *Id.* at 998.

[290] *Id.* at 1001.

[291] *Id.*

[292] U.S. Const. amend. IV.

[293] United States v. Jacobsen, 466 U.S. 109, 113 (1984).

[294] *Id.*

[295] *See, e.g.*, Zarmach Oil Servs. v. U.S. Dep't of Treasury, 750 F. Supp. 2d 150, 160 (D.D.C. 2010) (blocking action is not a seizure entitled to Fourth Amendment protection); Islamic Am. Relief Agency v. Unidentified FBI Agents, 394 F. Supp. 2d 34, 47-48 (D.D.C. 2005) (same). Some courts have taken the opposite view, finding that blocking orders are "seizures" under the Fourth Amendment. *See, e.g.*, Al Haramain Islamic Found., Inc. v. U.S. Dep't of Treasury, 686 F.3d 965, 994 (9th Cir. 2011) ("[W]e reject OFAC's argument that its blocking orders are *per se* reasonable under the 'general reasonableness' approach."); KindHearts v. Geithner, 647 F. Supp. 2d at 872 (N.D. Ohio 2009) ("An OFAC block interferes with possessory rights, and is, in Fourth Amendment terms, a seizure.").

[296] United States v. El-Mezain, 664 F.3d 467, 543 (5th Cir. 2011).

possessory interest.[297] In *Al Haramain Islamic Foundation, Inc. v. U.S. Department of Treasury*, the Ninth Circuit reached the same conclusion. The Ninth Circuit found that "designation [as a SDGT] is not a mere inconvenience or burden on certain property interests; designation indefinitely renders a domestic organization financially defunct."[298] Further, "[a] blocking order effectively shuts down the private entity."[299] However, in *Zarmach Oil Services v. U.S. Department of Treasury*, the District Court for the District of Columbia held that freezing assets was not a seizure under the Fourth Amendment.[300]

The courts that agree that asset-blocking is a seizure are divided on whether such action is unreasonable absent a warrant. In *El-Mezain*, the Fifth Circuit balanced the government's "extremely high" interest in preventing actions that could facilitate terrorism against the defendants' possessory and privacy interests.[301] The defendants failed to object to the blocking under the Fourth Amendment, so the court inferred that defendants had a "greatly reduced" possessory interest and consequently, a much weaker privacy interest in the blocked property.[302] The Fifth Circuit held that "[i]n light of the Government's strong interest in combatting terrorism, and the minimal intrusion here to the defendants' diminished interests," the government "did not infringe the defendants' Fourth Amendment rights" by moving the HLF's property from the HLF offices into a storage facility until it obtained a judicial warrant to search the materials.[303] However, it should be noted that the Fifth Circuit's ruling is narrowly tailored to the facts of the case. Because the initial seizure resulted in a meaningful interference with the defendants' possessory interests, the court likely would have found a Fourth Amendment violation had OFAC failed to subsequently obtain a judicial warrant to search the materials.

Some courts maintain that if OFAC's SDGT designation is not arbitrary and capricious, the blocking action is "reasonable" under the Fourth Amendment. In *Kadi v. Geithner*, the district court held that OFAC's decision to block Kadi's assets did not violate the Fourth Amendment.[304] Even assuming OFAC's blocking order constituted a "seizure," the court concluded that Kadi's designation as an SDGT was supported by "substantial evidence" and therefore it was "not issued unreasonably or without probable cause."[305]

---

[297] *Id.*

[298] Al Haramain Islamic Found., Inc. v. U.S. Dep't of Treasury, 660 F.3d 1019, 1032 (9th Cir. 2011).

[299] *Id.* at 1045.

[300] *Zarmach Oil Servs.*, 750 F. Supp. 2d at 160.

[301] United States v. El-Mezain, 664 F.3d at 544.

[302] *Id.* at 544-45.

[303] *Id.* at 545.

[304] Kadi v. Geithner, 2012 WL 898778, at *31 (D.D.C. 2012).

[305] *Id.*; *see also* Islamic Am. Relief Agency v. Unidentified FBI Agents, 394 F. Supp. 2d 34, 48 (D.D.C. 2005) (because OFAC's decision to issue a blocking order was not arbitrary and capricious, plaintiff could not state a cognizable Fourth Amendment claim); Holy Land Found. for Relief & Dev. v. Ashcroft, 219 F. Supp. 2d 57, 78-79 (D.D.C. 2002) (same).

Other courts have held that absent a warrant, an OFAC blocking action violates the Fourth Amendment. In *Al Haramain Islamic Foundation, Inc. v. U.S. Department of Treasury*, the Ninth Circuit found that OFAC's warrantless seizure violated AHIF-Oregon's Fourth Amendment rights.[306] The court held there was no Fourth Amendment exception that applied to OFAC's warrantless seizure of AHIF-Oregon's assets, therefore, the seizure was not justified under a "general reasonableness" test.[307]

Finally, courts that have considered this issue have all held that OFAC blocking actions do not fall within the "special needs" exception to Fourth Amendment requirement of probable cause and a judicially issued search warrant. The special needs exception was first articulated in *New Jersey v. T.L.O.*[308] In a concurring opinion, Justice Blackmun stated:

> Only in those exceptional circumstances in which special needs, beyond the normal need for law enforcement, make the warrant and probable-cause impracticable, is a court entitled to substitute its balancing of interests for that of the Framers.[309]

Three requirements must be satisfied for the special needs exception to apply. First, the seizure must be for important non-law enforcement purposes.[310] Second, a warrant and probable cause must be impracticable.[311] Third, there must be sufficient safeguards in place that act as a "constitutionally adequate substitute for a warrant."[312] In *Al Haramain Islamic Foundation, Inc. v. U.S. Department of Treasury*, the Ninth Circuit held that the special needs exception did not apply to the government's issuance of a blocking order under the IEEPA.[313] The court conceded that blocking orders are implemented for important non-law enforcement purposes, specifically, to prevent the funding of terrorist organizations.[314] However, the court disagreed with OFAC's assertion that it would be impracticable to obtain a warrant.[315] While the court acknowledged that the

---

[306] Al Haramain Islamic Found., Inc. v. U.S. Dep't of Treasury, 686 F.3d 965, 995 (9th Cir. 2011).

[307] *Id.*

[308] New Jersey v. T.L.O., 469 U.S. 325 (1985).

[309] *Id.* at 351. The special needs exception has been applied in various non-criminal search situations, such as searches of prisoners, parolees, probationers, border searches, immigration stops and searches, airport security, and administrative searches. *See* 2 JOHN WELSLEY HALL, JR., SEARCH AND SEIZURE, §38.2 (3d ed. 2000); *see also* KindHearts v. Geithner, 647 F. Supp. 2d 857, 880-81 (N.D. Ohio 2009) (special needs searches includes administrative searches, searches and seizures that occur at roadblock checkpoints and border crossings).

[310] *See* Ferguson v. City of Charleston, 532 U.S. 67, 81-86 (2001); City of Indianapolis v. Edmund, 531 U.S. 32, 41-47 (2000); Al Haramain Islamic Found., Inc. v. U.S. Dep't of Treasury, 686 F.3d at 990.

[311] *See* Griffin v. Wisconsin, 483 U.S. 868, 873 (1987); New Jersey v. T.L.O., 469 U.S. at 351 (Blackmun, J., concurring).

[312] New York v. Burger, 482 U.S. 691, 703 (1987).

[313] *Al Haramain Islamic Found.*, 686 F.3d at 993.

[314] *Id.* at 991, 993.

[315] *Id.* at 993.

issue of "asset flight" is a legitimate concern, it found that OFAC could protect its interest in stopping the funding of terrorism by seizing the assets *initially* pursuant to an emergency exception to the warrant requirement.[316] However, once "OFAC has blocked the assets so that asset flight is foreclosed," it would not be impracticable for OFAC to "obtain a warrant specifying the particular assets."[317]

In *KindHearts v. Geithner*, the court also found that the special needs exception did not apply to OFAC's blocking action.[318] In *KindHearts II*, the court further held that the appropriate remedy for such a violation was a *post hoc* probable cause determination.[319] However, because it was not a conventional criminal case, the court stated that the typical Fourth Amendment probable cause standard was inapplicable. Thus, the government need not show probable cause to believe that the seizure of KindHearts' assets would disclose evidence of a crime.[320] Instead, the government need only show that "at the time of the original seizure, it had probable cause—that is, a reasonable ground—to believe that KindHearts . . . was subject to designation under E.O. 13224 §1."[321]

4. Fifth Amendment Due Process Challenges

OFAC designations and blocking orders have been challenged on procedural due process grounds. Plaintiffs have advanced the following legal theories: 1) OFAC actions fail to provide meaningful notice and an opportunity to be heard; 2) use of classified information without disclosure to the designee violates due process; 3) OFAC's authority under the IEEPA and E.O. 13224 is unconstitutionally vague; and 4) OFAC blocking actions constitute an unconstitutional taking under the Takings Clause of the Fifth Amendment.

a. Notice and Opportunity to Respond

The Due Process Clause of the Fifth Amendment guarantees that "[n]o person shall . . . be deprived of life, liberty, or property, without due process of law."[322] "Due process requires notice 'reasonably calculated, under all the circumstances, to apprise interested parties of the pendency of the action and afford them an opportunity to present their objection.'"[323] Moreover, "[d]ue process is flexible and calls for such procedural protections as the particular situation

---

[316] *Id.*

[317] *Id.*

[318] *KindHearts*, 647 F. Supp. 2d 857, 878-84 (N.D. Ohio 2009).

[319] *KindHearts II*, *supra* note 57, at 648).

[320] *Id.* at 652.

[321] *Id.*

[322] U.S. Const. amend. V.

[323] United Student Aid Funds, Inc. v. Espinosa, 559 U.S. 260 (2010) (quoting Mullane v. Cent. Hanover Bank & Trust Co., 339 U.S. 306, 314 (1950)).

demands."[324] Courts have consistently held that due process does not require pre-deprivation notice in all cases. In *Calero-Toledo v. Pearson Yacht Leasing Co.*, the Supreme Court articulated a three-part test for determining whether the government is justified in delaying notice until after the seizure has already occurred.[325] To satisfy this test, the government must show "(1) the deprivation was necessary to secure an important government interest; (2) there has been a special need for very prompt action; and (3) the party initiating the deprivation was a government official responsible for determining, under the standards of a narrowly drawn statute, that it was necessary and justified in the particular instance."[326]

Courts applying the *Calero-Toledo* three-part test have uniformly agreed that due process does not require OFAC to provide notice *before* issuing a blocking order under E.O. 13224. First, OFAC's designation and blocking actions serve an "important government interest," namely "combatting terrorism by cutting off its funding."[327] Second, the potential for "asset flight" constitutes a "special need," which justifies OFAC's decision not to provide notice before freezing the assets.[328] Third, the blocking actions are taken pursuant to the IEEPA and E.O. 13224, both of which authorize such actions in limited circumstances.[329]

The Due Process Clause does require OFAC to provide meaningful notice and the opportunity for a hearing *after* the blocking action has occurred. Courts disagree, however, as to whether OFAC must provide the designated party a detailed statement citing the reasons for the decision. In *Holy Land Foundation for Relief & Development v. Ashcroft*, the D.C. Circuit held that notice and a meaningful opportunity to be heard are satisfied by a post-deprivation administrative remedy and the opportunity to present written submissions to OFAC.[330] In rejecting plaintiff's due process argument, the court posited:

> Treasury notified both Holy Land and the district court that it was reopening the administrative record and considering whether to redesignate HLF as an SDGT on the basis of additional evidence linking HLF to Hamas. Holy Land was then given thirty-one days to respond to the redesignation and the new evidence. Holy Land did respond and the Treasury considered its response as well as the new evidence before deciding to redesignate HLF. . . . Therefore, Treasury

---

[324] Gilbert v. Homar, 520 U.S. 924, 930 (1997) (brackets omitted) (quoting Morrissey v. Brewer, 408 U.S. 471, 481 (1972)).

[325] Calero-Toledo v. Pearson Yacht Leasing Co., 416 U.S. 663, 678 (1974).

[326] *Id.*

[327] Holy Land Found. for Relief & Dev. v. Ashcroft, 219 F. Supp. 2d 57, 76 (D.D.C. 2002) (*affirmed* Holy Land Found. for Relief & Dev. v. Ashcroft, 333 F.3d 156, 163-64 (D.C. Cir. 2003)).

[328] *See* Al Haramain Islamic Found., Inc. v. U.S. Dep't of Treasury, 686 F.3d 965, 985 (9th Cir. 2011); Holy Land Found. for Relief & Dev. v. Ashcroft, 333 F.3d at 163-64; Global Relief Found., Inc. v. O'Neill, 315 F.3d 748, 754 (7th Cir. 2002).

[329] *See* Holy Land Found. for Relief & Dev. v. Ashcroft, 219 F. Supp. 2d at 77.

[330] *Id.* at 163-64.

provided HLF with the requisite notice and opportunity to satisfy due process requirements.[331]

The court noted that the notice "need not disclose the classified information to be presented *in camera* and *ex parte* to the court."[332] Moreover, the court stated that the Due Process Clause does not require an agency to provide procedures that approximate a judicial trial.[333] Significantly, the sanctioned person does not have a right to confront and cross-examine witnesses.[334]

In *Al Haramain Islamic Foundation, Inc. v. U.S. Department of Treasury*, the Ninth Circuit reached the opposite result, holding that OFAC's notice violated the plaintiff's due process rights.[335] In February 2004, OFAC issued a press release stating that it had blocked the assets of AHIF-Oregon pending an investigation.[336] However, the press release did not provide the basis for the investigation.[337] Seven months later, in September 2004, OFAC issued a second press release declaring that it had designated AHIF-Oregon an SDGT.[338] The September 2004 press release alleged that AHIF-Oregon supported Chechen terrorists. In February 2008, OFAC redesignated AHIF-Oregon as a SDGT. AHIF-Oregon received a letter from OFAC specifying the following three reasons as the basis for the redesignation: "(1) being owned or controlled by [designated persons] Aqeel Al-Aqil and Al-Buthe, (2) acting for or on behalf of [designated persons] Al-Aqil and Al-Buthe, and (3) supporting and operating as a branch office of AHIF, and international charity that employed its branch offices to provide financial, material, and other services and support to al Qaeda and other [designated persons]."[339]

The court found that the 2004 press release issued seven months after the plaintiff's assets had been frozen failed to provide sufficient notice of the reasons for the blocking action.[340] More specifically, the press release gave notice concerning only one of the three reasons for OFAC's investigation and AHIF-Oregon's designation, and the notice was untimely because it was issued seven months after OFAC froze AHIF-Oregon's assets.[341] The court held that

---

[331] *Id.*; *see also* Kadi v. Geithner, 2012 WL 898778 (D.D.C. 2012) (holding that the requirements of due process were satisfied); Al-Aqeel v. Paulson, 568 F. Supp. 2d 64 (D.D.C. 2008) (the OFAC press release which cited a variety of sources and reports identifying Al-Aqeel as the Chairman, Director General and President of AHF and designating him as a SDGT, provided plaintiff adequate notice of the reasons for his SDGT designation).

[332] Holy Land Found. for Relief & Dev. v. Ashcroft, 333 F.3d at 164.

[333] *Id.*

[334] *Id.*

[335] Al Haramain Islamic Found., Inc. v. U.S. Dep't of Treasury, 686 F.3d 965, 988 (9th Cir. 2011).

[336] *Id.* at 973.

[337] *Id.*

[338] *Id.* at 973-74.

[339] *Id.*

[340] *Id.* at 986.

[341] *Id.*

"[s]uch a significantly untimely and incomplete notice does not meet the require-ments of due process."[342] Thus, according to the court, OFAC must provide a complete statement of its reasons for a blocking action to comply with due process.

The court also rejected OFAC's argument that it was impractical to provide all the reasons to AHIF-Oregon during its four-year investigation. The court stated that clearly OFAC had its reasons for investigating AFIF-Oregon, and providing plaintiff a summary of those reasons would not present an impractical burden.[343] The court stated:

> We can envision situations in which OFAC acts so quickly between the original deprivation and its decision to designate that it may be impractical to provide a statement of reasons. But the seven-month period of the original investigation, and certainly the four-year period of the entire redesignation determination, gave OFAC ample time to provide AHIF-Oregon with, at a minimum, a terse and complete statement of reasons for the investigation.[344]

In *KindHearts v. Geithner*, the district court also held that OFAC's notice vio-lated plaintiff's due process rights because any notice provided by OFAC was given in a piecemeal, untimely manner.[345] According to the court, the initial notice of the blocking order pending investigation simply recited the criteria from E.O. 13224 and referenced the IEEPA.[346] Further, OFAC did not disclose any of the unclassified administrative record to KindHearts or give it access to any of the document seized during a search of KindHearts' premises.[347] Approxi-mately one year later, OFAC notified KindHearts that it had completed its inves-tigation and provisionally designated KindHearts as an SDGT.[348] OFAC's notice of provisional designation included numerous unclassified documents, such as court opinions and indictments, articles on Hamas, OFAC press releases, newspaper articles, and KindHearts' newsletters as well as its organizational chart.[349] However, OFAC failed to explain how those materials related to Kind-Hearts' designation as an SDGT.[350]

The court held that "[t]o comply with due process requirements, OFAC should, at the very least, have promptly given KindHearts the unclassified admin-istrative record on which it relied in taking its blocking action."[351] Further, OFAC

---

[342] *Id.*

[343] *Id.*

[344] *Id.* at 986.

[345] KindHearts v. Geithner, 647 F. Supp. 2d 857, 906 (N.D. Ohio 2009).

[346] *Id.* at 901.

[347] *Id.* at 902.

[348] *Id.* at 865.

[349] *Id.* at 903.

[350] *Id.* at 902; *see also* Al Haramain Islamic Found., Inc. v. U.S. Dep't of Treasury, 585 F. Supp. 2d 1233, 1255-56 (D. Or. 2008) (holding that the government failed to provide constitutionally adequate notice when it provided documents supporting its designation and redesignation but failed to explain the significance of the evidence).

[351] KindHearts v. Geithner, 647 F. Supp. 2d 857, 905 (N.D. Ohio 2009).

should have also provided its estimate of the approximate amount of donations, or what portions of KindHearts' funds went to Hamas or individuals and entities related to Hamas, and which recipients of funds were fronts for Hamas.[352] Without such information, any challenge to the blocking action would be ineffective and unsuccessful.[353] However, it should be noted that no other court has interpreted OFAC's obligations under the Due Process Clause so broadly. The court also held that OFAC's procedures for challenging the blocking action failed to provide a meaningful opportunity to be heard.[354] OFAC waited 15 months after the blocking action pending investigation before making a provisional determination and providing KindHearts with access to an unclassified administrative record.[355] The court held that a party whose assets are blocked pending investigation is entitled to prompt notice of the reasons for the blocking action, and that a 15-month delay in notifying the plaintiff of these reasons is inconsistent with due process principles.[356]

However, the *KindHearts* district court rejected plaintiff's due process argument that a hearing before the Director of OFAC violates the due process right to a hearing before a neutral decision maker. In finding that the OFAC hearing satisfies due process, the court relied on *Withrow v. Larkin*,[357] where the Supreme Court held that members of administrative agencies typically receive the results of investigations and "approve the filing of charges . . . and then to participate in the . . . hearings."[358]

b.   OFAC's Use of Classified Information

Plaintiffs have also argued that OFAC's use of classified information in making its designation determinations violates due process. However, this argument has been rejected by every court in which it has been considered.[359] In *Holy Land Foundation for Relief & Development v. Ashcroft*, the D.C. Circuit held that due process does not prevent OFAC from designating a party as an SDGT on the basis of classified information disclosed only to the court *ex parte* and *in camera*.[360] The D.C. Circuit relied on its earlier ruling in *People's Mojahedin Organization of Iran v. U.S. Department of State*, where it rejected a claim that use of classified information for designating plaintiff a foreign terrorist organization violated due

---

[352] *Id.* at 904.

[353] *Id.* at 905.

[354] *Id.* at 907-08.

[355] *Id.* at 907.

[356] *Id.* at 908.

[357] *Id.* at 908 n.29.

[358] Withrow v. Larkin, 421 U.S. 35, 56 (1975).

[359] *See* Al Haramain Islamic Found., Inc. v. U.S. Dep't of Treasury, 686 F.3d 965, 982 (9th Cir. 2011); Holy Land Found. for Relief & Dev. v. Ashcroft, 333 F.3d 156, 164 (D.C. Cir. 2003); Global Relief Found., Inc. v. O'Neill, 315 F.3d 748, 754 (7th Cir. 2002); *KindHearts II, supra* note 57, *at* 660; *Al-Aqeel v. Paulson*, 568 F. Supp. 2d 64, 72 (D.D.C. 2008).

[360] Holy Land Found. for Relief & Dev. v. Ashcroft, 333 F.3d at 164.

process where that information was disclosed only to the court and not the plaintiff.[361] In that decision, the court justified withholding classified information from plaintiffs by "emphasiz[ing] the primacy of the Executive in controlling and exercising responsibility over access to classified information," as well as the Executive's "'compelling interest' in withholding national security information from unauthorized persons in the course of executive business."[362] In *Holy Land Foundation for Relief & Development v. Ashcroft*, the D.C. Circuit applied the reasoning in *People's Mojahedin Organization of Iran* with equal force to OFAC designations. The court opined:

> That the designation comes under an Executive Order issued under a different statutory scheme makes no difference. HLF's complaint, like that of the Designated Foreign Terrorist Organization in the earlier cases, that due process prevents its designation based upon classified information to which it has not had access is of no avail.[363]

In *Al Haramain Islamic Foundation, Inc. v. U.S. Department of Treasury*, the Ninth Circuit reached the same conclusion as the D.C. Circuit, holding that given the extreme importance of maintaining national security, OFAC may use classified information in making its designation determinations.[364] OFAC designations may therefore be supported by classified information not disclosed to the designated person or entity.[365]

c.   Unconstitutional Vagueness

Plaintiffs have also brought vagueness challenges to the ban imposed by E.O. 13224 on the provision of services to SDGTs. Section 1(d)(i) of the order permits the Secretary of the Treasury to designate individuals and entities who "provide . . . financial or other services to or in support of" acts of terrorism or to SDGTs.[366] Section 2(a) prohibits "any transaction or dealing by U.S. persons or within the United States in property or interests in property blocked" pursuant to E.O. 13224, "including but not limited to . . . services, to or for the benefit of" an SDGT. [367]

---

[361] People's Mojahedin Org. of Iran v. U.S. Dep't of State, 327 F.3d 1238, 1242 (D.C. Cir. 2003).

[362] *Id.*

[363] Holy Land Found. for Relief & Dev. v. Ashcroft, 333 F.3d at 164.

[364] Al Haramain Islamic Found., Inc. v. U.S. Dep't of Treasury, 686 F.3d 965, 980-81 (9th Cir. 2011).

[365] *Id.*; *see also* Global Relief Found., Inc. v. O'Neill, 315 F.3d 748, 754 (7th Cir. 2002) ("The Constitution would indeed be a suicide pact if the only way to curtail enemies' access to assets were to reveal information that might cost lives.").

[366] E.O. 13224, *supra* note 24, §1(d)(i).

[367] *Id.* §2(a).

III. Economic Sanctions Against Suspected Terrorists

"A statute must be sufficiently clear so as to allow persons of 'ordinary intelligence a reasonable opportunity to know what is prohibited.'"[368] Statutes that are insufficiently clear are void for three reasons: "(1) to avoid punishing people for behavior that they could not have known was illegal; (2) to avoid subjective enforcement of the laws based on 'arbitrary and discriminatory enforcement' by government officers; and (3) to avoid any chilling effect on the exercise of First Amendment freedoms."[369] While the Treasury regulations do not provide a definition of "services," they clarify the meaning of the term by providing a non-exhaustive list of various types of "services," including "legal, accounting, financial, brokering, freight forwarding, transportation, public relations[.]"[370] The examples make clear that educational services are prohibited, and that "one should not perform a useful professional or business task for a terrorist organization."[371] In *Humanitarian Law Project v. U.S. Department of Treasury*, the Ninth Circuit dismissed plaintiffs' vagueness challenge, holding that even if, standing alone, the term "services" is ambiguous, "the[se] examples alert a person of ordinary intelligence to the services that should not be provided to or for the benefit of SDGTs."[372]

5. Fifth Amendment Takings Claim

OFAC blocking orders have also been challenged as an uncompensated taking, in violation of the Takings Clause of the Fifth Amendment. The Fifth Amendment provides that no "private property [shall] be taken for public use, without just compensation."[373] Courts considering similar Fifth Amendment "takings" challenges have rejected them on two grounds. First, federal district courts lack subject matter jurisdiction over such claims, which must be brought before the Court of Federal Claims under the Tucker Act, 28 U.S.C. §1491.[374] In *Dames & Moore v. Regan*, the Supreme Court held that the Court of Federal Claims is the proper forum for claims alleging an unconstitutional taking.[375]

---

[368] Foti v. City of Menlo Park, 146 F.3d 629, 638 (9th Cir. 1998) (quoting Grayned v. City of Rockford, 408 U.S. 104, 108 (1972)).

[369] *Foti*, 146 F.3d at 638.

[370] 31 C.F.R. §594.406.

[371] Humanitarian Law Project v. U.S. Dep't of Treasury, 578 F.3d 1133, 1146 (9th Cir. 2009).

[372] *Id.* at 1146-47.

[373] U.S. Const. amend V.

[374] 28 U.S.C. §1491(a)(1) provides:

> The United States Court of Federal Claims shall have jurisdiction to render judgment upon any claims against the United States founded either upon the Constitution, or any Act of Congress or any regulation of an executive department. . . .

[375] Dames & Moore v. Regan, 453 U.S. 654, 688-89 (1981); *see also* Kadi v. Geithner, 2012 WL 898778, at *25 (D.D.C. 2012) ("Even if the Notice of Blocking constituted a 'taking,' pursuant to the Tucker Act, 28 U.S.C. §1491, jurisdiction would rest in the Court of Federal Claims, not here."); Islamic Am. Relief Agency v. Unidentified FBI Agents, 394 F. Supp. 2d 34, 51 (D.D.C. 2005); Holy

Second, courts uniformly hold that blocking orders under E.O. 13224 are temporary deprivations that do not constitute a "taking" within the meaning of the Fifth Amendment. Since blocking does not vest the blocked assets in the government, it does not constitute a cognizable "taking" under the Fifth Amendment.[376]

C. International Asset Freeze

The UN Security Council has adopted several resolutions to prevent and suppress acts of terrorism by requiring Member States to freeze the assets of suspected terrorists. The international asset freeze program has its origins in UN Security Council Resolutions 1267, 1333, and 1373.[377] While the Security Council has adopted a number of successor resolutions intended to strengthen the mandate of these resolutions, these three resolutions constitute the foundation of the international sanctions regime to freeze terrorist-related assets. Resolution 1267 imposes various obligations on Member States, including the duty to "[f]reeze funds and other financial resources, including funds derived or generated from property owned or controlled, directly or indirectly by the Taliban, or by any undertaking owned or controlled by the Taliban."[378] Resolution 1333 goes beyond imposing sanctions on state actors, such as the Taliban. Resolution 1333 imposes measures on individuals and nonstate entities, mandating a freeze on the financial assets of Osama bin Laden, Al Qaeda, and associated individuals and entities.[379] Under Resolution 1333, states are required to freeze "without delay" the funds and other financial assets of bin Laden, members of Al Qaeda, and their associates, and ensure that no funds or financial resources are made available to them or any entities owned or controlled by bin Laden, or individuals and entities associated with him, including the Al Qaeda organization.[380]

In the aftermath of the September 11, 2001 terrorist attacks, the UN Security Council unanimously adopted Resolution 1373, which imposes several important duties on Member States to combat the threat of global terrorism. Specifically, states are required to 1) prevent the movement of designated terrorists by

---

Land Found. for Relief & Dev. v. Ashcroft, 219 F. Supp. 2d 57, 78 n.32 (D.D.C. 2002); Global Relief Found., Inc. v. O'Neill, 315 F.3d 748, 754 (7th Cir. 2002) ("Global Relief Foundation's takings claim not only is premature—it must await decision on the validity of the Global Terrorist designation—but also is in the wrong court. It belongs to the Court of Federal Claims under the Tucker Act.").

[376] See Islamic Am. Relief Agency, 394 F. Supp. 2d at 51; Holy Land Found. for Relief & Dev., 219 F. Supp. 2d at 75.

[377] See S.C. 1267, UN Doc. S/RES/1267 (1999); S.C. 1333, UN Doc. S/RES/1333 (2000); S.C. Res. 1373, UN Doc. S/RES/1373 (2001). For a comprehensive discussion of the international sanctions regime developed pursuant to Resolutions 1267, 1333, and 1373, see GURULÉ & CORN, PRINCIPLES OF COUNTER-TERRORISM LAW, supra note 43, at 331-63; GURULÉ, UNFUNDING TERROR, supra note 26, at 233-75.

[378] S.C. Res. 1267, ¶ 4(b).

[379] S.C. Res. 1333.

[380] Id. ¶ 8c).

III. Economic Sanctions Against Suspected Terrorists

effective border controls and controls on the issuance of travel documents (travel ban), 2) prevent the supply of weapons to terrorists (arms embargo), 3) deny safe haven to those who plan, support, or commit terrorist acts (safe haven ban), and 4) afford states the greatest measure of assistance in connection with criminal terrorism investigations (mutual assistance).[381] Resolution 1373 further imposes certain obligations on Member States to prevent and suppress the financing of terrorism. First, states are required to criminalize the willful provision or collection of terrorist-related funds.[382] Second, states must ensure that any person who participates in financing terrorist acts is prosecuted and brought to justice.[383] Third, states must prohibit persons and entities from making financial assets, economic resources, and financial services available to persons who commit or facilitate the commission of terrorist acts.[384] Finally, Resolution 1373 authorizes states to "freeze without delay funds and other financial assets or economic resources" of terrorists, those who finance terrorism, and terrorist organizations around the world.[385]

The effectiveness of the UN sanctions program to deprive terrorists of funding has been dealt a devastating blow by a decision of the European Court of Justice (ECJ), the highest court in the European Union (EU). In *Kadi and Al Barakaat International Foundation v. Council of the European Union*, the ECJ ruled that the EU's application of UN economic sanctions against Yassin Kadi, a wealthy Saudi businessman, and Al Barakaat International Foundation, an international money remitter based in Sweden, violated their due process rights. As such, the ECJ held that the blocking actions were illegal under EU law[386] because including the appellants' names on the EU list of persons and entities whose funds are to be frozen violated the Charter of Fundamental Rights of the European Union—in particular, the right to be heard and the right to an effective judicial review.[387] According to the ECJ, appellants cannot be deprived of their property absent a hearing before an independent judicial officer affording them the opportunity to challenge their designation and any blocking actions ordered pursuant to UN Security Council Resolution 1267.[388]

---

[381] *See* S.C. Res. 1373, ¶¶ 2(a), (c), (f), & (g); *see also* ALISTAIR MILLAR & ERIC ROSAND, ALLIED AGAINST TERRORISM, 16 (Century Foundation Press 2006).

[382] S.C. Res. 1373, ¶ 1(b).

[383] *Id.* ¶ 2(e).

[384] *Id.* ¶ 1(d).

[385] *Id.* ¶ 1(c).

[386] *See* Joined Cases C-402/05 P and C-415/05 P, Kadi & Al Barakaat Int'l Found. v. Council of the European Union and Comm'n of the E.C. (E.C.J. Judgment), Sept. 3, 2008 [hereinafter 2008 ECJ *Kadi* decision], *available at* http://curia.europa.eu/en/conent/juris/index.htm. For a comprehensive discussion of the 2008 ECJ *Kadi* decision, see GURULÉ & CORN, PRINCIPLES OF COUNTER-TERRORISM LAW, *supra* note 43, Ch. 9: International Economic Sanctions.

[387] *Id.* ¶ 348; *see also* Joined Cases C-584/10 P, C-593/10 P and C-595/10 P, Comm'n of E.C., et al. v. Kadi (E.C.J. Judgment), July 18, 2013 (dismissing the appeal of the European Commission and holding that the EU blocking action against Kadi violated the Charter of Fundamental Rights of the European Union, including the right to be heard and right to ascertain the reasons upon which the decision was taken to block his property).

[388] *See* 2008 ECJ *Kadi* decision, *supra* note 386, at ¶ 348.

The legal controversy over the procedural protections afforded parties designated for asset freeze seriously threatens the future of the UN sanctions regime. Although the *Kadi and Al Barakaat International Foundation* judgment applies only to those two parties, the ECJ ruling has far-reaching implications. Unless the 28 EU Member States find a way to implement Security Council Resolutions 1267, 1333, and 1367 in a manner that satisfies the Charter of Fundamental Rights of the European Union, the UN sanctions regime may collapse.[389] Further, the *Kadi and Al Barakaat International Foundation* judgment could have a chilling effect on future designations and blocking actions. Finally, the ECJ judgment creates an untenable situation for EU Member States, requiring them to choose between implementing measures imposed by relevant Security Council resolutions or following the ECJ decision. Ultimately, noncompliance by EU Member States could lead to the demise of the UN sanctions regime.

IV.   FOREIGN TERRORIST ORGANIZATIONS

Section 2 of the Antiterrorism and Effective Death Penalty Act of 1996 (codified at 8 U.S.C. §1189), authorizes the Secretary of State, in consultation with the Secretary of the Treasury and the Attorney General, to designate an entity as a "foreign terrorist organization" (FTO).[390] To designate a foreign group as an FTO requires the Secretary of State to make three findings: "(1) the organization is a foreign organization, (2) the organization engages in terrorist activity, and (3) the terrorist activity threatens national security or the security of U.S. nationals."[391] In making an FTO determination, the Secretary of State compiles an administrative record and makes "findings" based on this record.[392] The administrative record may include classified information that may be withheld from the designated party.[393] Further, the Secretary of State is not required to

---

[389] *See* Richard Barrett, *Al-Qaida and Taliban Sanctions Threatened,* Washington Institute of Near East Policy (Oct. 6, 2008).

[390] Anti-Terrorism and Effective Death Penalty Act of 1996, *supra* note 222. As of December 31, 2012, 51 foreign organizations or groups had been designated as FTOs by the Department of State. *See Terrorist Assets Report, supra* note 29, at 5. These 51 FTOs include 11 of the 12 Middle East terrorist organizations designated under Executive Orders 12947 and 13099 as well as 40 other foreign organizations located in South America, Europe, Asia, and Africa. *Id.* at 5-6. All 51 of these groups also have been designated pursuant to Executive Order 13224. *Id.* at 5 n. 7.

[391] 8 U.S.C. §§1189(a)(1)(A)-(C). "The term 'national security' means the national defense, foreign relations, or economic interests of the United States." *Id.* §1189(d)(2).

[392] *Id.* §1189(a)(3)(A).

[393] *Id.* §1189(a)(3)(B); *see also* People's Mojahedin Org. of Iran v. U.S. Dep't of State, 327 F.3d 1238, 1240-41 (D.C. Cir. 2003); Nat'l Council of Resistance of Iran v. U.S. Dep't of State, 251 F.3d 192, 209 (D.C. Cir. 2001).

notify a foreign organization *prior* to designation as an FTO.[394] However, seven days before designating an organization as an FTO, the Secretary must submit a "classified communication" to key Congressional leaders and committee members detailing the Secretary's findings.[395] After congressional notice, the FTO designation is published in the Federal Register.[396]

Designation as an FTO carries severe economic consequences and criminal liability. First, financial institutions are required to freeze the assets of an FTO that are located in the United States.[397] Second, members and representatives of the FTO are banned from traveling to the United States.[398] Finally 18 U.S.C. §2339B imposes severe criminal penalties for knowingly providing "material support or resources" to an FTO.[399]

An FTO designation can be revoked in three ways: "(1) Congress blocks or revokes a designation, 8 U.S.C. §1189(a)(5); (2) the Secretary [of State] revokes the designation based on a finding that changed circumstances or national security warrants such a revocation, 8 U.S.C. §1189(a)(6)(A); or (3) the D.C. Circuit sets aside the designation under 8 U.S.C. §1189(c)(3)."[400] The D.C. Circuit has exclusive jurisdiction to review FTO designations.[401] However, the court may only review the Secretary's findings that the entity is a "foreign" organization and that it engages is "terrorist activity."[402] The court does not review whether the terrorist activity threatens the security of the United States or U.S. nationals. Finally, an FTO seeking to challenge its designation must do so no later than 30 days after the Secretary of State publishes the designation in the Federal Register.[403]

V. CONCLUSION

U.S. courts have upheld sanctions to serve foreign policy goals. Courts rarely second-guess the substance of sanctions decisions. However, they do police the borders of due process.

---

[394] *See* Nat'l Council of Resistance of Iran v. U.S. Dep't of State, 251 F.3d at 209 (holding that due process requires that entities under consideration be afforded notice that the designation is impending, but allowing such notice to be delayed until after designation if pre-designation notice would jeopardize national security or foreign policy).

[395] 8 U.S.C. §1189(a)(2)(A)(i).

[396] *Id.* §1189(a)(2)(A)(ii).

[397] 18 U.S.C. §2339B(a)(2).

[398] 8 U.S.C. §1189(a)(3)(B)(i).

[399] 18 U.S.C. §2339B.

[400] United States v. Taleb-Jedi, 566 F. Supp. 2d 157, 163 (E.D.N.Y. 2008).

[401] *Id.*

[402] *Id.*; *see also* People's Mojahedin Org. of Iran v. U.S. Dep't of State, 327 F.3d 1238, 1240-41 (D.C. Cir. 2003).

[403] 8 U.S.C. §1189(c)(1).

CHAPTER 12

National Security Law and Emerging Technologies

National security is big business in the United States, involving the expenditure of billions of taxpayer dollars. Major corporations have begun and remained vibrant almost solely due to the U.S. defense industry. How these businesses and the government interact plays a critical role in the national security of the United States; thus, the successful defense of the nation is inseparably interwoven with corporate America. Law often defines how these relationships work. This chapter will look at the nature of these relationships and the frictions that are inherent in a free market system that is directly tied to government requirements. The chapter will also consider the changing nature of national security threats, including advanced technologies and weapons systems, and how defending against those advanced technologies, as well as developing them, presents frictions for the current system of national security law and economic freedom.

I.   ENCOURAGEMENT AND REGULATION

Topic #1

Lockheed Martin, Boeing, Northrup Grumman, General Dynamics, and Raytheon account for almost $150 billion in arms sales annually. Not all of these weapons systems and services are purchased by the United States, but much of them are and that which is sold elsewhere is heavily regulated by U.S. law. This section will discuss ways in which the U.S. government both encourages and regulates development, production, and sale of weapons systems both to the United States and other countries.

A.   *Encouraging the Defense Industry*

US uses private industry

Unlike command economies where the government directs areas of production (including the development of weapons), the United States has to rely on private industry to supply the needs of the U.S. Department of Defense (DoD). Part of that approach is to allow market principles to drive production and innovation. These market principles are often supplemented by regulatory schemes or tax incentives, but private corporations do most of the development and production of weapons by responding to the needs of the military and other government agencies.

I. Encouragement and Regulation

In order to let market forces work for the benefit of both private industry and the government, lines of communication have to be established to allow the government to let industry know what it needs. These lines of communication are established in a number of ways, some formal and others informal. For example, as will be further discussed below, the DoD or its separate branches will publish a request for bids as part of the contract process. The request for bids will specify what the government entity needs, whether it is 1,000 tanks or 1 aircraft. Private industry will then have time to look at the request and put together a bid to supply that good or service. The government then selects a supplier based on specific criteria discussed below and contracts with that supplier.

Some needs are transmitted less formally. Suppose a contractor gets a contract to supply missile systems. That contractor will send maintenance and review personnel to the areas where that system will be used. As contract personnel deploy with members of the military, their proximity to military operations also provides them with a continual stream of feedback on developing needs experienced by military personnel. For example, as the missile system is used in actual military operations, potential modifications to the system that would benefit the military may become apparent. These needs can then be addressed by the contractor.

Of course, the biggest incentive for private industry is profit. As the DoD expresses needs and contractors fill those needs, the profits can be sizable. The same five contractors listed above experienced more than $12.5 billion in profit from those same sales in that year. Government contracts can be very lucrative, even in an era of fiscal austerity. Because national defense is not an area most politicians like to cut, money continues to be available to defense industries who appropriately tailor their offerings.

B. Regulating the Defense Industry

Though the contracting system is a great incentive to defense contractors because it is one way that the DoD's needs are transmitted, it is also a significant regulator of the system. Government contracting and procurement law is a highly detailed and intricate portion of national security law that requires careful study and attention to detail. Many of the rules are contained in the United States Code,[1] the Federal Acquisition Regulation,[2] the Defense Federal Acquisition Regulation,[3] and Comptroller General Opinions.[4] Many civilian and uniformed

---

[1] For example, see 31 U.S.C. §1301, which is known as the "purpose" statute and will be discussed below.

[2] Federal Acquisition Regulation (FAR), GSA, DOD, NASA, March 2005, *available at* http://www.acquisition.gov/far/current/pdf/FAR.pdf

[3] Defense Federal Acquisition Regulation System (DFARS), DOD, last updated 11/18/2013, *available at* http://www.acq.osd.mil/dpap/dars/dfarspgi/current/index.html.

[4] See, e.g., Presidio Trust—Use of Appropriated Funds for Audio Equipment Rental Fees and Services, B-306424, 2006 U.S. Comp. Gen. LEXIS 57 (Mar. 24, 2006), for a discussion of the "necessary expense" rule.

lawyers are completely dedicated to ensuring the contracting and procurement practices are done well and in compliance with the law.

To help illustrate the process, assume the DoD determines that it needs a large number of rifles to supply its soldiers. A military commander can rarely walk into a local weapons store and purchase rifles for his soldiers. Instead, he will work through the contracting and procurement processes mentioned above. Numerous constraints exist on spending government money. Initially, the right kind of money must be spent. In other words, Congress gives or appropriates money to the DoD for specific purposes. When the money arrives, it is put into specific "pots," which can then only be used for those purposes. For example, Congress gives money to DoD for construction projects that DoD tells Congress it needs to accomplish. DoD cannot later decide to take the construction money and spend it on buying a new weapon system. Rather, that new weapon system would have to be funded out of money set aside by Congress for procurement.

Even if the right pot of money is available, other restrictions apply. Congress gives money for a specific amount of time, and that money will eventually "expire." If it is not used within the designated time frame, it goes back into the Federal Treasury. Also, even if Congress has allocated money for a specific purchase, there must be a bona fide need for that purchase to occur or the money cannot be spent. So, if circumstances change, making that expenditure no longer necessary, the purchase cannot be made.

Finally, the enforcement of fiscal constraints is backed by the Anti-Deficiency Act,[5] which provides for individual criminal and civil penalties for persons who violate contract and fiscal constraints on government spending.

These are just a few general principles that apply to spending government funds, but they highlight how regulated this area of the law is. Though these rules do serve to notify private industry of government needs, they also provide constraints and restraints on the freedom of commerce. Some businesses will not qualify to do work with the government because of specific business practices or relationships. Others will accrue benefits, such as the small business preference, that are not applied equally to all. All businesses will have to comply with significant regulation or open themselves up to discrimination from competition or even potential criminal prosecution.

And this is just for defense contractors who want to do business with the U.S. government. Doing business with non-U.S. entities carries even more regulation.

C.   Arms Export Controls

As mentioned above, industries that provide goods and services to the DoD also provide them to other nations and entities. In fact, the United States has consistently been the number one or number two supplier of arms worldwide. Again, this is big business and American companies want to be heavily involved.

---

[5] 31 U.S.C. §§1341-42, 1511-19.

II. The Emerging Threat

The government regulates the sale of defense goods and services by U.S. companies through the Arms Export Control Act (AECA).[6] This Act gives the President the authority to apply "restraints and control measures" and to approve sales "only when they are consistent with the foreign policy interests of the United States." As with contracting and procurement, the rules of the AECA are intricate and require in-depth study, providing good jobs for lawyers both in the government and in the defense industries. Importantly, violations of the AECA carry severe penalties.

Each year hundreds of potential violations are investigated, followed by arrests, indictments, and convictions. A recent case involved a University of Tennessee professor who was convicted of violating the AECA and sentenced to 48 months in prison for sharing defense data with Chinese and Iranian graduate students who were working for him.[7] The professor had a contract with the U.S. Air Force to research plasma technology to reduce drag on airplane wings and having his graduate students work on his research, even though the information was not classified, was a violation of the AECA.[8]

The AECA and similar restraints apply equally to U.S. corporations. In a completely free market, these companies would be able to sell goods and services to whomever they wanted. Even in regulated markets, most transactions are based on profit. Here, the transaction that otherwise would be executed is proscribed by law, and the sale simply foregone. Additionally, the transaction costs to hire sufficient expertise to protect against violations of these rules are also a major inhibitor to the free market. Such rules are often debated but seldom contested in any meaningful way. Congress and the President accept that these constraints are necessary and appropriate in the furtherance of national security.

This balance between encouraging weapons development and production and the constraints on free trade necessary to assure national security is becoming even more difficult in an age of advancing technologies. As new technologies emerge, creating new weapon systems, national security law and policy must find the right place to strike that new balance.

II. THE EMERGING THREAT

The process of law creation is inherently reactive and produces laws that respond to events or situations that have already occurred. In many cases, this leads to better, more well-considered laws that sufficiently take into account

---

[6] 22 U.S.C. §2751 *et seq.*
[7] United States v. Roth, 628 F.3d 827; *cert. denied*, 2011 LEXIS 6705.
[8] United States v. Roth, 628 F.3d 827; *cert. denied*, 2011 LEXIS 6705.

the actions the laws are trying to proscribe or authorize. However, in the case of advancing technologies, it may be that the consequences of waiting until these weapons are employed will prove too catastrophic. In order for national security law to provide adequate protections, national security law and processes may need to look into the future and anticipate some of the possible threats and opportunities these advances provide.

This section will first look at advancing technologies that are likely to play a role in armed conflict in the near future, some of which are already partially in use and others that are in the very early stages of development. It will then look at the new range of actors who might employ these and other technologies and how the new range of actors also cause potential national security law issues.

A. *Technologies*[9]

Technology is continuously advancing and providing new benefits and opportunities to society. It is also creating weapons that were not previously possible. And as U.S. Deputy Secretary of State William Lynn once said, "Few weapons in the history of warfare, once created, have gone unused."[10]

Weapons technology has played an important role in national security throughout the ages, providing considerable advantage to those nations who possess advanced technology and causing great concern among those who didn't. For example, when the Spaniards arrived in Mexico with gunpowder and different rules of warfare, the Aztec nation quickly fell. Interestingly for this chapter, the greatest destruction brought by Europeans came from viruses as opposed to military arms, but the superior technology would also have eventually allowed the Europeans to prevail. The use of advances in cannons and the rifled barrel by Western forces during the Boxer Rebellion is another example of the benefits of militarily superior technology.[11] More recently, the use of radar allowed the outnumbered British planes to defeat the Luftwaffe during World War II.[12]

The benefits of leap-ahead technology need no real justification. And the international community is on the cusp of great leaps in innovative technology that will find its way into weapons systems. The following sections will highlight some evolving technologies and discuss how they create weapons that are qualitatively different than those of the past.

---

[9] For a much more detailed and referenced article on this subject, see Eric Talbot Jensen, *The Future of the Law of Armed Conflict: Ostriches, Butterflies, and Nanobots*, 35 Mich. J. Int'l L. 253 (2014), *available at* http://papers.ssrn.com/sol3/papers.cfm?abstract_id=2237509.

[10] John D. Banusiewicz, *Lynn Outlines New Cybersecurity Effort*, Fed. Info. & News Dispatch, Inc., (June 16, 2011).

[11] *The Boxer Rebellion and the U.S. Navy, 1900-1901*, Department of the Navy—Naval History and Heritage, http://www.history.navy.mil/faqs/faq86-1.htm (last visited Nov. 20, 2013).

[12] *See* David Zimmerman, Britain's Shield: Radar and the Defeat of the Luftwaffe (reprint ed. 2011).

II. The Emerging Threat

1. Cyber

It seems like every day there is a new news story of some cyber event where technology was stolen or bank accounts were hacked or web pages defaced. Some are more serious than others. A recent crime ring hacked into ATMs in major cities, stealing over $45 million from 20 countries.[13] The FBI recently added cyber-crime hackers to their most wanted lists, including Alexsey Belan, a Russian national who stole millions of identities from U.S. e-commerce companies.[14] Among the most significant cyber-attacks is the recent STUXNET malware, which infected more than 100,000 computers worldwide. STUXNET managed to destroy almost 1,000 centrifuges at an Iranian nuclear facility.[15] Similarly, the Flame malware was one of the most sophisticated and persistent pieces of malware that has ever been discovered.[16]

As a result, cyber capabilities have become the topic of interest amongst politicians as well as military leaders. In an age of shrinking defense budgets, money sought for anything "cyber" seems to still get funded. The law surrounding cyber operations has been written about extensively, including the new Tallinn Manual on the International Law Applicable to Cyber Warfare, which provides guidance on the application of the current law of armed conflict (LOAC) to cyber operations.[17] Over 140 nations have responded to the increase in cyber events by developing their own cyber capabilities.

Cyber weapons have many attractions. One is their potentially bloodless nature. For those who want to do great harm but not cause typical kinetic effects such as heat, blast, and fragmentation, cyber weapons offer a perfect alternative. They also offer an expanded array of targets. As demonstrated by the attacks described above, using cyber tools allows an attacker to reach financial and other targets that would otherwise not be readily available.

However, probably the most impactful aspect of cyber tools is their general accessibility to a growing range of actors. With many of the technologies discussed herein, the resources of a state are necessary to research, develop, and employ. But cyber tools are available and currently being used by the full array of possible actors from individuals to nations. As Symantec has noted, it does not take the resources of a nation to create something even as technical as STUXNET. The fact that cyber tools put state level violence in the hands of just about anyone is a significant development to which national security systems must respond.

---

[13] Joe Palazzolo, *More Arrests in ATM Cybercrime*, Wall St. J. (Nov. 18, 2013), http://online.wsj.com/news/articles/SB10001424052702303985504579206161498537516.

[14] Samuel Gibbs, *FBI Adds Five New Hackers to Cyber Most Wanted List*, The Guardian (Nov. 6, 2013), http://www.theguardian.com/technology/2013/nov/06/fbi-hackers-cyber-most-wanted.

[15] John Markoff, *A Silent Attack, But Not a Subtle One*, N.Y. Times (Sept. 26, 2010), http://www.nytimes.com/2010/09/27/technology/27virus.html?_r=0).

[16] CrySyS Lab, *sKyWIper (a.k.a Flame a.k.a. Flamer): A Complex Malware for Targeted Attacks* 1-3, CRYSYS LAB, http://www.crysys.hu/skywiper/skywiper.pdf (last updated May 31, 2012).

[17] The Tallinn Manual on the International Law Applicable to Cyber Warfare (Michael N. Schmitt ed., 2013).

Chapter 12.   National Security Law and Emerging Technologies

2.   Drones, Robots, and Autonomous Systems

The recent use of both armed and unarmed drones has been widely documented in the media. Drones have played a major role in the fight against terrorists in Afghanistan, Iraq, Pakistan, and Yemen, as well as less publicized roles in various other places such as in Africa. These drones are distinct from robots or other autonomous weapons because they currently require flight and weapons guidance and direction from a human, though that human may be many thousands of miles away.

As technology advances, drones will increase in capability while decreasing in size. Drones are already being developed that are as small as caterpillars and moths that replicate flight mechanics so they can "hide in plain sight."[18] Eventually, drones will be measured in terms of nanometers and will take on more and more autonomous characteristics. In addition to decreasing in size, drone lethality will increase through innovative technologies such as those discussed below.

As with cyber tools, another evolving aspect of drones is their increasing accessibility to many nonstate actors. Currently, you can build your own drone for less than $1,000. As drones miniaturize and become more lethal, many of these same capabilities will be available to the general public.

The recent use of robots in armed conflict has also been well documented. Though not as far progressed as drones and cyber operations, the use of robots is clearly increasing. They have been used in mine and bomb discovery and detonation, to provide advance warning of potential threats (particularly in room clearing operations) and in the transportation of goods in conflict zones. Some robots fit into a broader category of weapons known as autonomous weapon systems. This category also includes unarmed and armed unmanned aerial and underwater vehicles, auto-response systems such as armed unmanned sentry stations, and a host of other developing weapon systems. Robots have been and will continue to be used both for lethal and less than lethal operations. Future robotics will be fast, small, and too numerous for humans to adequately direct.

More than 40 nations are building, buying, and using military robotics today. In 2005, a U.S. Joint Forces Command report projected that autonomous robots would be commonplace within 20 years,[19] and a recent report written by the U.S. Department of Defense (DoD), titled *Unmanned Systems Integrated Roadmap FY2011-2036*, stated that it "envisions unmanned systems seamlessly operating with manned systems while gradually reducing the degree of human control and decision making required for the unmanned portion of the force structure."[20]

---

[18] *See, e.g., Nano Hummingbird*, Aerovironment, http://www.avinc.com/nano/ (last visited Nov. 15, 2013) (demonstrating a hummingbird-like drone weighing less than a AA battery).

[19] Staff, *In the Loop? Armed Robots and the Future of War*, DEF. INDUSTRY DAILY (Jan. 28, 2009, 20:09), http://www.defenseindustrydaily.com/In-the-Loop-Armed-Robots-and-the-Future-of-War-05267/.

[20] U.S. DEP'T OF DEF., UNMANNED SYSTEMS INTEGRATED ROADMAP FY2011-2036 3 (2011), *available at* http://www.defenseinnovationmarketplace.mil/resources/UnmannedSystemsIntegratedRoadmapFY2011 .pdf.

II. The Emerging Threat

DoD also recently issued a directive titled "Autonomy in Weapon Systems"[21] that applies to the "design, development, acquisition, testing, fielding, and employment of autonomous and semi-autonomous weapon systems, including guided munitions that can independently select and discriminate targets."[22] In the directive, "[i]t is DoD policy that . . . [a]utonomous and semi-autonomous weapon systems shall be designed to allow commanders and operators to exercise appropriate levels of human judgment over the use of force."[23] Many who work in the area are skeptical about the longevity of this policy and see both future armies and law enforcement relying heavily on autonomous systems, including those with lethal capabilities.

3. Virology and Genomics

Though biological agents have seldom been used on the battlefield and are generally prohibited under international law,[24] many believe they are a significant potential threat in the future. Advances in laboratory technology have made these potential weapons accessible to a much broader group of people and hundreds of "biohacker communities" have established themselves around the world. When combined with recent advances in nanotechnology, biological agents become an even greater threat, making them self-replicating, self-transmitting, remotely operable, and extremely lethal.

In addition to biological agents, there are two emerging technologies whose status under international law is unclear: virology and genomics. The rapid advances in genomics have had a multitude of benefits for modern medicine and science in general but can also be put to dangerous purposes, especially as costs decrease and accessibility increases. What used to take decades and cost hundreds of thousands of dollars in terms of sequencing and cloning DNA can now be done in three days for less than $1. And experts argue that for a few

---

[21] Department of Defense, Directive No. 3000.09, Autonomy in Weapon Systems, Nov. 21, 2012. The directive followed a DoD Defense Science Board Task Force Report on "The Role of Autonomy in DoD Systems" that was issued in July of 2012. DoD Defense Science Board, the Role of Autonomy in DoD Systems (July 2012), *available at* http://www.fas.org/irp/agency/dod/dsb/autonomy.pdf.

[22] Department of Defense, Directive No. 3000.09, Autonomy in Weapon Systems, para. 2a(2), Nov. 21, 2012. The directive does not apply to "autonomous and semi-autonomous cyberspace systems for cyberspace operations; unarmed, unmanned platforms; unguided munitions; munitions manually guided by the operator (e.g. laser- or wire-guided munitions); mines; or unexploded explosive ordnance." *Id.* at para. 2b.

[23] Department of Defense, Directive No. 3000.09, Autonomy in Weapon Systems, para. 4a, Nov. 21, 2012.

[24] 137 Nations are parties to the Protocol for the Prohibition of the Use of Asphyxiating, Poisonous or Other Gases, and of Bacteriological Methods of Warfare, and in 1972, the Convention on the Prohibition of the Development, Production and Stockpiling of Bacteriological (Biological) and Toxin Weapons and on their Destruction was signed and there are 170 parties as of April 2013.

thousand dollars, someone can order subsets of select agent DNA and assemble them to create entire pathogens.

The range of nefarious possibilities through the use of genes and viruses is very broad, particularly when combined with other innovations such as nanotechnology discussed below. The potential weaponization of genes and viruses is still new and difficult to accurately project or regulate but poses a distinct national security threat.

4.   Miniaturization and Nanotechnology

Nanotechnology allows for the use of matter at the nanoscale. It has already yielded amazing results, including the potential eradication of the hepatitis C virus in laboratory testing. Nanotechnology is a development with almost unlimited applications to future armed conflict. It will make weapons smaller, more mobile, and more potent. It will provide easier, quicker, and more accurate means of collecting information. It will give weapons greater range, effect, and lethality. It will eventually allow for the creation of microscopic nanobots that can be controlled and used as sensors to gather information or as weapons to carry lethal toxins or genomic alterers into the bodies of humans. In other words, it will make everything better and more capable.

Unlike some of the other technologies discussed, nanotechnology remains expensive and complex, requiring state-like apparatus to develop and weaponize. However, Russia and China have joined the United States in investing heavily in this area and it is unclear what innovations the future will bring. The potential capabilities presented by nanotechnology are a significant threat to national security.

B.   Actors

As mentioned above, many emerging technological advances will be available generally. As these technologies are weaponized, their use will not be limited to national militaries. Rather, a broad spectrum of actors will have access to their destructive effects. Advanced technologies in the hands of an enlarged spectrum of actors represent a significant threat to national security.

1.   Fighters

The term "fighters" is used here to describe those who organize themselves to openly fight with weapons in an armed struggle. This category would include traditional militaries, as well as other armed groups such as terrorists. Of course, the militaries of advanced nations will have access to all of these emerging weapons as their governments develop them; the use of these advanced technologies even by state militaries presents difficult issues that will be discussed below.

II. The Emerging Threat

But other fighters, such as terrorists, expanded private security companies, corporate armies, and global criminal networks such as drug cartels, will also have access to some of these weapons. In the hands of these groups, advanced weapons pose even greater national security threats because neither law nor practice seems to provide adequate disincentives or controls on their actions. Because these fighters do not function within the accepted legal construct for the use of state-level violence, they challenge the norms of predictability upon which national security law is predicated. As these fighters gain greater access to advanced weapons, the United States will have to adjust to counter the threat.

2. Civilians

Under the LOAC, some of the fighters listed above will be considered civilians for targeting and treatment purposes. However, the term is used here to denote those who are not engaging in armed conflict in the traditional way. In other words, they are not on the battlefield with weapons. Nevertheless, with access to advancing technologies, these "non-fighters" will be able to have a significant impact similar to more traditional fighters.

a. Transnational Communities of Interest

The potential impact of the recent rise of social networking as a forum to gather individuals and groups from across the globe around particular areas of interest is just beginning to be understood. These "transnational communities of interest" allow people to create an identity that is tied to global ideologies rather than geopolitical affiliations. People will begin to view themselves less as Americans, or Germans, or Iranians, and more as members of worldwide activism created, maintained, and mobilized over social media.[25]

Social media will allow individuals to recruit, provide financial support, collect intelligence, pass strategies and information, forward ideas and instructions for munitions, create and solidify plans of action, and coordinate attacks. These events will occur in disparate locations but their impacts may be felt at the point where it will have the greatest effect on security interests.

Perhaps the best current example of these social transnational communities of interests revolves around cyber hackers. Hacktivists have already played a significant role in armed conflict during the conflicts between Russia and Estonia and between Russia and Georgia.[26] Additionally, the global collective "Anonymous" has had far-reaching effects on both nations and nonstate actors in its attempts to

---

[25] Thomas J. Holt & Max Kilger, *Examining Willingness to Attack Critical Infrastructure Online and Offline*, 58 CRIME & DELINQUENCY 798 (2012).

[26] Clay Wilson, *Botnets, Cybercrime, and Cyberterrorism: Vulnerabilities and Policy Issues for Congress* 5-7, CRS Report for Congress, http://www.fas.org/sgp/crs/terror/RL32114.pdf (last updated Jan. 29, 2008).

influence government behavior. The trends in technology will only make organizing through social media around particular ideologies easier and allow a much broader spectrum of actors to play significant roles in influencing national security.

b.   "Arms" Dealers

Another emerging actor around new technologies is the new age "arms dealer." These are individuals or groups who will develop and market new technologies to the highest bidders. There is already a large market for cyber "arms," where someone can ask to purchase something that will accomplish a specific task against a specific target and receive a made-to-order piece of malware.

For many new tech arms dealers, this will be nothing more than a business opportunity. For others, they will not only develop and market but also determine targets based on their own social agendas. They will recruit allies with the same agendas from around the world. They will use others as innocent transmitters of genetically coded viruses or nanobot sensors. Certainly arms dealers are not a new phenomenon, but the spread of technology to new types of arms will open this line of work to a much broader and previously innocuous group of individuals. At some point, the law will have to determine how to deal with these creators of modern arms.

These are just examples of threats and actors that will likely represent threats to national security. Predicting the future is not a reliable career. However, to the extent that many of these developments are already under way, it is important to assess how well the current national security system responds and what changes if any might be needed. Certainly these developments will cause frictions within the government and between the government and the private sector. As discussed below, those frictions already exist and are likely to get worse over time.

III.   PROTECTIONS

The U.S. federal government is already aware of many of these emerging technologies and the risks they pose. As discussed below, the U.S. government is deeply involved in developing its own capabilities in these areas, to be used as needed. However, the fact that the government is aware and involved does not mean that the corporate world is equally informed and focused. Even if the government is capable of protecting itself from these threats, that will be insufficient to maintain our national security. Corporate America also needs to be safe from these emerging threats. And the government knows it. How the government gets corporate America to respond to these threats is a potential source of great friction between appropriate levels of regulation and corporate freedom.

III. Protections

A. *Government Initiatives*

Because cyber-technology is the most prevalent of the emerging technologies discussed above, analyzing the government's methodology for ensuring national security interests in the private sector with respect to computer and digital security will be most useful. Numerous events have demonstrated the lack of good security on government computer systems, but especially on corporate systems, even those involved in providing and maintaining critical infrastructure systems and in the development of our most sensitive weapons systems. The need to secure these is obvious, but true security (to the extent that it can even be achieved) would raise the specter of government intrusion into civil liberties and corporate freedoms. As a baseline for governmental balancing of these important, and often competing interests, President Obama has made the following statement:

> Let me also be clear about what we will not do. Our pursuit of cybersecurity will not—I repeat, will not include—monitoring private sector networks or Internet traffic. We will preserve and protect the personal privacy and civil liberties that we cherish as Americans. Indeed, I remain firmly committed to net neutrality so we can keep the Internet as it should be—open and free.[27]

With this as the policy background, a review of what the government has done and how effective their methods have been is in order.

1. Critical Infrastructure Protection

One of the most serious concerns in the area of cyber-security is critical infrastructure. As early as President Clinton in the 1990s, Presidents have been aware of potential vulnerabilities in these systems. Richard Clarke, the "cyber czar" for two Presidents, famously warned of an impending "cyber pearl harbor" where our critical infrastructure would be compromised and result in similar devastating effects as the Japanese attack on Pearl Harbor during World War II. Numerous separate studies have established dangerous exposures in critical computer and digital systems that, though not catastrophic, clearly present a national security risk.

In response, successive Presidents have taken numerous steps, including creating task forces, issuing presidential directives and executive orders, and seeking legislation from Congress to ascertain the extent of the problem and recommend increased security measures. The 1998 Presidential Decision Directive 63, for example, makes it the policy of the U.S. government to "take all necessary measures to swiftly eliminate any significant vulnerability to both physical and

---

[27] Barack Obama, U.S. President, Remarks on Securing Our Nation's Cyber Infrastructure (May 29, 2009), http://www.whitehouse.gov/the_press_office/Remarks-by-the-President-on-Securing-Our-Nations-Cyber-Infrastructure.

cyber-attacks on our critical infrastructures, including especially our cyber systems."[28] Directive 63 goes on to state that "[s]ince the targets of attacks on our critical infrastructure would likely include both facilities in the economy and those in the government, the elimination of our potential vulnerability requires a closely coordinated effort of both the government and the private sector."[29]

In 2002, Congress passed the Homeland Security Act, which contained critical infrastructure protections and in 2003, President George W. Bush issued Homeland Security Presidential Directive 7,[30] which directed the creation of the National Infrastructure Protection Plan (NIPP). The NIPP was created in 2006 and subsequently updated. In 2003, President Bush also issued the National Strategy to Secure Cyberspace.[31] President Bush further issued the Comprehensive National Cybersecurity Initiative in 2007, which became NSPD 54/HSPD 23, Cyber Security and Monitoring in 2008.[32]

President Obama has continued executive focus on cyber security. Shortly after entering office, President Obama ordered a comprehensive review of U.S. cyber strategy. This review resulted in the Cyberspace Policy Review.[33] The Review argued that

> [t]he Federal government cannot entirely delegate or abrogate its role in securing the Nation from a cyber incident or accident. The Federal government has the responsibility to protect and defend the country, and all levels of government have the responsibility to ensure the safety and wellbeing of citizens. The private sector, however, designs, builds, owns, and operates most of the digital infrastructures that support government and private users alike. The United States needs a comprehensive framework to ensure a coordinated response by the Federal, State, local, and tribal governments, the private sector, and international allies to significant incidents.[34]

The Cyber Policy Review made strong statements about government cooperation with the private sector. For example, the report argued that "[t]he common

---

[28] Presidential Decision Directive NSC-63, Critical Infrastructure Protection (May 22, 1998), *available at* http://www.fas.org/irp/offdocs/pdd/pdd-63.htm.

[29] Presidential Decision Directive NSC-63, Critical Infrastructure Protection (May 22, 1998), *available at* http://www.fas.org/irp/offdocs/pdd/pdd-63.htm.

[30] *Directive on Critical Infrastructure Identification, Prioritization, and Protection*, 39 WEEKLY COMP. PRES. DOC. 1816 (Dec. 22, 2003), *available at* http://www.dhs.gov/xabout/laws/gc_1214597989952 .shtm#1.

[31] The White House, *The National Strategy to Secure Cyberspace* (2003), *available at* http:// www.dhs.gov/xlibrary/assets/National_Cyberspace_Strategy.pdf. In 2004, President Bush issued National Security Presidential Directive (NSPD) 38, also called the National Strategy to Secure Cyberspace. The 2004 document is not available to the general public due to its classification.

[32] White House, Cyberspace Policy Review 4 (2009), *available at* http://www.whitehouse.gov/ assets/documents/Cyberspace_Policy_Review_final.pdf.

[33] White House, Cyberspace Policy Review (2009), *available at* http://www.whitehouse.gov/ assets/documents/Cyberspace_Policy_Review_final.pdf.

[34] White House, Cyberspace Policy Review iv (2009), *available at* http://www.whitehouse.gov/ assets/documents/Cyberspace_Policy_Review_final.pdf.

III. Protections

defense of privately-owned critical infrastructures from armed attack or from physical intrusion or sabotage by foreign military forces or international terrorists is a core responsibility of the Federal government."

In response to the Report, President Obama stated:

> From now on, our digital infrastructure—the networks and computers we depend on every day—will be treated as they should be: as a strategic national asset. Protecting this infrastructure will be a national security priority. We will ensure that these networks are secure, trustworthy, and resilient. We will deter, prevent, detect, and defend against attacks and recover quickly from any disruptions or damage.[35]

Some important steps have been taken and progress continues to be made, but many still believe that until the government establishes clear regulations and incentivizes compliance, the private sector will not find it economically useful to invest in sufficient cyber-security measures. With a burgeoning cyber insurance market, it may be easier to insure against cyber disaster than to prevent it. Unfortunately, insurance does not protect the integrity of the data or the critical information it may have contained.

2. Defense Industrial Base

One area where the government has increased oversight and regulation is in the area of government defense contractors. These government contractors, who produce most of the United States' weapons systems and care for most of the critical data that is maintained outside of DoD computer systems, are collectively known as the Defense Industrial Base (DIB). In response to HSPD-7 and as part of its responsibility under the NIPP, DoD issued its sector specific plan for the DIB (DIB SSP) in May 2007.[36] One of the key points in the plan is that "[p]rivate sector participation in executing the NIPP is voluntary." However, the government has begun requiring more in-depth security assurances and procedures for companies within the DIB in order to be awarded government contracts.

The DIB may represent a good test for government regulation of and assistance to private corporations. Certainly the government will feel freer to impose specific security measures and then verify compliance when this can be done as a matter of contract. However, the specific measures used and the methods of verification will be the foundation upon which any larger government outreach will be based.

---

[35] Barack Obama, U.S. President, Remarks on Securing Our Nation's Cyber Infrastructure (May 29, 2009), http://www.whitehouse.gov/the_press_office/Remarks-by-the-President-on-Securing-Our-Nations-Cyber-Infrastructure.

[36] U.S. Dep't of Def., Defense Industrial Base: Critical Infrastructure and Key Resources Sector-Specific Plan as Input to the National Infrastructure Protection Plan (2007), *available at* http://www.dhs.gov/xlibrary/assets/nipp-ssp-defense-industrial-base.pdf.

B.   *Public Private Partnership*

As mentioned in the Cyberspace Policy Review, partnership between the private sector and the government is vital to the overall success of any security program and to national security as a whole. Both the President and Congress have been active in trying to promote this partnership, and progress is being made. However, there is still much improvement that is needed. The government must find ways to incentive corporate America to work with the government and minimize the potential risks of doing so.

1.   Carrots and Sticks

Private sector priorities are often different than those of the public sector. Corporations must always be conscious of their profits and shareholder confidence and satisfaction. Because of this, a combination of carrots and sticks is required to incentivize the private sector to maintain adequate cyber-security.

Carrots can come in the form of tax incentives, access to information, relief from other regulatory requirements, and other benefits that further corporate goals. Many varieties of benefits have been proposed in Congress and the Executive, and some have been implemented to varying degrees of success. This will need to continue to be an area for focus.

2.   Information Protection

One of the continuing concerns of the private sector when considering partnership with the government is the amount of disclosure that would be required. Inherent in this partnership, companies and the government would share information about security issues, including intrusions and breaches. Corporate representatives continually express skepticism about the government's ability to safeguard their information, both from competitors and from the general public. Competitors may gain competitive advantage from disclosures about the corporation and the public may lose faith in the corporation as information about security breaches emerges. It seems clear that one step the government must take as part of any meaningful partnership with industry is assuaging those concerns.

C.   *Government Sector*

The government is obviously a significant target for cyber activities. Each government agency is responsible for its own cyber-security, with the ability to work together where cooperation creates efficiencies. The DoD obviously has very robust cyber and counter-cyber capabilities with the National Security Agency (NSA). Other governmental agencies are in various stages of developing their own capabilities. The Government Accounting Office routinely grades each government agency on its cyber-security and so far, the results have generally been abysmal. However, it is a work in progress and progress is being made.

In terms of overall national cyber-security and the government's role in that, the Department of Homeland Security has primary responsibility to protect government systems, with DoD prepared to provide assistance as necessary. DHS and DoD have created a joint command center and are building institutions and processes to facilitate their cooperation in the event of a major cyber incident.[37]

D.   Other Emerging Technologies

The discussion above has focused on protection from cyber activities, but other emerging technologies present similar concerns. Just as cyber tools are used to gather information and intelligence from both government and civilian sources, nanosensors could be used to collect and transmit data sought by both state and nonstate actors. Micro and nano drones and robots could be used for similar purposes as well as to conduct sabotage or cause destruction. The methods for protection against other emerging technologies may be different to protecting against cyber-attacks, but the approaches to protection and paradigms for accomplishing it may be quite similar. The government must determine the threat, provide its own protection, and then consider how to encourage protection for industries, corporations, and other entities that affect national security.

In some cases, adequate protection will come in part through offensive capabilities. The government must determine to what extent having an active offensive capability is necessary to deter or even interdict potential adverse actors. It is to this offensive capability that the next section now turns.

IV.   OFFENSIVE ACTIONS

Whether as part of or in addition to efforts to protect national security interests, the United States is also likely to develop a multitude of emerging technologies in the near future, including those discussed above. The research, design, development, production, and employment of these advanced technologies require both coordination and cooperation within the government and also between the government and the private sector.

---

[37] U.S. Dep't of Homeland Security and Dep't of Def., *Memorandum of Agreement between the Department of Homeland Security and the Department of Defense Regarding Cybersecurity* (Sept. 2010), *available at* http://www.dhs.gov/xlibrary/assets/20101013-dod-dhs-cyber-moa.pdf.

A.   *Encouraging Weapons Development*

Weapons, and particularly innovative weapons, do not just appear. This desire for states to sponsor emerging technologies creates friction concerning the allocation of resources and state-sponsored incentives. Just as traditional military expenses draw funds that could be used for other public goods, such as medical care and social security, funding of emerging technologies also draws from these public goods. In the case of research and development of advanced technologies, however, the returns are much less apparent and often quite speculative. Governments, particularly democratic-style governments, often struggle to convince the polity that such investments are a wise use of limited resources. This is particularly true of offensive capabilities, especially during times of relative peace. Nevertheless, maintaining a technological advantage requires research and development, and protecting national security in the future is also likely to require research and development of emerging weapon systems.

Additionally, the development and use of emerging technologies often create legal and ethical concerns over their actual employment in armed conflict. These concerns force a discussion concerning the balance between national security policy within the government and between the government and the public. These issues will be highlighted below.

B.   *Offensive Use of Emerging Technologies*

Many of the same emerging technologies that were discussed above in section II are also being considered as potential offensive capabilities. In many of these areas, the United States is already quite advanced in its efforts. In other areas, progress is just starting. What seems clear is that the efforts to research, develop, and produce advanced weapon systems based on emerging technologies will be a major part of U.S. national security in the near future.

1.   Cyber Weapons

The line between offensive and defensive cyber tools has been blurred since their development. Often the same cyber tool will enable access to information necessary to defend U.S. national interests and access to conduct offensive cyber actions to disrupt, deny, degrade, or even destroy adversary capabilities. Recent disclosures of classified documents have detailed U.S. operations to gain access to information not only on adversaries but also allies. These disclosures have also pointed to offensive actions taken by various U.S. government organizations. Computer analysts have also speculated that the STUXNET and Flame malware packages were created and used by the United States (potentially in conjunction with Israel).[38]

Further, General Keith Alexander, the former director of the NSA and commander of Cyber Command, stated publicly that he was developing offensive capabilities, and in a request to the Pentagon for funding, the Air Force disclosed that they have designated a certain number of cyber tools as "offensive." In response, section 954 of the 2012 National Defense Authorization Act authorizes the use of offensive military capabilities in cyberspace.

SEC. 954. MILITARY ACTIVITIES IN CYBERSPACE.

Congress affirms that the Department of Defense has the capability, and upon direction by the President may conduct offensive operations in cyberspace to defend our Nation, Allies and interests, subject to—

(1) the policy principles and legal regimes that the Department follows for kinetic capabilities, including the law of armed conflict; and
(2) the War Powers Resolution (50 U.S.C. 1541 *et seq.*).[39]

Offensive cyber capabilities present a number of significant benefits but also raise significant issues in consideration of how these weapons might be used both outside of armed conflict and once armed conflict has begun.

Looking first at national security frictions brought about prior to armed conflict, the law governing the resort to armed conflict, or *jus ad bellum*, makes it illegal under international law to take actions that amount to a "use of force" and allow a victim state to respond with countermeasures as well as other unfriendly but lawful acts (see Chapter 4 for further detail). Countermeasures are otherwise unlawful acts that are designed to bring an offending state's conduct back into compliance with international law. There are many cyber actions that might qualify as a countermeasure, such as cyber interference into the electronic polling of a neighboring country in order to cast doubt on a particular election.

For acts that amount to an "armed attack," states can respond in self-defense, including the use of proportionate force. Offensive cyber capabilities increase dramatically the options available to a government both in taking such actions and in responding to them. For example, consider the case of the STUXNET malware that infiltrated an Iranian nuclear facility and damaged almost 1,000 centrifuges. Most commentators seem to believe that this action amounted to a "use of force" and many believe it was an "armed attack" because of the damage that resulted from the malware. Those who believe so, usually consider the effects

---

[38] Ellen Nakashima, Greg Miller & Julie Tate, *U.S., Israel Developed Flame Computer Virus to Slow Iranian Nuclear Efforts, Officials Say*, WASH. POST (June 19, 2012), http://www.washingtonpost.com/world/national-security/us-israel-developed-computer-virus-to-slow-iranian-nuclear-efforts-officials-say/2012/06/19/gJQA6xBPoV_story.html; Dave Lee, *Flame: Israel Rejects Link to Malware Cyber-Attack*, BBC NEWS (May 31, 2012), http://www.bbc.co.uk/news/technology-18277555.

[39] National Defense Authorization Act for Fiscal Year 2012, Pub. L. No. 112-81, §954, 125 Stat. 1298, 354 (2011).

of the STUXNET and determine that the resulting property damage was sufficient to qualify as a use of force (or even an armed attack).

Whether a "use of force" or an "armed attack," Iran would have had the legal
authority to respond in some way to the action, including a proportional use of
force if it was considered an armed attack. However, the malware was only discovered after it had done its damage, it was more than a year before the first factual
allegations were leveled against the United States and Israel, and there is still no
solid proof of who it was that created and deployed the malware. The nature of the
internet and cyber tools makes attribution very difficult and allows an attack to
remain anonymous, potentially for a very long time.

In addition to anonymity, the amount and types of targets that can be hit are
much broader with cyber capabilities. Effects that were not available before cyber
operations can now be achieved, such as raiding bank accounts and spoofing
emails. Operations can include things from as small as just interfering with
access to the web, to as large as destroying generators or interfering with the
air traffic control system. The United States wants to not only be able to defend
against these capabilities, but also possess them, even if it chooses not to use
them.

The majority of cyber actions, including those accomplished by state
actors, currently involve actions that do not rise to the level of the use of
force. In those cases, states must resolve their disputes through other
means, such as criminal sanctions. The recent indictment by the United States
of five Chinese military members for violations of U.S. domestic law is an
example of this.[40]

Such weapons and their use present significant national security issues. As
discussed in much more detail below and was previously discussed in Chapter 4
concerning national security and the use of force, it is unclear how these emerging
weapon systems and their non-traditional employment will be understood under
constitutional and statutory allocations of power within the government. Can the
President authorize the use of such weapons, even though they may lead to war,
without consulting Congress because they do not have the typical effects of heat,
blast, and fragmentation that are normally associated with armed conflict?
Current practice seems to indicate that the President thinks he has such authority.

In addition to potential cyber actions outside of armed conflict, cyber capabilities offer many increased targets after armed conflict is initiated. Obviously, if
the United States and Iran were at war, the use of a STUXNET-style weapon would
be equally useful against many potential targets in an effort to destroy or degrade
enemy forces and capabilities. For example, using cyber operations to take down
an enemy's air defense systems or to interrupt communications systems are both
actions that have been used in recent conflicts. Other potentially effective cyber
actions might include the destruction of data on servers containing logistics information, causing a breakdown in the delivery of personnel and materiel to the

---

[40] Ellen Nakashima & William Wan, *U.S. Announces First Charges Against Foreign Country in
Connection with Cyberspying*, WASH. POST (May 19, 2014).

conflict zone. All of these actions would certainly be governed by the applicable LOAC, but how that law applies is not yet clear in many cases.[41]

One of the issues that has already emerged from growing cyber capabilities and their perceived bloodless nature is a call to make their use mandatory in certain circumstances. In other words, some have argued that if a nation has a choice of using a cyber weapon to accomplish a military task or using another weapon, both of which would be lawful under the circumstances, that nation must use the cyber weapon because it would result in less damage and death to civilians and civilian objects. The United States and many other countries have rejected this notion but it continues to cause friction in the development and employment of military capabilities.

Regardless of these frictions, there is no doubt that cyber capabilities will continue to be considered an important part of overall national security. Many cyber capabilities are currently developed within the government, either at the NSA, Cyber Command, or some other government agency. However, it is entirely possible that elements of the government have already taken advantage of the new cyber "arms dealers" discussed above. And the likelihood certainly exists in the future. Additionally, the time may come when industry begins to produce cyber tools, like it does rifles and airplanes.

2.   Drones, Robots, and Autonomous Systems

Even clearer than in the case of cyber tools, the United States is engaged in an extensive use of drones for offensive purposes. Drones have become the tool of choice in the war on terror. Discussions abound as to the long-term impacts of armed drone attacks, but the capability is lawful, effective, and on the rise. Drones will only become more prominent in national security as nanotechnology makes them smaller and more capable.

Like drones, robots are already well integrated into current operations. Remotely piloted robots first began being used in Iraq in 2007, and their numbers and variety have steadily increased. Future robots will use "brain-machine interface technologies" or "whole brain emulation" in their operations. The potentially autonomous nature of robots means that they will not only be used in warfare by humans, but also become actors on the battlefield themselves.

Finally, autonomous weapon systems are still in the early stages of development and deployment. The DoD currently has several systems that have varying levels of autonomy, but as discussed above, the current position of the DoD is to maintain a human in the loop for actions. Many believe that this policy cannot survive continued innovation. The speed of information processing, the increased survivability, the ability to react in significantly shorter periods of time based on facts rather than emotion, all will push autonomous weapon systems to the fore.

---

[41] *See generally* THE TALLINN MANUAL ON THE INTERNATIONAL LAW APPLICABLE TO CYBER WARFARE (Michael N. Schmitt ed., 2013).

In all of these cases, it is clear that the United States has and will continue to embrace innovative technology. It is also clear that the private sector will play a key role in the research, design, and development of these advanced weapons. Recalling the discussion at the beginning of this chapter, the government needs to ensure that its law and processes are agile enough to respond to innovation as it occurs. Contracting and funding methods may pose limitations that will hamper technological development.

Further, these developments, along with cyber capabilities, have also sparked questions about the legal and ethical ramifications of these weapons. Ethical questions revolve around the fairness and equitable nature of employing weapons systems against enemies who do not have similar technology. There is also concern that the bloodless nature of such conflict will increase the likelihood of its use as an instrument of national policy. Legal questions include issues of attributability and criminal responsibility. In other words, when an autonomous weapon acts in a way that is in violation of the law of armed conflict, who bears responsibility—the designer, the producer, the commander who employed it? These are legal questions of some consequence and will certainly cause frictions within the national security realm as emerging technologies continue to develop.

In addition to these questions, DoD will have to work under other specific legal constraints as they develop advanced technologies. These constraints will undoubtedly produce continuing national security friction.

C. Constraints

As DoD and private industry work together to develop new offensive weapons based on emerging technologies, there are at least two fundamental constraints that must be addressed. The first is the legal requirement for a weapons legal review of new weapons, and the second is the potential impact (or not) of the War Powers Resolution.

1. Weapons Reviews

Both international law and domestic regulation require a legal review of any new weapon introduced into a military inventory. The international law requirement is found in article 36 of the 1949 Additional Protocol I to the Geneva Conventions (API).[42] The article states:

---

[42] Protocol Additional to the Geneva Conventions of 12 August 1949, and Relating to the Protection of Victims of International Armed Conflicts (Protocol I) art. 48, June 8, 1977, 1125 U.N.T.S. 3. *See also* International Committee of the Red Cross, A Guide to the Legal Review of New Weapons, Means and Methods of Warfare: Measures to Implement Article 36 of Additional Protocol I of 1977 (Jan. 2006), *available at* http://www.icrc.org/eng/assets/files/other/irrc_864_icrc_geneva.pdf

IV. Offensive Actions

> In the study, development, acquisition or adoption of a new weapon, means or method of warfare, a High Contracting Party is under an obligation to determine whether its employment would, in some or all circumstances, be prohibited by this Protocol or by any other rule of international law applicable to the High Contracting Party.

Note that the requirement for a legal review is triggered at the point of studying a new weapon, not just prior to its employment. That means that the United States is required to do a legal review of any new weapons based on emerging technologies very early in the stage of weapon design. Though the United States is not a party to API, it accepts this provision and its legal requirement as customary international law and binding on all nations, including the United States.

Perhaps one of the reasons the United States accepts article 36 as binding is because it had its own requirement to perform legal reviews of new weapons even before API. This same requirement exists today. It is the policy of the DoD[43] that the Judge Advocate General of a sponsoring military department, or the DoD General Counsel, perform a legal review of every weapon, weapon system, and munition that will be used to meet a military requirement. The legal review must at least determine 1) whether there is any treaty or customary prohibition on the intended use of the weapon, 2) whether the weapon is calculated to cause unnecessary suffering or superfluous injury, and 3) whether the weapon is capable of being directed at a specific military objective.

New weapons such as genetically tainted viruses that may travel through innocent hosts but only have lethal effects on one specific individual will tax the current understanding of the application of this law. As DoD seeks, and corporate America responds by developing, advanced weapons systems based on emerging technologies, it would be wise to do legal reviews early in the process to not only give the "yes" or "no" but to guide developers in the process.

2. War Powers Resolution[44]

Another potential constraint on the development and use of new technologies is the War Powers Resolution (WPR), which has been discussed in Chapter 3.

---

[43] Review of Legality of Weapons Under International Law, U.S. Department of Defense Instruction 5500.15, 16 Oct. 1974 (updated Jan. 1, 1979); Legal Reviews of Weapons and Cyber Capabilities, Air Force Instruction 51-402, July 27, 2011 [hereinafter U.S. Air Force Instruction]; Legal Services: Review of Legality of Weapons under International Law, U.S. Department of Army Regulation 27-53, Jan. 1, 1979; Implementation and Operation of the Defense Acquisition System and the Joint Capabilities Integration and Development System, U.S. Department of Navy, Secretary of the Navy Instruction 5000.2C, Nov. 19, 2004; Policy for Non-Lethal Weapons, U.S. Department of Defense Directive 3000.3E, April 25, 2013; The Defense Acquisition System, U.S. Department of Defense Directive 5000.01, May 12, 2013.

[44] War Powers Resolution of 1973 (50 U.S.C. §§1541-1548).

As Congress made clear in §954 of the 2012 NDAA quoted above, it believes that any use of advanced technological weapons is subject to the WPR. In pertinent part (and extremely simplified), the WPR places two main requirements on the President. One is a reporting requirement and the other is a requirement to withdraw the armed forces in 60 (or 90) days unless Congress authorizes their continuing deployment. Both provisions are triggered by the same basic language.

The WPR begins by stating that its purpose is to "fulfill the intent of the framers of the Constitution of the United States and insure that the collective judgement of both the Congress and the President will apply to the introduction of United States Armed Forces into hostilities."[45] This purpose would presumably apply equally to the use of all future technologies by the President, to the extent that they are covered.

The WPR goes on to require the President to report to Congress within 48 hours "any case in which armed forces are introduced . . . into hostilities."[46] The same trigger also starts a 60 (or 90) day clock where at the end of that time, if Congress has not taken action approving the President's deployment of armed forces, "the President shall terminate" the use of the military.

The WPR raised numerous issues, not the least of which is its basic constitutionality. However, for the purposes of this chapter, it is important to determine how that triggering language would apply to future technologies. In other words, is cyber conflict "hostilities?" If the President sends a squadron of armed drones into a combat situation, is this a "case in which armed forces are introduced"? Does it make a difference if they are remotely piloted or completely autonomous? What if they are micro or nano drones and are indiscernible by the naked eye?

These questions are unlikely to be answered in the near future but will undoubtedly begin to be discussed by both the President and Congress as emerging technologies are weaponized. If the President thinks he can avoid WPR reporting requirements by using advanced technologies, such a determination will incentivize him or her to do so. If Congress thinks that advanced technologies are not currently covered by the WPR but should be, they will need to address that issue through amended legislation.

Other legislative issues will arise with the advent of advanced technology weapons. National security law and process will need to be reexamined to insure that they provide sufficient control and authority for their research, design, development, production, and legitimate use.

---

[45] 50 U.S.C. §1541.
[46] 50 U.S.C. §1543.

V. CONCLUSION

Emerging technologies and their potential weaponization create many opportunities for frictions both between the government and private enterprise and also within the government. The strictures of the contracting process, combined with statutory considerations such as the AECA, create strong non-market disincentives to provide necessary national security goods and services. Since the government must rely on the private sector, these disincentives deserve some reflection to ensure they are necessary and useful.

The continued cooperation between the government and the private sector is vital, especially given emerging technologies and their development into advanced weapons systems. The threat includes many advances in technology that are accessible to nonstate actors and can allow individuals and groups to control what has previously been state-level violence. The ability for the United States to adequately defend itself will require close coordination with the private sector, particularly in the area of critical infrastructures where the public sector controls most of the vulnerabilities.

In order to ensure protection of vital national security interests, the government must consider the role of regulation in setting standards for safety and security of national assets. The current work with the DIB is useful but will likely need to be expanded to include non-defense contractors who also provide important services to the nation as a whole. The current administration's unwillingness to do this may only continue until a catastrophic breach and resulting major event occurs.

Finally, the government is already actively pursuing the development of these emerging technologies for its own offensive purposes. Current statutory restrictions on executive action will need to be reviewed and an understanding reached that will facilitate the research, design, production, and employment of emerging technologies that will advance national security interests.

CHAPTER 13

Law and Domestic Security Operations

I. OVERVIEW

Protection from domestic natural and manmade dangers is a core function of any government. The federal structure of the U.S. government significantly impacts the execution of this government responsibility. Unlike response to threats arising externally, authority to respond to domestic emergency implicates a complex mosaic of local, state, and federal capabilities and authorities. The federal government, although vested with constitutional and statutory authority to respond to certain domestic threats on its own initiative, normally performs an augmentation role, assisting local and state authorities in their response and consequence mitigation efforts. This division of authority, with its varying powers and restrictions, is central to understanding the complicated federalism aspects of domestic national security operations.

Federal disaster and emergency response, relied upon to augment state police power and inherent authorities, is generally limited, falling within three broad categories: 1) federal disaster assistance and consequence management efforts; 2) use of federal resources (most notably the armed forces) to enforce law and restore public order; and 3) an imposition of martial law. This area of national security law also involves unique considerations related to the domestic use of the armed forces, as both the state and federal governments will often resort to the use of military resources to respond to domestic emergencies. The permissible use of these forces is framed by their operational status: Are they in state or federal service?

It is clear that the federal government is a government of limited powers, derived from the consent of the people.[1] The federal government, in contrast, must ground any action affecting the states' exercise of the police power on one of its enumerated federal powers, such as the war power or power to suppress insurrections. As expressed by the Supreme Court in *Bond v. United States,*

> [i]n our federal system, the National Government possesses only limited powers; the States and the people retain the remainder. The States have broad authority to enact legislation for the public good—what we have often called a "police power." United States v. Lopez, 514 U.S. 549, 567, 115 S. Ct. 1624, 131 L. Ed. 2d 626 (1995). The Federal Government, by contrast, has no such authority and "can exercise only the powers granted to it," McCulloch v. Maryland, 4 Wheat. 316, 405, 4 L. Ed. 579 (1819)[.][2]

In contrast, the states are vested with general police power, limited only by the state's self-imposed legal constraints and by constitutional provisions applicable to the states (such as due process and equal protection).[3] This fundamental distribution of power in large measure determines the allocation of domestic response authority to natural or manmade emergencies.

The first step in understanding this critical division of authority requires an exploration of the broad and plenary nature of the state police power. Extending beyond the traditional response to criminal threats, this authority permits the states to impose measures reasonably necessary to protect the health and welfare of the local or state population. In *Kansas v. Hendricks,*[4] the Supreme Court upheld a state's statute providing for involuntary civil commitment of certain violent sexual predators. The Court indicated that the public protective purpose upon which

---

[1] The Declaration of Independence para. 2 (U.S. 1776) ("Governments are instituted among Men, deriving their just Powers from the Consent of the Governed").

[2] Bond v. United States, 134 S. Ct. 2077, 2086 (2014).

[3] It may also be limited by the exercise of federal powers that preempt otherwise proper areas of state activity.

[4] 521 U.S. at 366.

the statute was based fell within a different scope of authority than criminal incapacitation, and therefore was not to be considered a "punitive" measure. Because such laws protect the public from individuals who posed a danger to the public health and safety—an exercise of state authority the Court had historically and consistently endorsed when exercised pursuant to proper procedures and evidentiary standards—the measure fell within the scope of state police power.

This non-punitive exercise of the general police power is central to responding to emergencies and crises resulting from both manmade and natural causes. For example, a major terrorist incident may necessitate the imposition of a quarantine or other restrictions on the free movement of the population of a given area; or a natural disaster may necessitate the compelled evacuation of an affected area. In these situations, the imposition of mandatory restrictions or other measures upon the population would be the operational manifestation of this inherent general police power (although the level of emergency might very well influence the assessment of whether a sufficient federal interest existed to justify a federal response based on either statutory authority or an assertion of inherent constitutional authority).[5]

Although recognizing this general state power, Supreme Court decisions have also emphasized due process and equal protection based limitations on its exercise. In *Jacobson v. Massachusetts*,[6] the Court considered whether a mandatory vaccination requirement ordered by local health officials, and the accordant criminal conviction for failing to comply with the requirement, violated constitutional due process. The Court held that protecting the public from the imminent spread of a contagious disease fell clearly within the general police power of the Commonwealth.[7] According to the Court,

> [t]he authority of the state to enact this statute is to be referred to what is commonly called the police power,—a power which the state did not surrender when becoming a member of the Union under the Constitution. Although this court has refrained from any attempt to define the limits of that power, yet it has distinctly recognized the authority of a state to enact quarantine laws and "health laws of every description"; indeed, all laws that relate to matters completely within its territory and which do not by their necessary operation affect the people of other states.[8]

The Court emphasized, however, two critically important qualifiers on the legitimate exercise of this state power: First, the claim of necessity must be objectively reasonable and must be rationally related to the necessity; and second, any measure must account for situations where the harm caused by the measures would be more than the harm avoided.[9] While state authorities need not predict

---

[5] *See* 521 U.S. at 25.
[6] 197 U.S. 11 (1905).
[7] 197 U.S. 11, 24-25.
[8] 197 U.S. 11, 24-25.
[9] 197 U.S. 11, 27-28.

the necessity of the imposed measure with absolute certainty, there must be some reasonable basis for the measure.[10] In Jacobson's case, this was especially relevant, as the feared outbreak never came to fruition. Nonetheless, the Court held that even assuming the public health prediction had been in error, the state officials' prediction was based on a reasonable assessment of the situation at the time the measure was imposed.[11] The Court's reliance on the assessment made by state officials entrusted with such judgments suggests that although a determination of necessity to impose measures based on the general police power may not be arbitrary, the Court will accord substantial deference to such determinations. So long as these judgments are made by officials with competence over the relevant issue of concern, and are based on some objectively verifiable and credible criteria, they will not be considered arbitrary, even if the judgment later proves erroneous.

Conversely, where police powers are exercised without an objectively valid necessity—most notably measures with no rational relationship to the alleged risk—the deprivation of liberty or property will violate due process. This was the conclusion reached by a federal circuit court of appeals in another important decision, *Jew Ho v. Williamson.* This case involved the quarantine of an entire neighborhood due to concerns of a plague, despite a lack of any evidence that the disease had been identified in such a large area.[12] The court struck down the quarantine, noting (as in *Jacobson*) that a measure imposed pursuant to an assertion of police power will violate due process where "the means prescribed by the state to [address the public danger] have no real or substantial relation to the protection of the public health and the public safety."[13]

The second limitation on the exercise of the general police power is that a measure must account for situations where the harm caused would be greater than the harm avoided.[14] Thus, in *Jacobson*, the Court addressed Jacobson's assertion that the vaccination might cause him injury. The Court rejected this aspect of Jacobson's challenge to the vaccination requirement, noting that the potential harm was speculative at best.[15] However, the Court did suggest that exemption from such a mandatory measure based on a meaningful risk that the measure would cause more harm than it would prevent—for example, *where* the risk of harm from a vaccination was more than mere speculation—was an important consideration when assessing constitutionality.[16]

Where a state-imposed emergency response comports with these due process considerations, the cases suggest a very broad range of permissible

---

[10] *Id.*

[11] 197 U.S. at 27.

[12] 103 F. 10 (N.D. Cal. 1900).

[13] *Jacobson*, 197 U.S. at 31.

[14] West Univ. Place v. Ellis, 134 S.W.2d 1038, 1040 (Tex. 1940).

[15] 197 U.S. at 37.

[16] *Id.* at 38.

response measures. It is certainly true that invocation of this broad police power to respond to a threat to public health or safety is not nearly as common today as it was during prior eras of our history when pandemic disease was a much more common experience (for example, the Spanish Influenza pandemic of 1918 claimed more victims than all the casualties of World War I, including an estimated 675,000 victims in the United States). Nonetheless, the Supreme Court's periodic endorsement of the general police power to respond to public dangers remains an important foundation for state measures in response to threats to the public, whether natural or manmade. Of equal importance, the locus of this broad response power in state (and not the federal) governments will inevitably impact implementation of measures in response to such public safety threats.

II.   LOCAL AND STATE POLICE AUTHORITY AND FIRST RESPONSE

The term "first responder" is used in common parlance to refer to local law enforcement and emergency response personnel expected to respond to domestic natural or manmade emergencies. The term also reflects the legal locus of emergency response powers. Because the state retains primary responsibility for ensuring law, order, and public safety within its sovereign territory, the response to such threats should and must logically begin with state and local authorities.

Ideally, local and state resources will be capable of dealing with a domestic emergency. However, it is always possible that these capabilities will be overwhelmed by a natural or manmade emergency, necessitating reliance on federal resources to assist, or in some situations assume responsibility for, public protection and consequence management. While each domestic emergency will undoubtedly involve unique characteristics that may impact the "who, what, where, when, and how" of the government response, law will define the permissible activities of state and federal authorities, to include the armed forces under the command and control of each of these sovereigns.

Emergency response planning is based on the assumption that local and state authorities will assert an initial and primary emergency response role. Unlike the states, federal authority to assert primacy in response to a domestic emergency is limited to very narrow situations, most notably an attack or invasion of the United States triggering the federal government's war powers. In such a situation, federal military forces (and other federal resources) could be utilized pursuant to the authority vested in the President to respond to an attack against the homeland. This authority is derived from Article IV of the U.S. Constitution, which provides that "the United States . . . shall protect [every state] against Invasion; and . . . against domestic Violence." This response authority was endorsed by the Supreme Court in *The Prize Cases*,[17] where the Supreme Court concluded that "if a war be made by invasion of a foreign nation, the President is not only authorized but bound to resist force by force. He does not initiate the war, but is bound to accept the challenge without waiting for any special legislative authority."[18]

Of course, the President may determine that state and local capabilities are sufficient to address a situation that ostensibly triggers federal response authority—perhaps with limited augmentation by federal resources—in which case reliance on the first responder concept might still be the order of the day. What is more likely is that a response to a domestic emergency would progress along a continuum from purely local response to substantial federal support to state authorities, and perhaps even a predominant federal role responsive to the gravity of the emergency.[19] Should, however, the emergency render state and local resources totally incapable of responding to the situation, it may be necessary to resort to a far more robust federal role. The authority for such a domestic federal response will be addressed in more detail below, but generally involves augmentation with military and civilian assets.

III.   SUPPORT FROM STATE MILITARY: NATIONAL GUARD AUTHORITY

If and when a domestic emergency situation overwhelms civilian response capabilities, governing authorities at both the state and federal level will likely consider utilization of military forces to augment or replace civilian response assets. Understanding the distinct roles and legal authorities of federal and state military forces—active duty and reserve forces of the United States and the state National Guard—is essential to implement and comply with statutory restrictions on the domestic missions such forces may be assigned to execute.

---

[17] 67 U.S. 635.

[18] *Id.* at 668.

[19] *But see* CHARLES DOYLE & JENNIFER K. ELSEA, CONG. RESEARCH SERV., R42659, THE POSSE COMITATUS ACT AND RELATED MATTERS: THE USE OF THE MILITARY TO EXECUTE CIVILIAN LAW 49-50 (2012) [hereinafter DOYLE & ELSEA].

It is arguable that Congress's authorization for the use of force against those responsible for the September 11 attacks has mooted some of the limitations on the use of the military for law enforcement purposes by recasting them as military operations. Soon after the attacks, the Office of Legal Counsel advised the White House and Defense Department that the Posse Comitatus Act imposed no constraint on the President's use of military forces domestically for anti-terrorism operations against international or foreign terrorists operating within the United States. This conclusion rested on the determination that the act only applies to the domestic use of the Armed Forces for law enforcement purposes, rather than for the performance of military functions.

III. Support from State Military: National Guard Authority

It has become almost routine to observe military forces deployed into areas of major manmade or natural disasters to perform a wide array of functions, ranging from provision of essential humanitarian needs—food, water, shelter, and medical care—to provision of security in afflicted areas. However, while a soldier in uniform may look the same regardless of which of these components of the armed forces she belongs to—federal military force or state National Guard—her authority will frequently be contingent on this distinction.

The U.S. military is composed of three components: active federal forces, reserve federal forces, and the National Guard. Federal forces are under federal command and control at all times they are in service (for active forces, this means at all times; for reserve forces, this means when they are called into active service). In contrast, the National Guard is normally under the authority of the state government,[20] with each governor serving as the commander for his or her state's National Guard. The National Guard, however, is also subject to being called into federal service.[21] When this occurs, the affected units shift from state to federal command and control—in effect becoming national military forces. Federalized National Guard forces are then subject to the same limits applicable to other federal military forces.

Significant legal consequence flows from this status distinction. So long as National Guard units are in Title 32[22] or State Active Duty status, and have not been called into service of the nation, they are not subject to legal limitations imposed on federal military forces. Most notably, when in a state controlled status, the National Guard is not prohibited from engaging in law enforcement pursuant to the Posse Comitatus Act (law that prohibits such activity, with limited exception, by federal armed forces).[23] As a result, they may be used to enforce state law like any other state law enforcement entity responding to an emergency.

However, once called into service of the nation, or "federalized," National Guard units become identical to any other federal military unit for purposes of command, control, and legal authority. This means that the governor no longer exercises command over these forces, and federal authorities will dictate when, where, and how they are utilized. It also means that these forces fall under the scope of the Posse Comitatus Act (PCA), and therefore may no longer engage in law enforcement activities unless the activity falls within one of several narrow exceptions to the PCA discussed below.[24]

---

[20] *See* U.S. Dep't of Defense, Dir. 3025.1, Military Support to Civil Authorities (MSCA) para. 4.4.6.1 (15 Jan. 1993).

[21] *See* 10 U.S.C. Ch. 1211 (2012).

[22] 32 U.S.C. §§101 *et seq.*

[23] 18 U.S.C. §1835 (2012). There may be some fiscal limits on the use of federal Title 32 funds.

[24] *See* Judge Advocate Gen.'s Legal Ctr. and Sch., Domestic Operational Law 2013 Handbook for Judge Advocates 42 (Dave Sherry & Robert Pirone eds., 2013) [hereinafter Judge Advocate Gen.'s Legal Ctr. and Sch.] (discussing the importance of the distinction between Title 10 and Title 32 status).

When a governor mobilizes the National Guard to respond to a crisis or emergency, his or her assertion of command authority indicates the forces are acting in their state capacity. This status may change during the course of the mission. If at any point during the deployment the President orders the forces into federal service, they will at that point fall under federal command and control. However, an emergency response mission will frequently involve armed forces in different statuses: Even where active duty federal forces are deployed to support the state, the President may choose to leave the National Guard forces under state status. This decision may be motivated, at least in part, by a desire to allow National Guard personnel to continue to enforce state laws, even where other federal military forces are deployed for non-law enforcement related support operations. For example, active duty forces may be deployed to establish logistics support areas to feed, shelter, and provide medical care to impacted civilians, with National Guard forces responsible for establishing security in the area. Fiscal considerations may also influence such a decision—National Guard forces operating in a Title 10 or Title 32 status are funded by the federal government. National Guard operations in a State Active Duty status are funded by the state.

It is also important to note that deployment of National Guard forces outside the territory of their home state does not automatically indicate they are acting in federal status. In fact, one important homeland security initiative implemented following the September 11, 2001 terrorist attacks was the development of agreements between states facilitating the use of interstate National Guard assets in a State Active Duty status. When deployed to another state in a State Active Duty status, they remain under state authority, command, and control. This method was used with positive effect during the response to Hurricane Katrina, where a number of governors ordered their National Guard personnel to deploy to Louisiana to augment the response effort. These forces were, pursuant to agreement, placed under the operational control of the Louisiana National Guard and were, as a result, permitted to engage in the same type of activities as their Louisiana National Guard counterparts. Congress specifically authorized such interstate operations in Title 32 of the United States Code.

IV.   FEDERAL EMERGENCY RESPONSE SUPPORT

While state response measures may be conducted pursuant to the broad police power vested in the state government, federal response measures, like the authority of the federal government itself, are more limited.

A.   The Federal Emergency Management Agency

In response to an emergency, the federal government will often intervene to mitigate the consequence of the incident by providing what is in essence domestic humanitarian relief and assistance. As more fully explained below, Congress has provided for the provision of such assistance in the Stafford Act of 1988. Title IV of the Stafford Act enumerates the President's authority once the Act is triggered. The essence of this federal response power is to call upon all agencies of the federal government—to include the Department of Defense (DoD)—to contribute to the disaster or emergency response effort. A Federal Coordination Officer (FCO), appointed by the President, will coordinate the federal response effort. The Federal Emergency Management Agency (FEMA), in turn, will be the lead federal agency managing this federal response. FEMA's role in such situations is both to coordinate the contributions of other federal agencies, and to procure resources from the private sector utilizing federal funds made available by the Act.[25]

Because of DoD's rapid response capability and readily available resources, it is common for FEMA to call upon the DoD to contribute to the federal response. When DoD assets are employed pursuant to Stafford Act authority, their function is to provide relief support, and *not* to engage in law enforcement type activities (such as providing security or law enforcement support). While National Guard units in a state status may, as noted above, engage in such law enforcement type activities, federal forces supporting FEMA efforts normally may not.

However, some domestic emergencies or disasters may necessitate a more robust role for federal military forces. This is especially the case when the incident is perceived as a threat to national security, such as a terrorist attack. In such situations, the Stafford Act may be only one of a number of federal response authorities invoked to authorize a federal military role. Federal military forces may take a more robust role in two situations of special federal concern: 1) mitigating the risk and/or effects of a chemical, nuclear, biological, radioactive, or explosive (CNBRE) attack; and 2) situations triggering the use of federal military forces to engage in law enforcement type activities.

B.   CNBRE Response

In 1996, Congress directed the Department of Defense to establish a joint service Chemical and Biological Rapid Response Team (CB-RRT). The congressional goal was to ensure that the unique capabilities of the armed forces—capabilities developed in preparation for conducting military operations in a

---

[25] *See* Military and National Guard Roles in Disaster Response: J. Hearing of the H. Subcomm. on Emergency Preparedness, Sci. and Tech. of the Comm. of Homeland Sec. and the Subcomm. on Terrorism, Unconventional Threats and Capabilities of the Armed Serv. Comm., 109th Cong. 12 (2005 (statement of Paul McHale, Asst. Sec'y Homeland Defense) (indicating effective response management of major disasters affecting counties not multiple states simultaneously); *see generally* Drabek, *Managing the Emergency Response*, 45 Pub. Admin. Rev. 85, 85-88 (1985); (exploring the roles of various levels of government in disaster response); Saundra Schneider, *Governmental Response to Disasters: The Conflict Between Bureaucratic Procedures and Emergent Norms*, 52 Pub. Admin. Rev. 135, 136 (1992).

battle-space involving the use of these types of weapons—was made available to support civil authorities responding to threats or incidents involving such weapons.[26] In response, DoD established a joint rapid response team, placing it under the command of the U.S. Army Soldier and Biological-Chemical Command. The CB-RRT's mission is to provide specialized and military capability in support of civilian authorities responding to an incident or anticipated incident involving a CNBRE weapon. The CB-RRT may also be utilized in support of "designated national security events"—high-risk gatherings, such as presidential inaugurations and major sporting events.[27]

As will be noted is greater detail below, the PCA[28] generally prohibits federal military personnel from engaging in any activity that would qualify as law enforcement. This prohibition does not, however, extend to activities that fall outside the scope of law enforcement or are otherwise authorized by statute or the Constitution. Accordingly, assistance to detect the presence of a CNBRE threat or to mitigate the consequences of a CNBRE attack are not restricted by the PCA, so long as it does not involve activities that would fall within the "law enforcement" prohibition. These include traditional missions of such military units, such as employing personnel and equipment to detect the presence of a CBRN agent, decontamination operations, and dispersal modeling. The authority to utilize federal military forces in response to a weapon of mass destruction incident was expanded following the terrorist attacks of September 11, 2001. Under 10 U.S.C. §382, the military personnel used to respond to an incident are allowed to engage in law enforcement type activity so long as such activity is "considered necessary for the immediate protection of human life, and civilian law enforcement officials are not capable of taking the action."[29]

Congress also expanded the Attorney General's authority to request Department of Defense support in response to other types of weapon of mass destruction. Pursuant to the PATRIOT Act,[30] the Attorney General may request federal military assistance in response to an emergency caused by the use of *any* weapon of mass destruction, thereby expanding the type of emergencies that may result in federal military intervention. This authority is found in 8 U.S.C. §2332e, which provides:

> The Attorney General may request the Secretary of Defense to provide assistance under section 382 of title 10 in support of Department of Justice activities relating to the enforcement of section 2332a of this title during an emergency situation involving a weapon of mass destruction. The authority to make such a

[26] Public Law 104-201, §§1414 *et seq.*

[27] *See generally* STEVE BOWMAN, CONG. RESEARCH SERV., RL31615, HOMELAND SECURITY: THE DEPARTMENT OF DEFENSE'S ROLE 6 (2003) [hereinafter STEVE BOWMAN].

[28] 18 U.S.C. §1835 (2012).

[29] 10 U.S.C. §382(d)(2)(B) (2012).

[30] USA PATRIOT Act, Pub. L. No. 107-56, 115 Stat. 272 (codified in scattered titles 8 U.S.C., 12 U.S.C., 15 U.S.C., 18 U.S.C., 20 U.S.C., 31 U.S.C., 42 U.S.C., 47 U.S.C., 49 U.S.C. & 50 U.S.C.).

request may be exercised by another official of the Department of Justice in accordance with section 382(f)(2) of title 10.

Weapons of mass destruction are defined in 18 U.S.C. §2332a and include:

(A) any destructive device as defined in section 921 of title 18 [18 U.S.C. §921(a)(4)]; (B) any weapon that is designed or intended to cause death or serious bodily injury through the release, dissemination, or impact of toxic or poisonous chemicals, or their precursors; (C) any weapon involving a disease organism; or (D) any weapon that is designed to release radiation or radioactivity at a level dangerous to human life.

18 U.S.C. §921(a)(4) defines destructive device as:

(A) any explosive, incendiary, or poison gas—(i) bomb, (ii) grenade, (iii) rocket having a propellant charge of more than four ounces, (iv) missile having an explosive or incendiary charge of more than one-quarter ounce, (v) mine, or (vi) device similar to any of the devices described in the preceding clauses;

(B) any type of weapon (other than a shotgun or a shotgun shell which the Secretary finds is generally recognized as particularly suitable for sporting purposes) by whatever name known which will, or which may be readily converted to, expel a projectile by the action of an explosive or other propellant, and which has any barrel with a bore of more than one-half inch in diameter; and

(C) any combination of parts either designed or intended for use in converting any device into any destructive device described in subparagraph (A) or (B) and from which a destructive device may be readily assembled.

Federal military support may also be utilized at the request of the Attorney General to assist in enforcing federal statutory prohibitions on the transfer of nuclear materials.[31]

Within the National Guard, teams analogous to the federal military CB-RRT provide state governors their own WMD response capability. These teams are designated as Weapons of Mass Destruction Civil Support Teams (WMD-CST).[32] National Guard personnel who make up these teams serve on full-time active service (AGR) status, meaning that, although they are on full-time duty, they

---

[31] The authority to request such military support is intended to facilitate enforcement of 18 U.S.C. §831, which prohibits the intentional unauthorized receipt, possession, use, transfer, alteration, disposal or dispersal of any nuclear material or nuclear byproduct material when the party responsible for the transaction knows the material is likely to cause the death or serious bodily injury to any person, or substantial damage to property or to the environment. 18 U.S.C. §831(e)(3)(B). Like 10 USC §832, §831 is also a limited exception to the PCA, as the statute includes the authority to arrest persons and conduct searches and seizures, as well as "such other activity as is incidental to" its enforcement or to protect persons or property from the proscribed conduct. *Id.*

[32] *See* JUDGE ADVOCATE GEN.'s LEGAL CTR. AND SCH., *supra* note 24, at 112-13 (discussing authority for WMD-CST support and composition of WMD-CST teams).

are not in federal military status. To date, Congress has authorized the creation of 55 such teams.[33]

V. POSSE COMITATUS AND THE GENERAL PROHIBITION AGAINST FEDERAL MILITARY INTERVENTION IN DOMESTIC AFFAIRS

Some domestic emergencies may unfortunately necessitate the use of federal military forces to engage in activities to enforce law, restore and maintain public order, or respond forcibly to a threat. In such situations, use of these forces must comply with the Posse Comitatus Act (PCA),[34] a federal statute prohibiting use of the Army or Air Force as a posse comitatus or to otherwise participate in law enforcement activities, unless authorized by statute or the Constitution. A posse comitatus is composed when all able bodied citizens in a given jurisdiction are called upon to assist in enforcing the law.[35] The PCA was enacted to prevent the use of federal military forces to participate in law enforcement activities—in short to be called to participate in a posse comitatus—unless the use was authorized by Congress or otherwise constitutionally authorized. The PCA was responsive to concerns that arose in the post–Civil War era that federal military forces had become far too involved in the maintenance of public order by routinely engaging in local law enforcement activities in the defeated Southern states. Accordingly, the PCA provides:

> Whoever, except in cases and under circumstances expressly authorized by the Constitution or Act of Congress, willfully uses any part of the Army or the Air Force as a posse comitatus or otherwise to execute the laws shall be fined under this title or imprisoned not more than two years, or both.[36]

---

[33] According to a Congressional Research Service Report,

[t]heir mission is to assess a suspected CBRN incident, advise civilian authorities, and expedite the arrival of additional military personnel. Each team consists of 22 personnel and is equipped with CBRN detection, analysis, and protective equipment. Congress has authorized 55 WMD-CSTs, ensure that each state and territory would have a team.

STEVE BOWMAN, *supra* note 27. There are obvious advantages to utilization of the National Guard to complement the federal military CNBRE response capability. First, these units are subject to the authority of state governors, which allows for utilization during events and potential incidents that do not, or might not yet, trigger federal response authority. Second, developing state level CNBRE response capability disperses these units and their expertise throughout the country, potentially facilitating a more timely response to these highly destructive weapons.

[34] 18 U.S.C. §1835 (2012).

[35] BLACK'S LAW DICTIONARY 1281 (9th ed. 2009).

[36] 18 U.S.C. §1835 (2012).

V. Posse Comitatus and the General Prohibition

This restriction has been extended by DoD policy to apply to the Navy and Marine Corps,[37] and reflects the traditional restriction on domestic use of federal military forces.

The PCA does not, however, impose an absolute prohibition against using federal military forces in a law enforcement capacity. Instead, the PCA is best understood as establishing a powerful, albeit rebuttable, presumption against such use. As the PCA provides, this presumption is rebutted whenever such use is authorized by statute, or when otherwise authorized by the Constitution. Accordingly, the PCA endeavors to align permissible domestic use of federal military forces with the underlying constitutional reticence towards military involvement in domestic affairs.

In practical terms, the two PCA exceptions will be implemented through one of three legal mechanisms: 1) invocation of the Insurrection Act[38] for the "authorized by statute" exception; 2) invocation of constitutional war powers to respond to an attack on the homeland;[39] or 3) invocation of martial law to respond to a domestic emergency resulting in a total breakdown of civil function.[40] Each of these exceptions will be addressed in turn.

If, however, federal military forces were used in violation of the PCA, there are two probable consequences. First, the government authority responsible for ordering such use could be subjected criminal liability, or some lesser form of disciplinary action (for example, an official reprimand issued to a military commander ordering use of her forces in violation of the Act).[41] Second, it would provide individuals impacted by the action with a basis to seek civil damages for a violation of their civil rights. In order to mitigate the risk of a violation, Department of Defense Instruction 3025.21 limits a military commander's authority to respond to domestic emergencies so that it will comply with the PCA.[42]

This Instruction incorporates a judicially established test for assessing when military activities fall within the scope of the PCA's prohibition. This test is based on the federal court decision, *Bissonette v. Haig*.[43] That case involved a lawsuit seeking damages against the United States asserting that the use of federal military resources to assist with the response to the siege at Wounded Knee on

---

[37] *See* U.S. DEP'T OF DEFENSE, INSTR. 3025.21, DEFENSE SUPPORT OF CIVILIAN LAW ENFORCEMENT AGENCIES (Feb. 27, 2013) [hereinafter U.S. DEP'T OF DEFENSE, INSTR. 3025.21] (implementing the direction by Congress to prohibit members of the armed forces from participating in searches, seizures or arrests). *See also* 10 U.S.C. §375 (2012).

[38] 10 U.S.C. §§331-335 (2012).

[39] *See* 10 U.S.C. §§331-335; Res. 116, 77th Cong. (1941). *See also* Authorization for Use of Military Force, S.J. Res. 23, 107th Cong. (2001); Maj. Kirk L. Davies, *The Imposition of Martial Law in the United States*, 49 A.F. L. REV. 67, 83 (2000).

[40] *See* Maj. Kirk L. Davies, *The Imposition of Martial Law in the United States*, 49 A.F. L. REV. 67, 83 (2000).

[41] 18 U.S.C. §1835 (2012).

[42] *Supra* note 37 at 2.

[43] 776 F.2d 1384 (8th Cir. 1985).

the Pine Ridge Indian Reservation in South Dakota violated both due process and the Fourth Amendment.[44] The Eighth Circuit Court of Appeals reversed the district court's decision to dismiss the lawsuit for failing to state a claim.[45] According to the circuit court, use of federal military forces in violation of the PCA would qualify as "unreasonable" within the meaning of the Fourth Amendment, thereby triggering government liability for a civil rights violation.[46]

Determining what qualifies as a PCA violation, however, was more complex. The *Bissonette* court endorsed a test for assessing when the actions of military personnel amount to "execut[ing] the law" within the meaning of the PCA. Relying on an earlier decision related to military action at Wounded Knee, *United States v. Casper*,[47] the court concluded that the PCA is violated only when "military personnel subject[ed] the citizens to the exercise of military power which was regulatory, proscriptive or compulsory in nature, either presently or prospectively."[48] The court then remanded the case to the district court to determine whether the use of federal military assets to support establishing a perimeter around Wounded Knee met this definition.[49]

This "regulatory, proscriptive or compulsory" test is incorporated into the DoD Instruction[50] and many other derivative Service regulations, instructions, and manuals, and provides the standard by which any request for support to civil authorities will be assessed. Accordingly, violations of the PCA are very rare, as compliance with DoD and Service authorities will normally ensure compliance with this test.

This is not, however, the only test that has been applied by the federal courts to assess whether military action violated the PCA. Other decisions emphasized an additional requirement of willfulness, even if military forces are used in a proscriptive, regulatory or compulsive function. For example, in *United States v. Walden*,[51] enlisted Marines, working with an ATF agent, entered the defendants' store under the pretense of purchasing weapons, which led to evidence used against the defendant at trial.[52] The Fourth Circuit Court concluded that the role of the Marines was prohibited by a Navy regulation extending the PCA

---

[44] *Id*. at 1386.

[45] *Id*. at 1392.

[46] *Id*. at 1386-87.

[47] 541 F.2d 1275 (8th Cir. 1976).

[48] 776 F.2d at 1390.

[49] *Id*. at 1391.

[50] *See* U.S. Dep't of Defense, Instr. 3025.21, *supra* note 37, at 22, which provides:

g. Other Permissible Assistance. These forms of indirect assistance are not prohibited by law or DoD policy:
   (3) Such other actions, approved in accordance with procedures established by the DoD Components concerned, that do not subject civilians to the use of DoD power that is regulatory, prescriptive, proscriptive, or compulsory.

[51] 490 F.2d 372, 372-73 (4th Cir. 1974).

[52] *Id*. at 373.

V. Posse Comitatus and the General Prohibition

restriction to the Navy and Marine Corps.[53] However, the court denied the appeal, based in part on the conclusion that exclusion of evidence required the additional finding that "there was a conscious, deliberate or willful intent on the part of the Marines or the Treasury Department's Special Investigator to violate the Instruction or the spirit of the Posse Comitatus Act."[54]

As noted in *Walden*, the DoD has implemented policies extending the PCA to the Navy and Marine Corps through Department of Defense Instruction 3025.21.[55] Instruction 3025.21 also extends the prohibition on direct involvement in civilian law enforcement activities to "all actions of DoD personnel worldwide."[56] This policy-based extension of the PCA was recently relied upon by the Ninth Circuit Court of Appeals in *United States v. Dreyer*,[57] reversing a federal conviction for distribution of child pornography based on its determination that much of the internet evidence used against the accused in that case came from Navy investigation activities that blatantly violated the PCA. According to a summary of the opinion prepared by the court's staff:

> The panel reaffirmed that NCIS agents are bound by Posse Comitatus Act-like restrictions on direct assistance to civilian law enforcement, and held that the agent's broad investigation into sharing of child pornography by anyone within the state of Washington, not just those on a military base or with a reasonable likelihood of a Navy affiliation, violated the regulations and policies proscribing direct military enforcement of civilian laws.[58]

While these cases indicate the potential consequences of use of military personnel in violation of the PCA, the Act's restrictions apply only to official activities. Accordingly, the PCA does not restrict activities of a member of the Army, Navy, Air Force, or Marine Corps if the member is "off-duty and acting in a private capacity,"[59] for example, when military personnel volunteer to participate in a search and rescue operation conducted by local law enforcement agencies.

---

[53] *Id.* at 373-74.

[54] *Id.* at 376.

[55] *See* U.S. Dep't of Defense Instr. 3025.21, *supra* note 37, at 23:

> By policy, Posse Comitatus Act restrictions (as well as other restrictions in this Instruction) are applicable to the Department of the Navy (including the Marine Corps) with such exceptions as the Secretary of Defense may authorize in advance on a case-by-case basis.

[56] *See* U.S. Dep't of Defense Instr. 3025.21, *supra* note 37, at 3.

[57] United States v. Dreyer, 767 F.3d 826 (9th Cir. 2014), *available at* http://cdn.ca9 .uscourts.gov/datastore/opinions/2014/09/12/13-30077.pdf.

[58] *Id.* at 2.

[59] *See* Judge Advocate Gen.'s Legal Ctr. and Sch., *supra* note 24, at 71(discussing the PCA applicability to the various branches of the armed forces).

VI. FEDERAL MILITARY HUMANITARIAN SUPPORT AND THE STAFFORD ACT

A common form of federal involvement in response to a natural or manmade emergency or disaster is the provision of what is in essence humanitarian assistance. When these events adversely impact lives and property, federal resources will often be utilized to mitigate the suffering of the population and assist in the restoration of normalcy, to include providing varying forms of compensation and financial assistance to individual victims of the event.

This type of humanitarian assistance is provided primarily pursuant to the Stafford Act of 1988.[60] The law provides federal funding for disaster relief and defines events that trigger this humanitarian assistance authority. The Act also calls for the establishment of the Federal Emergency Management Agency (FEMA), and defines FEMA responsibilities.[61]

Relief available pursuant to the Stafford Act is triggered by a "major disaster[62] or emergency."[63] Consistent with the first responder domestic emergency response concept, the declaration of a major disaster or emergency is normally contingent on a request for federal support by the governor of the affected state based on a determination that state resources are insufficient to deal with the crisis.[64] At that point, the President is authorized to declare a disaster or emergency, thereby triggering the Act, to include the cost-sharing arrangements that allow the federal government to fund 75 percent of the federal response (with the state responsible for 25 percent). A visit to FEMA.gov will show that at any given

---

[60] The Robert T. Stafford Disaster Relief and Emergency Assistance Act, 42 U.S.C. §§5121 *et seq.*, as amended by the Post-Katrina Emergency Management Reform Act of 2006, Pub. L. No. 109-295 (2007), and the Sandy Recovery Improvement Act of 2013, Pub. L. No. 113-2 (2013).

[61] *Id.*

[62] 42 U.S.C. §5122(2) (2012) provides the definition of major disaster as:

any natural catastrophe (including any hurricane, tornado, storm, high water, snowstorm, or drought), or, regardless of cause, any fire, flood, or explosion, in any part of the United States, which in the determination of the President causes damage of sufficient severity and magnitude to warrant major disaster assistance under this Act to supplement the efforts and available resources of States, local governments, and disaster relief organizations in alleviating the damage, loss, hardship, or suffering caused thereby.

[63] 42 U.S.C. §5122(1) (2012) defines emergency as:

any occasion or instance for which, in the determination of the President, Federal assistance is needed to supplement State and local determination of the President, Federal assistance is needed to supplement State and local efforts and capabilities to save lives to protect property and public health and safety, or to lessen or avert the threat of a catastrophe in any part of the United States.

[64] Requirements for an emergency declaration are enumerated in 44 C.F.R. §206.35 (2012), and the requirements for a major disaster request are enumerated in 44 C.F.R. §206.36 (2012). *See also* Judge Advocate Gen.'s Legal Ctr. and Sch., *supra* note 24, at 32-33 (discussing the different assistance available for emergencies and major disasters as well as the differing authority for each).

time there are a number of existing federally declared disasters or emergencies. The Act also authorizes the President to declare an emergency without such a state request when he "determines that the emergency falls within the primary responsibility of the United States exclusive or preeminent responsibility as governed by the United States Constitution or laws."[65]

VII.   FEDERAL MILITARY LAW ENFORCEMENT SUPPORT AND THE INSURRECTION ACT

Throughout the nation's history, there have been incidents that, in the judgment of state and/or national leaders, required intervention of federal armed forces to ensure compliance with domestic law. These incidents have fallen into two general categories: 1) local disturbances that exceeded the law enforcement capability of local and state authorities; and 2) incidents involving a refusal of state authorities to ensure compliance with federal law.

Recognizing the possibility that federal military resources may, in extraordinary situations, be needed to respond to such a domestic crisis, the first Congress enacted the Militia Act. This law implemented the authority vested in Congress by Article I, §8 of the U.S. Constitution "[t]o provide for calling forth the Militia to execute the Laws of the Union, suppress Insurrections and repel Invasions." In 1807, the Militia Act was replaced with the Insurrection Act,[66] a law intended to provide the same statutory implementation of this constitutional authority.

The Insurrection Act establishes a limited number of situations in which the President may order federal military forces to engage in activities otherwise prohibited by the PCA. These are broken down into two general categories: 1) providing military augmentation to state authorities; 2) and using the military to ensure enforcement of federal law. The first situation is addressed by §331 of the statute, which provides:

> Whenever there is an insurrection in any State against its government, the President may, upon the request of its legislature or of its governor if the legislature cannot be convened, call into Federal service such of the militia of the other States, in the number requested by that State, and use such of the armed forces, as he considers necessary to suppress the insurrection.[67]

It is important to note the absence of a definition for the term "insurrection" in the statute. As a result, it is error to assume that this triggering event requires some type of direct challenge to the governing authority of a state—what might be

---

[65] 42 U.S.C. §5191(b) (2012).
[66] 10 U.S.C. §§331-335 (2012).
[67] 10 U.S.C. §331 (2012).

considered an insurrection in common parlance. Instead, the term has a much broader meaning, and includes any disturbance that challenges the capacity of state authorities to maintain law and order. Accordingly, an "insurrection" within the meaning of this provision may be triggered by any number of natural or man-made incidents. There is simply no touchstone for assessing what is or what is not a "genuine" insurrection within the meaning of the statute. Instead, it is the collective judgment of the state and the President that will result in a determination of a triggering insurrection within the meaning of the statute.

This implicit concurrent judgment requirement is reflected in the plain terms of §331, which does not permit the President to invoke its authority without first receiving a request to do so from the state.[68] Even then, the invocation is not automatic, as the authority vested in the President is discretionary and not obligatory. If the President "may" invoke §331 in response to such a request, then by implication he may not. Accordingly, only when a situation is perceived first by state authority, and then also by the President, as necessitating this extraordinary action to restore law and order will federal military forces be authorized to intervene for such a purpose.[69] Finally, §334[70] requires the President to issue a proclamation demanding the "insurgents" disperse prior to exercising federal intervention authority, although in practice this provision of the statute has been understood as relatively ceremonial.

A useful example of an invocation of §331 occurred in 1992 during the Los Angeles riots following the verdict in the trial of the police officers accused of beating Rodney King.[71] Those riots quickly overwhelmed the capacity of local and state police to maintain law and order in Los Angeles. Governor Pete Wilson first ordered California National Guard units to intervene to bolster law enforcement capability. However, it quickly became apparent that the situation required a more robust military response, and Wilson requested federal military intervention from President George H.W. Bush.[72] President Bush responded by invoking §331, issuing a proclamation to disperse, and ordering U.S. Army and Marine Corps units stationed in California to intervene to support the restoration of law and order. Because this intervention was ordered pursuant to the Insurrection

---

[68] *Id. See aslo* DOYLE & ELSEA, *supra* note 19, at 32-33 (discussing requests from governors under §331).

[69] *Id.* at 33:

> The first request by a governor for troops after enactment of the Posse Comitatus Act appears to have occurred in 1879, when the governor of Nebraska requested a company of troops to help protect a local court where the trial of a prominent outlaw was taking place, which had occasioned concern that the courthouse would be the scene of a rescue attempt by the portion of the band of outlaws still at large. This request was denied.

[70] 10 U.S.C. §334 (2012).

[71] *See* DOYLE & ELSEA, *supra* note 19, at 36.

[72] George H.W. Bush, Address to the Nation on the Civil Disturbances in Los Angeles, California (May 1, 1992), George Bush Presidential Library.

VII. Federal Military Law Enforcement Support and the Insurrection Act

Act, these federal military forces were authorized to conduct law enforcement activities, such as seizures and searches.

The federal response to Hurricane Katrina indicates the importance of state initiation of a §331 response. President George W. Bush came under criticism for failing to respond to the deterioration of law and order in New Orleans as his father had done in response to the Los Angeles riots. But unlike his father, President George W. Bush never received a state request to invoke section 331. Accordingly, this provision never provided the legal authority to order an analogous federal military intervention.

The Insurrection Act does, however, provide an alternate basis for ordering a federal military response to a domestic emergency or crisis that is not contingent on a request from the state. Where the state government is essentially unable or unwilling to ensure respect for U.S. law, to include the constitutional civil rights of U.S. citizens, the Act authorizes the President to order a federal military response. This requires a determination that the "insurrection" results in a denial of a constitutional right, or the inability to enforce federal law. In such situations, there is no requirement for a state request for intervention. Instead, the President is vested by the Act with independent authority to invoke the Act. Accordingly, §332[73] provides:

> Whenever the President considers that unlawful obstructions, combinations, or assemblages, or rebellion against the authority of the United States, make it impracticable to enforce the laws of the United States in any State by the ordinary course of judicial proceedings, he may call into Federal service such of the militia of any State, and use such of the armed forces, as he considers necessary to enforce those laws or to suppress the rebellion.

Section 333 of the Insurrection Act[74] also granted the President authority to invoke the Act in the absence of a state request, providing that:

> The President, by using the militia or the armed forces, or both, or by any other means, shall take such measures as he considers necessary to suppress, in a State, any insurrection, domestic violence, unlawful combination, or conspiracy, if it—
>
> (1) so hinders the execution of the laws of that State, and of the United States within the State, that any part or class of its people is deprived of a right, privilege, immunity, or protection named in the Constitution and secured by law, and the constituted authorities of that State are unable, fail, or refuse to protect that right, privilege, or immunity, or to give that protection; or
>
> (2) opposes or obstructs the execution of the laws of the United States or impedes the course of justice under those laws.
>
> In any situation covered by clause (1), the State shall be considered to have denied the equal protection of the laws secured by the Constitution.

---

[73] 10 U.S.C. §332 (2012).
[74] 10 U.S.C. §333 (2012).

In an apparent effort to provide enhanced domestic military response authority following the crisis created by Hurricane Katrina, Congress amended §333 in 2007. This amendment provided for the use of the armed forces in response to a "major public emergency."[75] Specifically, the Act provided that:

> (1) The President may employ the armed forces, including the National Guard in Federal service, to—
>> (A) restore public order and enforce the laws of the United States when, as a result of a natural disaster, epidemic, or other serious public health emergency, terrorist attack or incident, or other condition in any State or possession of the United States, the President determines that—
>>> (i) domestic violence has occurred to such an extent that the constituted authorities of the State or possession are incapable of maintaining public order; and
>>> (ii) such violence results in a condition described in paragraph (2); or
>> (B) suppress, in a State, any insurrection, domestic violence, unlawful combination, or conspiracy if such insurrection, violation, combination, or conspiracy results in a condition described in paragraph (2).
> (2) A condition described in this paragraph is a condition that—
>> (A) so hinders the execution of the laws of a State or possession, as applicable, and of the United States within that State or possession, that any part or class of its people is deprived of a right, privilege, immunity, or protection named in the Constitution and secured by law, and the constituted authorities of that State or possession are unable, fail, or refuse to protect that right, privilege, or immunity, or to give that protection; or
>> (B) opposes or obstructs the execution of the laws of the United States or impedes the course of justice under those laws.
> (3) In any situation covered by paragraph (1)(B), the State shall be considered to have denied the equal protection of the laws secured by the Constitution."

It is significant that this amended provision of the Act included an express reference to a range of domestic incidents that allowed the President to invoke the Act to order a federal military response. And like the original version of §333, this authority was not contingent on a determination that judicial process is ineffective for enforcing law, and therefore provides the broadest grant of federal domestic emergency response authority.

This amendment certainly enhanced and clarified federal military response authority in an era of increasing concern that terrorism may create a domestic emergency. However, it also generated substantial concern that Congress has overreached in its effort to provide for a federal military response to domestic emergencies. This generated a backlash to the amendment, which was repealed

---

[75] 10 U.S.C. §333 (2012).

in 2008, returning the Act to its pre-2007 language, eliminating the term "major public emergency" and the definition of that term.[76]

Even pursuant to the reversion to the pre-2007 version of §333, the President is vested with substantial authority to order a military intervention absent a state request for assistance. If the President determines that the judicial function is ineffective, he may invoke §332; and even without such a determination, his assessment that U.S. law is not being enforced, either due to inability or unwillingness on the part of state authorities, triggers his authority pursuant to §333.[77] And, because this authority is triggered by the *consequence* of a domestic incident, and not the *cause* of the obstruction, there appears to be no reason why the President could not rely on one or both of these authorities to order a military intervention in response to a manmade crisis, such as a terrorist attack.

No matter what provision of law is invoked to justify the use of federal military forces to engage in law enforcement activities, the forces will be subject to civilian command and control. Pursuant to 32 C.F.R. §182.6, the Attorney General may (and will normally) appoint a Senior Civilian Representative of the Attorney General (SCRAG).[78] This representative will be a civilian federal officer

---

[76] HR 4986: National Defense Authorization Act for Fiscal Year 2008, SEC. 1068: Repeal of Provision in Section 1076 of Public Law 109-364 Relating to Use of Armed Force in Major Public Emergencies, which provides:

(a) Interference With State and Federal Laws—
(1) IN GENERAL—Section 333 of title 10, United States Code, is amended to read as follows: "Sec. 333. Interference with State and Federal law
The President, by using the militia or the armed forces, or both, or by any other means, shall take such measures as he considers necessary to suppress, in a State, any insurrection, domestic violence, unlawful combination, or conspiracy, if it—
(1) so hinders the execution of the laws of that State, and of the United States within the State, that any part or class of its people is deprived of a right, privilege, immunity, or protection named in the Constitution and secured by law, and the constituted authorities of that State are unable, fail, or refuse to protect that right, privilege, or immunity, or to give that protection; or
(2) opposes or obstructs the execution of the laws of the United States or impedes the course of justice under those laws.
In any situation covered by clause (1), the State shall be considered to have denied the equal protection of the laws secured by the Constitution.
(2) PROCLAMATION TO DISPERSE—Section 334 of such title is amended by striking 'or those obstructing the enforcement of the laws' after 'insurgents.'" H.R. 4986: National Defense Authorization Act for Fiscal Year 2008. *GovTrack.us*. 2008. Retrieved 2008-01-24.

[77] A notable example of such an invocation was President Eisenhower's decision to order the 101st Airborne Division (a federal U.S. Army unit) to deploy to Little Rock, Arkansas to ensure compliance with the Supreme Court's desegregation decisions. Not only did President Eisenhower order these forces to enforce federal law, he also nationalized the Arkansas National Guard so that they would be under his command and not that of the Governor. Doing so, Eisenhower told the nation, was necessary to prevent "anarchy." See DOYLE & ELSEA, *supra* note 19.
[78] See JUDGE ADVOCATE GEN.'S LEGAL CTR. AND SCH., supra note 24, at 96 (explaining the role of a SCRAG in domestic operations).

responsible for coordinating the federal response among federal agencies (including the DoD) and between the federal government and the states. Federal military forces will remain under a military chain of command,[79] but it will be the SCRAG who will coordinate the role these forces will play.

The military chain of command for federal military forces committed to a domestic emergency response will be organized like that of any other operational mission.[80] The individual military services will be directed to provide forces for the mission. These forces will be integrated into a joint (multi-service) task force (JTF). This JTF will most likely be designated as "JTF Civil Disturbance," commanded by an officer appointed by the Commanding General of U.S. Northern Command (NORTHCOM). Normally, a senior commander of one of the units forming the JTF will be designated as the JTF commander. This JTF will fall under the operational command and control of NORTHCOM, the unified combatant command responsible for homeland defense. Commanded by a four star general, NORTHCOM operates under the direct command of the National Command Authority: the President through the Secretary of Defense. Thus, all military forces participating in the operation will always fall under civilian control. But at the operational execution level, the JTF Commander will be under the direct supervision and authority of the SCRAG, thereby ensuring civilian control of military operations at every level of command.[81]

At the tactical or ground level, the missions and responsibilities assigned to federal military forces will be dictated by a range of considerations, to include the situation, available state and federal resources, the suitability of military forces in relation to different mission needs, and most importantly, the legal authority under which these forces operate. The two latter considerations generally result in a preference that civilian or National Guard personnel execute law enforcement functions, with federal military personnel providing what might best be characterized as tactical "backup" to these personnel. This is because federal military personnel are rarely trained to engage in law enforcement activities, such as seizures and searches. There are, of course, exceptions to this (for example, military police units), but utilizing forces trained and normally tasked to conduct combat operations in a domestic law enforcement capacity poses risk of overzealous response.

To mitigate this risk, certain tactical "best practices" will be considered during the preparation and execution of a domestic military utilization. One example of this is to establish teams of personnel composed of civilian law enforcement and

---

[79] 32 C.F.R. §182.6(b)(5)(i)(C) (2013), which provides:

The President may provide, through the Attorney General or other Federal official, a personal representative to communicate the President's policy guidance to the military commander conducting [Civil Disturbance Operations]. That representative may augment, but shall not replace, the military chain of command. In addition, an individual may be designated by the Attorney General as the Senior Civilian Representative of the Attorney General.

[80] *See generally* Judge Advocate Gen.'s Legal Ctr. and Sch., supra note 24, at 96.
[81] *Id.*

federal military assets. Such combined teams will frequently engage in patrolling operations in an effort to establish and maintain law and order. Combining federal armed forces with National Guard and even local police forces allows law enforcement officer to conduct any seizures and/or searches with the military personnel providing support. This method was utilized to great effect in Los Angeles during the 1992 riot response. Additionally, federal military forces will operate pursuant to Rules for the Use of Force (RUF), command directives that establish the conditions for permissible uses of force. Unlike wartime Rules of Engagement, these rules will reflect the type of use of force restraint central to the law enforcement function. These forces will be instructed and trained on these rules as best as possible within the time constraints of the response. Finally, because a federal military intervention will almost always be conducted as a measure of last resort, efforts will be made to shift the law enforcement function to civilian and/or National Guard personnel as rapidly as possible.[82]

VIII. OTHER EMERGENCY RESPONSE AUTHORITIES

A. Martial Law

As noted above, the Insurrection Act[83] provides broad statutory authority for the President to order federal military forces to intervene in a domestic crisis or emergency. It is not, however, the exclusive authority for such action, as there may be situations that trigger the President's and/or federal government's inherent constitutional authority.

The federal government is obligated pursuant to the Constitution to protect the states against both foreign invasion and, at the request of the state, domestic violence. Article IV, §4 of The Constitution provides:

> The United States shall guarantee to every State in this Union a Republican Form of Government, and shall protect each of them against Invasion; and on Application of the Legislature, or of the Executive (when the Legislature cannot be convened) against domestic Violence.

This obligation indicates that when executing missions conducted pursuant to this authority, the federal government may use military forces without violating the PCA.

It is generally accepted that the President is vested with inherent constitutional authority to respond to an attack on the United States with military

---

[82] *Id.*
[83] 10 U.S.C. §§331-335 (2012).

force.[84] This authority was affirmed by the Supreme Court in *The Prize Cases*[85] during the Civil War. Furthermore, this inherent executive authority was explicitly acknowledged by Congress in the War Powers Resolution,[86] a law that sought to limit the exercise of presidential war powers to only those situations consistent with Congress's view of the President's constitutional authority. Accordingly, should the President determine that a state or nonstate group had or was about to conduct an attack against the United States, he or she might very well assert Article II war powers as the legal basis for the mission.[87]

How the federal government would respond to a catastrophic incident that totally disabled civil function raises the prospect of martial law.[88] The precise parameters of martial law are difficult to identify, although imposition of martial law would likely result in the military assumption of law enforcement and public order responsibilities resulting from a situation of extremis disabling the capacity of civil authorities. In this regard, martial law would probably manifest many characteristics of a wartime occupation of enemy territory, with a military commander asserting the full range of governing authorities, to include law enforcement, in order to restore and maintain public order and basic government services.[89]

The Constitution does not provide express authority for declaring or imposing martial law. However, the Supreme Court has in several decisions indicated that this authority is inherent in the federal government, although strictly limited to situations of imperative necessity in response to a complete breakdown of civil function. In *Ex parte Milligan*,[90] the Court emphasized this necessity requirement for the imposition of martial law, specifically indicating that such a measure could only be permissible when federal courts are unable to perform their normal function. Nearly a century later, the Court struck down trial by military tribunal of a civilian in Hawaii pursuant to the imposition of martial law following the Pearl Harbor bombing because these conditions were not satisfied, although the Court again indicated that in some extreme situations martial

---

[84] U.S. Const. art. II, §2.

[85] 67 U.S. 635 (1863).

[86] 50 U.S.C. §§1541-1548 (2012).

[87] An ostensible example of such response authority is provided by the initial response to the September 11, 2001 terrorist attacks. During the initial hours following the attacks, Vice President Cheney ordered U.S. Air Force fighter assets to conduct combat air patrols over New York and Washington, D.C. airspace. The aircraft scrambled to conduct these missions were ordered to prevent the unauthorized intrusion of any other aircraft into the airspace. Although they were unarmed, the 9/11 Commission Report indicated that several of the pilots were prepared to ram any aircraft violating the prohibition. The order that might have produced that outcome was based on the determination that the nation was at that moment under attack, and therefore an exercise of the inherent authority of the President to repel such attacks.

[88] *See generally* Harold C. Relya, Cong. Research Serv., RL31615, Martial Law and National Emergency (Jan. 7, 2005).

[89] *See generally* Maj. Kirk L. Davies, *The Imposition of Martial Law in the United States*, 49 A.F. L. Rev. 67, 83 (2000).

[90] 71 U.S. 2 (1866).

law may be valid.[91] Finally, in *Youngstown Sheet & Tube Co. v. Sawyer*,[92] Justice Jackson, although rejecting the assertion that emergency creates power,[93] qualified that rejection in a footnote to his opinion noting that he excluded from this rejection "the very limited category by itself, the establishment of martial law."[94]

A catastrophe or emergency of sufficient magnitude to require imposition of martial law would, of course, also justify invocation of the Insurrection Act. However, this does not render martial law as a source of potential government authority superfluous. First, martial law may result in the imposition of measures beyond those justified pursuant to the Insurrection Act, for example, the establishment of military tribunals to adjudicate violations of military orders and directives. Second, as an exercise of constitutional authority—particularly inherent executive authority—martial law does not seem contingent on the invocation of statutory authority.[95] As a result, martial law might be continued even following revocation or modification of the Insurrection Act.

It is, however, almost impossible to predict what type of emergency might result in an imposition of martial law, or what measures might be taken under the rubric of martial law. The military would almost certainly play a central role in implementing martial law, which would almost certainly involve the imposition of domestic military authority. Like occupation of belligerent territory in time of war, the military would fill the ungoverned vacuum with military authority, establishing military government and exercising all powers necessary to restore and maintain public order, provide for essential needs of the population, and mitigate the consequences of the incident that triggered martial law.

B.   A Military Commander's Immediate Response Authority

Military commanders may also feel compelled to respond to an emergency in the locality of the military base or installation they command even in the absence of a declaration of martial law or invocation of the Insurrection Act. What authority, if any, does a military commander possess to use her forces for an immediate

---

[91] Duncan v. Kahanamoku, 327 U.S. 304 (1946).

[92] 343 U.S. 579 (1952).

[93] Jackson's opinion provided that,

> [t]he appeal, however, that we declare the existence of inherent powers ex necessitate to meet an emergency asks us to do what many think would be wise, although it is something the forefathers omitted. They knew what emergencies were, knew the pressures they engender for authoritative action, knew, too, how they afford a ready pretext for usurpation. We may also suspect that they suspected that emergency powers would tend to kindle emergencies. Aside from suspension of the privilege of the writ of habeas corpus in time of rebellion or invasion, when the public safety may require it, they made no express provision for exercise of extraordinary authority because of a crisis.

Id. at 560.

[94] *Id.*

[95] *See generally* RELYA, *supra* note 88.

response to such a local emergency? Department of Defense Directive 3025.18 answers this question—at least in terms of departmental authority—and indicates that federal military commanders may, on their own initiative, order their forces to respond to such an emergency as an exigent measure. According to this directive:

> Federal military commanders have the authority, in extraordinary emergency circumstances where prior authorization by the President is impossible and duly constituted local authorities are unable to control the situation, to engage temporarily in activities that are necessary to quell large-scale, unexpected civil disturbances because:
> (1) Such activities are necessary to prevent significant loss of life or wanton destruction of property and are necessary to restore governmental function and public order; or,
> (2) When duly constituted Federal, State, or local authorities are unable or decline to provide adequate protection for Federal property or Federal governmental functions. Federal action, including the use of Federal military forces, is authorized when necessary to protect the Federal property or functions.[96]

This emergency response authority is narrow in its scope, applicable only to situations of true exigency, where a local military commander concludes that the necessity for immediate response outweighs the necessity of obtaining national level authorization. While invocation of this authority is therefore uncommon, and increasingly unlikely in an era of almost instant communication to national level command, it is notable that the directive does not seem to restrict or limit the type of measures a commander could order pursuant to this authority.

This latter omission might be understandable based on an assumption that the PCA would apply to such a response, thereby prohibiting any action that would qualify as law enforcement. This would imply that an immediate response must be limited to humanitarian action. However, when the directive is considered in its entirety, such an implicit limitation is difficult to support. This is because the directive specifically addresses authority for humanitarian action, explicitly prohibiting *in that section* any action inconsistent with the PCA. Specifically, paragraph 4(g) of the directive provides that:

> In response to a request for assistance from a civil authority, under imminently serious conditions and if time does not permit approval from higher authority, DoD officials may provide an immediate response by temporarily employing the resources under their control, subject to any supplemental direction provided by higher headquarters, to save lives, prevent human suffering, or mitigate great property damage within the United States. *Immediate response authority does not*

---

[96] *See* U.S. Dep't of Defense, Instr. 3025.18, Defense Support of Civil Authorities (Sept. 21, 2012), at 5.

permit actions that would subject civilians to the use of military power that is regulatory, prescriptive, proscriptive, or compulsory.[97]

The absence of any analogous restriction in relation to an emergency response suggests that both humanitarian and law enforcement type actions could fall within the scope of this immediate response authority.

Because this immediate response authority is not derived from statute, it must be based on the President's constitutional authority to protect the nation from dire emergency, implemented by a local military commander. The requirement that this authority may be exercised only when prior authorization from the President cannot be secured reinforces this conclusion. It is therefore unsurprising why the directive applies only in the extremely unusual situation where communication with national level authorities is not possible. Nonetheless, the lack of a clear statutory authorization for the implementation of an immediate emergency response could result in legal challenges to a commander and/or the United States for actions conducted pursuant to this directive.

C. Public Health Emergencies

One especially frightening domestic national security threat is a pandemic involving the rapid spread of a contagious disease. Whether caused naturally or by a terrorist or other manmade act, the consequence of such a pandemic could challenge the ability of local, state, and the federal governments in a way that has not been experienced for nearly a century. The range of potential response requirements is so broad that it would very likely require substantial federal involvement to contain the disease and mitigate the consequences of for afflicted areas.[98]

Like any other domestic threat that does not trigger federal defensive war powers, State governments would most likely take the lead in responding to a contagious disease threat to the health of the population. Measures available to the state would flow from the general police powers. Historical examples of such measures include quarantines, movement restrictions, and mandatory vaccination programs. It is likely, however, that the states may request or require federal support to any pandemic response. Furthermore, restrictions on movements between the states and at international borders would fall within federal, and not state, responsibility.

In order to enhance the efficacy of state response measures and federal support for such measures, the Department of Homeland Security proposed to the states a Model State Emergency Health Powers Act (MSEHPA), which

---

[97] *Id.* at 16.

[98] *See generally* LAWRENCE KAPP & DON J. JANSEN, CONG. RESEARCH SERV., R40619, THE ROLE OF THE DEPARTMENT OF DEFENSE DURING A FLU PANDEMIC (June 4, 2009).

establishes a range of response measures available to state officials. Proposed following the terrorist attacks of September 11, 2001,[99] MSEHPA provides a framework for state government response to bioterrorism and other public health threats.[100] While MSEHPA is intended to advance the valid interest of maximizing the effect of local, state, and federal government response to a public health threat, it has been criticized because of the potential impact it might have on civil liberties. According to the ACLU, MSEHPA fails to provide a system of checks and balances that would protect individuals from the extraordinary power given to state governments. Furthermore, MSEHPA's definition of "public health emergency" is very broad, potentially reaching beyond incidents of bioterrorism or pandemic to include diseases such as HIV/AIDS, which may not warrant extraordinary response measures. Finally, MSEHPA does not include a provision that would protect individual privacy, and would actually undercut existing privacy protections related to sensitive medical information.[101] Despite these concerns, a version of MSEHPA has been enacted by 38 states, as well as the District of Columbia.[102]

Federal pandemic response authority is vested primarily in the Surgeon General, who is authorized to impose quarantine and other interstate movement restrictions.[103] However, enforcing such measures would require support from either state officials, or other federal agencies, to include use of the armed forces. Accordingly, it must be anticipated that either state governments, or the Department of Homeland Security, might request support from the DoD in response to a pandemic emergency. Any such support would fall within the scope of the authorities explained above: Humanitarian type assistance would be provided pursuant to the Stafford Act, enabling leverage of DoD resources to provide medical and other logistical assistance to the response effort; law enforcement type support for quarantines or other movement restriction enforcement would almost certainly necessitate invocation of the Insurrection Act. Such an invocation would permit the use of federal military forces to act in the capacity of any other law enforcement agent for purpose of implementing response measures. Thus, any major epidemic or health threat poses a genuine likelihood of triggering invocation of both the Stafford and Insurrection Acts, enabling federal military assets to provide a full range of responsive support.

---

[99] Model State Emergency Health Powers Act, ACLU (Jan. 1, 2002), https://www.aclu.org/technology-and-liberty/model-state-emergency-health-powers-act [hereinafter ACLU].

[100] Model State Emergency Health Powers Act (Ctr. for Law & the Pub. Health, Draft for Discussion 2001), *available at* http://www.publichealthlaw.net/MSEHPA/MSEHPA2.pdf.

[101] ACLU, *supra* note 99.

[102] The Model State Emergency Health Powers Act (MSEHPA), Ctr. for Law & the Pub. Health, http://www.publichealthlaw.net/ModelLaws/MSEHPA.php (last updated Jan. 27, 2010).

[103] SEC. 364. [42 U.S.C. 267], 2011 WL 485333. *See* Swine Flu Memos ("The Department of Justice has established legal federal authorities pertaining to the implementation of a quarantine and enforcement. Under approval from HHS, the Surgeon General has the authority to issue quarantines.")

IX. CONCLUSION

While the United States homeland has fortunately rarely suffered the direct consequences of war and other national security emergencies, the terrorist attacks of September 11, 2001 served as a painful reminder that there is no immunity from such dangers. It is a simple and unfortunate reality that the homeland is always a potential target for those who seek to threaten our people and our national security. As a result, the legal authority to respond to domestic emergencies is an increasingly relevant and important aspect of the study and implementation of national security law.

Unlike the legal framework for directing national power to address threats outside our borders, our system of federalism significantly alters the paradigm of federal supremacy when the nation is confronted with domestic emergencies. States have and will continue to exercise their primacy in responding to emergencies within their territory. This is the legal foundation for the "first responder" concept.

Some threats will, however, necessitate a federal role—in some cases including a military role. In response to this reality, federal statutes authorize the leverage of federal resources, both civilian and military, for humanitarian and law enforcement type missions. Implementing these authorities involves compliance with a range of derivative statutes, regulations, directives, instructions, and other policies. Ultimately, however, all uses of federal power must be tethered to a statutory or constitutional authority, which unlike the states does not include a general police power.

How any given emergency is characterized will substantially impact the legal basis for the federal response. This could range from a naturally created emergency necessitating support to the state pursuant to a state request, to an attack from abroad triggering the nation's defensive war powers. Finally, although unlikely, a catastrophic incident disabling civil function might even trigger invocation of martial law, a power ostensibly vested in the federal government that involves extreme uncertainty as to scope, implementation, and duration.

Table of Cases

Table of Cases

Table of Cases

Table of Cases

Table of Cases

Index

Index

Index

Index

Index

Index

Index

Index

Index

Public health emergencies, 477–478
Public Interest Declassification Board
 (PIDB), 335–336
Public officials, suits against
 detainees' suits for damages, 297–299
Public-private partnership, 440
Public safety exception, 186–188
Public trials
 functions of, 190–191
 jurisdiction and, 189–190
 limitations on, 190–193

Qualified immunity doctrine, 298–299
Quarantines, 477, 478

Randolph, Edmund, 4, 5
RAS. *See* Reasonably articulable suspicion
 (RAS)
Ratification of treaties, 128
Reagan administration, 32, 52, 77, 382, 383
"Realpolitik," 95
Reasonably articulable suspicion (RAS), 229
Rendition, 121–122. *See also* Extraordinary
 rendition
Repatriation of Guantanamo detainees,
 challenge to, 289, 290–292
Reserves, 118, 119, 120
Responsibility to protect (R2P), 102–103
Restatement (Third) of Foreign Relations Law
 customary international law, and last-in-
 time rule, 138
 extraterritorial criminal jurisdiction,
 166–167
 international law, description of, 126, 127,
 167
Revolutionary War, 118, 148, 303
Right to Financial Privacy Act, 244, 245, 246,
 247, 248, 256
Ripeness doctrine, 44, 47–48, 143, 144
Robots, use of, 432
 micro robots, 441
 nano robots, 441
 offensive use of, 445–446
Roosevelt, Franklin D., 13, 267, 372
R2P. *See* Responsibility to protect (R2P)
RUF. *See* Rules for Use of Force (RUF)
Rules for Use of Force (RUF), 473
Rules of Engagement, 473
Russia, nanotechnology in, 434

Sabotage, 198, 200
Sanctions, enforcement of
 financial institutions, 398–399
 individuals, 399
 legal challenges, 399–400

Saudi Arabia, 188, 294, 385, 408
SCRAG. *See* Senior Civilian Representative
 of the Attorney General (SCRAG)
SDN List. *See* Specially Designated Nationals
 (SDN List)
Sea, law of, 134
Search and seizure, 170, 173–177. *See also*
 Fourth Amendment
 arrest, search incident to, 177
 body cavity searches, 182
 border searches. *See* Border searches
 computers, 182
 destruction of property, 182
 exigent circumstances, 177
 plain view, 177
 probable cause, 176, 177, 178
 warrant requirement, 176, 177
 warrantless, 177
Self-defense, 98–101
 anticipatory, 99–100
 Article 51 of UN Charter, 99, 307
 interceptive, 100
 preemptive, 101
 preventive, 101
Self-incrimination, privilege against, 185
Senior Civilian Representative of the Attorney
 General (SCRAG), 471–472
SEPA. *See* Single Euro Payment Area (SEPA)
Separation of powers
 Japanese-American internment and, 268
 military commissions and, 302–305
September 11, 2001, terrorist attacks. *See*
 9/11 terrorist attacks
Serbia, conflict against, 62, 63, 64, 77, 82
Shackling, 286
Shah of Iran, 381
Shahid Hemat Industrial Group (SHIG),
 393, 395
SHIG. *See* Shahid Hemat Industrial Group
 (SHIG)
Sierra Leone, "unusual and extraordinary"
 threats emanating from, 381
Silent witness rule, 191
"Silver Platter" doctrine, 172, 188
Single Euro Payment Area (SEPA), 257
"Sister city" agreements, 146
Sixth Amendment, 170, 323
 confrontation right, 243
 fair trial, 11
 jury trial right, 303, 305
 public trial, right to, 190–193
Slavery, 288
Snowden, Edward, 215, 326–327, 338–339,
 348
Sobriety checkpoints, 182

507

Index

Index